Grandma Never Lived
in America

Grandma Never Lived in America

The New Journalism of Abraham Cahan

Edited with an Introduction by
MOSES RISCHIN

INDIANA UNIVERSITY PRESS

Bloomington

Manufactured in the United States of America

Library of Congress Cataloging-in-Publication Data
Cahan, Abraham, 1860–1951.
Grandma never lived in America.
1. Jews—New York (N.Y.)—Social life and customs—
Addresses, essays, lectures.   2. Lower East Side (New York,
N.Y.)—Social life and customs—Addresses, essays,
lectures.   3. New York (N.Y.)—Social life and customs—
Addresses, essays, lectures.   I. Rischin, Moses,
1925–   .   II. Title.
F128.9.J5C333   1985   306'.08992407471   85-42541
ISBN 0-253-32614-1

1 2 3 4 5 89 88 87 86 85

For our daughters,
Sarah, Abigail, and Rebecca

CONTENTS

CONTENTS

CONTENTS

CONTENTS

CONTENTS

CONTENTS

ILLUSTRATIONS

EDITOR'S NOTE AND ACKNOWLEDGMENTS

The selections in this anthology have never before appeared between the covers of a book. Most of them were published in the *New York Commercial Advertiser* between 1897 and 1903. The others appeared in the Sunday supplement of the *New York Sun*, the *Atlantic Monthly*, *Ainslee's Magazine*, the *Bookman*, the *Century*, *Cosmopolitan*, *Harper's Weekly*, and *Scribner's Magazine*. Eight are original Cahan stories. Five are his translations from the Russian of stories by Anton Chekhov, Vsevolod Garshin, and Ignaty Potapenko. Included as well is his translation of a memoir by Vera Mikulich. Unless otherwise indicated, the *Commercial Advertiser* may be assumed to be the source for the selection.

Save for his stories and translations, which generally were signed or initialed, Cahan's work appeared, with rare exception, without a by-line. Most of his "bits of living writing," as Hutchins Hapgood called them, therefore had to be "discovered" and identified by a painstaking, thorough, day-by-day examination of the files of the *Advertiser* and the *Sun* from the years when Cahan was associated with those newspapers. Only a careful scrutiny of his subject matter, diction, style, and literary mannerisms—what might be called a virtual textual analysis, informed by many years of study of Cahan's life, letters, memoirs, and published writings of all kinds—as well as a close examination of the idiosyncrasies and writing habits of his colleagues, made attribution possible. Only when his imprint appeared unmistakable have we ascribed authorship to him.

Fortunately, a small collection of newspaper clippings in the YIVO Archives in New York proved strategic in launching us on our way. On the verge of disintegration, these fragile, fragmentary, often illegible or barely legible, and misdated or undated remnants of what once must have been a formidable Cahan collection, had fortunately been rescued from the oblivion to which newsprint has been fated. Thanks to the marvels of the microfilm, photocopy, and copy-flow reproduction processes, we were able to decipher, authenticate, and, with two exceptions, date the newspaper clippings precisely by tracking them down in the original files in the New York Public Library and in a microfilm copy of the *Advertiser* for the Abraham Cahan–Lincoln Steffens era acquired by the San Francisco State University Library.

The texts of Cahan's writings have been reproduced in their entirety, except, in rare instances of illegibility, where we were compelled to omit a line or two. Typographical errors of course have been corrected, and oddities in spelling and punctuation and occasional grammatical slips have also been rectified. None of these trivial revisions is so indicated, for they would only distract the reader and serve no good purpose. For the same reason, we have provided essential background information in the introduction, limiting ourselves in the text itself to an occasional explanatory note.

The transliteration of Russian spelling follows the guidelines set forth in *A Manual of Style*, 12th ed. (Chicago: University of Chicago Press, 1969). In the transliteration of Hebrew and Yiddish, we have adhered to the accepted conventions.

After a long and arduous task, it is a distinct pleasure to acknowledge my obligations to those who lightened my way: I am deeply indebted to Joy Johannessen, who proved to be an utterly resourceful and totally superb editor; to Marek Web, who faithfully put at my disposal the rare resources housed at the YIVO Archives; and to Moira Anderson, who typed the manuscript with care and devotion.

Above all, my wife, Ruth, has played a critical role in the making of this book. Her assistance in selecting representative pieces and her editorial acumen based on her keen understanding of the Russian literary context have been indispensable throughout. Finally, the presence in our lives of our three daughters—Sarah, Abigail, and Rebecca—has invested all our days and years with the unquenchable vitality that is the mainspring of Abraham Cahan's new journalism.

INTRODUCTION

At the height of his fame, Abraham Cahan (1860–1951) described himself as "the best foreign language editor in the United States," an "important" American novelist, and a former "feature writer for various English language newspapers."[1] Had one of America's most original journalists elaborated further, he would have made special mention of his seminal years with the *New York Commercial Advertiser* (1897–1902). There, given free rein, he brought readers their first authentic glimpses into a vital new America in the making, an America Cahan foresaw as the vibrant world cultural center that it has become in our time.

Neither the star reporter for Lincoln Steffens's avant-garde *Advertiser* nor his gifted associates would ever forget those years. Nearly half a century later, when the newspaper was long defunct, Cahan would revel in recounting spirited stories of his tenure with the *Advertiser*. In those days, when every assignment held the potential for new literary adventure and inspired creation, when every vignette was the seed of a story and every story an incipient novel, Cahan had seen himself on the threshold of a new American literature, equal in its humanity to the unfulfilled promises of American life. Had circumstances been different, he would occasionally speculate, his major book, *The Rise of David Levinsky*—"the most remarkable contribution of an immigrant to the American novel"[2]—might have been surpassed in range, complexity, and literary power by still others. "A gifted writer," as Saul Bellow has reminded a later generation of readers, Cahan might then have gained the recognition he so avidly coveted, to be counted among America's great novelists, the peer, perhaps, of Theodore Dreiser, the American writer whose raw genius he most admired. At times, Cahan may have dreamed of serving, even if briefly and tenuously, in apostolic succession to William Dean Howells, along with Van Wyck Brooks, Randolph Bourne, and H. L. Mencken, as a recognized spokesman of a new transnational American literature, unencumbered by the genteel tradition.

More compelling public demands, however, whirled Cahan back into the Jewish immigrant maelstrom, where he became the central civic and cultural presence and the most influential Jewish tribune in the country, as he daringly transformed an unreadable sectarian Yiddish daily into an American journalistic landmark, no less than the world's greatest immigrant, socialist, and Jewish newspaper. In the strenuous opening decades of the twentieth century, Cahan had not the time, the solitude, or the freedom to pursue a major American literary career. The ever accelerating rate of change in an ever more beleaguered immigrant and Jewish world, and the automatic identification of the *Forward*'s editor with a Yiddish-speaking public, dimmed perceptions of Cahan's remarkable pioneer role as an important American novelist and virtually obliterated all traces of his *affaire de coeur* with the *Advertiser*, which had proclaimed his the first luminous inner voice of the nation's pluralistic new ethnic and urban worlds.

At the turn of the century, Cahan's carefully crafted stories, his "genuine artistic transcripts from life," and the "implicit literature" of his "hastily conceived and written newspaper reports," as his close friend Hutchins Hapgood described them, had been much admired by the discriminating few but had generated no broad-based response. By contrast, Finley Peter Dunne, whose satiric genius informed Mr. Dooley's acerbic political commentary in Irish brogue, had become a national institution. But the popular American columnist's readers were not likely to find in Cahan the Hester Street counterpart to the Irish sage of Chicago's Archey Road saloon. Even had the Russian immigrant Cahan been sufficiently ingenious to invent a cracker-barrel literary persona with as profound, as witty, and as quotable an ethnic perspective as spouted by Messrs. Hennessy and Dooley, he would have been powerless to overcome prevailing attitudes stigmatizing those for whom he spoke.

In these years, in any case, an inchoate new ethnic and Jewish America simply could not muster the cultural poise, much less the group esprit, that might somehow have generated a larger American ethnic voice. Out of step with the rhythms of a new land unattuned to their ways, young immigrants, eager for American acceptance, were without that sense of unwitting belonging that had been granted—if grudgingly—an earlier generation of newcomers like the municipally regnant American Irish. Inhabiting culturally strategic terrain between an older and newer America, Irish America's most gifted writer was able to endow a uniquely urbane, explicitly ethnic, seriocomic genre with a courtly dignity irresistible to a larger American public. Unlike the columns of thick Dooley dialect piping an elegant New World Celtic polyphony graced with a knowing, adversarial note, the green Yiddish idiom was as yet ill equipped to blend and resonate in familiar counterpoint with American speech, too undomesticated to insinuate its way onto the printed page. "When we Americans are through with the English language, it will look as if it had been run over by a musical comedy," was one of Dunne's shrewd philological quips that did not quite allow for historical contingency.[3]

Only with the waning of the immigrant generation, as the lives of Jewish and other more recent ethnics have come to be seen as integral to the American condition and deeply important in their own terms as well, have their experiences found authentic spokesmen and wide self-accepting audiences. True, in the early years of the twentieth century, the nation began to see its new ethnics with increasing familiarity, but it remained a dumb and patronizing familiarity. Only recently have we been able to accept the portrayal of the actual lives of strange others as central to our own enlarged humanity and deeper self-knowledge. Only in our time have the stories of ethnics and immigrants, written by one of their own in the impassioned yet detached spirit of Abraham Cahan at his best, won an honored place in our literature.

This anthology of Cahan's English-language journalism, therefore, is no simple commemorative response or belated tribute to a great American newspaperman over a century after his coming to America. Rather it is the first effort to recover an unknown stratum of his writings that indisputably places him at the vortex of twentieth-century American literary and journalistic culture, bringing to New York's Newspaper Row, and to all America, a rare quality, range, freshness, verve, and sense of discovery. With an acute and penetrating feeling for history, this sentient literary journalist probed American ethnic and cultural consciousness as had no one before him. Since Cahan resorted to dialect only rarely, and almost never for mere effect, his prose is not barnacled with the "Dooleyisms" that, ironically, have made Finley Peter Dunne's rollicking topical anthologies incomprehensible to a latter-day public. Combining craft, prescience, crystalline candor, and a deep compassion for everyday humanity, Cahan gave even his least-finished writings a universality and accessibility that defy fashionable literary and ideological strictures and bridge the generations even more effectively in our time than they did in his.

Cahan entered the world of American journalism at a most auspicious time. Two decades and more before the ascendance of the movies, radio, and television, no more potent instrument of mass communication was to be found than the metropolitan daily press. Scanning, canvassing, and exploring an ever more startling universe, the newspapers alone gave graphic concreteness to the quotidian deluge of events, experiences, and perceptions that assaulted the consciousness of every city inhabitant. To assure the perpetual flow of copy demanded to quench an insatiable public appetite for the latest news, newspaper editors were continually driven to recruit a numerous, enterprising, and sophisticated corps of reporters who, winning the admiration of the crowd, became instant national heroes as they daringly relayed enchanting new worlds of reality to increasingly vaster audiences.

In no time or place did newspaper reporters play so salient and so dramatic a role in shaping the popular mind as they did in New York between 1897 and 1902, when Joseph Pulitzer and William Randolph Hearst drove the "new journalism" to unprecedented heights of influence, virtuosity, and extravagance. Almost overnight, these two titans of the press appeared to validate the spirit of the new century and the hegemony of the nation's greatest city. Masters of the emerging popular idiom, they became the new American tribunes and guides for millions of perplexed new city people. Morning, noon, and night, they competed to make unlanguaged urban realities comprehensible to readers intimidated by the dense gray columns of fine print in the older papers. To bridge the growing gap between new facts and perceptions, opaque old-fashioned terms, and untrained audiences who missed the hard words, as Mencken had it, the *World* and the *Journal*, in their battles for circulation, ran ingenious line sketches and eye-catching woodcuts; introduced snappy features, saucy cartoons, comic strips, and Sunday color supplements; and let pass no stunt, crusade, promotional technique, or news invention that might further swell their mass voyeurships. Ever thicker and flashier, at one cent per copy, these bargain-basement packages of newsprint run riot, with their scare headlines, trick headlines, and headlines all in black, wauled and howled to be read.

Fortunately for Cahan, these years also spawned a radically different and little recognized "new journalism" singularly suited to his special needs. Aspiring to quiet art, this genre aimed to penetrate beneath surfaces, and to educate and extend reader sensibilities and perceptions, rather than to titillate and inflame their imaginations. In many respects, it was the direct ancestor of the piercing but often factually unreliable reporting of Tom Wolfe, Norman Mailer, and other notable contemporaries who have adopted fictional techniques to capture reader interest. The new journalism of the 1890s, like its successor of the 1960s and after, was "powered by feeling as well as intellect." [4] If it did not become emblematic of a mass revolution in manners and morals, as did the later new journalism, it too proposed to open windows on new realities, clearing the way for an era when the distinctive inner worlds of all the nation's peoples would increasingly be incorporated into an ever enlarging American public consciousness.

Cahan, of course, did not acquire his fire-line badge on Hearst's "Yellow Peril" or Pulitzer's "Hellhound of the Opposition," as sardonic newspaper people dubbed the *Journal* and the *World*, with their audiences running to a million and more. Instead, he joined the staff of the pitifully low-circulation, conservative, and decorous *Commercial Advertiser*, New York's oldest paper, founded by Noah Webster in 1793 and affectionately known as "Grandma." Thanks to the daring and imagination of a young Californian who became city editor in the fall of 1897, "Grandma" swiftly was being transformed from a blanket of dull type that incredibly had run to as many as ten columns per page, into a bright-eyed journal of culture and sensibility. Unlike the jaded mass-circulation dailies that stridently featured the aberrant, the brutal, and the bizarre in their shallow coverage of city life, the *Advertiser* proposed to portray everyday experience simply, honestly, and directly. To attain that goal, Steffens replaced shopworn professional reporters with alert inexperienced young college graduates eager to become poets, dramatists, and novelists. Urging them to write what they heard, what they saw, and as they spoke, the new city editor spiritedly solicited sketches, fiction, and special articles for New York's most distinguished Saturday supplement in the making. In addition to the array of features, feuilletons, and stories that gave the *Advertiser* distinction, Steffens daily extracted from his reporters bits and pieces of culturally informed news that captured the habits, manners, emotions, and color of the great unknown city's assorted representatives of humanity. So successful was Steffens in his efforts at high journalism that the elder statesman and cultural arbiter of American letters, William Dean Howells, insisted that no writer or artist could afford not to read the *Commercial Advertiser*.

The new paper was made for Cahan. Just a year earlier, in 1896, Howells's front-page rave review of *Yekl*, the Russian immigrant's first novel, had appeared in the Sunday *New York World*, bringing Cahan overnight fame. Along with Stephen Crane, Howells hailed Cahan as a "New Star of Realism" for rendering "the Truest Pictures of East Side Life." Steffens also admired "the original American Jewish novel,"[5] and its author promptly became the unmitered senior oracle of a brilliant band of new journalists in whom the city editor took intense pride. "Nearly all of those I have brought to the paper with me are writers, educated, thoughtful fellows with character and ambition, who are hand and glove in the conspiracy with me to make a newspaper that will have literary charm as well as daily information, mood as well as sense, gayety as well as seriousness," boasted Steffens to his father. "We are doing some things that were never done in journalism before, and I think some of our issues are better in quality and higher in spirit than any of the magazines. . . ."[6] In the *Advertiser*'s dirty city room, around a long table lighted by naked bulbs dangling from ceiling cords, the recognized novelist and cultural ambassador from the Lower East Side regularly lectured, goaded, and debated half a dozen of his young colleagues on the meaning and purpose of art. To this group dominated by Harvard graduates with literary ambitions and esthetic ideas that differed from his own, Cahan continually preached on the need for "sincerity, realism, purpose, and unity," and above all else upon the virtues of the great Russian realists—Tolstoy, Dostoyevsky, and Chekhov—whose hero was truth. "I love you . . . clever good fellows, but you are children in the fields of art,"[7] rang the cautionary refrain of the Russian immigrant writer, socialist, and former Yiddish newspaper editor, whom Steffens had hired, immediately upon assuming the city editorship, to breathe the spirit of an uncharted New York into the pallid gray columns of the city's oldest newspaper.

Along with allowing his reporters total freedom—to write as they pleased as long as they wrote interestingly, sympathetically, and naturally—Steffens nursed an overarching vision of the *Advertiser* as the self-appointed educator of its genteel readers in the everyday arts of metropolitan living. In Steffens's calculations, the special foil for his running critique of proper New York was the improper Lower East Side and the satellite immigrant quarters, which he perceived not as regions for reform, as Jacob Riis of the *Sun* viewed them, but as revolving showcases of human possibilities that challenged the assumptions of late Victorian America and intimated that life might be lived more interestingly, more generously, and more openly.

Since nothing seemed more ridiculous to respectable Americans than the public display of emotions, Steffens resolved to report incidents of gaiety in New York as conspicuously as most newspapers reported incidents of murder—on the front page—and to do the same for indignation, surprise, cunning, rage, and all other expressions of human feeling. Two composite feature articles, printed in the early months of Steffens's editorship and jointly prepared by members of the *Advertiser* staff, vividly illustrated his method of learning from life, from people who, perpetually oblivious to one another, lived their private selves in public. In a two-column article entitled "Lovemaking in New York," Steffens posed the question, "How does European expressiveness modify Puritan or Anglo-Saxon repression?" Although the article failed to explain why "Teutons" are universally prone to public squeezing or kissing while American men "drive all expressiveness of the tender mood to some invisible social recess," it succeeded in presenting a series of simple incidents, documenting what Steffens regarded as "genuinely American" love styles, which escaped the etiquette manuals and the unseeing eyes of correct New Yorkers.

In the first vignette, a portly German piano teacher, determined to marry, gallantly rushes down from his small third-floor tenement room into a tiny courtyard between his building and the adjacent one to retrieve the hat of a Fräulein whose room, directly opposite his, looks out on a common airshaft, but whose face has eluded his gaze ever since he first became aware of her presence. Glancing upward, hat in hand, the lonely forty-year-old bachelor sees for the first time what he has long hoped would please him. Catching the Fräulein's eye, he boldly asks her name and a few days later they are married in the little German church around the corner. Then there is the story of a dashing young Italian lad who sells coal on Sundays to Irish, Germans, and Italians. Wearing work clothes covered with coal dust, he is all the while carrying on a spirited flirtation with an Italian girl colorfully attired in her Sunday best. Two months later, they too are wed. Less happily, a third story focuses on a Swede's abrasive and apparently ill-fated courtship of an American-Irish girl one wintry Sunday afternoon on nearly deserted Fifth Avenue. Finally, the fourth sketch tells of a month-long daily romance between a Third Avenue cable-car conductor and a young woman passenger, a love affair so discreet in its unfolding that it entirely eludes the watchful gaze of the *Advertiser*'s reporter. Only when the conductor explains one day why the girl is no longer to be seen does the reporter learn of their marriage.

Appearing on the same page, the second composite article, "Expressions of Grief," conveys in authentic vernacular tones the heartrending grief of an Italian, a Polish, a Russian, and a Jewish mother, each mourning over the death of her child. "Alessandrino! My Baby! My active little Angel! My clear little soul with two twinkling stars for a pair of eyes . . . Poor Bambino, you have died so young! Oh how smart he was! And how well he spoke! . . . Dio! Madonna! He is dead. He is really dead," laments an Italian mother. "It were much better if I took your place. . . . Why did we take care of you? Why did your young mother sit up nights at your crib? Oh, how unjust you are, God! Such a young bird, such a sweet swallow—and here you have taken him away! What for?" grieves a Polish grandmother. In the case of the Polish, and surely in the case of the Russian and Jewish mothers, the reporter is Cahan, whose simple but powerful renditions into English project his remarkable ability to convey the cadence and idiom of Russian and Yiddish speech. A distraught Russian woman, on the verge of cutting her throat, Cahan notes, had been on the way to a mining town in Pennsylvania to join her husband when her four-year-old daughter fell sick and died in an East Side boardinghouse. "What is the trouble, little mother?" asks the sympathetic reporter. Astonished to hear Russian in the strange land to which she has come, the distressed woman forgets herself and smiles momentarily before pouring out her indescribable woe.

Why did you desert me, my bright dove? Did I not pamper you enough? Did I not caress you? Did I ever take my eyes off you? Did I not pray to you, God? Did I not keep you under my heart for nine months? Did I not guard you—did I not cherish my lovely one? Awake! Open your eyes, dovey! Get up, hope of the family! Come, we shall feed you—we shall catch your little fingers as before! Oh, why did you not take counsel with us? Why, oh, why, did you confide your secret to none but the damp earth?

Similarly, but in an entirely different idiom, the Jewish mother gives vent to her despair. "My crown, my kingdom, my wealth," she moans, as the casket containing the body of her firstborn is carried out of the room.

> The temple I have been building has suddenly fallen to pieces. Ai, the crown has been torn off my head. Woe! The shine of my eyes is put out and it is all dark, dark, dark around me! What shall I do except to dig a pit and descend into it? But if Thou doest a thing it must be right, Lord of the World, for Thou art right and Thy judgment is just and I must accept Thy lashes with love and contentment! Oi, oi, I am dying. Save me, good people—come and save me or I shall swoon away![8]

Abraham Cahan arrived in America on June 6, 1882, a banner year in the epic of immigration. One of nearly 800,000 newcomers—the greatest number to enter the country in a single year before the twentieth century, and the heaviest immigration in history from Germany and Scandinavia—he also came in the vanguard of the great Jewish migration that would transform New York in less than two decades into the greatest, most vibrant, and most diverse center of Jewish life in all of Jewish history. Singularly attuned to the immense drama of uprooting, Cahan became the first new American to make his life and work into a total expression and instrument of what the distinguished American sociologist Robert Park called "a new literature and a new culture based on the life of the common man."[9]

Upon reaching New York, Cahan was a Russian immigrant, not yet twenty-two years old, with, at best, half a dozen newly learned English words on his lips, yet he was to become more rooted in that city than any American writer of his time. By comparison, Cahan's contemporaries—Howells, Crane, and even Dreiser—were mere sojourners, ever lodging in an alien terrain, for whom the inhabitants of the city remained strangers, just as the people they portrayed in their fiction were invariably visitors or victims in a city they never came to know and were eager to desert. Cahan, however, had already spent most of his adult life, before joining the *Advertiser*, learning the ways of the living city from the ground up. True, his experiences had been largely confined to the

Lower East Side, but by 1897 he had thoroughly assimilated the ethnic, the American, and the cosmopolitan components of that district's turbulent spirit. By the time the *Advertiser* offered him the chance to do so, he was better equipped to tackle the greater immigrant metropolis than were any of his contemporaries.

One of tens of thousands of immigrants and Americans who had found a home in New York in the expansive eighties, Cahan had shared personally in every aspect of that experience. Despite the distance his artistic temperament and Russian education put between him and most of his fellow immigrants, he saw his future inseparably identified with theirs. He had worked in factories, had founded labor unions, had played a leading role in socialist politics and, as a popular Socialist party speaker, had repeatedly toured the larger and smaller cities of the Northeast, addressing American as well as immigrant working people in a score of factory towns and industrial centers from the Boston Common to the South Side of Chicago. He had also edited and written for four Yiddish journals—two weeklies, a literary monthly, and the newly founded daily *Forward*—had taught fellow immigrants English for over a decade at the city's adult evening schools, the first to do so, and over the years, had intermittently contributed reports, sketches, and translations to the American socialist and general press. In the early nineties, Cahan had gone abroad three times, twice as the sole representative of the Jewish labor movement at the second and third congresses of the Second Socialist International. To cap it all, he was the author of the first authentic novel of the immigrant city, which, despite its flaws, came closer to portraying the real people of New York than did the work of any other novelist.

In the course of fifteen years, Cahan had witnessed the New York ghetto evolve from a scorned, ragged, down-at-heel quarter into a great cosmopolitan and Jewish crossroads at the heart of the world's greatest and most diverse immigrant metropolis. Out of such intimacy with his surroundings would come Cahan's singular capacity for writing about flesh-and-blood people of a dozen different nationalities. Distinctive in their names, addresses, and mannerisms, as well as in their speech, dress, diet, and behavior, Cahan's people were real human beings with complex lives and feelings. Here were not to be met the skeletal, wraithlike creatures of Crane's *Maggie* or the manikins of Steffens's Jewish stories or the cartoons of Richard Harding Davis's and Edward Waterman Townsend's faddish Gallegher and Chimmie Fadden Bowery dialect tales.

In Cahan's writings, one does not hear the tireless roar of electricity and steam, the endless whirl, clang, and clatter of trolley car, ambulance, and fire engine; one does not experience the hopelessness and impersonality of the totally secular city of flickering streetlights, damp pavements, and looming tenements, factories, and warehouses without end. What one does encounter is a glowing sense of life, sustained in voice, language, nuance, and especially situation—of a tumultuously varied ethnic, religious, and human milieu where people emerging from age-old constraints inhale the alternately liberating and intimidating air of the great American city. Mingling the most exalted expressions of the human spirit with the peddler's cry and the urchin's bawl, Cahan wrote in the vernacular rhythms of the people. Despite recurrent tragedy, loneliness, desperation, and bewilderment, his people were not pauperized remnants without familial supports and community associations. Ultimately, Cahan's New York and theirs was no urban wasteland or wilderness but a new cosmopolis of the spirit, where a journalist struggling to assimilate the ways and woes of the city's many peoples to his own understanding, virtually through his pores, might lift his experiences, and theirs, into words.

Cahan, it must also be remembered, wrote for the *Advertiser* in the years when the United States was emerging as a world power with New York at its epicenter. The ringing out of gas-lit old New York and the ringing in of the incandescent greater city came just as the arrival of the twentieth century appeared to release new nationalizing forces and expectations, crowned by spectacular events that contributed to a sense of high drama, of precipitous change, of the rapid passing of the old and the dashing advent of the new. More so than any other American, New York's own Teddy Roosevelt became the flamboyant embodiment of the energetic, all-embracing, youthful world nation of the new century. In six dramatic years, Roosevelt rose successively through the offices of president of the New York Board of Police Commissioners, assistant secretary of the Navy, colonel of the Rough Riders, governor of New York, and vice-president of the United States, and, at forty-two years of age, he became the youngest president in American history. While the expansive Manhattan-born young Knickerbocker aimed to weld the newer American West to the older American East, Rocky Mountain tough with New York tenderfoot, in the name of an all-embracing American world nation, the Lower East Side American and Russian-Jewish newspaperman, just two years Roosevelt's junior, labored to bridge the chasm between newer immigrants and older Americans, between Old World and New, in the name of a more complex and deeply felt American world civilization.

Rarely has a great city's consciousness of itself as the dynamic confluence of old and new intruded so poignantly into the bone and marrow of a writer. In the final years of the nineteenth century, a whole American chapter of Cahan's life was coming to a close. The tiny, lovingly remembered attic home on Clinton Street, where he had lived during his first three years in America and where he had celebrated his first American New Year with fellow Russian intellectuals, had given way to a massive tenement; the old ghetto milieu at Bayard and Catherine Streets, the setting for his novella, *The Imported Bridegroom*, had become extinct; and the school where the unflappable Chrystie Street schoolteacher, as he was known, had taught English to fellow immigrants for a dozen years, had been reduced to rubble. Suddenly it appeared that even the immigrant epic of Russian pioneers like himself was destined for oblivion. It was time to take stock before it was too late—and to write. While the old still remained altogether vivid and the new appeared totally fresh, memories, affections, and the crosscurrents set in motion by adventure upon adventure would flow together in Cahan's columns, stories, and articles, leaving rich tracings of that larger voyage of spirit and sensibility. With near Tolstoyan amplitude, Cahan would reach out to embrace the new world of Americans-in-becoming, a world that eluded the older American imagination and that he felt compelled to impress upon the American consciousness with all of his integrity and art.

In the course of assembling and identifying Cahan's varied writings, we have aimed first to unravel the design that the hustling reporter had neither the time nor the impulse to contemplate. Second, we have attempted to convey to the reader the cool excitement that surges through Cahan's unique journalism, where the stumbling interview with its immediacy of revelation becomes a study in character or the vehicle for a totally unanticipated experience, while an incident rich in human interest becomes the germ of a sketch or story. This was the way of the Russian newspapers, where, as Cahan noted, "the quintessence of the matter" was stressed, leaving "the reader to supply the rest from his imagination."

Inevitably, in choosing among hundreds of items, we have had to be highly selective. We have not included the columns Cahan wrote on wheelmen (bicyclists), rapid transit and Barge Office investigations, and the extension of the Long Island Railroad to Port Washington; on the cross-eyed in Europe and America; on the Hudson River Valley as seen from the deck of an Albany Day Line steamer; and on his first day at the races. Nor have we included his interviews with the surviving crew members of a sunken French steamship or the shipwrecked sailors rescued in the wake of a hurricane off Barbados. He clearly was responsible for dozens, perhaps scores of columns that totally eluded our net, including an interview with Roosevelt and another with McKinley aboard a Hudson River ferry. In almost all cases, the criteria that guided us were those we felt would have guided the author—human interest, variety, representativeness, a sense of the larger pattern—and, of course, space.

The anthology has been organized partly along topical and partly along chronological lines so that the reader is provided with both a larger intellectual portrait and a dramatic running account of Cahan's new journalism. Topically, it is divided into six parts, each subdivided into chapters. Within each chapter the pieces are arranged chronologically, except where a piece serves to frame a chapter at beginning or end, or where several pieces have been grouped around themes within a chapter. In this way, the anthology portrays primarily the inner lives of the new peoples of the pulsating New York metropolis, as mediated through "the fresh staring eyes" and the trifocal lenses of a Jew, a Russian, and a new American—new in sensibility and artistic tact, no less than in his choice of subject matter. It projects as well the inner and outer worlds of one of America's most original citizens and most extraordinary newspapermen.

Part One: Tremors of the Twentieth Century

The book opens with the Spanish-American War, the Dreyfus Affair, and the Kishinev massacre—three events of international significance that provide the public historic frame for Cahan's *Advertiser* years. If the war profoundly affected all Americans, the Dreyfus trials and the notorious tsarist pogrom especially affected Cahan and his fellow Jews. All three events were of pivotal importance for the shaping of Cahan's life and of things to come, and his coverage of them is crucial to an understanding of his journalism.

No event more dramatically signaled both the opening of the twentieth century and the onset of modern newspaper history than did the Spanish-American War. Officially, at least, it broke out six months after Cahan joined the *Advertiser*. Unofficially, the war had been brewing for decades, as Cuban rebels, abetted by American sympathizers, struggled to free the island from Spanish rule. As is generally known, the unsparing efforts of William Randolph Hearst drove Joseph Pulitzer's *World* and much of the American press to bring the "*Journal*'s war" home to their readers in a suicidal battle for circulation that is without parallel in American newspaper history. Within weeks, hundreds of reporters, artists, and photographers were dispatched to the Caribbean war theater. Hearst himself led a personal expeditionary force of newspapermen to Cuba, which included a crew of typesetters equipped with their own portable printing press. While the swashbuckling Richard Harding Davis became the war's most celebrated correspondent as he reported the exploits of the Rough Riders in heroic Kiplingesque prose, a faltering Stephen Crane, who would be dead in two years at age twenty-eight, brought to the battlefront his rare if not fully appreciated talents for realism and truth.

Without the resources of the newspaper giants, the *Advertiser* made only modest efforts to cover the fighting directly. Instead, it devoted major attention to documenting those aspects of the war that could be reported closer to home. Cahan's assignments reflected *Advertiser* priorities and the spirit of Lincoln Steffens's new journalism, as is evident in chapter 1, The New World Power. After inquiring, listening, and recording, Cahan wrote of Germans and Hungarians uninhibitedly debating the war in Second Avenue cafés; of immigrant patriotism, heroism, and skepticism; of the attitudes of Jewish immigrants and their children toward the war; and of the immigrant passion for books about war heroes, especially the romantic new naval heroes Richmond Hobson and George Dewey. Cahan also shared pallet and grub with soldiers at rest camps and took down their vividly recalled versions of the "Song of the Mauser"; he talked with the men of the Ninth "Immunes," one of four black regiments, and found that some had learned Spanish, others had brought brides home from Cuba, and still others, contrary to all expectations, had contracted yellow fever; and he interviewed Major General Wheeler, who looked like "Fighting Joe," but who turned out to be a courtly, soft-spoken southern gentleman. Indeed, the only genuine war pieces that Cahan contributed to the *Advertiser* were his splendid translations from two superb antiwar stories by the Russian writer Vsevolod Garshin (1855–88), "Blows and Bullets" and the tremendously popular "Left on a Battlefield," better known as "Four Days." Inspired by Tolstoy's Sebastopol tales, these stories were based on the author's experiences during the Russo-Turkish War twenty years earlier and depicted war through the eyes of the ordinary soldier. In their fidelity to reality, if not in their imaginative power, they surpass Stephen Crane's *tour de force*, *The Red Badge of Courage*, which portrayed the Civil War as seen by a bewildered American farm lad.

No less than the Spanish-American War, the Dreyfus Affair proved to be a harbinger of the twentieth century. Again Cahan and the *Advertiser* reported the reaction at home rather than covering the event firsthand. Though it has since been called "a kind of dress rehearsal for the performance of our own time" and "the only episode in which the subterranean forces of the nineteenth century enter the full light of recorded history,"[10] the Dreyfus Affair did not appear quite so demonic at the time, when no one, of course, could foresee the horrors of Nazism. In 1894, Captain Alfred Dreyfus had been arrested on charges of high treason, condemned to public military degradation, and sentenced to solitary confinement for life on Devil's Island, the notorious prison colony off the coast of French Guiana. Only four years later, in August 1898, did Americans of all kinds, not primarily Jews, become aware of the implications of that tragic travesty of justice. The confession and suicide of Colonel Hubert-Joseph Henry, a bungling careerist caught up in the coils of his own falsehoods, set in motion Dreyfus's second trial, this time by court-martial. For over a month in the summer of 1899, international attention, informed by the daily accounts of three hundred on-the-scene reporters, was focused on the returned prisoner from Devil's Island. To the world's astonishment, Dreyfus was again found guilty. Given a ten-year sentence by the court, he was abruptly pardoned a week later by the president of the Third French Republic.

On the Lower East Side, the Dreyfus Affair, which had been simmering for some years, ranked next to the war with Spain in the consciousness of Jewish immigrants. Both events reinforced their passion for their newly adopted country, the universal upholder of law, liberty, and the rights of the oppressed, as the Cahan pieces in chapter 2, The Old World Scourge, make clear. A few years after Dreyfus's pardon, on Russian Easter 1903, a barbaric attack perpetrated upon the Jews of Kishinev by suborned mobs aroused world indignation. In an article for the *Advertiser*, Cahan reported on that event by special invitation, for by then he was no longer with the paper. Writing in a personal vein, he related the terrible slaughter at Kishinev to that "chapter in the history of my unhappy people" which began with the pogroms of 1881–82 that first sparked mass migration. In Cahan's judgment, the latest massacre augured revolution.

Part Two: Faith and Tradition at Bay

If distant catastrophes framed the world of Jewish immigrants, more immediately threatening was the great world that crowded its way into their consciousness and assaulted their way of life at every turn. At no time or place was the "living, but rapidly crumbling relic of a musty past bubbling over with intellectual and emotional energy"[11] as nakedly visible as it was in turn-of-the-century New York. And no American wrote more knowingly and more felicitously of Jewish religious traditions, customs, and observances under siege than did Cahan in his *Advertiser* years, as is abundantly demonstrated in the pieces in chapter 3, Two Worlds and Two Souls.

Not unlike the scholarly old physician in the opening sketch, "Talmudism at the Brooklyn Bridge," which juxtaposes the two most fully realized contemporary symbols of the old Jewish and the new American worlds, Cahan was a modern man. But he was a modern man with a difference, for his unqualified apostasy in no way diminished his capacity to recreate in loving detail the most deeply felt religious emotions and experiences of his fellow Jewish immigrants. Hutchins Hapgood, that most sensitive of observers, refrained from directly describing Jewish religious life in his classic, *The Spirit of the Ghetto*,[12] for he was fully aware of how remote were Jewish ritual, liturgy, and inspiration from his own experience and well knew that only his Lower East Side mentor and friend, Abraham Cahan, could authentically portray so dense, textured, and intricate a religious world. Steeped in the old Jewish ways in early childhood and youth, in later life Cahan cherished Jewish graces and conventions, furtively and reflexively relived the old emotions, and inadvertently even relished talmudic allusions. In often glowing prose, he explored the immensity of an antique Jewish civilization, still in being but no longer in full sail, as it heaved and buckled before the sweeping winds of modernity. For example, in column and story, Cahan captured the disarming impact upon Jewish immigrants in the heart of the Lower East Side of an American Christmas totally devoid of anti-Jewish sentiment. In "Rabbi Eliezer's Christmas," he tells of the encounter between a poor, perplexed newsstand keeper and two condescending, good settlement house ladies who are unexpectedly generous to him on Christmas Day, leading Eliezer to fear that his acceptance of their gift might be interpreted as an acknowledgment on his part of the Christian God. The poignant private and public struggle of this obsolete former master scribe of sacred Hebrew literature with his conscience reflects Cahan's unfailing sense of the moral complexity of the total immigrant experience.

The religiously ordered Jewish calendar that Cahan had lived with in Vilna, the Jerusalem of Lithuania and the city of his boyhood, was reincarnated in New York, where fasts and feasts alike leapt from the pages of the *Advertiser* in often lyrical and always authoritative columns, as they did in no other newspaper in the English-speaking world. Indeed, Cahan's career with the *Advertiser* had been launched by a series of articles on the coming of the Jewish New Year that had been published in the *New York Evening Post*, the city's most prestigious and most literary daily. The *Post*'s assistant city editor, Lincoln Steffens, had immediately recognized the difference between Cahan's authentic copy and his own often stilted reports of the Jewish holidays and somewhat supercilious stories of Jewish tenement life. The opening paragraph of Cahan's first column, "When the Shofar Blows," sang in almost metered liturgical prose of an intense religious civilization, singularly awesome and ecstatic in this holy season, which commemorated the biblical creation of the world in an age of geological and Darwinian time.

> The ghetto is all bustle and hurry, preparing for the great season of song and prayer which begins Monday. It is the Jewish New Year, the 5658th anniversary of the creation of the world. Ushered in by ten days of penance, the approaching holidays are to cover a period of

more than three weeks, in the course of which the neighborhood will ring now with sobs of worshippers for a happy new year, now with "Rejoicing of the Law!"[13]

Cahan's High Holiday columns for the *Post* set the stage for dozens more on Jewish religious life that were to follow in the *Advertiser* in the next few years. Some of the best of these are collected in chapter 4, Seasons for Song and Prayer. Annually, as the holidays came due—beginning with Rosh Hashana and Yom Kippur and followed by the Feast of Tabernacles, the Rejoicing of the Law, Chanukah, Purim, Passover, Shavuot, and the Ninth of Av—Cahan would recreate each observance in his column. Without fail, he would elaborate on some little-known ceremony or prayer by relating a colorful legend or incident or by explaining a historical allusion or a newly detected nuance that brought depth, freshness, and resonance to his account.

Unlike the leading examplars of modern journalism and literature for whom religious matters were incidental, Cahan celebrated a heroic Jewish civilization that he considered obsolete intellectually but that emotionally and culturally remained inseparable from his sense of self and from that transcendent Jewish community for which the Sabbath was recurrently the most momentous festival of all. In his columns heralding the Sabbath day's coming, Cahan invariably invoked the Hester Street fishmonger's pre-Sabbath sales pitch, first heard late Thursday afternoon, which shouted the virtues of the Lower East Side's most prized Sabbath dinner delicacy in the street's most familiar and oft-heard refrain, "Fish, fish, living, floundering, jumping, dancing fish!"

Part Three: The Chasm

The inspiration for many of Cahan's most genuine and unaffected columns derived from his daily association not only with the inhabitants of the Lower East Side but with the throngs of "green" immigrants who continually debarked at the Battery. From the middle of 1897 to the end of 1900, while the Ellis Island buildings that had been destroyed by fire were being rebuilt, the readily accessible Barge Office served as temporary receiving station and halfway house for the latest newcomers to America. At the foot of Manhattan Island, near Castle Garden, where immigrants had come ashore since the seventeenth century, the Barge Office was within easy walking distance of Newspaper Row and the *Advertiser* offices, making it possible for Cahan to meet the boatloads of immigrants as they landed and to write about them regularly. Chapter 5, The

Barge Office, contains some of these renowned *Advertiser* sketches, which were the most informative evocations of the newcomers' initial reactions to their new country to appear in the daily press and in the whole literature of immigration.

Voraciously interviewing every kind of immigrant to come his way, Cahan faithfully transcribed their words in their own voices. Kaleidoscopic in his coverage, he portrayed Armenians, Greeks, Syrians, Germans, Italians, Poles, Lithuanians, Slovaks, Czechs, Hungarians, Russians, Ruthenians, Georgians, Russo-Germans, Swedes, and virtually every species of East European. All emerge not as types but as distinct individuals, sharing similar experiences in their special way as they hopefully await friends, relatives, sweethearts, fellow townspeople, and representatives of immigrant societies who will relieve them of the agonies and anxieties of being total strangers in a new land.

In these columns, Cahan was unerringly successful in conveying the sense of the American wonderland as seen through the bewildered eyes of immigrants, who invariably looked up to all Americans, beginning with the uniformed immigration inspectors, as noblemen—though by all means American noblemen—whose blessed company they clearly aspired to join. For these newcomers, a change of headgear especially worked miracles. A battered old derby in place of a cap instantly seemed to transform a European peasant into an American gentleman. Bonnet in place of kerchief, a jacket, and Grand Street shoes proved equally wondrous in turning wife or sweetheart into an American lady, at least in her eyes. The proverbial role of the famed Barge Office mother in straightening out marital and legal problems, the Rumanian exodus that recalled its Russian forerunner, the indignities and perplexities experienced by detained immigrants never quite certain that they had indeed reached the mythic new land, and Cahan's recollections of his own image of America upon arrival—all were part of the range of intimately felt experience that Cahan regularly injected into the columns of the *Advertiser*.

The area of human relations that obsessed Cahan above all others is the subject of chapter 6, Love and Marriage. Inevitably a major preoccupation for an author of stories and novels, the relations between the sexes provided Cahan with an unusual challenge. No sphere of immigrant life seemed more threatened by radical modification in the encounter between Europe and America, and nowhere was the change so disconcerting. It was the "international situation," as Henry James called it, the Europe-America relationship, not as seen from the cozy niche of an observer of the leisured international set in Paris or London, but the Jamesian drama as portrayed from within the eye of the New York maelstrom, where Old World conventions of love, courtship, marriage, and family relations were being shaken to their core. Cahan's reports, sketches, and stories abound with the maneuvers of matchmakers, marriage brokers, and matrimonial agents as "thick as huckleberries"; with the stratagems of arranged, proxy, and diploma marriages; with the dilemmas of imported brides, if not the famed Japanese picture brides, and college bridegrooms; with the stresses and strains of unexpected romances, love matches, and intermarriages. The jumble of calculation, confusion, affection, agony, and frustration that coursed through every immigrant breast and tenement flat was the stuff of a new international literature of psychological realism, spurring Cahan to transform his human-interest pieces into over a dozen love stories that found their way into the *Advertiser*'s Saturday supplement, *Scribner's*, the *Atlantic Monthly*, and other well-known national magazines.

In sketches and stories, Cahan knowingly portrayed men and women of varied antecedents as they groped for one another in transit between continents and civilizations, attempting to find their bearings by overcoming the loneliness in their own hearts. Cahan was especially drawn to the plight of exiled European noblemen who, under American conditions, found themselves ordinary immigrants, the Noblemen No More of chapter 7. More acutely and dramatically than others, they suffered the pangs of social displacement and isolation, feeling estranged from the American and ethnic worlds around them no less than from the countries of their birth. Some of them were like his fictional Georgian nobleman, Tzinchadzi of the Catskills, who was inspired by Cahan's meeting with David Kadzbaya, leader of the Georgian horsemen who performed with Buffalo Bill. Prosperous and successful, Tzinchadzi, who renamed himself Jones, bemoaned his lost integrity of soul. Other, less exotic aristocrats found themselves ennobled by work. No longer cutting the figure of the moneyless baron, "the worst kind of hunchback the world ever saw," noblemen regarded as the "shiftless good-for-nothings" of Europe were delighted to be known simply as "plain" citizens. Cahan even wrote of a poor German immigrant, churlishly nicknamed Count Long-or-Round, who managed to live down that handicap by sheer hard work.

Chapter 8, Living in the Public Eye, focuses on the street and tenements of the Lower East Side, an area of the city once thickly settled with German residents but becoming pronouncedly more Jewish. This was Cahan's turf, its people the fellow immigrants whose lives he shared. Unlike the *Journal* and *World* reporters, Cahan was never tempted to descend to the "take the roofs off the house" school of shudder journalism. Where the walls between the public domain and individual privacy were permeable or virtually nonexistent, Cahan had almost unlimited entree to the lives of his neighbors. He wrote with zest of the perennial landlord-tenant altercations that reached their climax on the first of every month. He made note of the artifices to which tenants resorted to avoid payment of rent and of the strategies employed by rent collectors and real estate agents to track down truants and defaulters. He clambered up the common stairwells, walked the hallways, and peered down the airshafts in search of good stories. Amidst the babble of many tongues and dialects, Cahan insistently recorded the everyday drama in the lives of close-living people. He recreated incidents, odd, tragic, often quietly heroic ones, that routinely obtruded in quarters where birth and death were almost as readily observable as fires, family quarrels, and the pushcart trade. His mildly censorious tale of a slumming visitor from the country, eager to be titillated by an excursion through the "sodden depths" of the subworld of the "other half," pointed its own moral. After attending a Saturday night dance in the company of a "slumologist" friend, she departed, disappointed, "with not one honest shudder to carry home."

Part Four: The Bridge

In the fifteen years that he had lived in New York before joining the *Advertiser*, no one had been more deeply implicated in the cultural and intellectual life of the Lower East Side than had Abraham Cahan. It might have been expected, therefore, that so widely acknowledged and influential a figure would have reported extensively on the Yiddish rialto and Yiddish Newspaper Row, where the new American immigrant culture was most readily observed and admired. This did not prove to be the case. Since Hutchins and Norman Hapgood were especially drawn to the higher manifestations of immigrant life in Yiddish as well as in German, Italian, and Chinese New York, and wrote about them with much sympathy, insight, and enthusiasm, Cahan had no difficulty in vigilantly maintaining his critical distance from the Yiddish cultural scene. As an insider, he was freed to write articles like those in chapter 9, Daily Arts and Letters, on subjects that were uniquely accessible to one with his sensibility, cultural intelligence, and journalistic method. Cahan's columns on the drama and the press, the professional letter writers, the vendors and writers of pulp romances, and his profile of pioneer Yiddish lexicographer Alexander Harkavy radiate his singular angle of vision, illuminated with flashes of wit, pathos, and empathy.

With little taste for but much curiosity about ideological politics, *Advertiser* readers also perused columns like those in chapter 10, Ideologues of the Left and Right—informative interviews with anarchists, socialists, and positivists, as well as with the business tycoon Russell Sage, often mixed with elegiac personal reminiscences of Cahan's first years in New York. In columns on an old Polish revolutionary and on the Danish-born author of *The Cooperative Commonwealth*, Laurence Gronlund, one of the first to write on Marxism in English, Cahan paid his respects to those who had been unable to change with the times and had fallen into obscurity or were no more. On the other hand, in an interview with his close friend Louis Miller, the acting editor of the *Forward*, Cahan made it evident that the "new nihilism" in Russia bore little resemblance to the old, and that Russian Social Democracy shared the same principles and ideals that informed its equally new American counterpart. Cahan proved especially solicitous of the much-maligned and harassed anarchists Errico Malatesta, Emma Goldman, Johann Most, and Peter Kropotkin, as well as of a self-proclaimed anarchist disciple of the only true philosophical anarchist, Herbert Spencer. These interviews reflected the continued popular fascination with the shocking expounders of violence, but more important, they revealed Cahan's unswerving dedication to promoting a courageous press and informed public mind. Cahan was particularly attentive to the fate of the prematurely aged Most, the most defiant and persecuted radical of them all, who, as publisher of a German anarchist paper, had been arrested for absentmindedly reprinting on the day of President McKinley's assassination an ancient editorial on the use of dynamite. Although absolutely no one other than the arresting detective had even read the editorial, the hapless anarchist was sentenced to a year in jail. Cahan's laconic report of the hearings and the failed efforts of his friend and fellow socialist Morris Hillquit to win his first civil liberties case was statement enough of the tragedy.

If major party politics interested Cahan only incidentally, their everyday human dimensions fascinated him mightily. Chapter 11, Affairs of State, includes his interview with poker-faced Boss Richard Croker after the defeat of Tammany Hall's gubernatorial candidate by Theodore Roosevelt; his columns on the orators and spellbinders of the East Side, and on German and Jewish voting patterns; and best of all, his wry sketch of the beneficence of American ward politics as seen through the uncomprehending eyes of Jewish immigrants. These pieces especially reflect Cahan's direct way of perceiving reality. As a loyal supporter of the new Social Democratic party, however, he clearly revealed his sympathies in his interviews with that party's first officeholders. For Cahan, the mayors of Brockton and Haverhill and the two state legislators, solid Americans all, and Massachusetts Yankees to boot, projected the new promise of American life.

The labor movement, no less than socialist politics, found in Cahan, the former labor organizer and labor editor, its faithful reporter and conscientious historian. Chapter 12, The Rights of Labor, reviews labor developments in the course of Cahan's fifteen-year involvement and illuminates the working conditions, organization, and psychology of Jewish immigrants as they became less exuberant and more practical and "American" in their behavior. Whether writing of cloakmakers, jacketmakers, tailors, bakers, or cigarmakers, Cahan left no doubt that secular and religious impulses were inextricably bound together. An annual strike by coatmakers on the ninth day of the Jewish month of Av, when the faithful mourned the fall of the First and Second Temples in Jerusalem, had special meaning for the heirs of an antique religious tradition bursting with summonses to social justice, and its significance may not have been altogether lost on *Advertiser* readers.

In virtually all of Cahan's writings, real women appear as a central presence. The pieces in chapter 13, Females and Feminists, however, focus on women in distinctive roles. Whether writing of them as employers, landladies, factory hands, strikers, servants, plaintiffs or witnesses in court, housewives, or inspired synagogue celebrants on the one day of the year when they were admitted to the main sanctuary, Cahan portrayed women as people. In his stories and especially in his two novels, *The White Terror and the Red* and *The Rise of David Levinsky*, women are Cahan's most fully realized characters, with the moral strength, endurance, capacity for self-sacrifice, and idealism that mark them as beautiful in the tradition of Turgenev's heroines.

Part Five: The Arena

The Lower East Side in its every mood and phase gave resonance to Cahan's columns, articles, and stories, and remained the hub of his universe. But in chapter 14, Fancy Free, the whole metropolis is his "beat." He went out to a Long Island village near Newton to describe the critical role played by Mike and Mikova, a Polish-Jewish couple, in easing the entry into American life of a colony of industrious Polish immigrants. He attended a Russian church service honoring the czar's cousin on his visit to New York. He wrote of a lost old American on the Upper East Side, "a foreigner in his own birthplace," who, isolated and alone among Czechs, Hungarians, Germans, and Italians, acted out his ambivalent emotions. He dropped over to lower Washington Street, where young Syrian revolutionaries plotted and dreamed, almost like Russians. At Madison Square Garden, he covered a traditional cakewalk contest, where blacks gracefully mimicked white plantation styles, and he also interviewed Buffalo Bill's Cossacks, recruited to perform in Bill Cody's Wild West Congress of Rough Riders, who proved to be no Cossacks at all but the first proud Georgians to reach the United States. And in richly peopled classroom sketches like "Two Boys from Asia" and "Cats, Rats, and Mats," Cahan wrote, with freshness, a keen ear for speech patterns, and restrained humor, of the public adult evening classes for immigrants, where he long had served as American preceptor.

Criminal trials, the most sensational of all newspaper stories, found Cahan in sober attendance. The whole courtroom drama, often humorous and with unexpected possibilities for human interest, not to mention the verbatim testimony, which spoke for itself, was ideally suited to Cahan's reporting style. Of the six major criminal trials he covered for the *Advertiser*, Cahan was most fascinated by the thirteen-week-long trial of socialite chemist Roland B. Molineux on the charge of poisoning Mrs. Katherine Adams, a case that Dreiser planned to transform into literature in his discarded novel, *The Rake*. So intrigued was Cahan by the Molineux case that after he left the *Advertiser* he doggedly attended the retrial on his own for weeks. The criminal Passions on Trial in chapter 15, as well as the absurd arraignment of the renowned actress Olga Nethersole for indecency in her performance of Daudet's *Sappho*, the case of the Yiddish parrot, and a series of East Side district court trials gave scope to Cahan's unrelenting curiosity, his characteristic sobriety, and his eye for the revealing remark or telling detail.

Part Six: The Frame of Soul

Cahan inhabited a terrain of the spirit that was as central to his writings as it was to his person. Both Russian and universal, it inspired him with an unbending belief in himself and in his role as an apostle of Russian literature and of the Russian struggle for freedom. Recognized as America's best-known Russian writer, its most ardent literary disciple of Tolstoy, and its preeminent spokesman for Russian literary culture, Cahan at times readily slipped into the persona of a *barin* or Russian nobleman, as in the fictionalized reminiscence in Chapter 16, Life in Russia: A Backward Glance. "The Young Pomeschik" portrays a boyhood not like his own but like that of Peter Lavrov, the Nestor of revolutionary Russia, to whom he paid high tribute and with whom he so readily identified. In "The Share of Count Brantsev," Cahan experimented with a romantic story that was to be central to his novel *The White Terror and the Red*, published four years later. The book deserves more attention than it has received, for it is the only novel in any language to portray the revolutionary plot culminating in the assassination of Alexander II, the ensuing anti-Jewish riots, and the moral crisis that overtook Jewish university students and others when the revolutionaries failed to condemn the pogroms. Their dilemma in having to choose between migrating to America or Palestine or holding fast in Russia marked one of the great turning points in Jewish history. However flawed as a work of art, the novel portrays the Russian revolutionaries as models of heroic virtue, as historians generally have known them to be, and not as the subterranean grotesques who people two of Joseph Conrad's most brilliant novels.

Long acknowledged as the pioneer Chekhov critic in the United States, Cahan was also the first to introduce—prematurely as it proved, for the public was as yet unprepared—all the new Russian writers: Vladimir Korolenko, Ignaty Potapenko, Maxim Gorky, and others.[14] At a time when no American magazine editor was at all interested, Cahan translated some of the best contemporary Russian short stories for the *Advertiser*. His renditions of the two Garshin war stories reprinted in chapter 1 were followed by translations of three memorable stories by the long-since-forgotten Potapenko, ranked only after Tolstoy, Chekhov, and Korolenko by contemporary critics, and especially admired by Cahan, as by Chekhov, for his stories of university and intellectual life. Cahan also translated the first important Chekhov story to be published in the United States, which he called "The Fated Functionary" ("Smert' chinovnik"). Regarded as a minor masterpiece, the story most recently has been rendered as "The Death of a Civil Servant," and its two characters, Cherviakov (worm) and Bryzhalov (spray), have adroitly been dubbed with their onomatopoetic English name equivalents, Kreepikov and Shpritzhalov.[15]

For Cahan, literature, the new journalism, and the battle for the good society were all inseparable from the quest for the "truth in life and letters," which linked the American reform tradition and the best in the new Russia with the universal struggle for justice and freedom. Opening chapter 17, Literature and Truth, is "Howells on Zola," an interview with Cahan's sponsor and friend, which provides a vivid commentary on the bonds that united these two American writers, as well as a rare and revealing snapshot of Howells, and incidentally of Cahan. A few days earlier, Émile Zola (1840–1902) had been condemned to a year in prison for his brilliant open letter *J'accuse*, which denounced the key members of the French general staff for their complicity in the Dreyfus Affair. Although Howells had failed to persuade the Author's Club to officially extend its sympathy to the great French novelist and crusader for justice, he remained as optimistic as ever regarding the ultimate triumph of right. Cahan clearly shared that faith with him.

INTRODUCTION

Like Howells, Cahan was obsessed in his literary criticism with the fidelity of literature to life, for realism, of course, was central to their conception of truth, as is implicit in Cahan's verbatim reports of Israel Zangwill's and Hamlin Garland's lectures and in his translation of Vera Mikulich's reminiscences of Dostoyevsky. When *Cosmopolitan* serialized Tolstoy's new novel, *Resurrection*, the widely circulated national magazine, which had published two of Cahan's stories, outraged him by altering Aylmer Maude's authorized translation, changing the title to *The Awakening*, and distorting the meaning and moral intent of the novel. In a review article of a new twelve-volume American edition of Tolstoy's works, Cahan paid tribute to Tolstoy's unmatched talent for arriving at truth through the keenest and most unflinching observation, the gift of his universally recognized genius. In an especially astute piece summing up the long-term trends of modern Russian literature, Cahan rejoiced in the still little-known Chekhov, seeing in the solitary great heir of the glorious age of Russian realism hope for another brilliant era of Russian social and artistic creativity.

In these years, as far as can be ascertained, Cahan reviewed only one work of American fiction, I. K. Friedman's *By Bread Alone*. Published in 1901, it was the first radical American novel of the twentieth century. Cahan called the fictionalized account of the Homestead Strike of 1892 "a novel with a serious purpose and a big canvas," although he ultimately judged it a failure. Curiously, a truly pathbreaking novel did not elicit a response from him, even though the *Advertiser*, unlike any other paper, carried not one but two appreciative reviews lauding *Sister Carrie* for its "extraordinary power" and proclaiming it "one of the strongest and best-sustained pieces of fiction that we have read for a long time." [16] Certainly Cahan was aware of the publication of Dreiser's remarkable first novel. Some fifteen years later, he would in great part emulate its realism in his best book, *The Rise of David Levinsky*. In 1901, however, it appears that neither he nor Howells—whom Dreiser, ironically, had hailed reverentially as "the lookout on the watchtower straining for a first glimpse of American genius"—was ready for it.

A self-conscious immigrant, Jew, Russian, and American, Cahan struggled continually to write unselfconsciously about the intersecting worlds that he observed with rare acuity each day as he ventured in and out of the *Advertiser* offices off Newspaper Row. Writing in a newly fashioned American English that mixed at least three English dialects—those of the street and shop, the school, and the study—with German, Italian, Russian, Yiddish, and old Hebrew words, Cahan forced brilliant advantage out of seemingly insuperable obstacles to communication. What sometimes appear to be awkward turns of phrase, unfelicitous lapses in syntax, or inept usages of words, influenced unconsciously by conflicting Russian, German, Yiddish, and old Hebrew rhetorical mannerisms and linguistic habits, in fact lift his prose, so heavily flavored with the living languages of the city, to heights of authenticity and power that are notably absent in the pale columns of his contemporaries.

A veteran teacher of English to immigrants of all nations, obsessed with the spoken as much as with the written word, Cahan found himself a newspaperman and fiction writer familiarly spinning live stories right out of the mouths of the peoples of New York. If he cannot be credited with inventing the personal interview and the extended-dialogue form of reporting, the *Advertiser*'s star reporter certainly employed those techniques more steadily, more faithfully, and more imaginatively than had any newspaperman before him. Bringing to his work a cultivated ear for the varied voices and language sounds of the city and an assurance that went with a long naturalization in multilingual New York, Cahan was without rival in his ability to transform the hot spoken vernacular into vibrantly authentic printed American languaged equivalents. Cahan got both the words and the tune, as Mark Twain would have said—the rhythm, the flavor, and the imagery—and his columns, at their best, can be savored fully only when read aloud, so that they reverberate in the mind's ear.

For the first time, the nation had a newspaperman who was passionately committed to and able to write about the real metropolis, about the ethnic congeries that had been in the making for at least half a century but that had remained uncelebrated, even in the songs of Walt Whitman. At last, in Cahan, a spokesman of the new New York emerged, able to portray the city's people in their own words and voices, making manifest the simple dignity of human diversity and individuality. When Abraham Cahan appeared on the horizon in the 1890s, Americans for the first time were beginning to write seriously, or at least half-seriously, about an ethnically, regionally, and socially segmented America that had surfaced with a new salience. When Howells and Hamlin Garland spiritedly called for a genuine American literature, repeatedly exhorting local, regional, and ethnic voices to sing out, Cahan was the first to respond in full register, the only immigrant to do so, and the only novelist, other than Dreiser, to survive into the early decades of the twentieth century with an integral literary vision still intact.

Cahan migrated to the United States on the crest of the greatest wave of German and Scandinavian immigration in history and on the threshold of the mass migration of Poles, Italians, East European Jews, and many others. Sensing himself to be singularly situated and equipped to interpret the new ethnic America to older Americans, Cahan wrote of all the peoples of New York as well as of the Jewish immigrant world that was central to his experience. He wrote not of a glamorous, fairytale city but of real people who had been blocked out of American consciousness by "a certain blindness in human beings," as William James would have it. As the selections in this anthology attest, few aspects of the lives of immigrants escaped Cahan's intent gaze. Almost every piece centers on a theme that had never before been given such detailed attention or been elucidated with such candor, with "lifelikeness clothed in the simplest forms of expression and artistic sincerity," as Cahan often would say. This spirit of probity, art, and purpose Cahan brought to even his slightest journalistic pieces, his pen almost invariably transmuting the raw stuff of front-page sensationalism and cliché into the rare stuff of literature. If he fell short of the standards of his household gods, Tolstoy and Chekhov, he did not fail to convey to his readers that fidelity to truth of which they were the masters.

A century after Abraham Cahan happened upon a new America in the making, we have come to see ourselves more candidly, more perceptively, and more generously than ever before, even as we continue to be perplexed by the mystery of what it is to be an American. In column and story, *Grandma Never Lived in America: The New Journalism of Abraham Cahan* captures that spirit of perplexity with a buoyant sense of contemporaneity that links his America to ours. Cahan's sensitive evocations of a complex condition, aptly designated "pluralistic integration," project a classic complementarity—*Omnia in pluribus* joined with the familiar *E pluribus unum*—that embodies our best sense of what the ongoing American ethnic experience has been all about.[17] In an era when a resurgent immigration has brought to our shores the most variegated people in all of American history, new and old and in between will surely see and hear themselves anew through the eyes and ears of Abraham Cahan.[18]

NOTES

1. *Who Was Who in Journalism 1925–1928* (reprint, Detroit, 1978), p. 74.
2. Nathaniel Buchwald in William P. Trent et al., *Cambridge History of American Literature* (New York, 1921), 3:607. Bellow in a review of a reprint of *The Rise of David Levinsky* (New York, 1960), with an Introduction by John Higham, in *The New York Times*, Jan. 15, 1961, VII, 10. Also see Jules Chametzky, *From the Ghetto: The Fiction of Abraham Cahan* (Amherst, 1977), and Moses Rischin, "Abraham Cahan: Guide Across the American Chasm," in *The Legacy of Jewish Migration: 1881 and Its Impact*, ed. David Berger (New York, 1983).

3. See William V. Shannon, *The American Irish* (New York, 1966), pp. 145–50; and Charles Fanning, *Finley Peter Dunne and Mr. Dooley: The Chicago Years* (Lexington, 1978). In *The Discourses of Keidansky* (New York, 1903), which appeared originally in *The Boston Transcript*, Bernard G. Richards wanly imitated the Dooley style.

4. Nat Hentoff, "Behold the New Journalism," in *The Reporter as Artist*, ed. Ronald Weber (New York, 1974), p. 52.

5. See Edwin Cady, ed., *W. D. Howells as Critic* (Boston, 1973), p. 257.

6. Ella Winter and Granville Hicks, eds., *The Letters of Lincoln Steffens* (New York, 1938), 1:130.

7. *New York Commercial Advertiser*, May 21, 1898. See Ashbel Green, "Book Publishing and the Émigré Writer," in *The Third Wave: Russian Literature in Emigration*, ed. Olga Matich with Michael Heim (Ann Arbor, 1984), pp. 244–50, for an acute assessment of the continuing gap between the American and the Russian literary traditions.

8. *New York Commercial Advertiser*, January 29, 1898.

9. Robert E. Park, *The Immigrant Press and Its Control* (New York, 1922), p. 109.

10. Hannah Arendt, *The Origins of Totalitarianism* (New York, 1951), pp. 10, 120.

11. Abraham Cahan, "Zangwill's Play 'The Children of the Ghetto,'" *Forum* 28 (December 1899): 505.

12. Cahan was the silent collaborator who aided Hutchins Hapgood in writing *The Spirit of the Ghetto*, ed. Moses Rischin (Cambridge: John Harvard Library, 1967), "the first authentic study by an outsider of the inner life of an American immigrant community" (vii). In his last letter to Cahan (May 21, 1942), Hapgood fondly acknowledged his obligation to his old friend. "I have felt indebted to you for many years, as I think you know. You gave me one of my most interesting experiences, that of the Jewish East Side. I met there your interesting friends, and listened to your elucidating talk about them. And you helped me to write a considerable part of the manuscript. So I have always had a good reason to know your generosity. . . ." (Hutchins and Neith Boyce Hapgood Papers, Beinecke Rare Book and Manuscript Library, Yale University), quoted with the permission of Beatrice Hapgood Faust.

13. *New York Evening Post*, September 26, 1897.

14. See Michael Henry Heim and Simon Karlinsky, eds., *Letters of Anton Chekhov* (New York, 1973), pp. 362–63. Cahan's pioneer article, "Younger Russian Writers," subtitled "Especially Anton Chekhov, The Short Story Teller," appeared in the *Advertiser* on January 29, 1898, and was expanded and revised for publication eighteen months later in *Forum* 28 (September 1899): 119–28. See reprint in *Chekhov: The Critical Heritage*, ed. Victor Emaljanow (London, 1981), pp. 59–63.

15. For the latest version, see *Chekhov: The Early Stories, 1883–1888*, chosen and translated by Patrick Miles and Harvey Pitcher (London, 1982), pp. 11–14. For the first translation to follow Cahan's, see "The Death of An Official," in *Stories of*

INTRODUCTION

Russian Life, trans. Marian Fell (New York, 1914), pp. 118–22. Isabel Hapgood, who wrote on Russian literature and culture for the *Nation* and the *New York Evening Post*, was the first to translate Tolstoy and others directly into English, anticipating the work of England's Constance B. Garnett by a few years. See Stefanie Von Susich Foote, "Isabel Florence Hapgood," in *Notable American Women 1607–1950*, ed. Edward T. James (Cambridge, 1971), 2:129–30. Miss Hapgood's rendition of Chekhov's "Philosophy at Home" was published in *Short Stories* (October 1891) and apparently went virtually unnoticed, even by Cahan. See Kornei Chukovsky, *The Art of Translation*, trans. and ed. Lauren G. Leighton (Knoxville, 1984), pp. 219ff., for an appreciation of Garnett.

16. See Alfred Kazin and Charles Shapiro, eds., *The Stature of Theodore Dreiser* (Bloomington, 1955), pp. 55–58 and 65, for the *Advertiser* reviews of December 19, 1900, and September 18, 1901.

17. See Moses Rischin, "Creating Crèvecoeur's 'New Man': He Had a Dream," *Journal of American Ethnic History* 1 (Fall 1981): 26–42; John Higham, *Send These to Me: Immigrants in Urban America* (Baltimore, 1984), pp. xii–xiii, 242–45; Moses Rischin, "The Jews and Pluralism: Toward an American Freedom Symphony," in Gladys Rosen, ed., *Jewish Life in America: Historical Perspectives* (New York, 1978), p. 64.

18. See Thomas Kessner and Betty Boyd Caroli, *Today's Immigrants. Their Stories* (New York, 1981).

PART ONE

Tremors of the Twentieth Century

Park Row: *World* bulletin board announces sinking of *Maine*. (Photograph by A. Witteman, 1898. *Courtesy of the Museum of the City of New York*.)

1

THE NEW WORLD POWER

EAST SIDE TALKS MAINE
February 22, 1898

The *Maine* disaster is the all-absorbing topic of conversation on the East Side. At several cafés the talk at most of the marble tables turned upon the national calamity and the question of war with Spain. Some of the remarks were characteristic.

A large table at one of the cafés frequented by the better class of Germans was occupied by half a dozen well-dressed young men intently following the strictures of a heavily bearded, spectacled old gentleman.

"The American people are all right," he was saying, sawing the air with his long-stemmed German pipe, "but they give some of their papers too much license. If this country is to have war, let us have it, by all means. Old as I am, I shall not stay at home. I knew how to fight for the good old fatherland yonder, and when it comes to business I shall recall my military drill and fight for the fatherland of my children. But these things must be decided by the elected representatives of the people, and not by a self-constituted authority in the form of a sensational press. The Yankee strikes me as a fighter par excellence. He is used to fight, and to win, and nothing seems easier than to precipitate war upon this nation. Why, look at my boys. They are Germans by parentage, but they were born here, and yet they are full of fight, and ever since the *Maine* catastrophe was reported they have restlessly talked of nothing but war and of their inclination to join the navy. All you want is to fan this feeling, to stimulate it by foolish war cries, such as some of the papers have been shouting to raise their circulation."

3

One of the old man's auditors expressed the opinion that war would be a godsend to the trade of the country. "Apart from the immediate stimulus it would lend to business," he said, "it would tend to further the commercial activity of the United States in other lands, but the conflict would be sure to result in the taking of Havana and Madrid by Uncle Sam's soldiers and so give rise to favorable mercantile treaties."

"Is that so?" a voice broke in from a corner. "You are positive the United States would smash Spain to dust, are you?" The speaker was a bilious-looking man of fifty. His reputation at the café is that of a misanthrope—woman-hater and Yankee-hater. "The Americans are a lot of braggards and bluffers, and that's all. They can fight the whole world—with their tongues." Then he burst into a lonely laugh and lashed himself into such a fury at the Americans that he was choked with rage and could not speak.

"Why do you live in America, then, if you don't like the country?" asked two voices in duet.

"I didn't say I disliked America, did I?" the sickly man returned, finding his voice. "The country is not the Yankee's property. He has no title deed for it. Columbus discovered it for all."

A leading Hungarian citizen was found haranguing an assemblage of his fellow-countrymen in a Houston Street café.

"The time of colonies is gone," he argued. "Cuba must belong to the United States and be free. Canada, too, will be annexed. The shackles of royalty must be cast off. My father died fighting under Kossuth for the independence of Hungary, and I am ready to die fighting for the independence of an oppressed people. Glory to the United States for the noble stand it takes on behalf of downtrodden Cuba. War is inevitable. I think it would be in bad grace for this country to leave the Cubans to their fate. It would be like the man who, after eating a good dinner, turns a deaf ear to the hungry fellow who is begging for a penny. Uncle Sam shook himself free long ago. Shall he leave his Cuban brothers in bondage?"

The others in the room were indifferent to the entire question. They listened to the enthusiast with an air of lukewarm curiosity, never interrupting him with a sound of approval or objection. The only exception was a dark-eyed young woman of thirty, the wife of one of the gathering.

"You men cannot do without bloodshed. If you were mothers, you would not be in such a hurry about sending your children, the flower of the population, to the battlefield."

Whereupon the champion of liberty bowed deeply, and with a broad smile of gallantry supplanting the look of martial enthusiasm on his bewhiskered face, he said:

4

"Madam, love is the vocation of your sex. I may feel like remarking that it is for the sake of love that I advocate war, but who dares oppose you?"

An Italian grocer was fairly raging with impatience because the people at Washington did not send troops to Cuba at once. Asked for his reasons, he said:

"Spanish people bad people. A Spaniard lived in this house, owed me $4, ran away, never paid me. All Spain bad."

ALL AGAINST SPAIN
April 30, 1898

The volunteer regiments in process of formation in this city are composed of a dozen different nationalities. Not to speak of such an organization as the Lafayette Post's regiment of Germans, who speak no English, every enlistment bureau in this city attracts as many foreign-born applicants as natives. There are Irishmen among the recruits and Englishmen, Swedes and Austrians, Prussians and Frenchmen, and a sprinkling of other European nationalities, even a few Spanish—a polyglot, piebald multitude of all classes and antecedents.

The greater part of these aliens have borne arms before, having served in the army or navy in their native countries.

"All Europe is going to fight Spain for us," said someone. "Every nation has sent us some of its soldiers to join our ranks in the present conflict."

What actuates these foreigners in rushing into the enlistment tents, is a question more easily asked than answered; however, from the bombastic replies of some of them, one would be thrilled to think that a new-fangled American patriotism, a warm gratitude and a close attachment to the country which offers them a better home is the real source of their readiness to join the American army.

"Why do we enlist?" asked, in an East Side café, a dashing young German, who expects to return from the war with the rank of colonel. "We are proud of this country, and we are ready to shed every drop of our blood for its glorious flag."

Carried away by the force of his own eloquence, the man launched into

5

an endless German sentence, but before the predicate was reached another German, a well-known philosopher of the Second Avenue cafés, interrupted him.

"You have said enough, old man!" he addressed him, shoving his spectacles to his forehead. "We all know that you have the gift of speech, but you had better keep your rhetoric for a better purpose. Much do the boys who come to enlist care for the flag and its glories! They are simply glad to get a job and some excitement, that's all."

"Excitement? And how about the enemy's bullets?" retorted the orator. "Excitement, forsooth! Don't we know that our chances of coming back are meagre? It is into the jaws of death we are to march. War is anything but a child's play. War, my dear sir, is ruthless destruction of human life; war is the offering up of one's life on the altar of one's—of one's—" The eloquent man was desperately fumbling for a word when his hoodoo came to his rescue:

"On the altar of one's rot and rubbish!" he broke in. "Those who enlist don't think of the battlefield. They never try to imagine the real business for which they enlist. If they did they would stay home and look for another job. I have watched them at the saloon on the corner of Fifth Street and Second Avenue, where the enlistments were going on, and I have spoken to lots of them, so I know what I am talking about. Cool down and listen, my friend. They don't think. Very few people do. They are either out of work or they get poor jobs and are not sure of them. Now here is a chance of the government taking care of them and freeing their minds of all trouble about food, rent, clothing. All that will be furnished them, and that in itself is enough to induce thousands of men to enlist. Then again there is the great social instinct which makes a man seek the company of his fellow-men, and the more of such fellow-men the higher the sense of security. Yes, the sense of security. With all the dangers which war entails and with all the discipline which transforms the individual man into a cog of a wheel in a monstrous machine, the soldier is happy to think of the thousands of his comrades who are linked to him and who fight for him as he does for them. The dangers are great, but people never picture them vividly until it is too late. Did you ever pause to think of your own death? You know it is inevitable, yet you hate to dwell on it.

"As a matter of fact we never can get ourselves to believe in real earnest that we are actually going to die. This is also the case with the dangers of war. The man who enlists does not actually realize them. He regards them as something hidden in the vague indefinite future, and threatening anybody but himself.

6

"Add to all that the sportsman's instinct of young men and the fact that most of our German recruits are used to look upon war as their trade, and you will understand why so many of them are so anxious to join."

"So you deny all patriotism?" asked the phrasemaker, halfheartedly.

"Who says I do? Patriotism is all right enough, and it will get into the hearts of the foreign volunteers as well as into the souls of the native fellows in due course. Wait till the first real danger, till some bullets buzz past your ears and some of your chums drop by your side; wait till you get so fagged out and your senses are so blunted as to leave no room for your instinct of self-preservation; wait till then for the real patriotic, ferocious, bloodthirsty soldier in you. Not until then will you curse the Spaniards and mean it; not until then will you be filled with the genuine desire that your flag will be victorious."

The other customers were gravely attentive. The philosopher fell silent, and for a minute stillness reigned in the room, which is used to incessant noise. Presently a band made itself heard in the distance. "Yankee Doodle" came floating through the street. There was a flutter outside. Crowds were heard scurrying in the direction of the musicians. Everybody in the café stood up, and there was a rush for the windows.

"Music helps a good deal in infusing patriotism into the soldier," somebody observed.

"I don't know but it may," the philosopher returned, musingly.

"THE GOD OF ISRAEL IS GETTING EVEN WITH THEM"

May 14, 1898

The ghetto never does things by halves, and its war feeling manifests itself with an oriental exuberance which keeps the neighborhood in a constant effervescence of excitement. The crowds in front of the bulletin boards of the four Yiddish dailies in this world within a world are not quite so large, perhaps, as the throngs on Park Row, but this numerical inferiority is more than made up in violence of gesticulation and vehemence of verbal expression. The Jews are glad to see Spain defeated. They have a double reason for it. Apart from considering themselves Americans and loving their adopted country as the only one in the world where the unhappy children of Israel find a home, they have an old account to settle with the Spaniards.

"Serve them right! Serve them right!" said a patriarchal old tailor, speaking of Manila. "They tortured the Jews and banished them from their land, and now the God of Israel is getting even with them. It is an old story, more than four hundred years old, but the High One never forgets, you know. You see, the Lord could have smashed them long ago, and even now He could have made some other power the messenger of Spain's ruin. Why, then, did it fall to the lot of the United States to settle her? You don't know? Well, I'll tell you. Who should avenge the blood of Israel? Russia, which is just as bad to the Jews as Spain was? Germany, Austria or any other country which is eaten up with anti-Semitism as a bad apple is with worms? England isn't a bad country, but what good does she do our people? The United States is the only land that has been a real mother to us. So God thought He might as well give the Americans the job. The friends of Israel getting square on His enemies, see?"

The younger and more educated part of the East Side population are against Spain because they are Americans and because they sympathize with the cause of free Cuba, but to the older folks, especially such as are initiated into the intricacies of Talmudic lore, a victory like Dewey's is as much of a triumph to the Jewish race as it is to the American people.

Perhaps the most interesting things in this connection are the prayers offered in behalf of American arms in the synagogues of Russia. The Saturday service usually includes a prayer for the health of the ruler of the country in which the worshippers dwell, and according to letters received from Russia and Poland, some of the Jewish congregations in these countries have now added to the benediction which they chant for the health of the Czar a hymn blessing President McKinley and the American nation and praying for their triumph over Spain.

As to the synagogues of this country, where the President of the United States is the object of a prayer every Sabbath, the present war has called forth a special hymn which is chanted in the orthodox synagogues of the East Side.

The war news is conveyed to the people of the ghetto in a manner which the Yiddish papers have borrowed from English papers of the "yellow" type. The race for the size of headlines was caught up with a will, and the result is a display of scare-heads which turns the first page of every Yiddish daily into something like the show-cards which advertise the performances at the two Jewish theatres.

"End of War! Peace!"—this in the largest Hebrew type to be found in any foundry, and followed by "Such Is the Desire of Helpless Spain" in pica—is an illustration of the new journalistic methods for which the ghetto is indebted to some English newspapers. The Yiddish dailies translate their news as well as heads from these papers.

When the first report of Dewey's victory reached the ghetto the joy expressed in the streets, tenement houses and sweatshops reached a pitch of excitement the like of which was perhaps unknown in any other part of the city. Business was interrupted, and the whir of sewing machines came to a halt; everybody was shouting and gesticulating over the glad tidings.

Thousands of Jews have enlisted in the various volunteer recruiting stations. Many of these can now be seen drilling at Peekskill or Camp Black, and many more are impatiently waiting to be called. A characteristic episode was related by one of the well-known lawyers of the East Side. A poor tailor of forty-five, who had seen fire in the Russo-Turkish War, became so excited over the conflict between the United States and Spain that he made up his mind to go to the front.

"Are you crazy?" asked his wife, pointing to their four children.

"I can't help it, my dear," was the old soldier's reply. "God and good people will take care of you and the young ones. My blood is up. If I had to face death for Russia, which has done nothing but evil to our people, how much more readily ought I to fight for this country, which has been so good to us? Ah! you are only a woman. What do you know about these things? I am going to enlist." And he did.

One old housewife, who has been some ten years in this country, without seeing anything of it beyond her tenement house and the Hester Street markets, was slow to understand what the whole trouble was about.

"War?" she asked in amazement. "America going to shed blood, too? Why, they have no Czar here, so who has quarrelled with the King of Spain?"

After the situation was explained to her at length she asked again: "Cuba? And where is Cuba? Did you not say yourself that Cuba was also America, and don't I know that America belongs to the President, so where does the Spanish King come in after all?"

Another old matron, whose Americanized son had enlisted, thought it was only a joke. "No, mother, it is not a joke," the boy declared in English, to which she answered in Yiddish, as usual: "It is not a joke? What then is it? Is that what we came away from Russia for—to become soldiers here? We might as well stay at home."

The boy explained that Russia never was the home of the Jews, while in America they were as good as the Gentiles, and that being an American he must fight for his country.

BLOWS AND BULLETS

A Story by Vsevolod Garshin*

Translated from the Russian by Abraham Cahan

May 28, 1898

Bad roads, dust, exhaustion, bleeding feet, short halts during the day, heavy sleep at night, the hateful bugle sounding reveille at the first peep of dawn; ever the same interminable fields, so unlike those at home, covered with the tall, green, loudly rustling husks of corn, or with yellowing wheat. The same faces, the same marches, the same life, the same talks of home, of the last town, of the officers. Of the future the men spoke rarely, and with reluctance. Of the object of the war they had but a vague idea. The army had lingered near Kishinev for six months, so that there had been plenty of time to explain to the men whom and why they were going to fight, but this was apparently deemed unnecessary. I remember being asked by a soldier how soon we would reach Bokhara.† At first I thought I did not catch the name, but when he repeated the question I explained that Bokhara lay beyond two seas, some two thousand *versts*‡ away, and that we should hardly get there. He said:

"Well, you are wrong this time, Mikhaylych. The regimental clerk told me all about it. 'We are going to cross the Danube,' says he, 'and then we'll be right in the Bokhara land'—that's what he said."

"Well, well—you mean Bulgaria, then, not Bokhara!" I exclaimed.

"Call it Bulgaria—Bokhara or Bulgaria—what is the difference?"

All the men knew was that they were going to fight "the Turk," because he had shed a great deal of blood. And they were willing to whip him, too, but not so much because he had spilled somebody's—they did not know whose—blood, as because he disturbed the peace of so many Russians, causing them to leave their homes and families and to march hundreds of miles in order to present their breasts to bullet and cannon ball. The Turk

---

*A Russian novelist—famous at home, unknown abroad—who hated war and therefore joined the army. Most of his work is, like this sketch, fiction in form only.—*A.C.*

†A region in central Asia.—*Ed.*

‡A *verst* is equal to three-fifths of a mile.—*Ed.*

appeared to them as a rebel, a troublesome fellow who was to be subdued and silenced.

The gossip of the regiment and the little domestic troubles of the various companies interested us much more than the war. Our company got along very well, but the state of affairs among the *strelki* (sharpshooters) went from bad to worse. Ventzel, their commanding officer, seemed to grow more cruel and heartless every day, and the discontent of his company increased in proportion.

We had just passed a town and emerged on a meadow, where our first regiment was already resting. The spot was an inviting one, being flanked on one side by a river and on the other by an old oak grove—presumably the picnic ground of the little town nearby. It was a beautiful warm afternoon. The sun was setting. The regiment halted; guns were stacked. Zhitkov and myself busied ourselves with our tent. We had staked out a plot, and I was holding one end of the flap while he was driving the pegs into the ground.

"Tighter, tighter, Mikhaylych!" he urged me. "That's it!"

At this moment there came from behind me a succession of strange slapping sounds. I turned around.

The *strelki* were lined up. Ventzel, yelling in a husky voice, was beating one of his men in the face. Pale as death and trembling all over, the soldier stood, gun in hand, not daring to dodge the blows which his commander was raining on him, while the latter, his small, gaunt form writhing and wriggling with the effort, was striking his victim with both fists—now on the right cheek, now on the left. Everybody around was silent. Nothing was heard except the slapping noise and the husky gasps of the infuriated officer. My eyes grew dim, and I made a movement in his direction. Zhitkov saw what I was about and gave a violent tug at the canvas in my hand.

"Hold tight, handless devil that you are!" he screamed, swearing in the foulest manner at me. "Your hands ain't paralyzed, are they? What are you looking at? Something you never saw before, is it?"

The blows continued. The soldier's upper lip and chin were bleeding. At last he fell on the ground. Ventzel turned his back on him, and sweeping his company with a glance, he shrieked out:

"If anyone dares to smoke while in line I'll give it to him worse than that, the beast. Pick him up, wash his mug and carry him into his tent. Let him lie there till he gets over it. Stack guns!"

Ventzel's hands were swollen, bloodstained and trembling. He wiped them with his handkerchief and walked away pale, gnashing his teeth, his eyes shooting fire. As he passed me and met my fixed glance, his thin lips relaxed in a forced smile of derision, and whispering something which I could not make out, he proceeded on his way.

"The blood-drinking cur!" said Zhitkov, in a voice full of hatred, and then addressing himself to me: "But what is the use of sticking in your nose? You don't want to be shot, do you? Don't be uneasy. The men will get even with him, depend upon it."

"Will they complain? To whom?" I asked.

"That they won't; but we will be in some engagement with him, won't we?" And he added something in a murmur, the meaning of which I dreaded to guess. By this time, Fyodorov, who had gone to the *strelki* to find out the cause of Ventzel's anger, came back to us.

"Torturing people for nothing!" he said. "While we were still on the road, Matushkin—that's the name of that soldier that was licked, you know—lit a cigarette. When we halted he left it between his fingers. He forgot all about it, the poor fellow. Well, Ventzel saw it and got wild."

"The brute!" he added, after a while, as he lay down in our tent, which was by this time ready. "The cigarette was out, too. Anybody could have seen he had forgotten all about it. . . ."

I have but a dim recollection of the beginning of the fight. As we reached the summit of a hill, in plain view of the enemy, who could see our companies break up column and fall into skirmishing line, the report of a cannon rang out, grim and lonely, from the Turkish camp. Our men gave a sudden shiver. Everybody's eyes were fixed upon the melting puff of white smoke which was quietly rolling down the opposite hill. At the same instant the sonorous screeching sound of a shell which seemed to be flying over our very heads made us all duck. The shell did pass over us, hitting the ground near the rearmost company. I remember hearing the dull thud with which it burst and then the piteous cry of a man. My ear heard it—that was all. I learned later that a fragment of the shell tore off the leg of that company's sergeant, but at that moment I did not understand the meaning of the cry. All my senses were merged in that vague, indescribable feeling which takes hold of one under fire for the first time. It is said that no one is absolutely free from terror on the battlefield—that every candid man who is not given to boasting, if asked whether the enemy's fire causes him fright, would say, "It does." It was not, however, the physical terror which you experience upon coming face to face with a gang of robbers in a deserted lane in the dead of night. It was a complete and clear feeling that death was near and unavoidable. And, strange and unnatural as it may seem, this feeling, far from holding the men

12

back or making them think of flight, urged them on. There was no awakening of bloodthirsty instincts, there was no desire to kill anybody, but there was an irrepressible impulse to go ahead, to move onward, happen what might, and our notion of what we were to do during the fight would have found expression in the words "We must die" rather than in the words "We must kill."

While we were passing the clearing the Turks kept firing at us. We were separated from them by the last expanse of underbrush. Presently we were hidden by the bushes. Silence fell over the place.

Our march was impeded by a thick growth of underbrush. The *strelki*, who were in the lead, had already broken ranks and were advancing in skirmishing order, now and then calling to one another to keep from straying apart. Our column still held together.

A deep stillness reigned in the thicket. Presently there came a noise, not very loud, and ringing like the sound of a lumberman's axe. The enemy had begun firing at random. The bullets were whizzing high overhead and rattled through the bushes, snapping off branches but doing no harm to the men. The noise became thicker and thicker till it was one monotonous chorus of crackling sounds. We could not hear any separate bullet. The whole air was now whistling and wailing around us. We walked on at a double-quick step. Everybody about me was safe and sound and so was I. This surprised me very much.

All at once we emerged from the thicket. The road was intersected by a ditch with a tiny rill trickling on its bottom. We rested awhile and took a drink of water.

The companies were marched off in various directions, to surround the enemy by a flank movement. The sharpshooters were to go straight ahead and, after passing through the bushes, to make a dash into the village. The Turkish guns kept booming as thick and as fast as before, but much louder.

Ventzel took his men across the stream. He was now saying something to them which I could not hear.

"We will try our best!" they shouted.

I stood looking at him from below. He was pale, and as it seemed to me, sad, but quite calm. As his eye fell on two of our officers he waved his handkerchief to them and then began to search our company with his glance. I understood that he was looking for me to bid me good-bye, and I rose to my feet to catch his eye. Ventzel smiled, nodded to me several times and commanded his company to advance in skirmishing order. The line broke into groups of four, and they marched off, some to the right, some to the left, and then forming a long line, they disappeared behind the bushes—all except one man, who suddenly jerked himself forward and, throwing up his arms, fell heavily to the ground. Two of our company rushed out of the ditch and soon came back with the corpse.

An agonizing half-hour of suspense followed.

The battle waxed hot. The air was filled with the fierce wail of bullets, to which was soon added the roar of cannon. Presently bleeding men began to appear from the bushes, some walking, others crawling. We helped them down the bank, gave them water and laid them down to await the arrival of stretchers. One sharpshooter with a crushed wrist, his face livid with pain and loss of blood, came groaning fearfully and rolling up his eyes, and sat himself down by the stream. We bandaged his hand and put him to bed on his overcoat. The blood was stanched, but he had a violent attack of fever. His lips quivered and his frame shook with nervous, broken sobbing.

"Oh, my dear mates! Dear fellow-countrymen!" he moaned.

"Many killed?" somebody inquired.

"Oh, lots, lots!" the wounded man answered.

"Is Ventzel alive?"

"So far he is. If it were not for him we should be sure to be repulsed for good. With him at the head our men will take the village—with him they will," the wounded soldier said faintly. "He led us three times, and we were repulsed each time. He made a fourth attack. Then our boys went to bivouac for a spell. What a lot of cartridges they must have; they are sowing them like seed, the devils—but no! no! You won't! I say you won't, curse you!" he suddenly began to shriek, sitting up and jerking his wounded hand. "No! no!" And rolling his infuriated eyes, he yelled out a terrible oath and fell back in a swoon.

Suddenly an officer appeared on the bank, shaking his clenched fists in the air.

"Advance, Ivan Platonych! For God's sake, advance!" he shouted at the top of his voice. . . .

Smoke, cracking sounds, a fierce "Hurrah!" . . . The smell of powder and of blood. . . . Strange-looking, unfamiliar faces, pale and wrapped in smoke. . . . A savage, an inhuman scrimmage. . . . Let us thank God that such moments can be recalled but as through a haze.

When we came up, Ventzel was leading the remainder of his company for a fifth attack on the Turks, who were showering lead on him. This time the *strelki* took the village. Few of the Turks had time to escape. In two hours Ventzel's company had lost fifty-two men.

Toward evening we were in camp. Ivan Platonych invited me to tea. "Have you seen Ventzel?"

"Not yet," I answered.

"Go to his tent and bring him here. He is going crazy, the poor fellow: 'Fifty-two! fifty-two!'—that's all you can hear from him. Go fetch him out, will you?"

I found Ventzel alone. His tent was faintly illuminated by the thin stub of a candle. As I came in he was crouching in a corner, with his head on a box, and sobbing quietly.

LEFT ON A BATTLEFIELD
A Story by Vsevolod Garshin
Translated from the Russian by Abraham Cahan
June 11, 1898

I

I remember how we were running through the grove, how the bullets were whizzing and the snapped-off twigs falling all around us, how we were pushing and tearing our way through the bushes. Shots came thick and fast. Glimmering here and there through the interstices of the trees were dots of red. Sidorov, a little private of our first company ("What is he doing in our line?" flashed through my mind), suddenly sat down on the ground and fixed a frightened stare at me. Blood was streaming from his mouth. Yes, I remember it all clearly. I also remember how I caught sight of *him* among the bushes. A big stout Turk he was, but I at once made a dash at him, forgetting that I was so much smaller and so weak. There was a loud boom, and something big seemed to sweep by; in my ears there was a roaring.

"He has shot at me," I said to myself. With a scream of horror the Turk cowered down against a thick shrub. It would have been easy for him to get around it, but he was out of his wits with terror and tried to climb over the prickly twigs. With one blow I knocked the rifle out of his hand and with another I stuck my bayonet somewhere.

The next moment I heard something between a shriek and a groan, and ran on. Our men were cheering, firing, falling. I recollect discharging several shots—that was when we were well out of the woods. All at once the

15

cheering became louder, and with a sudden start we pushed on—not I, that is, but they, our men, for I remained behind. I thought it queer. Still queerer was the fact that everything had suddenly disappeared and the cheering and firing ceased. I heard not a sound and saw only something blue—the sky, I should think. And then that, too, vanished.

II

I had never been in such a queer condition. I must have lain with my face to the ground, for a small bit of sward was all I could see. A few grass blades, an ant crawling down one of them with its head downward, some rubbish of last year's grass—that was all my world. I could look at it with only one eye, for the other was held shut by something hard—probably a branch upon which my head was leaning. I was awfully uncomfortable. I wished to stir, and was at a loss to understand why I could not do so. Some time passed. I could hear only the buzz of bees and the stridulation of grasshoppers. With an effort I disengaged my right arm from under me, and propping both elbows against the turf, I tried to raise myself. A sharp, shooting pain rushed through my frame from the knees up to the heart and the head, and I fell once more. Again there was darkness.

III

I woke up. How is it that I can see the stars glittering so brightly in the Bulgarian sky? Is it possible that I am out of my tent? Why did I crawl out of it, then? I try to move and feel an excruciating pain in my legs.

Yes, I have been wounded in battle. Is it serious? I feel the painful spot with my hand. Both legs are covered with dry blood. When I touch them the pain becomes still worse. It is something like a toothache, tugging at my very soul, unrelenting, ruthless. My ears are tingling and my head has grown heavy. I have a vague idea that I am wounded in both legs. What has happened, then? Why don't they pick me up? Can it be that we were beaten? I begin to recall what took place, vaguely at first, then more and more distinctly, until I become convinced that we were not beaten. Indeed, it was in the clearing on the top of the hill that I fell, although that I do not remember, and can only recollect seeing our company rushing onward, while I could not follow them.

"We shall get there, boys!" our little commander had shouted to us, pointing at that hilltop, and there we were presently. Consequently, we had not been repulsed. But, then, why have I been left to lie here? This is an open spot, so that they could not miss me. And I cannot be lying here alone, either, seeing that the Turkish fire came so thick and so fast. I think I had better turn my head and see. This is much easier now, for as I fell the second time, while trying to stand up, I came down on my back. That's the reason I see these stars.

I raise myself and try to sit up. My crushed legs will not let me do so. I make several futile attempts, and am in despair, but finally, with tears starting in my eyes, with the frightful pain that the effort caused me, I succeed.

Overhead there is a bit of dark blue sky, with one big star and a few smaller ones burning on it, while all around me I see something tall and black. I am surrounded by bushes. They did not find me.

I feel the roots of my hair stirring on my head.

But how in the world do I come to be lying here among the brush, seeing that I was shot on the open hilltop? I must have crawled over here after I was wounded and when I was half unconscious with pain. However, is it not strange that I cannot budge now, while then I managed to creep up here? Perhaps I started out with only one bullet and got another on my way.

Faint blotches of rose-color are fading away around me. My big star has grown pale, and smaller ones have vanished. It's the moon rising, is it not? How lovely it is at home now!

I hear some terrible sounds, something like a man groaning. Yes, it is a groan. Is there another forgotten soldier hereabout, an unfortunate fellow with crushed legs, like myself? No; the groans seem to be so near, and yet there is nobody here. It must be something else. But, heavens, it is myself. Those faint piteous groans are my own. Can it be that my pain is really so awful? It must be. Only I cannot understand that pain, for my head is full of fog, or lead. I had better lie down again, fall asleep and sleep, sleep, sleep. But will I ever wake up? Oh, that does not concern me.

As I try to lie down a broad streak of moonlight falls across me, and I discern something bulky and dark sprawling on the ground five paces away. Here and there it is mottled with bright spots. These are brass buttons. It must be a wounded soldier, or the corpse of one. Anyway, I shall lie down.

No, our men cannot have gone from here. They must have routed the Turks and are holding the conquered position. But then, why do I hear neither voices nor the crackling of campfires? Well, I am too weak to hear anything.

"Help! Help!"

Savage, husky shrieks break from my breast, and meet with no answer. They ring loud and die away on the night air—everything else is silent. Only the grasshoppers keep rattling as monotonously as ever. The moon looks at me sadly.

If *he* were only wounded my screams would have waked him. It is a corpse. Is he a Russian or a Turk? But, God! as if it made any difference! And a heavy slumber descends upon my inflamed eyes.

IV

I am lying with my eyes shut, although I have been awake for a considerable time. I am loath to open my eyes, because I can feel the sunshine through my eyelids, and if I open them the light will be too sharp for me. I had better not stir, either, I think. Yesterday—was it really yesterday?—I was wounded. A day has passed; more days will follow, and I shall die. It does not matter to me. No, I won't stir. Let my body lie motionless. How good it would be if I could put a stop to the work of my brain, too. But the brain won't be stopped. Thoughts, memories, come crowding into my head. However, this won't last long. The end is near. A few lines in the newspapers is all that will remain of me. These will state that our losses, if you please, were slight: so many wounded and one killed—a volunteer private named Ivanov. Well, no, they won't print my name. They will simply say, "Killed, one."

Will anybody come to pick me up? No, it looks as if I were doomed to lie here till I die. And yet how sweet it is to live! How happy I was once, how intoxicated with happiness! But away with you, memories! Leave me in peace. . . . Oh, my yearning heart! You give me more pain than my wounds.

It is getting hot, however. I open my eyes and behold the same bushes, the same sky, only in the daylight. Ah, here is my neighbor. I can see him now. It's a Turk—a corpse. What a giant! I do recognize him: it is the same Turk . . .

Yes, it is the man I killed. What did I kill him for? He is dead, covered with blood. Why should fate have thrown him in my way? Who is he? Maybe he has an old mother, like myself? Many a long day will she sit in front of her hut looking to the far north for her dear one, her breadwinner. And I? Here I am ready to change places with him. He does not hear anything, and he feels neither pain nor thirst, nor the pangs of yearning. How happy he is! . . . The bayonet went right into his heart. There is a black hole in his coat; it is surrounded with blood. It was I who did that.

I did not mean to do it. I bore no one any ill feeling when I went to the war. The thought that I would have to kill people somehow escaped me. I

18

only thought of how I should present my own breast to the bullets. And I did. . . . And this unhappy fellah (he wears the Egyptian uniform) is still less to blame. Before the troops were crowded on board the steamer to be taken to Constantinople, he had never even heard that there was such a country as Russia or Bulgaria in the world. He was ordered to go and he went. If he had disobeyed he would have been killed. He marched all the way from Stambul to Rustchuk. We attacked them, and he defended himself. But seeing that we are terrible people, that we are not afraid of his patent rifle, made in England, and that we keep pushing ahead, his heart grew faint within him. As he was about to escape, a little man, whom he might have killed with one blow of his black fist, leaned up to him and thrust a bayonet into his breast.

Where is his fault, then?

And where is my fault, even if I did kill him? How am I to blame? Why should the thirst torment me so? Thirst! Does anybody understand what the word really means? Even while we were marching through Rumania at the rate of fifty *versts** a day in the scorching heat, even then I did not feel what I feel now. Ah, if somebody would come along!

But there must be some water in that huge canteen. But I would have to creep up to him, and what will it cost me? Well, I don't care, I'll try.

I set out to crawl, my legs drag along, my emaciated arms are hardly able to support my body. The corpse is some fifteen feet away, but to me the distance is dozens of *versts*. But it cannot be helped. I must see if I cannot find some water in the canteen. Oh, my throat, it is burning like fire. Death would come much quicker if I had nothing to drink; I would soon be rid of my agonies. . . . Still, maybe . . .

And so I am dragging myself along, and each motion gives me unbearable pain. I scream, I shriek, but keep crawling. At last, here it is. Here is the canteen. Yes, there is water inside, and what a lot, too! It is more than half full. Oh, I have got water enough to last me a long time—until my very death!

You have saved my life, my dear victim. Leaning on one arm, I open the canteen, when, suddenly losing my balance, I fall with my face on the breast of my benefactor. It is already emitting an odor. . . .

*See p. 10.

V

I have taken a drink. The water is warm, but it is not bad. I can live a few days longer. I remember reading in *The Physiology of Everyday Life* that you can live more than a week without food, provided you have water. Yes, in the same passage there is a story of a suicide who starved himself. He lived quite a long time because he drank water. But what of it all? Suppose I do live five days more? Our men have gone, the Bulgarians have abandoned their villages, and there is no highway near. I shall die anyhow—with this difference, however, that instead of three days I may have to be tortured a whole week.

Had I better not put an end to it? Here, by my neighbor's side, is his rifle—an excellent piece of work. I have only to reach out my hand for it, then—one second—and it will all be over. And here are cartridges, too—quite a pile.

Well, shall I do it, or shall I wait? Wait for what? Death, or help? Shall I wait till some Turks come to pull the skin off my broken legs? Had I not much better finish it myself? . . .

No, I must not lose heart. I shall struggle to the bitter end, to my last breath. Indeed, if I am found, I may be saved. Who knows but what the bones are intact, and I shall soon be well again? I shall see my native place, mother, Masha. . . . I hope to God they may not learn the whole truth. Let them think I was killed outright.

I feel dizzy. The trip to my neighbor has completely exhausted me. And here is that terrible smell into the bargain! How black he has grown! What will become of him in a day or two? After I have rested a little I shall try and crawl back to my former place.

I lie faint, unable to stir for exhaustion. The sun is burning my face and hands. I wish I had something to cover myself with. Would that night came sooner, at least. This will be my second night here, will it not?

My brain is in a maze. I fall into a stupor.

VI

I must have slept very long, for when I woke it was night. Everything is the same as before; my wounds pain me excruciatingly, my neighbor lies stretched as big and as motionless as ever. I cannot help thinking of him. Can it be that I have left everything that is dear to my heart, marched thousands of *versts*, borne hunger, cold, tantalizing heat—all in order that this wretched man should cease to live? Did I accomplish anything more important from a military standpoint? What have I done except to murder a man?

When I determined to enlist and to go to the war, mother and Masha did not dissuade me, although they wept over me. Blinded by my lofty ideas, I did not see their tears. I did not understand (now I do) what I was doing with my dear ones. . . . But what is the use of dwelling on it all?

And how strange was the way many of my friends treated me! "What a crank!" they exclaimed when they heard what I was going to do. How could they say it? How does it accord with their notion of valor, patriotism and the like? I only acted in compliance with these notions of theirs, and yet they called me a crank.

And so I arrive in Kishinev at last, get a heavy load on my back and set out, together with thousands of others, among whom only a few march of their own will like myself. The thousands would much rather have stayed at home. Still, once they are compelled to go, they do so like ourselves, "conscious warriors" that we are; they march thousands of *versts,* and fight as well as we, if not better.

A fresh morning breeze has broken out. The bushes are bestirring themselves; a little bird, half awake, has fluttered off her perch. The stars have gone out. The dark-blue sky has grown gray, with here and there a feathery cloudlet floating across. The gray twilight is lifting from the ground. This is the third day of—what shall I call it?—my life? My agony? The third? And how many more? Not many, at any rate. I have grown fearfully weak, and I don't think I have strength enough to move away from the corpse. It won't be long before I shall be like him, and he will be no more offensive to me than I am to him.

I think I shall take a drink. I shall drink three times a day: in the morning, in the afternoon and in the evening.

VII

The sun is up. Its huge disc, all intersected and criss-crossed with the black twigs of the bushes, is red as blood. This threatens to be a hot day. What will become of you, neighbor? You are terrible enough as you are.

Yes, he was terrible. His hair began to drop out; his skin, naturally dark, grew pale and sallow. His feet, encased in leather shoes, were swollen so that you could see enormous blisters protruding from the shoes, while his whole figure was puffed up into frightful dimensions. What more is the sun going to do with him today?

To be so near to him is unbearable. I must crawl away. But can I do it? I

21

can raise my arm, open the canteen, and take a drink, but shall I be able to drag my heavy body? I must, if only a pace each hour. It is impossible to remain near him.

The whole morning is spent in this crawling process. The pain is fearful, but what can I do? I have forgotten and cannot so much as imagine how it feels to be well. It even seems as if I had become used to my pain. I have crawled on some fifteen feet, however, and got to my former place. Still, I did not enjoy the fresh air long, if you can call fresh air the atmosphere within a few feet of a fast-decomposing corpse. The wind has veered around and once more brings me the nauseating odor. I cannot stand it. I am in despair. I burst out crying like a baby.

VIII

Overcome with exhaustion I lay in a state of semi-consciousness, when hark! Is it an illusion of a diseased brain? No, it is not. I hear human voices, there is no mistake about it—human voices and the tramp of horses. I came near crying out but checked myself. Suppose they are Turks! What then? In addition to my present agonies they would inflict upon me tortures the very description of which in our newspapers makes one's hair stand erect. They would skin me, roast my broken legs. It would be a lucky thing if that was all. Indeed, they are quite inventive in these things. Is it not better to die here alone than to be tortured to death by them? But suppose they are Russians? Oh, accursed bushes! If it were not for you I might now be able to see the horsemen.

All I can see through a little window in the bushes is a little brook in the far distance. It must be the same from which we drank a few minutes before the fight. Yes, so it is. I can see the flagstones lying across it for a bridge. The horsemen will probably cross it there. The voices sink to a lower pitch. I cannot discern the language. Besides, my hearing is weak with exhaustion. What if it is some of our people? God! I shall cry out; they will hear me from the brook, too. If they are Turks I will keep quiet. But why are they so long in coming out. So great is my impatience that I forget the fearful odors around me, although they are as strong as ever.

All at once, behold! a detachment of Cossacks is looming up on the stream yonder. Blue coats, red trousers—stripes, lances. . . . It looks like a half-hundred. Heading them is an officer with a black beard, on an excellent horse. The half-hundred had barely crossed the stream when he suddenly faced about in his saddle and shouted:

"Tr-r-r-r-t!"

"Hold on! Hold on, for God's sake, hold on!" I scream at the top of my voice. But the tramp of the sturdy horses, the clang of swords and the noisy talk of the horsemen are louder than my feeble voice.

Heavens! . . . Completely broken down, I fall with my face to the ground and burst out crying. The canteen is upset, and the water, my life, my reprieve from sure death, is trickling out on the grass. I do not become aware of it until all but half a glassful has been swallowed up by the thirsty earth.

How can I recall my state of mind at that terrible juncture? I lay motionless with half-shut eyes. The wind kept changing its course, now blowing fresh and pure air at me, now overpowering me with a wave of foul odors. My neighbor was by this time beyond description. Once, as I opened my eyes to glance at him, I was horror-stricken. His bony grin, his everlasting grin, seemed to me more ghastly and hideous than anything I had ever seen. At the medical college I had handled dozens of skeletons, yet none of them had repelled me as much as this neighbor of mine. Yes, this skeleton in the Egyptian uniform with brass buttons made me shudder. "It is the image of war," I said to myself.

Meanwhile, the sun is burning as fiercely as ever. My hands and face are blistered. The water is all gone. So tantalizing was my thirst that, having decided to swallow a few drops only, I could not help making away with all there was in the canteen. Oh, why did I not call out to the Cossacks when they were so near me! Even if they had turned out to be Turks I would have been better off than I am. What if they had put me to torture? How long would it have lasted? An hour or two, and my agonies would have been over, while now, there is no telling how long they will last. Mother, dear! I can see you, tearing your gray tresses and striking your dear head against the wall, as you curse the day when you gave me birth—curse the whole world for having devised that source of distress and horror called war.

Neither you nor Masha will ever hear of my sufferings. Good-bye, mamma, dear; good-bye, my sweetheart, my love! Death, where art thou? Come and take me!

But death does not come, and here I am lying under this fearful sun, without a drop of water to refresh my parched throat, while the corpse nearby spreads its pestiferous odors around me. Poor fellow; what a horrible sight he has become! And when nothing is left of him but his bones and uniform, then my turn will come, and after a while I shall be just as he is now.

The day passes and the night. Everything is the same. Another day . . .

The bushes are swaying and rustling, as though whispering: "You shall die, die, die."

"Can't see them, can't see them, can't see them!" return the bushes yonder.

"The bushes are so thick, you can't see them!" I suddenly hear a loud voice.

With a tremble I come to. Looking at me from the bushes I see the kindly blue eyes of Yakovev, our lance corporal.

"Up with your spades!" he shouts. "Here are two more. One of ours and one of theirs."

"Never mind the spades! Don't bury me. I am alive!" I am trying to cry out, but a faint groan is all that comes out of my parched lips.

"Heavens! He is alive, isn't he? Our master, Ivanov, I declare! Eh, boys, hurry up! Our master is alive. Fetch the surgeon at once!"

IX

Half a minute later they pour into my mouth some water, vodka and something else. Then everything disappears. Rhythmically swaying to and fro, the stretcher moves along. This lulls me to sleep. Every little while I wake up, only presently to become unconscious again. My bandaged wounds give me no pain. An indescribable sense of bliss is spread through my whole body.

"Ha-lt! Let down! Fourth relay, forward! Stretchers, lift!"

It is Peter Ivanovich, our hospital officer—a tall, gaunt, good-natured fellow—commanding his men.

"Peter Ivanovich!" I whisper to him.

"Well, my little dove," he says, bending over me.

"What did the doctor say? How soon am I going to die?"

"Come, come, Ivanov! Don't be talking nonsense. You are not going to die at all. Your bones are all right. What a lucky fellow! But how did you pull through those four days? What did you eat?"

"Nothing."

"Did you drink?"

"That I did. I helped myself to a Turk's canteen. Oh, Peter Ivanovich, I cannot speak now. Afterward."

"Well, God be with you, little dove; sleep away."

Again I am unconscious.

It was at the division hospital that I next regained consciousness. Standing by my bedside I saw surgeons, Sisters of Mercy, and among them I recognized the face of a celebrated St. Petersburg professor. He was bending over my legs. His hands were covered with blood. For some time he works without looking at me. At last he says:

"Well, yours is a lucky star, young man. You are going to live. One leg we have taken from you—that's true, but what does it amount to! Can you speak?"

I can, and I tell them all I have written on these pages.

"A BOOK ON DE HERO OF DE MANILA"
July 2, 1898

A young hopeful of the Upper East Side wandered into the Aguilar Free Circulating Library on East 110th Street a few days ago and demanded "a book on de hero of de Manila." The librarian with considerable difficulty convinced him that no such book had been printed. He then requested "de udder book by Hobson on 'Wid Sampson before de Merrimac.' " It took the librarian ten minutes to convince the stubborn youth that Hobson's book had not yet reached the publisher's hands.

In another East Side library not long ago a youngster of eleven or twelve years, who was known as "Peter," asked for a "Life of Dewey." The librarian told him that there was no such book on the shelves.

"That's too bad," said Peter. "I don't see why you don't have his life when you have his classification."

The "classification" was the regents' scheme for arranging books on the shelves, which was posted in a conspicuous place in the library. It was devised by Mr. Dewey, one of the regents, who, as the librarian said, "everybody knows is one of the most peaceful of men."

These are fairly typical examples, the librarians at the circulating libraries say, of the demands for books made almost every day. Ever since the war broke out there has been a run on the free libraries for books relating to Spain, Cuba and the Philippines, and works on military and naval tactics. And as soon as there began to be any fighting the demand extended to lives of military and naval heroes, stories of battle and sieges and anything that might be expected to thrill persons whose fighting blood was up. First come the children. The boys of the East Side go to the libraries to draw books about the men whose names they see in large type in the "war extras." Failing to get these, they content themselves with *The Red Badge of Courage* or King's *Cadet Life*. And if these books have already been loaned, one resource still is left them. "Please, may I enjoy the library?" is the next request, which means, the librarians have to learn, that the youngsters want to revel among the illustrated weeklies. But the children are not the only readers who want to be thrilled with tales of blood and daring. The novel readers have also come under the spell of war.

"There are not nearly so many calls for novels as there used to be," said the librarian of a small circulating library on the East Side; "and a good many people draw novels who, I am sure, never read them now. How do I explain it? Oh, the force of habit. They've been used to drawing novels regularly, and so they keep on drawing novels. But I am morally certain that if they open them at all they don't read many pages of them. They think they have read them perhaps, but they have really been talking about the war all the while."

Another class of readers are those who read books relating to war and military affairs, not for the sake of the excitement and the thrill, but because they are seeking information. A juvenile member of this class astonished a librarian a few days ago by asking for the "Handbook of Subsistence Stores." He explained that he wanted the book because he had a brother in one of the regiments in the South, and "he wrote home dat dey didn't get nothing but beans to eat." There is a great demand for reference books which treat of tactics in both the army and the navy. The applicants for such books are mostly young men, whom the librarians usually class as volunteers that are making the best of their time before orders are received to go to the front. Such books as Patterson's *Naval Dictionary,* Captain Mahan's *Influence of Sea Power on History,* and *Military Laws of the United States* are favorites with these young men. Other information seekers are curious chiefly about the enemy. These are mostly women and children, and they are constantly asking for books which will throw further light upon the government of Spain and her colonies and upon the ways of life of the Spaniards. Among these the books in greater request are Robertson's *History of the Reign of Charles V,* Harrison's *Spain,* Prescott's *Ferdinand and Isabella,* Cabria's *Cuba and Cubans* and Rowan's *Island of Cuba.* The three or four books which have been written about the Philippines and all works relating to Don Carlos, the Spanish pretender, are also in great demand with these information seekers.

Curiously enough, all the preceding incidents and facts were gathered at East Side libraries. In the corresponding quarters on the West Side of the borough the librarians say that they have observed no extraordinary demand for books. Things were proceeding on the even tenor of their way, and no unusual excitement or interest was manifest. On the East Side, on the other hand, the interest in all phases of the war is described by a librarian as intense and absorbing.

"In fact," continued this librarian, "we find that the people around here are always interested keenly in the great topics of the day. Not only the war, but every event of national importance interests them and excites their curiosity. And they turn at once to the libraries." It would be a difficult sociological problem to determine the cause of the difference between the West Side and the East, if there really is a difference in this respect. The librarians, at any rate, are not able to explain it.

In the great free libraries, such as the Astor and the Lenox, another class of readers may be found—a class that is not so much in evidence now as it was during the early days of the war. This class comprises the writers for magazines and newspapers, who are preparing special articles relating to the war. They come armed with paper and pencils, and spend hours in transferring facts and figures from the books of reference to their notebooks.

"LET YOUR COUNTRY BE
DEARER TO YOU THAN YOUR LIVES!"
July 6, 1898

Five hundred boys and girls, each with a pair of little American flags crossed on his or her breast, yesterday morning sang and marched, recited and applauded patriotic speeches at the large hall of the Hebrew Institute, East Broadway and Jefferson Street. It was at once the celebration of the Fourth of July and the closing exercises of the Hebrew Educational Alliance.

"Don't be surprised at our celebrating the Fourth on the 5th," said one speaker. "The Fourth of July is every day. It is the day of American glory, and I want you to consider yourselves Americans. Forget that you are Russians. Remember only that this country is your country, and that the Jewish faith is your faith. Let the two—your country and your religion—be dearer to you than your lives."

Other speeches eulogized Hobson and Dewey and glorified the American victory over Cervera's fleet; and although many of the little immigrants did not seem to understand what the speakers meant, they all knew that they were saying something good about America and the way the American soldiers are licking the Spaniards, and the hall every little while rang with applause and cheers.

The most patriotic member of the Hebrew Free School was a little fellow of about seven or eight, with glittering black eyes and glossy curls. He listened to the speeches with absorbed attention, every minute putting his hand to his breast to make sure that his flags were all right, and anxiously waiting for an opportunity to applaud and to cry "Hurrah!" Once he did so out of place, whereupon another boy by his side pinched him to order. One girl of ten kept nodding assent to nearly every word of the speakers, and when the girls on the platform began to applaud she would face about as if to give her schoolmates the signal.

"What were you applauding, sonny?" was asked of an eight-year-old boy when the exercises were over.

"Sampson," he answered bashfully.

"Who is he?"

"He is President United States. No, sir, Mr. McKinley is President. Mr. Sampson lives in Manila. The teacher says he is a brave man."

"Are you a brave man?"

"No, sir. I am a boy. When I'm big I'll be a brave man."

"Like Sampson or like Dewey?"

"I want to be like Mr. Hobson."

"Why?"

"Because."

SONG OF THE MAUSER
July 30, 1898

What does a flying bullet sound like? The question was asked of each of a group of wounded soldiers on the hospital ship *Relief,* as they lay chatting in their neighboring bunks on the main deck.

"St—st—st!" said Private Wilhelm F. Volimar of the Eighth Infantry, who was shot through the femoral artery in the battle of San Juan. "I remember marching with the other boys up the road. Some of us were whistling, others were joking or asking questions, when suddenly I heard something like a—what shall I call it?—like an insect pass by me. It seemed to be buzzing or whispering. 'St—st—st!' it was saying, or something like it.

Of course, I knew what it meant, and it gave me the chills. I'd been expecting it all along, and I thought I wouldn't care a bit. But when that first 'st—st—st!' came it struck me cold. Afterward I got so used to those bullets that I didn't mind them. They whizzed all around me and still I did not care a button.''

When the question was put to Private Darby, Company D, Thirteenth Infantry, who was shot through both lungs while charging up the hill at San Juan, he said, with a smile of intelligence, as though he had been interested in the subject himself and given it some consideration:

"Png—png—png! but sometimes it's like 'pwow—pwow—pwow!' It all depends on what kind of bullet and how it scoots through the air, I think.''

William Young of Company F, Sixth Infantry, who was wounded in the right leg in the same engagement and whose face and beard gleam dark amidst the lighter complexions of his neighbors, was sure the sound made by a Mauser bullet was "Dz—dz—dz!''

"I can just hear it ringing all around me,'' he said with the air of one trying to recall a dear moment in his life. "It was before Santiago on July 11. We were only a few hundred feet from the Spaniards, and the fire was too terrible for anything. The full strength of our regiment was 450, and about one-third of that number fell in that hail of bullets. 'Dz—dz—dz!' they went.''

Privates McCue, Oscar Baucum, Henry Brett, Walter Buck, Frank Manning and Joe Sullivan, all of whom are down with wounds received while fighting the Spaniards in Cuba, agreed with the others, one of them adding philosophically that it was hard to define exactly how a flying bullet sounded, since it is no human being, and its voice can no more be imitated by man than the language of birds.

Fred Shockley, colored, of Troop D, Tenth Cavalry, however, thought the question the easiest thing in the world to answer.

"How do a bullet sound?'' he asked, as he raised his bandaged head with an air which seemed to say, "You might as well ask me the color of grass,'' and then said in the most matter-of-course way:

"Like a trolley.''

Shockley was shot through the head near Santiago de Cuba on July 2. The bullet came out over his left temple, entered the shoulder and pierced its way through the breast. The wounds are healing well, and he is rapidly approaching complete recovery.

"I stood fire from 5 in the mornin' till 3 in the afternoon,'' he said. "It was a regula' hail an' I thought I don' neba' be hit. Why? 'Cause I stood it so long an' day couldn't strike me.''

"So you felt sure you could not be hit?" was asked.

"Indeed I did," Shockley answered with some resentment, his eyes glowing beneath his snow-white bandages.

"But finally you were hit, were you not?"

"Sure I was, but I didn't feel it. They picked me up half-dead like. It was this way. I was layin' down to shoot an' raised my head an'—an'—an' dat's all, sah."

Asked how it feels to be afraid of death, Shockley said in the same matter-of-course manner in which he had answered the question as to the sound of a bullet:

"Don' be afraid o' death, sir."

"But didn't you think you might be killed? Didn't you try to imagine how it feels to be dead?"

"When a fella' be dead he don' feel nothin' nohow; so it ain't no use thinkin'," he concluded, triumphantly.

Private Darby, the man who had been shot through both lungs, said in answer to the same question:

"You get a kind of 'I-don't-care' feeling and you don't care a damn. You get reconciled to it. How did I feel before I got reconciled to it? I was afraid. No, it was not like any other fear I'd ever felt before. It was something different. It was like—but I'll be hanged if I can explain it."

Previous to the war Darby was stationed on Governor's Island, and a short time before he left for the South he was a member of the company of soldiers who gave military performances in Madison Square Garden. He is a track athlete and a sharpshooter, and soldiering was a pleasant occupation with him, and so he went to the front willingly, he says, and held himself in readiness to kill and be killed. While he was speaking one of the occupants of the neighboring beds said to the other:

"I was not afraid of death a bit."

"I was—like hell," remarked the other.

Private Young told of a young recruit who was so green that he did not know how to use the sight of his rifle.

"He was an Ohio boy," he said, "only eighteen years old, but a luckier fellow I never saw. Once, as we stood firing, he came up to me. 'Say,' says he, 'I can't get my d——d sight fixed. I don't know if I shot over the hill or under it.' And he was as cool as a cucumber."

The wounded men all laughed, and, elated with the success of his story, Young went on to tell them how his company was commanded to retreat while he was so excited firing at the enemy that he did not hear or see anything.

"All at once I found that I was all alone and near the Spaniards. Talk of being afraid of death! If I did not drop dead for fear it was because I was somebody else, not myself. My, how I ran! When I reached my company and all danger was over for the time, at least, I was more afraid than ever. It strikes me that after the battle a fellow is more afraid than while he is right in it. Then he is too excited."

"I guess you're right," said one of Young's wounded listeners.

NEW YORK'S 71ST COMES HOME
September 3, 1898

A group of foreigners sat in a Second Avenue café discussing the homecoming of the Seventy-first and the war in general. They had just been to Broadway, where they had seen the regiment and the crowd.

"To look at those wan, haggard-looking fellows one would be inclined to doubt that they could shoot at all," said a hatchet-faced Czech, as he poured himself out a cup of tea from a gleaming little tin pot. He said it in good German, which he spoke with a bad accent, and his listeners at the same table and at others followed him with apparent respect.

"Of course, we all know that they are fever-stricken and exhausted, and all that, but—I don't know," he faltered, with a shamefaced smile, "I have been here now twelve years, and yet I cannot get used to the idea that the American soldier is really what he is called, and not a schoolboy, playing soldier. You see, we Europeans are used to the sturdy, burly type of warrior. It is not in vain that we say he is big and strong as a soldier. And so, when we are shown a slender, boyish-looking Yankee, and we are asked to believe that he is a fighter, that he can endure the fatigues and privations of war, and conquer countries, we cannot help smiling skeptically."

One of the men who shared the Czech's table and teapot was an elderly, genial-faced German, who looked as though his only part in the conversation was to agree and to corroborate the opinion of his companion. All the while the Czech spoke he kept nodding and smiling happily, as much as to say, "Exactly, exactly! I have always thought that way." Presently there was a pause, the Czech being busy lighting his pipe, which was so short that it seemed a wonder the tip of his nose escaped uninjured; and eagerly catching up the conversation, the German said:

"Why, look at their uniforms, knapsacks, hats! If they came to Germany they would be taken for a lot of tramps, wouldn't they?" he appealed to the Czech, whose pipe was by that time hiding his nose in a cloud of smoke.

"Exactly," assented the Czech. "There is nothing soldierly in their uniforms nor in their general bearing, nothing to strike terror into one's heart."

"They look like a lot of Polish peasants on their pilgrimage to a celebrated image of Our Lady," came from a neighboring table, with a laugh, which was lost on the others, however, who did not seem to know anything about Poland and its peasant pilgrims. The man who spoke German with an accent of his own seemed somewhat rattled, and to work himself out of his awkward position he went on: "The Americans make me sick anyhow. It is all very well to talk of beating a weak nonentity of a nation like Spain. Let them tackle us Germans [as he articulated the last words his accent and pronunciation seemed more Polish than ever]. Why, we would make dough of the whole lot of them, wouldn't we? One of our soldiers would manage a whole regiment, I think."

At this, a sallow-faced little German, with piercing black eyes, who sat alone in a bleak corner, fixed his terrible glance on the man from Posen. The sickly-looking German is known in the cafés for his sharp tongue and quarrelsome disposition, although nobody seems to mind his outbursts of temper, while some are said to like him all the more for them. In the present instance, it appeared as if he did not care whether the American soldier was as good as the German or worse, but the Pole's manner, the way in which he boasted of "us Germans," and, it may be, his accent, roused his ire, and he instantly took a stand against him.

"One of you Germans could lick a whole regiment of Yankees, did you say?" he broke out. "Fiddlesticks, you can! How many German fighters have you to face a Corbett or a Fitzsimmons, hey? We Germans—oh, I beg your pardon, sir, you Germans—are fat and big and good for nothing. We have a lot of flesh, and we can drink a lot of beer; that's all we are good for. Don't you make fun of the boyish-looking Americans. They are not big, because they have no superfluous flesh to hamper them. Whatever their size, it is all strength and fight. You ought to thank your German stars Kaiser Wilhelm did not run up against them. He would find it a tougher job to get rid of them than the Frenchmen."

Everybody listened and smiled—everybody except the man from Posen. He shifted uneasily on his seat and blushed and paled, and was so overwhelmed that all he could say was to ask:

"Why, are you not a German yourself?"

"Never mind what I am. If you are a German, I am an American. I live here anyhow, don't I? And if you don't like this country, I don't see why you live here. Why don't you go back to your Germany?"

The poor Pole was about to retort, but the others signed to him, and little by little he caught their facetious mood, and laughed at his own expense.

———

YELLOW FEVER HITS THE NINTH
July 3, 1899

"Santiago is a pooty folly place," said one of the colored "immunes" on board the *Meade,* "only it's jess chockfull o' yellah fevah an' dat knocked de life outen me."

There were other fever-stricken "immunes" on the main deck, and when they were asked how they accounted for their sickness, one man said that it did look "kind o' funny that the blamed yellow thing should go back on an immune fellow," while another gave the questioner a melancholy stare of his big jaundiced eyes, shrugged his shoulders, and remained silent. These men, however, were all well enough to be about and help keep the ship clean, so that the only member of the Ninth regiment actually on the sick list was a man with a broken leg. But then, the "immunes" had no sooner recovered from yellow fever than they fell victims to homesickness, and so they sat or lay about or stood leaning on their guns, each with a yearning look in his eyes and each communing with his own thoughts.

One of the buglers of the regiment is of a scholarly turn of mind. He was found sitting in a snug corner, his bugle in one hand and a Spanish grammar in the other. While in Cuba he picked up enough Spanish to make his way about, he said bashfully, but he did not think he used good grammar, so one of the things he bought before leaving was the textbook on his knees.

"It's quite an easy language to learn," he said. "Much easier than English," and when asked whether he thought his Spanish better than his English, he answered, with another bashful smile:

"Pardon me, sir, I mean that English must be a much harder language for a foreigner to pick up. Our people all learned to speak Spanish, but the Cubans could not get much English into their heads. We tried to teach them,

33

but it was no use. Maybe the colored people of this country are a brainier lot than the colored Cubans, but I think it's all in the language.''

The bugler's slouch hat was covered with inscriptions and pictures. The name of every Cuban town, castle or camp which the Ninth regiment had visited was inscribed upon it, and the pictures, in red and blue ink, represented the American and Cuban flags, a Cuban soldier and an American soldier, both colored, with their hands clasped and some of the scenery in the suburbs of Santiago.

''What are you going to do with this hat?'' was asked.

''When I get home I will hang it up and keep it,'' answered the bugler. Then he added in his embarrassed way: ''I wouldn't part with it for a hundred dollars.''

The son of ex-Governor Pinchbeck of Louisiana, one of the colored officers of the regiment, expressed himself as anxious to have the public know that in the recent skirmish with Cuban brigands it was the colored regiment that captured the marauders.

''Let me introduce you to Lieutenant Wakefield,'' he said, pointing to a tall colored man in an officer's uniform. ''He played an important part in the affair. It was he and Hanna who rounded up the brigands, but, of course, we colored people don't get the credit that is due us.''

The white officers, and particularly the quartermaster, also dwelt on the conflict with the Cuban outlaws.

''One thing is certain,'' said Quartermaster Swobe, ''the United States is going to have a lot of trouble in Cuba. These brigands are all mustered-out soldiers of the revolutionary army of Cuba. They go about holding up trains, looting villages and keeping the peaceful population in constant terror. You see, they have been so long in the business as soldiers that they cannot get out of it.''

On a bench near the entrance to the quartermaster's office sat a young Cuban couple with their three little girls. They had lived in Philadelphia for ten years until the war was over, when they returned home. But they found the business outlook in Cuba so unfavorable that they had to come back.

''You can't make a living there,'' said the father, ''and the fever and all kinds of other troubles drove me back. The Cubans are all upset, and it will be a long time before things settle down. Besides, I am used to this country, and I just simply had to come back.''

When six-year-old Gracie, the eldest of the three girls, was asked whether she would go back to Cuba, she opened her flashing black eyes wide and said in good American kindergarten English:

''No, sir; I am afraid of the fever.''

"And where would you like to live?"

"In Philadelphia."

"Why?"

"Because I am an American girl."

Captain Wilson spoke in warm commendation of the regiment, describing it as the hardest-working and cleanest body of men he had ever seen, adding that if he had to travel with a regiment around the world he would select the Ninth immunes.

Colonel Crane also spoke highly of his men, but when asked about the state of things in Cuba, he said bluntly:

"That question is beyond me. I've no right to express an opinion. I'm a soldier."

2
THE OLD WORLD SCOURGE

DREYFUS AND HAMAN
September 1, 1898

Business on Hester Street was not suspended on account of Colonel Henry's confession, but the market women and men who had no customers at their pushcarts talked nothing but Dreyfus and Haman this morning. Haman is the Hester Street nickname of every "fiend of Israel" in general and Esterhazy and Colonel Henry in particular.

Next to the war with Spain the pushcart peddlers have kept track of the Dreyfus affair. The five Yiddish papers print the news of the matter in their biggest type, and this is read and reread over the pushcart, to be discussed and commented upon at the synagogue after prayer or perhaps during the half-hour or so when the Master Reader is busy chanting the Bible from the central platform.

The names of every actor in the Dreyfus case, from the unhappy prisoner of Devil's Island himself down to the assistant of the lawyers on either side, are well known, therefore, to every *cheder* (school) boy in the ghetto, and when yesterday's news of the colonel's confession burst upon the crowded streets of the Jewry, the name Henry was caught up as that of an old acquaintance, and was accompanied by curses such as none but a ghetto market woman could invent.

"Henry? That knave, Henry?" the women shouted, glaring at each other and slapping their smutty aprons with mixed triumph and despair. "And what did I say, Sarah? I knew all along it was he who had forged all those papers against the poor Jewish boy. Henry, may he be shaken with ague and hurled from one end of the world to the other!''

"She knew!" another pushcart woman retorted, with a high shrug. "As if it was not plain as day that the rogue—grant, O Lord of the Universe! that he and all the enemies of Israel be burned with all the pests the world has ever tasted. Dreyfus a traitor! A son of Israel betray the secrets of his King to the King's enemy!''

"Crazy woman that you are," broke in a tall grey-bearded herring peddler. "Have you fogotten that the French have no king? Don't you know that they have a president like the Americans?''

"What? A president?" asked the woman. "On my part they may have kings and presidents and devils and be choked. But no. A president like the Americans, did you say? What have those rascals, fiends of Israel, to do with America? This is a good country, a righteous country. You don't see children of Jewish parents sent to prison on false charges, do you?''

The soda water stands, particularly of the circulating library variety, were besieged by knots of men, young and old, discussing the great news of the day.

A portly red-bearded man, with his spectacles on his forehead, who took a hand in the debate on the corner of Allen and Division Streets, was of the opinion that Dreyfus would not profit by Henry's confession one whit.

"Do you suppose those Gentiles will let Israel triumph?" he exclaimed with a violent twirl of his sidelock. "The Gentiles will perjure themselves and commit suicide rather than let it be known that our people are pure and good.''

"You say so because you don't read the papers," objected a younger man. "I read the Gentile papers as well as the Yiddish journals, so I know all about it.''

"Well, what do you know?" the bystanders asked, some seriously, others with a glimmer of sarcasm. "Go ahead, it would not do to keep one's knowledge to one's self.''

"Well, what I know is this, that Dreyfus will come out clear and that the whole business will do an immense amount of good to all Israel. The Gentiles will now see that all charges against us are false, and that we are the best and most honest people on earth. Mark my word, my rabbi, the Jews will fare better even in Russia now.''

"May it please the Lord of the world to make it so," sighed several men dubiously.

"It is a black eye to the anti-Semites, anyhow," observed a little man of fifty or thereabouts, with a sparse black beard, which somehow made him look even smaller than he was. "But is it not interesting the way the whole world is excited, and France is in spasms and on the verge of an upheaval, and all on account of whom? Of a mere Jew!" He answered his own question with a glow of exultation in his black, melancholy eyes.

"Oh, they can't pooh-pooh the Jews. Even if there were only a handful of us left we would amount to more than a Gentile nation."

"But you forget that God preserves the children of Israel only to give them their reward in the world to come," interposed the red-haired man. "Suffer here in this world, that the recompense may be the brighter in Heaven—such is the rule, and all your talk about better plans on earth is mere nonsense. No, children, the Gentiles will not come around, and fiend Henry's confession will only serve to embitter and to spur them on to further malice. The redemption of Israel cannot come before the advent of the Messiah, children, and all we can do now is to accept our lot as Jews, that is with love and reverence."

A DREYFUS CRANK
AND A PIOUS LUTHERAN WIDOW
September 9, 1899

The tenants of a certain house on the East Side are following the progress of a love affair, which had its origin in the interest of the two young people in the Dreyfus case. The young man, whom we shall call Aaron Jacoby, is a graduate of the Berlin University. He came to this country some three years ago at the invitation of a rich uncle, who offered to assist him to a business career. The young man had not been a week in his relative's store, however, before he made up his mind that his natural vocation lay in other directions. The atmosphere of a clothing warehouse did not agree with him.

Among his chums and college mates at home he was known as a promising mathematician, and he told his uncle that his ideal occupation was to teach his favorite subject at some American college. The uncle asked him if he was not crazy. His head drummer made more money than three professors put together, he urged. The nephew answered that he did not care, and that he would much prefer to earn one thousand dollars a year as a teacher of mathematics than ten times that sum as a business man.

The uncle was good-natured but vain: the nephew, proud, stubborn, and morose. Some hot words followed, and the young man went away to shift for himself. He peddled, he worked in factories, he canvassed for instalment companies. Things have gone hard with him. His uncle has made him several peace offerings, but they have all been rejected.

At first Aaron found consolation in his mathematics. He was working on some new theorems in celestial mechanics, and often dined on a couple of pretzels without minding it. Recently, however, the Dreyfus case dethroned the theorems in his brain and heart. At first he paid but slight attention to the case. He even had a lurking suspicion that the captain was guilty. Little by little he became interested in the details of the case. He was loath to take the statements of the American and German papers on trust. "All foreign countries are hostile to the generals," he reasoned. "Mercier, Roget and the rest of them are certainly guilty of conspiracy. That's clear from their own assertions, and that's the reason the foreigners are inclined to take sides with the prisoner. But is Dreyfus really innocent? Is it all a plot based on nothing except the fact that the nationality of the prisoner suited him of all other officers of the general staff for this terrible part?"

Aaron wanted to hear the other side. With some difficulty and a considerable pecuniary sacrifice he procured sets of newspapers such as *Le Petit Journal, L'Intransigeant* or *L'Autorité*. These he read and reread, marking salient points with his pencil, collating them with the corresponding passages in the articles of the Dreyfusard papers and filling scrapbook after scrapbook with clippings.

The upshot was that Aaron became firmly convinced of Dreyfus's absolute innocence, and that he took the case of the unfortunate captain so close to heart that he could attend neither to his theorems nor to his instalment business.

The people at the café where he takes his meals call him a Dreyfus crank and consult him on the obscure points in the history of the case. Since the present trial was begun he has been in a continual fever of excitement. He reads every newspaper he can get and spends more than he can afford on "extras." He is so wrapped up in the case that his friends are discussing the probable effect which a verdict of guilty would have on his health. He has come to think of Dreyfus as a near relative, as a close friend. He curses Mercier and his allies as if they were his personal enemies, and often, as he harangues the customers or the residents of the tenement house on the suffering of the famous prisoner, tears come into his eyes, and his voice is choked with sobs.

"I'll commit suicide if the rogues get the best of it," Aaron said the other evening in the course of a talk on his favorite subject on the roof of the house where he lives.

One old man told him he was a fool, that Dreyfus was not the only innocent man that was sent to prison or even to the gallows.

Aaron was wild. The whole world was made up of brutes, he said, of people without hearts, without a sense of pity or of justice.

A young widow, the daughter of the janitor, said he was right, and Aaron poured out his tale of woe upon her. She proved an appreciative listener. He went over the whole case for her benefit, and she listened with the closest attention, sighing over the captain's fate and seconding the curses which the young man called down upon the heads of the anti-Dreyfusards.

Since then the two of them are seen every evening reading the Dreyfus news together. The young woman takes the matter to heart as closely as Aaron. An infatuation is said to have sprung up between them; they are described as being madly in love with each other, and what quickens the curiosity of the neighbors is the fact that the widow is a pious Lutheran, while Aaron is a Jew.

THE CAPTAIN BEFORE HIS JUDGES
Harper's Weekly / September 23, 1899

Rosh Hashana found the Jewish captain before his judges. The *shofar* blew in the synagogue, its every note an angel-advocate soaring heavenward to plead for the wandering people. It was New Year, one of the Days of Awe, the season of broken hearts.

When the patriarchs, enveloped in their praying shawls, chanted the ancient hymn with which Rabbi Amnon, the martyr, sang himself to eternal sleep, there were sobs in the house of God.

One's soul revels in grief on these Ten Days of Penance, stifled woes bestir themselves; silenced pangs clamor for tears. It is as if every sorrow which has been overlooked in the rush and scramble for bread had been put off to a time especially set aside for "hearts to have their cry out." Every Jew has his own "bundle of misery" to pray to be delivered from, but this time there was the image of a brother in Israel bent with untimely age to wring a sigh from one's breast.

The people of the ghetto had heard the story of the man who had been degraded, tortured, crushed for a crime which another had committed. They had been told that he suffered because he was their brother. The six Yiddish dailies of New York were filled with details of the struggle which has rent a great nation in two and turned the rest of humanity into a host of breathless spectators. Captain Dreyfus had been likened to the "birds of redemption" which the worshippers were to put to death as a ransom for themselves on the eve of Atonement Day. He was the scapegoat of wicked Gentiles because he was a Jew, and every child of the ghetto saw in his emaciated body a harrowed lump of his own flesh.

The unenlightened and unlettered, those whose imaginations had not been trained to paint people and scenes beyond the seas in the colors of their own life, gathered from all the talk about the man on trial at Rennes that "a lot of heartless Gentiles were tapping the blood of a Jew who had done nobody any harm." They were sure it was all because the race was in exile and that there was no help for it, and they sought consolation in the curses which they invoked upon the heads of the French generals.

"What is there to think about?" said a fishwife who had been asked for an opinion on the Dreyfus case. "A plague in their every limb for every pang they give him. As if it were the first time a Jew had been trampled upon! Wait till Messiah comes round. Then our sufferings will be at an end."

Those who had learned to think and to imagine, however—the readers of the papers who had been drinking in the reports of the court-martial—took something like a personal interest in the trial. For two years the face of the un-happy man had never been absent from their minds.

"Who shall be at rest, and who shall be wandering; who to remain tranquil, and who be disturbed; who shall be cast down, and who exalted?"

As the cantor sang these words in his doleful, awe-stricken recitative, the worshippers beheld an innocent man in irons over his bleeding wounds, and in the outburst of prayer which followed their voices spoke as much of the pain of a martyr in Israel as of the accumulated anguish of their own hearts.

A few days had gone by. It was Penance Sabbath in the ghetto. The morning service was over, yet the synagogues were alive with people, the men in the vestry-rooms, the women in the "women's synagogue." With humbled mien, as befits the season of broken spirits, they were studying Talmud, chanting psalms, or reading the Book of Tears. Every minute was precious, for it was one of those days when prayer, divine study, charity, and penance will erase one's sins from the heavenly book of records, and obtain for one an enrollment in the Book of Life. Yet now and again the patriarchs would pause to listen to the noise of the street. Boys were crying English and Yiddish "extras." At a distance their voices rang stern, portentous.

"Maybe it is the verdict!" someone would whisper, as if frightened.

"God knows what news they have!"

But the noise outside did not seem loud enough, so the old men went on swaying and chanting more earnestly, more passionately than ever.

The tallest man in the group was Rabbi Jacob, "of the exile of Moscow," whence he was banished, with his numerous flock, in 1892. Stroking his gray earlocks as he rocked his stalwart figure to and fro, he was absorbed in the open folio before him.

The others joined in a chorus of soft sing-songs. Somebody asked the rabbi a question of sacred law. The venerable man began to explain the point.

All at once there was an outcry in the street: "Extra! Extra!"

Silence fell over the room. Faces turned pale. The rabbi's arms dropped to his sides. He was about to send somebody out for information, but at the same moment a man came in, pale and panting.

"They have found him guilty, the brigands!" he said, with his hand to his breast.

"What? How do you know? Maybe you are mistaken?" asked the rabbi, starting to his feet, aghast.

While the newcomer was telling how he had heard the grim news read in a Gentile paper, the rabbi of the exile sank into his seat, and leaning his head in his hands, he burst into tears.

"*Oi! oi! oi!*" wailed the pious people, wringing their hands.

A bewigged head peeped out of one of the windows of the women's synagogue.

The next minute the women's synagogue rang with sobs.

"My heart told me they would do it," said the rabbi, "but I would not give up hope, and now gloom and void have come upon us. It is because he is a Jew that they have sacrificed him, the murderers, yet I would weep as much if he were a Gentile, for do not the Gentiles of the world outside of France mix their sighs with ours? It is for truth and justice we are grieving. Yes, the fall of sinful France is complete. She was the most exalted; now she wallows in the mire, as it is written: 'He raises one high, and He throws one into the depths.' The higher up one is perched the more violent is one's fall. Ah, but why should the poor son of Israel be made to pay the penalty of a nation's wickedness? What has the poor child done to be tortured so cruelly? Why should our people suffer for everybody else's sins? When, oh when, will come the end to our exile?"

The rabbi's voice was choked with sobs.

42

THE DIABOLICAL MASSACRE
OF JEWS IN KISHINEV
May 23, 1903

At the request of The Commercial Advertiser, *Abraham Cahan has written the following description of the conditions in Russia, of which the massacre at Kishinev is symptomatic. Mr. Cahan is probably the best known Russian writer now in this country. He has contributed articles concerning his country and people to many of our leading reviews and is now engaged on a novel dealing with the nihilist movement in Russia, the anti-Jewish riots and the consequent great influx of Russian Jews to this country. He has written two other novels which have met with great success in this country and in England, Mr. Howells having referred to him as one of the best of the younger representatives of American realism. He has kept in constant touch with the affairs of his native country, especially the "underground movement," and is probably as well qualified as anyone can be to tell the truth about the situation.*

Russia is quivering on the brink of a revolution, and the diabolical massacre of Jews in Kishinev is one of those political "electric rods" which the present minister of the interior, M. von Plehve, first learned to employ in 1881, after the killing of Alexander II by the "terrorists" of the Narodnaya Volya ("Will of the People"). The anti-Jewish riots of those days, which spread from district to district, laying waste an aggregate of some 200 towns and villages, and covering a period of nearly a year and a half, were ushered in six weeks after the death of the Czar. The assassination of the Czar by the revolutionists was followed by a general state of unrest. The new Czar, Alexander III, feared a general uprising, and was prepared to sign what has since been known as the "undersized constitution of Loris Melikov," when the first and mildest of all the anti-Semitic riots of the period broke out in Elizavetgrad, a city in the near neighborhood of Odessa and Kishinev. This outbreak had been organized by local anti-Semites, and had nothing to do with the general state of things, except in so far as it had given rise to a vague feeling that the government was in trouble and that the foundation of "law and order" (as the term is understood by Russian officials) was shaken; but once this riot had taken place the notion of having the popular "fidget" spend itself on a racial crusade of this sort, was seized upon. Count Loris Melikov, the liberal-minded and progressive minister of the interior, was replaced by a champion of blind oppression named Ignatyev, and the "undersized constitution" was buried in the archives unsigned. M. von Plehve was head of the police department under Ignatyev, and in that capacity he had much to do with the enforcement of that policy of making a scapegoat of the Jew which his then-superior carried to perfection.

In his circular to the governor of Bessarabia, sent a few days before the recent slaughter and which refers to it as an expected event, Minister von Plehve shows himself to be a faithful follower of his old master. In this official communication, it will be remembered, he not only enjoins the governor from using drastic measures against the prospective rioters (frankly explaining that such a step was apt to arouse anti-government feeling in the masses), but also, by referring to the Jews as "the principal fleecers of the region," throws out an unmistakable hint that the best thing to do in case of riot is to "let our boys have some fun with the Jews," as the anti-Semitic phrase runs in the land of the czars.

This is precisely the kind of circulars that were addressed to governors by Ignatyev in 1881. As a result, the governor of Kiev, during the atrocities which took place in the capital of his province (the most inhuman that were committed in 1881), drove around among the hoodlums and their well-dressed brothers-at-arms, smilingly exhorting them to "quiet down, boys." Then, as now (in Kishinev), the streets were full of police and troops who, far from protecting the victims, were encouraged by their officers to take a hand in the work of pillage, destruction, rapine and murder; then, as now, every attempt on the part of the Jews at defending their property and the honor of their wives and daughters was prevented by the soldiers dispersing every band of these would-be champions at the point of the bayonet and driving them indoors to await the coming of the drink-crazed rioters.

The governors of other riot-ridden provinces acted in a similar manner. The natural upshot was an impression which rapidly spread among the blind, illiterate peasantry that this crusade had been ordered by the Czar and that the ukaz to that effect was in the hands of local officials. It was a common incident of the period for the people of a village to best the government of the place, demanding to know how soon "that paper" was expected to reach their district, or for the inhabitants of the suburbs of a city to come to town with their wagons, sacks and implements of destruction and ask policemen in the street when they would be "wanted by the authorities."

"What for?" asked a policeman in one case.

"Why, to smash the houses of those un-Christian fellows" was the answer. "Look, sir, we have our wagons ready to carry off their wares and treasure in. Tell his honor, the master of police, that we are all ready and only waiting for his word of command."

In numerous instances, an honest, good-natured peasant living on the best of terms with his Jewish neighbors and doing odd jobs for them, told them, tearfully, that he would have to demolish their furniture, but that the authorities could be fooled by the furniture being carefully concealed, only the windows being smashed "for a ruse."

The object of that "imperial ukaz" was, in the opinion of these primitive masses, "to turn over the ill-gotten wealth of the anti-Christs to the beloved children of the Czar, the peasants," and Ignatyev, assisted by M. von Plehve, helped these rumors to spread and gain ground by having the rioters everywhere encouraged in their fiendish work.

This chapter in the history of my unhappy people ought to be of special interest to the American reader, because it was these riots of 1881 and 1882, which started that immigration which has since increased the Jewish population of this country by more than a million, and has made New York by far the largest centre of Jewish residence in the world. The overflowing Jewish immigration, which was begun by the arrival of shiploads made up of victims of those riots, has now received a new stimulus from the slaughter in Kishinev. Efforts will be made by the older Russian refugees to systematize this new influx, directing it toward the less densely populated sections of the country.

To return to the riots and the political situation of 1881, the revolution of those days was mere child's play to the crystallized and well-organized political agitation of our time. A Berlin dispatch quotes the *National Zeitung* as saying that the massacre at Kishinev is "only a symptom of the deep, latent dissatisfaction among the peasant classes in Russia, the causes of which are well known. The fury of the mob happened to be vented chiefly on the Jews. The Russian newspapers, however, have been compelled to suppress the facts that 'during the riot the windows of the government palace were smashed, the house of a nobleman named Krupensky was looted, a Christian church plundered, and that many of the dead and injured were Christians.' "

Still more to the point is the following Associated Press dispatch of the same date:

The government fears serious outbreaks next week Friday at the city's [St. Petersburg's] bi-centenary. The police have asked owners of factories not to give their employees a holiday, but the men probably will refuse to work. Revolutionist emissaries have been flooding the workshops with seditious literature.

The two concluding sentences contain the sum and substance of the situation. In 1881 I had an opportunity to study the revolutionary movement in Russia at rather close range, and I have kept track of its development from this side of the Atlantic all these years. The long and short of it is that while in the early eighties the movement was practically confined to a handful of college students (of both sexes), the organized political struggle embraces great numbers of the working population of the cities, and in its blind, elemental form, the spirit of discontent finds vent in the form of frequent agricultural riots, of which the western world is allowed to hear but a faint distant echo. It was as a consequence of one of these rural uprisings and the unthinking iron-handed repressions following them that the governor of Uffa was killed four days ago. An attempt upon the life of two other governors having been made since the assassination of M. von Plehve's predecessor, Minister Sipyagin, and of a minister of public education.

The Russian Social Democrats, one of the rival revolutionary organizations now at work in the empire and which has obtained a firm hold upon the factory population in many cities, is opposed to assassination or to acts of violence in any form, and the demonstrations which are held under its flag are often half a million strong. The country is literally flooded with revolutionary literature, and the pages of the underground papers are filled with the names of new political prisoners, exiles to Siberia.

I have before me the latest issues of several organs of this kind, all but two of them issued in Russia, and their columns are seething with the signs of a feverish revolutionary activity. Unfortunately, this part of the empire, its "underground," is almost unknown to the people of this country, or western Europe, or they would be aware that if there ever was the spectacle of a monarch sitting on the crater of a volcano, such a spectacle is to be seen now in Russia.

Aye, Russia is on the verge of a revolution, and if there was need of an outlet for the popular feeling of discontent in the form of anti-Jewish riots at the time of Ignatyev, this is certainly the case now, when his one-time subordinate and pupil is in charge of the Interior Department.

As to the attitude of the revolutionists toward "anti-Jewish riots," they do much toward making such racial outbreaks impossible. Indeed, in every place where their movement has obtained a firm footing, the two races live in perfect harmony and good feeling. Jew and Gentile belong to the same secret trade organization, attend the same "underground" gatherings and go to Siberia surrounded by the same forest of bayonets. In this respect there is no distinction between the two revolutionary bodies, and upon the whole the movement which makes for free speech and the beginnings of parliamentary government is an active force against racial or religious prejudice. In several instances where anti-Semitic riots threatened to break out the revolutionary Gentiles have succeeded in warding off the calamity.

Unfortunately, however, Kishinev is not a revolutionary stronghold, and the incendiary agitation of the *Bessarabets,* the anti-Semitic organ of Kishinev, finding encouragement in the attitude of the authorities, brought about those scenes of human butchery the very description of which is enough to drive one mad. The government is badly in need of this "electric rod" for turning off the thunder which is gathering over the roof of the Winter Palace. But then the miscreants of Kishinev went too far. One could allow thousands of Jewish houses or shops to be demolished or pillaged, with a few score violated women and a dozen or so of corpses into the bargain, as the case was with the riots of Ignatyev's time, but when the streets are strewn with mutilated dead bodies or crowded with cripples, when children are torn to pieces and women about to become mothers are made the objects of savage sport, then the voice of the civilized world is sure to be raised, and to let the game pass from city to city becomes impossible.

The anti-Semites of Kishinev have overdone it: the governor had to be removed (a thing unheard of during the entire period of the Ignatyev riots), and M. von Plehve is a disappointed man.

Nor is this the only instance of M. von Plehve's practice of aping the policy of his old master. Because, in 1881, the government succeeded in breaking up that handful of self-sacrificing college students, he has been endeavoring to break up the multitudinous movement of today by applying the methods of 1881, and that his efforts in this direction have so far been crowned with anything but triumph is clear, even from the scanty bits of information that steal their way to the foreign press.

Count Cassini, the Russian minister at Washington, has put forward the statement that the usurious tendency of the Russian Jews was at the bottom of the Kishinev pandemonium. He has characterized the Jews of his country as a population shirking useful work and gravitating toward money lending and the fleecing of Gentiles generally. In reply to this, I wish, to begin with, to let the reader see what another Russian anti-Semite—one who is far better informed on his country than Count Cassini—has to say on the subject.

The *Kievlanin* is the leading newspaper in Kiev. It is one of the two anti-Semitic periodicals that lamented all the trouble between Jew and Gentile during Ignatyev's administration, and is easily the most influential daily in the south—the classical district of anti-Jewish disturbances. This is what it says in an editorial which I find quoted in the St. Petersburg *Novosti* of April 30.

47

We cannot refrain from saying that the root of that popular anti-Semitism which gives rise to those appalling outbreaks is to be sought in the depths of history and of economic relations, to analyze which would be out of season just now. It is proper, however, to call attention to the fact that the Jews, who have been the target of all sorts of accusations, should not, as a body, be held responsible, directly or indirectly, for those objectionable elements which are to be found among Jews and Christians alike. Considered collectively, the Jews of southern and western Russia form an energetic, enterprising class of merchants and tradesmen, contenting themselves with modest earnings, including an enormous element of industrious, frugal and sober artisans, who, living in our towns and villages, earn their scanty piece of bread by the hardest toil, scarcely making both ends meet.

We are all aware of the fact that western and southern Russia and the kingdom of Poland, where lives the bulk of the Jewish population, so far from growing poorer or being ruined, are in a much better economic condition than many of the other sections of the empire. Indeed, with the development of credit, means of communication and a broad system of commercial competition, the question as to the fleecing and oppression of the rest of our population by Jews is rapidly losing ground. Even business pursuits have no easy profits to offer nowadays.

When the savage passion of hatred and the lust of destruction awaken in the masses, then it is the duty of every honest man to counteract these inhuman instincts and remind the people of the fact that the Jews are not only fellow-citizens of ours, but that by their energy and industry they materially contribute to the welfare of our region.

Such is the opinion of the best-informed and most influential anti-Semitic publication in south Russia as to the economic makeup of the Jewish population in that country. As to the Jewish usurer, who is hated by his own people as much as he is by their Gentile neighbors, he represents but an insignificant percentage of the Jewish population of the south. As to the central and northern provinces, the vast area of Russia proper or Great Russia, Jews have no right of settlement there, but then this "truly native" part of the population is blessed with its own species of economic parasite, the so-called *kulak* ("fist" usurer). The best representatives of Russian literature have been interested in this creature, and they make him out even a more loathsome specimen of humanity than the anti-Semites do the "usurer of Mosiac faith." Nor has Great Russia a monopoly of the *kulak*. Little Russia and the rest of the south has its own version of this "Christian usurer," and a most interesting character of this type of human leech forms one of the two heroes in a celebrated story by Vladimir Korolenko, one of the three leading Russian writers of today. The other hero of the tale ("The Day of Atonement") is a Jewish usurer, and the trend of the narrative is to show that one is "just as bad as the other."

Korolenko is not a Jew. He is a Slav and a Christian, but then he is no "Anti" of any kind, and knows his country well, particularly the riot district, which is his native place.

PART TWO
Faith and Tradition at Bay

Engraving on front cover of the first edition of *The Spirit of the Ghetto* (1902)

3

Two Worlds and Two Souls

TALMUDISM AT THE BROOKLYN BRIDGE
January 20, 1900

A crowd gathered in front of a picture store window on the East Side. It was a large, cheap painting which attracted them. The painting represented an old rabbi bent upon his Talmud, and the crowd seemed to admire it more for the memories of their old home which it aroused in them than for its art. Ignorant as most of them appeared to be, they knew enough to understand that the man "did not look like a man," as an old tradesman said with scorn and regret. A scholarly old physician, well known in the neighborhood, chanced to pass the store. He paused, smiled, and pointing at the picture, said to the writer:

"It's a very poor picture of a very interesting idea."

A little later the two sat in a Grand Street café, discussing the subject over glasses of Russian tea.

"The man absorbed in his Talmud is a symbol," said the physician. "It is the epitome of a great world, beautiful and gloomy, poetic and common-place, which is, but is doomed not to be. The book is not merely a book. It is a soul, the soul of a whole people. But another soul, that which is called the modern spirit, is crowding it from the bosom of life to the dust-covered shelves of history.

"The twenty-odd volumes of the Babylonian Talmud, the Alfas,* the

---

*An eleventh-century compendium of the legal discussions of the Babylonian Talmud assembled by Isaac Ben Jacob Alfasi (1013–1103), generally known as Rif.—*Ed.*

'Midrash,' the Jerusalem Talmud, this living monument of the life of our people some seventeen centuries ago, is not merely a library to be found in every orthodox synagogue and in the parlor of every honored householder in the old ghettos of Europe; it is really the sun which gave light and life to our race during centuries of oppression. In the advanced countries of our time the struggle for existence is at once the end and the means of existence. Time was when people worked, traded, feathered their families' nests in order that they might live—live intellectually, spiritually, emotionally. That was the time when the woes of Israel were at their height. But Israel found comfort in his Talmud. His tormentors could debar him from the pleasures of the flesh. But by so doing they only intensified his thirst for the delights of the mind, of the heart, of the soul.

"Says the fool to the fish he has caught: 'I hate thee; I shall not let thee breathe the air which my privileged lungs enjoy. Thou shalt be drowned.' And the fish heaves a sigh of relief, breathes freely in the living waters and is happy. The Gentiles barred our ancestors out of their tournaments, of their orgies, did they? No harm done, my friend. The fish was not thrown out of the air. It was only thrown into the stream of fresh water. Neither were the Jews driven from anything. They were driven into the synagogues, the synagogues which were their libraries, their intellectual and emotional exchanges, the distilleries—not of brandy, for they were kept out of those places where one may learn to drink it—but of the lofty spirit, of the noble enthusiasms which are the real hallmark of Judaism.

"I am not of the Old World," the physician went on. "Behold, my coat is short, my beard is shaved; I smoke on the Sabbath and I dine on Yom Kippur; I neither study the Talmud nor snap my fingers to express my religious fervor. But I am only what my time has made me. My childhood was spent in the past, in the ancient past of our people. In Russia, Poland, Rumania, where medievalism holds sway over the Gentiles, the Talmud holds sway over us. I burst through the barrier; I left my birthplace. I found myself surrounded by the blessings and the curses of the New Era. I am still a Jew, but there the twentieth century is upon the Gentiles and the ghetto; my cradle is treasured in the archaic museums of humanity. I am still a Jew, but I am a Jew of the twentieth century.

"Poor old Talmud! Beautiful old book! My heart goes out to thee. The old ghettos are crumbling, the old world, childlike, beautiful in its simpleheartedness, is waning. I hear they are translating the Talmud into modern languages. It cannot be done. They may render the old Chaldaic or Hebrew into English, but the spirit which hovers between the lines, which goes out of the folios spreading over the whole synagogue, and from the synagogues over the out-of-the-way town, over the dining table of every hovel, over the soul of every man, woman or child; that musty, thrilling something which should be called Talmudism rather than Talmud can no more be translated into English or German or French than the world of Julius Ceasar can be shipped from the Rome of the last century before Christ to the Brooklyn Bridge.''

FOREVER A JEW

October 29, 1898

A carriage came rumbling down Essex Street and drew up in front of the Hebrew bookstore near Allen. A carriage is a rare sight in the neighborhood, so this one at once became the centre of a crowd.

"Who is sick?" everybody whispered. "What is the doctor's name?"

"It ain't no doctor at all. It's a rich uptown gentleman."

"A Gentile in a Jewish bookstore. Does he want a *sidur* [prayerbook]?" some of the idlers joked.

"Maybe it ain't no Gentile. Maybe it's a Jew—an uptown Jew."

Meantime the people within were in a flurry. The crowd guessed right. The newcomer was really a brother in Israel from uptown, and although he was shaved and spoke nothing but English his face bore the stamp of Judaism, and what is more he asked for some *lulovs, ethrogs, hosannas* and *machzors** for the holidays. But then he did not speak Yiddish, and the way he pronounced the Hebrew names of the sacred things he came to buy was so queer, so un-Yiddish, that other customers, mostly old men with sidelocks and women in wigs, could not get it into their heads that it actually was "one of our brother Jews," and not some Gentile nobleman.

The stranger was alive to it all and relished the situation keenly.

"Let me have a Pentateuch, if you please," he asked the proprietor, with a merry twinkle in his eye. "I don't mean an English one. Give me one in *lashan hakodesh* [the holy tongue]."

"Do you hear, Sarah? He says *lashan hakodesh* just like a plain Jew," and one customer nudged her companion.

Lulovs are palm leaves; *ethrogs*, citrons; *hosannas*, willows; and *machzors*, holiday prayer-books.—*Ed.*

The well-dressed old man got a Hebrew Bible, and opening it at random, he fell to reading it.

"Do I read correctly?" he paused to ask the old women who stood gaping at him. His English was translated by the bookkeeper into classical Yiddish. Sarah blushed like a little girl as she said:

"Would that no Jew read worse than that. Once a Jew, forever a Jew. Never mind that you . . ." She halted and dropped her eyes.

"Out with it, my good old woman," the stranger encouraged her. "Never hesitate to tell the truth."

"I am not afraid at all," said Sarah, suddenly mustering more courage than was necessary. "You shave your beard, I mean. You are a Jew all right, but if you think this going about without a beard makes you look handsomer you are mistaken. All Gentiles and all hogs are beardless."

"Hush, foolish woman, or I'll put you out," broke out the proprietor and several customers.

The woman looked guilty. The well-dressed man was shaking with laughter.

When he was gone everybody heaped strong Yiddish on Sarah.

"He is a better Jew than your husband—than anybody you know," said one. "He spends thousands of dollars on charity," said another. "He does enough pious deeds to atone for his shaving," added a third.

"And he knows a word or two of Judaism after all," broke in a fourth.

Sarah seemed dazed. For some time she stood looking as if she were about to run. Suddenly, however, she colored deeply, and turning upon her accusers she fired out:

"You may be talking till tomorrow, and I will stick to my opinion that he is a Gentile. If he were a Jew he would not look like that. You don't see many Jews like him in a pious, God-fearing town in Poland, do you?"

————

"PILLELU, PILLELU!"
April 1, 1899

To those who stood on the corner of Hester Street and Ludlow last night the two intersecting marketplaces looked like a vast cross of flaring gold. It was the eve of the "second days" of the Jewish Passover. The sidewalks and the asphalt pavements were crowded with pushcarts, each with a torch dangling and flickering over it, and the hundreds of quivering flames stretched east and west, north and south, two restless bands of fire crossing each other in a blaze and losing themselves in a medley of fire, smoke, many-colored piles of fish and glimmering human faces.

"Get a move on you, housewives! Time is not waiting for you. It is flying. The holiday is in front of your noses. Buy fish—living fish, screaming, dancing fish!"

"Carrots, carrots, carrots! Buy carrots, good women! Carrots in honor of the holiday!"

"Passover prunes! Why tarry? The prunes melt in one's mouth. They are an ornament to the Passover table, a health to the stomach, a blessing to the family. Prunes, prunes—they are huge diamonds and pearls, not prunes! Prunes, good women! Buy them and be blessed!"

In one place, at the junction of Ludlow, Canal and Division Streets, there was a commotion. A knot of girls crowded about a consumptive street organ, and the market women were hurling curses at the spot.

"May his Passover be disturbed and darkened even as he disturbs and darkens our holiday trade. Beets, good women; blood-red, vivifying beets in honor of the second days! May he spend on doctor's bills a dollar for every cent of business we lose on account of his defiled bones. Beets, young women; beets, young and old!"

"Who is he?" asked a snooper.

"Who? The black and the bitter years know who he is, the Evil Visitation! Beets, sir? Beets that taste like wine, gentleman?"

The Evil Visitation proved to be a dashing young fellow in charge of fortune-telling mice and parrots. He wore a sack coat and trousers of gray corduroy, which, he said, he had bought in London; a collarless shirt, embroidered in the red and black of Little Russia, while glittering from under his coat sleeves were Rumanian cuffs, made of beads of half a dozen colors. His organ he bought at Algiers, and the "fortune tickets" in all languages were printed in Budapest, Hungary.

"Muy spake ulla laynguage!" he said, wagging his head in all directions and flashing his black eyes and dazzling teeth. "Aynd may balong to ulla countray. But excusay may, sayr, baseness bayfore playsure."

Here he went on jabbering in a sort of Yiddish, which the girls said was of the same quality as his English. As he spoke he gnashed his great teeth and squinted his eyes at the torch. This was his way of making himself look weird and wizardlike. But the girls never ceased laughing. The flickering light fell on his eyes, on his teeth, on his plump, dusky cheeks, but even this did not terrify them, they said. A newcomer, a little girl of fifteen, with a big hat, paid him two cents for her fortune. The young fellow screwed up his face to look like a Hungarian gypsy woman and said in a gentle, cooing voice, as he picked up one of the mice on his box:

"*Pillelu, pillelu, pillelu!* Dear little life, dear little soul, dear little sage! Go draw the lot of this little girl. Tell her the truth! Pick her the future! Tell her her fate! Pick it out! Pick it out! Pick it out! Tralla-la tralla-la tralla-la!"

The mouse pulled out the ticket upon which the wizard had pressed its snout, and the bit of printed paper was handed to the little girl with the big hat.

"Who can read?"

"I can, I can, I can!"

"Go ahead, Fanny!"

Fanny read aloud:

"You are often unhappy. You have enemies. ["How correct!" shouted the little girl.] Your greatest enemy is jealous of you. ["Holy words, as true as I wish to be well!"] But all her intrigues will avail her nothing. The young man is not so very, very tall, but those who know a thing or two about looks will tell you he is handsome and suger-sweet. ["Never mind blushing; I know whom Mousie means and it is correct," declared the reader.] He is dead stuck on you. He is swooning away for you, but there are obstacles in your way. Never fear. Your enemy will burst with jealousy. The handsome man and the sweet girl will marry and be happy one hundred and twenty years. The wedding feast will be the talk of the town."

"*Mazel-tov*. [I congratulate you.] *Mazel-tov!*" laughed the maidens.

The next girl wanted an "English fortune," and she got a ticket which said, among other things, as follows:

"All this is because you kept part of the truth from your confessor. Still, your priest is your best friend, and it will all come right."

"What does it mean?" several girls asked, in consternation.

The wizard would not say. "Mousie ought to know what she is talking about," he answered.

"Who writes your tickets?" asked the snooper.

"They are not written, they are printed. *Pleellii—pleellii—li.*"

"Maybe you bought them of a Catholic or you got them mixed up with Catholic fortunes?"

"Mousie never mayx up nayting," the wizard answered, in haughty English. "*Trulilu-lu, trulilu-lu-lulu!*"

"Never mind your *trulilulu!*" screamed one of the girls. "What do you mean by working off ungodly fortunes on daughters of Israel?"

"I want my two cents!" stormed another.

"And I want mine!"

The wizard shouldered his burden, organ, mice, parrots, "Fortunes" and all, and fled.

"That's it! Let him fly to all the black years!" the market women shouted after him. "Now we will do some business in honor of the holiday."

"Carrots, carrots. Fish, living fish."

MAGISTRATE AS RABBI

September-October 1899

Mary Bloom of 175 Norfolk Street is quite a God-fearing daughter of Israel. She blesses her candles on Sabbath eve, salts and purifies her meat and lives with her husband according to the laws of Moses and the rabbis of the Talmud. It goes without saying that her kitchen is perfectly *kosher,* that the meat she buys is prepared according to the regulations of her faith, and that her dishes and cooking utensils are kept from contamination by anything which is unkosher or *treife.* Such is her rule of life every day in the year. This is the second day after Rosh Hashana, the fourth of the Days of Penance, when the sins of every child of Israel are weighed and his fate is decided by the heavenly tribunal.

This is the season of fasting, prayer and penitence. It is Mary's opportunity to set herself right before the Uppermost, to have her sins stricken out and her name and the names of her husband and children entered in the Book of Life. So she has redoubled her piety. She gets up at daybreak and prays and sighs and weeps; she inspects her dishes carefully, scours them with might and main to make sure that they are perfectly *kosher,* that there is not a crumb of *treife* food on them.

Having thus prayed and cried and cleaned her dishes this morning, she threw a kerchief over her wig to make sure that not one of "her own hairs" was visible to the passing men, and made her way, with slow, humble step, as befits the Days of Penance, to the butcher store of David Cornbloom, at 127 Suffolk Street.

"I want a chicken, but a good one, Reb David," she said.

Her face looked gloomy and her voice was unusually low, but David knew that it was one of the Days of Awe, and that the customer was a pious woman, so he was not surprised.

59

"Here is a chicken, fat as a goose and cheap as beans, my dear little missus," he said. "Take it and let your family relish it in honor of the holiday."

Mary felt under the chicken's wings, blew at the feathers, paid the price and left with the fowl in her basket, saying, with a sigh:

"Good-bye, Reb David. May you be enrolled in the Book of Life."

"I wish you the same. May you live to eat lots of such chickens, dear little missus."

Half an hour later Mary came back, but instead of looking gloomy, she looked daggers, and instead of speaking under her breath, she shouted at the top of her voice:

"Murderer that you are; sinner in Israel! Heartless wretch, you are worse than a Gentile, worse than a *meshumed* [convert Jew]," and flinging the chicken, which was by this time half plucked, into his face, she went on, with tears in her eyes: "To think of a Jew selling a Jewess a *treife* chicken during the Days of Penance! Suppose I did not notice that it had died a miserable natural death, and not been killed according to the laws of our faith, I would serve it, then, and my whole family would eat *treife* and be enrolled in the Book of Death. Oh, you heartless, godless man, give me back my money!"

The butcher swore the chicken was *kosher*: the woman swore she could see by the cut in the bird's throat and by the "heavy smell she gave off" that it was *treife*. Mary offered to submit the case to a rabbi, but the butcher preferred Magistrate Olmstead of the Essex Market Court.

"But he is a Gentile; what does he know about *kosher* and *treife*?" argued Mary. "He eats nothing but *treife* himself."

David was obdurate and the chicken was taken before the magistrate, who, after inspecting it carefully, decided in favor of Mary.

"I have had many cases of this kind," said his Honor. "This practice of substituting *treife* chickens for *kosher* ones must be stopped."

"Long live America!" said Mary. "Even the Gentiles are fond of *kosher*. May his Honor be enrolled in the Book of Life!"

———

"KNOWN AS MUCH FOR HIS POVERTY
AS FOR HIS SCHOLARSHIP"
June 3, 1899

Rabbi Abraham Dobsevage is one of the best-known men in the ghetto. He is known as much for his poverty as for his scholarship. He is too learned in Gentile books to be a strict orthodox, yet too fond of the old traditions of his race to pass for a reformed Jew. His friends say that he is like the husband of the Talmudic parable, whose young wife pulled out all his gray hair, while his elderly wife tore out his dark ones. And as the man of the parable was left bald-headed, so is Rabbi Dobsevage left empty-pursed.

He came to this country in the hope of seeing his book, the work of thirty-two years, in print. He has now been eight years in America. He has shown his manuscript to men of learning and to men of wealth; the drawer of the rickety kitchen table, which serves him for a desk, is jammed with promises and panegyrics, but the dream of his life—to see his great work in type—has not yet been realized. The time-worn package is still on the shelf, and the sight of it still grips the old man's heart.

Rabbi Dobsevage is tall and stately, with commanding dark eyes and two white tufts of beard, which become his sallow, scholarly face well, but his woes are making a decrepit, trembling old man of him. The red handkerchief which was tied around his head when the writer called at his house added to the inspiring effect of his strong, sickly, affectionate face.

"It's only a headache," he said, apologetically.

The room in which the visitor was received was at once the kitchen, the dining room and the parlor of the family. The walls were discolored, the bare floor in holes and the furniture of the cheapest to be found in the slums. Everything spoke of need and of a housewife's struggle to make it look clean and respectable. Mrs. Dobsevage is considerably younger than her husband. She is an interesting-looking woman of about forty, and her speech and manners remind one of the better days which she and her husband saw in Russia, their birthplace. She was found busy polishing her rusty kitchen stove, and as she turned around to take a look at the stranger she blushed and tried to hide her begrimed hands.

The rabbi's desk stands in the bedroom, and it was there that he unbosomed himself to the visitor.

"Look at this. It is from Rabbi Gottheil. As you see, he thinks highly of my work. So does Rabbi Hertz,* and scores of other rabbis and professors. But what good does it do my poor work—the fruit of my brain, the child of my soul? I have labored decade after decade. I have brought misery upon my patient wife and children—all in the hope of seeing the offspring of my mind and heart see the light before the light went out of my own eyes. Tell the world through your paper, sir; tell the world—" His voice was choked with emotion, and tears came into his black eyes. When he had regained composure he said:

"It will be an obligation to my family as much as to humanity at large if you announce it to the world that there is an important book of which the learned have been deprived by the black poverty of the author. So much money is expended by the open-handed friends of Bible study. Ah, if the world could only see what I have done in this line of scientific research. I have shown it to some well-known Gentile scholars, and they have all spoken enthusiastically of my discoveries, but what good does it do me?"

One chapter in Rabbi Dobsevage's unpublished book treats of a Hebrew word in the Old Testament whose meaning has, according to the Hebrew scholar, been distorted to suit the spirit of Christianity. The word is *koari,* and it occurs only twice in the whole of the Old Testament. The spelling is, in both instances, precisely the same, and so is the vowel punctuation under the word, which is the Hebrew substitute for vowel letters. The word means "like a lion," but it could also be twisted to mean "they pierced," explained Rabbi Dobsevage.

"The word occurs in verse 13, Chapter XXXVIII of Isaiah," he said enthusiastically, "but there the Gentile scholars have left it intact, for the real definition does not stand in their way. And so the translation of that verse in the Christian Bible is as follows: 'I reckoned till morning that as a lion so will he break my bones.' This is correct. This is honest. But then look here," he exclaimed, opening his English Bible on Psalm XXII, verse 16. " 'For dogs have compassed me; the assembly of the wicked have enclosed me; they pierced my hands and feet.' You see, the same word, *koari,* which they translate 'as a lion' in Isaiah—exactly the same word, letter for letter and vowel-mark for vowel-mark—they translate 'they pierced.' Now, if it is 'as a lion' in one passage why should it be 'they pierced' in the other? We Jews give the same meaning to the word in both cases, and it fits beautifully. We have it: 'They as a lion (broke) my hands and my feet,' as it stands written in

*Gustav Gottheil (1827–1903) was rabbi at New York's Temple Emanu-El, and Joseph H. Hertz (1872–1946) became chief rabbi of the British Empire.—*Ed.*

the other place. 'As a lion so will he break all my bones.' Why, then, should the Gentiles twist it? Why? Why? I'll tell you why. Because the Twenty-Second Psalm is the great psalm in which they see reference to Jesus. This is the psalm in which the celebrated exclamation occurs, 'God, my God, why hast thou forsaken me.' It fitted this general spirit of the chapter as they understand it to make *koari* mean 'they pierced' because then it reads 'they pierced my hands and feet.' ''

Rabbi Dobsevage was so carried away by his explanation that the little bedroom proved too close for him and his visitor. The two returned into the kitchen, where the old man with the red bandanna over his pale face began to pace up and down the rickety floor.

"I see you think it clever, don't you?" he said. "Well, it's only one of the many hundreds of equally important discoveries I have made in the Bible. The worst of it all is that the Gentiles have got their fine work into our own Masorah, which keeps count of every letter and every vowel mark in the Old Testament, to insure it from mutilations. While we translate the word *koari* the same way in both instances, our Masorah says of this word: 'twice in the Bible, but with two different definitons.' How do you like a trick like this?"

Besides the Masorah study of the Bible Rabbi Dobsevage has written a book on the humor of the Bible and the Talmud.

"I don't speak of this work because the good man who will help me publish the one will also help me publish the other," he said. "I have shown specimens to Zangwill and he liked them very much."

RABBI ELIEZER'S CHRISTMAS

A Story by Abraham Cahan
Scribner's Magazine / December 1899

One of the two well-dressed strangers who were picking their way through the ghetto—a frail, sharp-featured little Gentile woman with grayish hair—brought herself and her tall companion to a sudden halt.

"Look at that man!" she said, with a little gasp of ecstasy, as she pointed out an elderly Jew who sat whispering over an open book behind a cigarette stand. "Don't you think there is a lion effect in his face? Only he is so pathetic."

The other agreed phlegmatically that the man was perfectly delightful, but this was not enough.

"You say it as if the woods were full of such faces," the nervous little woman protested. "A more exquisite head I never saw. Why, it's classic, it's a perfect—tragedy. His eyes alone would make the fortune of a beginning artist. I must telegraph Harold about him."

"Yes, there is pathos in his eyes," the head worker of the College Settlement assented, with dawning interest.

"Pathos! Why, they are full of martyrdom. Just look at the way his waxen face shapes itself out of that sea of white hair and beard, Miss Colton. And those eyes of his—doesn't it seem as if they were looking out of a tomb a mile away? We must go up and speak to him. He looks like a lion in distress."

Miss Bemis was out with her list of "deserving cases," mostly Irish, which Miss Colton had prepared for her as she had done the year before. This time, however, her effervescent enthusiasm was not exclusively philanthropic. She had recently become infatuated with a literary family and had been hunting after types ever since.

When the two came up to the old man's stand they found that besides cigarettes it was piled with candy and Yiddish newspapers, and that part of the brick wall back of it was occupied by an improvised little bookcase filled with poorly bound volumes.

Miss Colton, who spoke German and had taken special pains to learn the dialect of the ghetto, acted as her friend's interpreter.

"How much are these cigarettes?" she asked, for a beginning, as she took up a package decorated with a picture of Captain Dreyfus.

"Cigarettes?" the old man asked, with a perplexed smile which made his sallow face sadder than ever.

"Yes, these cigarettes."

"How many? One, two, three, or the whole package?" he inquired, timidly.

"Of course, the whole package. Why, do you find it strange for women to buy cigarettes?"

"Not at all. Who says it is strange?" he answered, with apologetic vehemence. "Quite a few of my customers are ladies."

"Do they smoke?"

"They? What business has a woman to smoke? But then, she may have a husband or a sweetheart who smokes."

Miss Bemis bought the Dreyfus package and one bearing a likeness of Karl Marx. By this time the old man's bashfulness had worn off, and he said, in answer to questions, that his name was Eliezer (Rabbi Eliezer people called him, out of respect for his voluminous gray beard and piety); that he had been in America two years and that he was all alone in the world.

"And how much does your stand bring you?"

For an answer he drew a deep sigh and made a gesture of despair. After a short silence he said:

"I sit freezing like a dog from six in the morning to eleven in the night, as you see. And what do I get for my pains? When I make five dollars I call it an extra good week. If I had a larger stock I might make a little more. It's America, not Russia. If one would do business one must have all kinds of goods. But then it's a sin to grumble. I am not starving—praised be the All High for that."

Speaking of his bookcase, he explained that it was a circulating library.

"Silly stuff, that," he said with contempt. "Nothing but lies—yarns about how a lad fell in love with a girl and such-like nonsense. Yet, I must keep this kind of trash. Ah, this is not what I came to America for. Was I not happy at home? Did I want for anything? Birds' milk, perhaps. I was a *sopher.** I was poor, but I never went hungry, and people showed me respect. And so I lived in peace until the black year brought to our town a man who advised me to go to America. He saw me make a *misrach*—a kind of picture which pious Jews keep on the east wall of their best room. I fitted it up with beautiful pillars, two lions supporting the tables of the Law and all kinds of trappings, you know. Well, all this lots of people could do, but what nobody could do and I can is to crowd the whole of Deuteronomy into a circle the size of a teaglass." A sparkle came into his dark brown eyes; an exalted smile played about his lips; but this only deepened the gloom of his face. "I would just take a glass, stand it on the paper upside down, trace the brim and—set to work. People could hardly read it—so tiny were the letters; but I let everybody look at them through a magnifying glass and they saw every word. And how well written! Just like print. 'Well,' says that man, 'Rabbi Eliezer,' says he, 'you have hands of gold, but sense you have none. Why throw yourself away upon a sleepy town like this? Just you go to America, and pearls will be showered on you.' " After a little pause Rabbi Eliezer waved his hand at his wares and said, with a bitter smile: "Well, here they are, the pearls."

"And what became of your pictures?" asked Miss Colton.

"My pictures? Better don't ask about them, good lady," the old man

*A writer of parchment scrolls of the Pentateuch or some other section of the Old Testament. —A.C.

65

answered, with a sigh. "I sat up nights to make one, and when it was finished I got one dollar for it, and that was a favor. My lions looked like potatoes, they said. 'As to your Deuteronomy—it isn't bad, but this is America, and such things are made by machine and sold five cents apiece.' The merchant showed me some such pretty pictures. Well, the lions were rather better than mine, and the letters even smaller—that I won't deny—but do you know how they were made? By hand? Not a bit. They write big words and have them photographed by a tricky sort of thing which makes them a hundred times smaller than they are—do you understand? 'Ah, but that's machine work—a swindle,' says I, 'while I make every letter with my own hands, and my words are full of life.' 'Bother your hands and your words!' said the merchant. 'This ain't Russia,' says he. 'It's America, the land of machines and "hurry up!" ' says he, and there you are!" The old man's voice fell. "Making letters smaller, indeed!" he said brokenly. "Me too, they have made a hundred times smaller than I was. A pile of ashes they have made of me. A fine old age! Freezing like a dog, with no one to say a kind word to you," he concluded, trying to blink away his tears and to suppress the childlike quiver of his lips.

Miss Bemis was tingling with compassion and with something very like the sensation of an entomologist come upon a rare insect.

"Ask him how much money it would take to bring his stock up to the standard," she said, peremptorily.

Rabbi Eliezer's cadaverous face turned red, as he answered, bashfully:

"How much! Fifteen dollars, perhaps! I wish I had ten."

As Miss Bemis opened her handbag, the old scroll-writer's countenance changed colors and he looked as if he did not know what to do with his eyes.

The two Gentile women had no sooner left the cigarette stand than the market people came crowding about Rabbi Eliezer.

"How much did she give you?" they inquired, eagerly.

"How much! It is not quite a hundred dollars—you may be sure of that," he replied, all flushed with excitement.

"Why should you be afraid to tell us how much? We aren't going to take it away from you, are we?"

"Afraid! What reason have I to be afraid? But then—what matters it how much she gave me?"

One of the fishwives said she knew the taller of the two ladies.

"She belongs in that Gentile house on the next block where they fuss around with children and teach them to be ladies, you know," she explained.

"They are all Gentiles over there, but good as diamonds. How much did she give you, Rabbi Eliezer?" she concluded, confidentially.

Rabbi Eliezer made no reply. He was struggling to look calm, but he could not. The twenty-dollar bill in his bosom pocket was the largest sum he had ever handled. Every time a passerby stopped at his stand he would leap to his feet, all in a flutter, and wait upon him with feverish eagerness; and at the same time he was so absent-minded that he often offered his customer the wrong article. Again and again he put his hand to his breast to make sure that the twenty dollars were safe. Now it occurred to him that there might be a hole in his pocket; now he asked himself if he was positive that he had put the precious piece of paper into his purse. He distinctly remembered having done so, yet at moments his mind seemed to be a blank. "With these begrudging creatures around, one might truly lose one's mind," he complained to himself.

He pictured the increased stock and library, and the display he would make of it. All this would only take about fifteen dollars, so that he could well afford a new praying shawl for himself. His old one was all patches, and how could he expect any attention at the synagogue? Wouldn't his fellow worshippers be surprised! "I see you are doing good business, Rabbi Eliezer," they would say. Yes, he would get himself a new praying shawl and a new hat. His skullcap in which he worshipped at the synagogue was also rather rusty, but a new one cost only twenty-five cents, and this was now a trifle. Suddenly it became clear to him that he had no recollection of putting the twenty-dollar bill into his purse. His heart sank. Under the pretence of rearranging some books he hastily took out his dilapidated purse. The twenty dollar bill was there—green on one side and brown on the other.

"Been counting the money the Gentile woman gave you?" asked a market woman, archly.

"Not at all," he murmured, coloring.

"Foolish man that you are, does anybody begrudge you?" a carrot peddler put in. "Out with it—how much?"

This time Rabbi Eliezer somehow felt hurt.

"What do you want of me? Do I owe anything?" he flamed out.

"You need not be excited, nor stuck up, either, even if a Gentile woman did make you a Christmas present—in honor of her God's birth," snapped the other.

"That's what it was—a present in honor of their God," seconded a remnant peddler.

Rabbi Eliezer was in a rage.

"You say it all because your eyes are creeping out of your heads with envy," he said, with flashing eyes. "Well, she gave me twenty dollars. There now!"

The quarrel blew over, but Rabbi Eliezer was left with a wound in his heart. The green and brown piece of paper now seemed to smell of the incense and to have something to do with the organ sounds which came from the Polish church in his birthplace. He was horrified. Nestling in his bosom pocket right against his heart, was something *treife,* unholy, loathsome. And this loathsome thing was so dear to that heart of his—woe to him! . . . . What a misfortune that it should all have happened on Christmas of all other days! Had the good-hearted Gentile woman only come one day sooner, all would have gone well. Or, had there been nobody around to see him receive the Christmas present . . . Anyhow, she never said it was a Christmas present, did she? Rabbi Eliezer also reminded himself of the Christmas gifts which thousands of American Jews exchanged with their Christian friends, and even among themselves; but the thought had no comfort to offer him. What if so-called Jews who shave their beards and smoke on the Sabbath do exchange Christmas presents? Shall he, an old man with one foot in his grave, follow their godless example. Woe is him, has it come to that? He was firmly determined to return the Gentile woman her money, and felt much relieved. He knew all the while that he would not do it, however, and little by little his heart grew heavy again. "Ah, it was the black year which brought me the Gentile ladies and their twenty dollars!" he exclaimed in despair.

At last, after hours of agony, he hit upon a plan. He would call at the Gentile House, as he described the College Settlement to himself, and ask whether the money had been given to him in honor of Christmas. He would not say: "Was it a Christmas present?" for that would be too dangerous a question to ask. Instead he would put it like this: "I am a poor man, but I am a Jew, and a Jew must not accept any presents in honor of a Gentile faith. I took the money because the kindly lady gave me it. It wasn't meant for a Christmas present, was it?" To be sure, the good woman would understand his trouble, and whether it was a Christmas present or not, she would say that it was not.

It seemed such a trifling thing to do, and yet when he found himself in front of the little two-story building—the only exception in a block of towering tenement houses—his heart sank with fear lest the well-dressed lady should say, "Yes, it was a Christmas present."

"Why should I bother them, anyhow? Is it not enough that they gave me such a pile of money?" he said to himself, with an insincere sense of decency, and turned back. He had not gone many blocks when he retraced his steps. When he came in sight of the brownstone stoop he slackened his pace.

Never in his life had he called at the house of *pritzim* (noble folk), and he now felt, with a rush of joy, that he had not the courage to ring the doorbell. Finally when he had nerved himself up to the feat, his heart beat so violently that he was afraid he could not speak.

A minute later he was in the presence of Miss Colton. He recognized her, yet she seemed much younger and taller.

"Well, what can I do for you, Rabbi Eliezer?" she asked, with a friendly radiance which did his heart good.

"I come to ask you something, lady," he said, with a freedom of manner which was a surprise to himself. "People tell me it was a Christmas present that lady gave me. I am a Jew, you know, and I must not take any Christmas presents. I don't care if other Jews do or not."

He could not go on. He felt that it was not the speech he had prepared, and that it might cost him the twenty dollars. He was dying to correct it, but he could not speak. After a pause he blurted out:

"If I had received the money yesterday or tomorrow it would be another matter, but today—"

Miss Colton burst into laughter.

"Of course, it wasn't a Christmas present," she said. "The good lady never meant it for one, for didn't she know you were a Jew, and a pious one? But since you are worried about it let me have the twenty dollars and you call tomorrow morning, and I shall give them to you in the lady's name as a fresh present. Will that mend the matter?"

Rabbi Eliezer said it would, and left the College Settlement with his heart in his throat.

The next thing he did was to inquire of the Jews in the neighborhood whether Miss Colton was good pay. Everybody said she was good in every way, and Rabbi Eliezer went to the evening services at his synagogue in high spirits. Still, during the Eighteen Blessings he caught himself thinking of the twenty dollars and the Gentile God, and had to say it all over again.

By the time he got back to his stand the markets were in full blast. The sidewalks and the pavement were bubbling with men and women and torches. Hundreds of quivering lights stretched east and west, north and south—two restless bands of fire crossing each other in a blaze and losing themselves in a medley of flames, smoke, fish, vegetables, Sabbath loaves, muslin and faces.

"Fish, fish, living fish—buy fish, dear little housewives! Dancing, tumbling, wriggling, screaming fish in honor of the Sabbath! Potatoes as big as your fist! A bargain in muslin! Buy a calico remnant—calico as good as silk, sweet little housewives!"

Rabbi Eliezer, whose place of business was in the heart of this babel, sat behind his stand, musing. He was broken in body and spirit. That he should have been in a fever of anxiety, humiliating himself and deceiving his God—and all because he was so poor that twenty dollars appeared like a fortune to him—suddenly seemed a cruel insult to his old age. He burst out muttering a psalm, and whatever the meaning of the Hebrew words his lips uttered, his shaking voice and doleful intonation prayed Heaven to forgive him and to take pity on his last years on earth.

The reddish torchlight fell upon his waxen cheeks and white beard. His eyes shone with a dull, disconsolate lustre. As he went on whispering and nodding his beautiful old head, amid the hubbub of the market, a pensive smile overspread his face. His heart was praying for tears. "I am so unhappy, so unhappy!" he said to himself in an ecstasy of woe. And at the same time he felt that hanging somewhere far away in the background was a disagreeable little question: Will the Gentile lady pay him the twenty dollars?

KATIE AND LEAH
December 30, 1899

Two Jewish women had a debate in front of a Grand Street store last week. One wore an elaborate hat, and her name was Katie; the other had her hair carefully concealed under a wig, and Katie addressed her as Leah. The debate took place in front of a large window through which gleamed and glistened a heavily laden Christmas tree.

"Your mother was a pious woman," said Leah. "I knew her; she was a blessing in Israel. She would fast Mondays and Thursdays and never omit the service at the synagogue. To think of her daughter fixing up a Christmas tree like a Gentile! Why should you give your own dear mother so much pain in her grave?"

"I am not giving her any pain at all, Leah," Katie retorted with heat. "My mother's memory is dearer to me than it is to you, and all you say comes from your being green in America, Leah. Wait till you have learned the ways of this country. It is not Russia. It's America, my dear," she added, with some venom.

The other was shocked. "America? America? Is that reason enough why we should celebrate the Christian holidays and become Christians? May the All High forgive me for my awful words."

70

"But you are green, my dear, so you don't know what you are talking about. It is not the Christian holiday we are celebrating, not at all; you don't know what you are saying, for you are green, my dear."

"Don't call me dear when you don't mean it, Katie. I knew your mother, peace upon her—"

"Leave my mother rest in her grave; but you are only a greenhorn. So you think this is Russia, where our people are hated and persecuted."

"Ah, I see. The American Gentiles are good to us, so they wheedle us into changing our faith for theirs. Is that what you mean?"

"That's not what I mean. The trouble with you is that you are green, Leah, so you can't understand what I mean."

"If I can't, then what's the use of talking to me?"

"There isn't any, either; but I shall try to explain it to you. Maybe you will understand me after all." Somehow Katie smiled and Leah did the same, and the debate was continued in milder tones.

"A Christmas tree is only called Christmas tree. It has nothing to do with the Christian religion, Leah. I have been twelve years in America, so I ought to know. Christmas is simply a day when people are trying to be good to themselves and to everybody else. If it was a Christian holiday the Christians would not give presents to their Jewish friends, and the Jews would not do the same. Besides, it's the great children's day, Leah. They get their gifts, and how can you let your children go around without any presents while their Christian schoolmates are showing off theirs? In Russia our children and the Christian children did not see much of each other, but here things are different, Leah. The trouble is that you are so green. Besides, even in Russia the educated Jews and the educated Christians get along together."

"There you have it! The educated, indeed! You mean the ungodly. In our time, in your mother's time, people were not 'educated,' and they were better off. They had God in their hearts and He helped them. So they had no need to leave their birthplace and to go to live in a strange place beyond the sea. God knows where it will all end."

"It will end well," said Katie, with a smile. "Our people have suffered enough. It's high time to be treated like human beings. Nobody prevents us from professing our faith as our fathers and mothers did. You go to synagogue regularly, don't you, Leah? And you spend hours reading your commentary. Does anybody stand in your way? Does anybody compel you to bow to the images of the Gentiles? They do that in Russia in some cities. Do they do it here?"

Leah had nothing to say, so she interlocked her hands and sighed.

"A BACK NUMBER"
January 24, 1901

The leading orthodox Jewish congregations on the East Side have joined to provide for the family of Rabbi Jacob Joseph, who has been an invalid for the last five years. Rabbi Joseph was called to this city by eighteen of the largest orthodox synagogues in 1887, from Vilna, Russia, where he had acquired renown as a preacher as well as for his unusual Talmudic erudition.

His arrival in this city was looked upon as one of the most important events in the history of orthodox Judaism in America. His sermons were attended by crowds of enthusiasts: he was named chief rabbi, and all the Jewish slaughterhouses and butcher shops, where meat is expected to be prepared according to the laws of Moses and the Talmud, were placed under his supervision. There is no hierarchy in the Jewish Church, yet Chief Rabbi Joseph was installed as a sort of bishop with a force of minor rabbis attending the killing of cattle under his authority.

He was a beloved religious teacher. The older people of the East Side, those who hold the traditions of the synagogue dear, looked upon him as the centre of a religious regeneration, as the hope of an orthodox revival. The new rabbi was easily the profoundest Talmudic scholar in America, and this, added to his sincere piety and affectionate, gentle nature, endeared him to all those who clung to older forms of the faith.

"At last we have procured a rabbi who is worthy of this great, wealthy city of ours," said the orthodox people on the East Side. The New York ghetto is the largest and wealthiest Jewish community in the world, and it prides itself upon the array of celebrities it has imported from the older Jewish ghettos of Europe. The East Side has the greatest Yiddish wedding band, the greatest synagogue singers, the greatest Yiddish actors, one of the leading Hebrew poets; and in persuading Rabbi Joseph to come and preside over their religious life they congratulated themselves upon cutting the ancient town of Vilna of their celebrated exhorter. The people of the East Side are quick to pick up American ideas, and one of the first things they learn is to reach out for everything that's "the biggest in the world."

Chief Rabbi Joseph was happy, but his happiness was not destined to last long. He had not been here many months before he found himself confronted with conditions which disturbed his peace of mind and made him wonder whether he would ever feel at home in the turbulent American city. This was the beginning of a quiet tragedy which is said to have been the original cause of his failing health and to have resulted in his present helplessness. It is the sad story of an unspoken struggle between two worlds. Rabbi Joseph is the victim of this struggle.

The rapidity with which the Jewish immigrant falls in with the spirit of his new environment, his readiness to learn English and the manners of his new environment, makes itself felt in the life of the ghetto at every turn. Old-fashioned Jews from the old European ghettos soon learn to shave their beards, to go to the theater, to read newspapers and to look down upon all those who remain true to their sidelocks as "a lot of greenhorns." Circumstances alter cases, but Rabbi Joseph could not see that. Hence the tragedy. The same sermons that evoked the admiration of the old people in Vilna were criticized here, even ridiculed. The learned Talmudist was satirized as "a greenhorn," "a back number," "a man who makes funny speeches." Some of the very people who drank in his words thirstily in Vilna left the synagogue in the middle of his sermon here. They had been two or three years in America. They had heard speakers, read newspapers. The celebrated preacher proved a disenchantment. The rabbi looked around him in surprise, then in dismay, and was sorry he had ever left Vilna.

True to his mission he insisted upon a strict observance of the law, and this brought him into conflict with various elements whom he neither understood nor was understood by. There was some trouble about the *kosher* certificates he issued to the butcher shops. This gave rise to a conflict of business interests. The inexperienced rabbi, the helpless "son of the law," was embroiled with people of whom he had not the remotest idea, and the tragedy of his life in the strange country became deeper and deeper.

Now that he is a hopeless invalid there is nothing but sympathy and love for Rabbi Joseph. His bitterest enemies have become his warmest friends. The quiet struggle of which he is the victim is regarded as something symbolic of the sad history of the whole race.

The work for which Rabbi Joseph was called to this country is now partly done by a board of rabbis. These issue certificates to the butcher shops which recognize their authority and answer questions of law which the faithful call at their homes to propound. There are some learned rabbis on the East Side, and the lives of some of them are as sad as was that of Rabbi Joseph during the first year of his stay here.

KADDISH FOR PRESIDENT MCKINLEY
September 19, 1901

The hundreds of synagogues on the East Side mourned the death of President McKinley today, each in its own way. In comparatively few instances the congregations united in anything like a formal service, but there were crowds of worshippers in every house of prayer, and these gave expression to their grief by chanting psalms in mournful intonations, reading appropriate selections from the Talmud, praying or listening to sermons.

This being one of the Ten Days of Penance, which include the Hebrew New Year and the solemn fast day of Yom Kippur, the usual number of synagogues in the five ghettos of Greater New York have been multiplied several times by the opening of hundreds of temporary houses of prayer. It is the season of contrition, and the thousands of men and women who flocked to the synagogue to pray for a happy New Year devoted much of their time to a prayer in behalf of the country at large.

In the large auditorium of the Educational Alliance, East Broadway and Jefferson Street, the Rev. Dr. Radin read the mourner's Kaddish before a congregation of several hundred worshippers at 10 o'clock. This Kaddish is a prayer in Chaldaic which is usually offered by the bereaved in Israel for the souls of their dead. To say this sacred prayer for a Gentile is a most uncommon proceeding, but so unanimous and ardent is the feeling of the people of the ghetto in the present instance that McKinley is spoken of in that quarter as "the loving brother of all of us," as one who "died a martyr to the freedom of Jew and Gentile," and as one "so dear to our hearts that we say Kaddish for him just as we do for our own fathers or mothers."

In the vestry rooms of the great synagogue, Norfolk Street, near Broome, a group of elderly men were studying the Talmud this morning. As they sang out the Hebrew and Chaldaic words in subdued, melancholy accents, their bodies swayed to and fro over the open folios before them, and their fingers gesticulated to suit the meaning of the sentences they were intoning. In one corner an aged man, with an immense snow-white beard, which seemed too heavy for his cadaverous little face, was mumbling a psalm with inarticulate fervor. In another corner, near the entrance to the adjoining study room, two younger men were engaged in debate upon a passage in the holy books relating to the death of a beloved ruler.

"You see, there were no presidents at the time of the Talmudists," said one of the two scholars to the reporter, "but there was something like the republican regime in certain respects, and we can deduce from the sayings of the ancient rabbis principles applicable to the death of President McKinley. Israel is in tears, my friend. You can say that to the readers of your paper. Israel, the scapegoat of every evildoer in Europe; Israel, the victim of a thousand and one enemies all over the world; Israel, the homeless race, has found a home at last. That home is the United States. The Stars and Stripes? What are they? They are the wings which spread over our downtrodden people to protect us from the wiles of the anti-Semite, from the envy of the shiftless idler.

"That's why the heart of Israel goes out to the chosen representatives of the republic; that's the reason our souls melt in tears for the death of our beloved President."

As the man proceeded some of the Talmudists left off their melancholy studies to listen to his words, and as they sat listening across their venerable folios their heads kept nodding assent, while now and then a sigh expressed the emotion which seemed to fill their hearts.

"This is a day of sadness," said one of these old men, interrupting the younger worshippers. "It is a day of sorrow in Israel, not only in America, but all over the world. Our brethren in Russia are saying Kaddish for Mr. McKinley."

4

SEASONS

FOR SONG AND PRAYER

REJOICING OF THE LAW
October 19, 1897

"O Thou, who art pure and just!" sang the young cantor from the open book in his hand, as arrayed in his praying shawl and tall black cap and bearing a Sefer-Torah (scrolls of the Law) in his arms, he led the procession around the reading platform.

"Save us!" echoed a multitude of ringing soprano voices from the platform.

"O Thou, who compassionest the poor!" pursued the cantor.

"Send us prosperity!" rejoined the boy choir.

"O Thou who art clothed with righteousness!"

"Answer us!"

The tune was an adagio of joyous solemnity, and the *chazan*'s (cantor's) step kept time to it.

"O Thou who knowest our thoughts!"

"Save us!"

"O Thou who art mighty and glorious!"

"Send us prosperity!"

"O Thou who supportest the fallen!"

"Answer us!"

Following the young *chazan* were forty venerable men, each with a gayly robed Torah in his arms. Red Torahs, blue Torahs, white Torahs; Torahs with crowns and Torahs without crowns; some in grave humble silence with their silk mantles unadorned; others with tinkling, glittering shields of silver suspended from their "trees of life."

"O Thou Eternal King"

"Save us!"

"O Thou who art good and beneficent!"

"Answer us!"

As scroll after scroll passed by, daughters of Israel, young and old, standing on the pews, leaned forward to kiss each of them in succession; for it was the night of the Rejoicing of the Law, the only occasion upon which the orthodox synagogue will allow the two sexes to mingle during divine service.

After the scroll-bearers came a number of little boys or infants in their father's arms, each child carrying a paper flag with a lighted candle attached to the top of its staff.

"Make merry and rejoice on the Rejoicing of the Law!"

The older boys who could read the Hebrew inscription on their flags chanted it gleefully every time the *chazan* and his choir came to a pause, the babies prattling the words after their fathers or brothers.

"Hold your flag high, my son. God will grant you high luck for it!" called a beaming mother to a five-year-old boy as he passed her pew. The child's olive face was as rapt as some of the venerable countenances preceding him, and he obeyed his mother with grave mien and without turning his face toward her.

"O Thou who helpest the poor!" sounded the sweet baritone in the distance.

"Save us!" responded the sopranos from the platform.

"O Thou Redeemer and Deliverer!"

"Send us prosperity!"

"O Thou Former of Worlds!"

"Answer us!"

Presently the *chazan* and the Torah bearers reached the observers once more.

"Please, sir!" a dark-eyed maiden besought a gray-bearded old man. "May I ask you to pause a little and allow me to kiss your Purity scrolls, for I fear that I have missed it."

"That's right, my daughter," commended her a pious-looking lady who stood by. "Don't miss a single Sefer-Torah and the Uppermost will send you your predestined sweetheart next year."

The old man paused, with an affectionate smile, and held out his Purity as a mother does her babe. Blushing crimson at the lady's most earnest remark, the dark-eyed girl leaned forward and kissed the Torah, which then rejoined the procession.

There were not many women on the main floor of the synagogue, for the space was needed for the procession and the other men worshippers. But then the women's gallery was crowded, more even than on the Day of Atonement, with dark-haired maidens and wigged old matrons, who craning their necks and straining their eyes, watched the glorious spectacle underneath. Bathed in floods of light and flushed with the excitement of the great moment, they were all young and all beautiful, their enraptured faces blending into a fascinating expanse of living radiance that seemed like a visible accompaniment to the silvery voices which rose from the illuminated enclosure below.

When the scrolls had been carried seven times around the platform and restored to the Holy Ark, the congregation burst into a deafening hymn of welcome to the Law; for the two Torahs which had been left outside the Ark were now borne to the platform to be read.

A few minutes later the Master Reader, bending over the unfolded parchment, began:

"And this is the blessing wherewith Moses, the Man of God, blessed the children of Israel."

Presently his intonations were drowned in a hubbub of merriment, for it was the last section of the Five Books of Moses he was intoning, and to rejoice in the closing chapter of the Law is even a higher good deed than to attend the reading of them. The whole Pentateuch is divided into as many sections as there are weeks in a year, one section being read at the synagogue on each consecutive Sabbath, and the Rejoicing of the Law being the day when the Five Books, begun the year before, are finished and commenced over again.

"Make merry and rejoice in the Law!" broke out a hundred gleeful voices.

Encouraging kerchiefs were waved from the gallery, and other merry songs burst forth. Spirits ran high. Some old fellows, entwining their arms, launched out into a jumping, frisking, shouting chaos.

"What makes you so jolly, Reb Leizer?" someone chaffs a venerable pillar of the synagogue. "Wine has not come within four ells of your lips."

"No matter!" replies Reb Leizer. "It is the Rejoicing of the Law! You had better join in!"

And, intoxicated with the inspiration of the occasion, he goes on hopping and singing and drawing others into the boisterous company, till the floor fairly trembles with the trampling of a hundred feet and the Holy Ark flickers in a bounding, gesticulating maze.

"Mr. President, tomorrow at your house, mind you!" yells a husky, panting voice from the human whirlwind.

"Well said!" The president strives to overshout the rejoicing bedlam. "I hereby invite the whole congregation. The *chazan* and his brave choristers will sing and there will be plenty to eat and to drink. Come, brothers one and all, and let us have a good Law-rejoicing frisk as in the old country."

"That's right!" somebody rejoins. "If you acquit yourself well as behooves a president, we will vote for you once more."

FEAST OF CHANUKAH
December 20, 1897

"Have you got your Chanukah candles, Mrs. Cohen?"

"I have a Chanukah lamp; a fine silver thing which we brought over from the old country. You use candles, don't you, Mrs. Levy?"

That is now the general topic of neighborly chat among the housewives of the ghetto. The quaint feast of Chanukah which is to be observed by every faithful son and daugher of Israel during the eight days commencing today is the only Jewish holiday which is in celebration of a martial event in the history of the eternal people.

Away back in the second century B.C., Mattathias, a Jewish priest, withdrew with his five sons from Jerusalem to Modin to mourn over the devastation of the holy city and the desecration of the temple by the heathen conquerors of Judah. When a Syrian captain urged the venerable Cohen to espouse the faith of the Greeks, the old man answered by slaying a convert Jew who was on his way to a heathen altar. That was the signal for a sudden uprising of the faithful. Mattathias attacked the foe of Judah boldly and destroyed everything connected with pagan worship in Modin. Soon many more warriors rallied around his banner, and they invaded towns and villages, circumcising the children everywhere and re-establishing the religion of Moses. At the death of Mattathias, his son Judah took command of the army, and with 6,000 men against 70,000 (so it it written) he gained victory after

79

victory, until finally he reconquered the holy city, purified the defiled temple and reinaugurated the old service.*

Then it was that the great miracle was wrought. The conquerors found only one flask of undefiled oil; but, though it was barely enough for one evening, yet when it was lit for the great Reconsecration (Chanukah) it gave uninterrupted light during eight days and nights. And so "the men of understanding," in the language of the beautiful hymn which will be chanted tonight in all the synagogues on the East Side, "appointed these eight days for song and praises."

Work is not interrupted; the Sabbath clothes are left unmolested in the trunk; and how great are the joys which the good old feast has in store when one comes home after a long day's stooping at work at a sewing machine!

Chanukah! To the Yiddish-speaking the word smells of reeking buckwheat cakes and resounds with the buzz of spinning "Chanukah tops." By the way, do not confound the ordinary secular top, such as may be seen whirling and whirring under the lash of an American schoolboy, with the orthodox Jewish top. The latter is much smaller and is set in motion by its own stem. It is made of tin or lead, and bears the initials of the sentence, "There was a great miracle."

The main feature of this merry though unassuming holiday is the Chanukah lamps or Chanukah candles, which are lighted every evening during the feast, in commemoration of Judah's victory and the oil miracle. On the first evening one wick or candle is lighted, the number being increased by one each consecutive evening.

In good Yiddish the eight days of Chanukah are referred to as candles. Thus it is usual to speak of Haman's and Esther's marriage ceremony, for example, as having taken place on the third candle, or of Abraham having landed on the sixth candle. The kindling of the dedication lights is also invariably called consecrating the Chanukah candles, even when the great miracle is celebrated with olive oil.

The candles are made of wax or tallow. They are about four inches in length and very thin and flexible. The lamp has eight burners, all in a row, and a separate receptacle, opposite the centre, for the candle with which the lights are kindled and which is called the "sexton."

The Chanukah lamps and bunches of Chanukah candles can be seen in

---

*Mattathias (d. 167/166 B.C.) was the father of the Hasmonean brothers, and Modin was their home. His title, Cohen, denotes membership in the priestly class and descent from Aaron. After his death, he was succeeded by his son Judah the Maccabee. Each Chanukah a lighted torch is carried from Modin to Jerusalem by relay runners.—Ed.

the windows of every Hebrew bookstore or grocery in the Jewish quarter, where they are sold in great quantities.

Chanukah offers the only occasion when the service at the synagogue may be conducted to the accompaniment of a band of music. The organ music during Saturday service in some of the reformed synagogues uptown is frowned upon by the conformists of the ghetto. It is considered by them a downright desecration of the house of worship as well as of the Sabbath, instrumental music in any form being proscribed as part of the service since the destruction of the Temple. Nevertheless, for a synagogue reader to be assisted in the dedication of the Chanukah lights by a choir and band is the ideal of the most orthodox congregation in the region of Hester Street.

At home each householder dedicates the lights for himself, as follows: "Blessed art thou, O Lord our God, King of the Universe, who wroughtest miracles for our fathers in days of old in this season." As the head of the family solemnly chants the words, with the quaint old traditional Chanukah intonation, the other members of the household stand silently by, some devoutly, others, perhaps, with half-amused, half-solemn faces, but delight and sadness mingled are sure to thrill the chanter as well as his audience. Memories of the native place beyond the seas crowd upon one's mind at the sight of the Chanukah lights and at the sound of the peculiar, melancholy tones in which the benediction is recited; and should there be cause for regretting the old home, should life in the adopted country be one of toil, care and uncertainty, then the quaint scene may be accompanied with an occasional sigh, or if you watch the housewife closely, you may see the edge of her apron touching her eye furtively. Then the Chanukah lights seem to burn gloomily, and the "sexton," like the tallow candle placed at the head of the deceased, to be mourning the death of the past. Such a mood never lasts long, however, for soon after the dedication of the lights the table is set for supper, and although not a gala repast, it may be taken for granted that the housewife has exerted her every effort to make it worthy of the occasion.

As the family congregates around the table and the little room rings with the merry jingling of spoons, knives and forks and with everybody's ready appreciation of everybody else's joke or andecdote, the Chaunukah lights grow brighter, heightening the good humor of the group and adding solemn benignity to their mirth. After supper the assemblage is likely to be swelled by the arrival of visitors. At least, the children are ever and anon directing their little eyes to the door, for the chances are that some uncle or cousin will bring some Chanukah money. Card playing is regarded with anything but favor by the sedate denizens of the ghetto. Indeed, the pious elders look upon cards as something impure and sinful; and zealots are not far to seek who would literally refuse to handle a card for fear of being contaminated by contact; and yet to play cards on Chanukah is sanctioned and encouraged as one of the time-honored customs associated with the Feast of Dedication.

While the older folks are absorbed in their cards in the largest room of the set, the boys, if not too far Americanized to scorn the imported customs of their fathers, are grouped around another table spinning the Chanukah top. Nor is this a mere pastime, for the initials of the Hebrew sentence referring to the great miracle also happen to be head letters in the Yiddish words for nothing, all, half and cent, and this is utilized for determining the result of the play, the letter which occurs on the upper part of the top when it falls, or, to put it technically, when it terminates its prayer, indicating whether the one who spun it last is entitled to all the stakes, to half, to one cent, or to nothing.

The card playing and the top spinning are interrupted by the long awaited buckwheat cakes. There are buckwheat cakes and buckwheat cakes, and it would be the height of injustice to form an idea of the genuine Chanukah species from the flat, lean thing which is served in an American restaurant with butter or molasses. The Chanukah buckwheat cake or *latke* is much thicker and smaller and does not deserve its name unless, when served, it is fairly dripping with fat. It would be futile to attempt a description of it here, for the glories of a successful Chanukah *latke* defy the resources of the richest of Gentile languages. Even Zangwill, who sang the praises of the fried fish of the London ghetto, stopped short of the unrivalled, the incomparable Chanukah *latke*.

DEAD AFTER PURIM
March 9, 1898

Harris Freedman of 28 Orchard Street celebrated Purim like the good, pious Jew that he was. His religion bids the sons of Israel make merry on the fourteenth of Adar, and he did. In the morning he attended the reading of the Book of Esther at the synagogue. Willy, his twelve-year-old boy, Purim rattle in hand, was with him, and every time the Master Reader called out Haman's full name, Harris nudged the little fellow not to miss his chance. "Give it to him, my child!" he would say. "Make it hot for the enemy of the Jews, my darling." And as Willy's rattle joined the deafening noises around, Harris looked on beamingly and rubbed his hands for delight.

The dinner and the three-cornered Purim cakes, full of poppy seeds and covered with honey, were more than satisfactory. Harris had given gifts to the poor, according to the Book of Esther, and interchanged presents and felicitations with his friends. When night fell it found him in the best of spirits. He was pleased with the world, with his faith, with his family, with himself. He was ready for the great feast.

"Rosy," he said to his daughter, a comely damsel of nineteen Purims, "go and fetch your married sister, with her husband, and your married brother, with his wife. Purim does not take place every day. I want all my children at my table. Let it be a Purim feast worthy of a king."

Accordingly, Harris's married children, Joe and Bertha, came with their little families: Willy and Rosy joined them, and, with Harris at the head of the table in the front room on the second floor, and with Mrs. Freedman hovering about between the table and the kitchen stove, the picture was as Purim-like as it could be. The supper, if possible, was still better than the dinner; the *Hamantaschen* (Purim cakes) were the best Willy had ever tasted, and there was wine with which to get so drunk as to "confound Mordecai with Haman." Harris looked at his family, drank a toast to his happiness, and sang Purim song after Purim song. The Chaldaic words were Greek to him, but he knew that they spoke of the downfall of the enemies of Israel, and the melody was so dear—the same which his father had sung in Poland when Harris was as big as Willy—and his heart was thrilling and thrilling and tears of joy welled up in his eyes.

It was midnight when the little gathering broke up.

"It is late. We must go to work tomorrow," said Joe.

"Yes, my son," Harris seconded. "You must go to work and I must get up to see that the hands have something to do." For Freedman was a boss, a "kneepants" maker, with a small sweatshop, employing two machines, at 96 Canal Street. "Well, thanked be God for His mercy," he said, rising from the table. "May we be together next year, my children."

"Amen, thou Lord of the Universe!" Mrs. Freedman whispered, lifting her eyes to heaven. And ten minutes later the little apartment was immersed in sleep, Willy sharing the cot in the front room with his father, as usual.

At 10 o'clock this morning there was a crowd of people in front of the house at 28 Orchard Street. A gaunt patriarch was jingling a tin box half filled with coins, as he called out to the passersby in sepulchral tones, "Alms, deliver from death! Alms, deliver from death!" The tin box was filling up rapidly. Housewife after housewife on her way to the market stopped to put down her basket, drop a nickel and to say, devoutly: "Blessed be the true Judge!"

In the little courtyard within, a knot of men and women stood around two pools of blood. Some of the women were wringing their hands and crying bitterly as they looked, while one middle-aged man with enormous red sidelocks was murmuring psalms.

From the hallway on the second floor came the heartrending sobs of Willy.

"What's the matter, sonny?"

"Oh, my papa! He was such a good papa!" the boy answered. "I did not even hear him get up. Oh, *papale, papale,* dear!" He relapsed into half Yiddish.

A pretty young girl who stood swaying to and fro in mute despair was pointed out as Rosy.

"She is a *kalle* [betrothed]," whispered the informant, "and she had some money saved from her work for a marriage portion, but her father borrowed it all for his shop, and as things went wrong with him and he could not raise the sum, he took it so close to heart that he committed suicide. He was the best father you ever saw."

Inside the house a bundle wrapped up in a white sheet lay on the floor. Three candlesticks, each with a lighted candle in it, stood on a chair at the head of this bundle. The room was full of old Jews—members of the Synagogue "Men of Sochachov," to which Freedman had belonged, for like the other members he hailed from Sochachov, in Poland.

"The coroner? No," said one of the old men, tearfully, in answer to the question. "We have sent for a doctor to have the body examined. You see, if it is a case of suicide we have no right to bury him in a *talith** and *tachrichim* [burial clothes] nor to perform any of the rites. Poor Harris! He was a good man, and I hope it will prove to have been an accident, so that we can bring him to the 'Burial of Israel.' "

Presently Dr. Alexander Rosenthal of 89 Henry Street made his appearance, and with his hat on like the rest knelt down and unwrapped the bundle, revealing the remains of Freedman all covered with blood. The old Jews looked on anxiously. "No fracture anywhere. Only the nose is broken. He could not have flung himself from the roof. I don't think it is a case of suicide."

"Of course it is not. He was a sickly man," somebody interposed. "He had frequent fainting spells. He must have dropped dead. So we can bury him like a Jew, Doctor?"

"I think so."

*Prayer shawl.—*Ed.*

84

"A good year upon you!" the men of Sochachov shouted, in grim triumph, while through the open window could be heard the mournful jingle of the tin box and the solemn monotone of "Alms, deliver from death! Alms, deliver from death!"

PASSOVER ON CLINTON STREET
April 6, 1898

Heyman Berkovitz last night left his sweatshop an hour or two earlier than usual. It was the eve of the fourteenth day of the month of Nisan, when, in the language of Heyman's prayerbook, "It is requisite for the master of every family to search after leavened bread in every place where it is usually kept, gathering all leaven lying in his way."

"Beware of the floor!" Rebecca warned him angrily, as he opened his door on the top floor of a Clinton Street tenement house. "I have broken every bone in my body scrubbing and cleaning in honor of the feast, and here you are with your dirty boots! What did I cover the floor up for? Can't you tread on the rag, Fifth Avenue nobleman that you are?"

Heyman never touched the bare floor, but he knew that the good old woman was fagged out tidying up their three little rooms for the greatest and most expensive of holidays, so it was excusable for her to be out of temper, and he took it in good part.

"Hush, don't grieve, my crown," he said. "You had better rest yourself. But wait till I have gathered the leaven, my comfort."

In point of fact, there was nothing to "gather," for not only had every bit of leavened bread been carefully removed, but the "leaven dishes" had all been packed away out of sight and the Pesach (Passover) plates, bottles, glasses, spoons, forks, knives and what-not—everything that had lain in the cellar intact during the last twelve months—were out in their dazzling Pesach array on the bureau and in the kitchen closet, more spick and span than ever, and adding a touch of unwonted splendor to the apartment. There were the *kosses* (wine glasses) from which every member of the family, as well as the spirit of Elijah the Prophet, will drink tonight; and as Heyman's eye fell upon his glass his heart leaped with joy as if at sight of an old friend. A pretty little thing it was, finished in gold and red, and sparkling with the memories of a quarter of a century. It was the same dear *koss* which Rebecca had bought for

85

Heyman for the first Passover feast after their wedding. Every Pesach it had made its glad appearance to partake in the joys of the liberation from the bondage of Egypt, only to return, at the end of seven days, to its gloomy hiding place for another long twelve months. When the family had been compelled to leave the old home in Russia the *koss* was carefully put away in the big trunk among the choicest things Rebecca had to take with her to the unknown land beyond the seas. Heyman had not seen the dear little thing since last year, and as it now greeted him with its roseate and golden twinkle, as he came from the American workshop, it spoke to him of bygone days, of the days of his youth, of the old home where he sat at his father's Pesach table. Heyman's heart went out to the *koss,* and he was about to speak of it and the golden memories it stirred in his careworn bosom; but, behold! Rebecca, poor thing! was out of humor, and she might get angrier than ever. So, in order to cheer her up, he said:

"Oh, how fine the house and the dishes! How nice and clean and Pesach-like! Truly mine is the best housewife in New York. Praised be the Lord of the Universe for His goodness!"

"All right! You had better hurry up!" Rebecca replied, more morosely than ever, to hide her delight.

Not a bit of leavened bread had been left in the house, but a Jew must fulfill the commandment and gather the leaven on the eve of the fourteenth of Nisan. So Heyman procured a crust of rye bread, and breaking it into ten crumbs, he placed these in as many nooks of the little apartment. Arming himself with a feather brush, a wooden ladle and a lighted candle, he then proceeded to search for leaven, reciting as he did so, "Blessed art thou, O Lord our God! King of the Universe, who hast sanctified us with thy commandments and commanded us to remove the leaven."

After a ten minutes' search, during which he carefully kept his eye from falling upon the crumbs, he at last discovered them, one by one, sweeping them off into the ladle, with pious mien, and leaving Rebecca's questions unanswered so as not to break the sanctity of the search with worldly speech.

The next morning the ten crumbs, ladle, brush and all were thrown into the bonfire fed with the *chomets* (leaven) of the other tenants in the dingy little courtyard; whereupon Heyman recited another appropriate passage in Chaldaic, which he knew by heart.

"Benny, my son, make sure that you know the Four Questions," he said to his youngest boy as he saw the little fellow on the street. Benny is an American boy; he speaks not a word of Yiddish and is proud of it, too, although when his papa or mamma speaks to him he understands what they say, and his English answers to their Yiddish questions are always to the

86

point. He is at the head of his class at the Norfolk Street Grammar School, is Benny, but in the afternoon he attends a private class in Hebrew, and for Pesach his *rebbe* (teacher) had taught him to ask the Four Questions in the tongue of his father and mother. Indeed, he is the *mesinrik* (the youngest in the family), and it is upon him that the duty of asking the questions devolves. Nor is Benny loath to perform the task. Indeed, it is the only occasion when he wishes he could pronounce the words in the genuine Yiddish style, like papa and mamma, and not say them in his American way, like a "Gentile speaking Hebrew," as his greenhorn of an uncle once put it.

Tonight, then, when the good Jews return from the synagogue after the *maariv* service,* the great First Seder (Passover feast) will be spread. The table, covered with speckless cloth, will be set with a bottle of wine for the men and a bottle of mead for the women; clustering about these will be the *kosses* (glasses) of the household—from father's tall, dignified *koss* and mamma's dumpy blue *koss* to Benny's fancy little decanter emblazoned in three colors of the American flag, which the little patriot selected a few days ago on Hester Street. Rising at the head of the table there will be a little mound of *matzos* (flat cakes of unleavened bread), snugly concealed under a large napkin. A bunch of bitter herbs, symbolizing the bitterness of bondage; a gelatinous substance called *charoset*, denoting the clay which the sons of Israel used in building two cities for Pharaoh, will occupy the centre; while glistening in their Pesach-like splendor at the other end of the table will be the three brass candlesticks which Rebecca has burnished with might and main, with three stout candles spreading their warm Pesach rays over all. Two huge pillows, in snow-white cases, will be ready in the corner of the sofa near where the *matzos* are. For it is Seder night, the night of liberation from bondage, and Heyman, the freeman, is not to sit up at table as on ordinary days, but to partake of his *matzos* in reclining position as behooves the freeman and the king that he is tonight.

"*Gut yom-tov* [good holiday]," says Heyman as, attired in his Sabbath clothes, he enters the house with the boys and an *orach* (a homeless man invited to the feast) in tow.

"*Gut yom-tov*," echo the children and the *orach*, the former as joyously as the head of the family, the latter with humble solemnity.

"*Gut yom-tov!*" return the housewife and the girls in merry, tinkling chorus.

Every eye sparkles; everything seems brand-new and radiates good will

---

*The daily early-evening prayer service.—*Ed.*

and happiness. Heyman's heart trembles with joy, a tear creeps into his eye; but he overcomes his emotion with a frown and says, grimly:

"Well, it is not early, my wife. One must wash one's hands and set to the Seder."

A few minutes later, amid breathless silence, he takes off his high hat, replacing it with a velvet skullcap, dons the snow-white *kittel,* which he has not worn since the Day of Atonement, and takes his place in the corner of the sofa, dignifiedly reclining on the pillows in front of the *matzos.*

"Lo! this is the bread of affliction which our fathers ate in the land of Egypt." Heyman bursts out singing, the *orach* and the boys joining in at the top of their voices; the women accompany them all in a bashful murmur. "And now let all those who are hungry enter and partake of the feast, and all who are in need come and celebrate the Passover!"

Presently all fall silent. Resting their hands each on the open Haggadah (story of the Liberation) before him, they fondly look at Benny. It is his great moment. It is time to ask the Four Questions. Rebecca cannot help a smile of joy.

"Out with it, my son; don't be bashful, my ornament!" she urges him.

Benny begins. "Papa, dear, permit me to ask you four questions: Wherefore is this night distinguished from all other nights? On all other nights we may eat either leavened or unleavened bread, but on this night only unleavened bread. On all the other nights we may eat any kind of herbs, but on this night only bitter herbs. On all the other nights we do not dip even once, but on this night we dip twice. On all other nights thou eatest and drinkest either sitting or leaning, but on this night thou eatest only leaning."

To this the whole company answers: "Because we were slaves unto Pharaoh in Egypt, and the Eternal, our God, brought us forth from thence, with a mighty hand and an outstretched arm. Therefore it is meet that we tell the story of our Liberation."

As this story is told, Rebecca, overworked and having passed many a sleepless night in preparing for the great week, may serenely doze off over her Haggadah book, while the children, growing impatient for the supper and the *kneidlach* (cakes made of *matzo* flour and goose fat) gradually drop their voices to a less and less enthusiastic note. Phrases are slurred over, words are skipped.

"Don't skip, thieves that you are!" shouts papa, missing the merry chorus. "Read honestly or you will forfeit your *kneidlach!*"

At last the end of the first part of the Haggadah is reached. The royal repast is placed on the table, and presently the room rings with the merry jingle of knives and forks and with the gay chat of the hearty eaters. Everybody's appetite is active; only Rebecca is too fatigued and sleepy to care for the tid-bits she had overstrained herself to prepare. The fish and the roast chicken are sure to be a success, and if the *kneidlach* are well browned and brittle and "melt in your mouth" the praises of the supper will brace her up, so that when Benny steals the *affikomon* (a piece of *matzo* temporarily concealed by the head of the family under his cushion) she will join in the general outburst of merriment greeting the exploit.

Still, after the repast is over and each has drained four glasses of wine or mead, and Elijah, entering through the door left ajar for him, has helped himself to the glass especially set aside for him, and Heyman goes on with the second part of the story, not only Rebecca, but even the children, one by one, drowse off over their books.

Only Heyman's and the *orach*'s voices keep lingering in melancholy duet:

"A little goat! A little goat! Father bought a little goat for two *zuzim*.* And there came a wolf and ate up the goat that father had brought for two *zuzim*. A little goat! A little goat!

"And there came a dog, and he bit the wolf that had eaten up the little goat that father had bought for two *zuzim*. A little goat! A little goat!

"And there came a stick and it beat the dog that had bitten the wolf that had eaten the little goat that father had bought for two *zuzim*. A little goat! A little goat!

"And there came a flame and burned the stick that had beaten the dog that had bitten the wolf that had eaten the goat that father had bought for two *zuzim*. A little goat! A little goat!"

"WE MOURN THE LOSS OF OUR TEMPLE"
July 27, 1898

Tomorrow is the ninth of Av—the anniversary of the fall of Jerusalem and the destruction of the Temple by Titus.† It is a day of sighs and tears in the ghetto, of fasting and covering one's head with ashes, of sitting on the ground and mourning the bygone glories of Israel.

---

*"A little goat [or kid]!" is the title of an Aramaic song known as *Had Gadya* that concludes the Passover Haggadah. *Zuzim* are pieces of silver.—*Ed.*

†The Roman emperor Titus destroyed the Second Temple in 70 A.D. after a five-month siege.—*Ed.*

The fast and the mourning begin tonight, when the synagogues, their floors covered with hay, will be crowded with the faithful, who, seated on the ground, will follow the reading of the "Book of Lamentations" by the Master Reader and tearfully recite *kinoth* (elegies).

The Jewish bookstores were this morning busy selling *kinoth* books and "Lamentations," while the housewives had as much as they could do to prepare for the solemn repast preceding the fast.

It was after 12 o'clock when a stout woman in a great black wig came into the bookstore of Mr. Katzenelenbogen, Canal Street, near Allen. She carried a huge paper bag of bagels (ring-shaped cakes), eggs, and a pitcher of milk.

"Give me two *kinoths* and a "Book of Lamentations""; hurry up, mister; do me a favor. I have left the baby alone," she said anxiously, as she waddled up to the counter, amid piles of sacred books just imported for the approaching Days of Awe.

Mr. Katzenelenbogen, a well-built man of thirty, with one of the blackest beards and the saddest faces on Canal Street, was busy waiting on other customers, but he has the reputation of a good-natured man and he bore it out by asking a bewhiskered old man to wait while he went to attend to the woman.

"It's too bad to let a baby cry," he said, as he turned to her with a pleasant smile, which banished every vestige of sadness from his dusky face.

"Yes; if the mother needs a 'Book of Lamentations,' why should the baby be made to lament?" joked the bewhiskered old man.

"This is one of our most important fasts," said Mr. Katzenelenbogen, when he was left alone with his interviewer. "We bewail the lost independence of our people; we mourn the loss of our Temple, after whose destruction we became the victim of endless persecution. We sit on the ground reciting our tale of woe. Is there anything strange in the way our hearts break at the thought of the atrocities perpetrated on us in Russia, Rumania, Austria? Some of the poems to be chanted amid sighs and tears in our synagogues tonight are from the pen of the great Hebrew poet Jehudah Halevy, who lived in Spain in the days of Columbus, and who is extolled by Heinrich Heine in some of his most beautiful verses. Here is a passage in one of them."

Mr. Katzenelenbogen opened a *kinoth* book and read from an English translation of the text:

Oh, city of the world, beautiful and majestic.
For thee I long from distant Western home.
Oh, that on eagle's wings to thee I might come nigh;
That with my tearful face I could but touch thy dust.

Though kingless, crownless, now, yet do I yearn for thee,
Though serpents will be now where erst sweet honey flowed.
Oh, could I kiss thy dust, or tread thy ground!
I'd ask no more, my longing would be stilled.

"You are probably aware of the anti-Jewish riots which are now just going on in Galicia, Austria. Well, when we sit down barefooted on the ground to tell the tale of famine and desolation of the loss of our home, many a worshipper will think of Galicia and perhaps also of the riots in Russia which drove him to this land of freedom. Come to our synagogues tonight. They will ring with genuine sobs—with sobs that will echo the woes and the tears of our unhappy people since it became a prey to the brutal instincts of the scum of the earth. Ah, dear sir, you do not know what Israel has been through. Come to our synagogue tonight or tomorrow and you will hear the outpourings of woebegone hearts. You will see centuries of distress pent up and held in check suddenly let loose.

"But unrelieved tears are forbidden by our law. To enjoy life is one of the duties of the Jew. And so even in this day of sighs we have our relaxation—at least in the old country, where, after prayer and before leaving the house of God, while the congregation is still seated on the hay-covered floor, the youngsters and some of their gay elders will throw burrs at one another, as well as at the elders of the synagogue, and while the burrs stick and the good people joke or scold as they try to get them out of their beards or hair the rest of the congregation has plenty of time to laugh and to jest.

"The feast tonight before commencing the fast will consist of bagel, hard-boiled eggs besprinkled with ashes and milk. No meat has been eaten for the last nine days and will not be tasted before the fast is ended tomorrow after sundown."

Rabbi Beinish Zalkind Rabiner, whose office on the first floor of the tenement house at 24 Orchard Street is indicated by a huge sign bearing the inscription, "Here is the House of Law," was asked how he reconciled Jewish love for America and their patriotism as shown during the present war with their yearning after their old home in Jerusalem.

"What a strange question!" he exclaimed, shrugging his shoulders, and his cadaverous face taking on a look of astonishment. "If we are comparatively well off here, are we to forget that the race as a whole is in bondage? How about our brethren in Russia, in Poland, in Rumania? We are in exile, my son, we are in exile. True, America is our home; true, we love it and our children have given their lives for it in the present war, but—but, do you know what the Talmud says? 'He who mourns the fall of Jerusalem,' saith the Talmud, 'also sees the joy of Jerusalem.' There are many interpretations of this saying, but one of them is: 'He who is pious enough to think of the past glories of Jerusalem will see the happiness of a modern nation'—like the people of the United States whose glory is of an emancipated Jerusalem. Think of Cuba and think of the land of Israel, my son, and you will understand what I mean.''

———————

DROWNED THEIR SINS
September 19, 1898

Two of Roosevelt's Rough Riders, accompanied by an admiring civilian, were crossing the Brooklyn Bridge yesterday afternoon when their attention and progress were suddenly arrested by the sight of a knot of old women nodding and murmuring over the rail. Some of them wore heavy wigs on their heads, others had their hair carefully concealed under white silk kerchiefs, but they were all bent upon open books over which they were swaying to and fro as they whispered and sighed to the gleaming water below.

"What in —— is that?" asked the Rough Riders in duet. The question was addressed to the civilian, who was apparently their guide about town, but instead of an answer he stood gaping at the old women himself.

"You've got me this time," he muttered, as his eyes ran from one woman to the other. "Look, there are others and over there some more. They are Jew women, that's all I can tell you."

A bridge policeman who had been watching the movements of the cavalrymen with lazy interest noticed their perplexity and with an affected yawn dropped the explanation that it was "the Jewish New Year and them Jew women come to chuck their sins into the river."

The Rough Riders did not quite understand what he meant, and they stood gazing at the growing crowd of worshippers and expressing their astonishment in their own way, when they saw some of the women shake their skirts over the water.

"See that?" said the policeman. "That's the way they shake their sins off into the river."

"Gee!" exclaimed the Rough Riders.

The women went on shaking their skirts, murmuring and swaying more fervently than ever. Their number grew. Men, old and young, with shaggy beards and without, came along, and opening their books, joined the women, who, however, remained an overwhelming majority.

By 5 o'clock the bridge was swarming with these people. In one place a cluster of women were sighing and sobbing or nodding their heads dolefully, while they were repeating the words of prayer recited from a book by one of their number.

"They cannot read it themselves," an intelligent Jew explained, "and the one who can is their *sogerke* [reader]. The original prayer they are saying now is in Hebrew, of which they don't understand a word, but the *sogerke* reads a Yiddish translation. Still they will shed tears, even when they don't understand what they say. Tears are simply in the air in a 'Day of Awe' like this. It is the day of judgment, when one's account with God is settled and when one's fate for the coming year is determined."

"Today Thou sittest upon Thy throne of judgment," reads a passage of the prayer over which the good pious women were sighing and weeping, "to judge the whole world, the great and the lowly, the rich and the poor—to award them happiness or misery, life or death—each according to his or her deeds and desserts. We know that we are filled with wickedness. We have not fulfilled what Thou didst write in Thy holy laws. We have sinned against Thee and against one another. Therefore we are awed on this day of judgment, and we tremble for fear lest Thou judgest us according to our evil deeds. Therefore do we come to the edge of the water to shed tears like water and to pray for Thy mercy which flows in its abundance like this river. We pray Thee, Lord of the Universe, to erase all our sins from Thy book. Heartbroken we pray Thee to grant us a year of health, peace, and happiness; not to take away a father or a mother from their children, nor a child from its parents. Hear our sighs today and let there be no sighs and no tears during the new year. We know we have sinned but now our hearts are pure even as this water is pure. Help us, O God, that we may serve Thee, guard us against hunger and distress, against illness and grief. Amen."

Another part of the rail was occupied by a crowd of men and women, who recited their prayer aloud and shook their skirts more violently than the others. Conspicuous among these was an elderly man in a high hat and short sack coat. He was neatly dressed, his beard was well kept and he wore no sidelocks. He looked more prosperous and intelligent than the others, yet he read from his prayerbook louder and gesticulated more vehemently than the rest. Gentiles passing by stopped to look at him and to pry into his book, but he heeded nobody and nothing, and went on singing and jerking himself as fervently as ever.

"What is that you want?" he suddenly faced about to say to a bystander angrily. "I have finished, and now I can satisfy your curiosity. No, I am not angry at all. I am glad to explain it to you. Well, we call it *tashlich,* which means 'casting'—the casting of the sins upon the waters, as it stands in Micah, verse 19, Chapter VII, 'He will again have mercy on us; he will suppress our iniquities; yea, thou wilt cast all their sins into the sea.'

"Now, I don't want you to run away with the idea that we are fools enough to think that you can get rid of your sins by shaking them off your coat or skirt, as if they were a lot of fleas clinging to you. It's only some of these foolish old women who take the verse in its literal sense and come here to shake themselves clear of all sins. The Jew who understands his holy books takes it as a beautiful figure of speech," he went on, the vigorous, angry look on his face somewhat relaxing as he spoke. "Yet it is an old custom and a pretty custom, and why should I not pray here over the waters, rather than in my suffocating rooms in the tenement house?" he shouted again, taking on a wrathful look. "Here is God's flowing river, His pure, flowing, peaceful water. Here I feel nearer to Him, and my prayer seems more ardent to me. That's why I come to the river. But all talk about throwing your sins to the fish is stuff and nonsense. You don't see many men here, do you? It's all women, silly creatures who take everything literally."

The docks were also crowded with people going to *tashlich,* and the lakes at Central Park, especially near the 110th Street end, in which neighborhood the new uptown ghetto lies, were surrounded with Jewish men, women and children nodding and murmuring over their prayerbooks as did the people on the bridge. But the true women of piety preferred to walk many blocks to throw their sins into the river.

"You want flowing water, my son," said a little woman of seventy. "The stagnant water of a pond or a lake is not fresh enough, nor pure, nor does it move like a living creature. It's only in a country of sinners like this that people will put up with a lake for *tashlich,*" she concluded with a sigh.

At the Pike Street dock the worshippers had a good deal of trouble with some "Gentile rowdies," as they characterized them, who pelted the devout old women with stones. One Christian boy stole up to an old Jewess as she stood weeping over the waters as if her heart would break and tore off her wig. The commotion which ensued bade fair to develop into a riot, for the older Christians present, including some laborers or watchmen of the dock, relished the practical jokes of the boys and encouraged them. The police were rather slow in making their appearance, and so at one time stones and other missiles flew thick and fast. The news spread through the Jewish district like wildfire, and the devout people, armed with their prayerbooks, carried their sins to other docks. Some of these people seemed to take it all as a matter of course, as if it was the most natural thing in the world that "Irish *shegotzim*" (Gentile boys) should molest Jews with prayerbooks on the street.

"Still throwing stones?" asked one man of another on Pike Street, with the air of one who asks whether the rain is still falling.

Police Headquarters was notified, and the disturbance was soon stopped by the appearance of several bluecoats. Then the crowd at the Pike Street dock began to grow rapidly. Toward the evening it was literally thronged with *tashlich* worshippers.

When dusk was gathering on the dock it was so crowded that many belated had to go back. Presently strains of song and music rang out near the praying multitude. It was Gentile music, and as it was first heard many of the worshippers turned about with a pained air. It was a detachment of Salvation Army workers. A knot of sailors and dock hands surrounded them. The Jews after a little resumed their prayer. The hum and buzz of *tashlich* mingled with the song and prayer of the Gentiles, the caps of the latter gleaming red amid a sea of white kerchiefs and wigs.

"FISH, FISH, LIVING, FLOUNDERING, JUMPING, DANCING FISH!"
September 24, 1898

The fish market on Norfolk Street, between Grand and Division, did a rushing business yesterday. It was the eve of the Sabbath of Penance, and the housewives wanted fish for two great days. For next to the Sabbath of Penance, which is today, comes Atonement Eve (tomorrow), when about half an hour before sundown the pious people are to enjoy the great feast which is to fortify them for the twenty-four hours of fasting and praying of Yom Kippur.

"Fish, fish, living, floundering, jumping, dancing fish!" called the tradeswomen, trying to outshout each other and all but sticking their wares into the faces of the housewives.

"Look here, missus! You want God to give you a good year, don't you? Can't get it unless you buy my living fish, dancing fish, screaming, frisking fish. Fish, fish, fish, for Sabbath of Penance."

One fishmonger, a big burly fellow, whose store is in a cellar, rushed out of it into the street above, armed with a large pike and screaming at the top of his husky voice as if calling for the police, and asked the women who were pushing their way through the crowd whether they knew of the bargains he had in store for them.

"Good wo-men! Good wo-men!" he yelled. "This pike is for you. I sell it at a loss, but I am not going to let my stock rot in my basement. Today it is full of life, good women, so full of life that my whole store is pitching and rolling with the scrambling of the fish. Pike! Pike! Pike! Take pity and buy the living pike!"

The housewives smiled but could not help stopping, and one after the other they filed down into the basement. Half a block away two pushcart women were wrangling over a customer, whom each of them was pulling to her side, while she showered the most peppery Yiddish at her adversary.

"She never meant to buy any of your rotten fish. I know this lady, and she always buys fish of me. May I sink five miles into the earth and have a black inscription and seal for the new year if she does not."

"She buy fish of you," retorted the other. "It's dirt, poison, cholera that you are selling, not fish. You are an old customer of mine, dear little missus, are you not? Spit at her."

The *casus belli* meantime was struggling to disengage herself, and when she had succeeded at last, she screwed up a pious look and said to the two belligerents:

"You ought to be ashamed of yourselves, fighting like that two days before the Day of Atonement, when everybody must make peace with his enemies. You know it's only those sins which we commit against the Uppermost which He will forgive on Yom Kippur, but those between man and man—never."

"I did not start the fight," began one of the two rivals, with contrition.

"Yes, you did . . ."

"Hush!" interposed the devout housewife. "Better make peace and be friends, and God will help you both. I'll tell you what, if you kiss right before me I shall buy a pound of fish of each, and God will bless us all for your sake."

The offer was accepted, and the women who had two minutes ago been invoking damnation upon each other bashfully kissed.

"Forgive me, Leah," said one.

"Forgive me, Sarah," said the other.

The devout customer wiped her eyes with her sleeve. Some of the other women nodded their bewigged heads reverently.

WHEN ANGELS SHUDDER
September 26, 1898

This is Yom Kippur, the Day of Awe and of Atonement. The synagogues—from the rich Temple Emanu-El on the corner of Fifth Avenue and Forty-third Street to the humblest temporary praying room on the top floor of a ramshackle tenement house—are and will all day be crowded with men, women and children confessing their sins and praying for atonement, for a new account with the High Tribunal, for a favorable decree for the coming year. It is a terrible day in Israel, the day of days upon which depends the fate of every living creature, and with few exceptions it is observed and spent in fasting and prayer by every adult Hebrew in town. Whatever one does the whole year, however neglectful one may be of his religion on any other holiday, on this day of Yom Kippur one is sure to be at his synagogue and, *machzor* (prayerbook) in hand, follow the *chazan* (singer) and his chorus, strike his heart while enumerating the sins he has committed and pray for mercy and an enrollment in the Book of Life. Even the lonely visitors of the East Side cafés, those for whom even Yom Kippur has no terror, even their faces reflect the gravity of the day.

The Jewish population of Manhattan Borough is estimated at about a quarter of a million. It is the greatest number of children of Israel ever gathered in a single city. It is larger than the combined population of the ghettos of Warsaw, Berdichev and Vilna—the three largest centres of Jewish population in the world. And this multitude which constitutes one-sixth of old New York, and is made up of representatives of every country on the face of the globe, is today directly or indirectly joined in that reverence and melancholy which the Day of Judgment casts upon the sons of Israel.

"A Jew may smoke on the holy Sabbath or even eat pork, but show me the Jew who will stay away from the synagogue on Yom Kippur," says a pious patriarch.

"I know some," retorts his companion. "My cousin, for instance, passed last Yom Kippur in a café. So, you see, your rule is not much of a rule."

"Did your cousin really eat and drink last Yom Kippur? If he did, he is no Jew at all. Not at all. And it is of Jews alone that I speak. So, you see, my rule holds good."

This is one of the jokes of the week in the ghetto, and it expresses the mood of nine-tenths of its denizens. Another characteristic anecdote in circulation relates to the *appikorsim* (infidels) in Israel who will rather eat pork than fast on Yom Kippur. A Gentile proprietor of a delicatessen store asked a Jew what day it was when the Mosaic faith required the sons of Israel to dine on pork.

"What day!" roared the Jew, in bewilderment. "There is no such day."

"Ah, but I know what I am talking about," insisted the Gentile. "My place is crowded with your people on that day. It is my best day in the year."

Upon inquiry the pious Jew was shocked to find that the day the delicatessen man referred to was Yom Kippur, and that his store was then crowded with *appikorsim,* who, unable to find anything to eat in the Jewish quarter, are compelled to resort to a *treife* (impure) Gentile place.

The most important part of the service in the synagogues today is the chanting of a series of hymns, *unetaneh tokef.*

"The great trumpet is sounded," reads a passage of these; "a dull, murmuring noise is heard; the angels shudder; fear and trembling seize them. 'Ha!' they cry; 'it is the day of judgment,' for in justice even they are not found faultless before Thee. All who are about to enter into the world now pass before Thee, as a herd of sheep; as a shepherd numbereth his flock and passeth under his crook so dost Thou cause to pass, number and appoint every living soul, fixing the limitation of all creatures, prescribing their destiny. But Penitence, Prayer, and Charity can avert the evil decree!"

This is first sung by the cantor and his choir in a melancholy tune of his own composing, but the underlying theme of the melody is borrowed from the sweet and heartrending songs composed in the "Exile of Spain" in the reign of Isabella, when the Jews had to hide in caves and forests to serve their God without incurring the risk of the *auto-da-fé*. The songs speak of centuries of persecution, of streams of tears and blood, the cantor's voice dies away in a deafening outburst of fervent prayer, sighs and sobs.

Every married man wears today the long white gown called *kittel,* the praying shawl, the skullcap of white or black satin, and stands before his Judge in his stocking feet. The women in the galleries above are arrayed in their best dresses, wigs, kerchiefs and bonnets, but few of them have their finery on. It is a day of humble prayer and broken hearts. It is no time for exhibiting one's diamond earrings or gold watch and chain. There will be plenty of time for that, for following close upon Yom Kippur is the great merry Feast of Tabernacles.

THE SOOKA BUILDERS
September 29, 1898

The scene of the Yom Kippur riot, at the junction of Canal and Division Streets, where some Jews were mobbed by their coreligionists last Monday because they had been dining on the great Mosaic fast day, was this morning blocked with wagons heavily laden with fir trees. A number of men and boys were hovering about among the wagons, unloading them and dragging the trees into the courtyards of the surrounding tenement houses.

"*Sehah! Sehah!*" sang a little boy, clapping his hands for delight. "Papa is goin' to put up a *sooka* an' I'm goin' to help him."

"What? You don't know what *sehah* and *sooka* mean?" asked a bewildered old man. "*Sehah* means the covering, the roofing of the *sooka,* and a *sooka*—well, a *sooka* is a *sooka*. Did you ever hear!" he exclaimed, unable to define the word or to realize that there could be people who needed such a definition at all. But a bystander with an English newspaper in his pocket knew better, and with a superior smile he volunteered the explanation that a *sooka* was a booth or a tabernacle.

"Our forefathers, in the course of their peregrinations on their way to the land of promise, once stopped in booths, and so we commemorate the event by taking our meals in little makeshift dwellings or tents during the eight days of the Feast of Tabernacles, which is to begin next Saturday.

"In point of fact, this merry holiday of ours is intended to celebrate the ingathering of the crops. It is the Jewish thanksgiving week at the close of the summer season, but the leading features of the feast are the tabernacles which the faithful among the tenants of each house club together to put up for a sort of public dining room. The roof must not be of solid material, and while the booth is not to be covered with glass it must admit a view of the sky. So we cover it with fir branches, through whose interstices we can see bits of blue. A pious Jew, one who is an ardent observer of our complex and exacting faith, will even sleep in the booth during the week of the coming feast, but this is not strictly obligatory."

At one courtyard nearby several of the tenants were busily engaged putting up their *sooka*. They could afford to hire a man to do the work for them, and it might have been more economical to do so, too, for they were all tailors or peddlers, and they were stopping their daily occupations to build the booth. But then the very work connected with the building of one's *sooka* is a good deed, and the pious tailors would lose a dollar or two at their trade rather than the chance of performing such a good action at the opening of the year.

"That ain't the way to drive in a stake!" shouted one of the *sooka* builders as he paused with the board he was dragging to wipe the perspiration off his begrimed face.

"I am not going to learn how to build a *sooka* of you," answered the other, angrily. "In the old country I used to put up better *sookas* than you ever ate in."

The speaker's wife sighed. "In the old country! There was plenty of room for a decent *sooka* for good Jews to eat and to make merry in. But here, the yard is too small for a hen coop. I can't see where we are going to put the table and chairs. Woe is me, how crowded it will be."

"Don't you like it?" asked her husband, his mouth full of tacks. "You won't have to use it anyhow," he added with a wink at the other men. "You women folk ain't in it."

"I know we are not," said the woman with high defiance, as she put her bare stout arms akimbo. "Our religion does not count us in, and we have no seat even in the booth, but then what would you men eat in the *sooka* if we women did not get the dinners for you?"

"Well said! A woman with the head of a man!" shouted the *sooka* builder, cheerily.

THE GIVING OF THE LAW
May 15, 1899

The stores of the East Side are closed today, and some of the sweatshops and dancing schools have been turned into synagogues. Grand Street, Canal Street and East Broadway are swarming with promenaders in new holiday clothes, the matrons in shining black wigs and *tzipsiks* (bonnets), their pious husbands in long-skirted coats and tall "stovepipes," the younger people in the most stylish cutaway coats, derbies, spring jackets and spring hats Canal Street and Division Street have produced. Hester Street is deserted, strangely clean, quiet and gloomy—not a pushcart to bar one's way, nor a fishwife to sing the praises of her "living, jumping, laughing and dancing" wares into his ear.

It is the first day of the Pentecost—the "season of the giving of the law"—one of the three merry festivals in the Jewish calendar. It is one of the serious holidays, too, and to desecrate it by doing business or going to work would be as grave a sin as to smoke a cigarette or to write an address on the holy Sabbath. But then, it is one of the jolliest feasts of the year, and the milk dinner and milk *blintzes* (cheese tarts) without which Shavuot (Pentecost) would be like *Hamlet* without the prince, are sure to be a success, so the day is willingly observed by the delinquents as well as by the faithful in Israel. Altogether, counting the combined population of the four great ghettos of Greater New York (two in Manhattan and two in Brooklyn) more than 200,000 orthodox Jews are celebrating the giving of the law today.

A milk diet in all the varied forms which tradition has handed down to the orthodox housewife is strictly enforced, though meat is not proscribed, provided the two are not mixed. What affinity there is between the giving of the law and milk does not seem to be clear even to the rabbis of the ghetto. One of them advanced a theory, drawn from a musty volume in Chaldaic, but he gave it out for an hypothesis rather than for a positive statement.

"When we suddenly found ourselves with the law on our hands," he said, by way of interpreting the Chaldaic passage, "we did not know what we were to eat on the day of Pentecost. You see, our religion is very strict on the subject of diet, and you know, I suppose, that we draw a sharp line between meat-food and milk-food. Our religious laws also determine other details of our table, and we are so used to those specifications and restrictions that in each new case unprovided for by our books we are apt to feel helpless. Now on Passover our ancestors were ordered to eat unleavened bread; on the Feast of Tabernacles they were commanded to take their meals in booths; only the Feast of Pentecost, the third of the trilogy, was left unprovided with any prescriptions, so our people were at a loss. 'What shall we eat on this day?' they wondered. 'Alas!' the Torah [the law] is silent.' 'I tell you what,' said a sage, 'let us eat milk things,' and very likely he found something between the lines of the Scriptures which bore him out. Unfortunately, his discovery has been lost, as has many a gem of the law, and all that is left is the custom. But then, 'A custom breaks a law,' as we say."

Another man of learning said he was aware of the theory referred to, but did not take much stock in it. He had one of his own, and he cited authorities in support of it.

"What is the color of milk?" he asked. "White," he answered himself. "And what is the meaning of whiteness? The purity of the soul. Now what makes our soul pure as the driven snow? The Law which our fathers received from Moses on Mount Sinai."

The learned man has a learned son-in-law who wears no sidelocks and reads English papers. The young man followed his father-in-law with a superior smile, and when the old man was through, he said to the visitor:

"Mister, don't take it for a good coin, or you won't be able to pass it. The holy books are like a big store. You can get anything you want there. If you want a quotation showing that milk is the purity of the soul, just apply at the counter."

The old man flared up, but the son-in-law did not mind him.

"You want to know why we eat milk soup and milk cakes, mister, don't you? Well, because this is just the season for milk, and a Jew is not much of a Jew unless he knows a good thing from a bad one. The grass is so green and so fresh that the cows enjoy their dinners. Now, why shouldn't we enjoy ours? Why should we be worse off than cows. Well, the cows eat green food and they give us white food. That's all there is to it."

Tonight the faithful will stay in the synagogues all night, reading *tikkon Shavuot* and chanting psalms. To sleep when the children of Israel "saw the thunder" which resounded from Mount Sinai on the day of the giving of the law is considered unseemly. Besides, one wants time to study the law, and as the day is spent in enjoying the *blintzes* and exchanging visits, the reading of the *tikkon Shavuot* is postponed till after supper.

"The book which we read on Pentecost night," said the rabbi who expounded the more elaborate theory regarding the milk diet, "is made up of fragments of the various parts of the Five Books, the prophets and of almost every rabbinical book in the later ages. As it would be impossible to read through the entire law, we confine ourselves to specimens of each book, and the Uppermost in His mercy accepts it for the complete law.

The son-in-law of the other pious man took a different view of the matter, and when told about the specimens of the law, he said with a smile:

"Yes, indeed, they are specimens. One of our greatest preachers in Russia was a man who taught the law in the town of Dubno. He was great for his parables, and this is what he said of the book we read on Pentecost night: 'It's like the samples of cloth, silk and satin, which a rich man once showed the sweetheart of his son. "Be his wife and you shall have dresses made of these stuffs," he urged her. "You see, time is too short for me to buy the material, but here you see the specimens." The girl married the rich man's son, and the samples were all she ever got. Some Jews say to the Lord: "It's only one night, and we cannot read all the law, so we shall show Thee samples of all the holy books that we are going to read during the coming year." ' You understand the rest, don't you?" concluded the son-in-law, rubbing his hands, merrily.

THE NEW YEAR
September 5, 1899

The crowds in the ghetto were decked out in their best clothing this morning. The markets and the sewing machines were silent, but there was plenty of noise on the larger thoroughfares. The cafés swarmed with men in new Prince Albert coats, high hats and white four-in-hand neckties. An air of lightheartedness and even gaiety enveloped Grand Street. It looked like Sabbath, ordinary Sabbath in a season when work is plenty and wages are high, when one has a sneer for the immigrant fresh from Europe and is at peace with Columbus, the man who had the good sense to discover the land of milk, honey, and gold.

But, hark! a tune bursts forth from the fourth floor of that tenement house yonder. It is a sad tune; it speaks of tears and sighs, and some of the gay faces on the sidewalk in front of the café across the street darken. A white-bearded patriarch, his trousers tucked into his long snow-white stockings, scurries anxiously past, hugging his praying shawl to his bosom. There is no mirth in his face. His bleached brow is contracted. He is a belated worshipper on his way to the great morning service of the great day of Rosh Hashana. We have lived to see the Days of Awe again!

"A merry holiday to you, grandma!" says a well-dressed fellow from the doorway of a café. He is a stranger to her, and he utters the greeting partly in jest, partly succumbing to the Awe Day atmosphere of the neighborhood. "Mayest thou be inscribed for a year of life, little grandmother."

"I wish you the same, my son," the old woman stops to answer with a sigh. "Mayest thou be inscribed for a year of happiness, my child. God grant that neither you nor any child of Israel knows evil during the coming year. Our people need God's mercy. The enemies of Israel are raging. May Captain Dreyfus, too, be enrolled for a year of life, freedom, and happiness, for is he not the sacrifice of Israel, poor child that he is?"

There were tears in the old woman's eyes. She wiped them hurriedly with the end of her gay silk kerchief.

"I must not be late for the service," she said. "And you, my son, can it be that you are taking your breakfast before you have heard the *shofar* blow? Come, my son. Don't let our poor people suffer for your sins. Have you not bought a seat in some synagogue? You don't mean to tell me that you went to a café before you attended the song and prayer of the great day? *Unetaneh tokef,* at least you must attend, must you not?"

The young man shamefacedly assured her that he had a seat in a house of worship and that he was going there at once.

"May you live long in health and in happiness, then," she blessed him, hurrying away in the direction of the Eldridge Street synagogue.

Unetaneh tokef is the most important prayer on the two days of Rosh Hashana and the Day of Atonement. It is known as the "song of a martyr in Israel." The story of this prayer is one of the prettiest of Jewish folk tales. It is the song of Rabbi Amnon, who was the rabbi of Metz in the days of Bishop Ercembud (1011–1017). Rabbi Amnon was of an illustrious family, of great personal merit, rich and respected by Jew and Gentile alike. The bishop frequently pressed him to abjure Judaism and embrace Christianity, but to no avail. It happened, however, that on a certain day, being more closely pressed than usual, and somewhat anxious to be rid of the bishop's importunities, he said hastily: "I will consider the matter and give thee an answer in three days."

As soon as he had left the bishop's presence, however, his heart smote him, and an uneasy conscience blamed him for having, even in the remotest manner, doubted his faith. He reached home overwhelmed with grief. Meat was set before him, but he refused to eat, and when his friends visited him he declined their proffered consolation, saying:

"I shall go down mourning to the grave."

On the third day, while he was still lamenting his rash concession, the bishop sent for him, but he failed to answer the call. Finally the bishop's messengers seized him and brought him before the prelate by force.

"Amnon," said the bishop, "why didst thou not come to me, according to thy promise, to inform me of thy decision in regard to my request?"

"Let me pronounce my own doom for this neglect," answered Amnon. "Let my tongue which uttered those doubting words be cut out. It was a lie I uttered, for I never intended to consider the proposition."

"Nay," said the bishop. "I will not cut out thy tongue; but thy feet, which refused to come to me, shall be cut off, and the other parts of thy obstinate body shall also be punished and tormented."

Under the bishop's eye the toes and thumbs of Rabbi Amnon were then cut off, and, after having been severely tortured, he was sent home in a carriage, his mangled members beside him.

Rabbi Amnon bore all this with the greatest resignation, firmly hoping and trusting that this earthly torment would plead his pardon with God. The Days of Awe came round while he was on his death bed, and he desired to be carried to the synagogue. He was conveyed to the house of God, and during the service he asked that he be permitted to utter a prayer. The words, which proved to be his last, were as follows:

"I will declare the mighty holiness of this day, for it is awful and tremendous. Thy kingdom is exalted thereon; Thy throne is established in mercy, and upon it Thou dost rest in truth. Thou art the Judge, who chastiseth, and from Thee naught may be concealed. Thou bearest witness, writest, sealest, recordest and rememberest all things, aye, those which we imagine long buried in the past. The Book of Records Thou openest; the great *shofar* is sounded: even the angels are terrified, and they cry aloud, 'The Day of Judgment dawns upon us,' for in judgment they, the angels, are not faultless.

"All who have entered the world pass before Thee. Even as the shepherd causes the flock he numbers to pass under his look, so Thou, O Lord, causest every living soul to pass before Thee. Thou numberest, Thou visitest; appointing the limitations of every creature, Thy judgment and Thy sentence.

"On the New Year it is written, on the Day of Atonement it is sealed. Aye, all Thy decrees are recorded. Who is to live and who is to die. The names of those to meet death by fire, by water, or by the sword; through hunger, through thirst, and with the pestilence. All is recorded. Those who are to have tranquility, those who are to be disturbed. Those who are to be troubled, those who are to be blessed with repose. Those who are to be prosperous, those for whom affliction is in store. Those who are to become rich, who poor; who exalted, who cast down; but penitence, prayer and charity, O Lord, may avert all evil decrees."

When he had finished this declaration Rabbi Amnon expired, dying in God's house, among the assembled sons of Israel.

GHETTO FULL OF SIGHS
September 14, 1899

All day yesterday the ghetto was astir. There was a babel of excitement at the markets, an unusual rush and bustle on every street. Everybody was in a hurry, every housewife in a fever of agitation. Faces were overcast, the noise rang doleful. The sidewalks in front of the larger synagogues were crowded from early morning. Men and women with a humbled look in their eyes were coming and going. The lobbies were taken up with long tables, around which sat patriarchs, each with a plate and a card in printed Hebrew, naming the charity for which he solicited the worshipper's contribution. There were the cantors and their choristers, too, for the coins put into their plates on Yom Kippur Eve were part of their stipulated income. Altogether the long table in the vestibule of a prosperous downtown synagogue, with the score of venerable men around it, reminded one of the *sanhedrin,* the High Court of Judea.

As the worshipper came out of the synagogue, his sad face grown sadder, and his movements more subdued and humble than ever, he would take out his purse, pour out part of its contents on the palm of his hand, and stepping softly, almost on tiptoe from plate to plate, put a coin in each. There was melancholy and solemnity in the very jingle of the copper and silver. As hand after hand was held out over the plates, the beadle, the cantor and the choristers watched the proceeding from the corner of their eyes, and if the coin was smaller than expected the pious look on their faces had to struggle with one of disappointment or indignation. But there are no observers of human nature on Yom Kippur Eve, and the plaintive hum that came from the synagogue filled the lobby with an atmosphere of "crushed hearts and broken spirits."

The service within was not conducted by the principal cantor. It was only *minchah,* the prayer of the eve of Atonement Day. The House of God was full of sighs. The worshippers, bent over their prayerbooks, swayed to and fro as they murmured fervently and struck their hearts with their fists, but all this was evidently preparatory to a far greater event. The congregation suggested an army on the eve of a great battle.

Outside, in a little room between the synagogue and the vestibule, the pious old people prostrated themselves on the floor to receive the thirty-nine lashes of *molkoth,* administered with the thong of the beadle's old phylacteries. The huge wax candle which was to burn until the night service of the next day had by this time been lit; at home the birds of redemption had been "beaten," swung three times around one's head and then killed according to sacred law, and ready to be served at the feast which was to be the last until the great day of fasting and prayer was over. The graves of the dead relatives had also been visited; everything was ready for the tears of the Erev Yom Kippur supper, which makes one ready for the tears of Kol Nidre—Kol Nidre, the song of awe, the beautiful and terrible awe; ready for the moment when the synagogue should ring with voices from the caves and forests of Spain, where the downtrodden people served their God at the peril of the stake.

It was sundown. The last pushcarts were hurriedly being taken away from the marketplace. Hester Street was deserted, gloomy. It looked like a Polish town in ruins. The noise had died down. Men and women with prayerbooks and packages containing shrouds under arms were quietly scurrying hither and thither. Here and there a pair stopped to fall on each other's shoulders, tearfully to beg forgiveness.

"Let us make peace, forgive me," said people who had not spoken for months, or perhaps years. "I wish you an inscription in the Book of Life with all my heart."

Half an hour later, at sunset, was Kol Nidre. The synagogues were white with shrouds and a-glitter with the silver-laced praying shawls and skullcaps. The doors of the Holy Ark stood open, the silk vestments of the scrolls within looming in many colors. The wax candles in front of the worshippers burned dim and mournful, the women in their gallery above were nodding over their Books of Tears.

At last the beadle in a white shroud, glittering shawl and cap, like the substantial men by the east wall, mounted the steps of the reading platform and slapped the desk. Silence fell. The women raised their bewigged heads from their books and looked down upon the *omud** against the centre of the west wall, where stood the cantor, surrounded by his chorus of men and boys. A sigh broke from an elderly matron. Again the beadle slapped for order. There was another pause, and then softly, cautiously, as though looking around to see if some spy of the Inquisition were not hidden in bushes nearby, the cantor began in Chaldaic:

"All vows and self-prohibitions, vows of abstinence and promises!"

The melody was the same which the sons of Israel sang in the days of Queen Isabella. The words were of the time when they were compelled to betray the faith of their fathers at the point of the sword. Some gave up their lives rather than their belief; others escaped death by making promises and vows of which they prayed God to be absolved. The prayer is out of touch with modern conditions, but its strains retain the subdued whisper of the hiding worshippers, their suppressed sighs and their broken hearts. It comes from the very heart of the race's sufferings in the Middle Ages, it bears likeness of the weeping people. It is one of the holiest relics of Israel. It is the song of songs in the ghetto.

*Prayer stand—*Ed*.

PART THREE
The Chasm

Americanized by a Hat. (Augustus F. Sherman Collection, American Museum of Immigration. *Courtesy of the National Park Service, Statue of Liberty National Monument.*)

5

THE BARGE OFFICE

BARGE OFFICE MOTHER
July 9, 1898

Amalia Mahr came here from Silesia, Germany, to marry Karl Vogt, her sweetheart. She had never seen him in the old country, and he had been in America before she first heard of him, yet he was her sweetheart. About a year before she was landed at the Barge Office they became acquainted and he began making love to her—all by mail. Karl is an engineer and has $2,000 in the savings bank and, to judge from his photograph, he is a handsome man. As to Amalia, who is not quite eighteen, she was the belle of her village and by far the prettiest girl at the Barge Office.

People who knew Karl said he was an honest, good-natured fellow and that Amalia would be happy with him; and so when she showed his love letters to her parents and asked them what to do, they put their heads together and then said:

"Well, daughter, go to America and use your own judgment. You have been a good girl, so we can trust to your own common sense."

To America, then, she came, and she had only been a few hours at the Barge Office when she was brought face to face with her intended husband. His photograph proved a correct likeness of him, but he was an older man than she had pictured him to be, and in answer to her questions he frankly said that he was thirty-nine. That did not seem to make any difference to her. Still, the clerks of the Barge Office, and especially the matron, took such an interest in her and were so kindly that she thought she might as well lay her story before them and seek their advice. This she did in the same confiding,

111

loving manner in which she had consulted her parents. The joint verdict of the officials was that she should be in no hurry to marry Karl, but should take a position as a servant in some respectable family, let Karl call on her and wait for developments.

"You are so young and he is thirty-nine," said the chief clerk to Amalia, who sat listening, with bent head, like a dutiful daughter. "He could be your father, could he not?"

Amalia nodded her head sadly.

"Well," pursued the chief, dropping deeper and deeper into the manner of a loving father lecturing his child, "you see that there is no hurry. Maybe you will come to like him and he will make you an excellent husband. But you must first wait and find out the state of your own feelings. Do you understand?"

Amalia nodded her head.

"Ask her how she felt when she first met him," suggested a bystander. The chief did so, and the immigrant girl said, blushing:

"He looks to be an honest man."

"But how did you feel?" the chief insisted. "Did you like him? Do you understand?"

Amalia hesitated a moment and then responded:

"I thought that when we got to know each other he would be good to me and that he would be satisfied."

"And would you be satisfied with him, Amalia? Do you think you could like him and be happy? You must know that marriage is an important matter. Upon it depends the whole life of a person, and you had better know whether you like Karl before you marry him. Now you have seen him. Do you think you like him?"

"He looks to be an honest man, and people who know him say he is a good-natured man," said Amalia, with drooping head.

"Well, we shall get you a nice place. You will make a few dollars—do you understand? And meantime you will become better acquainted with Karl," decided the chief, with which he left the girl to the matron, and for some time the two women were talking confidentially, like mother and daughter.

"You see, I think Karl will make her a good husband," said the matron to a visitor. "We know the people for whom he works, and they speak well of him. More than twice as old as she? What of it? A husband may be twenty years older than his wife, and the couple may still live happily together. I want this poor girl to take time. She is so young and inexperienced, and they know so little of each other."

Asked about the general nature of her work, the matron said:

"Well, as you see, I have to be a mother and a sister and sometimes a detective and a judge to the immigrant women that are landed here. Most of them are so green that we must take care of them as of little children. We would not let them fall into a trap or take a step that might prove fatal to their happiness. They need fathers and mothers to look after their interests, and that's what we try to be to them. Others, on the other hand, are full of cunning and are as bad as they can be, and then it is our business to find them out, to get their true story out of them and, if it is against the law to admit them, send them back.

"Recently I had in my charge a middle-aged woman, who came here with a young man of about twenty-five. She could have been his mother, but they gave themselves out for man and wife. Somehow I suspected that there was something wrong in their relations, and after repeated talks with the woman I learned that she had a husband in Germany. 'We shall wait till I get a divorce,' she said, 'and then we shall get married.' Was she pretty? No. But she had character and he had not. Of course, we sent them back.

"Many young men will come to America in advance of their sweethearts, whom they get over after they have made themselves self-supporting in this country. But sometimes they forget their vows, and in many instances the girls come to remind them."

"CAN'T GET THEIR MINDS ASHORE"
November 11, 1898

A score of immigrants of half a dozen different nationalities were this morning clustered about a young Italian who sat on one of the long benches at the Barge Office. His name was Farneti Albano, and he was quite a handsome fellow, but he spoke with a painful stutter, and as he went on answering the questions of his fellow-countrymen his ruddy cheeks twitched and his flashing black eyes blinked in a manner which made some of the bystanders smile, and made some others shake their heads sympathetically.

"What is the matter?" asked a visitor.

"Oh, he is an idiot," somebody answered. "Can't you see?"

A buxom Italian woman with a baby in her arms stood behind Albano

113

chuckling. She was striving to catch the visitor's eyes, and when she succeeded she put her index finger to her forehead, saying, with a fresh giggle:

"He has no sense, *signore*. No more than a baby, *signore*. Si, *signore,*
he is a born fool. God has punished his parents, *signore,* and he's the
punishment."

Another woman, in a green kerchief, stood smiling and nodding assent.
The visitor addressed himself to Albano.

"When did you arrive?"

"Day before yesterday, *signore,*" he stammered. "I have a father here.
I have written to him and now I am waiting for his answer."

"How do you like America?"

The young immigrant smiled. "How do I know whether I like it or
not?" he said. "I have not seen America. I have not been out of here since I
came. The officers won't let me."

"Why, he is as sensible as any of the people I have seen around here,"
exclaimed the visitor.

"Of course," assented the green kerchief, ardently. "He is more sensible than she, anyhow," she added, with some indignation, as she pointed at
the buxom woman with the child.

One of the other women in the crowd was a stout young Lithuanian, in a
kerchief of red, yellow and white and a loose-fitting jacket of flaming blue.
Her big fleshy face seemed to be bursting with fullness.

"What are you doing here?" was asked through an interpreter.

An ample grin overspread her massive face as she said:

"I am waiting for Joseph."

"Who is Joseph?"

"The son of Martin the blacksmith."

"Where is he?"

"In the smithy at home, far away from here."

"Who is in the smithy? Joseph?"

"No, Martin, his father. Joseph is in America. I am waiting for him to
come for me."

"What is he to you?"

"My sweetheart," she said, the grin broadening over her flaming face.

"Is he going to marry you?"

"If he was not, why then did he send me a ticket? He has a good job in
America, and he has saved lots of money. We shall live like noble folk in
America."

Seated on their baggage by the wall were some Ruthenians, men,

114

women and children. They looked forlornly about them from time to time, whispering to one another timidly.

"What makes you so downhearted?" was asked.

The eldest of the group, a portly, pleasant woman of fifty, getting up from her seat, folded her hands as if in prayer, and said, beseechingly:

"Good, merciful sir! Will our troubles ever come to an end? Will my husband and this woman's father, and the father of these girls, will they all come to us and take us out to America? The bailiffs here have been so kind to us, and they feed us well, but when, oh, when, will we see our husbands and fathers?"

A bench nearby was occupied by several men in broad caps with huge visors and in heavy coats which had the effect of a tight-fitting jacket with a loose dangling skirt attached at the waist. They spoke good German, but they came from the Teutonic colonies in south Russia. The clerks at the Barge Office spoke of them as the most desirable class of immigrants.

"Our forefathers emigrated from Germany to Russia," said one of them, as he took snuff from an old "birchbark." "And now we are emigrating from Russia to a still better place—to America."

In a corner, a yard or two off, nestled a Jewish family from Volhynia, Russia. It was made up of a father, mother, and five daughters, all handsome, and all almost as robust as the Lithuanian girl. The eldest sister was a young woman of about twenty-six, and she sat with a beautiful little girl in her arms who bore striking resemblance to her.

"Are you married?" the visitor asked.

"No, sir. This is mamma's baby," was her reply.

"Oh, my dear little *Herr*," sighed the old man, "we have been over a week in this terrible place. They say I have not money enough, and they want to send us all back. God in heaven! I have ruined myself. I have sold my house and everything I had to pay my way, and now they will send us back a lot of beggars. But God will not forsake us. I have cousins in Philadelphia. They are good—ah, may God help them, they have the hearts of true Jews in them—and they came all the way from that city—is it a large town?—to try to get us out into the wide world, but—"

"But the officers here say the bonds they offer are not enough," the old woman interrupted him, anxiously. "They would have richer men to guarantee that we will earn our living in America. Don't we want to make a living ourselves?" she asked with a smile. She was about to say something else, but there it was her turn to be interrupted.

"Didn't we make a respectable living at home?" the eldest daughter broke in. "Father is a good tailor, and we all helped him. May no Jewish family fare worse than we did at home. They say America is a clever country. If they were clever they wouldn't keep us here for fear we might be poor. What fools they are! They want us to make money, and at the same time they won't let us go out and make it. They can't expect us to earn money here, can they?''

At this point dinner was announced, and the motley crowd threw itself at the long table, which was set with tin plates of soup and meat and long loaves of bread. There was no scramble. There was plenty of room and plenty to eat, and presently the room rang with jingling spoons and smacking lips.

"The soup is good! Very good! Would they had given us such soup on board the ship," a young Pole said to his neighbor. The neighbor was an Italian, and the Pole knew it, but he had to unbosom himself to somebody.

The Jewish family alone remained in their corner.

"Why don't you go to eat? Are you not hungry?" was asked. The girls smiled. The old man shook his head impressively. "We are Jews. The dinner is not *kosher*," he said. "But we are not starving. We can live on bread and some *kosher* things, which we buy with our own money."

"We don't starve!" the eldest girl protested. "How can you live without a drop of soup? No wonder we look like corpses. Look how thin we are! There is not a drop of blood left in us, is there?''

As the visitor surveyed her plump, florid cheeks he felt like saying that there was, but he did not.

The large waiting room was thronged with people come for their newly arrived friends. The best-dressed woman in the crowd was a German servant girl. She wore a huge hat with a forest of ostrich feathers and a brand-new jacket of blue cloth overladen with trimmings of every color in the rainbow. Her landlady, a Bohemian, dressed much less majestically, was with her. The girl never ceased laughing, and every little while changed her place, dragging her landlady with her.

"What is she laughing about?" the visitor asked.

"Her brother has come, so she is glad," said the landlady, sympathetically.

Five or ten minutes later the young man came out, with his baggage. He was a husky-looking fellow, with some dignity in his walk and look.

"Here he comes! Here he comes! Hugo!" the servant girl said, with a ringing chuckle, and flinging herself upon her brother's shoulder, she burst out crying.

———

ILYA THE FORSAKEN
April 4, 1899

A young Russian peasant has been detained at the Barge Office because he has not money enough to pay his way to his friend. Yesterday afternoon he was the only Russian in the overcrowded detention pen. The other immigrants in the room were Italians, Poles, Germans or Hungarians. Some of the Poles have been in the Czar's army and know some Russian, but they don't like to speak the language of the "Muscovite blood of dogs." Besides, each had his own troubles to keep him busy. And so the lonely Russian moped around, vainly seeking a companion or someone to hear his tale of woe.

Presently a visitor came in who had been in St. Petersburg and could make himself understood in the language of the friendless peasant.

"Do you really speak Russian, master?" asked the young fellow. He did not seem to believe his own ears. "I am so unhappy, sir," he went on. "My brother-in-law, he has been in America two years. 'It is a good land,' he says in his letters. 'Come, Ilya, I'll get you a job and God will see to it that you make as much money as I do.' He sent me some money and I bought a ticket, but I did not know enough to take care of my rubles, so I came here penniless, sir. Take pity, master—God, the Lord, will take pity on you—get me out of here and send me to my brother-in-law. My name is Ilya Sorokvash. I am a White Russian and I come from Molodechny."

"Where does your brother-in-law live?" asked the visitor.

"In America."

"But what is the name of the place?"

"How should I know?"

"Have you got his address?"

"Sure. Here it is."

He thrust his hand far down into his bosom and, after some fumbling, he brought out a piece of paper.

"Here, master; everything is written on this paper; his first name, his family name, his address—everything. The scribe of our village wrote it himself."

The visitor could not make out the address, and called upon some of the clerks to help him. Several of them knew Russian well, but they all gave it up

117

as a bad job. The address was scribbled in Latin characters, mixed with Russian, and altogether it looked like a line of Chinese rather than either Russian or English.

The inscription on Sorokvash's immigrant card was: "Address illegible."

"What is to be done?" asked the peasant in despair, when the situation had been explained to him.

"The clerks are too busy just now. Don't you see the rush? Have patience, my lad," said the visitor. "When they get time they'll get about looking up your brother-in-law. It may be quite a job, though."

"Quite a job? Why, he is in America!" said the bewildered peasant.

Somebody suggested that Father Chotovitsky of the Russian Church be notified. "It is not every day that a Russian peasant comes here. The Polish priests have all they can do, but Father Chotovitsky, he will be glad of the opportunity."

The few Poles who understood Russian and were standing by looked envious.

"But what brought him over here? You know it is against the Russian law to leave the country," suggested one of these. "The Russian priest may not want to have anything to do with him."

"Have you been in the army?" the visitor asked Sorokvash.

"No, sir; but they let me go because I was the only son of an aged mother, sir. I have all my papers, sir. Do you want to see them?"

BLACK HOLE OF CALCUTTA
April 10, 1899

The bulk of the crowd in the detention pen of the Barge Office yesterday afternoon was made up of Polish peasants from Austria, Galicia and the western provinces of Russia. There were scores of them, besides the Italians, Germans and the few Jews who shared the same suffocating pestiferous room. It will be some time—a year, perhaps—before the new immigrant station now building on Ellis Island will be completed and ready for use. Meanwhile hundreds of unkempt immigrants, each with the insupportable steerage odors which he brings with him from the steamship, are packed together in a "pen" hardly large enough to hold dozens.

It is New York's nearest approach to the Black Hole of Calcutta. Some of the Poles found there yesterday had been in the "pen" as long as sixteen days, while the number of those who had been confined in this atmosphere from five to ten days was much larger. How anyone can stay there one day and be alive is beyond the comprehension not only of the occasional visitor from the outside world but also of some of the officials of the Barge Office.

Yesterday afternoon one of the visitors to the detention pen was a man who was able to communicate with the Poles through those of their number who had learned to speak Russian in the Czar's army. He was at once surrounded by an eager crowd.

"Take pity, sir, take pity!" they begged him with deep bows, taking off their caps, their faces a picture of misery and supplication.

Each asked that his card be read and his case explained to him. Some had no addresses; others had not money enough to take them to their final destinations; still others had telegraphed or written to their friends in New York or other points in the United States without receiving a reply; and all were anxious about their fate, perplexed, frightened. Few of them seemed to have a clear notion of the place—whether the overcrowded, filthy room, with these overworked, nervous, yelling clerks in blue coats with brass buttons running in and out, was America or something else.

"How far are we from America?" asked one cowed, haggard-looking peasant.

"Does nobody come to speak to you, to offer you advice and to explain things to you?" Peasant after peasant was asked this question. Only three mentioned the agent of the Polish Immigrant Society of 3 Murray Street. He had promised to get them out, they said, with a dubious shrug of their shoulders. The others looked perplexed, and sighed or kissed the visitor's hands, beseeching him to help them. A word of consolation was enough in most cases to bring a cheery look into the immigrant's face. But there were scores and scores of them, and it was all the clerks could do to perform the strictly official part of their duties.

Chief Clerk Lederheiger was found at his desk in the large registration room upstairs, burrowing into a pile of telegrams, letters and post-cards. These were from people in various parts of the country, who had been communicated with in behalf of the detained immigrants, he said.

"We do all in the power of man to straighten out things for these ignorant people, and to help them get out of here, but if you think you want special men to be with them to speak to and advise them you are mistaken. You must know them without speaking to them. For they are so ignorant that you can't rely upon their own statements or explanations about themselves. They are detained, and it is only too natural that they should be anxious to get out. That's why they seize upon everyone who comes to see them, as a drowning man seizes upon anything that drifts his way. But they are only detained to wait for money or until we disentangle things for them.''

Ksavere Wanlusky, the agent of the Polish Immigrant Society, has been one year in this country and does not speak English. He thinks himself competent to take care of all the Polish immigrants in the Barge Office, however, and sees no ground for complaint on their part. He accompanied the visitor back to the detention room, where he got three peasants to admit that he had spoken to them before, but as the other Polish immigrants came crowding up, each praying to be heard, it was clear that the solitary agent was anything but equal to his task.

The Italians seemed to fare much better. Yesterday, at least, when their number at the Barge Office was small—much smaller than that of the Poles—Agent Rossa and his three assistants were able to attend to every one of them.

Agent White of the United Hebrew Charities and his assistant had only five or six cases on hand.

"It is only one week after the Jewish Passover," they explained. "That's why there are so few Jews here. This is just the time when thousands of them leave their home for America. Come in a few weeks and you will see crowds of them."

Mr. White said that he had never seen a Jewish immigrant sent back because of a defective address or lack of money to pay his way from New York to his or her destination. "We usually communicate with the fellow-townsmen of the person to whom the immigrant is going, and through them we generally solve all our knotty problems. In some cases, however, we find it necessary to advertise in the Yiddish papers."

"WHAT ABOUT THE BABY?"
July 7, 1899

The crowd in the detention pen of the immigrant station was made up this morning of Poles from Russia and Austria, Germans from the southern provinces of Russia, Ruthenians and Slovaks from the northern districts of Austria and Jews from everywhere. The heroine of the company was Elizabeth Sienkewicz, a young peasant woman with a baby in her arms. One of the railroad agents had told her there was a ticket for her in his office, and that she would soon be released and sent to her uncle, somewhere in Chicago, Forest City, Pennsylvania, or Oswego, New York, she did not know which, so the other immigrants stared at her enviously or fondled her baby.

They all knew her story, and that increased their sympathy and envy. To a visitor who spoke through an interpreter to Elizabeth, or Azbeta, as she calls herself, she explained that baby's father was dead and that her uncle had sent her money to come with the child to him; and when she was asked how long she had been married the young woman blushed and then, dropping her eyes, she said, after a pause:

"We were just going to be married, sir. The priest had announced to the village people that the wedding would come off in a few days, and everything was ready for the feast when the Lord was pleased to take Vladyk away from me."

Here Azbeta was interrupted by one of the bystanders, also a Polish peasant woman, who suggested that she tell the nobleman why Vladyk did not marry her before.

"He was going to be called for military duty," said Azbeta. "He was not to be a soldier, though, for he had an old mother to support, so he said to me: 'Azbeta, my darling, my dove,' says he, 'let us wait till I am free, and then I'll marry you.' "

"He must have been a bad fellow, anyhow," put in another bystander. "He was only trying to put you off."

Azbeta flared up.

"He was much better than you!" she said. "If he had meant to fool me he wouldn't have asked the priest to announce the wedding. Vladyk was not the kind of fellow to cheat anybody. Besides, he was dying to have me. If I had not been sure of it I wouldn't have agreed to marry him."

"Did you love him?" asked the interpreter.

"How could I help it? He was the best fellow in the village."

"Was he handsome?"

"Was he! He was so tall, so strong, his shoulders were that broad, and his face shone so that he looked like a regular *panych* [young nobleman]."

Continuing, Azbeta told how she and Vladyk wrote to her American uncle, inviting him to the wedding, and how the uncle drew a thousand rubles from the American bank and went to visit his birthplace and see his niece married.

"Uncle Joseph is a very rich man," she explained. "He is so rich! So rich! He is a carpenter and he wrote me that he made $25; only I don't remember whether it is $25 a week or a month. Well, he is rich, and he has no children and he is a good man, and he loved me, because my own father and mother died when I was a baby, and he used to bounce me in his arms and frisk about with me. So he came and said: 'Azbeta, you are a bad girl, but since he is going to marry you, it's all right.' He said that Vladyk was also a bad fellow, but he liked him, too. Well, everything was ready for the wedding, and Uncle bought a lot of whiskey and good things for the feast, when Vladyk took sick and died. When Uncle saw me crying, he said: 'You are a fool. What are you crying about? I'll take you to America. There are fellows there who are a heap better-looking than Vladyk was.' 'But how about the baby that will be born to me?' I asked. 'What about the baby?' 'God has given me no children, so I will be a father to your child, Azebeta.' ''

Uncle Joseph was in a hurry to get back to America, it seems, so he left Azbeta money and told her to come to join him as soon as she and baby were well enough to undertake the journey. A week after he left Azbeta gave birth to a girl, whom she christened Marysia, or Maria. This was two months ago. Last week Azbeta and Marysia arrived in the Barge Office. Her uncle's address, which she had on a crumpled piece of paper, was so illegible that the Barge Office clerks were at a loss where to send her. Some of them even doubted her story, and her card was marked "A case for matron." Azbeta was in despair. She was told she might be sent back, but she said she would commit suicide first.

"What shall I do at home with this child whose father died before the wedding?" she wailed. "The village people would call me names and life would be death to me."

The officials of the Barge Office wrote letters to several points, trying to discover Azbeta's uncle and to verify her story. Day after day passed. Azbeta was growing pale and haggard.

"Will the nobleman send me and Marysia to Uncle Joseph?" she would ask each time an official passed by. The answer was sometimes advice to be patient and wait, sometimes an angry shrug of the shoulders.

This morning Azbeta stood in a corner of the pen quietly crying and swinging Marysia in her arms, when the railroad agent called out:

"Elizabeth Sienkewicz?"

She gave a start and turned pale.

"That's me, dear nobleman. Anything from uncle?"

"Yes, he sends you a ticket and he wants you to start at once."

"Oh, good nobleman! I shall pray to the Saint Mary for you!" she cried, seizing his hand and trying to kiss it.

"Don't do that," the nobleman said, releasing his hand. "Such business don't go in America."

A KISS THROUGH THE NETTING
September 6, 1899

A fresh shipload of immigrants had arrived at the Barge Office. There were Italians, Slovaks, Magyars, some Syrians and some Armenians in the consignment. As the detention pen was filling up, green, yellow and black asserted themselves as an extemporaneous tri-color in a mass of fluctuating hues and shapes. There was the usual rush and hubbub in the room. Everybody was on pins and needles to get out "into America." Everybody asked questions, pleaded, cried, cursed, or kissed the clerks' hands.

One of the few who seemed resigned to their fate was an old Armenian woman. She stood gazing around her and hugging an oblong sort of blanket which at a distance might have been mistaken for a baby. Her eyes were so dark and so sad that they stood out of the whole black-hued host which surrounded her, and the noble cut of her olive face and the gray hair which strayed out of her reddish bonnet made some of her excited neighbors stand reverently back.

"Do you speak French, madam?" asked the reporter in that language.

She smiled, shook her head and shrugged her shoulders. Her smile was as sad as her eyes, and the gesture added to the effect of her face.

The interpreters were all busy at the registration desks and in the rooms of the special inquiry, so the reporter and the immigrant woman stood helplessly smiling, murmuring and gesticulating to each other. There was pathos and a touch of poetry in her looks and her movements. The reporter could not get away from her, and, being unable to do anything for her, he stared around him in despair. He was as comical as she was touching.

Presently she gave a start. One of the clerks called out: "Kazarosian Mahourba!" It was her name. A tall, well-formed and well-dressed young woman stood on the other side of the wire netting. The old woman ran up to her. They cried, they threw up their arms, they kissed the wire which separated their lips. They scratched the partition like cats. They were in despair. They cried again and again, they fell to kissing each other and the netting.

The younger of the two could speak English. She has been ten years in this country. She is a trained nurse and makes a comfortable living. Kazarosian is only a distant relative of hers, but the sight of her brought dear memories to her heart, and through her tears she declared herself ready to care for her as for a mother as long as she lived.

"We are from Alexandria, Egypt," she explained. "We are a very unfortunate people, we Armenians. This woman and my mother were born and raised in Constantinople. But they were true to God and Jesus: for an Armenian who is not a member of the Greek Catholic Church and a faithful worshipper of the Lord is not an Armenian. Well, the Mahometans persecuted this woman and my mother, robbed them of their wealth and of their peace, so they fled to Alexandria for safety, where they have lived more than ten years. This woman belongs to a noble family, as you can see by the way she holds her head. Her son is a learned man, and she herself can handle a pen. But Alexandria is not her home. Like a flower plucked from its stalk, she withered away under the strange sky. So her beautiful daughters—yes, sir, they are beautiful as roses—who are married and happy and live in Massachusetts, sent her a letter, which read: 'Mother, darling, come to us. The God of our people has been with us; come you also to live with us. Our husbands make lots of money; come to share our prosperity.' "

All the while the nurse spoke the old woman nodded assent in her dignified, touching way. She did not understand a word of her friend's English, but "she knows that whatever I say is true," as the young woman explained.

ALL READY FOR HIS FAMILY
October 30, 1899

About two months ago David Kreisel, a teacher of Hebrew on the East Side, received a letter from his wife, who was at that time in their own home in Balta, Russia. She said:

"At last it has pleased God to let me and our children go to join you. We shall leave home tomorrow. In two days we shall reach Bialystok, whence the steam ticket agent is to take us across the frontier and then across the seas to America. The children are all well, thank the Uppermost. They mention you every little while. The agent assures me through letters that we will have no trouble. God grant that his words come true, and that our family be reunited in peace and happiness. Amen."

David Kreisel was in a fidget. "My wife and children are coming," he said to every friend and townsman he met. He was so bubbling over with his happiness and impatience that for want of any other listeners he would talk of it to his pupils. But his pupils are "American loafers," as he often complains. They take to their English books much better than to their Hebrew grammar, and show Mr. Kreisel as little respect as they do his subject. He had lost all patience with them, in fact, and made up his mind to quit teaching and learn suspender-making, but his wife and children were coming, so he had no mind for anything but the preparations for their welcome.

The first thing he did was to rent a room-and-bedroom apartment on the second floor of an old tenement house at 144 Eldridge Street. It was $9 a month, and Mr. Kreisel invited thither several of his intimate friends to show them what a nice, cozy home he had prepared for his family and what a bargain it was.

"It is the best thing you can get for the money downtown," he said to the father of one of his pupils. "When she comes she will find it all furnished."

The next thing he did was to buy a second-hand table, some chairs, two bedsteads, a lounge and a gas stove. It took him so long to buy these and he talked of them so much that he neglected some of his lessons, but that did not matter. "If their fathers don't like it, let them suit themselves. I am going to be a suspender-maker anyhow."

Rosh Hashana passed. Kreisel was awaiting his family every day. He was getting impatient. He went to the Barge Office, he inquired at the office of the steamship company. There was no news.

Yesterday morning he received a telegram from the Immigration Bureau that his family had arrived. He slapped his hands together, he laughed, he cried for joy. He was so excited that he forgot to put on his Sabbath clothes in which he had planned to meet his wife.

"Hannah! Rivka! Abram!" he cried out as he embraced them all in a bunch. "Where is Mamma?"

Hannah, the oldest of the three, who is fourteen, disengaged herself and dropped her head. There were tears in her eyes, but she said nothing. Then Mr. Kreisel saw that seven-year-old Abie's arm was bandaged.

"What does it all mean? Where is Mamma?"

"The soldier killed her," said Abie, knuckling his eyes. "He shot me and Mamma. Mamma died and me they took to the hospital."

Mr. Kreisel dropped his arms and stared. Hannah told the story:

"The agent brought us to Myshenitz near Lornsy, where we were to be smuggled over the frontier, he said. They would not give Mamma a governor's passport because you forgot to leave a kind of paper about the children, they said. So she had to get across the border on the sly, and the agent said it would be all right. When we got to Myshenitz he put us in the hands of two Gentiles—Polish peasants—and said to Mamma: 'These two men will take care of you.' The peasants then took us far out of town. We walked and walked and walked until we came to a big swamp. Mamma wanted to stop because she had no strength to carry the baby, but the peasants told her to go on and to keep still. So we waded through the swamp, Mamma with little Moses in her arms and Abram by her side, and I with Rivka in my arms. There were some more people with us, and one of them, an old man, took pity on us and took Mosey from Mamma. It was so dark we could hardly see each other. It must have been 12 o'clock. The other people had more strength, so they ran ahead and crossed the frontier. Mamma was so weak that she could hardly drag herself along. Suddenly we heard somebody behind us cry to us: 'Stop! Stop!' The peasants signaled to us to keep still and to walk faster. Then they said to Mamma: 'See that light yonder? It's a house; make straight for it. We have some business to attend to. Good-by.' They ran away in the dark. Mamma wanted to call to them not to leave us alone, but she was afraid to raise her voice. We walked on, all as quiet as we could be. Abie wanted to say something, but Mamma signaled to him to keep still. My heart beat so that I thought I would drop dead.

"Then we heard a noise and the report of a gun. We stood still. 'Our end has come,' said Mamma. The man who shot at us came up and began to curse Mamma, who stood holding Abram by the hand. She begged him to let her go, but he said he would shoot every one of us if we stirred, and as he said it he discharged his gun. The bullet hit Abram's elbow and went through it right into Mamma's heart. Mamma dropped dead, and I caught Abram in my arms. He was all bleeding. Moses was left in a little town. They will send him to us."

This morning Mr. Kreisel was found, tending three-year-old Rivka, at the home he had prepared for his family. The other two children sat nearby. Abram, his left arm bandaged, was learning to write the English A-B-C on some telegraph blanks.

"Thanked be God for having sent me my children," the father said, mournfully. Then, pointing to a pile of old books in a corner, he added: "That's the library my wife took with her. I did not expect all these books, but my wife knew how dear they were to me, so she wanted to surprise me."

The gas stove stood on the floor near the cupboard. When Mr. Kreisel saw that his visitor was looking at it he nodded his head sadly. Then he burst into tears.

"WILHELMINA HAD NEITHER MONEY
NOR FRIENDS"
February 16, 1900

Wilhelmina Praast was detained at the Barge Office because she had neither money nor relatives to claim her. She was in despair. At home, in Bavaria, she had left an ill-natured stepmother and a father too busy and too much under his wife's thumb to take Wilhelmina's side in the eternal quarrels between the two. Wilhelmina is robust of figure, rosy and dark-eyed. She is decidedly pretty, but she is twenty-eight, and Frau Praast often told her she was an old maid, and that the young men of the village fought shy of her as they would of the plague. What particularly stung Wilhelmina was when her enemy alluded to Franz.

"Where is he?" the second Frau Praast would ask, with a sneer which set the girl's blood boiling.

"Stop, or I'll kill you!" she would shriek.

"I know you are up to murder. That's why Franz was afraid of you. That's why he married Elsie and went to America."

An old woman who came to the Barge Office with Wilhelmina assured the visitor that she was a good soul, and that it was only because her stepmother's gibes cut her to the quick that her temper would give way. Frau Praast was a virago, a termagant, the worst-natured woman in Bavaria, said the old woman. As to Franz and Elsie, she explained in a smiling whisper that "Wilhelmina was pretty, but that Elsie was prettier still." Besides, Wilhelmina and Franz had been engaged too long, and the old woman did not believe that long engagements did young people any good. She had seen men fall in love with their wives after the wedding, but if there was a fellow and a girl who were engaged for three years without either of them getting sick of the love affair, she had not heard of them.

All this the officials of the Barge Office were ignorant of. All they knew was that Wilhelmina had neither money nor friends, and her card was marked "deferred."

The old woman had no trouble in getting out. She had a daughter in New York. On bidding Wilhelmina good-bye, she said:

"Don't grieve, child. I'll be out, so I'll see what can be done for you."

The girl burst into tears.

"Don't cry, don't cry, my baby," the other said, petting and kissing her. "I swear to you I'll get you out of here." She was going to say something else, but the detention pen was overcrowded and the officials were exhausted, hoarse, impatient. They see tears every minute, and they have little time to feel sorry for those who shed them. It is as much as they can do to attend to their own work. So Wilhelmina's friend was hurried out of the pen and the girl was left where she was, her rosy face buried in her apron.

Two days later one of the overworked officials called out Wilhelmina's name. She trembled. Were they going to send her back home to Bavaria, to her stepmother? Or was it her friend come with some angel to get her out and help her to find work and a home in America? Franz and Elsie were far away, in a place called Milwaukee, so that she could live in New York, earn her living, get married and be happy.

"A friend of yours wants to take you out," explained the official. "He says he knew you at home and he is willing to go before the board of special inquiry and pledge himself to keep you until you can support yourself."

Wilhelmina's face clouded.

"He? What he? Who? What's his name?"

The official told her. It was Franz. He had moved with his family back to New York.

Wilhelmina shook her head emphatically. She would rather go back than be befriended by Franz and his wife. She would rather be taunted by her stepmother than give Elsie this kind of satisfaction.

The stranger who took an interest in the case saw Franz. He turned out to be a fleshy, rather shabby-looking workman of thirty-five, with a few days' growth of beard and not a hint of romance.

"Oh, that was a long time ago," he said, simply, when the story of his first love was broached. "Who ever remembers such foolishness? Wilhelmina has no other friends in America, and Elsie and I knew her when she was a baby. You tell her not to be a fool and to come along, will you?"

The request was made so earnestly, Franz was so anxious about the matter and so far from the point of view Wilhelmina took of the situation, that the stranger could not help delivering the message to the girl.

"Never," said Wilhelmina, morosely.

"But Elsie won't think she is getting her satisfaction," pleaded the stranger. "She says you are her girl friend and it would break her heart to have you sent back because you have no friends in America."

"I don't want her friendship."

"But it is all sincere."

"I don't want her sincerity, nor her husband's. Tell them I have no ill feeling. For my part, he may love her more than life. I don't care a bit. If he thinks I do, tell him he is mistaken."

"But there is no question of your caring one way or the other. They are almost elderly people, and they have four children to feed. He works hard in a factory, and she is always busy about the house. To judge from her looks she could be your mother." Wilhelmina's dark eyes lit up, but she said nothing. "She hardly ever goes out, and he has grown so fat and bloated that you would hardly recognize him," added the visitor.

A wistful look came into her face.

"Is that so? Is that so?" she murmured. Then she was silent and, after a little, when the stranger had renewed his plea and assured her that Elsie had the best feelings for her, and repeated that she looked twice as old as she (Wilhelmina), the girl yielded.

"Tell her I, too, have the best feelings," she said. "It happened so long ago. I am awfully sorry for Elsie. I thought they were rich in America, and she wore nice dresses and all. Poor Elsie!"

THE RUMANIAN EXODUS
August 7, 1900

The "new exodus" from Rumania is ever increasing, and although many of the newcomers are detained by the Barge Office authorities as paupers, these are sooner or later released and allowed to join their friends in the ghettos of the large cities. The United Hebrew Charities and the Rumanian Immigrant Society have much to do with the admission of these penniless people, but the law is complied with in each case. Pauper-assisted immigration is forbidden, so that the help given to the impecunious Rumanian by an eleemosynary institution renders him ineligible, but there is a considerable colony of old Rumanian settlers in each town, and there is not a newcomer but some relative or friend of his may be found willing to stand his sponsor and secure his admittance according to law.

The persecution of the Jews in Rumania, the virtual boycott of all mechanics and tradespeople of the Mosaic faith by citizens of Moldavian or Wallachian blood, has aroused the sympathies of the Hebrew population of this country, and the relatives of the detained immigrants vie with one another in trying to get them into their houses and to keep them until they are self-supporting. All that is necessary in most instances is to discover these relatives and to bring them in touch with the inmate of the "detention pen," and this is done by the Barge Office clerks, aided by the societies.

One of the gathering places of the newly arrived Rumanian immigrants is at 112 Eldridge Street, where one of their fellow-countrymen keeps a café. At 9 o'clock this morning the sidewalk in front of this café was crowded with robust-looking men. They had all come from Rumania a few days before and were waiting to be sent to a place in Pennsylvania where their friends had secured work for them. They all looked healthy, strong and in the best of spirits, and when asked what made them so happy, one of them, an intelligent-looking man of forty, with a forked beard and nearsighted blue eyes, said:

"It does us good to see ourselves surrounded by Jews who are not downtrodden and by Gentiles who do not boycott human beings because they profess the faith of their fathers."

He said that there was a tacit understanding among the Christians of his native country to employ Christian labor only, to keep the Jews out of the public schools and make things generally disagreeable, so as to bring about a wholesale Jewish exodus.

"All this is done to make room for peasant mechanics and peasant tradesfolk," he explained. "The rural population has grown enormously, yet the *boyars,* our landowning class, our nobility, will not yield one square inch of their vast estates to enable their despoiled peasants to make a living. As a result thousands of farmers are flocking to the towns, clamoring for bread. There is a revolution in the air, and to save their own necks our aristocracy is anxious to get rid of the Jews, so as to have a safety valve for the revolutionary spirit—employment for the starving peasantry. Besides, it does the nobility good to have the illiterate, ignorant farmers see how anxious they are to do something for the 'poor Christian' at the expense of 'the fellow who does not believe in Jesus.' "

The Rumanian told of the "walking parties" that start from his country on their way to the ports where they are to take passage for America. A few days before he left a party of young women was being made up for the same purpose. They were expected to be about 200 strong, mostly working girls, with a sprinkling of educated women who could afford to ride, but preferred to walk and share the fate of their poorer sisters. These walking parties are intended as a demonstration calculated to attract the attention of the civilized world to the anti-Jewish policy of Rumania, and, according to the man with the forked beard, they have so scared the Rumanian government that an ordinance has been issued by several mayors forbidding any Jew from leaving his native place unless he shows a railroad ticket.

"But our people have no trouble in getting out. They can't keep us starving," said the immigrant. "The party which I joined, for instance, was formed outside the city limits of our town. Our wives, children and friends were there to see us off. Speeches were made, tears were shed, several of the wives and mothers fainted. It was one of those scenes which never fade out of one's memory, but our journey was full of similar scenes."

Here the Rumanian, surrounded by his fellow-immigrants, who listened to his story with absorbed, sad faces, told how his party wandered from village to village till night overtook them. Footsore and fatigued, the wanderers voted to seek shelter and rest in a small town which they reached at about 9 o'clock, but the delegation which they sent to find lodgings was stopped by the authorities.

"Who are you, and what brings you here?" asked the mayor.

"We are unhappy sons of Israel in search of a resting place," answered the spokesman. "We are going to America, but meanwhile we want to spend the night here, so that we can resume our journey tomorrow."

"So you have left your native towns, have you? In that case you don't live in Rumania any longer. You are foreign Jews, and I can't let you in. We have too many Jews of our own."

When the delegation had reported the mayor's decision, there were curses and tears in the camp outside the town gates.

"But where are we going to pass the night?" the wanderers asked one another.

"In the Jewish cemetery!" shouted a voice. "That's outside the city limits, and certainly the Gentiles can't forbid us to rest with our dead brethren."

To the cemetery the party went. There was no moonlight, but the sky was clear and full of stars and the headstones showed white and gray.

"Let us pray!" said an old man, sobbing. "Some of you don't believe in prayer, perhaps, but in the name of these tombstones, in the name of the rivers of Jewish tears flowing in our native land, I beg you to join me in saying our night prayers."

The old man was obeyed. A cantor took his stand in front of a high headstone, as though it were an *omud*,* and soon the still air rang with the tearful voices of fervent worshippers.

"And now let us swear over these graves to be faithful and devoted to

* See p. 107.

one another and to our unhappy brethren in Rumania till they, too, have shaken from their feet the dust of our beloved mother land, which has become worse than a stepmother to us.''

"We took the oath," concluded the narrator, "and amid handshakes, kisses and sighs, we pledged ourselves to consider ourselves one family. I am an atheist myself, yet I prayed heartily. I felt uplifted. I could have died for humanity at that moment."

SOAP AND WATER STATION
December 4, 1900

The new immigrant station on Ellis Island is ready for use and will be opened on Monday next. The clerks all say they will be glad to get out of the old place in the Barge Office, which, owing to lack of room and accommodations, has ruined the health of many officials, agents or missionaries whose business is to take care of immigrants. Thousands of these newcomers are handled daily, each bringing with him some of the filth and odors which they pick up in the steerage of the ship coming over, in addition to the uncleanliness which most of them bring from their homes in Europe or Asia.

The new building, which is in the style of modern renaissance and looks like a huge railroad station or exposition building, was built with a view to making it absolutely sanitary. There is plenty of room and air in every part of the structure, and it is amply equipped not only with ventilating and disinfecting contrivances, but also with bath accommodations for 500 persons. These baths are the particular pride of Messrs. Boring and Tilton, the architects. Among the innovations are dormitories, with the regular beds and mattresses, and no immigrant is to be allowed to use Uncle Sam's bedding without first taking a bath.

The first impression of the immigrant who must wait overnight for his friends' address or a railroad ticket, will be that this is a country of soap and hot water. Another thing these people will learn is that America is a country of pajamas or nightshirts, for before going to bed each detained immigrant will have to put on this sort of apparel furnished by the attendants. Accommodations have also been provided for those of the detained aliens who want to wash their own clothing. The two dormitories, one for men and the other for women, are two well-ventilated, spacious rooms running on either side of the big registration room, one story above its main floor.

The building is absolutely fireproof, and is arranged for convenient administration, the offices being separated from the immigrants, but occupying points of vantage within easy access to the various parts of the structure. Visitors will be able to see immigrants without coming in contact with them. The new hospital stands on a separate little island nearby, and is not connected with the main building.

Besides steerage odors, filth and vermin, the immigrant is in danger of falling prey to all sorts of sharks in the shape of ticket scalpers, boarding masters and fakirs of all trades and masters at none. The new building will guard the newcomer against these, as it will against dirt. Mr. Boring speaks enthusiastically of the special passageway which he has provided for immigrants passed upon by the clerks and ready to be shipped to some other American town. Here they will be isolated from every possible evil eye to await the boat which is to take them to the railroad station or steamship dock for which they are booked.

One of the spacious rooms in the building is known as the record room. Here will be kept the record of every immigrant landed at this port within the last thirty or forty years.

"WHO EVER MARRIED A PENNILESS GIRL?"
January 19, 1902

The landlady of a German boarding house on the Upper East Side says that two of the girls who are stopping with her at present have come to this country for the express purpose of earning a marriage portion and that she knows of many other cases in which young women from Germany and Austria have been led to cross the ocean by a similar purpose.

One of the two girls is a native of a German-speaking town in Hungary. She is a flower maker, and there was plenty of work for her at her trade in her birthplace, but wages were so low that her pay was scarcely enough to support herself and her sister who is a deaf-mute. She is forever telling her landlady and fellow boarders of the young fellow who she says is in love with her. When anyone expresses surprise that he should have let her come all the way to America to make money for him, she rejoins:

"Oh, well, who ever married a penniless girl? I wouldn't have agreed to marry him even if he had been willing. I don't want him to throw it up to me when we are married that I was as poor as a church mouse when he married me. There is no blessing in such a marriage."

Her lover is a carpenter by trade, and she expects to stay here until she has saved enough money to start him in business on his own hook. She has been five months in this country.

She had no difficulty in obtaining employment at her trade, but it turned out that the methods which she learned in Hungary were not followed in the American shops, and her earnings were much smaller than she had expected. Things looked rather gloomy, although in her letters to the young carpenter she presented the situation in the most roseate colors.

"I don't want him to know the truth," she explained to her landlady and the boarders. "If he does he may give up all hope of my ever getting a marriage portion, and begin to flirt with other girls."

"Are you sure he doesn't flirt with other girls as it is?"

"Not he. He's the most honest fellow you ever saw. He considers himself bound by our engagement to keep away from other girls, but when he sees that I am breaking my part of the contract he may think himself free to do as he pleases."

"And yet you say he loves you?"

"Of course he does. If you read his letters you wouldn't have any doubts about it. But then, men will be men, you know. When he hears I am making good wages and my bank account is growing he will be attached to me. He'll think of the workshop he'll fix up when we are married, and that will keep him from making a fool of himself with other girls.

"But if he sees that I am downhearted and there is little hope of his getting the money he needs to start in business, he, too, will get downhearted, and then he will begin to look for consolation from other girls. That won't do, you know. I have thought it all out."

She expected in course of time to pick up the American ways of her trade and to make better wages, but a girl friend got her a job in a laundry at better pay than she could hope to earn at making flowers. She has been two months in her new place, and her bank book shows progress.

All she needs is $200, and if she retains her present place she expects to return home in about a year. The only thing that worries her is the fact that the work is rather hard and the hours long.

"I am not used to working so hard. I am afraid it will spoil my looks," she often complained to her landlady.

The other girl referred to has no definite fellow to start in business. She has come to this country to earn money enough for a trousseau and for a marriage portion large enough to induce the clerk of some delicatessen store to make her his wife. To own a delicatessen business in her native town in Prussia is the ideal of her life.

She is an orphan and has any number of poor aunts. She is rather plump and cheerful and is confident that the delicatessen store with a husband into the bargain will come sooner or later. She is a bunch maker in a cigar factory.

One of the things that trouble her, as she merrily tells the landlady, is the fear of having some of the men in the factory fall in love with her.

"I would rather die than live away from my home after I get married," she said the other day. "But suppose one of the rollers who work in the same room with me makes eyes at me and says he can't live without me and that sort of thing, and he turns out to be a fine fellow and I want to marry him, but he can't or won't go to Germany with me? I dread to think of such a thing."

The landlady is sure that the bunch maker is in no danger of falling in love with a cigar roller.

"She is saying it all for fun," she says. "She is just full of fun. When she thinks she has money enough she will just go home and marry a delicatessen man."

Speaking of other girls who came to this country in quest of a dowry, the same woman described how one of them went back on her sweetheart.

"She was a good girl," she said, "and she would have returned to her native place, as she had promised to do, but the fellows around here turned her head. They told her she was too pretty to marry a man who could not provide for her without waiting for her marriage portion, and they laid themselves out to please her.

"Well, she married one of the boys on the block. Her husband turned out to be a worthless wretch. He drank heavily and beat her.

"Her old lover did not know she was married, but he missed her letters, and finally he came over to look for her. Then there was trouble without end.

"The young woman's husband was jealous and threatened to shoot her, although the former sweetheart never called, and there was not the slightest reason to suspect that they met secretly. She would just sit home brooding. She will never be happy."

One of the frequenters of a small café on Second Avenue is known among the other customers of the place as the father of the six daughters. He is an intelligent-looking middle-aged Austrian, and he earns his living by peddling.

"He was a schoolteacher at home," the owner of the café said to the reporter, in a whisper. "He is well read and can quote Goethe and Schiller by the hour. But he could not make enough at home to marry off his girls, so he came here to earn marriage portions for them."

"Is he making money?"

"I don't think so. Poor fellow, he is not made of the stuff of which successful immigrants are built. He is bashful and full of all sorts of foolish notions. Then, too, he is too fond of his newspaper and his poetry. He is a dreamer. That's why he came here, in fact.

"He imagined all kinds of things about America. He thought he would open a German school here, and make money hand over fist, but he found that there were enough German schools here to supply the demand and that many first-rate German teachers were vainly looking for jobs.

"He then took to peddling. At first he was quite enthusiastic about it. He expected to get rich in no time. You should have heard him dwell on the way he was going to surprise his daughters. He never gets tired talking about it.

"His hopes were soon shattered. He found that it was all he could do to make his own living here and that saving money by peddling was out of the question. Still, he does not despair. He is not the kind of man to cease dreaming.

"His present air castle is to import a certain article from his native town. He is sure he can make a fortune that way. All he needs is a little money and some time in which to arrange matters on the other side, he says. In the meantime his daughters support themselves by giving music lessons and sewing, I think."

A somewhat similar story is told of a Rumanian Jewess who came here to plead with her two well-to-do brothers for dowries for her own and her sister's daughters. Letters had proved powerless to move the brothers, so it was decided to send the sister as a representative of the family "to make life a burden to them" until the brothers gave her a suitable marriage portion for every marriageable niece of theirs.

The two brothers received the newcomer warmly, but said America was not the country where money could be had for the picking, and that they did not believe in Rumanian matches anyhow. Everybody was starving there, and to give a few hundred francs to a bridegroom who could not make his living would be foolish. Their plan was to have the girls come to America.

"We'll give you steamship tickets for them. That's the kind of marriage portion we'll give them," declared the elder of the brothers. "When they come we'll support them until they have learned a trade, and then they will find their predestined husbands here.''

The woman flew into a passion and reminded her brothers of the time when they would have starved if it had not been for the dinners she cooked for them. As her brothers remained obdurate she made up her mind to stay here until she earned the desired sum herself.

She took to peddling, and, unlike the father of the six daughters, she is a decided success. She has saved money enough to marry off her own two daughters, and she expects to save the rest in a very short time.

''I'll show my brothers I can get along without them,'' she says.

Whether she will take the money to Rumania is not certain, however, for whatever she may think of her brothers she seems to agree with them now that America is the only place in the world worth living in and that it is full of young men who are worthy of a pretty girl and a snug marriage portion. When not on her guard, she is fond of drawing a parallel between the young men of her native place and those she has met here, very much to the advantage of the latter.

''I think she'll wind up sending for her husband and her daughters,'' said the wholesale merchant with whom she deals. ''She has a remarkable business instinct. She will be very rich some day. The idea of her dropping all her chances in this country just to carry out her threat is preposterous.''

———

IMMIGRANTS WHO TELL FIBS
January 26, 1902

When an old official of the Immigration Bureau on Ellis Island was asked which of the immigrants were most difficult to handle, he answered with a smile:

''The liars.''

Being asked to be more specific, he continued:

''The liars are not confined to any particular district, country or language. They lie in Italian, Arabic, Greek, German, Polish, Ruthenian, Armenian—in any of the tongues one hears under this roof.

''Nor are they inveterate story-tellers as a rule. It is in answer to our official questions that they tell the fibs that are the bane of our life.

''Of the American immigration laws they have the most grotesque conception. All they seem to know clearly is that it is not quite so easy to get into America as it used to be. The upshot is an inclination to outwit 'the American nobleman.'

"In the great majority of cases, these falsehoods are easily discovered. They either involve some amusing contradiction or are so lacking in the element of what critics call artistic truth that the most superficial cross-examination is enough to break the author down."

About one hour after this conversation took place, a polyglot visitor saw a young Hungarian peasant woman in the detention pen.

"Be merciful, sir!" she implored him. "The nobleman won't let me out because I have been married only one year."

"Is that the only reason?" he asked, rather skeptically.

"My husband is in Detroit, sir. The Lords here asked me how long he had been in America, so I said five years."

"Have you been in this country before?"

"No, sir. Sickness befall me if I have."

"Has your husband been to see you during those five years?"

"No, sir! No, sir! I swear to you. It's the holy truth I am telling you. He has never been back since he left home."

"And how long has he been in America?"

"Five years."

"And how long have you been married?"

"One year. That's the truth, sir."

"Then you must have seen him last year?"

She looked puzzled, and then, bursting into tears, she said:

"Oh, I'm only a poor peasant woman and don't know anything about figuring, but it's the truth I'm telling you. Take pity, sir."

Finally, when the matron, otherwise known as the "mother of immigrants," had gained her full confidence, she said, vehemently:

"If I am to tell the truth, the truth it shall be. My cousin at home is a smart man and has been in America, so he said: 'You mustn't forget that unless your husband has been five years in America you'll be put in prison over there, do you hear?' That's the way he spoke, ma'am. My husband has only been six months here.

"It was like this: We got married, then we lived in my mother's house, and then he went to America. And now I, too, want to go to America—to Detroit. Do take pity, ma'am."

One Polish peasant, a big, strapping fellow, with a cunning look, gave his name as 'A,' while his sister, who came to meet him, asked for B. The officials were at a loss to understand what object he could have in telling a lie about his name, and he was detained. He soon made a clean breast of it.

"A fellow on the ship warned me that if I told the truth I would be sent back," he explained.

"But your sister didn't know you were going to fake your name, did she?"

"Of course she did not. She is only a woman, after all, even if she has lived in America."

An investigation was made, and it became clear that the only motive the peasant had in changing his name was an impression that unless one told the American authorities some sort of lie, one would get into trouble. When he was told by one of the missionaries on the island that the best thing to do was to tell the truth, he fell to scratching the nape of his neck dubiously.

"Where would a fellow be if he told nothing but the truth to officials?" he remarked.

A Jewish woman who gave her name as Chaya Weisberg was incessantly blessing the agent of the United Hebrew Charities for the interest he took in her and her baby; but he had a feeling that she was withholding at least part of the truth from him. The agent can speak Yiddish, but he does not pronounce it as Chaya did.

Presently there came a man whose dialect was of the same variety as hers, and to him she instantly unburdened her heart. Her real name was Chaya Lucovsky.

"I have a husband in New York, but, oh, how unhappy I am!" she wailed, hugging her child. "He wrote to ask me how much I would take for a rabbinical divorce, and I wrote back to tell him that his letter had struck me like a dagger.

"So I have come here under my cousin's name. I thought I would take my husband by surprise, but now I am afraid he may get angry and run away to some other city. What do you think, sir?"

The agent comforted her as well as he could and asked her what sort of letters she had received from her husband before.

"May every child of Israel receive such letters," she replied. "He sent me money and called me pet names and told me how he longed to see baby and myself. And suddenly, behold! darkness came on us."

She was so young and comely that some of the bystanders said her husband must be blind, while others expressed the opinion that he was one of those brutes who do not know a good woman when they see one.

While she stood talking and wiping her tear-stained face the agent was called out. When he came back he told her to stop crying.

"Your cousin and your husband are out there, in the waiting room. They say you're a fool," he said.

"Am I?" she asked, beamingly.

"Yes, it was an enemy of your husband's who wrote that letter to put up a job on him. I suppose your husband can't write himself, and has the letters written by other people."

Chaya had another cry, and then met her husband.

An Italian dressmaker called at the immigrant station for the daughter of an old friend. When the officials asked her whether she knew the girl, she said:

"She's an honest girl, you may take my word for it."

"How do you know she's honest? Have you known her in Italy?"

"I know her in Italy!"—resentfully—"I've been more than twenty years in America. Yes, sir."

"Then how do you know she is honest?"

"Because she comes from my town, and there are no dishonest people in my town. There was one thief once, so he got married. Well, then he became an honest man."

"So the girl tells the truth. You're sure of it, aren't you?"

"Yes, sir."

"Well, she says you're her mother."

The dressmaker took fire.

"She's a miserable liar! I'm not very much older than she, anyhow. I can prove it to you. And if you say it again I'll go to court and have a trial made. I'm no greenhorn, sir."

When she and the immigrant girl were confronted the newcomer burst into tears.

"Take pity, *signora*," she said. "I meant no harm, I only thought it would be quicker that way."

An amusing case came up on the same day, when the inspector who looks after contract labor cases thought he had extorted a confession from a Greek who was bound for St. Louis.

"What are you going to do there?"

"I'll work in fruit store. A friend of my father's aunt sent me money and a letter, and I wrote back to pledge myself that I would work for him and nobody else."

When he learned that his story barred his way to America, he took an oath that he had received neither money nor a letter from the Greek merchant.

"What did you mean by telling the lie, then?"

"You see, the agent of the steamship company who sold me the ticket told me that unless I had a contract with somebody in America I would not be allowed to land."

When the official explained that a contract of this sort was just the thing that was sure to bar an immigrant out, the Greek said:

"Then I suppose I have mixed it up, for the agent is a smart man. He told me to tell you a first-rate story. Only I don't remember how he fixed it up. Some fellows have their story written down, so they can't forget it."

A clerkly-looking young German said, in answer to the usual question, that he had $200, but when told to show the money it turned out that he had nothing to exhibit. To a man who subsequently saw him at the detention pen he said, forlornly, that it was a mere misunderstanding.

He took great pains to formulate his ideas in what he called classic German. Some of the big words he used were rather ill-chosen, and each time he became aware of this he would pause to fumble for the right word with inexhaustible patience.

"The worthy officers of this important establishment have detained me because I had no ready cash to produce," he said. "You see, I am not opposed to such a system. But I was going to inquire if things were as good as money, sir."

He went to his massive valise and soon returned with a big stock of German books, all gaudily bound, and two of them of the size of *Webster's Unabridged*. One was entitled *The Practical Business Man*, the other, *Commerce on a Scientific Basis*. The other books were on kindred subjects, one of them guaranteeing to make a successful business man of one in three months.

"They're all absolutely new, sir," the young man said. "I paid 120 marks for them two days before I left Berlin."

"You spent your last money on them, didn't you?"

"Exactly," the immigrant answered radiantly. "America is a land of commerce, and I wouldn't go there before I was sure I was going to make a success of it."

He also showed me two suits of clothes.

"I have only worn them a few times on Sundays," he said. "They are as good as new."

When it was pointed out that, at any rate, the two suits and the books did not amount to $200, he answered:

"No, but some friends in Berlin and Charlottenburg owe me some money. That is part of my assets. When I figured it all up it amounted to more than $200. Only I preferred to mention a round sum to save the worthy American officials trouble. Do you think they will admit me?"

He heaved a deep sigh, and gathering up his clothes and books, he clumsily carried the gleaming pile back to his valise. The German Immigrant Society undertook to provide him with work, and he was admitted.

A Lithuanian peasant of 40 and a Galician woman of 30 said they were man and wife; but the name on her ticket was Maryssa Kovalik, while his name was Kasimir Stendas.

"How long have you been married, Maryssa?" she was asked in the man's absence.

"Oh, an awfully long time. Such a long time, my lords!"

"How many years? Five, six, ten?"

"Maybe more. It's an awful lot."

"What's your name?"

"Maryssa, of course."

"And your other name?"

"Kovalik."

"And your husband's name?"

"Kasimir."

"And his other name?"

"I don't know. What do I care what his other name is, so long as he treats me well?"

She was taken out of the room and Kasimir was brought in.

"How long have you been married?"

"Four months, sir."

"Well, Maryssa says you're a liar. She says you have been married ten years, she says."

"She does, eh? Well, tell her she is the biggest story-teller I ever saw. There! I met her on the steamer for the first time, and I don't understand what she is talking about half of the time. She said she was going to her husband in Buffalo, and that he was not a nice-looking fellow. So I said: 'Come with me, I'll marry you. I have a brother and half a farm in America.' So she said, 'Yes, you're a nobleman compared to my husband.' "

When Maryssa's husband was notified he refused to receive her, and she was sent back to Galicia.

"ALL RIGHT! HURRY UP!"
The Sun / *February 2, 1902*

A polyglot visitor on Ellis Island has observed a number of cases in which people coming to meet immigrants have insisted that their newly landed friends shall be Americanized on the spot.

One day, for example, he saw a young Czech hand his newly arrived sister a list of English words and their definitions which he ordered her to get by heart by the time her case had been disposed of by the clerks. The girl looked alarmed, but her brother would not relent.

"If you want to be treated with respect you must know how to speak English," he explained to her. "It won't take you more than ten minutes, dear. When you have lived in America for some time you will understand how necessary it is to know how to say 'all right,' 'hurry up,' 'street' and such words."

It turned out, however, that so far from being able to read the English words written out for her, the newcomer could not even decipher their Bohemian definitions. Her brother was thunderstruck.

"Didn't you go to school?" he asked.

She shook her head, bursting into tears.

"I sent you money, didn't I? What did I do it for? To have you grow up a savage?"

"Stepmother said we were too poor to have me educated like a lady. She wanted me to mind the children and to help her in the kitchen."

"So you can't even read and write Bohemian? Heavens! What will the fellows say?"

An old woman sat with a little girl by her side. When the polyglot observer asked her, in Rumanian, whether it was her daughter, she interlocked her fingers and shook her head mournfully.

"Her father left for America six years ago," she said, "and when he sent a ticket for her—her name is Margiola—I brought her over."

About an hour later Margiola came face to face with her father. He looked her over, smiling curiously.

"What's the matter?" asked the linguist.

"No matter at all," the Rumanian answered, wistfully. "I recognized her at once. She is her mother all over. The very picture of her. I never saw a little bit of a girl look so much like a big one, did you?''

He smiled as he went on scanning Margiola from head to foot, now talking to the old woman, now eyeing the child silently. At one moment his eyes filled with tears. The next moment he started.

''But what is this I see?'' he shouted. ''Barefoot? That won't do. No barefooted children in America. I can't take her home this way. Is there a shoe store on the island?''

When told that there was not, he was in despair.

''I could take her to a shoe store on our way home,'' he said, ''but suppose somebody I know meets us in the car? My New York friends don't know anything about my old home, and when they see this little girl without shoes, they will say: 'Ah, you were a peasant at home.' So I want her to look like an American girl.''

The old woman had to wait the rest of the day on the island, so she volunteered to take care of the girl until her father should bring her a pair of shoes. An hour and a half later he returned with the shoes and a red dress.

''Will you be an American girl?'' he asked Margiola as the old woman took her into a corner to put on the new things.

Margiola nodded assent.

''Your name is not Margiola any longer. It's Maggy, do you hear?''

''Yes,'' answered ''Maggy,'' dazed and tearful.

Presently Margiola or Maggy made her appearance in shoes and a brand-new dress of flaming red. Her tears were gone. She was eyeing the floor with beaming bashfulness now.

On another occasion the polyglot visitor noticed a party of overdressed men and women who were merrily chatting in a mixture of Yiddish and English. It was in one of the waiting rooms of the immigrant station, and it was evident that they had put on their best clothes in order to make an impression on the immigrant they had come to meet.

The youngest and prettiest of the women held aloof from the rest. She was nervously pacing up and down the room. The observer soon learned that she was the daughter of an old woman who had arrived from Russia on a German steamer, and that the others were the newcomer's other daughters, sons, nephews, nieces, daughters-in-law and cousins.

''Pesha Anolick!'' shouted a blue-coated official.

There was a flutter in the overdressed crowd. The pretty girl trembled. The others made a dash for the railing.

A very old woman, wizen-faced but erect, emerged from the doorway.

"Mamma! Mamma darling! Grandma! Aunty! Look at her! How old she looks! Dear Aunty!"

"Children mine," the old woman sobbed out, hurrying to her youngest daughter.

While the two were hugging each other and sobbing with joy, the others were petting Pesha's back or kissing her withered hands.

At last, when the old woman was free to stand up and to dry her tears with the edge of the silk kerchief which covered her black wig, two of her daughters-in-law stepped forward, carrying a bonnet of black velvet trimmed with roses. The others stood back, radiantly.

"Wait," Pesha said, as she held out both her hands. "First tell me what you are after."

"We want to put it on your dear head," answered one daughter-in-law.

"So that you may wear it in health and joy and glory until you are 150 years old," put in one of the nieces.

"This is America, mother," added a son. "One must be dressed like a lady here."

The two daughters-in-law tried to put the bonnet on Pesha's head, but she would not let them.

"Let me die as I have lived so far," she said. "I don't care to be dressed like a rich lady. I am only an old-fashioned Jewess and I won't part with my wig. It's rather late to begin sinning."

"But you can wear it over your wig, Mamma. There are lots of God-fearing ladies in America who wear wigs, and those of them who can afford a bonnet wear one over their wigs."

"Do they? Well, I think I'd better not. Your grandma did not wear such an affair, did she?"

"But grandma never lived in America."

"Is there no God in America? Children mine! Hasn't God been good to me to let me see you all? Would you have me repay his goodness by beginning to wear finery in my old age?"

Some of the daughters-in-law and nieces looked disappointed.

"Tell her it's impossible to take her home without a bonnet," one young woman said to her husband, Pesha's son. "Tell her this America, not Russia."

The matter was settled by the pretty girl, who brought her sisters-in-law to terms by threatening to take her mother to her own lodging, a hall bedroom in a sweatshop. She was the only one in the throng who preferred to leave Pesha un-Americanized.

"I don't want her to look like an American lady," she said amid a fresh

145

flood of tears. "I want her to be just as she was at home, and if you are ashamed to take her into your Norfolk Street parlor, I'll take her to my room, my dear Mamma, my own darling Mamma!"

A similar scene took place between a Ruthenian girl and a young peasant of the same nationality. The girl came to the Immigration Bureau accompanied by a bevy of other girls.

"I want to see my sweetheart," she said, "and these young ladies are my friends. I am a cook in a doctor's house, and these young ladies are out of jobs, so they have time to see my sweetheart. They all knew him in the old country."

At last the young peasant was brought in. He was a tall, broad-shouldered fellow with a shock of unkempt, flaxen hair, and he wore a coat of coarse cloth and a cap to match.

The girls attacked him with squeaks and chuckles, pulling him this way and that, and chattering at him all together like a flock of magpies, while he let himself be jostled and knocked about, grinning with self-satisfaction. The doctor's cook stood back, her arms akimbo, her plump face aglow with bliss.

"Guess what I have brought you," she shouted.

"A lot of pretty girls," answered the cavalier, with a jaunty jerk of his locks.

"And what else?"

"A package of tobacco."

"That you will get when we get home. What else?"

"A piece of ham."

"Guess again."

The peasant shook his mane, whereupon one of the girls undid a package from which she took out a black derby hat and handed it to the newcomer's sweetheart. The doctor's cook smoothed it fondly, and then standing tiptoe, she tore off the peasant's cap.

"Hold on!" said the peasant, gripping her wrist. "Don't be in such a hurry. What's that for?"

"She wants to make a gentleman of you," the other girls shouted. "Everybody is a nobleman in America."

"That I know; only let me put it on myself. I am no woman to have somebody else clap a hat down on my head."

And taking the derby from his sweetheart, he held it before him for awhile and then plunged his head into it with the air of a man to the manner born.

The derby proved a trifle too small for his flaxen mop, but the girls were in a ferment of admiration.

"He'll be the nicest nobleman on Tompkins Square," said one.

"Wait till he gets into an American suit of clothes," remarked another.

But the newly made nobleman felt rather awkward in his derby.

"But it isn't Sunday," he urged, taking it off. "Whoever wore a hat on week days?"

"In America they do. Put it on again, I say," his girl commanded impatiently. "You must be an American nobleman, or I won't take you out of here. You don't think I'll walk through America with a peasant, do you? Why, we are all ladies," she argued, pointing at her own and her friends' hats.

And having convinced him, they carried him out.

IMAGINED AMERICA

August 6, 1898

I do not know through what association of ideas the image came into my head, but I remember distinctly that the word America would call to my mind a luxuriant many-colored meadow, with swarms of tall people hurrying hither and thither along narrow footpaths. They were all young and beardless and all men. Why the scene contained not a single woman I can explain no more than I can account for the color of the spring overcoats the men wore, which were exclusively gray.

When a child, I was fond of Cooper's and Mayne Reid's stories, which I read in a Russian translation, and it may be that something in some of these stories it was which painted the meadow and the gray-coated people in my mind. Later I read of Washington and Lincoln and liked them both. When Garfield was assassinated I read the news in a St. Petersburg paper. I can almost see the page and the upper part of the column in which the despatch was printed and the feeling of indignation with which I was discussing it with my classmates. We were all more or less "tainted" with nihilism, and while we applauded those who blew up the palace of our own Czar, the man who would lay his hand on the chosen representative of a free people was in our eyes nothing short of a demon.

By the time I had made up my mind to emigrate, the portraits of Washington, Lincoln and Garfield, as I had seen them in illustrated books and weeklies, had been added to the image of America in my head. By a strain of memory I can recall these portraits looming somewhere over my rich-colored meadow and my gray overcoats.

I knew some people who could speak English, but I do not think I ever heard them speak it. At all events, I never had any personal impression as to how that language sounded. But then, Turgenev says somewhere in his writings that English is the language of birds, so, accepting that, I would imagine Englishman twittering, warbling and chirping in their efforts to produce French words. This had nothing to do with my beardless Americans, however, whom I somehow could not get to speak the "language of birds." To be sure, I was aware that my gray-coated young fellows were of the same stock and spoke the same tongue as the inhabitants of Great Britain, but the composite picture of the English nation in my brain was so distinct from my image of an American that I could not get them to speak the same language either, and if the truth must be told, my gray-coated Yankee must have been a dumb creature, for I do not seem ever to have thought of him as speaking or singing or doing anything except push his way through that bright-hued meadow of his.

I set foot on American soil on a scorching day in June, and the first American I saw was an old customs officer, with a white beard and in the blue uniform of his office. The beardless men in gray vanished as if at the stroke of a magic wand, but then, gleaming green, fresh and beautiful, not many yards off, was the shore of Staten Island, and, while I was uttering exclamations of enchantment in chorus with my fellow passengers, I asked myself whether my dream of a meadow had not come true.

Still, pretty as America was, it somehow did not seem to be genuine, and much as I admired the shore I had a lurking impression that it was not the same sort of grass, trees, flowers, sod as in Europe, that it was more or less artificial, flimsy, ephemeral, as if a good European rainstorm could wipe it all off as a wet sponge would a colored picture made with colored chalk on a blackboard.

I remember joking of the seeming unreality of things in my new home. "The ice here is not cold," I would say, "the sugar is not sweet and the water is not wet." And a homesick German thereupon added in the words of a favorite poet of his that America was a country where "the birds had no sing, the flowers no fragrance, and the men no hearts." Why I should have doubted the actuality of things in the New World I do not know. Now that I try to account for that vague, hidden suspicion which the very sky and clouds of New York aroused in me, it occurs to me that it may have been due to my deep-rooted notion of America as something so far removed from my world that it must look entirely different from it. If Staten Island had the appearance which its reflection had in the water, if the trees and the cliffs were all upside down, I should have been surprised but satisfied.

However it may be, although I expressed my doubts as to the reality of nature in the strange land in jest, and although the logic of my mind and all I knew of things natural and artificial told me that the trees were trees and the grass grass, still these doubts remained intact, and from their remote corner in my soul they made me scrutinize the verdure to see if it was the genuine article. One of the first things I beheld on the pier as we were landed was a big Maltese cat. I can just see her squatting by the side of the gangplank and eyeing me as I came down. Nor shall I ever forget the queer sense of joy which the sight of her gave me. "Why, they have cats here!" I exclaimed to myself. "And just like ours, too!" I felt like flinging myself upon the little creature, hugging her, shaking her paw and introducing myself to her as a fellow-countryman. At the next instant, however, I was surveying that same cat to make sure that she was really a cat like our cats at home, a living creature and not a mechanical imitation of one; the more so since I knew of the prevalence of machinery in the United States, and of the inventive genius of its people. I had read of the artificial hatching of chickens, and by a stretch of imagination I could see artificial dogs and artificial cats. Of course, I knew that this cat was a genuine one, and I inwardly made fun of my suspicions as well as of my joy, but the suspicions held their own, and altogether I was two men in one.

"Oh, come, it's a cat; can't you see?" said one.

"Of course it is. Who says it isn't?" the other retorted with cowardly insincerity.

When I found myself on the street and my eye fell on an old rickety building, I experienced a feeling akin to surprise. I could only conceive of America as a brand-new country, and everything in it, everything made by man, at least, was to be spick and span, while here was an old house, weather-beaten and somewhat misshapen with age. How did it get time to grow old?

The first American who left an impression on me was a tall, gray-haired missionary whom I saw preaching from a bench on Union or Madison Square—I do not remember which. One of his hands was bandaged, and as he stood against the blue sky with the disabled member resting against his breast and his flowing beard looming dazzlingly white in a flood of sunshine, this picture at once moved me to pity and thrilled me with reverence. The old man's speech at first impressed me like the monotonous thrumming noise which is produced by playing upon the loose end of a thin, flexible strip of steel whose other end is made fast to some stationary object. A dignified, reverent sort of monotony it was at first, and I liked it as well as the metallic ring in the man's voice. As I stood listening to it I had a sense of being in the presence of self-denying piety, and again I was wondering whether it was not a sort of *fata morgana*. My idea of America had so little to do with what I now saw before me that I was timidly asking myself whether the man was a genuine man, his beard a genuine beard, the bandages on his hand real bandages. But presently he began to speak faster, and the illusion fled. His English now sounded in my ears like the snapping noise made by running a stick across the rods of a metal gate or fence. The sound at once became annoying to me, and the man was suddenly transformed into a heartless, vulgar, supercilious creature. His voice set my teeth on edge, and I remember the malicious feeling with which I set to analyzing it. "How does he get that confounded metallic sound of his?" I asked myself, and after listening a few minutes I made the discovery that he pronounced the "R" utterly unlike any people I had known. "Do they all speak like that?" I said to myself with disgust, trying to imitate him for sheer hatred, and getting all the more disgusted with him because I failed.

The preacher's manner, his scant gesticulations, the way he aimed his fist at the air and then brought it down on nothing, his projecting lower lip when he shut his mouth, his gray eyes, everything about him seemed to me intensely repulsive and anything but human. He struck me as a species of frog, and try as I would, I could not get myself to imagine that the sounds he uttered were words and that the crowd around him understood their meaning.

Subsequently, when I had mastered English enough to understand the old preacher and to make myself understood, more or less, to him, I made his acquaintance, and my original impressions gave way to others. I found him to be a very pleasant and interesting man. I liked him, and my second image of him is one of my dearest portraits in my mental album of American races.

6

LOVE AND MARRIAGE

A ROMANCE OF NEW YORK
A Story by Abraham Cahan
December 4, 1897

The habitués of a small French restaurant on the West Side were recently the guests at a humble wedding reception, which was the upshot of one of the most pathetic chance meetings that ever was brought about by the surging ocean of cosmopolitan life in this greatest of cosmopolitan cities.

The customers of the restaurant constitute one of the thousands of little worlds of which the American metropolis is made up, and for two or three months a Russian artist and a Polish piano teacher formed a separate microcosm in that world. The other frequenters of the place are Frenchmen, French Canadians, Swiss, and Belgians, but Aleksey Alekseyevich Smirnov and Panna (Polish for Mrs.) Rusheczka are natives of Russia. It was not until they had taken their supper at the same table every evening for several weeks that each of them became aware of the other's knowledge of Russian, and the fact thrilled them both like the sudden discovery of a close blood relationship. But there was a far more interesting, and, as it has since proved, a far more important revelation in store for them.

Panna Rusheczka was a woman of thirty-five, a well-preserved brunette, slender and stately, and with features somewhat irregular, but full of typical Polish grace. She had been educated partly in Russia and partly in Paris. She had come to New York, after losing her husband, with a small soprano voice and with great musical aspirations. The voice had deserted her before her ambitions were on the road to realization, and heartbroken and penniless, she was driven to take up piano lessons as a means of livelihood.

Smirnov was a bachelor, some twenty-three years her senior, though he looked fully ten years younger than his age. Tall and wide awake, with a brisk military carriage, a military steel-gray moustache and blond hair, unstreaked with silver save at the temples, he appeared in the prime of health and activity, while his never-failing good humor and hearty, sonorous, genuinely Muscovite laughter made one feel in the presence of a young man of twenty-five. That had been his actual age when he left his native country, and after some three decades of peregrination in western Europe he had at last settled down in New York. He is a jack-of-all-trades and master of quite a few, and although free-hand drawing is not one of his strongest points, he is clever enough with his pencil to meet the requirements of a small electro-engraving establishment, where he has steady employment at a modest salary.

The language of the restaurant is French, spoken with a dozen different accents. One day, however, when the soup was exceptionally satisfactory, and Smirnov, who is something of an epicure, was going off in ecstasies over it, a word of his native tongue escaped his lips. *"Slavny* [capital] *sup!"* he murmured to himself, as he was bringing the second spoonful under his moustache.

The piano teacher started.

"What is that you said just now—'*slavny sup*'?" she inquired, with a flush of agreeable surprise.

This was the way they came to speak Russian to each other, and from that evening on it was the language of their conversations at the restaurant table. Although there are many thousands of Russian-speaking immigrants in New York, the artist and the music teacher felt in the French restaurant like the only two Russians thrown together in a foreign country, and the little place which had hitherto drawn them by the quality of its suppers and its genial company now acquired a new charm for them.

They delighted to converse in Russian, and the privacy which it lent to their chats, in the midst of people who could not understand a word of what they were saying to each other, became the bond of a more intimate acquaintance between the two. They were reticent on the subject of their antecedents, but both were well read and travelled, and there was no lack of topics in things bearing upon Russia, Paris, current American life, the stage, art, literature, and the like. The gallant old Russian was full of the most interesting information and anecdotes, and their friendship growing apace, he gradually came to introduce into his talks bits of autobiography, though they were all of the most modest nature, and he seemed to steer clear of a certain event which formed a memorable epoch in the story of his life.

Panna Rusheczka neither asked him questions nor saw fit to initiate him into some of the more intimate details of her own life, though by this time it was becoming clearer to her every day that her Russian friend was in love with her and about to approach her with a proposal which she was by no means inclined to accept. And yet, like many another woman under similar circumstances, she was flattered by his passion, and, being drawn to him by the magnetism of sincere friendship, she had not the heart to cut their agreeable acquaintance short.

He procured some lessons for her, escorted her home after supper, and took her to theatres and public lectures. All of which attention she would accept with secret self-condemnation, each time vowing in her heart that on the following evening she would change her restaurant. Nevertheless, and perhaps unbeknown to herself, she even grew expecting, and on one occasion when she had expressed a desire to see Duse in *Magda,** and he remarked thereupon, with a profusion of impulsive apologies, that he was kept from the pleasure of taking her to the performance by a previous engagement, her face fell and for five minutes she did not answer his questions and witticisms except in rigid monosyllables. This augured well for him, he thought. He did not yield, but at the next walk they took together, he popped the question in a rather original way.

They stood in front of the house in which she had her room. He had bid her good-night and was about to doff his hat with that dashing sweep of his which makes him ten years younger, when he checked himself, and said, as though in jest:

"Is it not foolish, Panna Rusheczka?"

"What is foolish?" she queried, without a shadow of presentiment as to what was coming.

"Why, the way we go on living separately, each without what could justly be called a home. I am madly in love with you, Panna Rusheczka, and I feel like devoting my life to your happiness."

She stood eyeing the door of a house across the street and made no response.

"Panna Rusheczka!" he implored her tremulously.

"I'll give you my answer tomorrow," she whispered.

"Mme Rusheczka has not come yet, has she? Any letters for me?"

*Eleonora Duse (1859–1924) was regarded as the greatest actress of her time. *Magda* is a play by the German dramatist Hermann Sudermann (1857–1928).—*Ed*.

Smirnov asked the next evening, as he entered the little restaurant with his usual blitheness. Like some others of the customers he received his mail at the restauranteur's address.

The Frenchman handed him a letter. When he opened it he read, in Russian, the following:

"Much respected Aleksey Alekseyevich—I am the unhappiest woman in the world today. I confess I was not blind to the nature of your feelings toward me, but was too much of a woman and an egoist to forego the pleasure of your very flattering kindness to me. Forgive me, I pray you, dear Aleksey Alekseyevich, but my answer must be of a negative character. I have been crying like a baby since last night for having led you into a false position. Do forgive me. Your sincere friend, Mariya Rusheczka."

"Do you forgive me? I beg you again and again."

Smirnov had had too many successes and failures in life to let this defeat hurt his pride deeply. But he was overcome with a poignant sense of loneliness, coupled with a cruel consciousness of his old age. At the same time he sincerely regretted the pain he had caused the widow, and out of sympathy for her as well as for the opportunity of seeing her, he secured another interview with her, which took place in one of the remote nooks of Tompkins Square.

"I wish to reassure you, Panna Rusheczka," he said gravely, "and to restore peace to your mind. I love you, and your letter leaves me more wretched and desolate than I ever felt before, but believe me, your happiness is dearer to me than my own, and since you find that it would be disturbed by your marrying me, I am resigned to my fate."

The Panna was overjoyed and thanked him heartily for his friendship; and yet his ready surrender, the ease with which he was getting reconciled to her refusal, nettled her.

However, he did not seem as lighthearted as he was affecting to be, and the perception of it was a source of mixed exultation and commiseration to her. He was uncommonly effusive and sentimental, and as if by way of bidding her melancholy farewell, he launched out, describing his past, she listening to his disconsolate accents with heart-wringing interest.

"I know it is foolish of me to obtrude my personal reminiscences upon you. Why should you be bored with the humdrum details of the life of a man who is a perfect stranger to you? Yet I cannot help speaking of it at this minute. I feel sheepish, like a schoolboy, but it somehow relieves my overburdened heart. You will excuse me."

She was burning to offer some word of encouragement, to assure him of her profound respect and friendship, and of her interest in everything he had to say, but her tongue seemed grown fast to her palate and she could not utter a syllable.

"It was many years ago that I was torn from my dear native soil and from a splendid career," he proceeded, egged on by the very taciturnity of his interlocutor. "I was a young fellow and an officer in the army then, with a most promising future before me. It was during the Polish insurrection of the early sixties. My regiment was stationed at the government city of N."

The Panna gave a start, and a volley of questions trembled on the tip of her tongue, but she somehow could not bring herself to interrupt him.

"I had been recently graduated from the military school, and that was my first commission," he went on. "I had many friends in the regiment, and among them a young Polish officer named Staukevich."

Panna Rusheczka remained petrified. After a while she made out to inquire, "Staukevich, did you say?"

"Why, have you heard of him or some of his family?" Smirnov asked eagerly.

"No, I am simply interested in what you are relating. Proceed, please."

"Well, he was the most delightful fellow in the whole lot of us, but he did not know how to take care of himself and paid his life for it, poor boy. His heart was with the insurgents, and I knew it and begged him to be guarded, but he was too much of a patriot to allow the impulse of self-preservation to get the better of his revolutionary sympathies. One day when the Cossacks had locked the house of a Polish nobleman and taken the count and his family prisoners, my friend gave loud utterance to his overbrimming feelings to the Officers' Club, cursing the government and vowing vengeance.

"You must have heard how things were in those days. The city of N. was in a state of siege, martial law prevailed, and the most peaceful citizens were afraid of their own shadows. Well, poor dear Staukevich was court-martialled and sentenced to be shot within twenty-four hours by a line of soldiers from the very company of which he had been in command. And who was to take charge of the shooting and utter the fatal word to the soldiers but his best friend, who was ready to die for the man."

Smirnov said it with a grim sort of composure and then broke off abruptly and fell into a muse.

"Well," the widow demanded in a strange voice, which he mistook for a mere sign of interest in a thrilling story.

"Well," he resumed, "I did not, of course, utter the terrible word, but at the very moment I was to do so I fell on the ground in a feigned swoon. My place was instantly taken by another officer, and I was since then branded as a coward, and had no choice but to resign my commission and to become the rolling stone that I have been ever since.''

He went on narrating some of his subsequent experiences in foreign countries, but the widow did not hear him. All at once she interrupted him.

"Don't tell me about that, pray. Better tell me more about that friend of yours—Staukevich,'' and succumbing to an overflow of emotions, she burst out sobbingly:

"I know you. I have your photograph. Staukevich was my father!''

"Ma-ra-Marusya! Is that you?'' the old man shrieked, jumping to his feet and seizing her by both hands. "Dear little Marusya! Why, when you were a morsel of a thing I used to play with you.''

"I know,'' she rejoined, "and now that you say it I can recognize your face by the faded old portrait I have in my album. You were photographed together with my unhappy papa. Mama left me the picture. I did not remember your name, but I heard the story from mama when I was a child, and since then I have held the portrait dear for your sake as well as papa's. Of course it never occurred to me that it was you, but now the identity of it is as clear as day to me.''

She invited him to her lodgings, where she introduced him to her landlady as the best friend of her dead papa. They had a long and hearty talk over the portrait and about the persons and things it brought to the old man's mind. And on the following evening, when he came to the French restaurant for his supper, he found there a letter which read as follows:

"Dear Aleksey Alekseyevich—It was not yourself, but an utter stranger that I refused the other day. I have loved you my whole life without knowing you. The handsome officer who ruined himself for my father has always been my ideal of a husband, and, will you believe it, I never gave up a vague sort of hope that he would be mine. Your loving Marusya.''

A STORY OF COOPER UNION
A Story by Abraham Cahan
December 11, 1897

A curious friendship, which led up to a still more curious Christmas present, sprang up between two frequenters of the reading room at Cooper Union a year or two ago. Both were in the habit of spending the better part of every evening there, and both had developed a preference for a particular table. At first it was the location of that table alone which attracted them, but in course of time they became accustomed to each other's company, and although perfect strangers, they felt acquainted, and as though they met by appointment.

One was a stout old Englishman, with a florid, stern face—one of those surly faces that usually go together with an honest and kindly heart. He was a well-read mechanic and a bachelor, and having, or pretending to have, an aversion to women and children, he passed his leisure hours either in the seclusion of his little hall bedroom or at Cooper Institute. The other was a dry-faced, beardless Dane of forty, with blue eyes of pellucid clearness, and long flaxen locks, which adhered close to his head and neck. It was the childish and yet penetrating look of those crystalline eyes of his which first cast a spell over the gruff-looking Englishman. He could not help glancing at them again and again, and as he tried to read his book or magazine he seemed to feel their soft, appealing gaze upon him. At one moment he was on the verge of a quarrel, but no sooner had he met the Dane's eye than instead of resentment he felt like asking if he could not be of service to him.

As for the Scandinavian, the crusty look of his neighbor, far from repelling, had a peculiar sort of glamour for him. And so the two passed two or three hours at the same table six nights in the week until they came to greet each other, at first with a slight nod, then with a more demonstrative one, and finally with a bland "good evening."

One night as they sat reading, the Dane handed the Englishman a note which read as follows:

"Dear Sir—My heart is full tonight, and I wish to speak to some good man. Will you be my listener? I like you without knowing who you are; but so much the better. Would you mind having a cup of coffee with me?"

"With pleasure," was the Englishman's written reply.

Some five minutes later they were seated at a marble table in one of the Vienna cafés on Second Avenue.

The Dane spoke English with perfect fluency, and although his pronunciation was labored, and often incorrect, his grammar was irreproachable.

"I beg of you, don't set me down for a crank," he began. "I am tired of being called that."

"Whether you are one or not, I'm not goin' to call you names, sir," grumbled the Englishman.

"All right, then. This is my day of misery. Just a year ago Fate dealt me a blow—or, rather, played me a trick—under which I have been squirming and writhing ever since. Today is the anniversary of an incident which may,

157

after all, drive me mad. By the way, when you know me better you may find that I am no crank—not as yet, at least. Well, then, it is a love story I am going to recount to you—a love story of which I am the unhappy hero. Is it not amusing—a hero and yet defeated and miserable? Well, some three years ago I fell in love with a poor but accomplished Swedish girl in Copenhagen. Have you ever been in love, sir?''

"That's neither here nor there. You just go on," snarled the Englishman.

"I beg your pardon, sir. I meant no offense. As to myself, I had been in love a dozen times before I met the Swedish young lady, and when I saw that I was infatuated with her I thought it was something like my previous romances—a passion of a week or a month, after which there is nothing left but 'smoke, smoke, smoke,' as the hero of one of Turgenev's novels puts it. Are you fond of Turgenev? But excuse my impertinent questions. Well, I had made up my mind to be a bachelor. You wish to know why? Because I was the most forlorn fool in creation. In the first place, I had taken it into my head that I had been born to fill the universe with a new sort of sunshine— with the dazzling rays of my poetry. Accordingly, for me to marry and be bothered with a wife and children and the sordid details of family life would be a crime against the interests of humanity, don't you know. In the second place, I should get tired of my wife before the honeymoon was half over, and marriage would be eternal torture. I drew my conclusions—do you know from what? From the brevity of my former passions. I was an idiot; the greatest on earth.''

"No, you weren't," the Englishman interrupted him.

"Yes, I was. I believed in the *Kreutzer Sonata*—have you read it? I think it ought to be burned. But at that time I had the same idiotic views as the man in that story. Well, the last girl I fell in love with was a singular sort of woman. She was not pretty. No. I wish she had been, for then I should have forgotten her long ago. But she was good—a genius of kindliness—and it goes without saying that she was also called crazy. She loved me desperately, and I knew it and that helped to spoil it all. I had a frank explanation with her and told her I liked her, but that my life belong to humanity. Oh! the idiot that I was. She gave me a sad look and bade me farewell, and that is the last I have seen of her—in Europe at least.

I reluctantly learned that she had immigrated to America, and that was what brought me over here. Why? Because I could not live without her, because when she was gone I became aware of the real nature of my love for her. Ah, dear friend! I found when it was too late that I had never loved before. No other woman left an impression so deep, so cruel, so ineffaceable. And the feeling itself, too, seemed novel, unprecedented, so entirely unlike anything I had ever experienced before. It is still there [he pointed to his heart] and will be there to make life hell to me as long as I exist.

"I abandoned a thousand things that I held dear and came over here in search of her—in a quixotic search for her. Was it not foolish, seeing that I knew not even in what city she had settled? And yet—and here I come to the most appalling part of it—I did meet her in this city, and at the same time I did not; but I hope to come across her again, although I may be chasing a golden sunset. But be it as it may, I neither have the courage to give it up and to return to my home, nor do I enjoy a single hour's rest in this city.

"I had searched high and low for her in New York and Chicago, where the Swedish colony is much larger, but all in vain. I had abandoned all hope and was nerving myself up to leave this country and to try to forget the whole episode as a romantic tale, which could never become invested in flesh and blood, when this very day a year ago I caught sight of her in an elevated train on Second Avenue. Yes, I saw her seated by an open window—it was a beautiful day in September, like this. But it seemed Fate had only intended it for a joke on me—for the most cruel joke it had ever played upon a helpless being. Ah, only Tantalus and myself are familiar with this kind of torture.

"Yes, she was in an uptown train while I was in a car on the opposite track. I looked at her back without recognizing her, but just as the two trains began to move in opposite directions, she faced about, and—and—it was she! Excuse me, stranger, you don't see me crying, do you? And there is no lump in my throat, either. I am not overcome as I tell you this—no more, at least, than usual, than every day, for my poor heart is always crushed every time I think of it—and when don't I think of it?"

"Did you call to her?" the Englishman queried.

"Did I! I came near jumping out of the window. But she did not hear me—at least, she did not seem to. I rushed out of the train at the very next station and idiotically boarded an uptown one, and—and I have been a wretch ever since.

"I have spent many whole days and many dollars riding up and down the same road in the hope of meeting her once more, but in vain, in vain, in vain."

The Englishman was deeply touched, although he tried not to show it. He came away with the Swedish girl's full name in his memorandum book and with a secret determination to do what he could for his eccentric friend. He thought the Dane had not conducted his search in a practical manner, and he decided in his mind to see if he could not be more successful.

The idea of discovering the young woman and presenting her to his lovelorn friend took a firm grip upon the misanthropic bachelor's mind, and little by little became the great ambition of his lonely days. He had a little independence of two or three thousand dollars, and half of it he set aside for advertisements and other expenses which the pursuit of his all-absorbing object might involve. Having learned from the Dane that his beloved had taught French and embroidery, he framed his advertisements in the "want" columns of English and German dailies accordingly, in addition to having "personal" notices inserted in the various Scandinavian weeklies of this country.

A month passed, another and a third. Every evening his landlady would hand him a pile of letters. They bore all sorts of signatures and plenty of Swedish names in their number, but the one name which had become his *idée fixe* was not there.

The two friends met at the library as usual and frequently took supper together. Their intimacy grew apace, though the Englishman listened more than he talked.

"You aren't a crank at all," he once reassured the Dane. "You're queer a little bit, that's all. If you met your good lady and got married you might settle down."

"Ah, dear fellow," sighed the other, without the remotest suspicion of what the Englishman was doing for him.

One evening as the mechanic sat rummaging through his bulky mail, he suddenly leaped to his feet. "Good! I've got her," he exclaimed, so loudly that his landlady heard him through the door of his room and whispered to her husband that their boarder was getting crankier every day.

He at once dispatched a letter to the Swedish young lady, and next evening he called to see her.

When she heard the Dane's name she dropped her gaze.

"What is he doing in America?" she then inquired.

"He has come for you."

"For me?" she said with a disconsolate shake of her head.

"Yes, for you. Why, are you married?" the blunt Englishman demanded, his heart sinking within him.

She shook her head more sadly than before.

"Very well then," her interlocutor fairly shouted. "Do you still love him? Will you marry him? He will die if you don't."

"How do you know?" She burst into tears and then pursued, sobbingly, "Is it really true, sir? Are you sure of what you say? Why did he not come himself? Where is he?"

"He is safe and sound: but look here, my friend, it is two weeks to Christmas—will you have patience to wait that long? Then I shall give the

160

two of you the nicest dinner I ever ate. But promise me that you'll keep quiet and let me see you every once and awhile.''

''But where is he?''

''No questions, or you won't see him at all.''

When he met the Dane at the library that evening he thrust a note into his hand:

''Would you mind having Christmas dinner with me? Accept no other invitations.''

At last the anxiously awaited day arrived, and the Englishman with a fast-beating heart received his Danish friend in his little bedroom.

''We shall have dinner with my landlady today,'' he said to him, ''but first I want you to accept a Christmas present which I have prepared for you as a token of our friendship. Come, it is in the parlor.''

With this he opened the door and ushered his perplexed visitor into the presence for which his heart had been pining and yearning without cessation.

The two were married the same week and immediately left for Copenhagen, where, judging from the long epistles which the Englishman receives from both, they live as happily as any couple that ever belied the strictures of Tolstoy's *Kreutzer Sonata*.

As for our British friend, he still persists in inveighing against marriage, but when he sits reading the endless rhapsodies on matrimonial felicity in his Danish letters, his crusty face becomes overspread with radiance and he seems to feel as if the writers of the effusive missives were his beloved children.

"I AM A JEW
AND MY WIFE IS A GENTILE"
March 14, 1899

Morris Sarner, fifty-one years of age, short in stature and frail in build, Mrs. Sarner, several years her husband's junior and taller and stouter, and their seven children filed into the Harlem Police Court this morning. When they reached the rail Mrs. Sarner and the children turned to the right and sat down. Mr. Sarner presented a summons to a policeman. The paper had been made out at the request of Mrs. Sarner. It called for Mr. Sarner's appearance in court.

When the case was called Mrs. Sarner stepped forward. She said that her husband had been acting in a most reprehensible manner of late. He had been coming home late in an intoxicated condition and used profane and abusive language to his children. She continued:

"Why, judge, it has become impossible for my children to receive any company in the house. His language, to say the least, is positively indecent. Just think how it must seem to a young lady to have a gentleman call and then have her father come into the house and indulge in such language."

Sarner listened quietly to all his wife had to say, and when asked by Magistrate Brann for an explanation, he replied:

"Your honor, all this trouble is brought about because I am a Jew and my wife is a Gentile. My wife has never allowed me to worship as I pleased, and she has got all the children on her side. Whenever I come into the house all my children cry out in chorus: 'Here comes the sheeny.' If I am held on this charge, the first thing my wife will say to me will be: 'Didn't I tell you I could fix you, you sheeny?' Your honor, I am treated like a dog in the house and fed like a pig. Here is what they give me to eat."

Sarner drew from his pocket a package done up in a newspaper, unwrapped it and disclosed a piece of meat four inches in length, two inches wide and one inch thick. He put it on the bench under Magistrate Brann's nostrils. The magistrate pushed it aside.

"That, together with a few dry crusts and a cup of coffee, is what they give me for my meals," said Sarner.

"That looks like prime roast beef," said the magistrate.

"Don't, don't, don't!" cried Sarner, "don't insult roast beef. That is not roast beef. It is fried steak. It took me ten minutes to cut it, and I had to sharpen the knife before I did it. Smell it, judge, smell it and see if you can eat it: I'll wager the meat the soldiers got wasn't as bad as that.

"Your honor, my wife has put all my children against me. I have a grown-up son and he is very strong. He belongs to some athletic club. He said he was going to use me as a punching bag. He showed me his muscles one day, and said: 'Look here, sheeny: this is what you are going to get pretty soon.' "

The magistrate adjourned the case until next Monday and ordered both sides to bring witnesses.

———

THE PREDESTINED ONE
June 27, 1899

Lina Copelovich came to this country from a small town in the province of Grodno, Russia, about a year and a half ago. She has relatives in New York, and it was at their advice that she left her native place.

"God has been merciful enough to give you good looks," they wrote to her, "and in America girls like you can make a better match than in Grodno. Come to us. You will have no trouble in finding work in America—it is a great land and there is enough to go around—and so you will earn your own living until the All High sends you your predestined one."

Lina was of a quiet, meditative disposition; she was fond of her relatives, particularly Aunt Leah, the wife of Joseph Trainovich, "20 Chrystie Street, New York America" as she knew by heart from the addresses which the educated young man in the village wrote for her. And so she followed their advice and went to the land where dwelt the vague image of her predestined one.

When her aunts and cousins went to claim her at the Barge Office they were delighted to find her prettier than when they had left her. Her cheeks flamed, her black eyes sparkled, her tresses hung like two well-tarred ropes. Besides, she was a strong and healthy girl. Who would refuse such a girl a job? Those of the aunts who went to the Barge Office with a frown on their bewigged brows were now all smiles.

In vain had their hearts misgiven them. Lina would hardly cost them a cent. She would make her living at once. And so she did. She went out to service at first with the family of a sweater, and then in the house of a tradesman named Carp, at 12 Delancey Street.

Her employers and her aunts were charmed with her. She was a girl of few words, obedient, respectful, handy, and diligent, and Mrs. Carp came to regard her as her own child. The only fault Aunt Leah found with her was that she was apt to take things too hard, which was not good for her blooming cheeks.

One day she met a young fellow at Aunt Leah's house. It was Abraham Abramovich, a blacksmith who came from a village near Lina's birthplace. He was tall, broad-shouldered, and his cheeks were as red as hers. Mrs. Trainovich is sure now that she saw at once that the young man and her

163

niece "got stuck together like a window and putty." At all events Lina confided to her later on that she felt that Abram was her predestined one the moment she set her black eyes on him. It appeared that she had been dreaming long dreams of the unknown fellow who had been foreordained to be her husband ever since she received the letter calling her to America. Often when she met a young man she would ask herself: "Is this he?" But no one seemed to be he until she saw Abram. He was he, sure enough; she felt it at once, and her heart beat so violently that she had to take a chair, she said.

As to Abram, he felt that she was she, and so he took her to the next soda stand, treated her to a penny glass of strawberry, and then to the Jackson Street Park, where, amid the rumble of baby carriages and the laughter of other predestined couples, they called each other "little crown," "little treasure," "little lamb" and "little kitten."

Abram works in Hoboken, but every Saturday he would come to New York to spend the day with Lina, without whom life was darkness to him, he said. The old Chrystie Street women who watched the progress of his courtship would nod their heads affectionately. "God bless you, children," some of them would say. "The Uppermost give that when you are united you may live like a pair of doves even as you do now."

One day Abram came with a cloud on his ruddy face.

"What's the matter, my consolation?" asked Lina.

"My family is against the match," he answered, and after a good deal of hesitation he added:

"It's all because you are a servant girl, Lina. My sisters say it is a disgrace for the family."

Lina nearly fainted, but Abram assured her that he would rather renounce his sisters than his predestined one, and so she braced up.

Abram's sisters never relented. They, too, were looking for their predestined ones, and what if these fellows got wind of the fact that there was a former servant maid in the family? It turned out that the heart of the robust blacksmith was anything but robust. He could not stand their tears and their complaints. He swore some, but he gave in and promised to break the engagement. But his heart "pulled him to Lina," as Lina's aunt put it, and so he would visit her stealthily and keep his anguish from her as well as he could. Lina suspected trouble, and "her heart told her" that she would never live to stand under the canopy by Abram's side, but she kept her own counsel, and her love grew stronger and more desperate every day. "The surer I am that I can't have him, my predestined one, the dearer he is to me," she said, subsequently.

At last the secret leaked out, and it came to an open fight between

Abram's family on the one hand and Lina's aunt and Mrs. Carp, her employer, on the other.

"What, a servant girl is not good enough for your brother?" shouted Mrs. Carp. "And who is your brother? A blacksmith! I would not take five blacksmiths for one servant girl like Lina."

"And, besides," Lina's aunt added, "her father, too, was a blacksmith, and a better blacksmith than Abram."

At this the young man's sisters wrought themselves to such a pitch that one of them made a dash at Lina and wrenched the engagement ring off her finger.

"There! That settles your engagement with my brother, servant maid!" she shouted.

"You are mistaken," retorted Lina's aunt. "We have the *tenoim* [engagement contract]; it is right in the bureau."

As to Abram, Mrs. Trainovich says he proved himself too cowardly to visit Lina after this combat, so that the girl could not sleep nights and went for days without food.

"She wasted and wasted until she became as thin as a shadow," said Lina's aunt. "Then she began to say foolish things and to chuckle to herself. Finally she became so violent that she had to be taken to Bellevue. Poor Lina, America has done her no good," concluded Mrs. Trainovich, wiping her eyes with her apron.

THE APOSTATE OF CHEGO-CHEGG

A Story by Abraham Cahan
The Century / *November 1899*

I

"So this is America, and I am a Jewess no longer!" brooded Michalina, as she looked at the stretch of vegetable gardens across the road from the threshold where she sat. "They say farm-hands work shorter hours on Saturdays, yet God knows when Wincas will get home." Her slow, black eyes returned to the stocking and the big darning needle in her hands.

She was yearning for her Gentile husband and their common birthplace, and she was yearning for her father's house and her Jewish past. Wincas kept buzzing in her ears that she was a Catholic, but he did not understand her. She was a *meshumedeste*—a convert Jewess, an apostate, a renegade, a traitoress, something beyond the vituperative resources of Gentile speech. The bonfires of the Inquisition had burned into her people a point of view to which Wincas was a stranger. Years of religious persecution and enforced clannishness had taught them to look upon the Jew who deserts his faith for that of his oppressors with a horror and a loathing which the Gentile brain could not conceive. Michalina's father had sat seven days shoeless on the ground, as for the dead, but death was what he naturally invoked upon the "defiled head," as the lesser of the two evils. Atheism would have been a malady; *shmad* (conversion to a Gentile creed) was far worse than death. Michalina felt herself buried alive. She was a *meshumedeste*. She shuddered to think what the word meant.

At first she seemed anxious to realize the change she had undergone. "You are a Jewess no longer—you are a Gentile woman," she would say to herself. But the words were as painful as they were futile, and she turned herself adrift on the feeling that she was the same girl as of old, except that something terrible had befallen her. "God knows where it will all end," she would whisper. She had a foreboding that something far more terrible, a great crushing blow that was to smite her, was gathering force somewhere.

Hatred would rise in her heart at such moments—hatred for her "sorceress of a stepmother," whose cruel treatment of Michalina had driven her into the arms of the Gentile lad and to America. It was owing to her that Rivka (Rebecca) had become a Michalina, a *meshumedeste*.

The Long Island village (one of a dozen within half an hour's walk from one another) was surrounded by farms which yielded the Polish peasants their livelihood. Their pay was about a dollar a day, but potatoes were the principal part of their food, and this they got from their American employers free. Nearly every peasant owned a fiddle or a banjo. A local politician had humorously dubbed the settlement Chego-Chegg (this was his phonetic summary of the Polish language), and the name clung.

Wincas and Michalina had been only a few days in the place, and although they spoke Polish as well as Lithuanian, they were shy of the other peasants and felt lonely. Michalina had not seen any of her former coreligionists since she and her husband had left the immigrant station, and she longed for them as one for the first time in mid-ocean longs for the sight of land. She had heard that there were two Jewish settlements nearby. Often she would stand gazing at the horizon, wondering where they might be; whereupon her vague image of them at once allured her and terrified her.

The sun shone dreamily, like an old man smiling at his own drowsiness.

It was a little world of blue, green, gray and gold, heavy with sleep. A spot of white and a spot of red came gleaming down the road. Rabbi Nehemiah was on his way home from Greyton, where he had dined with the "finest householder" and "said some law" to the little congregation at the afternoon service. For it was Sabbath, and that was why his unstarched shirt-collar was so fresh and his red bandanna was tied around the waist of his long-skirted coat. Carrying things on the seventh day being prohibited, Rabbi Nehemiah *wore* his handkerchief.

The door of the general store (it was also the inn), overlooking the crossroads from a raised platform, was wide open. A Polish peasant in American trousers and undershirt, but with a Warsaw pipe dangling from his mouth, sat on a porch, smoking quietly. A barefooted boy was fast asleep in the grass across the road, a soldier's cap by his side, like a corpse on a battlefield.

As Michalina glanced up the gray road to see if Wincas was not coming, her eye fell upon Rabbi Nehemiah. A thrill ran through her. She could tell by his figure, his huge white collar, and the handkerchief around his waist that he was a pious, learned Jew. As he drew near she saw that his face was overgrown with wisps of silken beard of a yellowish shade, and that he was a man of about twenty-seven.

As he walked along, he gesticulated and murmured to himself. It was one of his bickerings with Satan.

"It's labor lost, Mr. Satan!" he said with a withering smile. "You won't catch me again, if you burst. Go try your tricks on somebody else. If you hope to get me among your regular customers you are a very poor business man, I can tell you that. Nehemiah is as clever as you, depend upon it. Go, mister, go!"

All this he said quite audibly, in his velvety, purring bass, which set one wondering where his voice came from.

As he came abreast of Michalina he stopped short in consternation.

"Woe is me, on the holy Sabbath!" he exclaimed in Yiddish, dropping his hands to his sides.

The color rushed to Michalina's face. She stole a glance at the Pole down the road. He seemed to be half asleep. She lowered her eyes and went on with her work.

"Will you not stop this, my daughter? Come, go indoors and dress in honor of the Sabbath," he purred on, with a troubled, appealing look.

"I don't understand what you say, sir," she answered, in Lithuanian, without raising her eyes.

The devout man started. "I thought she was a child of Israel!" he exclaimed, in his native tongue, as he hastily resumed his way. "Fie upon her! But what a pretty Gentile maiden!—just like a Jewess—" Suddenly he interrupted himself. "You are at it again, aren't you?" he burst out upon Satan. "Leave me alone, will you?"

Michalina's face was on fire. She was following the pious man with her glance. He was apparently going to one of those two Jewish villages. Every step he took gave her a pang, as if he were tied to her heart. As he disappeared on a side road behind some trees she hastily took her darning indoors and set out after him.

II

About three quarters of an hour had passed when, following the pious little man, she came in sight of a new town that looked as if it had sprung up overnight. It was Burkdale, the newest offshoot of an old hamlet, and it owed its existence to the "Land Improvement Company," to the president of which, Madison Burke, it owed its name. Some tailoring contractors had moved their "sweatshops" here, after a prolonged strike in New York, and there were, besides, some fifty or sixty peddlers who spent the week scouring the island for custom and who came here for the two Sabbath days—their own and that of their Christian patrons. The improvised little town was lively with the whir of sewing machines and the many-colored display of shop windows.

As the man with the red girdle made his appearance, a large, stout woman in a black wig greeted him from across the street.

"Good Sabbath, Rabbi Nehemiah!" she called out to him, with a faint smile.

"A good Sabbath and a good year!" he returned.

Michalina was thrilled once more. She was now following close behind the pious man. She ran the risk of attracting his attention, but she no longer cared. Seeing a boy break some twigs, Rabbi Nehemiah made a dash for him, as though to rescue him from death, and seizing him by the arms, he shook the sticks out of his hands. Then, stroking the urchin's swarthy cheeks, he said fondly:

"It is prohibited, my son. God will give one a lashing for desecrating the Sabbath. Oh, what a lashing."

A sob rose in Michalina's throat.

A short distance farther on Rabbi Nehemiah paused to remonstrate with a group of young men who stood smoking cigarettes and chatting by a merchandise wagon.

"Woe! Woe! Woe!" he exclaimed. "Do throw it away, pray! Are you not children of Israel? Do drop your cigarettes."

"Rabbi Nehemiah is right," said a big fellow, with a wink, concealing his cigarette behind him. The others followed his example, and Rabbi Nehemiah, flushed with his easy victory, went on pleading for a life of piety and divine study. He spoke from the bottom of his heart, and his face shone, but this did not prevent his plea from being flavored with a certain humor, for the most part at his own expense.

"The world to come is the tree, while this world is only the shadow it casts," he said in his soft, thick voice. "Smoking on the Sabbath, staying away from the synagogue, backbiting, cheating in business, dancing with maidens, or ogling somebody else's wife—all this is a great pleasure, is it not? Well, the sages of this world, the dudes, the educated, and even a high-priced adornment like myself, think it is. We hunt for these delights. Behold, we have caught them. Close your fist tight! Hold the precious find with might and main, Rabbi Nehemiah! Presently, hark! The Angel of Death is coming. 'Please, open your hand, Rabbi Nehemiah. Let us see what you have got.' Alas! it's empty, empty, empty—*Ai-ai!*" he suddenly shrieked in a frightened, piteous voice. While he was speaking the big fellow had stolen up behind him and clapped his enormous high hat over his eyes. The next moment another young man slipped up to Rabbi Nehemiah's side, snatched off his bandanna, and set it on fire.

"Woe is me! Woe is me! On the holy Sabbath!" cried the devout man, in despair.

Michalina, who had been looking on at a distance, every minute making ready to go home, rushed up to Rabbi Nehemiah's side.

"Don't—pray don't!" she begged his tormentors, in Yiddish. "You know he did not touch you; why should you hurt him?"

A crowd gathered. The learned man was looking about him with a perplexed air, when along came Sorah-Elka, the bewigged tall woman who had saluted him a short while ago. The young men made way for her.

"What's the matter? Got a licking again?" she inquired, between a frown and a smile, and speaking in phlegmatic, articulate accents. Her smile was like her voice—pleasingly cold. She was the cleverest, the most pious, and the most ill-natured woman in the place. "Serves you right, Rabbi Nehemiah. You look for trouble and you get it. What more do you want? What did they do to him, the scamps?"

"Nothing. They only knocked his hat over his eyes. They were only fooling," answered a little boy.

Sorah-Elka's humor and her calm, authoritative manner won Michalina's heart. Oh, if she were one of this Jewish crowd! She wished she could speak to them. Well, who knew her here? As to Rabbi Nehemiah, he did not seem to recognize her, so she ventured to say, ingratiatingly:

"He didn't do them anything. He only talked to them and they hit him on the head."

Many eyes were leveled at the stranger. The young fellow who had burned Rabbi Nehemiah's handkerchief was scanning her face.

Suddenly he exclaimed:

"I shan't live till next week if she is not the *meshumedeste* of Chego-Chegg! I peddle over there."

The terrible untranslatable word, the most loathsome to the Yiddish ear, struck Michalina cold. She wondered whether this was the great calamity which her heart had been predicting. Was it the beginning of her end? Rabbi Nehemiah recognized her. With a shriek of horror, and drawing his skirts about him, as if for fear of contamination, he proceeded to describe his meeting with Michalina at the Polish village.

"What! this plague the *meshumedeste* who has a peasant for a husband!" said Sorah-Elka, as she swept the young woman with contemptuous curiosity. "May all the woes that are to befall me, you, or any good Jew—may they all strike the head of this horrid thing—fie upon her!" And the big woman spat with the same imperturbable smile with which she had drawled out her malediction.

Michalina went off toward Chego-Chegg. When the crowd was a few yards off behind her somebody shouted:

"Meshumedeste! Meshumedeste!"

The children and some full-grown rowdies took up the cry:

"Meshumedeste! Meshumedeste! Meshumedeste!" they sang in chorus, running after her and pelting her with stones.

Michalina was frightened to death. And yet her pursuers and the whole Jewish town became dearer to her heart than ever.

"Where have you been?" Wincas asked, shaking her furiously.

"Don't! Don't! People are looking!" she protested, in her quietly strenuous way.

The village was astir. Children were running about; women sat on the porches, gossiping; two fiddles were squeaking themselves hoarse in the tavern. A young negro, lank, tattered, and grinning, was twanging a banjo to a crowd of simpering Poles. He it was who got the peasants to forsake their accordions, or even fiddles, for banjos. He was the civilizing and Americanizing genius of the place, although he had learned to jabber Polish long before any of his pupils picked up a dozen English words.

170

"Tell me where you have been," raged Wincas.

"Suppose I don't? Am I afraid of you? I felt lonesome—so lonesome! I thought I would die of loneliness, so I went for a walk and lost my way. Are you satisfied?"

They went indoors, where their landlady had prepared for them a meal of herring, potatoes, and beef stew.

Half an hour later they were seated on the lawn, conversing in whispers amid the compact blackness of the night. The two tavern windows gleamed like suspended sheets of gold. Diving out of these into the sea of darkness was a frisky host of banjo notes.

"How dark it is!" whispered Michalina.

"Are you afraid of devils?"

"No—why?"

"I thought you might be," he said.

After a pause he suddenly pointed at his heart.

"Does it hurt you?" he asked.

"What do you mean, darling?" she demanded, interlacing her fingers over his shoulder and peering into his beardless face.

"Something has got into me. It's right here. It's pulling me to pieces, Michalinka!"

"That's nothing," she said. "It's only homesickness. It will wear off."

Wincas complained of his employer, the queer ways of American farming, the tastelessness of American food.

"God has cursed this place and taken the life out of everything," he said. "I suppose it's all because the people here are so wicked. Everything looks as it should, but you just try to put it into your mouth, and you find out the swindle. Look here, Michalinka, maybe it is the Jewish god getting even on me?"

She was bent upon her own thoughts and made no reply. Presently she began to caress him as she would a sick baby.

"Don't worry, my love," she comforted him. "America is a good country. Everybody says so. Wait till we get used to it. Then you won't go, even if you are driven with sticks from here."

They sat mutely clinging to each other, their eyes on the bright tavern windows, when a fresh, fragrant breeze came blowing upon them. Wincas fell to inhaling it thirstily. The breeze brought his native village to his nostrils.

"Mi-Michalinka darling!" he suddenly sobbed out, clasping her to his heart.

THE CHASM

III

When Michalina, pale, weak, and beautiful, lay in bed, and the midwife bade her look at her daughter, the young mother opened her flashing black eyes and forthwith shut them again. The handful of flesh and her own splitting headache seemed one and the same thing. After a little, as her agonizing sleep was broken and her torpid gaze found the baby by the wall, she was overcome with terror and disgust. It was a *shikse* (Gentile girl), a heap of defilement. What was it doing by her side?

She had not nursed the baby a week before she grew attached to it. By the time little Marysia was a month old, she was dearer than her own life to her.

The little railroad station about midway between the two settlements became Michalina's favorite resort. Her neighbors she shunned. She had been brought up to look down upon their people as "a race like unto an ass." At home she could afford to like them. Now that she was one of them, they were repugnant to her. They, in their turn, often mocked her and called her "Jew woman." And so she would often go to spend an hour or two in the waiting room of the station or on the platform outside. Some of the passengers were Jews, and these would eye her curiously, as if they had heard of her. She blushed under their glances, yet she awaited them patiently each time a train was due.

One morning a peddler, bending under his pack, stopped to look at her. When he had dropped his burden his face seemed familiar to Michalina. He was an insignificant little man, clean-shaven, with close-clipped yellowish hair, and he wore a derby hat and a sack coat.

All at once his face broke into a broad, affectionate smile.

"How do you do?" he burst out in a deep, mellow voice which she recognized instantly. "I once spoke to you in Chego-Chegg, do you remember? I see you are amazed to see me in a short coat and without beard and sidelocks."

"You look ten years younger," she said in a daze of embarrassment.

"I am Rabbi Nehemiah no longer," he explained bashfully. "They call me Nehemiah the Atheist now."

"Another sinner!" Michalina thought, with a little thrill of pleasure.

Nehemiah continued, with a shamefaced smile:

"When my coat and my sidelocks were long my sight was short, while now—why, now I am so saturated with wisdom that pious Jews keep away from me for fear of getting wet, don't you know? Well, joking aside, I had ears, but could not hear because of my earlocks; I had eyes, and could not see because they were closed in prayer. Now I am cured of my idiocy. And how are you? How are you getting along in America?"

His face beamed. Michalina's wore a pained look. She was bemoaning the fall of an idol.

"I am all right, thank you. Don't the Burkdale people trouble you?" she asked, reddening violently.

"Men will be men and rogues will be rogues. Do you remember that Saturday? It was not the only beating I got, either. They regaled me quite often—the oxen! However, I bear them no ill will. Who knows but what it was their cuffs and buffets that woke me up? The one thing that gives me pain is this: the same fellows who used to break my bones for preaching religion now beat me because I expose its idiocies. I am like the great rabbi who had once been a chief of highwaymen. 'What of it?' he used to say. 'I was a leader then, and a leader I am now.' I was whipped when I was Rabbi Nehemiah, and now that I am Nehemiah the Atheist I am whipped again. By the way, do you remember how they hooted you? There's nothing to blush about, missus. Religion is all humbug. There are no Jews and no Gentiles, missus. This is America. All are noblemen here, and all are brothers—children of one mother—Nature, dear little missus." The word was apparently a tidbit to his tongue. He uttered it with relish, peering admiringly into Michalina's face. "Go forth, dear little missus. Go forth, O thou daughter of Zion, and proclaim to all those who are groveling in the mire of Judaism—"

"S-s-s-sh!" she interrupted imploringly. "Why should you speak like that? Don't—oh, don't!"

He began a long and heated argument. She could not follow him.

Marysia was asleep in her arms, munching her little lips and smiling. As Michalina stole a glance at her, she could not help smiling, too. She gazed at the child again and again, pretending to listen. For the twentieth time she noticed that in the upper part of her face Marysia bore a striking resemblance to Wincas.

Michalina and Nehemiah often met. All she understood of his talk was that it was in Yiddish, and this was enough. Though he preached atheism, to her ear his words were echoes from the world of synagogues, rabbis, purified meat, blessed Sabbath lights. Another thing she gathered from his monologues was that he was a fellow-outcast. Of herself she never spoke. Being a mystery to him made her a still deeper mystery to herself, and their secret interviews had an irresistible charm for her.

One day Michalina found him clean-shaven and in a new necktie.

"Good morning!" he said, with unusual solemnity. And drawing a big red apple from his pocket, he shamefacedly placed it in her hand.

"What was it you wanted to tell me?" she inquired, blushing.

"Oh, nothing. I meant it for fun. It's only a story I read. It's about a great man who was in love with a beautiful woman all his life. She was married to another man and true to him, yet the stranger loved her. His soul was bewitched. He sang of her, he dreamed of her. The man's name was Petrarch and the woman's was Laura."

"I don't know what you mean by your story," she said, with an embarrassed shrug of her shoulders.

"How do you know it is only a story?" he rejoined, his eye on the glistening rail. "Maybe it is only a parable? Maybe you are Laura? Laura mine!" he whispered.

"Stop that!" she cried, with a pained gesture.

At that moment he was repulsive.

"Hush, don't eat your heart out, little kitten. I was only joking."

IV

Michalina ventured to visit Burkdale once again. This time she was not bothered. Only here and there someone would whisper, "Here comes the apostate of Chego-Chegg." Little by little she got to making most of her purchases at the Jewish town. Wincas at first stormed, and asked whether it was true that some Jew had bedeviled his wife's heart; but before long she persuaded him to go with her on some of her shopping expeditions. Michalina even decided that her husband should learn to press coats, which was far more profitable than working on a farm; but after trying it for a few days, he stubbornly gave it up. The soil called him back, he said, and if he did not obey it, it might get square on him when he was dead and buried in it.

By this time they had moved into a shanty on the outskirts of the village, within a short distance from Burkdale.

At first Michalina forbade Wincas to write to his father, but he mailed a letter secretly. The answer enclosed a note from Michalina's father, in Yiddish, which Wincas, having in his ecstasy let out his secret, handed her.

> Your dear father-in-law [the old man wrote] goes about mocking me about you and his precious son. "Will you send her your love?" he asked. "Very well, I will," said I. And here it is, Rivka. May eighty toothaches disturb your peace even as you have disturbed the peace of your mother in her grave. God grant that your impure limbs be hurled from one end of the world to the

other, as your damned soul will be when you are dead like a vile cur. Your dear father-in-law (woe to you, Rivka!) asks me what I am writing. "A blessing," say I. May similar blessings strew your path, accursed *meshumedeste*. That's all.

"What does he write?" asked Wincas.

"Nothing. He is angry," she muttered. In her heart she asked herself: "Who is this Gentile? What is he doing here?" At this moment she felt sure that her end was near.

Nehemiah and Michalina had taken root in the little town as the representatives of two inevitable institutions. Burkdale without an atheist and a convert seemed as impossible as it would have been without a marriage broker, a synagogue, or a bathhouse "for all daughters of Israel."

Nehemiah continued his frenzied agitation. Neglecting his business, half-starved, and the fair game of every jester, but plumed with some success, the zealot went on scouting religious ceremonies, denouncing rabbis, and preaching assimilation with the enlightened Gentiles. Nehemiah was an incurably religious man, and when he had lost his religious belief disbelief became his religion.

And so the two were known as the *appikoros* (atheist) and the *meshumedeste*. Between the two there was, however, a wide distance. Disclaim Judaism as Nehemiah would, he could not get the Jews to disclaim him; while Michalina was more alien to the Mosiac community than any of its Christian neighbors. With her child in her arms she moved about among the people of the place like a lone shadow. Nehemiah was a Jew who "sinned and led others to sin"; she was not a Jewess who had transgressed, but a living stigma, all the more accursed because she had once been a Jewess.

Some of the Jewish women were friendly to her. Zelda the Busybody exchanged little favors with her, but even she stopped at cooking utensils, for Michalina's food was *treife** and all her dishes were contaminated. One day, when the dumpy little woman called at the lonely hovel, the convert offered her a wedge of her first lemon pie. It was Zelda who had taught her to make it, and in exultation and shamefacedness Michalina forgot the chasm that separated her from her caller.

"Taste it and tell me what is wrong about it," she said, blushing.

Zelda became confused.

---

*Not prepared according to Mosaic law, proscribed; the opposite of *kosher*.—A.C.

"No, thank you. I've just had dinner, as true as I'm living," she stammered.

The light in Michalina's eyes went out. For a moment she stood with the saucer containing the piece of pie in her hand. When the Burkdale woman was gone she threw the pie away.

She bought a special set of dishes which she kept *kosher,* according to the faith of the people of Burkdale. Sometimes she would buy her meat of a Jewish butcher, and, on coming home, she would salt and purify it. Not that she expected this to be set to her credit in the world to come, for there was no hope for her soul, but she could not help, at least, playing the Jewess. It both soothed and harrowed her to prepare food or to bless Sabbath light as they did over in Burkdale. But her Sabbath candles burned so stern, so cold, so unhallowed. As she embraced the space about them and with a scooping movement brought her hands together over her shut eyes and fell to whispering the benediction, her heart beat fast. She felt like a thief.

"Praised be Thou, O Lord, King of the world, who hast sanctified us by Thy commandments and commanded us to kindle the light of Sabbath."

When she attempted to recite this she could not speak after the third word.

Michalina received another letter from her father. The old man's heart was wrung with compunction and yearning. He was panting to write to her, but, alas! who ever wrote a *meshumedeste* except to curse her?

> It is to gladden your treacherous heart that I am writing again [ran the letter]. Rejoice, accursed apostate, rejoice! We cannot raise our heads for shame, and our eyes are darkened with disgrace. God give that your eyes become so dark that they behold neither your cur of a husband nor your vile pup. May you be stained in the blood of your own heart even as you have stained the name of our family.
>
> Written by me, who curses the moment when I became your father.

Michalina was in a rage. "We cannot raise our heads"? Who are "we"? He and his sorceress of a wife? First she makes him drive his own daughter to "the impurity" of the Gentile faith, and then she gets him to curse this unhappy child of his for the disgrace she brought on her head! What are they worrying about? Is it that they are afraid it will be hard for Michalina's stepsister to get a husband because there is a *meshumedeste* in the family? Ah, she is writhing and twitching with pain, the sorceress, isn't she? Writhe away, murderess! Let her taste some of the misery she has heaped on her stepdaughter. "Rejoice, apostate, rejoice!" Michalina did rejoice. She was almost glad to be a *meshumedeste.*

176

"But why should it have come out like this?" Michalina thought. "Suppose I had never become a *meshumedeste,* and Nehemiah, or some handsomer Jew, had married me at home. . . . Would not the sorceress and her daughter burst with envy! Or suppose I became a Jewess again, and married a pious, learned, and wealthy Jew who fainted with love for me, and my stepmother heard of it, and I sent my little brother lots of money—wouldn't she burst, the sorceress! . . . And I should live in Burkdale, and Sorah-Elka and the other Jews and Jewesses would call at my house, and eat, and drink. On Saturdays I should go to the synagogue with a big prayerbook, and on meeting me on the road people would say, 'Good Sabbath!' and I should answer, 'A good Sabbath and a good year!' "

Michalina began to cry.

V

Spring was coming. The air was mild, pensive, yearning. Michalina was full of tears.

"Don't rail at the rabbis—don't!" she said, with unusual irritation, to Nehemiah at her house. "Do you think I can bear to hear it?"

She cried. Nehemiah's eyes also filled with tears.

"Don't, little kitten," he said; "I didn't mean to hurt you. Are you sorry you became a Christian?" he added, in an embarrassed whisper.

For the first time she recounted her story to him. When she had finished the atheist was walking up and down.

"Ai-ai-ai! Ai-ai!" All at once he stopped. "So it was out of revenge for your stepmother that you married Wincas!" he exclaimed. Then he dropped his voice to a shamefaced undertone. "I thought you had fallen in love with him."

"What's that got to do with him?" she flamed out.

His face changed. She went on:

"Anyhow, he is my husband, and I am his wife and a Gentile woman, an accursed soul, doomed to have no rest either in this world or in the other. May the sorceress have as much darkness on her heart as I have on mine!"

"Why should you speak like that, little kitten? Of course I am an atheist, and religion is humbug, but you are grieving for nothing. According to the Jewish law, you are neither his wife nor a Gentile woman. You are a Jewess. Mind, I don't believe in the Talmud; but, according to the Talmud, your marriage does not count. Yes, you are unmarried!" he repeated, noting her interest. "You are a maiden, free as the birds in the sky, my kitten. You can marry a Jew 'according to the laws of Moses and Israel,' and be happy."

His voice died away.

"Lau-au-ra!" he wailed, as he seized her hand and began to kiss its fingers.

"Stop—oh, stop! What has come to you!" she shrieked. Her face was crimson. After an awkward silence, she sobbed out: "Nobody will give me anything but misery—nobody, nobody, nobody! What shall I do? Oh, what shall I do?"

Under the pretense of consulting a celebrated physician, Michalina had obtained Wincas's permission to go to New York. In a secluded room, full of dust and old books, on the third floor of an Orchard Street tenement house, she found a gray-bearded man with a withered face. Before him were an open folio and a glass half filled with tea. His rusty skullcap was pushed back on his head.

The blood rushed to her face as she stepped to the table. She could not speak.

"A question of law?" asked the rabbi. "Come, my daughter, what is the trouble?"

Being addressed by the venerable man as a Jewess melted her embarrassment and her fear into tears.

"I have married a Gentile," she murmured, with bowed head.

"A Gentile! Woe is me!" exclaimed the rabbi, with a look of dismay and pity.

"And I have been baptized, too."

Here an old bonnetless woman came in with a chicken. The rabbi was annoyed. After hastily inspecting the fowl, he cried:

"*Kosher! Kosher!* You may eat it in good health."

When the old woman was gone he leaped up from his seat and bolted the door.

"Well, do you want to do penance?" he demanded, adjusting his skullcap.

She nodded ruefully.

"Well, where is the hindrance? Go ahead, my daughter; and if you do it from a pure heart, the Most High will help you."

"But how am I to become a Jewess again? Rabbi, a man told me I never ceased to be one. Is it true?"

"Foolish young woman! What, then, are you? A Frenchwoman? The God of Israel is not in the habit of refunding one's money. Oh, no! 'Once a Jew, forever a Jew'—that's the way He does business."

"But I am married to a Gentile," she urged, with new light in her black eyes.

"Married? Not in the eyes of our faith, my child. You were born a Jewess, and a Jewess cannot marry a Gentile. Now, if your marriage is no marriage—what, then, is it? A sin! Leave the Gentile, if you want to return to God. Cease sinning, and live like a daughter of Israel. Of course—of course the laws of the land—of America—do you understand?—they look upon you as a married woman, and they must be obeyed. But the laws of our faith say you are not married, and were a Jew to put the ring of dedication on your finger, you would be his wife. Do you understand, my child?"

"And how about the baby, rabbi? Suppose I wanted to make a proselyte of her?"

"A proselyte! Your learning does not seem to go very far," laughed the old man. "Why, your little girl is even a better Jewess than you have been, for she has not sinned, while you have."

"But her father—"

"Her father! What of him? Did *he* go through the throes of childbirth when the girl was born to you? Don't be uneasy, my daughter. According to our faith, children follow their mother. You are a Jewess, and so is she. She is a pure child of Israel. What is her name? Marysia? Well, call her some Jewish name—say Mindele or Shayndele. What does it amount to?"

As Michalina was making her way down the dingy staircase, she hugged the child and kissed her convulsively.

"Shayndele! Shayndele! Pure child of Israel," she said between sobs, for the first time addressing her in Yiddish. "A Jewish girlie! A Jewish girlie!"

VI

The charitable souls who had joined to buy the steamship tickets were up with the larks. At seven o'clock Sorah-Elka's apartments on the second floor of a spick-and-span frame house were full of pious women come to behold their "good deed" in the flesh. It was the greatest event in the eventful history of Burkdale. Michalina, restored to her Hebrew name, was, of course, the center of attention. Sorah-Elka and Zelda addressed her in the affectionate diminutive; the other women, in the most dignified form of the name; and so "Rievele dear" and "Rieva, if you please" flew thick and fast.

Nehemiah kept assuring everybody that he was an atheist, and that it was only to humor Rebecca that he was going to marry her according to the laws of Moses and Israel. But then nobody paid any heed to him. The pious souls were all taken up with the young woman they were "rescuing from the impurity."

179

Rebecca was polite, grateful, smiling, and nervous. Sorah-Elka was hovering about, flushed and morose.

"You have kissed her enough," she snarled at Zelda. "Kisses won't take her to the ship. You had better see about the lemons. As long as the ship is in harbor I won't be sure of the job. For one thing, too many people are in the secret. I wish we were in New York, at least."

The preparations were delayed by hitch after hitch. Besides, a prosperous rescuer bethought herself at the eleventh hour that she had a muff, as good as new, which might be of service to Rebecca; and then another rescuer, as prosperous and as pious, remembered that her jar of preserved cherries would be a godsend to Rebecca on shipboard. Still, the train was due fully an hour later; the English steamer would not sail before two o'clock, so there was plenty of time.

As to Wincas, he had gone to work at five in the morning and would not be back before seven in the evening.

Zelda was frisking about with the little girl, whom she exultantly addressed as *Shayndele;* and so curious was it to call a former Gentile child by a Yiddish name that the next minute everybody in the room was shouting: "Shayndele, come to me!" "Shayndele, look!" "Shayndele is going to London to be a pious Jewess!" or "Shayndele, a health to your head, arms, and feet!"

"Never fear, Nehemiah will be a good father to her, won't you Nehemiah?" said one matron.

Suddenly a woman who stood by the window gave a start.

"Her husband!" she gasped.

There was a panic. Sorah-Elka was excitedly signing to the others to be cool. Rebecca, pale and wild-eyed, burst into the bedroom, whence she presently emerged on tiptoe, flushed and biting her lip.

"What can he be doing here at this hour? I told him I was going to the New York professor," she said under her breath. Concealing herself behind the window frame, she peeped down into the street.

"Get away from there!" whizzed Sorah-Elka, gnashing her teeth and waving her arms violently.

Rebecca lingered. She saw the stalwart figure of her husband, his long blond hair curling at the end, and his pale, oval face. He was trudging along aimlessly, gaping about him in a perplexed, forlorn way.

"He is wandering about like a cow in search of her calf," Michalina remarked, awkwardly.

"Let him go whistle!" snapped Sorah-Elka. "We shall have to tuck you away somewhere. When the coast is clear again, I'll take you to the other railroad station. Depend upon it, we'll get you over to New York and on board the ship before his pumpkin-head knows what world he is in. But I said that too many people were in the secret.''

Sorah-Elka was a fighter. She was mistaken, however, as to the cause of Wincas's sudden appearance. Even the few Poles who worked in the Burkdale sweatshops knew nothing of the great conspiracy. Water and oil don't swap secrets even when in the same bottle. It was Michalina's manner during the last few days, especially on parting with him this morning, which had kindled suspicion in the peasant's breast. What had made her weep so bitterly, clinging to him and kissing him as he was leaving? As the details of it came back to him, anxiety and an overpowering sense of loneliness had gripped his heart. He could not go on with his work.

There was a cowardly stillness in Sorah-Elka's parlor. Nehemiah was rubbing his hands and gazing at Rebecca like a prisoner mutely praying for his life. Her eye was on the window.

"What can he be doing here at such an early hour?" she muttered, sheepishly. "Maybe he has lost his job."

"And what if he did? Is it any business of yours? Let him hang and drown himself!" declared Sorah-Elka.

"Why should you curse him like that? Where is his fault?" Rebecca protested feebly.

"Look at her—look at her! She *is* dead stuck on the lump of uncleanliness, isn't she? Well, hurry up, Rievele darling. Zelda will see to the express. Come, Rievele, come!"

Rebecca tarried.

"What has got into you? Why don't you get a move on you? You know one minute may cost us the whole game."

There was a minute of suspense. All at once Rebecca burst out sobbing:

"I cannot! I cannot!" she said, with her fists at her temples. "Curse me; I deserve it. I know I am doomed to have no rest either in this world or in the other, but I cannot leave him—I cannot. Forgive me, Nehemiah, but I cannot. What shall I do? Oh, what shall I do?"

The gathering was dumbfounded. Sorah-Elka dropped her immense arms. For several moments she stood bewildered. Then she said:

"A pain on my head! The good women have spent so much on the tickets!"

"I'll pay it all back—every cent—every single cent of it," pleaded Michalina. Again her own Yiddish sounded like a foreign tongue to her.

"You pay back! From the treasures of your beggarly peasant husband, perhaps? May you spend on doctor's bills a thousand dollars for every cent you have cost us, plaguey *meshumedeste* that you are!''

A bedlam of curses let itself loose. Michalina fled.

"Let her go to all the eighty dark, bitter, and swampy years!" Sorah-Elka concluded, as the door closed upon the apostate. "A *meshumedeste* is a *meshumedeste*.''

HERR ZIMMEL'S MEMENTO
A Story by Abraham Cahan
May 26, 1900

I

Wagner II was so tall, the front part of his ceiling was so low, and at the present moment he was in such a hurry that he often hit his head, but this didn't take much time, so he really didn't mind. Far worse was his having to search his attic for things which he had put away so carefully that he could not find them himself. He had been two hours dressing. It was getting well on to 7 o'clock, and at the thought that he might be late and have to turn back with his composition unplayed and his love unavowed, his heart sank with despair. His shirt and his collar were satisfactory, but the white four-in-hand necktie—devil take it—gave Herr Wagner no end of trouble. He lost half an hour tying it, and the operation left it all crumpled and anything but snow-white.

At last he was ready. The second-hand frock coat which he had bought in the morning for the great occasion was rather too short in the sleeves—so short, indeed, that it required constant vigilance to keep them from catching in his huge detachable cuffs. Still, the coat tails were big enough, and it was the best coat Herr Wagner had ever worn in America, and he was in good spirits.

He had barely time to get to his destination, yet he sat down to his piano for a last rehearsal of his declaration. It was a declaration without words, a love message in melody. Herr Wagner was sure it would speak to her heart, that she would feel its meaning. And not only was it his message of love, but also an epitome of his great system, the grand total of his life-work, the sum and substance of a new theory which was to revolutionize the world of sound.

But of this later on, and at this moment it may be of some use to know that Herr Wagner's attic was on East Seventh Street, that it was a fair-sized, trapezoid-shaped room full of books, music, musical instruments and dust. He paid by the month, and his dropsical landlady cleaned the room on rent day. There were plenty of furnished rooms where the sweeping was done every Saturday, but this was the only place where one was allowed to play his piano, violins, flutes, or clarinets after midnight. So Herr Wagner was willing to do part of the cleaning himself.

He had lived there until he came to look upon it, sloping front wall, dust and all, as part and parcel of his genius. And truth to tell, it did become him well. As he sat fingering the keyboard, writing or pacing the floor, now and again throwing back his long light hair and half-shutting his small blue eyes in a hazy, far-off gaze, the piles of dust-covered books, the instruments and the sloping wall seemed to be as essential to his work as his cigarette-stained fingers or his discolored clerical face.

Herr Wagner slammed the door behind him and faced a chilly November night. He had no overcoat and he shivered, but while passing the barber shop he saw through the window that it was even later than he was afraid it was, and his terror warmed him up. On and on he strode, crossing streets diagonally (on the principle, which he whispered to himself, that a straight line is the shortest distance between two points); jumping over boxes and knocking down little children; diving under horses and leaping over streams of coal; murmuring "*Ach,* pardon!" to the animals as well as to the ladies he whisked past, running, puffing for breath, perspiring.

II

"Annchen, don't talk so much."

"*Ach,* Mamma, don't you talk so much. You know I don't."

"Annchen, you can't keep a secret, you leak like a sieve."

"I leak like a sieve? That's rich! You leak like our old coffee can, Mamma. You can't keep a secret half an hour, Mamma."

"And you can't keep it ten minutes."

"And you two minutes."

An altercation of this kind took place nearly every day, and nearly every day each of them unburdened herself of her most private thoughts or feelings not only to the boarders, but also to some of the men who came to inquire about board.

One day Annchen had a secret which she made up her mind to keep from her mother. Well, she did not giggle, nor even smile to herself, but there must have been something which showed that she had a secret, after all, for Frau Binde was restless and every little while said:

"Won't you tell it to me, Annchen? It won't go any further, I assure you."

"But who says I have anything to tell?" Annchen would return, and as she did so she would give her mother a look which said: "I can keep a secret, can't I?"

"Do tell me what it is, Annchen, darling." But molasses was of no avail. It took vinegar to catch this fly.

"Herr Zimmel is a good-for-nothing," Frau Binde said, "and he owes me a month's rent. He is a rogue."

"I don't want you to talk like that, Mamma. Herr Zimmel is a gentleman," said Annchen. "I won't let you call him names in my hearing."

"Why, are you—? Is he—?"

"Never mind what he is. Well, he is my sweetheart. There!"

The old woman's eyes sparkled. "Did he make a formal declaration of love, a proposal of marriage?"

"That's my own affair, Mamma."

"Foolish girl that you are; but I am your mother."

Annchen wilted down, and, blushing to her ears, she said:

"There is nothing to tell, after all. We love each other; he loves me and I love him—that's all."

"Well, if he loves you, it means that—"

"Of course, he never said so, but he does; I know he does."

"How does he act? What does he say? Does he call you 'my treasure'?"

"Of course he does. Besides, he kisses me and I kiss him," she added, blushing once more. "But mind you, if you ever say a word."

"I say a word! You know how good I am at keeping secrets."

That very night, when her oldest boarder came home, she confided to him that her daughter was engaged.

"And who is the valiant knight whose heart Annchen has conquered?" asked the lodger.

"Oh, that's a secret," answered the old woman. And the next morning, when a talkative man asked to see a room on the second floor, Annchen said:

"Oh, that room! That room—my sweetheart has had it for a long time."

Herr Zimmel, a broad-shouldered fellow of twenty-eight, had a big brown dog which he usually left home when he went to work. Annchen took the dog wherever she went, patted him, spoke of Herr Zimmel to him till Leo was as fond of her as he was of his master.

One gloomy morning Herr Zimmel told his landlady and her daughter that America was a bad country and that he was going back to Koenigsberg.

"I say he's a rogue. He ought to be sued for breach of promise," said Frau Binde, when she and Annchen were alone.

"Sh-sh—I won't let you say anything bad about him, Mamma," retorted the girl. "Did I ever say he promised to marry me? Did he ever do anything wrong? He is a fine gentleman; and—and—what do you want of me?" She burst into tears.

"But he has deceived you."

"It isn't true. He never said a word about marriage. He only kissed me because he loves me, and now he must go back to Germany."

"It's a nuisance and a great expense to take dogs across the ocean," said Herr Zimmel. "Take Leo and keep him as a memento, Fräulein." He took his leave of mother and daughter in terms of the warmest friendship, heartily thanking them for their kindness and begging their forgiveness for any wrong he might have done them. He was a kind-hearted, honest fellow, and his words brought tears to the eyes of both women.

On her way from the steamer Annchen kept patting Leo.

"Now we, you and I, are lonely. He has left us. Isn't it terrible? Isn't it awful to live in this world?"

Leo made no answer, but he pranced and fidgeted around in a manner which convinced Annchen that he understood her and felt exactly as she did.

Two days had passed. Annchen and Leo were sad and restless as ever. In the evening of the third day they went out for a hearty talk about Herr Zimmel. They turned into Second Avenue. Annchen's eyes were full.

III

Herr Wagner was striding along Second Avenue, looking at the clocks in the stores, and apologizing to the ladies he brushed aside, when suddenly he felt a tug at his coat. A big dog bounded away and—low and behold! a fair-sized piece of cloth was dangling from his "Prince Albert"—a rugged, triangular piece with a hole—a black hole of precisely the same size and shape—over it. Herr Wagner's blood ran cold; his arms dropped to his sides. His eyes were looking for the dog, but it was a block away, capering about and barking like mad. The next moment he beheld a young woman. She was rosy-cheeked, blond and fleshy.

"*Ach du lieber Gott!*" she said, clapping her hands together, as she looked down at the rent in his frockcoat. "Leo! Leo! Whatever have you done?" The dog came dancing back, and she took him in her arms. "What

185

have you done, Leo?'' she repeated, with sympathy for the low-spirited dog, as much as for the young man.

"It's terrible, it's simply terrible," murmured Herr Wagner, his face red as his bleeding heart.

"I'm very, very sorry, sir, but the dog is out of sorts. His master has left for Germany, you know."

"It's simply terrible."

"It's not a new coat, is it?"

"What matters it? I have a very important appointment, and now I can't go there at all. It's simply terrible."

"I could mend it for you, sir. We live over there, on Eighth Street—oh, you naughty boy! I'll write to Herr Zimmel about it—I can mend it for you, sir."

"But it will show, and it's a very fine place I am going to. Oh, it's simply terrible!"

"It won't show a bit. Leo's master once came home with his overcoat all torn, and I mended it for him so well that nobody could see the seam."

"Yes, but what good will it do me? It will be too late to go there, anyhow."

"Ach, mein Gott!" she exclaimed, with genuine anguish. She assured him that the operation would not take more than fifteen minutes, and, as she spoke, her voice and her face were so full of sympathy that he could not help yielding. He had nothing to lose, anyhow. As he took a closer look at her he saw the traces of weeping in her eyes.

IV

They found a bright fire in the parlor stove. A warm twilight filled the room. Herr Wagner's face was all aglow. He sat in his shirt sleeves, while Fräulein was plying her needle on his unfortunate "Prince Albert."

"Excuse my coat sleeves," he said.

The dinner to which Herr Wagner had been invited was out of the question; it was nearly 8 o'clock. So it seemed something far away, something seen in a dream.

Frau Binde offered him a cup of coffee and a piece of cake. He tried to decline, but the room was so warm and comfortable, Frau Binde insisted so sincerely and he was so hungry that he accepted, with thanks and apologies. The old woman went back to her work. Fräulein Binde sighed again and again. So did Herr Zimmel, between sips and bites. At last she said:

"Leo's master was one of our boarders."

"Was he?"

Annchen's story was not slow in coming.

Herr Wagner was interested. "Did you cry?" he asked. She nodded several times. There was a sob in her throat; she could not speak. Presently she said: "He is gone, gone, gone, and all that remains of him is Leo—dear Leo. I'll never part with him. When I look at him I think of Herr Zimmel, and when I think of Herr Zimmel I feel both sad and happy." She burst into tears once more.

"Don't cry," Herr Wagner said tenderly. "He'll come back to you, mark my word."

He began pacing the floor, and then, suddenly stopping in front of her, he said, with great agitation:

"It's something like my own case, Fräulein. I am in love, Fräulein. Yes, I'm in love. Every fibre is aflame in me." Annchen looked up from her sewing, completely absorbed. "It was to play my declaration to her that I was going to her father's house. She would have understood me. I know she would. Every note would have addressed itself to her heart. It is based on my theory. Richard Wagner is all the rage nowadays. Even the French who hate us because we are better than they, even they play him. And yet, and yet—the last word has not yet been uttered. Verdi is naive. His melodies express—what do they express? Nothing. Absolutely nothing! They convey neither the character, nor the sentiment of the persons. It's candy music. But Wagner fell into the opposite extreme. His music is expressive. It's art. But it's heavy, dull, indigestible. So I say, let us combine the two, let us produce operas of expressive melody, of melody which should speak for itself, unaided—nay, untrammeled, by words.

Annchen said "Yes." She did not know what he was talking about, yet she laid down the coat for a minute, and running down to her mother, she said:

"That gentleman talks so nicely, Mother! It's all about operas and flowers and wise things. He is a music teacher, and he's awfully smart." And without giving the old woman time to put in a word, she hurried back to the parlor. A few minutes after she said:

"The song you were going to sing to your sweetheart must be awfully pretty."

Herr Wagner sat down to the old piano and hammered out his declaration.

"Wunder schoen! Wunder schoen!" she exclaimed, lifting her eyes to the ceiling.

"Well, I owe it all to myself," he said. "My father was a poor school teacher. I had to starve for it. I couldn't afford to engage a teacher. I was my own conservatory. I have shown some of my music to publishers. They send it back. Some musicians call me idiot, but that's because they envy my genius, because they are afraid of me. Others say it's pretty good, but they are a lot of liars. They only want to get rid of me. Only one man was honest. 'Look here, young man,' he said. 'There's some good stuff in you, but you need training and systematic study. I see snatches of melody in your compositions that are gems of art, but they are twisted. They might make an excellent waltz.' A waltz! He's honest, but he, too, is afraid I'll eclipse him. I don't care. I am bound to succeed. This poor body is used to privation.''

His voice broke, and as Annchen looked at him she thought she saw tears in his eyes.

"Don't cry," she comforted him.

The next afternoon he called on them again. He played to Annchen, spoke of his operas to her, wept to her. When the shades of evening were beginning to creep into the room, and a streak of gold gleamed through the window, she heaved a deep sigh, and before they knew why, they threw themselves into each other's arms, and their lips clung together.

When they resumed their seats both looked at the floor. Annchen was the first to break silence.

"But you love that young lady," she said, pouting.

"But you love Leo's master," retorted Herr Wagner.

"Oh, that was only imagination. I don't care for him a bit."

"Well, my love for that young lady was pure imagination. I feel it—I love you, and nobody else. Let me play my declaration to you. It's yours by right. Let me be your slave.''

A year has passed. Herr Wagner is still preparing to overwhelm the musical world with his operas, but if you met him in Tompkins Square, on his way to his pupils of an afternoon, you would see that his face has gained in flesh and color, and that his clothes are new and neat. Annchen, now Frau Wagner, takes good care of her husband, and her mother, who lives with them, takes care of both. She knows many people in the neighborhood of Tompkins Square, and while his own head is taken up with his future glory, she sees to it that he has lessons enough to keep them all in comfort. The two women are as confident of his ultimate success as he is, and, thanks to them, his fame is spreading far and wide, so that, instead of 25 cents for a lesson, he now charges 50 cents.

TWO LOVE STORIES
August 18, 1900

The crowd—a frowsy, dingy mass, dappled with gay kerchiefs and ruddy cheeks—was made up of Italians, Poles from Russia, Ruthenians and Slovaks from the northern districts of Austria and Jews from everywhere.

"Take pity, sir! Take pity!" the peasants prayed, with deep bows, snatching off their caps. They wanted to have their cards explained to them. This had been done by the government officials and the agents of the benevolent societies many times before, but most of the newcomers seemed too ignorant and frightened to grasp the situation. Some had bad addresses, others had not money enough to take them to their final destination; still others had telegraphed to their American friends without receiving an answer; and all were anxious about their fate, stupefied, terror-stricken. Some of those who had landed that day did not seem to have a very clear idea as to the nature of the place, whether the thronged noisy barn, with those overworked, nervous, yelling clerks in blue coats with brass buttons jostling their way in and out, was a house or a ship.

"How far are we from America?" asked one cowed, haggard-looking young Pole, named Vladyk. And when I told him that America was right there he stared at me in bewilderment and despair.

He was a tall, broad-shouldered fellow, and as he had been in the Czar's army we spoke in Russian. His features have faded out of my memory. All I can see when I think of him is a light forelock, a large mouth and a vague look of grim resignation. I have a better recollection of his voice than of his face, and as I write this the echo of its soft, hollow sound fills me with a strange desire to hear it again. At first he listened to me suspiciously, answering my questions in wary monosyllables, but when the ice was broken at last, his story leaked out at one gush.

Six years ago the father of a girl in his native village, which is near Grodno, had said to him:

"Vladyk, you know I have a fine piece of land. My horse is worth ninety rubles and my cow gives me plenty of milk. I have only Antoska in the world. Marry her and all that is mine will be yours. Antoska, she is a good girl and she has set her heart on you, Vladyk. Do take her in marriage and be a son-in-law to me."

189

"Maybe I would, and maybe I wouldn't," said the young immigrant, continuing his narrative. "But because he begged me so much I got kind of disgusted with his girl. She was so pale and sickly-looking, anyway."

One day Vladyk, taken into the army, was bidding his weeping old mother good-by when Antoska called him to a place behind an old fir tree, and falling to his feet, said:

"My darling! My nobleman! I cannot live without you. Tell me to wait till you come back from the army."

But this only increased Vladyk's impatience with her, and he said, angrily:

"Leave me alone, will you?"

Years had passed. Vladyk returned home. From a spare, frail little girl Antoska had become a buxom, well-formed young woman, her face flushed with health, her eyes full of life.

Vladyk fell in love.

"Darling! Queen!" he once said to her.

"Very well. Come," she answered, leading the way to the old fir tree.

Arrived there, she put her bared plump arms to her sides and said:

"Oh, leave me alone, will you?"

She broke into a giggle which went to his heart like a shower of needles, and said again:

"Oh, leave me alone, will you?"

In the afternoon of the same day, as he met her by the well, she set down her pail, put her arms akimbo, and said:

"You know what I mean."

Vladyk writhed, cursed, begged, but she only flashed her eyes at him, laughed and told him that Stassuk was her darling.

"Is that the reason you left? Couldn't you get over it?" I inquired.

"Maybe I could and maybe I couldn't," he replied. "I dreamed I had mixed her up with some logs and chopped her in two. Since then I was afraid I might do it for fair. She was drying up my heart, so." Then raising his arm above his head and hurling it down with a look of wild despair, he resumed: "There was nothing to do at home, anyway. What is a fellow who has seen large cities to do in a village, sir? My brother is in America and he wrote me a letter. 'Come to America,' said he. So I came."

"You'll soon forget her," I comforted him.

"Well," he returned, sheepishly. "When I get rich in America, I'll go back for a visit. Let her see my nobleman's clothes and the lots of money I have. Why did she tease me?"

About a quarter of an hour later, in the same corner of the pen where

190

Vladyk had told me his story, I made the acquaintance of an elderly Ruthenian with a wrinkled face and small blinking eyes full of sad humor. He had been in this country twice before and he had twice gone back to his old home, expecting to end his days there; but he could not live away from his daughter.

"I used to think that the best place to be buried in is where a fellow was born," he said. "But each time I get home I feel neither dead nor alive, so I thought I might as well give my son-in-law a chance to attend my funeral. What a fool! If he were not so anxious to keep me off, I might not be so hard up for a sight of her. Do you understand me, sir? When I am in Paterson he treats me so badly that I begin to feel homesick, but when I get back home I feel that where my daughter is, there is my home. So he keeps me going backward and forward like that dangling thing of a clock, you know."

"And your daughter?" I asked.

"Oh, she's a fool," he answered impatiently. "She thinks everybody is as straight and as good as she is. One would think I cost them a lot. Why, my daughter says she doesn't spend an extra penny on me. He hates me. That's all. He just can't bear the sight of me," he murmured, pensively.

"Well, I hope he'll treat you better this time," I comforted him, for something to say.

"Oh, he's a serpent, sir," he answered bitterly. He contracted his gnarled forehead, threw a grim look on the floor, and then raising his eyes again, he said with a sudden laugh which I thought more touching than a sob: "He won't get rid of me this time. He can't do more than kill me, can he? Well, he'll kill me near my daughter, at least."

DUMITRU AND SIGRID

A Story by Abraham Cahan

Cosmopolitan / March 1901

A fresh shipload of immigrants had arrived at the Barge Office. It was made up of Slovaks, Magyars, Poles, Jews, some Syrians, some Armenians, and a few lone representatives of other nationalities. The bay outside was overhung by a colorless, sullen sky. The "detention pen" was filled with depressing twilight. Red, yellow and black declared themselves a fluctuating tricolor in a mass of tints and shades. There was the ordinary rush and hubbub in the room. Everybody was on pins and needles to get out "into

America." Some wondered how far off America was; others knew from their relatives' letters that they were in "Castle Garden" (the name of the old immigrant station clings to its successors) and that Castle Garden was in America. Everybody asked questions, pleaded, sobbed, cursed, kissed the clerks' hands. The blue-coated officials were hoarse, exhausted, nervous. A Polish woman was crying and wringing her hands because she had an illegible address and there was nobody to get her out. An aged Jew was trembling with excitement at the thought that he had reached America and was about to see his son from whom he had been separated for six years. A sickly-looking man who had been excluded as an invalid and a pauper was tearfully telling other immigrants how he had sold everything he had in the world to take his family to America. A Slovak woman was scolding her husband because she wanted some more beef stew and he hadn't the courage to ask for it. Peasants, crouching against the walls, were whispering, sighing, waiting. At one table a young polyglot clerk, whose business it was to write telegrams for such of the newcomers as had legible addresses, was the center of a throng which was yelling to him in six languages at once.

In one corner of the room, a slender, dark-complexioned young man stood speaking to a bald-headed official, in French. It was not his mother tongue, for he was a Rumanian, but, like most educated people in his birthplace, he spoke the language of fashionable society with ease.

"I won't be a burden to the Americans," he said. "I'm willing to do the hardest work there is."

"Have you no money at all?" the official interrupted him, gruffly. He stood with his head cocked toward the immigrant, who was barring his way, and with his indifferent eyes on the wall.

"No, sir," answered the young man. "The journey took all I had."

The clerk still looked morose, but the immigrant had evidently touched a tender chord in his heart, for, although it was a case for the Board of Special Inquiry, he stopped to hear his story.

"I thought I had enough to get to New York and to show to the authorities here," the young man went on, in a low, refined voice. "But the ship agent in Bremen kept me waiting in his boarding house until I had spent my last penny."

"What was your occupation at home?" asked the clerk, the gruffness all gone out of his voice and confined to the wrinkles of his forehead.

"I was an officer in the army," replied the young man, dropping his eyes. "There was some trouble—a misfortune—I had to leave."

The official pricked up his ears. The Rumanian told him very briefly and very reluctantly how a superior officer (the young man was an ensign, just graduated from the military school) had slandered his sister and how he had slapped his face in the presence of other officers and men. The Barge Office clerk explained to Dumitru Robescu (the young immigrant's name) that it was not in his power to get him out, and that even the special board could not go behind the law, but he promised to get some society interested in his case and told him to cheer up.

Dumitru's spirits rose. He resumed his seat on his rusty valise in the corner, and taking out his grammar, he settled down to give himself a lesson in English. He could not muster attention, however, and little by little, as he made an effort to memorize the strange words, his heart grew heavy. Try as he would, he could not take these queer words seriously, as parts of real human speech, and as he grappled with their unmanageable sounds, his sense of desolation grew and grew upon him. The large city outside and the whole country into which he was begging to be admitted was a stirring mass of vague, hard faces in his brain. They chilled his heart, and, writhing with homesickness, he mentally called to his mother and sister to think of him. For many minutes he sat looking in front of him, seeing nothing but his black despair. Could it be that he was doomed to life-long exile? Was it possible that he should never see his home again? He was an affectionate, tender-hearted fellow of twenty-two. He looked eighteen or nineteen, and in his present trouble he felt like a boy of ten.

When the rush of anguish had subsided and he became aware of the sounds and the faces around him, his eye fell upon a pink-faced, light-haired girl in a blue dress and hat, who sat on a parcel, reading a small Bible. Her pretty head was bent and her puckered-up lips were moving with quiet fervor, as if she were confiding to the book the secret of her pining heart. Dumitru leaned slightly forward and watched the play of her mouth with unobtrusive interest. After a little he made another attempt to read his grammar, and again he recoiled before its hostile words. His heart failed him to face the awful reality of which their impossible echo spoke to it. His eyes fled to the comely immigrant, who was still murmuring over her Bible.

An hour had passed. The two had scarcely exchanged a glance, but she seemed to be conscious of his gaze and not to resent it.

Presently, the sky having cleared up, the attendants of the pen pulled up the window. A flood of April air and April sunshine glided into the dingy, suffocating room. The immigrant girl raised her glance to the window. A dreary look came into her face. Her eyes filled.

Dumitru stepped up to her and asked, in French, why she was detained. She shook her head, shrugged her shoulders and smiled through her tears. He smiled back. After standing in front of her awhile, he moved his valise close to her side.

"What language do you speak?" he asked, in despair.

"I don't understand what you say," she replied, with a distressed look, in Swedish, and both broke out laughing.

Later in the afternoon, when the detained immigrants were removed to the barges off Ellis Island for the night, they were separated, but the next morning they met again.

From that day on they were mostly together. He brought her her breakfast, picked out the best piece of meat in his stew and put it on her plate, and once got into a fight with a Hungarian who had placed a baby on her parcel.

Every now and then the stately, bespectacled young matron, on her way to the Board of Special Inquiry, stopped to speak to the Swedish girl in her mother-tongue.

"Well, Sigrid," she would say, "still reading your Bible? That's good. It keeps you from worrying, and God will soon get you out of here for your piety." As the matron turned away Sigrid would give Dumitru a look of intelligence, and he would respond with a fond smile, as though he understood what had been said.

Sigrid took things patiently. She was often seen moping or reading her Bible in a disconsolate intonation, but she never appeared irritated. Even the seven hours daily spent in the pestiferous pen failed to tarnish the bloom of her cheeks or the soft luster of her trustful eyes, and since she had made the mute acquaintance of the Rumanian her pensive moods had become very rare indeed. As to Dumitru, he grew thinner and more haggard every day. Sigrid noticed this, and once she expressed her sympathy by clasping her hands and bending upon him a look of great pity. His reply was a puzzled simper. Whenever she wanted a drink she smilingly put her fist to her lips, and then he was sure to jump to his feet and bring her a cup of fresh water.

One day, as the two sat exchanging glances and smiles, the young man's face suddenly took on a fierce look, and thrusting his index finger in his breast, he shouted: "Dumitru! Dumitru!" Then, all tenderness once more, he pointed his finger at her in a gesture of inquiry. The meaning of it all was: "My name is Dumitru. What is yours?" To his cruel disappointment, however, a perplexed stare was all the answer he obtained.

The matron got used to seeing the swarthy Rumanian beside the fair Swedish girl. Sometimes, when she found them smiling upon each other, or merrily gesticulating like two deaf-mutes, she would smile, too, and pass on. Lovemaking was strictly forbidden in the "pen," and the matron's motherly smile said, among other things, "Mind that you always behave like this, for if you only touch her hand, I'll have to separate you."

194

Whenever Dumitru took up his grammar, Sigrid would pout, in her mild, easy way, or bend over and join him in his studies playfully until he laid down the book. Nevertheless, when she opened her Bible and he mimicked her piety, she would sign to him that it was a sin to do so, and he had to desist. Besides a grammar, Dumitru had a dictionary. When he took it out of his valise for the first time and showed it to Sigrid, her face brightened up. She gave him to understand, in their sign-language, that she knew what it was and wished she had such a book in her own tongue. As Dumitru was glancing over page after page, Sigrid looked on over his shoulder with an air of reverence. He found many words that were almost the same in both languages, and every time he came across one of these he welcomed it with a little thrill of pleasure, as he would a fellow-countryman unexpectedly come upon in the land of his exile.

All at once he raised his head and clapped his hands in excitement. It was his own inspiration he was applauding. It had flashed upon his mind that if the girl had an English dictionary for her native tongue, they might be able to carry on some sort of conversation through the language spoken in America. He was all in a flutter. It seemed such an ingenious idea to hit upon, and promised such good sport, that he did not rest until he got Sigrid to ask the matron if she couldn't lend her a Swedish-English and English-Swedish dictionary.

A few minutes later they sat over their books, engrossed in the game which he was trying to explain to her. He began by searching his dictionary for the English words which he wanted to address to Sigrid. These she was to look up in the English-Swedish part of her dictionary, and, once his message was clear to her, to compose her English answer by means of the other section of her book, so that Dumitru might translate it into Rumanian and go on with the conversation. Sigrid, who had scarcely ever handled a dictionary before, was rather slow to grasp the process. Little by little, however, she began to see light, and after an hour's exercise she found her words as quickly as Dumitru and showed as much intuition in unriddling his sentences as he did in deciphering hers.

Oh, what a delight it was to make sense of the funny words he copied out and to see him understand those she dug out of her dictionary! Her cheeks glowed. Every time she unraveled his missive, she burst out laughing and jerked her arms. Not so Dumitru. He turned over the leaves of his dictionary, wrote down his words, or watched her face as the meaning of his communication began to dawn upon her, with the rapt, morose mien of a man absorbed in a game of chess. It seemed as though a deaf-mute had all of a sudden begun to speak. On the other hand, the words seemed to proceed from some mysterious source, and the weirdness of it gave a peculiar zest to his interest.

Some of the other immigrants crowded about them, watching their curious occupation, but Dumitru and Sigrid were too deeply immersed in their correspondence to feel annoyed.

"You have relatives in America?" wrote Dumitru.

"I have aunt. You?" returned Sigrid.

"Where your aunt?" he further asked; and the answer was:

"Know no. Lose address. American dame say she find mine aunt."

The clerks were working on a clue which seemed to lead to Sigrid's final destination. Her aunt had left Sweden when Sigrid was two years old and her mother was still living. All the girl knew about her relative was that she was childless and that her husband's name was Dansen. As long as Sigrid's father remained a widower, Mrs. Dansen had contented herself with sending her five dollars for Christmas and five dollars as a birthday present. A few months ago, however, when he married an old maid, his daughter's aunt had flown into a passion and sent her niece passage money.

All this Sigrid conveyed to the Rumanian as well as she could, piecing out her English with gesture-speech. Dumitru told her his own tale of woe. Upon discovering that he had been an officer in the army, her manner toward him suddenly grew reserved and respectful. This soon wore off, however, so much so that when she saw him help a pretty Polish girl with her packing her face clouded, and it was not until he had wormed out of the two dictionaries Swedish for "No be angry" that she smiled.

"You have a sweetheart!" he next wrote.

When she discovered what he meant, she slapped his hand.

"Say truth," he insisted.

She put her hand to her heart and shook her head.

One morning when a batch of immigrants had been discharged and the room looked empty, Dumitru wrote to her:

"Sad! Sad! Sad!"

Tears started to Sigrid's eyes as the meaning of the word was revealed to her. He told her she was "good angel," and while she was rendering it into Swedish, he watched her with bashful side glances. At last her face lighted up, and snatching the lead pencil from his hand she set to work on her answer.

"And you bad man," she declared.

Seeing a gleam of intelligence spread over his face, she gave a titter.

"I not joke, Sigrid," he wrote. "Know not where I be and where thou be, but I eternal remember thou."

Without raising her head, she proceeded to make up her reply.

"I also never forget thou," it read. "Never, never."

Two days later the detention pen was swarming with Italians. The bulk of them were disposed of swimmingly, but there was plenty to do and the hum and buzz of the many-colored multitude was pierced by the husky shouts of the clerks. Dumitru and Sigrid sat in their wonted corner, their dictionaries in their laps, their eyes on the open window; their thoughts thousands of miles apart, their hearts linked together by the sense of insecurity which the breath of spring brought over both.

Suddenly she started. Her name had been called. The next minute the chief clerk and the matron, both too busy and fatigued to smile, were by her side. Mrs. Dansen was waiting in the reception room, so Sigrid was hurried out of the pen.

Dumitru was left gaping. He flung himself toward the door through which the Swedish girl had disappeared, but the gateman pushed him back. During the dinner hour, when the other immigrants were busily dispatching spoonful after spoonful of soup, he sat curled up on his valise, brooding.

"Why don't you eat your dinner?" asked the bald-headed clerk.

"Take pity, sir!" Dumitru begged, leaping up. "If you keep me here another day I'll die, and if you send me back I'll jump overboard."

That afternoon the agent of the German immigrant society procured for him work as a laborer in a West Side photograph gallery, and the Inquiry Board voted to admit him.

During his first months in America, when the Scotch photographer often lost patience with his inability to understand what was said to him; when he was treated like a servant and was in constant dread of losing his job; when the American city impressed him as a world of savages and the strange tongue he heard around him seemed to speak of his doom—in those days of heart-wringing desolation he neither dared nor, indeed, knew how to find his way to the Barge Office to ask about the young Swedish girl. Yet she was never absent from the group which filled his daydreams and to which he addressed the outpourings of his yearning soul. "Where are you, dearest?" he would say to Sigrid, as he lay in his lonely attic, speaking in whispers, as if she were actually listening to him. "Are you true to your pledge, angel? As to me, your sweet likeness is never out of my thoughts." And remembering how she had repeated the word on paper, he added, "Never, never!" Then, addressing himself to his family—"This is Sigrid, mother. Kiss her, for she is a dear creature. This is my mother and this is my sister, Sigrid. Let me embrace you all, let me press you to my aching heart—tight—tight—tight!"

Sometimes, as he walked in the streets, a passing profile would make him start. "Sigrid!" he would say to himself, outrunning the young woman, only soon to pause with a pang of disappointment. Once, in a cable-car, he saw a girl whose resemblance to the Swede seemed so striking that he was about to accost her, tentatively, when she chanced to smile, which changed her face so completely that Dumitru thanked his stars he had remained silent. After this, he began to doubt whether he would know Sigrid if he really met her. Her image had waned to a pale blur in his mind.

At last he called at the immigrant station. The bald-headed clerk recognized him at once. He was so glad to see him in a new suit of clothes that he spared no pains to unearth the address for him.

Dumitru at once rushed to the place, but all he found was a row of unfinished new tenement houses. As to the other tenants on the block, they had never heard of a Mrs. Dansen. Tenement people seldom live in the same place long enough to know much about their next-door neighbors, much less about those of another house. The little community to which Mrs. Dansen had belonged had been wiped off the block together with the old houses which were torn down to make room for the new. Not a trace was left of the world which had laughed, cried, quarreled and gossiped on this spot a few months ago—nothing but a silent, cheerless expanse of brick and mortar pierced with rows of boarded windows. A lump rose to Dumitru's throat as he looked at all this.

The next morning he inquired among the members of a Swedish church and of some Scandinavian societies, but all in vain.

The elevated trains and cable-cars were overcrowded. The streets were deserted. The sweltering, Sunday-clad, wretched population was fleeing from the stone-bound city for breath. Dumitru, dressed in a cheap summer suit, negligee shirt and soft gray hat, was on his way to the uptown station of the elevated railroad at Fourteenth Street and Third Avenue. His face, his step and swing as he walked, the way he wore his clothes and the way he held his head—everything about him bespoke many months of life in an American city. The Scotchman had discharged him long ago. He had next obtained a job in a toy factory; then in a drugstore, and finally with another photographer, an Americanized Frenchman, who took a liking to him and let him learn his trade. As a result, Dumitru was now earning from ten to twelve dollars a week at retouching.

His acquaintances were two or three Frenchmen, but he never felt quite at home with them. The thirty-odd months which lay between him and his birthplace seemed so many years. The Barge Office episode he remembered as a mere joke, at once sweet and touching, of a half-forgotten past, and Sigrid, stripped of her flesh and blood, shone in the center of a far-off fancy.

Still, unreal as she had become, there she was, dwelling in his golden air-castles beside his mother, his sister and his country.

The train which he boarded was so jammed that he was glad to find standing-room on a platform. Crowded hard against the farther gate, which was for the most part left shut, he stood eyeing the tracks, the windows of houses, the passing trains, and musing to the lumbering rhythm of the cars. At one point a train moved out of a station across the road at the same moment as Dumitru's train started in the opposite direction. As his eye struck one of the crowded platforms sliding past, he beheld Sigrid. It was she. They seemed to have parted only the day before.

"Sigrid! Sigrid!" he shouted, flinging out his arms. But his voice was smothered by the rumbling duet of the two trains which were carrying them apart, and she never looked round. Dumitru felt that every inch he proceeded separated him from her two inches. He was tempted to jump off. When the helplessness of his position fully came home to him, his heart stood still.

He got out at the next station and boarded a downtown train, in a nerveless, perfunctory sort of way. Besides vexation and despair, he felt something like the shame of one who finds himself the victim of an ingenious practical joke.

The next morning he went to the Barge Office. When he reached the door, he called himself a fool and turned back.

From that Sunday on he preferred the elevated to the surface cars whenever he had occasion to travel. One Sunday he went from one end of the road to the other, on the chance of falling in with the Swedish girl. Her face was a living image once more. It was his symbol of nobleness and bliss.

"Oh, I will find you, Sigrid dear!" he often murmured to it.

One afternoon in August, more than a year after the elevated train incident, the young Rumanian was walking along East Seventy-second Street. His sister had married a widower. His mother had been dead for several months, yet he didn't seem to be able to realize the fact to the full. Not having seen her otherwise than living, he could not conceive of her as resting in a grave with damp earth all about her. "Impossible! Impossible!" his heart protested. At the same time he had a feeling that everybody and everything he used to know at home had vanished.

Otherwise things went well with him. His intelligence and his natural taste stood him in good stead. He now had the choice between employment in one of the finest photographic studios in New York and a half-interest in a modest establishment which a former roommate, a Czech, who had saved some money, offered to open. Inherited indolence and lack of enterprise inclined him to the former. Besides, the gallery which his friend was planning would have to cater to grosser tastes. Still, he was considering the matter seriously, and it was to reconnoiter the uptown Bohemian quarter with regard to a place for the projected studio that he was now prowling about Seventy-second Street. He was decently dressed, went to the American theatres and was a frequenter of the opera. On the whole he was getting to like his new home, so that during the Spanish war he went wild over every victory of American arms. And yet he felt lonely, gnawingly lonely, and his greatest pleasure was to pull the quilt over his head before falling asleep, and to imagine his mother alive, with himself, Sigrid and his sister by her side. Or else he would go to the Russian church on Second Avenue (he didn't understand the language, but there is no Greek-Catholic house of worship for Rumanians in New York) and, amid clouds of incense, pray for the soul of his mother and for the health of Sigrid and his sister.

He was at this moment trudging along Seventy-second Street, surveying the houses on either side, when a strange voice called out:

"Mr. Dumitru!"

It was Sigrid. She sat on the front steps of a new tenement house, with a baby in her lap, the brass baluster gleaming over her bare blonde head. Her face had broadened out and grown somewhat milky, but her maidenly comeliness of yore was gone only to make room for the good looks and ripe loveliness of young motherhood.

" 'I do you do?" he asked, reddening, and not daring to call her by her first name.

"I am ull righd, dang you," she answered. "I didn't see you since ve vas dere [pointing in the direction of the Barge Office]. I ulvays dought I vill see you sometimes," she said, radiantly.

Such was the first oral conversation they had ever held, the English in which it was carried on being mispronounced by each in his or her own way—his hard Rumanian accent set off by the flabby consonants of her Swedish enunciation. She told him she was married, that her husband was a piano maker and that he had come from Sweden when he was a boy. She was apparently very glad to see her old friend.

Dumitru felt keenly ill at ease. Her speech made another woman of her. It was not the Sigrid of his daydreams.

"Vat your business, Mr. Dumitru?" she asked. But she did not let him answer her question. "Say, Villie, Villie!" she called out to a young man in shirt-sleeves who at this moment came out of a cigar store nearby and stopped to talk to a neighbor on the sidewalk. When her husband came up, she introduced the Rumanian, saying, with a joyous little laugh:

"Dis is de gentleman vat mashed me in Castle Garden. I tol' you—you remember?" Husband and wife smiled as at a good joke.

Dumitru felt like one listening to the scratching of a window pane. He could see that the young couple were wrapped up in each other, and both in their baby, but all three were equally uninteresting and incomprehensible to him, and he hastened to take his departure.

He walked down the street with burning cheeks. The first pedestrians he met seemed to be laughing at him. He made an effort to think of his studio.

The next Sunday morning he went to the Russian church and prayed for the soul of his mother and the health of his sister.

IMPORTED BRIDES

October 12, 1901

"While we boast of our increasing exports," said an official of a transatlantic steamship company, "we should not forget a certain class of human imports which seems to be getting larger every year. I am speaking of the imported wives who come in the steerage of the big ships. Their number grows with the growth of our prosperity, and we have heard of towns in Norway, for example, which have been drained of their marriageable girls by well-established immigrants in America. A man who has made a study of the situation tells me that many of these immigrants prefer to marry a girl fresh from their native place. They don't take much stock in the Americanized immigrant girl, he says.

"I remember selling a ticket to a German farmer for a girl he was going to marry. He was a talkative fellow, and he told me all about himself and his prospective bride. He was a man of forty-five, while she was scarcely out of her teens, but he looked upon the match from a matter-of-fact, business-like point of view.

" 'I left my native village when she was a baby, but I know her family,' he said. 'There is not a bad-looking woman among them, nor one who is not a hard worker and a first-rate housekeeper. Besides, I received her picture a few months ago. They had taken her to the next town, where there is a photographer, so as to let me see what she looks like. She is pretty; there can be no mistake about that. I am sorry I have not the picture with me. I should like to show it to you. There are lots of girls near my place on Long Island,

German girls, but what are they good for? They only know how to eat candy and giggle.' It was the man's stepsister who played the matchmaker. She lives in his birthplace and she sang the praises of that girl in her letters to him until he opened negotiations.''

The usual way in which a marriage of this sort is brought about is for the immigrant to go to his old home for a visit and to take back a wife. An interesting case of that kind came under the observation of the proprietor of a hotel in Washington Street.

"Business was dull and that couple were the only guests we had that day," he said. "I saw at once that something was wrong between them, for he was dancing attendance on her in a way to make one sick, while she looked morose, downhearted, and scarcely answered his questions. Finally he took me into his confidence. The point was that she was in love with a fellow at home. When I asked him why he had married her he said:

" 'Well, I was crazy. They made so much fuss over me because I was a rich American and spent money freely that I made a fool of myself. I knew she had a sweetheart, but her parents did not care for him, and as I liked her looks they got her to accept me. At first it was all right. While she saw the two of us she thought she would rather be the wife of a rich man, but later, on the steamer, she became homesick and cried day and night. She tells me plainly that she does not care for me; that she loves that fellow and wants to 'go home.'

"I told him she would get used to him, but in my heart I doubted whether she would. She did not look like a woman who changes her mind easily. I was afraid my guest was in for it. If he had a strong will she might have given in, but he has not. He is a quick-tempered fellow without a bit of backbone. How it all ended I don't know.''

An officer connected with the Italian Immigration Bureau told the writer of a man who went to visit his birthplace for the express purpose of showing off his American gold to a married woman who had rejected him six months before. He found his successful rival dead, however, and the matchmaker had no trouble in getting him to marry the widow. She had three children and it was arranged that they should remain with their aunts, but the American proved "dead easy," as the agent of the bureau put it, and before he left his native town he agreed to take them along.

Instances of marriages arranged by correspondence, without the couples knowing each other, are common on Ellis Island, although the authorities of the immigration station do everything in their power to keep "imported brides-elect" from taking the important step before they are sure they will have no reason to regret it. The matron of the place, who has come to be known as "the mother of immigrants" because of the interest she takes in the foreign women under her care, usually counsels delay. As a rule, she tries to persuade the brides-elect to get some employment in this city, which she offers to provide for them, so as to have time to make the acquaintance of the men who import them and to decide for themselves whether they want to marry them.

"Very often we are successful," said the matron, "and it sometimes happens that a girl will come to thank us for saving her from making an undesirable match. Others marry the men who send for them, after a short interval, during which the girl goes to work, seeing her suitor from time to time. But there have been cases where our advice has been disregarded and the girl seemed anxious to marry the stranger at once. Sometimes it is a case of love at first sight, but generally such haste is due to the sense of insecurity and fear which fills the foreigner on suddenly finding herself amid strange people, so far away from home. Of course, we do all we can to make sure that the man means well, that he is honest and can support a wife."

A story is told of a prosperous cigar dealer in the Bohemian district whose wife exacted a pledge from him, on her deathbed, that he would not marry again unless it was a "green" girl. She was jealous of every Czech woman who could speak English, which her husband could use with facility, but of which she did not understand a word; so she had him promise that he would get his second wife from their native country.

"When she died," said one of the Czech's neighbors, "he was so broken up that we were quite uneasy about him. We watched him for several days for fear he might do some harm. He got over it, of course, and little by little he began to think of a second marriage. He is a good, warm-hearted fellow, and I think he would have waited much longer if it had not been for his two little children, who needed the care of a woman.

"Finally he made up his mind to go to Bohemia for a wife. He was quite sentimental about it. His first wife was a native of a town near Brunn, so he determined to marry some girl from that district. He wanted his second wife to speak the same dialect as the first, he said. When I remarked that that was more than he had promised, he answered bashfully that it might please her in her grave to know he thought of her so much.

"One day a friend of his came to bid him good-by. He was going to Brunn. The cigar dealer could not leave New York then, so he said, in fun: 'If you come across a good girl who would be willing marry a widower like myself, let me know, will you?' A couple of months later the cigar dealer received a letter containing a description of a girl in the very village where his first wife had been born. She was at least ten years his junior, but that did not matter. Her parents had heard of his American successes and agreed to the match. It was impossible for him to get away, and the long and the short of it was that he left it all to his friend.

" 'Find out all about her,' he wrote to him. 'If you think she's a good girl and good-looking into the bargain, bring her along.' His friend did, and the marriage took place a few days after the two arrived in New York. The cigar dealer loves his second wife dearly. They are really happy, but he sometimes speaks of his children's mother in a way which makes me think he has not altogether forgotten her."

A rabbi of a small Jewish congregation in Jersey told of a peculiar incident in which he was called upon to perform a marriage ceremony as well as to decide a question of Talmudic law.

"It was a case of *halitza,* as we call it," he said. "When a man dies his brother is expected to marry the widow, you know, and if he cannot or will not do so he must be released by going through a certain ceremony prescribed by our religion, in which the untying of some shoestrings is the main proceeding. It is quite a complicated and difficult ceremony. The devout people in the old country observe it, of course, but sometimes it is performed here, too.

"One day a stranger called at my house and said: 'Rabbi, my brother has died in the old country and his wife wants me to give her *halitza* (or release). She is willing to pay my way there and back, but I am a poor man, and how can I leave my job?' He wanted to know whether it would be a sin for him to decline the request. I told him it would not, and that if his sister-in-law was well-to-do she could come here for the ceremony. Correspondence ensued and finally the woman arrived. There was some delay as other questions of the law had to be settled, but preparations for the ceremony were under way and many people were looking forward to it with a great deal of interest.

"Meanwhile the man and the woman saw each other often, and when the appointed day came around I received a note from the widow's brother-in-law. 'Excuse us, rabbi,' it read, 'but if it is no sin we should like to be married instead of going through *halitza.* My sister-in-law is willing to stay in America, and when I sent her a marriage broker she said it was all right.' "

———

MARRIAGE BROKERS
November 9, 1901

One of the oddest of the Old World institutions to find a home on American soil is the profession of marriage broker, or matchmaker. Scores of them ply their vocation on the East Side, notwithstanding that American institutions and American ways all militate against the system, and many of them make a comfortable living.

A Slovak woman on East Fifth Street is kept busy arranging marriages among her country people in New York and New Jersey. Most of her girl clients go out to service in restaurants or private houses on the East Side, while the men who apply to her for wives work in factories. She is a shrewd woman, with much insight into human nature and a pleasing twinkle in her eye, and she owes her success as much to her tact and experience as to her personal magnetism.

"Some of my clients work in out-of-the-way places where there are no Slovak families around," she said. "They have no chance of making the acquaintance of a desirable girl of their class. Besides, many of them prefer a girl with a marriage portion, and girls of that sort—respectable girls who would make good wives—are not to be had for the picking, of course. One man who makes good wages wrote to me about a month ago that he wanted a girl of this sort, but he added that she must not be too blonde, because an old gypsy woman had told him that he was going to marry a very fair woman and that she would be the ruin of him. I set to work hunting for the kind of wife he wanted, and, as ill-luck would have it, the one who seemed to suit his needs was as yellow as a pumpkin. She was a first-rate girl, a hard worker, sweet tempered, of fine figure and not bad-looking, either, even if she has some freckles on her face.

"I made up my mind that the man ought to marry her. I wrote to him to come over and to see the girl for himself, hoping that he would get stuck on her. But I was mistaken. He was in a rage, the fool. 'Do you want me to marry a woman who will be the death of me and to pay you for it?' he said. I tried to reason with him. I told him gypsy women are a lot of humbugs, and that it was a sin to believe in witchcraft, but he was too ignorant to understand what was good for him, and now I am looking for another girl for him. Some men are very hard to suit."

THE CHASM

A man who does business as a banker and agent for steamship companies in one of the Italian settlements on the Upper East Side runs a matrimonial bureau as an adjunct to his establishment. He makes a point of asking his customers about their daughters or sisters, thus keeping track of the marriageable girls in his neighborhood.

The other day a man of about forty years called at the banker's place of business to have some money sent to his old home. It was during the forenoon, and there were no other customers present. The banker engaged the stranger in conversation. The latter said he was a musician in a small town in Connecticut, and that he made about $20 a week.

"It must be awfully lonely to live in a place like that," remarked the banker. This was expected to bring out a statement as to whether the stranger was married or single, and, sure enough, he agreed that his was a very lonely life indeed, and that it was particularly so because he was a bachelor, and there was not a single Italian family in his town.

There is a woman on Stanton Street who pretends to make her living by peddling tea, but who in reality uses this business as a pretext of making the acquaintance of hundreds of families with an eye to matrimonial alliances. Her *shadchan* business is said to yield her what among the people of her class is considered a large income. As to the goods she peddles, she often sells them at cost price and sometimes to people whom she knows to be bad pay.

This woman is also known as a skillful peacemaker. When a couple who have been married through her efforts cannot get along together she will lecture the woman and try to get her to please her husband. When the two quarrel she tries to get them to make up and to take an oath to be good to one another. Her clients know of her powers in this direction, and they often call on her to straighten out their domestic troubles for them. Her enemies say she does it all for the sake of her matchmaking, and that she is anxious to have her couples live happily lest she should get the reputation of a marriage broker on whose marriages "there is no blessing"; but she has more friends than enemies.

In the ghetto the *shadchan's* commission is usually paid after the engagement. It sometimes happens that the marriage broker is unable to collect his fee, and then a civil action is brought. Sometimes, too, the *shadchan* will try to part the couple before it is too late.

"If you don't pay me my commission in a week," said one *shadchan* to a young man, "your sweetheart will drop you."

"And how are you going to make her do so?" asked the young man, with a sneer. He seemed so sure of his girl, but the *shadchan* got the better of him. He called on the girl, and used all the eloquence for which he is celebrated in the profession to persuade her that the man was unworthy of her, that he had received fresh information about his antecedents, and that there were all kinds of shady stories afloat about him. The girl was devoted to her fiancé and was willing to marry him after all, but her relatives prevailed on her to give him up.

One *shadchan* beats the record by what he calls "enforced marriages." He is the most eloquent man in the fraternity, and when he makes up his mind that a certain man ought to marry a certain girl the marriage is almost sure to take place, whether the two want it or not.

"There is a very large number of men who are all alone in this country," said an East Side physician, who is familiar with this clever *shadchan* and his methods. "Many of them are tired of their boarder's life and crave a home of their own. The *shadchan* keeps track of such fellows, and when he thinks he has a suitable girl for one of their number he sounds her praises until the man agrees to call on her. Often he is disappointed, of course, and then it is that the talents of the *shadchan* are called into play. If he decides in his own mind that it is a 'predestined match' he describes to the man the girl's charms and tries to explain away her shortcomings. Why, that man is quite a poet. When he starts to praise some of his clients his imagination runs away with him, until he believes himself that all he says is true. Recently a man objected to a girl because she was not pretty enough. 'Ah, my friend,' said the *shadchan*, 'I see your eyes tell you a false story. You are the first man I have met who doesn't think her a beauty. Indeed, hasn't she the loveliest eyes in the world?' So speaking, he analysed every feature of the girl's face and painted her in the most glorious colors until the candidate for matrimony, a weak fellow who was tired of his loneliness, agreed to have a betrothal."

"GOD IS EVERYWHERE!"
January 11, 1902

When Sarah, the devout wife of David, heard of her niece's hopeless love for a young Galician she stroked her plump cheek, which, by the way, was getting less plump every day, and said:

"There is a saint on Pitt Street; call on him, Annie."

"A saint?" asked Annie, a smile breaking through her tears.

"Yes, a saint; and you needn't laugh, either. Your mother, peace upon her, did not make fun of saints."

"But my mother, peace upon her, never lived in America, auntie."

"No matter. This is a muddied country, it is true. It is full of business, dancing schools and cable-cars. So there cannot be so much piety. But God is everywhere, my child, and even on Pitt Street you can find a saint."

Annie had heard of the *hasidim*, a Jewish sect full of fervor and queer beliefs, who predominated at the place of her birth, but then, she was brought to America so long ago that all she remembered of her native town is the well in front of the synagogue and the goat which once knocked her down. Her father and all her uncles had belonged to the sect, and all the surviving members of the family who have not yet emigrated to America are still ardent followers of the local saint.

All this Annie knew in a dim, general way, but that there was a saint on Pitt Street and that he could work wonders she had never heard, and now that her pious aunt told her about it, she could not help smiling. The notion of *hasidim* and a saint carrying on their ceremonies in America struck her as one of the funniest things she had come across.

"What does he do here, that saint of yours?" she asked, hugging her aunt fondly.

"He does what a saint does in Poland, in Russia—wherever there is faith. He prays to the Most High, and his soul is so pure that the Most High attends to his prayer."

"Is that all?"

"Don't sneer, child," the old woman said, shaking her finger. "If you want Joe to care for you, you had better give up this obstinacy of yours and go before the saint."

"But what can he do for me, auntie? Pray? Prayers won't help me. They won't melt Joe's heart. Do you think they will? If my face didn't, prayers won't."

"You talk like a foolish child. Nothing is too great for a saint. Do you know that when he becomes transported with pious thought his soul becomes so light that it takes wing and soars up to the Divine Throne itself?"

"And what does it do there?"

"Hush! You are making mock of the Divine Throne, Annie. Beware of your words."

"But what can the saint do to make Joe love me, auntie?" the girl asked. She was getting impatient. While she continued to sneer at the saint she was obviously bent upon giving him a chance to see what he could do for her.

"What can he do? He can do everything, provided you come with a pure heart to him. Tell him all, my daughter, and bear in mind that he is a man of righteousness—a holy man."

The members of the sect are distinguished for their "passionate restlessness" during divine service. They jump, they snap their fingers, they clap their hands, they sigh, they toss about in a thousand different "contortions of limb and voice." Some people speak of them as "Jewish shakers." As to the saint, or *tzaddik,* everything he touches is supposed to carry a blessing with it. One of the regular things at the synagogue, where such a saint expounds divine law and sets a feast to his disciples, is for these disciples to fight for the fish, meat or pastry which the holy man has touched with his fork or spoon. Usually he eats very little at the feast in question, just tasting every dish and then pushing it from him for the *hasidim* to sweep upon in a mad struggle for a bit of the holy food.

The members of the sect in this country complain of the difficulty which they encounter in following their customs on American soil. They can observe their holidays as they did at home, of course, but the very atmosphere here is laden with ideas inimical to their creed, they say. Of course, saints are born, not made, but then, the saint who arrived from Austria recently finds it rather difficult to run things in a place where everybody is "on worldly manners bent," as he puts it.

Annie called on him on an evening. It was her own secret. Even her aunt did not know she had gone. She was just going to try the saint, and in case he helped her, it would not do to have Joe find out how she managed to charm him at last. On the other hand, if the saint proved to be powerless to do anything for her, nobody would have any additional reason to make fun of her.

The saint occupies an apartment of several rooms in an old tenement house. When Annie reached his floor her heart began to beat faster. Nailed to the door was a strip of parchment containing a passage from the Pentateuch. Annie touched it with her finger and then kissed the finger fervently, as she had seen her aunt do before entering her own house. Then she knocked at the door and, in answer to a voice, opened it and found herself in a dirty room crowded with bewhiskered men, some of whom were snapping their fingers and humming all sorts of tunes, while others sat around smoking pipes, gossiping or meditating "upon the communion of the soul with the Most High."

"What dost thou seek, daughterling?" asked a little man with a shaggy beard.

"I wish to see the saint, sir."

THE CHASM

The old man, who was a scribe, wrote a line or two in Hebrew on a slip of paper and asked Annie her name and the nature of her business.

"Can't I see him personally?" she asked.

"Thou mayest, although the saint does not see women, as a rule. He certainly doesn't look at them. Still, if he deigns to give thee an audience he will. But one must write down the nature of his business if he wants the holy man to offer a prayer for him."

"I'll tell it all to him when he lets me see him," Annie insisted.

About a quarter of an hour later she was ushered into the holy man's presence. He was a robust-looking man, in a coat and belt of black satin and with a flat cap trimmed with sable on his head. As the girl entered he shut his eyes.

"Be seated, my child," he said. "What ails you?"

"I wish to speak to you about a man. His name is Joe and I would like to marry him, rabbi."

"Is he not an ungodly man? Does he follow in the path of Judaism, daughterling?"

"I think he does as much as the average young fellow in this country. Neither more nor less."

"Oh," sighed the saint.

"But why should I be more religious than all the other girls?" Annie urged. "Why should I bother about the piety of my lover more than they do about the religion of their fellows? This is not Galicia, rabbi. This is America. People are educated here. They wear nice neckties and go to the theatre."

"I know this is America, my child. I know people don't think of God much in this country, but will one take his neckties and theatres into his grave?"

"But why should I worry more than anybody else? I want to marry Joe, and that's all there is to it, rabbi. Can you do something for me?"

"Ah, you are impatient and you talk in anger. This is just the kind of girls they bring up in America. How can you expect me to help you, seeing that you have no respect for me? At home people tremble at the very mention of the holy man. Here they have no faith in anything. To think of a young girl speaking harshly to a man in my position. Cursed be the day when I set foot on American soil!"

"Pardon me, rabbi. I meant no offense. If the Galician girls, those of the little towns, I mean, if they went to school as I did, and could understand an English newspaper, they would not believe in everything either."

"But if you don't believe in me what brings you to me, then?"

"I wish to tell you frankly, rabbi. My heart is so full of woe that I am willing to try everything. Who knows but you may help me after all. If you do, I shall never forget you, rabbi. I am so miserable. You must bear with an unfortunate girl like myself."

The saint took pity on her.

"Be calm, my child," he said. "Tell me what ails you. Why don't you marry Joe? What stands between you and him? Do the parents object to the match?"

"No, sir. Not they. For they are good people, his parents. They know me and my people, and they know that I should make him happy—far happier than Rosie would. She is a regular virago, rabbi. She will make him miserable. She'll be the death of him."

"But who is Rosie? Has he another sweetheart?"

"Yes, rabbi. She has charmed his heart with all sorts of tricks, rabbi. She only cares for his money, while I care for his shining eyes, his rosy cheeks and for his kindly nature, rabbi. Can you do anything for me, rabbi? If you can, I shall remember you as long as I live."

The rabbi is really a very good-natured, kind-hearted man. He was touched and interested. America is not the place where a saint can afford to stand on his dignity anyhow, so he opened his eyes, stole a glance at the maiden, and said in a voice tremulous with emotion:

"Tell me all, my child. I once had a daughter as big as you. But our Heavenly Father in His wisdom took her away from this world. Tell me all, my child, as if you were speaking to your own father."

"It was like this, rabbi. Joe and I used to visit the same house—the house of a fellow-countryman of my aunt's—and we used to go home together. When I got home I used to lie awake for hours thinking of him. He's so sweet, rabbi, so stately, so manly-looking and so good. We used to meet at that house on Saturdays, but I thought of it the whole week. Saturday was my great day, because I knew that on that day I should see Joe."

"Blasphemy!" whispered the saint, quoting from a holy book. "Sabbath, the holy day, is thought holy only because Joe can be seen on that day."

"What do you say, rabbi?"

"You would not understand that, child. Go on."

"Well, my heart was filled with fire, rabbi. I could not live without Joe. He became the apple of my eye, the consolation of my life, and unless he was mine there was no apple to my eye, nor any consolation to my life—nothing but darkness and misery."

"That was magic, poor child. The impure love that you describe is magic and ought to be exorcised. It is a kind of devil, my child, and it must be driven out of your sweet being till you become free. I shall pray to heaven to have the evil force that has been darkening your brain chased out of you. And then you will not love Joe any more and—''

"What! You want to fix it so that I shouldn't love him any longer? No, sirree. I'll love him as long as I live, and I defy anyone to make me hate him.''

"Hush! don't get angry, my child. The children of America are an unruly lot. To think of a holy man having to humiliate himself before a girl, as I do. If I told it in Poland and Galicia people would hardly believe it. But look here, child. I don't really know what I can do for you. If you don't care to get rid of this disease, then what would you have me do to cure it?''

"Well, I was sure Joe cared for me, and I expected that he would declare his love and ask me to be his wife, and to make him happy as long as he lived. I thought he was bashful, but he was not. All the time he kept me company he thought of Rosie, whom he had known before he met me.''

"But if she was his sweetheart before you first set eyes on him, then what right have you to think of him?''

"Because Rosie is false, and she would have given him up long ago but for my love for him.''

"That is more than I can understand.''

"Don't you see, she is afraid I should marry him if she gave him up. She doesn't care for him herself, the serpent, yet she doesn't care to have anybody else marry him, either.''

"I cannot understand it.''

"She sets his brain on fire, and he neither marries her, nor gives her up. Pray for me, rabbi; pray to have Joe hate Rosie and fall in love with me. Can't you do it?''

"I can pray to our Father in heaven to bring peace and piety into your heart, my child.''

"I'll give you a dollar, rabbi.''

"I'll take no money from you. You can put some in the poor box.''

"All right. Pray to have Joe fall in love with me at once, will you?''

The saint shrugged his shoulders, as much as to say, "America is not the place for me," and explained once more that he could not comply with her request.

"But why? If you are a saint and you can do everything, as auntie says, you ought to be able to do this too. I'll put $2 in the poor box. I'll put $3.''

The holy man shook his head, and became thoughtful.

"Will you promise me to be a good girl?" he then asked.

212

"Yes; but what do you mean? I'm good enough as it is. Much better than Rosie, anyhow."

"I mean you should keep away from Joe for six months."

"Oh?"

"Hush. If you want me to pray for you, you must obey my orders."

"Very well. I will, but will he fall in love with me?"

"God will be merciful. Will you keep away from him?"

"How can I do it? How can I do it?" she asked, bursting into tears.

"If you want to gain your object you must bridle your love; hold it in check."

The rest of the story was told by one of the saint's most ardent followers.

"She has character, that girl," he said, "so she kept away from Joe for six months and by the end of that time she was so cured of her soul-inflammation that she married another fellow. She is a happy mother now. The holy man of Pitt Street is one of the mightiest men of his kind in the world; I can tell you that. All he did was to pray for the poor child, and his prayer was granted."

"But what was that long wait for?" ventured a man who is not quite sure about the supernatural powers of the Pitt Street saint.

"What do you mean?" asked the other resentfully.

"I mean that perhaps the six months did it, not the saint."

"Oh, if you are going to make fun of my holy rabbi I don't want to talk to you."

DRESDEN VS. MUNICH

March 1, 1902

There is a large, clean tenement house on the East Side of Harlem in which the population is about evenly divided between Bavarians and Saxonians. A café across the street used to be the gathering place of the tenants. Some two years ago, however, a feud broke out between the two elements which led to the opening of a new café around the corner. The proprietor of the new place was a native of Munich and his resort at once became the headquarters of his fellow country people, the two contending parties thus being divided into two well-defined camps in the form of two rival cafés.

THE CHASM

With the establishment of this concrete line of demarcation the feud grew in bitterness, affecting some of the love affairs which had sprung up at a time when the people of the tenement house still lived like a happy family and when Saxonian and Bavarian touched beer glasses and swapped yarns in the old little place across the street from the big "double-decker." Conspicuous among the cases of this sort is that of Louisa and her lover, Herr Bunge. In general outline it is the story of Romeo and Juliet over again, but in detail it is not, and one of its curious features is the fact that Prince Henry of Prussia unconsciously played a benevolent and decisive part in the matter, bringing it all to a happy ending without knowing anything about it.

Louisa's father is a sign painter by trade and a man of firm convictions. He is known in the tenement house as Little Michel, to distinguish him from Big Michel, who is built on much larger lines, but who has no convictions. They both hail from Dresden, yet Big Michel says he does not care two straws whether the Dresden picture gallery is the greatest in Germany or not. The case is altogether different for Little Michel. He knows every picture in that gallery as he does his wife, so he says, and the very thought of the Munich gallery being superior to it is enough to make him smoke his big pipe violently. It was over this very question, in fact, that the first serious quarrel between representatives of the two elements broke out about two years ago. Hans, a Bavarian, said he was willing to bet that the Munich gallery was by far the better and the more celebrated of the two. Whereupon Little Michel fell to smoking his pipe with might and main.

"Ah, you don't take up the bet," Hans said with a sneer. "If you were sure of your gallery you wouldn't be so timid about it."

Little Michel removed his pipe, looked daggers at his opponent and then answered:

"It's in America you have picked up this nasty habit of betting. It is not my habit."

"But what has that got to do with picture galleries?"

"Nothing. Neither have you got anything to do with it, seeing that you are only a knife grinder. What does a knife grinder know about the Sistine Madonna?"

"Just as much, or as little, as a sign painter."

This was the way in which the first breach occurred, and it grew and grew until it involved people like Big Michel, who did not care whether the Dresden gallery was the greatest or the smallest on earth.

Louisa was about thirty and in dread of remaining an old maid. She had had suitors before, and in each case the engagement had been broken, directly or indirectly, through her father. Herr Bunge, who was a bachelor of fifty, was passionately in love with her, and she fully returned his feeling. So she was forever trembling lest her father should somehow or other hoodoo this match as he had done many others.

"I am so happy, so happy," she once said to Herr Bunge, whose steel-gray locks were on her broad shoulders. "Only father is so whimsical, you know."

"What of it?" Herr Bunge urged. "I'll stick to you through thick and thin."

"But you don't know him. He is so sensitive, so easy to offend. He may take something into his head and make life miserable to himself and to me."

"But he seems to like me. He is a good old man, your father—true as steel. We are friends, and I don't see why he should go back on me."

"Well, you don't know my father. He has a heart of gold, and his mind is always taken up with the loftiest aims and dreams. But he is not a happy man. He has not always been a sign painter. As you can see from his manners and speech, he was born in a good family. He is a graduate of a classical high school and has spent three years at the university. But he thought he was going to be a great painter, so he gave up his studies at the university and devoted himself to the brush. Well, although he is my father and there isn't a thing I wouldn't do to make him happy, yet I must confess he does not seem to have been right in choosing painting as his vocation. Perhaps if he had taken it up at a much earlier period in his life he would have succeeded. At all events, he was not successful, and the less he succeeded the harder he tried and the more bitter he grew against the world.

"He married my mother when he was still full of glowing hopes. In course of time he had to do something for a living. He tried to give lessons, but that was a precarious occupation. He went from town to town, taking his family with him, but hard luck followed us wherever we turned. He could have earned good money as a sign painter. That, however, was out of the question. He took the very suggestion of it as an insult. Finally, after my mother died and my brother obtained a good position with a relative of ours, my father went to America, where I joined him soon after. Here he was not ashamed to work as a sign painter. He has been at it ever since, and those who don't understand him think he is fully reconciled to his fate. He is not. He is a very unhappy man. He spends most of his time reading on art and artists. Some of his former chums and classmates have become famous, so he reads about their triumphs to spite himself, as it were. He reads and suffers, finding a vicious sort of pleasure in his sufferings."

"But what has that got to do with you and my love for you?" asked the bachelor.

"Ah, well, he's a very peculiar man, my father."

"I don't quite understand you."

A shrug of her shoulders and a wistful smile was all the answer Louisa would make to a question of this sort. She had inherited from her mother a clear insight into human nature, and she understood her father much better than he understood her, but, of course, she could not tell her lover all she knew. The real secret of the situation lay in the fact that Little Michel was afraid of being left alone. He was simply jealous of every man who meant to become his daughter's husband. With all his love for Louisa and his readiness to sacrifice himself for her, he had not strength of character to face a suitor "to the bitter end" without flinching. Outwardly he seemed to be pleased with his lot. He associated with working people, lived with them and even affected their slang, but deep in his heart lay the heavy shadow of the man who looks upon himself as an unrecognized genius.

Louisa understood it all too well, but, strange to say, the better she knew it the keener became her pity for the old man and the greater her forbearance.

"I cannot, I cannot leave him," she had said to Bunge's predecessor. "If I left him he would die of loneliness."

When Little Michel had broken with the man who insisted upon the superiority of the Munchen gallery and then imperceptibly extended the wrangle to other Bavarians, Louisa's feminine intuition told her that it was the beginning of the end. For Herr Bunge was a Bavarian, and sooner or later the feud would reach him.

"Why does he dislike them?" she asked herself. At first the question remained unanswered. One day, however, it dawned on her that it was all because of Herr Bunge.

"My father is very nervous these days," she said to her lover. "He is down upon the world in general, and Bavaria in particular."

"That's all right, my darling girl," the bachelor answered with a knowing twinkle of his kindly blue eye. "I understand what you mean. You needn't be uneasy. He'll never get angry with me. I know how to humor him."

"But he may say harsh things to you."

"Let him. I can stand a lot for my darling baby," and the man with the steel-gray locks was off in an outbreak of German pet names, for which the most complete English dictionary has no equivalents.

Herr Bunge was true to his word. The more the old man ill-treated him the more affection he showed him, yet things went from bad to worse. The very patience and imperturbable devotion of the bachelor irritated Louisa's father. He became more morose and ill-tempered every day and never ceased nagging his daughter for taking up with a man who belonged to the enemy's camp.

"But Herr Bunge does not belong to the other side, father," the spinster pleaded, struggling to keep down her tears.

"He does. He's a hypocrite, that's all he is," the old man replied between puffs. "You're only a woman and a fool. Else you would see through him, as I do. He hates everything Saxonian. He hates the very sight of me. He wants to marry you because you have a few hundred dollars and because—well, because he's an old fogy and nobody else would have him. It takes a big fool like yourself to be in love with him."

"But you used to like him, father. Indeed, it was yourself who introduced him to me."

"That was before I really knew him. He's a hypocrite. He plays the angel, but he's an old devil, and when you're married and he has nothing to fear he will show his cloven foot."

Herr Bunge was forbidden to enter the house, and his meetings with Louisa had to take place in secret. His love seemed to grow all the stronger for being a forbidden fruit.

"Let's be married on the sly and be done with it, dear," he besought her.

"No, dear. I can't walk over my father's corpse to my happiness."

"But he'll give in when he sees it's too late to do anything else. He is a good man and he loves you dearly, Louisa. When you come to ask his pardon with a wedding ring on your finger, he'll burst into tears and embrace me as well as you. I am sure he will."

"Maybe he will, but I haven't the courage to try him."

One day she agreed to the plan, but at the last moment, when they were on their way to the minister who was to perform the ceremony, she suddenly lost heart and returned home.

The old man was aware of this clandestine lovemaking, but never alluded to it. He had become reticent, uncommunicative, morosely philosophical.

"Father has let himself adrift," Louisa once said. "He knows he is wrong, but he doesn't care to own it."

"So you think he'll soon surrender?" asked the eager bachelor.

"You never can tell what a man like father may do."

The affair dragged on. Herr Bunge's courtship became more insistent and ardent every day, but Little Michel was grim and taciturn as ever. There seemed to be no hope for the two lovers.

"I don't care," said the bachelor, with a gesture of despair. "I'll love you as long as I breathe, whether I am allowed to marry you or not."

A week or two after this it was announced in the papers that Prince Henry was coming to this country. From that day on the press was full of accounts of the preparations projected or under way which were calculated to make this nation's welcome to the amiable prince a glorious demonstration of the good feeling which binds the two great countries.

Little Michel became talkative. He spent his evenings reading of the preparations and praising the United States, as well as his native country. He looked twenty years younger. He took much pride in the "hyphen" between his two homes, as he called the friendship between Germany and this country. He could scarcely talk of anything else.

One day he said to Louisa:

"Every German ought to take part in it. On an occasion like this we ought to be all united. I'm glad it is Prince Henry who is coming. He is the best specimen of royal blood we could find. He is a perfect gentleman with the heart of an angel. Let the Americans see who we are." After some hesitation he added: "Every German neighborhood ought to do something to show its joy. The matter ought to be discussed."

"Shall I invite Herr Bunge to the house?" asked Louisa, blushing deeply.

"Yes, by all means, Louisa," answered the old man, coloring as deeply.

The bachelor and his fiancée's father are the best of friends again, and the entire feud which divided the tenement is a thing of history. The matter of Herr Bunge's courtship has not yet been broached, but it is an open secret that the wedding will take place soon after the departure of Prince Henry and that the painter will be present in the church to give away his daughter to the bridegroom.

The café around the corner is still open, only it is visited by Saxonians and Bavarians alike, and as the population of the block has increased through the appearance of two new tenement houses in place of the old stable, there is no lack of customers in either of the two rival establishments.

———

"GET A GIRL, YOUNG MAN!"
July 28, 1902

"One of the peculiar features of the life of our people in New York," said an educated Jewish East Sider, "are the so-called college marriages of the tenements. Scores of our youngest physicians, lawyers, dentists or pharmacists are the products of these alliances which seem to be getting more popular every year. In many instances they result in some of the tragedies or comedies which fill the swift-flowing life of the ghetto, yet their example is lost on our girls.

"The most common form of this arrangement is when a young man who is ambitious to obtain a college education, but is compelled to work for a living, promises to marry a girl who undertakes to support him through college. Usually the young woman is an illiterate sweatshop hand, and, in some cases, the young man is equally ignorant.

"I know a finisher girl who is working fourteen hours a day to support herself and her sweetheart and to pay his preliminary teacher. He was a tailor at home and he can scarcely read and write, but he has taken it into his head that he would make a nice-looking doctor. In this case the college marriage was an afterthought, for the two had been engaged for some time when the idea occurred to him. The scheme pleased the finisher immensely. She only wanted to make sure that her sweetheart was smart enough, and to ascertain this she took him to an elderly man who makes his living by preparing fellows of this class for the Regents' examination.

" 'I'll give you a dollar if you tell me whether Reuben is smart enough to be a doctor,' she said.

"The tutor tried Reuben on reading, spelling and arithmetic, and after some thinking he announced this verdict:

" 'Truth to tell, Reuben is a piece of raw material, but if he were willing to study hard I would undertake to prepare him for the Regents' examinations in less than a year.'

"This took place more than a year ago. Reuben is still taking his preliminary lessons. He has passed successfully in one of the minor subjects on the list, however, so his fiancée is satisfied.

"My grocer is a well-to-do man. His older daughters were all married in Russia, where he was poor. Rachel is his youngest and his pet. As she was brought up in New York, she speaks English better than Yiddish and has not many of the ways of the typical ghetto girl. When her father saw her take up with an American-born young man, he unbosomed himself to me.

" 'I don't like that fellow,' he said with anguish. 'He talks nothing but races and variety shows. I am getting old and weak. There is no telling when I may have to close my eyes, and before I am gone I should like to see Rachel married to a decent man.'

"He told me of a young immigrant, a graduate of a high school somewhere in Galicia, Austria, on whom he had an eye.

" 'He is crazy to continue his studies, the poor fellow,' he said, 'but of course he has no money. He peddles.'

"The long and short of it was that the grocer wanted me to play the part which in the case of Reuben was performed by his present tutor. I answered that passing upon matrimonial candidates was not in my line, but he begged me so hard that I had not the heart to refuse him. I liked the young man. We were afraid that Rachel might object to the match, but to our agreeable surprise she did not. The Austrian is at the City College now.

"One of the saddest cases I have heard of is that of a good honest young Talmudist. He was too weak to work in a sweatshop, and he knew too little of practical life to be a success as a peddler. He was planning to return to his native place when his landlady, a hard-working woman with two daughters, said to him:

" 'I have a better plan. Go to college and study Gentile things until they make a doctor of you. If you give your word of honor you will marry Clara when you are through with it, you won't have to worry about food or clothing or cash. Whatever the Uppermost sends me belongs to my children, and if you are engaged to Clara you will be as good as a son to me.'

"The young man consented, although, as he now assures his friends, not without a certain presentiment that he would some day regret the step. Well, he entered college, and the three women slaved to keep him in good clothes and to pay his bills. One day the old woman declared that he and Clara would have to go before the Mayor to be married. The neighbors were talking too much, she explained, and besides, what guarantee was there that he would not go back on Clara after he was through with his studies? The rabbinical wedding could be held later on, but the civil marriage must take place at once as a guarantee of good faith, she insisted.

"He obeyed. Subsequently he expressed a desire to study philosophy. He had no taste for medicine or law, he said. Of course, neither the old woman nor Clara knew what he meant. All they did know was that he did not care to be a doctor or a lawyer. This made them wild. You see, the family had been boasting right and left that Clara's bridegroom was going to be a doctor, that Clara would occupy a parlor floor and basement on East Broadway—the highest ideal known to women of their class—while here the young man was talking of being something which is connected in one's imagination neither with a large income nor with a parlor floor and basement in East Broadway.

"The former Talmudist is a backboneless, good-natured man. He gave in. Meanwhile the intellectual chasm between him and Clara grew and grew. The 'Gentile things' opened new vistas, a whole new world, to him. Formerly, although learned in the Talmud, he had looked upon his landlady's daughter as his equal. Now her ways and her ignorance were beginning to jar upon his susceptibilities. Little by little he came to consider himself a martyr, to curse the day when he became the victim of self-imposed bondage, and so forth and so on.

"The old woman, who has more common sense than her daughter, was the first to perceive the change in his behavior. The upshot was that all three women were continually nagging the student and throwing it up to him that they were putting up with all sorts of privations and drudgery in order to feed him.

"The young man was in despair. He had not the courage personally to broach the subject of divorce, so he wrote about it to the old woman, although, mind you, the young couple were husband and wife in name only, only in the eye of the law of the land, for they lived apart, and the Mosaic ceremony which alone can unite a man and woman of the Mosaic faith in wedlock, had not yet been performed. Well, Clara's mother only chuckled. She knew he would not have the courage to do anything out of the ordinary.

"The young man is practising medicine now, although his office is not on East Broadway. The Mosaic marriage took place immediately after he received his diploma, and I hear that the young couple are getting along very badly. Sometimes, when there are patients in the office, the old lady appears on the scene and tells the doctor for the benefit of his patrons and the people of the next floor that if it had not been for her and her daughters he would still be peddling shoelaces, and that he is the greatest ingrate in New York.

"When she cools down and her business instinct tells her that scenes of this sort may have an unhealthful effect on her son-in-law's practice, she tries to mend matters by advertising his virtues as a physician. She is forever sounding his praises and twisting medical terms by way of illustrating his erudition. The poor fellow is the personification of wretchedness. A chum of his tells me that he has not his heart in his profession, and has no ambition to work up a practice. He often neglects his patients to read or to play chess, and when the old woman gets wind of it, there is the devil to pay, of course.

"In many instances the young man backs out before he is married either by the Mayor or by a rabbi, and then there is a breach-of-promise suit. Sometimes the young fellow is locked up, and I know of one young law student who got out of jail by promising his girl's brother to marry his fiancée at once. He is a worthless scamp, and the girl, although uneducated, is liked by everybody who knows her. They have been married for some time now.

"He is practising law among the tradesmen of Rivington Street, I think, and he keeps reminding his wife that she is an illiterate sweatshop girl, while he is a college man. That it was her hard work in the sweatshops which paid his way through law school he seems to forget, while she is too timid to put him in mind of it. To his friends he is always complaining of the gulf there is between his wife and himself.

"As a matter of fact, however, there is no such gulf between them. He has plodded through some law books and he has acquired a full command of bad English, but he is not what you would call an intelligent man. He does not read books, anyhow, and his bosom friends are some of the crassest ignoramuses among his clients. One of them cannot sign his name. So you see, the lawyer is not badly in need of intellectual company. Oh, that gulf between himself and his wife is a fake. That's all there is to it.

"Another professional man of the Lower East Side who married on the same plan compelled his wife to study geography after their wedding. 'Bear in mind that your husband is no tailor now,' he would say to her. 'Unless you improve your mind there will be trouble, my dear.' The poor woman, who had never learned to read anything beyond the Hebrew prayerbook and the Yiddish commentary on the Pentateuch, didn't know how to go about the English textbooks which her husband forced into her hands.

"But he was inexorable. He gave her lessons, and the poor thing was so scared by the big words that she would nod assent to everything he said and repeat, parrot-like, his words without knowing what he was talking about. She made pretty poor progress, but he soon became so busy that he had no time to bother with her. Only from time to time it would come back to him that he was a man of refinement and learning with a college diploma on his office wall, and that he was married to a former necktie maker. Gradually he forgot this too.

"He is the most devoted father you ever saw, and in his enthusiasm over his children he has become attached to their mother also. I hear she has a way of bragging of her husband and of the bits of geography she has tried to learn which is quite amusing.

"There are all kinds of combinations and surprises in a vast city within a city like the New York ghetto. A friend of mine knows a couple who were married on the diploma plan, as the institution I have been describing is called by the wits, and in this case the young woman who paid her sweetheart's way through college by working at shirtwaists had so much natural intelligence and ability that she soon helped her fiancé with his studies, and now that he is practising dentistry she is preparing to enter the Women's Medical College. The two get along excellently, and the dentist is forever boasting of the assistance, mental as well as pecuniary, which his wife gave him at college.

"Upon the whole, I should say that these college marriages are about evenly divided between those which turn out well and those in which there is more or less trouble. A man who has been studying this question tells me that the number of happy couples resulting from these matrimonial contracts is on the increase, and after all is said, the institution tends to uplift many a working girl, as well as the young fellows who are helped to a college course in the manner I have referred to.

"There is many an able young man who would be doomed to a life of drudgery and ignorance if it were not for the arrangement by which he is enabled to educate himself, and if he is the proper sort of fellow he will educate his sweetheart also. My friend has paraphrased Horace Greeley's celebrated advice to young men to suit local conditions. His motto is: 'Get a girl, young man.'

"He tells me of many instances in which a diploma marriage has resulted in the moral and intellectual uplifting not only of the two persons immediately concerned, but also of some of their relatives. The sister, for instance, of a young woman who married a physician used to keep company with girls and young fellows of a rather shady character. No sooner had her sister become Mrs. Doctor than she discarded her old companions and began to behave in a manner becoming the sister-in-law of a doctor. In this case the marriage has resulted in perfect happiness.

"The young man has taught his wife to read and to attend lectures, and the general tone of their house has had its effect on several of their relatives who visit them. Among the friends of this doctor are two or three of the well-educated members of his profession, graduates of Russian colleges; so that his wife and her relatives have an opportunity to come into contact with the intellectual cream of the ghetto.

"One of the stories he told me is about a young woman, a cloakmaker, who took a student sweetheart primarily because a fellow townswoman of hers married a physician. One day she met her driving in the buggy in which her husband made his professional calls. The doctor's wife acknowledged her greeting with a majestic bow and drove on. This was more than the cloak finisher could stand. She vowed to herself to marry a doctor and soon found a young man who was looking for this kind of a match and was a handsome fellow into the bargain.

"The curious part of it is that this girl, who is a thin, nervous, super-sensitive creature, took it into her head that her intended husband did not care for her and that he was willing to marry her merely because he considered himself under an obligation to her.

" 'I don't compel you to marry me,' she once said to him. 'I know I am not worthy to be your wife, for you are an educated man, while I am only a factory girl. If I marry you I will be unhappy, anyhow. Something tells me I ought not to go out of my own class for a husband. You can pay me what I have spent on you later on. You are a free man.'

"The point is that the medical man actually loves her. He is a quiet, studious man and her devotion has won his heart. But she has made up her mind that he does not care for her, and the idea of sacrificing herself for his sake, as she calls it, seems to be growing on her. Of course, this does not prevent her from being insanely jealous. My friend is sure she will give in in the end and marry him."

7

NOBLEMEN NO MORE

IN QUEST OF THE GOLDEN GIRL
July 7, 1899

A retired hotelkeeper in this city the other day entertained some friends with stories of aristocratic immigrants in reduced circumstances. The man's establishment was the resort of foreigners from every part of Europe, and counted among its guests representatives of the nobility of about a dozen countries. It was a respectable, but rather humble place, and, of course, the counts or barons were not quite as flush with money as their titles would seem to indicate. Most of them were stranded adventurers. Having got through with their estates by burning their candle at both ends, they had come to the "land of dollars" to better themselves by going into business, or, perhaps, marrying an American heiress.

"As a rule they were sorely disappointed," said the hotel man. "The American heiress who wants to marry a title generally goes to Europe for it. She wants to see her duke or count in the place where he is a duke or a count. As to making money out of business, these noble fellows find it beyond their depth. They are only good for dancing and making monkeys of themselves. When it comes to earning their living they are a pitiful failure."

The retired hotelkeeper then told how one of his noble guests, an insignificant-looking Hungarian, lived at the expense of an elderly watch-maker from Budapest, who had once repaired a clock in the kitchen of the aristocrat's father.

"The watchmaker was tickled to death by his friendship with the little count and beggared himself to keep him in good clothes. But this didn't last

225

long. The nobleman had a weakness for horse races and spent all the mechanic could scrape together on betting. Finally he pawned two watches which he took from his friend's trunk in his absence. It turned out that the watches belonged to some customer of the watchmaker who was employed in a factory in Brooklyn, but who did an occasional private job in his leisure hours at home. The old man was wild, and once his temper broke out he swore at the poor count enough to make up for all the respect he had shown him, and turned him out. The watchmaker soon felt sorry for the titled wretch, and went to look for him, but he never found him.''

Another count, a Pole, whose title had been conferred on his ancestors by the Pope of Rome, was described by the hotelkeeper as a good-natured and handsome man of thirty-five. He was too good-natured, in fact, and that got him into trouble. His parents were never rich, his grandfather having squandered all he had in the world. The count came to America for the express purpose of marrying some rich girl. He was very slow in making the acquaintance of one, however, and meanwhile he had to leave the hotel because he could not pay his bill. He then went to live in a German boarding house. He ran up a big bill, but here he was not molested. The landlady, a widow of forty, as good-natured as the count, but not at all as handsome, fell in love with him. Her attention jarred on the poor aristocrat, and he was dying to move out, but being absolutely penniless he had to stay. She pressed her suit energetically, feeding the nobleman on the best things she could cook and supplying him with good cigars and bad champagne. This the count was too good-natured to decline, and the upshot of it all was a breach-of-promise suit.

"Poor fellow, he was locked up," said the hotel man. "I visited him in jail. It broke my heart to see him behind the iron bars, and he did not take it like a man, either. He was pale and scared to death, the fool, but I told him he had only himself to blame. Still, he wasn't a bad fellow, and so I got some of his people—Poles, I mean—to do something for him. Each of them chipped in a few dollars, and so we made up quite a little sum. But the German woman wouldn't take money. She wanted the count. The poor man was locked up for quite a few days, until finally the boarding-house keeper was put to shame by a stepdaughter of hers, and let him go."

Another nobleman whom the narrator once knew was a middle-aged Rumanian.

"The great misfortune of our family is that our father was a very rich man," he said. "My brothers are in the same fix as I am. We have run through all we had and now we are poor as church mice. I came to this country because nobody knows me here, and because you are all a hard-working, matter-of-fact people. I thought America was just the place for me to be broken to harness. Nobody is ashamed to make a living here, and so I thought I would make myself useful with the rest and live a new life. But I was mistaken. I am too old to begin at the bottom round of the ladder, and everything I have tried has proven beyond me.''

The impression left on the retired hotelkeeper by all these aristocratic immigrants was, upon the whole, rather favorable to them than otherwise. The only nobleman against whom he bears a grudge is a Bavarian to whom he did many a favor in this country, but who snubbed him when the two met in an Austrian summer resort.

"He came to me when he was on his uppers," said the hotel man, indignantly, "and I let him run up a bill as long as from here to Harlem. He paid me, all right. I won't say he didn't. But while he was here he acted as if I was good enough to be his friend. I certainly was good enough to borrow a few dollars of. Well, after I went out of business I went to Europe for the summer. When I struck a certain summer resort, whom should I run up against but my old Bavarian guest. 'Ah, how do you do?' says I, running up to him. 'Sir, you have the advantage of me,' he answered, with a face as hard as a steel rail. I felt like giving him a piece of my mind and asking if he had forgotten the few dollars I'd loaned him. But somehow or other I held my tongue, and the next morning I left the place. I couldn't bear the sight of it.''

CITIZEN OF EUROPE
July 29, 1899

One of the habitués of a certain café in the vicinity of Second Avenue is a tall, bald-headed old man whom the proprietor of the place reverently describes as "the baron whom Lincoln got out of Siberia." He and some of his other customers know the old man well, and they say that his title is centuries old. The baron is a quiet, good-natured and well-educated man. His ancestors who belonged to the nobility in the Baltic provinces emigrated to Russia soon after their birthplace was annexed to the dominion of the Czar. They subsequently settled in the province of Minsk, which is partly Russian and partly Polish, and became part of the local Polish-speaking aristocracy.

The baron who frequents the little café off Second Avenue has a younger brother in this country who is more Americanized than he is. He is a graduate of an American college, is interested in the politics of this country and has held various public offices in several western states.

The two brothers are separated most of the time, often for ten or twelve years together, but they correspond regularly every week and their letters are said to be full of the most tender affection. When the baron looks somewhat low-spirited his friends at the café know that more than a week has passed since he received a letter from his brother. If it were not for that brother of his the old man would have left this country long ago. As will be seen, the gates of his native country have been closed to him since the days of Abraham Lincoln, but he considers himself a citizen of Europe, and next to the Polish-speaking provinces of Russia, France is dearest to his heart. But then, how could he leave his younger brother all alone in the New World? True, the distance between the young brother and himself is usually larger than between New York and Paris. It is all land, however, and the old baron finds comfort in the thought that he and his brother tread upon the same ground.

When he is asked how long he has been in America he smiles in his good-natured, graceful way and says evasively:

"Oh, a very long time. Things have changed greatly since I came here," and then, to turn the conversation from his own antecedents, he goes on to describe New York as he found it and as it is now.

"Talk of the Polish revolt to him," the proprietor of the café whispered to the writer one day. The suggestion was followed, and the baron, warming up, proceeded to describe the stirring days in the early sixties, when the nobility and the representatives of culture in Poland fought for the independence of their country. In the ecstasy of his narrative the old man cast off all restraint and told the writer the history of his own life, including the curious episode in which Abraham Lincoln and Alexander II figure as leading actors.

"I was a young fellow then," he said, "and my brother was a mere boy. Although Germans by descent, we were Poles at heart, and when the movement spread we caught the general contagion. Oh, those were great times! I consider it the happiest period of my life. We would meet in the woods and discuss the various plans of our coming campaign in the firm belief that victory was near at hand. We were all ready to die for the cause at any moment, and were vying with each other to show our devotion and our willingness to sacrifice ourselves. Now that I look back upon it all over the stretch of years, it seems naive and childish. We were a mere handful compared with the Russians, and we had to cope with every difficulty conceivable. Yet in those sweet days, when one's blood was young and danced in one's veins, nothing seemed impossible.

"Well, my brother was the most restless and reckless fellow among the revolutionary youngsters in our province. He was simply bubbling over with revolutionary sentiment. When he saw a Russian policeman or officer it was all he could do to keep himself from making a demonstration of his disloyalty.

"One day there was a conflict between a group of soldiers and some members of a secret organization. My brother, who happened to be nearby, at once lost all control over himself, and exclaiming 'Long live Poland!' he threw himself into the fight. I followed suit, and of course both of us were wounded and arrested. I was in the hospital a long time, and although I recovered sufficiently to be able to make my way to Siberia, where we were subsequently exiled, yet I have never completely regained my former health, and I still suffer from the effects of that wound.

"In Siberia we were as miserable as we could be. There were many Polish noblemen there, in exile for participating in the revolt, like ourselves, but they were all much older than we. The government treated us as harshly as it could, and though our relatives sent us plenty of money we had to stand privation of all kinds. My brother tried to look happy, as if it was the greatest pleasure in the world to suffer for one's ideals, but at the bottom of his heart he was in despair. I could see his misery, try as he would to conceal it. One day when things looked particularly black we were summoned to the local chief of police, who told us that we were to be taken to the capital of the province, where we were to be produced before the governor. My brother and I were sure we were going to be shot or to be transferred to another more distant point, at least. I grew faint with fear, but I bore up. As to my brother, he threw his head back and sneered the chief of police in the face.

"When we were brought into the governor's room my knees trembled. I stood up before him with my arms by my sides, speechless with fear. 'Another hour or two and you will be dead,' I said to myself.

" 'Well, boys,' said he, after sweeping us with his eyes, 'you are to be taken to St. Petersburg. His majesty the emperor wants to see you.'

"In St. Petersburg we were taken before some high official, who examined us on our family connections. He was particularly interested in our elder brother, who had lived in America for many years. We answered all his questions in a straightforward manner. At last he said: 'Well, boys, do you promise to be good and not dabble in foolish things any more?' My brother was going to say something worthy of his revolutionary record, but as good luck would have it he did not, and the official went on: 'Well, if you promise to be good you will be sent to America. President Lincoln of America thinks you will be good boys there, and that's why his majesty has agreed to let you go.'

"We were sent to New York, where our brother came to meet us. It was he who got President Lincoln to intercede for us. The president and the Czar were on terms of friendship at that time, and the matter was settled in a private way through a letter which Lincoln wrote to Alexander II. Our brother, who is now dead, was deep in American politics, and was an intimate friend of Lincoln. He knew the great American president long before he became the ruler of the nation. I don't know whether I ought to be glad to have spent the better part of my life in this strange country, but Lincoln was surely one of the greatest men that ever lived, and I am proud to have been the object of his kindly attentions."

"I AM MY OWN FOOTMAN"
October 30, 1899

There is a Polish count in Brooklyn who hates to be addressed by his noble title. He came to this country many years ago, when he was much younger, and his mind was filled with ideals. Years were added to his age. They seemed to take the place of his dreams. He is a practical old man now. He takes things as they come, lives in the present, lets the future take care of itself, and looks back upon his past as a pretty tale.

"I don't care to be called count," he said, "because I hate meaningless titles. I leave these things to sentimental maidens. When one says 'count' he has a picture in his mind. It is the picture of a dignified man surrounded by footmen and butlers, a man coming out of a majestic old castle to enter a carriage which is to rattle past bowing, awe-stricken peasants, and so forth, and so on. Now, I live in a most prosaic little house in an obscure street, next door to a roaring machine factory. I am my own footman and my own butler, and when I come out of my castle, for which I have got to pay $20 a month to the widow of an Irish politician, it is to walk a few blocks to the trolley car, the only carriage I have ridden in for many a year.

"I came to this country when I was a fool. I had heard of the American republic, of the struggle for the emancipation of the slaves. I yearned to see my own country's independence. My father had died for it in Siberia. The hopes of the Polish revolutionists were shattered. Some of them fled to France. I picked out this country. It was the golden dream of my youth. I pictured the Americans a people of saints, every mother's son ready to die for a noble principle. I was impatient to become one of them, to live under the free, star-spangled sky of freedom and justice. I was anxious to fight for it.

"I came—I came, I saw and was conquered. At first I was so disenchanted, so disgusted with America and myself that I felt like fleeing from both. Later on, as I grew older, I found that my despair was as idiotic as the oversanguine forecast which had preceded it. I came to understand that human nature is human nature, and that although the nation is not made up of angels exclusively, the devils are not without some interest, and that upon the whole America is a pretty good place to live in.

"My first shock came when I saw a candidate for alderman treat a crowd of voters in the courtyard of a corner saloon. I was wild. I pleaded with the man in my broken English; I threatened to denounce him to the police. I harangued him on the sacredness of the ballot box. 'We in Europe are willing to die for a republic like yours,' I said to him: 'Rivers of blood have we shed to gain a particle of the freedom you enjoy, while here you, who have it all, are trampling it in the mire of corruption,' and so forth, and so on. Well, at first the man laughed and threatened to thrash me, and then—guess what he did—'I see you are an honest fellow,' he said. 'Come, let's have a drink.' I was furious.

"I rushed home and began packing my trunk. I must leave this country, I said to myself. Well, somehow I did not go. I saw other places. I went through several campaigns. I saw people who would rather die than vote against their convictions or the traditions that had grown into their hearts. I came to feel that it takes all kinds of people to make a people. I got to like the country for its faults as well as for its virtues.

"There is no use being a boy when one has grey hair on one's head."

———

TZINCHADZI OF THE CATSKILLS

A Story by Abraham Cahan

Atlantic Monthly / August 1901

I was gazing at the mountain slopes across an ear-shaped valley, unable to decide whether they were extremely picturesque or extremely commonplace, when a queer-looking figure on horseback dived out of a wooded spot less than a mile to the right of me. It was a man with a full beard, wearing what in the distance looked like a turban, a cassock, and a sword. He broke into a spirited trot along the main road, but was soon swallowed up by the shaggy gap.

In the insupportable monotony of summer hotel life, the appearance of a cat would have been an event. The odd-looking horseman produced a sensation on the veranda. When the landlord's son arrived with the mail, he solved the riddle.

"He's a Circassian, an' he sells Oriental goods," he said. "He c'n play all kinds o' tricks on horseback, and he makes money hand over fist."

We feverishly hoped he would get around to our "farm," but he was kept busy peddling among the more fashionable cottagers. I learned that he lived with "Pity Pete," an ancient hemlock peeler, whose rickety shanty and stable, once by the side of a busy road, were now ensconced in the bosom of a young forest, and the next Sunday I went to call on him.

I knew the road well, for it led from the boarding house of which I was so weary down to the lively town at the foot of the wooded hill; yet, as I thought of the man whose acquaintance I was going to make, the leafage which was thickening all around me took on a weird look. I had never spoken to a Circassian before, and the whole Caucasus was epitomized in my brain as a group of horsemen like those I used to see galloping after the Czar's carriage. They wore snow-white coats; the sun played on their gold and silver mountings, on the crimson silk of their fur caps, on the gilt lace of their purple shirts. Their horses almost touched the carriage; their heads hung over the Emperor's. It was glorious and it was terrible. As they bounded past, a hollow-voiced, awe-stricken "Hurrah!" lifted itself along either side of the street.

The young maples closed in on me, and the midday glare lapsed into a twilight of greenish gold.

Presently I heard the neigh of a horse. Then a sabre flamed, and a white figure glimmered through the gloom.

"Hay! Choo!" said a voice.

"Good morning," I said, in Russian.

"What? Who's there? Good morning!" came back from behind the trees.

The horse disappeared, and the white figure emerged from the darkness. I introduced myself to a stalwart, pale-faced man with a blond beard. He wore a long white coat, gathered in at the waist by a narrow girdle of leather and Caucasian silver. A white fur cap shaped into a truncated cone, its top covered with red satin and gold lace, was jauntily tilted back on his head. A shirt of cream-colored silk trimmed with gold showed through an opening at the bosom of the cassock, and dangling from the girdle were a dagger and a sabre. The silver tips of what looked like two rows of cartridges glistened at his breast. Things gleamed and sparkled all over him, but there was nothing obtrusively dazzling.

He welcomed me with joyous hospitality, and presently we sat on a fallen tree by the road, chatting of Russia. His Russian was thick with the velvety gutturals of his native tongue, but he spoke it with ease; and he threw himself into the conversation with the eagerness of one loosening his tongue after weeks of enforced silence.

When I asked him if he thought the Catskills pretty, he raised his clear eyes toward the peak looming blue between the trees, and said condescendingly, "They are good."

"Of course they don't come up to your mountains."

He smiled and held out both his index fingers as he said: "A butterfly is pretty, and the sea when sprinkled with sunshine is pretty. These mountains are a butterfly; ours the mighty sea."

He told me his name was David Tzinchadzi, that he was a Georgian nobleman, and that his grandfather once led his tribe against the Russians.

"See this?" he asked, passing his hand over the silver-tipped ornaments at his breast. "They are relics of our glorious past. They are mere sticks of wood, but they represent the powder boxes we used to carry in the mountains. We lost our independence in 1801, yet our horses are fleet, and our steel gleams undimmed. See this metal?" He unsheathed his sabre and cut a swath in the air. "Four hundred rubles, sir! A Georgian who deserves to be a Georgian will rather be without a wife than without a faithful steed and a brave piece of steel." He paused, smiled ruefully, and added, "I had the two comrades, and I reached out for the third."

"What do you mean?" I asked bashfully. "Did you fall in love?"

"Yes, sir. I loved a dark-eyed maiden, and that's why I am now roaming about these strange mountains. You don't mind my talking about it, do you? My heart has been overflowing so long, I need a listener. Have you ever loved a maiden? Have you ever been homesick? Ill luck has inflicted both wounds on me. They are burning me, they are stifling me, they are wringing my heart. Will you hear my tale, sir?"

His speech seemed to me oddly stilted, but, strange to say, I was beginning to feel its effect on my own.

"Even if it takes you three days and three nights," I answered; and he resumed:

"Well, if your eyes ever behold a maiden, and your heart begins to ache, bear in mind a rule: don't— But no, I won't tell it to you just yet. First listen. All I will tell you is that I didn't know that rule myself, or I should not be here, a shadow among mountains that are not mine. Well, it was in my native town where my heart was touched, in a town called Khadziss. Ah, it's a lovely nest, sir! There are mountains there, and they are high and beautiful. Our valleys are deep, immense, filled with the echoes of heaven. Our rivers glisten like a sword and wind like a serpent; they murmur words into the Caucasian's ear; and as he flies along their banks on his dear one they speak to him, and he listens, and he flies and flies, and listens and listens. O Lord, have mercy on a poor Caucasian! Carry me back to Khadziss!'' He dropped his head, in despair; then a dreamy look came into his eyes, and he went on in a whisper:

"And our horses—oh, you can't think how good they are. They are brave, the sweet ones, the best friends we have. Do you know what we say? 'A good steed is better than a bad wife.' But the wife I sought would not be mine.''

"Was she the belle of the town?'' I urged him on.

"Indeed she was—a true Caucasian girl, beautiful as a new sword drawn under a million sunbeams, and she can sit in her saddle like the best of men. Our children, boys and girls alike, say 'Zkhem! Zkhem!' [A horse! A horse!] almost on the same day as they first say 'Mamma!' but I never saw a girl who could ride like Zelaya.

"One evening I saw her ride past the bailiff's office. I signed to her to stop, and she did. 'Tell me to ride to the world's end for you, Zelaya,' said I. She gave me a sad look, and answered: 'I know you are good to me, but what am I to do? Azdeck says his heart, too, is sore, just like yours. Speak to my father. Let him decide. I know you are both good, but I am only a girl, so I am a fool!' That's the way she spoke, and, O Lord!'' He smote his breast, and drew a heavy sigh.

"Did you speak to her father?'' I asked.

"I did, but he said no, the wolf. He's a stern old man, her father. The neighbors say he's wise, but he's as fond of sport as a bad boy. When I asked him why he wouldn't be my father-in-law, he said: 'You talk too much, my lad, and your talk is too fine. Sift it through a sieve, and out of a dozen words one will be to the point. You will make a poor husband, and a worse father.' 'And Azdeck?' I asked, and as I said the word I felt a load in my throat; and even now, as I speak to you, I seem to feel it choking me.''

"And what was his answer?''

"He thought a little, and then he gave a laugh and said: 'Well, Azdeck is as bad as you, and as good. He talks to the point, but he is a fool. Yet a better fellow than you two I don't seem to see around. So run a race and the one who wins will win Zelaya. Is it a go?' 'It is!' I answered. I was sure I could beat Azdeck, so my heart danced in me. Oh, the fool that I was!

"Well, the holidays were drawing nigh, and the great games were to take place on the square in front of the village church. Every fellow was to show his smartest *dzhigits* [feats of horsemanship], and then Azdeck and I were to ride for Zelaya. So I thought to myself: 'Here is my chance. I will learn to ride so that the whole village will make the sign of the cross.' Away into the fields I went; on the mountain tops I hid; in deserted dales I passed my days—riding, riding, riding. Oh, how I labored! I had never trained so hard before, and I invented the cleverest tricks that ever were shown by a Caucasian on his steed. ' 'Tis for you, Zelaya!' I whispered to the wind, and the words gave wisdom to my brain and suppleness to my limbs.

"At last it came, the great day. We rode out—"

"How was the weather?" I could not help interrupting him. At first he started, with an annoyed look, but the next minute he smiled, saying:

"I see you want to know how it all looked, but it's all a blur in my own brain. I do remember that the sky was overcast and a sharp breeze was blowing—yes, and it blew the fire of my veins into a merry blaze. There were trumpeters on the mountain slope nearby, and their blare is still in my blood. The Caucasians were out in their best silks, gold, silver, and steel. I remember I wore a coat of purple, and the man by my side said it seemed to be all aflame. Well, we unsheathed our swords and—but wait."

He suddenly disappeared, and in a minute or two he came back leading his white horse by the bridle. He paused, looked me over with a shamefaced smile, and then, suddenly leaping into his saddle, he said to the horse: *"Tzadzacha! Tzadzacha!"*

His face was set with a look of fury, his brow was contracted, his eyes sparkled, his beard seemed grown in size.

"Tzadzacha! Tzadzacha!" he shrieked, flung himself forward, struck the animal a savage blow, and was off, the skirts of his cassock fluttering and his scabbard and buckles twinkling between the trees. He disappeared down the narrow road, but he soon re-emerged, and hurling himself down from the horse, he hung suspended by his feet as he was borne along and out of sight again. He rode with his feet in the air and his head on his saddle, and he rode facing his horse's tail; he turned somersaults and he jumped over the saddle; and he was about to perform a more complex *dzhigit*, when all at once he reined in the horse and dismounted.

"What's the trouble?" I asked.

"Nothing," he replied morosely. He clearly resented my failure to applaud, and I hastened to mend matters.

"It was wonderful," I said.

But he continued to frown, and after a little he murmured, with the air of an injured child: "Oh, you don't mean it; you needn't praise me if you don't like my riding. I don't ask you to say it's good, do I?"

"But it is. I was so absorbed watching your tricks that I omitted to tell you how I admired them," I assured him.

He brightened up.

"I know your circus riders can do better work," he said, with lingering resentment, "but perhaps if you had seen me ride in the Caucasus you would have liked it better. You mustn't forget that these mountains are not mine, and the beast doesn't know me. Anyway, the Caucasians did think I rode well; and Azdeck, he was so scared at sight of my *dzhigits* that he sat in his saddle like a fool, and never budged. Seeing that, I lashed myself to still hotter work, and flew off in a whirlwind of *dzhigits*. You mightn't have liked it, but the Caucasians, such as they are, were wild with admiration, and—and there is where my great mistake comes in. The Caucasians began to tease Azdeck, to make mock of him, till he dismounted, and with bowed head and weeping he took his beast home."

"And Zelaya?" I asked impatiently.

"What about her? She came forward and said: 'Tzinchadzi, you have won the race. I am yours.' "

"Did she?" I inquired, perplexed.

Tzinchadzi burst into a triumphant laugh.

"You see, sir, although you know much about horsemanship, you don't seem to be very deep in some other kinds of wisdom. I had no trouble in getting you to believe that I won her; yet it was Azdeck who got her, not I, and all because of that accursed victory of mine!

"I tell you what," he continued softly, as he thrust out his two index fingers, and a thoughtful smile animated his queer, bloodless face. "There are many ways of bewitching a maiden, but beware of casting the wrong spell. Whatever else you do, beware of casting the wrong spell! I thought I should kindle her blood with admiration for my victory, but I only kindled it with pity for Azdeck. I shouldn't have let the villagers hoot and jeer at him the way they did. As it was, she walked up to me, pale, gloomy, and said, 'You are without a heart, Tzinchadzi,' and then she sent to tell Azdeck that she was sorry for him, and that she would be his.

He hung his head, and was silent awhile. Then he continued quietly:

"I disappeared again. My horse was the only friend I had. I could not bear to stay near Zelaya, and I bade my friend, my steed, carry me away, away from my misery. Do you know how we speak to our horses? 'Speed, my oak! Run like a lion, tear mountains asunder for me, darling!' we say.

236

'Fly like an eagle, my love! Sweep over sea and waste, over mountain and dale! Can there be an obstacle where the freedom and glory of your master are at stake? Take wing, birdie, take wing!'

"That's what I said to my mount; only I bade him take me away from my love, from the sun of my soul, from my black despair. But how can you realize the beauty and the thunders of our tongue unless you hear its echo in the Caucasian mountains, where the gales, our horses, carry their riders uphill and down? So I flew over mountains, and flying I sobbed. You will say Zelaya's father was right, that I am really a fool. Maybe I am, but I am sure that my horse understood my tears—I am sure he did. Poor darling, where art thou now? Alas, I am torn from thee even as I am from our birthplace!" He gazed up at the sky as he added, under his breath: "I was nine years old when I first mounted a horse and drew a dagger, and they have been my mates ever since. Have you heard of Irakly, our youthful king? He led our people on the Persians when he was a boy of thirteen, and he crushed his enemy into powder. Why? Because his men knew how to make friends of a steed and steel. Well, my friend brought me to Batum, and there the American consul picked me out as a rider for the World's Fair. So you see, although you don't think much of my horsemanship, the American consul did. A man was making up a party of skilled riders, and I was accepted at once. We showed what a Caucasian could do in Chicago. Then the other men went home. I did not. A fellow who came with us brought along a stock of Caucasian goods. He sold some in Chicago, and the rest I bought of him for a low price. He was homesick, like me; only he had a wife and children at home, and I—there was a maiden who would not let me love her.

"A Jew said, 'I tell you what, Tzinchadzi: go to the summer resorts and sell your wares,' and I came here. The Catskills are not much, but they are mountains; so I let them listen to the sighs of my pining heart. The Americans saw me ride, and although you, sir, don't seem to care for my *dzhigits,* they did. They went wild over them, sir. Then I bought a horse, and let them see what a Circassian could do.

"I sell all kinds of goods now. The Americans are kind: they like my horsemanship and buy my trinkets. I make plenty of money, but can it buy me Zelaya? Can it turn the Catskills into the Caucasians? Oh!" He gnashed his teeth, smote the air with his fist, frowned, and compressed his lips.

I saw him often, but I confess his homesick outpourings began to pall on me. The next winter we met once or twice in New York, and then I lost track of him.

237

THE CHASM

Six years passed. Last summer, as I sat on the upper deck of an overcrowded ferryboat, watching the splinters of a shattered bar of sunshine on the water, and listening to the consumptive notes of a negro's fiddle, I felt a hand on my shoulder.

It was Tzinchadzi, but how changed he was! His beard was gone, and instead of his picturesque costume of yore he wore an American suit of blue serge, a light derby, and a starched shirt front with a huge diamond burning in its centre. He had grown fat and ruddy; he glistened with prosperity and prose.

He told me he had changed his name to "Jones," because he had a busy store and owned some real estate, and the Americans found it difficult to pronounce "Tzinchadzi."

"Are you still homesick?" I joked him.

"I wish I were," he answered, without smiling.

"And Zelaya?"

"She married Azdeck. They are happy, but I bear them no grudge."

"Are you married?"

"No, but my heart is cured of Zelaya. I bear her no grudge."

"So you are all right?"

"Yes. America is a fine place. I expect to go home for a visit, but I won't stay there. A friend of mine went home, but he soon came back. He was homesick for America."

I inquired about his business and his associations, and he answered my questions in a quiet, sober, rather nerveless way, in which I vainly sought to recognize my companion of the Catskills; but suddenly he interrupted himself.

"Shall I tell you the real truth?" he asked, with his old-time vehemence. "I have money and I have friends, but you want to know whether I am happy; and that I am not, sir. Why? Because I yearn neither for my country nor for Zelaya, nor for anything else. I have thought it all out, and I have come to the conclusion that a man's heart cannot be happy unless it has somebody or something to yearn for. Do you remember how sore my soul was while we were in the Catskills? Well, there was a wound in me at that time, and the wound rankled with bitters mixed with sweets. Yes, sir. My heart ached, but its pain was pleasure, whereas now—alas! The pain is gone, and with it my happiness. I have nothing, nothing! O Zelaya, where are the twinges your name used to give me when I roamed around in the mountains that were not mine? Sweet twinges, where are you? Well, sir, I have thought about it often. It amounts to this: I do enjoy life; only I am yearning for—what shall I call it?"

"For your old yearnings," I was tempted to prompt him; but as I looked at his half-shut eyes and rapt face, my phrase-making ambitions seemed so small, so far beneath the mood for which he was vainly seeking a formula, that I remained silent.

"I can't tell you what I feel," he finally said. "Maybe if I could I shouldn't feel it, and there would be nothing to tell, so that the telling of it would be a lie. I have plenty of money; but if you want to think of a happy man, think of Tzinchadzi of the Catskills, not of Jones of New York."

"MEAN ENOUGH TO EARN HIS LIVING"
December 21, 1901

The long, narrow room of the café was rapidly filling up, and many of the newcomers cast envious glances at a certain very comfortable seat in a snug corner, but a tipped chair silently warned them that the place had been preempted.

"It belongs to an old customer of mine," the proprietor explained apologetically to a man who was not an old customer. "He's a baron, in fact—a genuine German baron. Only it would go hard with me if he got wind of it."

"Got wind of what?"

"Of the fact that I told you he was a baron," whispered the shrewd proprietor, looking around to make sure there were no eavesdroppers around.

"Does he live here incognito?"

"Not exactly incognito. Lots of people know who he is. Only he won't have anybody address him as baron or refer to his title in any other way."

When the stranger expressed the opinion that the baron must be either cranky or the central figure of some story, the proprietor answered sagely:

"No, he is no crank. As to there being some story back of it, there is one—a love story, in fact, but that was not the reason he discarded his title. It was rather the result of it."

All this the proprietor tells every new customer. In fact, he makes an advertisement of his nobleman. All he says of him is true, but the object of these whispered confidences with strangers is to pique their curiosity. The rest is done by the baron himself, without knowing it.

It was a little after 7 o'clock when there entered a tall, middle-aged man with dark, short-sighted eyes, and, quietly marching up to the tipped chair, he stood it erect and sat down. It was the baron. There was nothing to distinguish him from the other customers. The place is frequented by Second Avenue merchants, musicians, German literati, and there is no lack of intelligent and refined faces there. Nevertheless the stranger could not take his eyes off the nobleman. He ordered a glass of wine, and on the pretense of sipping it he went on gazing at the near-sighted man in the snug corner and wondering why he had abandoned his title, what sort of story the proprietor had alluded to, and what connection there was between the story and the man's determination to bury his past.

The proprietor of the little café offered to introduce him to the former baron.

"He is a very pleasant man to talk to," he said, "and if he happens to be in the right mood he may tell you his story. Not at once, of course."

Half an hour later the nobleman and the new customer sat chatting as informally as if they had been acquainted for years. It was evident that the stranger had produced a favorable impression on the baron, and being of a very talkative turn, the latter was glad of his company.

"I know almost everybody in this place," he said, "and many of the people who frequent it are really nice fellows, but I have had so many talks with each of them there is hardly left anything to say. A chap of my type, one who is fond of babbling," he went on with a smile which accentuated the intellectual cast of his features, "a fellow who has a tongue that is itching for work, don't you know, is glad of an opportunity to tell an old story so as to make it sound new. This could not be done with those who have heard it from you fifty times before, so when one gets hold of a brand-new listener it is a godsend."

One of the first things the baron told his new friend was that he was an agent for a piano firm, and that business was better this year than it had ever been before. He dwelt on some details of his business, in his humorous way, and finally led up to the subject of the differences between Germany and the United States. He spoke with spirit and humor, like one who had given the matter considerable thought.

"My heart is still in Germany, but my head is here," he said, with a smile. "Everyone is attached to his birthplace. That's as natural as the love of children for their mother, but my brain prefers this country. The Americans know how to run this world, and they will soon run the whole of it, too. If I owned the globe I would farm it out to Uncle Sam to begin with; he would make it revolve quicker around its axis. He would find its present way of swinging around too slow. Then he might invent something which would do away with night altogether. There are lots of things which a Yankee could do. But, joking aside, the Americans are not merely a nation. They are a revelation. Columbus discovered America, and now the Americans are discovering the real way to live in this world. If we only understood them! There is a lesson in the life of the average American, a lesson which we Europeans ought to study with might and main. The point is that we of the Old World are a lot of milksops, ninnies, boobies, muffs. We don't know what to do with ourselves, while the Americans, they not only know what to do with themselves, but they have a knack of finding something to do for some of the most shiftless good-for-nothings in Europe.''

The stranger was in a quiver of expectation. The baron seemed to be on the very verge of his personal story. To the former's bitter disappointment he suddenly checked himself, switching the conversation to the subject of Italian opera.

The new customer called again and again, and an intimate friendship sprang up between him and the nobleman.

At last one evening, in a burst of confidence, the baron said:

''I see you are a man of discretion. You certainly know who I am. I can see that by your eyes. Yet you never asked me a question about myself. This is more than the people around here could boast of. They are very inquisitive.''

''Well, I admit I know something of your antecedents, but I don't think it amounts to anything,'' answered the other. ''I confess I am curious to know some more. There must be something interesting in your past life.''

''Nothing much. It is here in America where the interesting part of my life lies. At home I was as uninteresting and useless a booby as many another fellow of my class. I was strong and healthy, yet I could not make my living.

''It is the old story, in fact,'' he continued gravely. ''The family estate went to pieces and there was nothing to live on. There were a thousand and one different things I could have done to earn a living, but the idea of Baron So-and-So earning his livelihood! It would have broken my mother's heart, and my sister, who was engaged to marry a count, said it would ruin her chances with her lover if he got wind of the fact that her brother was mean enough to earn his living. You may laugh, but this is the point of view of the people of my class all over the Old World—'the out-of-date world,' it should be called. There are lots of ruined barons, dukes, counts and what-not who will rather starve than work and bring disgrace upon their name by earning their own dinner.

''Well, I came here. Nobody knew me and I knew nobody, so I was not ashamed to look for work—I had to, in fact. The first few dollars I made, well, they were not exactly sweet, for habit is second nature after all, and, while I was proud of my achievement, yet I could not help feeling ashamed of myself for doing something which none of my ancestors had ever done. I felt as if some of them might come to me in my sleep and remonstrate with me for desecrating their name. But that's all nonsense. The feeling soon wore off. It is really sweet to make money with your own hands or brain. What is more, when I sent $25 to an impecunious baron in Germany—a relative of mine—he accepted it with thanks without saying anything as to my having earned the money by my own work.

"I discarded my title because I can't afford to keep it. As a common mortal I am in comfortable circumstances. As a baron, however, I would be a miserable wretch. So I prefer to be a well-to-do common mortal. Perhaps, if I could afford to put up in the Waldorf-Astoria and to get into society I might be tempted to show my old colors, but this I cannot afford. And, to tell you the truth, I am perfectly happy as I am. I have been in this country now over six years. I am used to this city and I have made a number of new friends here. I live the life of an intelligent member of the lower middle class, but I find more pleasure in it than I ever derived from my exalted position at home. That exalted position was a torture to me, in fact. Imagine a man on the peak of a barren mountain. He is high up, he is in an exalted position, but he has nothing to eat. Now, I am way below, but there is life on this lowland— fertile meadows and murmuring brooks. The long and the short of it is, 'I can't kick,' as the Americans put it.

"And do you know, my friend, that there are scores of *declassé* people like myself in this country? I meet some of them quite often, and the funniest part of it is that we are trying to conceal our antecedents from one another. There are lots of titled wretches in Europe, and the best thing they could do would be to come to this country and learn to make a living. To be sure, there are all kinds of charlatans and adventurers who come in search of heiresses, or who pretend to have relics to sell, but I am speaking of the honest, self-respecting people with big, crushing burdens in the form of ancestral titles to make life miserable to them. A baron without money is the worst kind of hunchback the world ever saw. His title is his hump, and he has got to carry it wherever he goes. America is the only place in the world where such hunchbacks are cured. Why, look at me. Isn't my back all straight now? Of course it is, for I have thrown off my useless hump and live as a plain citizen.

"There was a woman in the case, of course, but she came in after I had shed my hump. It's a sad story, and I am not very fond of telling it. It was right here in this very café where I met her. She was not very pretty, but full of grace. It was not the grace of high life, the kind I had been used to. It was a housewifely, bourgeois sort of charm, in keeping with my new life. She came here with her father, an elderly widower. When we got to talking it turned out that they were from a town a few miles from my birthplace. I visited them at their humble home on Fifth Street, and when the old man was sick I used to sit at his bedside, reading to him and helping the girl to take care of him. He died, poor fellow.

"It was during the sad days that followed his death that I came to the conclusion I could not live without her. I had never fallen in love before, and this humble German girl I loved with every fibre of my being. I tell you, friend, there is nothing like a first passionate infatuation as an elevating, ennobling influence. I was in a sort of a trance all the time."

"And the girl?" asked the listener.

"Well, somebody has said that in love only one of the two participants does the actual loving, the other merely letting himself or herself be loved. I don't think that was the case with us two. If ever a woman was in love with a man that sweet girl was with me. I could see it in her eyes, in her voice, in everything she said or did. We were a sort of religion to each other. But our happiness was not destined to last long.

"She had an aunt at home, so she wrote her all about it. Now, that aunt, like most aunts, was a very foolish woman. In addition, she was a great braggart, so that she went around boasting of the great fact that she was going to be related by marriage to Baroness So-and-So, my mother. When it reached my old mother, she took it to heart so close she wrote me a letter full of tears, asking me to choose between her and the working girl. In other words, she threatened suicide. As a matter of fact, I attached very little importance to it all. There is not a woman in the world but has threatened suicide some time or other. One can't afford to take such things seriously. But in my passion for babbling I once blurted the whole thing out to the girl, and this was the end of it. I tell you, a woman is a sealed book. No matter how well you know her she is full of surprises for you. My girl turned out to be the most sensitive, unreasonable and stiff-necked woman I ever saw.

" 'If your mother thinks I am not good enough to be your wife I am not going to force myself into the family,' she said, and declared our engagement off.

"I pleaded, I reasoned, I argued, but all in vain. I knew how much pain it cost her. I knew of her sleepless nights. She would not give in, however."

"Well?" asked the listener.

"That's all," answered the baron sheepishly. "There was another fellow who had been in love with her for years. She did not care for him, but she hastened to marry him—to burn her bridges, as it were. She was a peculiar girl," he concluded in a whisper.

THE BAKE SHOP COUNT
February 8, 1902

The richest man in a certain locality on the Upper East Side is an elderly German to whom his old acquaintances sometimes refer as Count Long-or-Round. He never was a count nor pretended to be one, and the name dates far back to a period when he was neither a rich man nor lived on the Upper East Side. He was a poor, struggling, love-lorn, homesick immigrant then, and the story of how he won his fortune and his wife and lost his love for the old fatherland is often told by those who came to America together with him.

He landed in the seventies, a man of thirty, with beautiful Teutonic locks, but rather ungainly, awkward of figure and anything but magnetic of face. His features were regular and symmetrically arranged, in fact, and when he smiled his looks would change very much for the better, but then, he smiled very seldom. He was a morose, reticent man. People who knew him but superficially invariably set him down for a hard-hearted man. This, however, was a mistake. He was one of those exceptional cases in which a sulky misanthropic exterior hides a heart full of feeling.

He was very slow to make friends, but those who succeeded in winning his heart saw such a novel aspect of the man that it seemed as if they had never seen him before. He left his old home because the girl he loved would not have him. She did not care for him, and because she did not he was unable to bend in her presence, to show her that, although he looked an iceberg, he had a soul capable of the warmest affection, of the deepest and most steadfast devotion. During his first year in New York, when he was undergoing all sorts of privations and pining away with his passion for the girl at home, he once laid his heart bare to a fellow lodger, the only intimate friend he had here at the time.

"I don't know how to account for it, but whenever I found myself in her presence I used to contract my forehead and look daggers at everybody in sight. I suppose it was bashfulness. Anyhow, try as I would, I could never get myself to look the way I felt. There was sunshine in my heart and a heavy cloud on my face. That morose look of mine has been the great curse of my life. I have inherited it from an uncle, my mother's brother, and he was not a bad fellow by any means. Sometimes I go up to the looking glass and stand staring at my own face, trying to discover the cause of it all. But of course I never detect anything. I try to smile, just in order to see the effect of it, but you can't smile to order, you know. So I finally get away from the glass, disgusted, with my heart yearning worse than ever.''

He made very few friends here, and his homesickness seemed to be getting more acute every day. To kill time and to keep himself from thinking of his home and his girl he took to scheming. He had an observant eye and a clear, active mind. He lived downtown then, in what used to be the heart of the German quarter. One day he overheard a conversation between two men who were singing the praises of a certain kind of bread they used to eat at home in a German-speaking town in Bohemia. They referred to the bread by a special name, which the love-stricken German had never heard before. On another occasion, while he stood in a bakery waiting to be waited on, a woman came in asking for the same sort of bread. The woman behind the counter shook her head. She had never heard that word.

The German with the beautiful locks put two and two together, and went on with his observations. The result was that he discovered a whole block where most of the tenants were from the Bohemian province in which the bread in question was baked. "If I could get a good baker from that place and the two of us opened a bake shop in this neighborhood we might be kept busy.'' This is the way he reasoned, and without taking any of his two or three friends into his secret he began to look for the desired man. He proved hard to find. Indeed, if there had been such a baker in New York at the time he would have begun to bake the bread referred to on his own hook. The morose-looking German did not give up his search. One day he made the acquaintance of a Bohemian, who proved to be quite a garrulous fellow and was glad of every opportunity to talk of his old home. The morose man became an appreciative and ardent listener. He hung upon every word the Bohemian said and made a mental note of everything he said that might be of some use in the realization of his scheme.

As ill luck would have it this Bohemian came from a town in which the bread the German had in mind was unknown. Still he talked of other towns and all sorts of people and by a chain of inductions the grim-looking German discovered the name and address of a well-known baker in a town where the bread that had become the ideal of his life was much in vogue. The next thing he did was to find out the name of one of the baker's apprentices. Meanwhile he worked day and night at odds and ends of jobs, living on $2 a week and saving the rest of his earnings. Finally he sent the baker's apprentice a letter offering him a good position and his travelling expenses if he agreed to come to New York.

The apprentice baker came and the shop was opened. It was a one-horse affair at first, and the worst part of it was that the imported baker was not quite up to the standard. But so thrilled were the housewives of the neighborhood when they tasted the new bread that they overwhelmed the baker with all sorts of suggestions, some of which he adopted. The bread kept improving and growing in popularity. People came all the way from Brooklyn for it.

It was during this period that the German who attended to the store while the baker attended to the baking end of the business was dubbed Count Long-or-Round. His moroseness struck some of the girls as if he was "stuck up," setting up for a nobleman, while the peculiar way in which he would ask a customer whether she wanted a long loaf or a round one became the subject of all sorts of jokes and anecdotes among the boys of the block.

When he thought he had money enough to make an impression on his old love he wrote to her. She wrote back to him to tell him that since he left home she had rejected four suitors because she did not care for them, but that she did not care for him either. "But," she added, "my sisters are growing, and one of them ought to be married by this time, and would, perhaps, if poverty and I did not stand in the way. I hate myself for being the cause of trouble to others and to myself. So if you are willing to let me come to New York on a certain condition, I will. This condition is that you shall let me stay in your city until I have made up my mind whether I shall marry you or not."

He agreed to the plan, and she came. The rest of the story is best told by her humorous relative, an old Bavarian with whom she boarded here until she was married to "the man with the gloomy face and sunny locks," as he used to call him those days.

"It was quite a complicated affair, but money and conscience overcame all obstacles," the Bavarian said, telling the story for the thousandth time. "The girl actually did not care for the gloomy face, no matter what a forest of golden locks there was to apologize for it. But then, Count Long-or-Round was not the timid fellow he used to be. They say 'money talks,' but it smiles, too. Yes, money can do everything; it can smile and laugh and giggle, and, what is more, it can make you giggle, too.

"Well, the rising baker called on my niece (that's what I called her, although she is a more distant relative than that) very often. He used to come in his best clothes, and, instead of looking morose, he would talk gaily on all sorts of nonsense with that air of confidence and authority which an immigrant is sure to adopt when things go well with him. To look at him and to hear him talk those days one would have imagined him to be the president of some big railroad. Now, nothing succeeds with a girl like a manner of this sort. My niece was beginning to feel interested in the baker, and everything

246

looked quite promising, when, lo and behold! another fellow—a really handsome and dashing chap—loomed up on the horizon. He had been an officer in the German army, and was lionized by a certain set of people with whom my niece became acquainted. Before I realized it my niece was in love with the officer—in love like a kitten.

"Meanwhile the baker was making important changes in his business, and was too absorbed in his new ventures to look after the business of his heart. He was as deeply in love as ever, but he called on the girl only once a week. He bought a piece of real estate and became interested in a certain line of imports. He was successful in everything he touched. His face was still gloomy, but now that people knew of his prosperity they did not call it 'sulky,' as they used to, but 'preoccupied,' 'absorbed,' 'absent-minded.'

"My niece grew thin and haggard. Love is quite a dangerous thing to play with, you know. It gnaws at one's heart, as the novelists put it, but this is not the worst part of it. Suppose it does eat a girl's heart out. So long as her cheeks remain plump nobody is any the wiser for it. The real trouble with love is that sooner or later it begins to nibble at the face. At least that was the way it handled my poor niece. She thought she could have the officer without any difficulty. He was paying all sorts of attentions, and she thought he was paving the way to that great hour which girls think the sole object of life. In short, she was expecting a declaration. At the same time she was torn with qualms of compunction with regard to her rich suitor.

"It was about this time that I became aware of the state of affairs. I had a talk with my niece. She made a clean breast of it. I told her she was making a fool of herself; that she was going to throw away one of the best chances that could come in a girl's way, and that the fellow she was in love with was a liar and an all-round good-for-nothing. Of course, she flew into a passion and threatened to move out of my house, but my words were not altogether lost upon her.

"There was something about the former officer which made me suspicious of his antecedents. He seemed to be concealing something. Besides, the fact that he seemed to be in love with my niece and yet was in no hurry to propose was in itself enough to make one ask all sorts of questions. I began to investigate him, and my labors were soon crowned with success. The fellow was a married man!

"When I broke the news to my niece she fainted. I told her to marry the baker, or rather, the importer, for his old business was rapidly sliding into the background, and was attended to by hired salesgirls. She shook her head. 'I don't love him,' she said. 'Besides, if he knew that I cared for another man he would not want me, and I am not going to deceive him.'

"Two years more passed. The man who had made a success of the bake shop was getting richer every day. One afternoon he said to my niece, in the most businesslike manner: 'Well, will you marry me? I want to have a final answer, you know. You see, I have a large business to attend to and I need a wife to sweeten my life and also to help me look after my affairs.' My niece told him of her love for the officer. 'Have you got over it?' the importer asked. 'Yes, completely,' was her answer. 'And will you marry me?' She blushed as she replied, 'If you will have me. I will try to make you a good wife. But I want you to understand that I am not in love with you.' 'You don't hate me, though, do you?' 'Hate you? I never did.' 'Well, then, it's all right. When you are my wife you will be too busy about all sorts of important matters to think of such nonsense as love.'

"And his words came true. She went into his affairs heart and soul, and was soon in love with him as well as with his business. They have been a happy couple. They are very wealthy now, and the first nucleus of their fortune was made in that little bake shop where he became known as Count Long-or-Round."

8
LIVING IN THE PUBLIC EYE

"ACH WIE SCHOEN":
A TENEMENT HOUSE EMPRESS
November 13, 1897

"Zu dir ist mein liebster Gang, mein liebster Gang, mein liebster Gang!"

When the inmates of the tenement house of which Mrs. Gericke is in charge hear the song they know that their fat, chuckling housekeeper is scrubbing the staircase. She has a special tune for each kind of work, and this is her scrubbing song. *"Zu dir ist mein liebster Gang, mein liebster Gang, mein liebster Gang!"* she goes on, her soap and brush keeping time to her cheery notes and deriving zest from them. Her massive arms are bare and her blond hair is encased in a red bandanna.

"Good morning, Mrs. Gericke!" she is presently interrupted by a young Irishwoman hugging a tin basin full of garbage to her bosom.

"Gut morgen, gut morgen!" Mrs. Gericke returns, raising a beaming face from her brush.

"Who will be next—Mrs. Brandt or Mrs. Levy or Mrs. Mullbauer?" she tries to guess as she resumes her work and her song with redoubled gusto.

"Gut morgen, Mrs. Gericke!" says the husky bass of a dumpy woman with a package of waste paper under her arm and an ash pail in her hand. "Are the barrels out?"

"Gut morgen, gut morgen! yes, ma'am!"

Next comes Mrs. Levy. Her load consists of all three classes of refuse, separated according to the ukase of the Street Cleaning Department, and a milk pitcher and a kerosene can in the bargain.

"Ah, *guten morgen,* Mrs. Gericke!"

"Gut morgen, gut morgen!"

Mrs. Gericke has finished her task, but she is in no hurry. The morning procession has only started: there are thirteen other housewives to pass in review, that they may have a chance to pay their homage and receive her acknowledgment. *"Zu dir ist mein liebster Gang, mein liebster Gang, mein liebster Gang!"* she sings merrily on, plying her brush on a step of the staircase which is as clean as her table, when hark! footfalls make themselves heard on the second floor. By their sound she knows them to belong to Mrs. Barna, the Hungarian woman of the "right-hand side, back" and her florid, fleshy countenance becomes overcast. The Hungarian comes down with her garbage done up in three neat parcels, as if intended for a present. The housekeeper raises her head, but there is no salutation. Their eyes meet, "sparring for an opening" for a while, but neither of them will be the first to utter the word of greeting, and the proud Hungarian stalks silently out into the street.

The housekeeper is gasping with resentment. "I knew the nasty thing would not. I just felt it," she torments herself inwardly, while her brush moves reluctantly and her subdued voice hums sadly: *"Zu dir ist mein liebster Gang, mein liebster Gang!"*

An hour or two later Mrs. Gericke is again wreathed in smiles. She is regaling two of her loyal subjects with her complex breakfast of coffee, rolls, butter, cheese, steak and half a dozen sorts of sausages and bolognas. Her ruling passion is to eat and to see others eat. She has not bought a new dress or bonnet for years, but she does not feel any need in that direction, and nearly the whole of her husband's wages and of her own earnings as a washerwoman is spent at the grocer's, butcher's and the delicatessen dealer's. Her greatest ambition, outside of her love of power, is to have her large dining table look like the counter of the delicatessen store around the corner.

"Help yourself to some more leberwurst, Mrs. Mullbauer! And why don't you taste the ham?" she fairly screams at Mrs. Schroeter. "Do eat and tell me if it is not the best ham around First Avenue," she insists, with glowing cheeks and sparkling eyes.

"Yes, it is delicious!" assents Mrs. Schroeter. "You get your ham at the old man's, next block, don't you?" And the congenial company launches out, drawing parallels between the old man of next block and his competitors, between German and American ham, vinegar pickles and salt ones, wiener schnitzels and veal cutlets, and so on and so forth, until the hostess, remembering, by an inscrutable association of ideas, the unruly tenant of the second floor, suddenly lays down her knife and fork to slap her hands together and to roll up her eyes, as if in prayer, and exclaims:

"What do you think of the airs Mrs. Barna is giving herself?"

"Yes, she is awful stuck up," assents Mrs. Mullbauer, melodramatically.

"I never cared for her," chimes in Mrs. Schroeter, mumbling her words through a mouthful of delicatessen.

"She feeds her family on soup and goulash, and spends every cent on dress, the supercilious coquette that she is! She feeds her family on soup and goulash," repeats Mrs. Gericke, bursting into a ringing chuckle. "Before I got married I served in some of the toniest houses on Second Avenue, and I tell you I never saw a missus to be as puffed up as that miserable creature who lives on soup and goulash, ha-ha-ha!"

"On soup and goulash, ha-ha-ha!" the other two echo, appreciatively.

Next to things gastronomical Mrs. Gericke's favorite topic of conversation are ante-nuptial glories as a domestic, although even Mrs. Schroeter and Mrs. Mullbauer sometimes speak of her, confidentially, as "the housemaid," with rather a disparaging smile.

To tell the truth, these two ladies are rather unfair to the satrap of their tenement house, for besides her never-failing hospitality, she is ever ready to come to the rescue in time of need and to intercede in their behalf with the landlord when their husbands are out of work. All Mrs. Gericke exacts is allegiance to her sceptre, and when this is yielded, a more generous rule few monarchies ever saw. But then woe be to the rebel in her little kingdom!

"Mrs. Barna!" she flames out at the first opportunity that offers itself. "I see you have put your ash bundle into the barrel without taking away the paper. That won't do; that won't do. If you can't remember that paper belongs in the paper bag in the cellar, I shall have to report you to the landlord. You don't expect me to sort your rubbish for you."

"Excuse me," replies Mrs. Barna, without a hint of a smile, and her surly answer only pours oil on the fire.

"Mrs. Barna, you must have forgotten it is your turn to scrub the hallway floor!" thunders the vengeful commandress, fiercely knocking at the door of the refractory tenant.

"All right," the latter returns, testily, and struggling to keep herself from remarking that the other women are even less prompt in fulfillment of their duties, and yet they are treated with much greater leniency.

"Mrs. Barna, the new neighbors on the floor below complain of your chopping wood on your floor. That will have to be stopped"; or, "Mrs. Barna, you will have to teach your boy to shut the hall door when he comes in or out"; or, again, "Mrs. Barna, your company was too noisy last night. Nobody could get a wink of sleep in the house."

When the first of the month arrives it is the disloyal subject who is first visited for rent, while the others get a day or two of grace.

One day Mrs. Barna went to borrow a fan of Mrs. Schroeter. The German woman is usually quite neighborly, and never refuses her a loan. This time, however, she was compelled to disoblige the Hungarian, to please the housekeeper, who happened to be present. It was the fifth of the month and Mrs. Schroeter had not yet paid her rent, and to antagonize Mrs. Gericke would have involved some danger.

Mrs. Gericke's door is always open to her subjects, and it is one of the unwritten laws of her dominion that whatever one of them buys in the way of millinery or dress goods or some contribution to the household establishment, it must be submitted to her judgment. As a rule some other good subjects are then invited into the housekeeper's apartments to form a cabinet council or jury. The verdict is usually, *"Ach wie schoen!"* (Oh, how pretty!) and the event is generally celebrated with cups of coffee and some of Mrs. Gericke's delicatessen.

Needless to say that Mrs. Barna never submits her new bonnets to the housekeeper's criticism, and this is another source of chagrin to the latter.

Upon the whole, the Hungarian feels quite isolated and boycotted, and were it not for the fact that her rooms are all lit and the rent reasonable, she would have emigrated from Mrs. Gericke's kingdom long ago. But, then again, would she, with her independent spirit, fare better in another tenement house?

Mrs. Schroeter thinks not. "One must always be on the right side of one's housekeeper," she observes, philosophically.

————

"ONLY $7 AND TODAY IS THE 25TH"
December 18, 1897

It was the first day of the month when a young German woman with a huge parcel under her arm came stealthily out of a poor uptown tenement house. She paused on the stoop to look around, and seeing no one of her acquaintance, she hurriedly made her way to the next corner, and with another hasty glance backward she turned into the avenue. Presently, when a few blocks away from her starting point and in front of a pawnshop, she once more stopped to take her bearings; but this time her gaze was divided between the passersby and the large glass door emblazoned with three golden balls. At that moment her eye fell upon a corpulent German woman, and blushing to the roots of her hair, she suddenly resumed her course, pressing the package to her side as though in a vain attempt to conceal it from view. The next instant she brightened up with an apparent flash of inspiration, and greeting the older woman with effusive cordiality, she said:

"Don't you know of a good laundry? I want to have some blankets washed, and I hate to give them to the Chinaman on our block. He charges too much, and ruins the stuff into the bargain."

"Right there, on the other side of the street, is a German laundry—near the barber shop." But as the stout woman said this her voice, manner and the look in her good-natured, clever eyes seemed to remark: "I am up to your innocent little farce, poor thing; but I am glad to help you out of your embarrassment."

The young housewife at once proceeded to the indicated place, the other following her for some moments with sympathetic curiosity. Then the portly matron retraced the younger woman's steps, and reaching the door from which her friend had issued forth with her parcel, she disappeared in the dingy hallway.

A little later she whispered to her next-door neighbor: "Mrs. So-and-So must again be hard up for her rent. I saw her in front of a pawnshop with a big parcel. Poor thing, she got as red as fire when she noticed me. She said it was some blankets she wanted washed."

"Yes, her husband lost his job yesterday, she told me," the next-door neighbor observed sadly.

"Did he? I am very sorry for them. They are nice people, are they not? Only they somehow don't know how to manage. Even when he has a job, they are always short. He does not drink, nor play cards, and she does not spend much on dresses or anything like that, and they have no children, and yet they are always dead broke. Last month she came in to ask me if I could not change a five-dollar bill for her," the stout old woman went on with a smile. "It was rent day, and as she held out the bill there were two other fives in her hand. " 'I was waiting for the agent to come and give me change, she said, but it is late and I must go to the butcher.' Of course, it was a bluff. Could she not give the five dollars to the butcher and get change from him? She only wanted to show off that she was flush and had her rent, poor child."

"I think it was not that," the woman of next door retorted, with an arch smile. "She must have been afraid to give the butcher the five dollars, because she owed him some money, and he might ask for it."

As to the two gossips themselves, they paid their rent and their butcher bills regularly and without trouble. Their husbands and their grown children work steadily, and after deducting a small sum for pocket money, each turns over his wages to the mistress of the house. The result is a regular income, which suffices to cover all the expenses that the two families are accustomed to incur and to leave a small surplus for a rainy day. Not so with the young couple who were the object of their good-natured criticism. In their case there is only one man to earn the family's living, and as his work is very unsteady and his wages when he does work are so small that their rent takes nearly half of their monthly income, no amount of pinching and scrimping can save the youthful housekeeper from an occasional visit to the pawnshops and from the little ruses which her neighbors see through.

Their rent is $12, and a week or so after they have paid it they usually begin to save for the next month. When the agent's receipt is safe in the young woman's bureau, the next payment seems so far away in the vague future that she cannot help spending, by way of a few days' respite, the whole of the first week's wages. The money is generally and by mutual consent kept by the husband, his wife dreading the temptation of buying something beyond their means.

"How much have you got?" she often asks, when the first of the next month is drawing near. With which she thrusts her hand into his bosom pocket, and producing the bills, she proceeds to count.

"Only seven dollars, and today is the 25th. What's to be done?"

"Well, we have another week in which to bother our heads about the balance," he replies, with some annoyance.

On the following Saturday she blushes crimson as she informs her grocer that she will pay him next week, and if she has the ill fortune to find him out of mood, as a grocer is apt to be during rent week, a frown is all the answer she gets from him. After that you may see her every morning hesitating for a few minutes on her stoop before she plucks up courage to cross the street and to enter the store with a fast-beating heart.

When the $12 are all in the husband's pocket and it is yet a day or two before rent day, she is on pins and needles waiting for its advent. There is a constant burden on her mind, and she is often in a flurry of excitement and impatience. At last the long-awaited knock falls on the door, and her heart gives a joyous tremble. As the agent comes in he greets her with a pleasant "good morning," for he can tell by her face that this time she is not going to ask for a postponement, and the young woman welcomes him with a beaming face which seems to say: "You think I have not? You are mistaken, sir! Here it is!" "One, two, three," she goes on, audibly, "three, and two is five, six, eight and four half-dollars make twelve!"

The agent counts it over, pockets the money, hands her the receipt, and leaves with a "good-by!" which is even more effusive than his "good morning!"

The burden is off her mind, and for a moment she feels greatly relieved. But presently another feeling creeps into her heart. It is as if a lump had just been cut out of her flesh and she was left with a bleeding wound.

Still, for a day or two, whatever she does or says, she is full of the cheering consciousness of having paid her rent.

TRAGEDIES AND COMEDIES OF RENT DAY
April 5, 1902

A broad-shouldered, middle-aged man with Irish features, a Swedish complexion and a French smile, was telling a knot of men some stories to which they listened with rapt attention. It was at the close of a lodge meeting in a small assembly hall in the vicinity of Fifty-ninth Street.

The narrator had not a drop of Irish blood in his veins, nor was there anything French or Swedish in his make-up. He was an Americanized Scotchman with a peculiar sort of humor and a keen sense of human motive. He was a good storyteller, and his talks were the drawing card of the meetings in question. On the present occasion his theme was his own business. He is a real estate agent and collects rents for landlords in different parts of the city, so he told his listeners some of his experiences and observations.

"Some people don't pay rent promptly because they haven't got the money," he said. "But there are many others who have the money all right, but hate to part with it. The most extreme class is made up of those who don't pay at all. They have made a study of the situation, don't you know. They have brought their art down to a fine point and know how to get the best of the shrewdest agent. For instance, I know a woman who manages to live a whole year on about two months' rent and to be dispossessed only two or three times during the period. She has a peculiar passion for beating landlords out of their money and will pay the amount to some shyster lawyer rather than to the owner of the house in which she lives.

"She has a knack of finding houses whose proprietors are either generous and lenient or too neglectful and busy in other directions to collect their rents properly. There are lots of landlords of this sort. The woman I am telling you about usually pays her first month's rent and then she keeps the landlord running. She tells him all sorts of cock-and-bull stories, begs off from month to month, and when she finally gets notice to move she trumps up some damage suit or other against him.

"Another woman makes a specialty of new houses in the eastern part of Harlem, where one gets one month's rent free. If you take an apartment in one of these houses and pay for the first month you get a receipt for two months. When the agent comes to collect the rent for the third month he finds the tenant out. He calls again or he orders the janitor to get the money for him, but as ill luck would have it the woman's child is sick and her money is needed to pay the doctor and the druggist. If you are hard-hearted enough to notify her that she must either pay or move, she will tell you that she won't stay in the house of a cruel man like you if you paid her; that she will vacate the premises as soon as her poor child is well enough to be moved.

"The month is out before you get rid of her, and if you trace her movements you find that her next house is another brand-new tenement house where one lives the first two months for one month's rent. If she succeeds in leading on until about the middle of the third month she may gain two weeks extra. You see, in many instances the proprietors of a certain class of new tenement houses count the rent on their first tenants from the first of the month. Now, if you move in say on the 15th of August you pay one month's rent in advance and get a receipt until Nov. 1. The woman I have reference to is thus enabled to live in decent tenement house apartments twelve months for fifty or sixty dollars. The bother of moving? It is meat and drink to her. As I have said, she belongs to that class of tenants who have a passion for cheating landlords out of their money, and she will spend freely on expressage or replacing this or that piece of furniture which gets broken in moving rather than pay her rent and stay in the same place.

"I know another such family, but in this case it is the husband who is responsible for the nomadic life the family is compelled to lead. I know him very well, and the peculiar thing about him is that in everything else he is a thoroughly honest and conscientious man. He will rather go without his shave than delay paying his butcher or grocer. He draws the line on the landlord. At first I thought it was a matter of principle with him. I thought he might be an anarchist or Socialist or single-taxer, some sort of crank who doesn't believe

256

in private property in land, you know, but I soon found that he was nothing of the kind. It was like this. One of my best tenants in a West Side apartment house, who turned out to be a Henry George man, once tried to make a convert of me. It was then that I learned that my tenant did not believe in landlords and in paying rent; he had quite an elaborate system as to how the city could deceive every landlord by letting him collect rent and then taxing him out of it.

"Well, what surprised me about this man was the promptness with which he paid his own rent. When I expressed myself to this effect he answered with a laugh that he drew a sharp line of demarcation between theory and practice, and he added that, at any rate, it was for the city or the state, not for the individual, to rob the landlords of their rents. Next time I saw the man who would pay everybody but his landlord I asked him whether he was a Henry George man. He stared at me. I found that he was innocent of all such hobbies and that he hated to pay for the use of the rooms which he occupied simply—well, simply because he hated it.

"I shall never forget the fun I once had when one of my landlords recognized in one of his tenants an old deadbeat whom he knew but too well. It was a woman, and one of the sleekest rent-jumpers in the city. He had had some interesting experiences with her before. When he found her on his stoop carrying a scuttle of coal he turned pale. 'What is this woman doing here?' he asked between a rage and a scare. 'You don't mean to tell me she is one of my tenants?' I owned that she was, but pledged myself to get rid of her at the end of the month. The landlord shook his head. He was in despair. Finally he called on the woman himself and offered her $25 if she moved out of his house at once. She pretended to feel insulted by the offer, but little by little she yielded to his plea and asked for a deposit. 'I haven't a cent in the house,' she said with tears, 'and how can I look for other rooms unless you let me have enough for a deposit and other expenses.' The landlord consulted me. I insisted on her first moving out. 'When your apartment is vacant and your furniture is gone from the premises you shall get your $25,' said I in the landlord's presence, 'and if you don't accept our terms you'll have to move out on the first or a day or two after without getting a penny.'

"There was a peculiar twinkle in her eye at this. She sighed and dropped her arms in despair, but there was something in all this which seemed to say, 'If you think you can get the best of me in this game you are mistaken.'

"What do you think she did? She said she would consult her husband, and wailed over her poverty, which caused her to consider a humiliating offer like ours, and the next day she let us know that she was willing to move out within three days if the $25 was deposited with a certain saloonkeeper in an adjoining assembly district. Everything went off smoothly. She moved out two days after the money was placed in the saloonkeeper's hands. The landlord felt as if a heavy burden had rolled off his shoulders. Less than a week after, he called me up on the telephone. I thought the wire was going to melt. Didn't he yell! Well, the woman had moved into one of the other houses he owned in another part of the city.

"He was willing to spend $1000 to get square on her, but what are you going to do in a case like this? She had her receipt signed by himself. Yes, by himself, in his own handwriting. The point is that he never read the names of his tenants, or if he did he did so mechanically, and anyhow it is the janitor who receives the first month's rent, and the landlord is bound by what he does. Of course in the well-ordered houses, or where the business is entrusted to an agent who knows his business, it is easy to avoid mistakes of this sort. This landlord, however, was a busy, absent-minded man, and the three houses he owned in that section of the city were in the care of a relative of his who owned a dry goods store in the neighborhood, and who was anything but an expert in matters of this kind. This time, however, there was not much trouble. She was dispossessed four or five days after the end of the following month.

"Some families, who are really respectable and honest in every respect, even with regard to their landlords, find it extremely difficult to pay their rent on time. With these one is often lenient and sympathetic far beyond the hard and cold relations of landlord and tenant as described in the law books. To be sure, some landlords are rather inclined to be hard and unyielding. I used to know a landlady—a widow—who was the best soul in the world in her private life, but who would shut all feeling out of her heart the moment she set out to collect her rents. 'Business is business,' she used to reason. 'Besides there are so many rogues who can afford to pay, but won't, that one is apt to be kind to the wrong man.' So this landlady would give herself the benefit of the doubt, don't you know.

"On one occasion she found that she had made a grievous mistake, however. She had a family dispossessed, and the poor people's furniture lay in a pile in front of the house when she came around. She was so affected by the sight of the little children camping out that she offered their poor mother money to pay their next two months' rent in some other house. The dispossessed tenant proved too proud to accept alms, and not until she was told by the neighbors that they would pay the money back to the landlady and then collect it in installments from the poor woman did the latter agree to avail herself of what she insisted upon calling her neighbors' loan.

"A still more interesting case came under my observation in 1899, when a wealthy German recognized in the man whom his agent had dispossessed a former playmate. Landlord and tenant had been boys together, but had drifted apart about twenty years before the episode in question, the one going to America while the other remained in Germany working at his trade. When the wealthy landlord saw the chum of his younger days in front of a heap of family belongings he was so moved that he broke into a fit of sobbing in the presence of a crowd of sightseers. I needn't tell you that the furniture was all taken back to the rooms from which the poor family had been turned out. My friend, the German landlord, acted nobly. He supplied his old-time chum with money, bought him new furniture and fixed him up in every other way.

"In some of the poorer districts in the city the people have a peculiar custom. When an impecunious family is dispossessed and its duds are placed on the sidewalk, either the unfortunate family itself or some of the neighbors put a plate on a chair in front of the pile, and the passersby are asked to put in their pennies to help the poor people pay their next month's rent. In the great majority of cases this is all straight, but there are some curious exceptions.

"There are people in the slums who make a business of this charity-plate custom. They know how to appeal to pedestrians and thus make the whole affair quite a profitable venture. They refuse to pay rent for the double purpose of retaining the money due to the landlord and of making money through the charity plate or can which they will thus be enabled to put out. The janitor of one house on the East Side once told me of a woman who made her living in this way. Frankly speaking, I thought it somewhat exaggerated, but that there was a foundation of truth to the story I haven't the slightest doubt.

"Sometimes an impostor of this sort will profit by somebody else's trouble. In one case, for instance, the people who had been dispossessed were so overcome with shame that they disappeared from the place without removing their effects. Another woman, who did not even live in the same house, then placed a jug on one of the chairs left by the bashful family, and bursting into tears, fell to pleading with the passersby for pity. The janitor asked her what business she had to collect money on furniture that was not hers. 'It's my sister's,' the woman answered in great grief. 'She is too bashful to beg herself, and she asked me to do it for her. Take pity! Oh, do take pity upon a poor mother and four children!' As the family who had been put out actually consisted of a widow and four children the janitor felt sure the stranger told the truth. He let her go on until she had collected a little over four dollars. Then some of the neighbors turned up who knew the widow intimately. 'What, your sister?' one of them burst out. 'She never had any sister.' The janitor was for having the woman arrested, but it was not in vain she had learned the art of pleading. She pretended to make a clean breast of it, and told such a story of poverty and involuntary dishonesty through dire need and distress that he let her go.''

PUSHCARTS FULL OF WOE
June 29, 1898

Last night's meeting of the Social Science Club at 28 East Fourth Street was devoted to the study of the pushcart problem of the city. Many of the audience had never suspected there was such a problem, but before they left they became convinced that there was, and that the subject is as serious as it is amusing. The situation was described by Dr. Wolbarst, who had made a thorough study of its East Side phase, and by a young Greek, who spoke of the pushcart army, which is made up of his fellow-countrymen and Italians. The legal aspect of the question was stated by Mr. Cohn, Chairman of the Committee on Pushcarts, while Charles B. Stover confined himself to the matter of remedies.

Dr. Wolbarst estimated the number of pushcart peddlers, men, women, and children, on the East Side alone at 1500, and one of the first things he said was that most of these paid regular tribute to the police for being allowed to violate the city ordinance bearing on their trade.

"This practice of paying booty to the police," he said, "was interrupted when Mr. Roosevelt was at the head of the Department. I was familiar with the pushcart people in his time, and a thorough investigation convinced me that there was absolutely no corruption then. Now, however, things are as bad as they were during the ante-Roosevelt period. I know a widow who supports her family by her pushcart. One day she was arrested and fined $2. There were hundreds of other pushcart peddlers around her, and they obstructed the street as much as she did. Yet they were not molested. The poor woman found that they paid blackmail to the officer on the beat, and she had no choice but to follow their example. She pays her tribute religiously now, and she is not troubled. Sometimes the police would arrest as many as 200 peddlers at a time. Several streets would then be lined with pushcarts, whose owners were held in court to teach them the lesson of being on the right side of the police. Since the introduction of the patrol wagon system they can only arrest a few men at a time, but the peddlers pay their dues as regularly as they ever did. The income from the pushcarts is shared by the captains, sergeants, and patrolmen, and some of the highest officers in the Department have become rich and have attained to their present positions, perhaps, through the blackmail system.

"The pushcart peddler is a nuisance? If he is, he is a nuisance to himself as much as to the public. Time was when he could make a decent living. Now, however, he can hardly earn more than $5 a week, and in increasing his income he is compelled to hire another pushcart for his wife and a third for his boy. The rent is 10 cents a day and there are special pushcart livery stables whose owners have made money in the business.

"What cannot be bought on the pushcart market on Hester Street cannot be bought in New York. If you want your goods of a good quality and cheap, Hester Street is the place to buy them. A lady of my acquaintance was trying to have a valuable piece of drapery matched. She went to all the best uptown stores, but nowhere could she procure what she wanted. At last she tried Hester Street and she was suited.

"It once took Colonel Waring an hour and a half to pass through Hester Street from the Bowery to Attorney Street only a few blocks in a carriage. It would have taken him much longer were it not for the effectual escort he had in the person of the president of the Pushcart Peddler's Association, who led his horse.

"What are you going to do with this army of honest, hard-working people? They are innocent of any wrong-doing, and if they are a nuisance to the city, which charges them $25 a year for their license, the city is a party to it. They work from morning to night for a miserable income, which they must share with the uniformed blackmailer and with the wholesale merchant, who, to squeeze out as much as possible from their earnings, has introduced the system of selling fish at auction to the peddlers. Yes, this is the system in vogue in the fish trade, and the poor peddlers cannot buy a pound of fish without bidding for it as one of an army of buyers who put up the price till he has barely a chance of making anything. When the fish is condemned by the Health Department the loss is the peddler's exclusively. Sometimes as many as fifty tons of fish are seized from them in one single day. What with this clear loss, the booty they have to pay and the labor their trade involves, their life is anything but an enviable one."

The representative of the Greeks and Italians said that his men were even worse off than the Jews. When a Greek peddler is arrested the police will not allow any of his friends to take care of his pushcart, but send it to a livery stable, which charges the peddler $2 a day for storage. "The police get a share of this storage money, but that is not the worst of it. While the pushcart is at the stable the proprietor of the place helps himself and treats his friends to some of the peddler's bananas or apples.''

Mr. Stover's idea of a remedy was to build a vast shed on a park at Division, Hester, Norfolk and Essex Streets, for the double purpose of a playground and pushcart market. The plan as worked out in detail by its author was ingenious, but complicated. It made a favorable impression on the audience.

At the close of the meeting a man who shut his eyes every time he began a new sentence took up the cudgels for the American people, who are being fast crowded out of the pushcart business by the foreigners. As he went on enumerating the various nationalities competing with the American peddler, a voice asked:

"How about the Spaniards?"

"I am afraid they give us more trouble than the other foreigners," answered the man with the shut eyes; "but we'll manage them all right enough."

"THE ONLY MARRIED WOMAN IN THE HOUSE WHO UNDERSTANDS EVERY ENGLISH WORD"
June 3, 1899

If it were not for Frau Linde the second floor would be the happiest in the tenement house. She is the only woman in the building who goes to church. She is a religious enthusiast and extremely good-natured, but she is also extremely quarrelsome and jealous. Herr Linde, who is a slender, good-looking, effeminate man of thirty-two, is her second husband. Being about fifteen years his senior, and a dumpy, broad-shouldered woman with a gnarled, pug-nosed face, she is always in a quiver of anxiety lest he should be snatched from her. That's why she hates to see him visit her neighbors, or to have any of the women call on her when "papa" is in.

Once Frau Wahlteich, who is something of a wit, asked her why she did not keep "papa" in an icebox. She forthwith tried to swallow her words, assuring Frau Linde that she meant it for a joke, but it was too late, and the scene which followed embroiled the other two housewives of the second floor, one of the third and the housekeeper who lives in the basement. All these the infuriated woman accused of trying to flirt with her husband. As their bad luck would have it, Herr Linde was not the kind of man even to look at a lot of frights like them, she said.

The other women form a separate little world in the big tenement house, and the soul of that world is Mrs. McAllister. She is full of life and grace, and her two friends like her for this, and respect her for her polite, bass-voiced, lordly husband, and because she is the only married woman in the house who understands "every English word."

Mrs. McAllister does not speak English, she only understands it. Nor does Mr. McAllister speak a word of German, nor understand it when it is spoken by anyone except his wife. They have been married now eight years, and get along better than any other couple in the house, conversing in the two languages in the most matter-of-fact way, so that the Czech woman who lives on the stoop originally thought that they spoke two slightly different dialects of the same tongue. Their little girl speaks German to her mother and English to her father, although she seems to prefer the latter. Sometimes she forgets herself and addresses Mrs. McAllister in Anglo-Saxon, and then the young woman laughingly pretends to be deaf, and Lizzie must repeat her question or request in Hamburg Deutsch, pronounced with American r's.

Mrs. McAllister made several attempts to speak English to her husband, but she made a mess of it, and as he never encouraged her, and seemed to prefer good Hamburg slang to her bad English, she gave it up. As to Mr. McAllister, he never tried to speak German. People look funny when they use a foreign language, he thought, and he would rather be dumb than funny.

He is a tall, stately man of fifty, with close-clipped dark side whiskers and gold-rimmed spectacles. His bass voice, his grand bearing and soft, genteel manner toward everybody in the tenement house have won the hearts of all the neighbors. To be sure, he holds himself at a respectful distance from them, but then he could not speak to them if he would, and as he is the only man in the house who never passes any of the housewives without taking off his hat, the respect which he inspires knows no bounds.

At first the neighbors thought he was a bookkeeper in some big store downtown. Mrs. McAllister soon disabused their minds. Her husband was a watchman in a warehouse, one of the biggest on Wooster Street, she boasted. The revelation was a severe disappointment to her friends, but Mr. McAllister continued to raise his hat to them and to say, "Ah, good evening!" in his genteel soft basso, and so the respect for him is profound as ever. He is extremely polite to his wife, too, at least when strangers are near; and so while a man of very few words himself, he will listen to Mrs. McAllister's chatter by the half-hour, smoking his pipe and solemnly looking into her eyes, even when her chubby cheeks become dimpled and her blue eyes half shut with laughter. When they are alone she calls him *dalle* (darling), the only English word she uses outside of such phrases as "all righd" or "never min," which she and all the other tenants treat as part and parcel of their German. When there are strangers in the house she calls him Mr. McAllister.

"*Und warum den nicht*, Mr. McAllister?"

"Oh, I don't know, I don't think it's worthwhile," he answers, politely.

Mrs. Wahlteich is an elderly woman. Her husband is a carping old street musician. They have been about thirty years in this country, and all their children were born in New York, and are all well fixed. They have offered to support them, so as to free the old man from his occupation, but he prefers to make his own living. He does not believe in American children supporting their father, he says. If they were all in Europe it would be another matter. There one has genuine respect for one's father, but in America, in the land of loafers and fighters—'*Ist es alles humbug, un dat's all.*'

His sons are interested in politics and vote straight, but he won't even become a citizen of "the land of loafers and fighters."

He is a loyal subject of the Fatherland and curses every German who is not. Often upon reading of a murder he loses his temper and reviles the country of fighters and loafers for it.

Frau Wahlteich has a good deal of trouble with him. She treats him like a petulant child, and that's what he sometimes likes. She makes jokes at his expense, assuring her friends that "her old baby" is very fond of America, and that all he says against the country is mere goff.

"Why, we once had a good chance to go home and make a fine living there, but he wouldn't budge. He is so used to Sixth Street and his *saenger verein* and Klein Fritz's *kneipe* [beer hall] he could not get away from it."

Frau Koch is the most reticent of the triumvirate. She has nothing to say, except, perhaps, to praise her husband. But, then, she is a good listener, and when the other two babble she nods assent and smiles enthusiastically. Her husband is seldom at home. He is a Socialist, and has a meeting every night. When he does call on Mr. McAllister he talks of the social revolution to him. The Scotchman does not seem to understand his Vienna German, but he listens attentively. Often Herr Koch becomes furious and uses some vigorous language, but his pinched face and his dark, bespectacled eyes remain meek and childlike, so that Mr. McAllister sometimes wonders whether he is exalted or cross. The revolutionist is one of the quietest men in the house. He walks gently, almost on tiptoe, and when he speaks of things that have nothing to do with the revolution, his voice often sinks to a gentle whisper.

Mr. McAllister is the only temperance man on the floor. The other three drink beer, and the only one who is apt to take more of it than is good for him is Herr Linde. Once or twice a week he gets home two or three hours too late, and then he noiselessly slips into the kitchen for fear of waking "mamma," of whom he is in mortal fear.

"BE BAPTIZED OR MOVE!"
June 28, 1899

Houston Street is in a uproar once more. Another convert Jew story is going the rounds, but this time it is only the setting for a family drama. The story has nothing to do with Oscar Lemberger, whom Wilson Dunlap, the "paralyzed apostate of the East Side," hired to preach Christianity to his former coreligionists, although Isaac Markowitz, the central figure of the new troubles, happens to live at 214 Houston Street, only six houses from Dunlap's headquarters.

Mr. Markowitz is a tall Rumanian of commanding appearance. He shaves his chin, and his bushy gray whiskers give him the air, so say some of his neighbors, of a Gentile, or, at least, of an uptown Hebrew. He lives with his wife and his seven children, deriving his livelihood from the printing shop which he has on the ground floor of the two-story house. All his children, except one, get along well with him, some working in his shop, others doing something else for a living. The exception is Nathan. He is thirty years old, is married and has three small children. He is also a printer by trade, but of late he has been out of employment, and some eight months ago his father let him move into two of the rooms on the second floor of the house which the old man leases. Quarrels between father and son were frequent, and the climax came yesterday when Isaac had his son dispossessed.

In the afternoon Houston Street rang with the cries of Yiddish newsboys.

"Buy the Yiddish paper, which tells the story of Markowitz, the *meshumed* [convert Jew]," they shouted, "and how he turned out his own son and three little grandchildren because the son would not go back on the Jewish faith!"

The story in the Yiddish paper had it that the old man gave his son the choice between becoming a Christian and being put out.

" 'If you don't wish to have your furniture put out on the street, get baptized at once,' " the paper says the father threatened. "But the son wouldn't obey him," the *Ghetto* again continues, "and so he received notice to move. The judge of the First Street court was shocked to hear of a case where a father was arrayed against his own son, but he could not help it.''

Isaac Markowitz was at his printing office this morning. When he was asked whether there was any truth in the story of his conversion, he smiled, then burst into tears.

"Look at my gray beard, look!" he said. "This is what I have lived to see—my own son call me *meshumed*. It was he who spread the story out of revenge. He is lazy and he wants to fasten on his poor father, who can scarcely make a living himself. He has been a hanger-on in the family long enough, until finally we could not stand him any longer, so I put him out. He owes me six months' rent. If I knew he could not make his living I should have supported him, but he wouldn't work.''

Nathan's brothers and sisters all repeated their father's statement.

"He has ruined us," said the girl. "Now that the Jews have heard that my father is a *meshumed* they won't patronize us. My brother, who keeps a sausage store, feels it. 'Is this Markowitz, the *meshumed*?' they ask, and then they just run away, as if we were a pest.''

The story of Markowitz's conversion is based on the fact that he has Pastor Gablein of the mission house at 91 Rivington Street among his customers. This old Markowitz did not deny. He admitted printing the *Tikvath Yisrael* (the "Hope of Israel"), a Yiddish monthly published by the pastor for distribution among the Jews of the East Side, but then he also prints admission tickets for synagogues, some of which he showed to the reporter. One of these bore the inscription, "Congregation Sons of Abraham, 144 Ludlow Street," and the other had been ordered by the congregation of the Brotherly Tie, 46 Orchard Street. Miss Markowitz also calls attention to the fact that her mother "purified" her meat and prepared it *kosher* according to the Mosaic law.

When Nathan Markowitz, who was seen at the printing office where he obtained a job this morning, was asked about the story of his quarrel with his father, he also burst into tears. He was sure his father was a convert, he said, and could prove it positively in court.

"If he was not, how did he get the job of the missionaries?" he argued. "Besides, I know he was baptized five years ago. I know the date.''

"What date was it?''

"I don't remember.''

"What are your positive proofs?''

"Well, for one thing, he never prays, not even on the Day of Atonement. I don't pray regularly, either, but on that great day I should rather die than stay away from the synagogue.''

"Any more proofs?"

"Well, he attends the ceremonies of the missionaries. Once Dr. Warszawiak invited him to a meeting and he went there."

Nathan's wife, who was found in her new rooms at 66 Suffolk Street, said she knew that her father-in-law was *meshumed* from her husband. All she knew from personal experience was that the old man was so hard-hearted that he was "worse than a Gentile," and so she was glad to live apart from him, she said.

———————

WHEN BAUER LAUGHED
July 8, 1899

An elderly German, who had lost two fingers at the shop where he was employed, recently opened a candy store in the middle of a certain block between Avenues C and D. The accident had unfitted him for manual labor, but the lawsuit which he had begun against his employer yielded him, by way of compromise, $150, so he invested part of it in candy, toys, a soda water fountain, a counter and three tables and chairs "for ice cream customers."

The elderly German, whom we shall call Mr. Bauer, was anything but popular with the boys of the block. He had always been known as a grumbling, ill-natured neighbor, but since he met with his misfortune his temper seemed to grow worse every day. The noise of the children jarred on him, and he would often chase them away from his stoop and spoil their game. When they built a bonfire he would sometimes come down with a pail of water and put it out, cursing America and the wild children it produces. At first the boys tried to get fun out of their kill-joy. They made a point of annoying him, called him "crazy loon," and even pelted him with stones. But Mr. Bauer proved more than a match for them. It turned out that he could beat the best of the gang in running, and his blows, once he got hold of the enemy, made a deep impression. He is of middle height, heavily built, and with a bald circle at the center of his enormous head; but you should have seen him shoot off after some offending youngster. Pale, his teeth glistening and his high forehead wrinkled, he would enter the race with a mad joy which gave an uncomfortable feeling not only to his poor quarry but also to the older people on the stoops.

Bauer's young daughter, Clara, remonstrated with him, but this only

267

made him crosser than ever. He is very fond of the girl, whose mother died before she could speak, but he tyrannizes over her, and his very love for her sometimes leads him to cause her mental anguish. Still, she never leaves his naggings unanswered. The neighbors say that she is a chip off the old block, and as much of a grumbler as her father, and so the two are often heard quarrelling "like man and wife," as the janitor of the tenement house puts it. Sometimes they are not on speaking terms, "just like a married couple," and then it is always the girl who is the first to break the silence.

When they were making ready to open their candy and ice cream store, Clara warned her father not to antagonize the boys any more, lest they should keep away from the store. The old man turned pale, and at the first opportunity that offered itself he twisted a boy's ear so that his screams brought a crowd to the scene. Miss Bauer cried and scolded, and told her father he might as well shut up shop, for who would be foolish enough to patronize a man who twisted boys' ears? The old man told her to hold her tongue; some hard words were exchanged, and for a day or two father and daughter were dumb and deaf to each other. Then some of the fixtures of the store were delivered, and in the stress of preparations even the old man forgot that he was not on speaking terms with his daughter.

The store was opened. The shelves were glistening with jars half filled with candy, a stately fountain rose from the middle of the counter, the tables were covered with white oilcloths, the walls were freshly papered, the gas burned bright, the paper tidies gleamed red—everything was spick and span, and as though smiling upon the boys out on the asphalt pavement and pleading with them to let bygones be bygones and come in. But they wouldn't, and the only customers Mr. Bauer had the first day was a young man and his sweetheart. Clara, who did not go to work that week, was in despair.

"Here you have it," she snarled. "The ice will cost us more than the ice cream is worth; everything will get spoiled, and the money will be lost, and all because of your temper."

To her great surprise the old man made no reply. He only contracted his eyebrows and remained grimly silent. He was too overborne by his misfortune to talk back. Another day passed, and still the boys held aloof. They spent their pennies in the old store near the corner, and some of them even made a point of passing hard by the Bauers' place blowing on a new penny whistle or sucking a stick of candy. Now and then the widow who keeps that store near the corner would pass along the sidewalk, and as she stole a glance into the empty store of her new competitors a smile would overspread her florid, fleshy face. At this Clara would sink in her chair and drop her arms, while her father would gnash his teeth and clutch at the seat of his chair as if to keep himself from running out into the street and wreaking vengeance on the boys or the widow.

But Mr. Bauer is a thinker. Among the men of the tenement he is known as a reader of books on philosophical and sociological topics. He does not agree with any of the authors he reads, and it seems as if he reads them all for the express purpose of reviling them for a lot of idiots. One morning after a long silence he got up smiling, and without saying a word, he put on his coat and hat and went out.

Clara called after him to know where he was going, but he made no reply.

In the evening of that day the neighborhood was startled by some peculiar singing. It seemed to be an Irishman performing one of the latest songs at the top of his voice, but then that voice of his had a peculiar ring to it, and it was accompanied by what now sounded like a piano and now like the squeaking of a dog. The people in the tenements at once saw it was a phonograph, and the younger folk rushed out onto the street to see it. The crowd which gathered in front of the new store was enormous. All eyes were fixed on the huge mouth of the funnel, behind which sat old Bauer. It was from this funnel that the Irishman's voice came, loud and sonorous. The invisible singer performed song after song; then an orchestra was heard playing "Marching through Georgia," and some of the boys caught up the tune. The old man changed the cylinders with a preoccupied air, and while his little phonograph sang or whizzed or squeaked he sat behind it, his arms folded and his face grimly motionless as ever.

Little by little the crowd fell off, but there were always a few score of regulars in front of the store, and the bulk of them was made up of the boys of the block. Still, the bystanders contented themselves with looking at the machine and listening to its music and recitation from the sidewalk. The old man's business improved but slightly. The boys still bought their toys and their candy at the widow's. Clara was pale and haggard. She sneered at her father's abortive scheme to catch the boys' custom, and told him that twenty phonographs could not cure the effect of twisted ears, and that he had only added the price of the machine to the money he had thrown away. The old man was wild but controlled himself. He bought new cylinders every day, changing the programme of the concert every hour; but the effect was the same; the boys were willing enough to listen, but when one of them had a penny he went to spend it in that store near the corner.

One evening the crowd stood on the sidewalk waiting to hear a new piece which the old German had just put into his phonograph, when the machine burst into laughter. It was the laughter of a singer overcome with merriment while performing a sentimental tune. He went on singing, but his deep ringing basso was choked with laughter. The crowd on the sidewalk caught the contagion and joined in. Their mirth brought others to the scene, and presently there were from fifty to sixty people, all laughing at the top of their lungs.

Mr. Bauer looked morose, his eyes on the machine, but as he stole a glance at the chuckling throng a smile lit up his face: and then suddenly throwing his massive head back, he burst into a hoarse laugh which shook his whole bulky frame.

It was the first time the boys saw him laugh. When he had laughed till he could laugh no more, and he sat panting and wiping his merry tears, his eyes met the eyes of some of the boys. Mr. Bauer laughed again. The boys joined in.

"Come in, poys!" the old man then said, beckoning to them with his index finger.

The next moment the store was overcrowded.

"LOTS OF MILK AND EGGS"
September 25, 1899

One of the latest fashions among the poor people of the East Side is for the father of a family to send his wife and children to the mountains for the summer. Time was when the workingmen, peddlers or small tradesmen of what is known as the congested district would look up with envy at the residents of uptown flat houses, whose families spent the hot season in Greene or Ulster counties. Now many of them have come to look upon it as one of the necessities of life which they can well afford, and they ask each other "When will the old woman come from the mountains?" almost in the same matter-of-fact tone in which they speak of their employers or customers. Not that the prosperity of the East Side has placed some of the luxuries within the reach of the poor, although to some extent it has, but board in the Catskills has come down to a point where the "keep" of a workingman's family in a boarding house is almost as cheap as it is at home in the city.

An East Side physician, whose patients are almost exclusively sweat-shop people, said the other day that in many instances relief is brought to otherwise hopeless cases by sending the sufferer to the mountains.

"I know a man who earns $15 a week as a baster in a tailoring shop," he said. "He has a wife and two little children, one of whom was so sick last May that I almost gave up all hope of seeing it improve. What it needed more than anything else was fresh air, but this was just what the locality did not have. I then told the baster that unless he sent the child to some country place it would go hard with it. This did not scare him. His wife's sister and cousins and friends were going to Tannersville, he said, and if they could afford it he could."

Board at Tannersville, Greene County, runs all the way from $15 to $5 a week, and the baster's wife found a room for which she paid $9 a week for herself and her two children. If the board left something to be desired the East Side woman and her children did not know it. They found the dinner "uptown style," and the milk and eggs were so fresh and plentiful that she had to keep herself and her babies from overeating themselves. As to the air, she wrote her husband that it was "a regular paradise," and she could almost see baby growing strong and inhaling it.

Competition among the boarding houses of the place and in the neighboring town is so rife that board is sometimes offered at less than cost price. Some of the farmers in Ulster County, who are anxious to get started in the boarding business, which has crowded out almost every other occupation in the district, advertise board at $4 a week. But the East Siders prefer towns such as Tannersville or Pinehill.

"Them farmers will give you lots of milk and eggs," said a German grocer, whose family were spending the summer in the mountains, "but they ain't got no meat."

Another East Sider whose family were in Ulster County, and who had been to spend a Sunday with them, told how he was accosted on the road by an old farmer, who was trying to persuade him to move over to his place. He offered him all sorts of inducements, and only asked $4 a week, explaining that he could afford it all because he had his own cows and hens, while the woman with whom the East Sider's family was stopping had "to send out and get" everything for money. The same farmer was subsequently met by another man, whom he approached in a similar way, and altogether it was plain that he made it his business to drive around among the boarding houses and "to talk away their boarders."

THE CHASM

Tannersville, Pinehill and the surrounding towns swarm with East Siders during the summer months. As most of these people are Jews many of the boarding houses in question keep *kosher*, preparing their food according to the regulations of the Mosaic faith, and sometimes advertising that fact in Hebrew letters on the window.

TWO-HEADED BABY
October 18, 1899

The basement of 58 Montgomery Street, where the "two-headed" baby was born last Monday night, swarmed with neighbors this morning. Isaac Epstein, the father of the child, was so excited that one of the smart housewives told him that he had lost his head, so that baby's extra head was given him in advance to make up for his loss. But the smart housewife was told to shut up by another housewife, who had placed herself in charge of things in general and the "extra head" in particular.

All Epstein knows about her is that she lives in the same house, or block—he could not say which. The reporter, editor, and manager of a Yiddish paper explained that she was a busybody, as he could see from her face, and that if the reporter of the Gentile paper thought that the East Side type of a busybody was the same as that of the rest of the world, he was mistaken.

Be it as it may, the housewife ruled things with an iron hand, so much so that poor Mr. Epstein sat looking about him, sheepishly, as if he was wondering whether he had a right to be in the house, when Mrs. Busybody shouted at him:

"You ought to be ashamed of yourself, Isaac, sitting around like a lazy good-for-nothing, while there is so much misery in your house."

Epstein, who is a shoemaker, is idle most of the time. The family has often been in need and once or twice has been brought to the attention of the United Hebrew Charities. When Mrs. Epstein was well, she nagged him about their poverty, appealing to him in the name of their four starving children. Now that she can't nag him, Mrs. Busybody has taken her place.

Still, the busybody had other things to keep her body busy. There were reporters in the house, and the shoemaker was about to let them see the baby.

"What, let them see baby and make money on its two heads without doing anything for the poor mother and her starving four children?"

She planted herself in the doorway leading from the shoeshop to the bedroom, and began shaking her head violently. "Nobody shall see the baby without assisting the poor starving family while I am here."

The father looked dazed. Somebody tried to explain to him that he would make more money if the story of his misfortune was published in the papers, but the busybody told him not to let himself be cheated.

"Once God has punished you that your wife has given birth to a deformed baby, make the most of it for your poor children. Such things don't happen every day, do they?" she asked, with a look which seemed to imply that God's punishment was not an unmixed curse.

The father obeyed. The smart neighbor told him he was a half-headed fellow to let himself be bossed by a stranger, but the reporters did not get a chance to see the baby anyhow.

"Don't grieve," the smart neighbor said. "I have seen it, and I can tell you you have not lost much. I saw one head all right, and it sits right on top of baby's neck, just like mine or yours. As to the other thing, which is on baby's shoulder, well, it might look like a head or an undersized watermelon, or a big white carrot if you looked at it at a distance of two blocks. If it has a mouth it will never be big enough to hold a cigarette, I can tell you that."

HERO LATE FOR PRAYERS
October 26, 1899

Abraham Koslowitz is a peddler, very pious, very humble, very industrious. He never fails to go to the synagogue in the morning, and he is never late. Indeed, his whole life is regulated by law and business. Yesterday, the poor peddler's record was broken, and, strange to say, he was glad of it.

He went to a wedding on Tuesday night. It was a happy spot in the seething ghetto, and Koslowitz tarried late into the morning. Naturally he slept late; he was late at prayers; later getting back; late to business. It was 9 o'clock in the day when he returned, and he was running all out of breath up the stairs to his attic room in the tenement at 235 Broome Street, when he paused. Smoke filled his nostrils and he sniffed. The odor of burning cloth startled him. He went from door to door smelling till he came to the apartment of Mrs. Levine. There the smell was strongest. But the door was locked. He listened and the cry of a child came to him. It was remote as from a back room.

The pious peddler could not open the door, so he ran around through another apartment to a fire escape, and, picking his way along this, he got to a window of Mrs. Levine's flat. Peering in he saw a flame.

Ida, the two-year-old baby of his neighbor, was ablaze. She was terrified, screaming, thrashing at the flame which rose from her dress to her face; it played in her hair; it ran up her frantic little arms. And beside the baby stood Harry, the little boy, who is only two years older than his sister. Well, Koslowitz, seeing this, gave thanks that he was late that day, and he broke that window, sprang into the room and caught up the child in his arms. About her he wrapped his praying shawl, and he clasped his great, black coat over her. Yes, it burned a little, and Koslowitz cried out even as the children had done, so that the whole houseful of tenants gathered there. People from the street came also, and from the houses next door and across the street and from the rear. Somebody told Engine Company 17 about it and a fireman came. But they all found the pious peddler holding the burned baby, swaying as if in prayer with the little boy clinging to the skirt of the great man's black coat.

By and by the ambulance surgeon came. He took the baby away and laid her on a neighbor's bed. The policeman talked to the boy, learning that his mother was gone to market, his big sister, ten years old, to school, and that after the door was locked the little boy got the matches and that—here the policeman stopped asking questions. He knew the rest, he said. The crowd moved over to the neighbor's where the baby lay. The surgeon covered the pained body in oil, using towels, sheets, anything at hand, while the poor neighbor wailed. She was sorry, sorry for the baby, she said; sorry too, for her soiled linen. The other people explained that she was famous in the neighborhood as the "clean woman," so when she looked at the oil on the pillows, the oil over her bed, the oil-soaked sheets, towels, everything—her sorrow burst clear as sunshine on a rainy day.

As for Koslowitz, he soon hastened away, smiling, happy, a hero, to hawk his tailor trimming about the ghetto.

———

TWO DOCTORS
February 3, 1900

Two young men (Joseph and Lazar, let us call them) came to this country on the same German steamship seventeen years ago. Joseph had studied at the University of St. Petersburg, and was full of lofty purposes. His parents were well-to-do. His sole reason for leaving his home was his sympathy for his persecuted brethren. Lazar was a "man of earth," although he had picked up some broken Russian in the army. He was a barber and a kind of nurse by trade, and the reason of his going to America was the difficulty he found in earning a living at home. When he returned from the army he found his native town overcrowded with poor people banished from the central provinces, and there were more barbers among them than men who could afford to pay for a haircut.

"I envy you," he said, wistfully, to Joseph, as the many-colored American city hove in sight.

"Why?"

"Because you are an educated man, and I am ignorant. You will soon be rich in America, while I—God knows what will become of me in this strange land."

Most of Joseph's friends had picked up English, exchanged their factory jobs for work as insurance agents, newsdealers, teachers. They saved, and, partly with their own money, partly assisted by some wealthy brother in Israel, they entered the American colleges. Few of these refined immigrants did not. Joseph was one of them.

In those days the medical schools of New York were open to all. All that was required was the tuition fee, and that was reduced when the applicant had a certificate of poverty to present. Lazar, who had been a successful peddler for several years, found himself with $2,000 in his savings bank. What was he to do? Some friends advised him to go into clothing, others urged furniture, while one man thought there was more certainty about medicine. The Yiddish-speaking colony had grown enormously, and the number of Yiddish-speaking physicians was ridiculously small. Lazar's ambition was aroused. To think of him, a mere barber and male nurse, being called doctor! And, by the way, had he not handled bleeding cups and leeches and syringes at home? Think of the people in his native town when they hear of him as a doctor—a full-fledged doctor with a college diploma and all that sort of thing!

Lazar came, paid his tuition fee, learned his English in a standard work on anatomy, worked hard, was graduated, put on a high hat, grew side whiskers, began to speak his broken English with a dignified basso, and became known as a specialist of half a dozen diseases. His real specialty was connected with the life on Allen Street, but he had a trick of patting housewives on the back, flying into a passion every minute and receiving his fee with the air of one conferring a favor on a poor fellow; so the people of the tenements were sure he was an excellent doctor, and his practice grew and grew.

Joseph gave lessons and spent his free hours reading. At last he, too, entered an American college, but he studied philosophy, natural sciences, literature. He thought he would never have a family to support, so what was the use of studying medicine, law or dentistry—things he did not have his heart in. He was mistaken. He fell in love, and at the eleventh hour he entered medical school. Once in it, he took up the subject with all the thoroughness of his nature. He attended lectures, dissected, read all he could get, gave his lessons in the evening, and was happy.

"I never dreamed what an interesting subject medicine was," he would say, full of enthusiasm.

When he had received his diploma he did not at once start in to practice, as Lazar had done. "I have no right to take the fate of a human being into my hands," he said. "I am still raw; my mind is full of theory; I must first study my subject on real patients, under the direction of experienced physicians." So he procured a place in a hospital and went to work with fresh enthusiasm. "It is getting more interesting every day," he would tell his friends, his face beaming with delight.

Finally he opened an office. He wouldn't wear a high hat, because it was snobbish, he said. He did not pat the poor people on the back patronizingly, nor get angry, nor speak broken English to them. He just spoke plain Yiddish, so that he could understand thoroughly what they said to him about the case, and they understood what they were to do. When they were slow to pay his fee, he would hem and cough bashfully. So they all said he was a "lobster" and not much of a doctor; only called him when the doctors in the high hats were out, and were more slow to pay every time they called him.

The other doctors bought carriages and horses and hired colored manservants, who would dust the rugs on the stoop in the morning and drive the carriage when the doctor made his rounds.

"You must put on a high hat," said a friend to Joseph a few months ago. "There is no bucking against the stream. The housewives have no faith in derby hats."

Reluctantly, with a lump in his throat, Joseph complied; but it was too late. Besides, he could not speak with a dignified basso, nor get angry; nor could he afford a carriage.

Lazar and Joseph were seen on Norfolk Street the other day, the one in a carriage, his side whiskers, his high hat, his diamonds and his fat, florid face gleaming past the pedestrians through the window. Joseph plodded along on foot. His overcoat was rusty and his trousers a trifle too short. The only thing that was new on him was his high hat, but it was so woefully out of accord with the rest of him, so painfully at variance with his worn, haggard, intellectual face, that one wished he would take it off and go back to the derby he once wore.

AIR SHAFT DIALOGUE
November 17, 1900

A mild family quarrel in one of the new tenement houses in the vicinity of Tompkins Square recently revealed to the neighbors one of the curious love affairs of that polyglot locality. The windows of the room in which the quarrel took place gave out into an air shaft, and the dialogue could be heard by all the tenants who had windows in the same "conductor of foul air and darkness."

"I can't and I won't," said the voice of what seemed to be a young girl, in Bohemian.

"If you don't go to work there'll be no supper tonight," answered a much older woman, sharply.

"I don't care."

"Of course you don't. But if you weren't such a cruel, heartless thing you would."

"I'm as good as you any time, mamma."

"No, you are not. I never let my father and mother starve. He is getting well, and in a month or two he may be able to go to work, your father. All he needs is rest. But you won't let him have it. You are bound to make him go to the shop before he has strength to pick himself up. You'll be the ruin of him and of all of us, Martha."

277

The woman spoke calmly, in measured, clear-cut accents, as if telling a story. The girl was excited.

"Stop, mamma, stop talking like this or I'll commit suicide. I can't stand it. Was it not yourself who brought it all on? I never wanted to work inside. I had plenty to do at home, and when it was slack at neckties I could get something else to do. But you wanted me to look for a chance to get married. So, there you have it now!"

"I did?"

"Of course you did. You don't mean to deny it, do you? Didn't you say, 'Martha, I think you had better look for some job in a factory, because—' "

"Oh, shut up, you're talking too much," retorted the mother, with some annoyance.

"No, I won't shut up, and I'm not talking too much, either. If you did not deny it I would not say anything about it, but you hint that I am a liar—"

"Who says you're a liar?"

"I won't let you back out, mamma. Didn't you tell me that if I worked in a factory where there were fellows I might strike up an acquaintance with one of them?"

"Yes, and if you were not such an ill-natured, sour-tempered thing, you'd—"

"If I have a bad temper I have my mother to thank for it."

"When your mother was a girl she didn't make herself and everybody else sick. If you took things easy you would have found your predestined one long ago."

"I don't care," shouted the other tearfully, "and I want you to stop talking about my 'predestined one.' You make me sick."

"If you don't care, then, why should you be so worked up because that young man stopped seeing you home as he used to?"

"Shut up, or I'll—"

"You'll do what? Kill your mamma? I only want to show how all I tell you to do works for your good. You said yourself he was a nice fellow and could make a nice living. Well, you had not been many weeks there before he began to make love to you—"

"Shut up, I say."

"And if you were not so crazy and didn't take things so hard and didn't make a nuisance of yourself, he'd have proposed long ago."

For some time there was silence, then the girl was heard to break into a fit of quiet sobbing.

"Crying again?" her mother said. "You've cried enough. That won't mend matters. Men hate weeping girls. That's just the trouble with you."

Another pause, during which the girl continues to sob and moan quietly.

"Stop crying, I say. Haven't you had enough of it?" says the mother, this time softly.

Still another pause.

"I don't see why you should feel so worried about it, anyhow. The woods are not full of girls like you. He'll come to make up; see if he doesn't."

The girl's sobs grew louder.

"Sure he will. I'm older than you; I know men. When your father made love to me we quarrelled several times, too. I was awfully sensitive and nagging, and I often bothered the life out of him for nothing. But we made up every time, and it was all right again."

The sobs still grew louder.

"Hush, my darling. Don't spoil your beautiful eyes."

"If you didn't bother me I would never cry or feel bad," answered the girl, apparently wiping the tears from her eyes. "Did you see me cry or worry before you began to talk to me about him? I can get work somewhere else, and if he wants to make up he knows where I live."

"Of course, of course. But if I were you I wouldn't give him the satisfaction. I wouldn't let him think I'm afraid to be near him. Let him see you every day, and let him go crazy looking at your beautiful face. Let him make himself sick for treating you the way he did. He deserves to be punished for it. That's the way I look at it."

There was no answer. But the silence which followed seemed to give consent.

"NOT ONE HONEST SHUDDER
TO CARRY HOME"
The Sun / March 30, 1902

Like many young women who come to New York, either to make it their future home or to do the shops and the matinees for a week, a great yearning possessed her to "go slumming"; to see with her own eyes those undercurrents of the huge city that dragged men and women hopelessly beneath their sodden depths; to go into the hidden places where the slaves of opium dreamed away their lives in Gustave Doré attitudes.

THE CHASM

Now that she was in the city she recalled how the billboards of her unsophisticated native town had once been made tragic to her young eyes by the livid pictures of a beautiful woman, somewhat tousled and tarnished, to be sure, who was being rescued from one of these dens by a young man in a folded opera hat, a splendid Inverness cloak, and a lower jaw knocked two inches out of plumb by an inartistic bill poster. She did not expect to meet the tarnished lady nor the rescuer with the undershot jaw, nor was her desire to see these places inspired by a morbid fancy to look upon wretchedness and depravity.

She knew, however, how heroic—even devilish—her conduct would appear in the eyes of her friends, and of the delicious shudders with which a recital of her adventures would be received at home, and she was not averse to being looked upon as heroic or a bit devilish.

The great difficulty she found in the carrying out of her plans was the absolute indifference with which her host and hostess looked upon slumming— they were New Yorkers. When she hinted that a few gaslight glimpses of the city might prove more educating than a daily round of the shops and the theater, they merely laughed.

And then, after she had abandoned all hope, Ruggles came in for dinner one evening. Ruggles was an old young man who looked upon life through bowed gold spectacles and considered it a grave affair. He belonged to a class in society that is referred to by those who are not eligible as the over-rich, and he had passed some time in one of the university settlements over on the East Side. Those who admired him called him a young man of great moral character and spoke of his unselfishness and of his sterling worth. Those who did not approve the manner in which he spent his time and his money declared openly that he was a *poseur*, that his interest in the poor was merely an affectation, and they christened him the "Amateur Slumologist." It is probable that both his admirers and his critics were in a measure right.

The young woman from the country town did not find Ruggles interesting—he was not the type of the New York man she had pictured to herself—and it was only through a rather petulant desire to irritate him, that she discovered that after all he was the key by which the doors of the slums might be opened to her.

"I am surprised," she said to him, and there was the hint of a sneer in her voice, "that you New Yorkers take so little interest in—in things that are—well, not conventional—in the poor, for instance, or in the slums."

"I am disgusted but not surprised," he answered quickly, "that New Yorkers take the interest they do in such things. Why, slumming is—or was until the novelty wore off—the most conventional thing we did. People went to the slums in quite the same way they went to picture galleries or the shops. As a matter of fact slumming became so popular at one time that sham burglar dens and opium dives—as much like the real ones as the scenery in *Ten Nights in a Barroom*—were arranged, with property burglars and fiends, and New York's 'beauty and chivalry' was lured there and went home shuddering and delighted.

"What was it that appealed to them?" In his earnestness Ruggles had dropped into a pulpit pose, and the question was asked with ministerial severity: "What was it?" he repeated. "Nothing more than a morbid craving to look upon wretchedness and vice. Would they have put themselves to the same inconvenience to look upon the bright side of the Other Half; to learn how it finds its pleasure and happiness? Never!"

Ruggles was becoming excited. "Would you care yourself," he asked of her with something of a challenge in the question, "to see a little of the sunshine that comes into the lives of the Other Half? Because if you do," he added, eagerly, "I can show it you.

"There is going to be a dance tomorrow night in which some of my—my—er—pupils on the East Side are interested, and they have asked me to come. Will you go?"

The question was strict challenge now, and had the young woman so desired she could not have declined it.

"I would advise you," he said, as he was leaving, "to wear something—well, you know, just something plain and simple—not the sort you have on now. The Other Half, you understand," he ended rather feebly, "might—might think we were trying to look down upon them."

The next night Ruggles, with the young woman from the country town beside him, hailed a crosstown car going in the direction of the East River. "The Other Half," he explained to her, when they had found seats, "prefers to go to its balls in barouches, but it is wiser that we should go in plain horse cars. You will find they are inclined to be a bit intolerant of Our Half. Because they ride in the carriages is no excuse for our doing so. And I may as well warn you now," he added in the same tone he had used on the evening before, "that if you are expecting to find a foul room filled with wretched beings in paint and peroxide and low-browed villains in melodrama raiment you will be very much disappointed. The Other Half is eminently respectable at its social functions, and so are its manners."

It was nearly 10 o'clock before they left the car and made their way down a street from which the river lights were occasionally revealed. The hall, on the second floor of one of the buildings they were passing, confirmed Ruggles' warning, and the young woman was conscious of a sense of disappointment. The place was long and narrow, and a row of pillars down the centre supported the ceiling. These pillars were covered with green baize palms that quivered in tropical luxuriance. The rooms were almost brilliantly lighted, and cheap flags representing the nations of the world were tacked to the walls in undiplomatic groups. To the girl it seemed as if a large majority of the Other Half must already be in the ball room. And whatever else it may have been it was without doubt cosmopolitan. Surely there was at least one patriot for each flag on the walls.

As Ruggles escorted her across the floor to one of the chairs that formed an unbroken row around the hall, she was vaguely conscious of a sense of chagrin that their entrance had made no impression upon the dancers. A waltz was being played, and couples, all dancing full measure to the music, dodged her with a dexterity that was bewildering. When they had found chairs a man in an evening suit that obviously was used to working in night and day shifts, darted through the throng with agile and elaborate grace and stood bowing before them.

"They ain't really got together yet," he said, apologetically waving at the same time to the men leaning against the windows and the girls in the chairs. The men were smoking cigars and the girls were for the most part looking at their neighbors' jewels. "Youse wait till they gits warmed up. There won't be nothin' but things doin' then."

The agile man's prophecy was already being fulfilled, and when the music stopped there was a general "gittin' together." The men who had been dancing placed their partners in chairs and, standing before them, fanned them vigorously. One young man who could not find a seat for his partner, gently tipped her against one of the pillars and fanned her frantically with a handkerchief which he held by two of its corners. It was evidently looked upon as a great joke, and when another young man called across the hall, "Save your strength, Danny, she'll be side steppin' when you are dragged to your corner," the Other Half applauded uproariously.

The lancers were announced as the next dance by a pasteboard sign hung from the piano, and as the sets were being formed Ruggles calmly asked his companion if he "might have the pleasure of the lancers." He did not wait for a response, but took the girl by the arm and led her to a vacant place in one of the sets. The girl was surprised to find how very seriously everyone seemed to take the lancers. Even in her own town a square dance was looked upon as an occasion for unwonted levity which expressed itself in a universal grin and crude attempts at jig steps. Here, however, she found herself surrounded by men and women who went through the various evolutions with the stately solemnity of a minuet. A preternaturally solemn man and an icily haughty blonde made up the couple opposite her.

She was beginning, in fact, to look upon this man with a good deal of diffidence, when suddenly in a "forward and back" he clutched her convulsively around the waist, drew her close to him and with the ease and rapidity of a cream separator whirled her around eight times in a space that did not seem to her larger than a twenty-five-cent piece. When she had obtained her bearings once more she was surprised to find that the man still maintained his immobility.

Ruggles, in the meantime, was having trouble of his own. Theoretically Ruggles was a pretty fair slumologist, as his friends called him, but practically he was likely to become stampeded. And while his own partner was being whirled through space he committed a blunder which made his case hopeless as far as that particular dance was concerned. In the first place he had forgotten to embrace the frigid blonde opposite him in the formal catch-as-catch hold, and being unaccustomed to other holds, the lady had caught his foot in her skirt and torn the latter. Without thinking, Ruggles exclaimed in exaggerated courtesy, "Can you ever forgive me? I am so stupid at such things, you know."

The blonde lady gazed at him with scorn and contempt in her eyes, and almost in the same breath the temperature dropped 10 degrees.

"You ain't one o' us," she said with calm disdain, "an' I told Eddie you wuz only one o' them Fifth Avenoo dudes when I'se saw you comin' over here. Ain't that what I told you, Eddie?"

Eddie nodded gravely.

"Don't pay no 'tention t' them kind, Susie, they'se all counterfeits."

Ruggles did not attempt to argue the question; it may have occurred to him that it would be bad form.

"Such little pleasantries," he remarked after the dance, "tend to give one a broader view of humanity. There is no agency like the Other Half to make possible the wish to see ourselves as others see us."

"Such little pleasantries," the woman from the country added, "also seem to impress upon one the wisdom of silence."

Not long after the square dance one of the amateur slumologist's pupils discovered him and with grave courtesy brought one of his friends to be introduced to the slumologist's companion. From his manner and make-up the friend evidently was a young man of sporting proclivities. He wore a deep red stock, a thin striped waistcoat affected by coaching men, a short jacket and peg-top trousers. He appeared to be quite at home at such social affairs, and when the young woman, having apparently no alternative, acceded to his request for the next waltz, his hand went involuntarily to the side of his forehead. During the dance he talked to her in the gay persiflage of the world as he knew it. He told her that her dancing was just like stepping on eggs and that she was beautifully gaited and bitted, and when he found a place for her and she had thanked him, he replied gallantly, "Keep the change."

Beer and ale were sold at a counter in one corner of the hall, and between dances there was a spirited demand for these beverages.

At 1 o'clock in the morning the programme of thirty-four dances had been half completed and an intermission was announced. In this much-needed lull a young man with his hair parted in a waving curve walked to the platform and without being urged began to sing sentimental songs. Instantly the dancers grouped themselves silently around the platform.

"Now you will see the Other Half as it really is," whispered the amateur slumologist eagerly; "see it without its veneer and affectations."

The young man was singing, in a voice from which the iron filings had not been wholly removed, a song ending with the lines:

> Because I love you,
> Because I love you,
> Because I love you.

There were a great many verses explaining why he loved her with such ardent repetition and many more assuring her that he intended to keep right on doing so.

In spite of herself the girl found herself yielding—not to the influence of the song—but to that which it produced upon those about her. At the very first assertion of his devotion and the reasons for it a strange hush fell upon the Other Half. The bright animated faces of the young girls instantly relaxed into expressions of vacant reverie, and the heads of the men were tilted at an angle of reverence and appreciation. When the chorus was reached the room was filled with a united and passionate explanation of why the young man had acted as he had in the first verse. For more than half an hour the demands for songs that filled the eyes with tears were continued, and it was not until the orchestra returned and drowned the clamor that the Other Half resumed its dancing.

"Has this little glimpse of the bright side of the Other Half repaid you?" the amateur slumologist asked the young woman from the country town as they were returning home.

"I have not really one honest shudder to carry home with me," she answered.

284

PART FOUR
The Bridge

A Political Discussion. (Drawing by Jacob Epstein, 1902, which appeared in *The Century*, 1917)

9

Daily Arts and Letters

"THEY HAVE GOT SO USED
TO DAILY PAPERS"
February 12, 1898

"Ah, if I had a thousand dollars," sighed an East Side poet in a Grand Street café. "I should at once start a daily, and then the other four Yiddish dailies published in this city and the one in Chicago would have to say the dying man's prayer. Think of it, I should give the New York public a newspaper with every headline in it composed in rhyme and ablaze with the poetry of Isaiah, the twelve prophets and Heinrich Heine rolled into one. Every bit of news would be written in the classical Yiddish which has made my songs so famous. Ah, ill luck attends me! Time was when our people here had nothing but weeklies, and they were quite satisfied, too. Then it was easy to establish a paper with two or three hundred dollars. Now they have got so used to daily papers that if you can't give them one every day they won't read your publication, no matter how well it is edited."

The poet makes buttonholes for a living, and his machine is said to have listened to hundreds of sonnets which the East Broadway and Canal Street editors conspired to keep from the public. At one time he was employed on one of the Yiddish dailies, but lost his job during a political campaign, when he refused to write two editorials advocating the election of two opposing candidates, both to appear in the same issue of the newspaper. When this crisis was recalled to him he sprang to his feet, and with flaming cheeks shouted:

"How do you know? You read it in the English papers? It's all true, sir.

287

The beasts thought they hired my soul. But I gave it to them. I told them they did not have money enough to buy my spirit, nor power enough to enslave it, nor—''

"Did they get another man to do the job?"

The poet was sorely displeased by this interruption, but his sallow, emaciated face presently brightened up with a fresh smile as he said: "They got one man to write the Republican article and another man to write the Democratic leader, curs that they are."

"And how about the candidates? Don't they read the paper?"

"An Irishman read a language which runs from right to left, ha-ha-ha!" he chuckled, heartily. "But look here, if you mean to put it all in your paper for the Christians to read, I want you to be fair and to tell the other side of the story too. You see, bad as the publisher of that newspaper is, it was not his own invention. It was an Irish politician who gave him the tip. 'Print a good humming editorial booming the Democratic candidate,' he said to the publisher. 'We will pay you well for it.' 'That's all right,' said the publisher, 'but we are already booming the Republican candidate for the same office, and he does not want it for nothing, either.' 'Well, then, boom them both, and neither will be any the wiser, see?' "

"Is the practice kept up?"

"With modification it is kept up by two newspapers that are published in this city. Sometimes they print a Republican edition and a Democratic edition of the same number, sending to each candidate a copy containing what he pays for. I see you are smiling. That bespeaks the sense of decency and honesty which throbs in your heart. I should rather starve than traffic in my conscience. But I am afraid it is from some of the American papers that the publishers I have referred to have learned the trick. Don't your big papers often palm off paid advertisements for reading matter? And how about advance notices sent out by the press agents of theatre companies? Doesn't it amount to the same thing?"

The poet grew animated. He fell to pacing the floor of the café, his hands nervously tugging at his coat-tails, his deep, dark eyes flashing fire.

"They are honest people, after all, these publishers, who will not give me a job," he pursued. "If you weighed the good they do against the evil, the good will be the heavier of the two. And then you must not forget that we have two dailies which do not print any political advertisements nor any editorials to boom candidates, no matter how much gold you may offer them. They are Socialist papers, the *Vorwaerts* being the organ of the Social Democrats who follow Mr. Eugene V. Debs—you know him, don't you? He is an American—while the *Abendblatt* is controlled by the Socialist Labor

Party. These two are good papers, but they don't know how to make money. They don't belong to private individuals, but to two rival societies, who use them for the dissemination of their ideas.''

"Are you a Socialist?"

"Yes and no. You see, I hate anarchy because of the violence it preaches. Socialism, on the other hand, is too peaceful for me, so I went to work and thought out a social doctrine of my own which partakes of the qualities of both and which is peaceful and revolutionary at once. But you had better wait till the work upon which I am now engaged sees the light. It will make such a stir that it will at once be translated into all languages, and will sell a thousand times better than *Trilby*. Ah! it is a great idea—much better than the theories of Darwin, Karl Marx and Roentgen put together.''

Recalled to the subject of East Side journalism, the poet said:

"Well, the oldest and the most prosperous of our daily papers is the *Tageblatt*, although it comes out only once a day. The *Tagliche Herald* has a morning and an evening edition. Circulation? Well, I think they have from eight to twelve thousand. Advertising rates are a dollar an inch. Cheap enough, isn't it? But then, their editors don't get quite so much as the editor of your paper,'' the poet said, with one of his childish, honest laughs. ''From fifteen to twenty dollars a week is the market price for an editor, and about two dollars for an assistant. What! a managing editor, a city editor, a telegraph editor, a dramatic editor? Heavens! no. We don't know such things at all. Can it be that the American papers have so many editors? What for? One boss is enough. Of course a big American paper needs a lot of reporters, while one or two men are quite sufficient for our purpose. You fellows of the American dailies do the work for us.'' The poet smiled. ''All we have got to do is to know English enough to translate. Our morning paper comes out at 6 o'clock in the morning, and our afternoon dailies wait for the evening editions of the Christian papers. Besides, what does it matter if we do print today the news of day before yesterday?'' The poet smiled once more, as he continued:

"To make up for it, we sometimes publish on Friday the news that will happen next day. You see, Jews are not allowed by their faith to print a paper on the Sabbath, so they used to prepare the Sabbath paper on Friday, just as they prepare on Friday their Sabbath food. But the newsboys had no patience to wait for the holy day, and so it was the most common thing to hear them yell, 'Buy tomorrow's paper, all the latest news; one cent a copy!'

"And yet, after all, when you come to think of the many thousands of families who learn what is going on in the world through these papers, and who would otherwise be doomed to utter ignorance, you will agree that they

289

are of great use to the Jewish population. Our high-toned American brothers who live uptown and don't speak Yiddish are down on these papers. They prevent us from learning English, they say. But they are wrong. They know no more about our people than the Christians do. As a matter of fact, it is just because they read the Yiddish papers that they are interested in the world outside of their own district and become ambitious to know English in order to read the English papers. After they have learned that, they discard Yiddish altogether and read nothing but English. But, anyhow, is it not a curious fact that the United States, whose Yiddish-speaking population is about 400,000, should have five well-established Yiddish papers, while Russia, where the Jews number between four and five million, has never had a single daily in that dialect? There was published a Yiddish weekly in St. Petersburg some ten years ago, and it was struggling hard to make both ends meet when the Government put an end to its misery by suppressing it.

"There is, however, a Hebrew daily in Russia which is quite a success. It is printed in the language of the prophets, in real Hebrew, not in the German jargon which we speak. Lots of our people can write Hebrew with facility, and we have a Hebrew organ here too, but it is only a small weekly. The trouble with those who know Hebrew well is that they are more or less intelligent, and once they find themselves in this country where there is no difference between Jew and Gentile they take to learning English and have no time for the language of their forefathers. Ah, it is a beautiful language, the one in which Isaiah poured forth his fountain of liquid gems. And I am sure the day will come when all languages will perish to make room for the only, for the immortal tongue in which our race expressed its noble thoughts in the glorious days of our independence."

Daily journalism on the East Side is making rapid progress. Each newspaper has its own press by which it is enabled to produce a complete edition two hours after the appearance of the English journals upon which it depends for its news. Besides the regular editor and an assistant or two, each Yiddish daily has quite a number of contributors who supply it with humor, fiction, scientific articles, and what-not. There are several gifted and well-educated men among the writers, and some of their articles, sketches and poems deserve wider circulation than the Yiddish journals can give them.

"ROSY'S EYES WERE FULL OF TEARS"
April 9, 1898

"Good morning, madam," said the *colporteur*, as doffing his hat gallantly and giving a jerk to the load on his back, he entered the kitchen. "With your kind permission, I shall leave you a sample copy of *The Princess's Unrequited Love*, the novel which is keeping all the good housewives of Germany, Austria and Switzerland in tears just now. It is a story full of thrilling, heartrending, soul-stirring incidents—five murders, half a dozen suicides, sixteen love intrigues, most ingeniously woven into one. You get it in weekly installments, each week a book and each book five cents. Read the sample copy—I charge you nothing for it—and next week I shall come again and bring you the next number of the story."

The scene was "the third floor, back, right-hand side" of a tenement house off Avenue B, and the language in which the *colporteur*, a gaunt, long-haired bespectacled, sickly-looking young man, poured forth the rhetoric which he seemed to know by heart, was good Hanoverian German. Encouraged by the housewife's beaming attention, he was about to launch into a fresh torrent of eloquence, when the woman's face broke into a smile.

"No, sir, I am not interested in the Princess and her unrequited love," she said, returning the sample book to the *colporteur*, "nor in the dozens of murders and suicides. You will have to apply to the Yankees. They go in for this kind of literature, not we," she added, forgetting that *The Princess's Unrequited Love* was a German publication and that hundreds of *colporteurs* earned their living by selling just that kind of literature in the German quarter of this city, as well as in the cities and villages of Germany and Austria.

"Oh, I see; you are reading Sudermann, and you have Schiller and Goethe and Heine," said the *colporteur*, as his eyes fell on the open book on the kitchen table and on the little library on the mantelpiece.

He looked crestfallen, but forthwith braced himself and added, with some defiance:

"Schiller, Goethe and Heine I love to read myself. They are true poets. But what of Sudermann? They say he is a realist, don't they? Well, I don't care what he is, but he cannot write. There is nothing worth reading in his stories. I dabble in literature myself," the young man pursued, with a shamefaced blush which soon gave way to the radiance of self-admiration. "I have just finished a novel which is even more heartrending, more soul-stirring than *The Princess's Unrequited Love*. It will soon be published, and then it will make a furor such as New York never knew. Its name will be *Tears and Joys on Second Avenue*."

"And will you peddle it, too?" asked the lady, with uncharitable merriment.

"Laugh away, madame; you won't laugh much when the book is out. Whether you want it or not you shall have to cry over the fate of my heroine; you won't laugh then except at the unparalleled humor I got into the book. Adieu, madame!" he said morosely, lifting his load of *Princess's Unrequited Loves* to his shoulder.

"What is your business?" asked the Ellis Island clerk in Italian of the seedy, sallow individual in front of his desk.

"I am a novelist, *signore*," the newcomer answered with a queer mixture of hauteur and abject timidity.

"A novelist?" the clerk echoed in amazement.

"Yes, a novelist, and if you don't keep track of the literature of your native country you have only yourself to blame."

"But what are you going to do here for a living? Writing Italian novels is not much of a trade in this country, and as you have no money—"

"It's none of your business whether I have or not!" the man of letters thundered out with flashing eye.

The novelist was detained as a pauper, but somehow he managed to gain his freedom.

"What are you going to do?" the Italian clerk asked him, this time amicably, as the literatus was making his sullen departure.

"Do? I shall write novels, of course. Are there not enough Italians to support a novelist here? I know there are."

The immigrant was met two years later. It was in a rich uptown restaurant, and the novelist came up to the table in a white apron and overladen with dishes.

"You are a waiter?"

"Such is fate, *signore*! This is a terrible country. The Americans don't know Italian, and the Italians don't appreciate a good piece of literature."

"Have you published anything since we last met at Ellis Island?"

"I published a novel, but I lost on it what little money I had saved from my wages and tips—some $240 in all. Ah, it was a beautiful story, full of the sunshine of Sicily and throbbing with the passion and the poetry of its people.

And the plot? Why, once you began to read it you could not lay it down before you had read the last word. Two Counts have a duel, neither is injured, but the young lady—the cause of the feud—mysteriously disappears, and two villages engage in the search, and in a series of bloody encounters. Stilettos flash, blood trickles, houses are burned. Then one of the young Counts emigrates to America, and—but you must excuse me, the head waiter is looking daggers at me. I may lose my job."

There are some able journalists and literati among the Germans, Italians and Frenchmen of this city, and some of the best writers in Yiddish in the world are to be found in the tenement houses of the ghetto. The four Yiddish dailies published in New York—and, by the way, their number is soon to be increased by a new Yiddish daily, to be published by the Jewish members of Tammany Hall—have among their contributors some undeniably talented men. But these confine themselves to short stories, sketches or poems. The typical novelist of the Hester Street world is quite a different being. Dozens of Yiddish novels of thousands of pages each have been written, published, and met with success within the last few years. The authors of these are, for the most part, people who make a specialty of it, although the market is becoming overstocked and the author's fees grow smaller every year. The king of Yiddish novelists of this class is well known all over the world. He is the father of some 200 novels, all of which are held dear by the uneducated classes wherever the Yiddish tongue is spoken. He is said to be able to write three novels at a time, and the following was given as an everyday scene at the printing office where the fruit of his literary genius was transformed into pages of lead type:

"Mr. So-and-So! Mr. So-and-So!" calls a typesetter to the distinguished novelist, angrily. "I have not a bit of copy, and you know I have a large family to support."

"All right," says the author, who is characterized as the best-natured man on the East Side. "What are your last lines?"

The typesetter reads: "Rosy's eyes were full of tears; she stood wringing her hands and—"

"Is that all?" says the novelist. "Rosy? Who is Rosy? What story are you setting?"

" 'Rosy, the Unhappy!' Hurry up, Mr. So-and-So. It's nearly eleven, and I have hardly made 20 cents today."

"All right; go on, 'and she said my dear, my little heart, my little crown! I cannot live without you. I shall throw myself into the East River, unless you sweeten my life!' '' This the compositor scribbles down on the margin of the newspaper which contains his lunch.''

"Well?'' he urges on the novelist. He is anxious to take down enough to last him a few hours, but the man at the other case interrupts the proceedings.

"Mr. So-and-So! Hurry up, I am all out of copy. Moses has enough. Give me something to do. I am a man, too, and I must live as well as Moses.''

"Right away, my friend,'' says the kindly novelist. "I am coming. What are you setting up? 'The Queen's Daughter and the Jewish Minister'?''

"Why, that's being done by Charlie. I am on 'The River of Tears; or, The Unexpected Guest.' ''

"All right, read,'' etc.

One of Mr. So-and-So's most formidable rivals is said to have made a little fortune out of a novel called *The Mysteries of the Russian Court*, which he partly translated from a German *colporteur* edition, and partly drew from his own fertile imagination. The book was all the craze of the ghetto. It ran in some fifty or sixty weekly instalments, each in book form, and when the end was reached, and most of the characters had been hanged, shot, starved or drowned, the author and his publishers were in more genuine despair than the widows and orphans of the book.

"What is to be done? Suppose your next story does not take as well as *The Mysteries of the Russian Court*? Couldn't you spin the story out to fifty or sixty more instalments?''

"Spin it out?'' exclaimed the novelist testily. "I have been thinking of it myself, but what can I do, seeing that nearly all my heroes are dead. Spin it out!''

"Why didn't you let them live longer?'' asked the publisher.

"Don't put salt in my wounds, please,'' the author fired out. "I repent it sorely enough. I should have let them live.''

The man of fame fell to pacing the floor nervously. Presently he stopped short, his eyes aflame with sudden inspiration.

"I have hit it! I have hit it!'' he shouted, rubbing his hands with exultation. "Have you ever read a translation of *Ivanhoe* by the Gentile author Walter Scott? Well, I have; and in that story one of the leading characters—an old Saxon nobleman—comes to life again after having been dead for some time. The writer did not want to do it, but yielded to a request of his publishers. I shall do it for you. Rely upon my ingenuity and genius. All the dead men in my novel shall 'arise from the dead,' '' he said with a smile, quoting a piece of Hebrew. "And what is more, it will all come out smooth and natural, depend upon it."

"But where are you going to get the plot? The 'mysteries' you have translated from a German story, and there is no more of it. It ends where you have stopped," said the publisher, solicitously.

"Where will I take the plot? Leave it to me!" replied the novelist, radiantly. "It is not for nothing that I am considered to be a man of genius. Look here. You know *The Nile and the Victim*? It's a wonderful tale, as long as *The Mysteries*."

"But it's quite a different story!" the other protested. "The names are different and the thing has nothing to do with Russia."

"Of course it has not. But that's what my brains and talent are for. You don't expect me to translate it literally, do you? Names and places are changed easily enough. It will form an admirable sequel to *The Mysteries*." And it did. *The Mysteries* were continued without interruption for more than a year longer, and the author's name became more famous than ever.

PHILOLOGIST AND LEXICOGRAPHER
OF THE GHETTO
February 11, 1899

One of the celebrities among the Jewish immigrants in this country is Alexander Harkavy, whose residence is at 130 Madison Street, this city. He is the philologist of the ghetto, an indefatigable disseminator of English in its tenements and sweatshops, one of its most useful and most popular men. He came to this city from Novogrudok, Russia, his birthplace, in 1882. He was eighteen years of age then and many avenues seemed open to him, for he was an able and fairly well educated young man, and the many American cities where the Russian Jews began to settle in large numbers needed Yiddish-speaking doctors, lawyers, dentists, writers. But while Mr. Harkavy's friends took up the study of law, medicine or dentistry, he set his mind on the study of languages in general and English in particular.

"Our people must study the tongue of their new home," he reasoned. "They must have somebody to help them in that direction. I shall learn English myself and teach it to my fellow-countrymen."

The linguistic faculty runs in Mr. Harkavy's family, his uncle in Russia being a celebrated student of Oriental languages and literature. And so he had not been five years in America before he added to the command of Hebrew, Russian and Yiddish, which he brought with him, a thorough knowledge of English and German, as well as some familiarity with French, Spanish and Italian.

His sources of livelihood at this time were the private lessons in English which he gave to the workingmen of the East Side at the rate of 30 or 40 cents per hour. To increase both his income and the field of his usefulness he decided to write a textbook, enabling those who knew no other language than Yiddish to learn English words of everyday use and the rudiments of English grammar without a teacher.

His private lessons were all given in the evening when the sweatshop hands or peddlers are at home, and so Mr. Harkavy had plenty of time to devote to his book. Those who knew him at that time remember the absorbing interest and keen pleasure he took in his work. Some of his friends would banter with him on the dryness of definitions and conjugations, to which he devoted himself. For Mr. Harkavy, however, every English idiom for which he found a Yiddish equivalent, and every grammatical rule he was expounding in his mother tongue, possessed an irresistible charm and a poetry which he failed to find in the anatomy or law of contracts studied by his friends.

The book was published by a Canal Street printer, and so far as its usefulness to the Yiddish-speaking population was concerned it met with signal success. The author's income from its sales, however, was far from large. Still, Mr. Harkavy was happy. He pictured the many tenement-house families in which the textbook was studied by the younger people, fancied how hundreds of basters or cloakmakers were learning to say "What is your name?" for "*Wie ruft men dir?*" imagined himself the invisible teacher of hundreds and perhaps thousands of scholars scattered over the ghettos of America, and the picture thrilled him.

Mr. Harkavy's friends advised him to take up the study of some more profitable profession, but he paid no heed to them and went on writing textbooks, grammars, dictionaries and what-not, all devoted to the same subject, the object of his life—to teach the Jewish immigrants to speak, read and write English. All his works have been published, and all have met with the same sort of success as his firstborn. Altogether, Mr. Harkavy has brought out over twenty different books, his *chef d'oeuvre* being two dictionaries (English-Yiddish and Yiddish-English), which are said to have a large circulation not only in this country but also in Russia, where some Jews study English preparatory to leaving their birthplace for America.

Mr. Harkavy is today as poor as he was before his first book saw the light. A Jewish college offered him the chair of Hebrew and Chaldaic. It was a tempting offer, financially as well as in other respects. But he was afraid lest his duties at the college would leave him little time for his favorite work, and so he declined.

Mr. Harkavy is a spare, dark man of about thirty-four years, retiring and bashful. He speaks of his work reluctantly, but when interviewed on his favorite subject in the abstract, his answers are full of a quiet animation and a shamefaced sort of intensity. He occupies with his wife four rooms in a shabby old private house, their main furniture being Mrs. Harkavy's piano and several overcrowded bookcases. The little library includes some bibliographical rarities and a full set of the Babylonian Talmud.

When seen at his residence the other day, Mr. Harkavy said, in his bashful way, that his next textbook would probably be a manual of Spanish for the Yiddish immigrants of this country.

"I think many of our people will emigrate to Cuba, Puerto Rico or the Philippines, perhaps," he said. "When the Americans begin to develop these new possessions and to infuse new life into them, Jews here will probably be among the first to settle there. So a 'self-instructor' of the Spanish language may stand them in good stead."

Speaking of the Yiddish dialect, Mr. Harkavy said that it was spoken by the Jews all over Russian Poland, Galicia, Rumania and part of Hungary. He admitted that it was made up of several languages with a species of German jargon for its framework, but insisted that it had the vitality, the vigor and to some extent the beauty of a cultivated language.

"It is crude, of course," he said, "and lacks literary form and flexibility, but millions of people have spoken it for many hundreds of years, and so it is a living organism, robust, resourceful and worthy of the attention of the linguist."

Mr. Harkavy's textbooks and dictionaries are to be found in almost every Yiddish-speaking community in the United States. Many an immigrant has learned to read English newspapers and books by their aid, and the name of their author is held in high esteem in every ghetto of the country.

AN EAST SIDE EXTRA
April 6, 1899

Resnick, the foreman of the daily *Vorwaerts*, published at 35 Chrystie Street, was this morning nagging Louis Miller, the editor, for copy, when a man burst into the room.

"I have something important, Mr. Miller," he gasped, the palm of his hand pressed against his heart, for breath. "Something very important."

It is part of Mr. Miller's daily routine to be consulted by dozens of people (readers of his paper and others) upon their private affairs. Sometimes it is an affair of the heart, and as the newcomer was a young and dashing fellow, the editor mentally set him down for the hero (or the victim) of some tragedy, comedy, or tragi-comedy with a woman in the case. These stories never pall, but they make no copy, for they are strictly confidential. So the foreman frowned upon the newcomer and went on nagging the editor for copy. Mr. Miller, who is the leader of the East Side Social Democrats, is as celebrated for his imperturbable sense of humor as for his fiery eloquence. His followers also speak of his indomitable courage, but he himself admitted this morning that there was one man, at least, whose wrath is enough to leave him breathless with fright, and that man is Resnick, the foreman of the composing room.

"Give me five minutes' time, Resnick," he pleaded.

"Five minutes! It's 10 o'clock," grumbled the foreman ruthlessly. "You want the paper to be late once more, don't you? The other four Yiddish dailies will be out on time, and our circulation will fall off. If it does, it won't be my fault. Can't you sit down and write something?"

It is the foreman's sincere devotion to the paper and the principles it champions which lends so much poignancy to his suggestions.

"All right," smiled the editor.

"Excuse me, sir," the stranger broke in.

"Excuse me," the foreman checked him; "the editor is too busy."

"But I have got something which I want him to write. It'll make a first-rate article."

"We have plenty of articles," answered the foreman, peremptorily. "It's news we want. The article page is all set up and the form locked."

"But what I have got is just for the news page," insisted the visitor. "I

298

have received a letter this morning. It's from Bialystok and it tells about a spy that the nihilists of that town killed two weeks ago. It has not been printed in any paper. The censor would not allow it.''

The Yiddish dailies have not as yet found a correlative for "beat" or "scoop," but the editor of the *Vorwaerts* knows what it means, and his paper contains it quite often, he says.

"Got the letter?" he asked eagerly.

The foreman, too, changed front, and while the editor was reading the Russian letter he took out the piece of cord with which he measures the type for his forms.

"How much will it make?" he asked impatiently, measuring the atmosphere with his string.

"It's first-rate! A spread head! It will be the sensation of the day. Here, have it set up as it is, while I am dashing off the introduction." Resnick grabbed the letter and darted out. The letter was as follows:

Last Saturday night a vile wretch of a spy paid the penalty of his machinations. He had ruined many a faithful comrade. He had been instrumental in having some of the best workers for the cause of labor and freedom sent to Siberia. The spy's name was Mendel Kolner, a sweater in a weaving establishment in the city [Bialystok, Russia]. He was in the employ of the police and the gendarmes and betrayed some of the people who thought him a friend. Suddenly he disappeared. We looked for him a long time until finally we bagged him. You know we Russian Social Democrats do not believe in violence any more than our comrades of Germany or France or America. The days of terrorism are gone. What we want is a peaceful labor movement and a peaceful dissemination of the principles of liberty and fraternity. But in a case like this it is a mere matter of self-defense. The choice lay between that traitor and hundreds of honest, warm-hearted comrades. If he had been allowed to live they would have to die in Siberia—sooner or later. We decided the question in the only way which we thought logic, our conscience and the interests of humanity dictated. Traitors are shot in war. It is war we are carrying on, and the ruffian was shot. Eighteen bullets were put into his treacherous body. His death has cast a spell of deadly fright over his accomplices, and has infused fresh courage into the hearts of honest men.

An hour or two after the letter was snatched by the foreman, the streets of the ghetto were ringing with the voices of Jewish newsboys:

"Extra-a-a! Extra-a-a! A spy shot in Bialystok! Extra *Vorwaerts!*"

Mr. Miller was found at his desk reading Sienkiewicz's *Quo Vadis*, which he is translating for the paper, and smiling. The beat glistened in his eyes.

"This is the second fellow the nihilists of Bialystok have put out of the way within the last few months," he said. "As you see from the letter, we are bitterly opposed to the anarchists who preach violence or, for that matter, to anarchists of any sort. We are Social Democrats, law-abiding citizens. We achieve our purpose by peaceful preaching. Did you read in the papers about Mayor Jones of Toledo? He is a Social Democrat like myself, and he has been elected as such by a majority of 9,000 over the combined vote of his Republican and Democratic opponents. He is a rich man, and yet he is with the poor. Toledo is a large city, the centre of many industries. It is a great sign of the times. We are going to celebrate the election of Mayor Jones."

Mr. Miller spoke hastily. He was in a hurry, and the reason was that the foreman had once more made his appearance.

Resnick tried to look morose as ever, but the beat was shining in his dark eyes, too. It was copy for the "article page" for tomorrow's issue he was snarling for now.

"You had better tell this man about your trip to Siberia," Mr. Miller said. "He was prominent in the nihilist movement and was implicated in an important conspiracy and sent to the remotest districts. Tell us how you got away, Resnick."

The foreman colored. He hates notoriety.

"WHEN I WRITE YIDDISH,
IT IS PURE YIDDISH"
July 23, 1898

A bonnetless young woman with a letter in her hand was gazing about her, as if in search of something, as she leisurely proceeded on her way along Ludlow Street.

"Missus! Missus! Want an express?" asked half a dozen burly men.

The young woman blushed and shook her head.

"Buy fish? cucumbers? horseradish? Sabbath loaves?" several market women clamored in chorus, tugging the bashful pedestrian by the arm or skirt as she passed them.

"No," was the young woman's invariable reply.

"Oh, I know what she wants!" broke in a little boy, the son of one of the fishmongers. "She wants to have a letter written; don't you, missus?"

"Sure I do. How did you guess it?" the young housewife said gratefully. "Do you know of a letter writer around here?"

"My rabbi [teacher of Hebrew] writes letters cheap and good. He lives around the corner. Shall I show you where it is?"

His offer accepted, the boy led the way, the young woman and a snooper in the ghetto following him. Presently the boy stopped in front of a basement window with a little signboard which read: "Hebrew Taught. Letters Written in Yiddish, English, German, Russian and Hebrew."

The rabbi was found at the head of a class of dirty boys who were lazily singing over huge open books. He was an old man with a reddish little beard and a wrinkled, cadaverous face.

"Louder, or I'll break every bone in—" The threat was suddenly broken off by the appearance of the newcomers, and the rabbi, without relaxing the angry and distressed look on his face, asked:

"Do you want to have letters written? Can you wait till we finish a chapter? We have only a few verses. Be seated."

The boys resumed their singing, some of them casting furtive glances at the strangers.

"Where do you keep your eyes, Gentile boy that you are? Look at your Bible, or I'll make you look the angel of death in the face," said the old man in a perfunctory sort of way.

The chapter finished, the rabbi asked, as he reached out his hand for the woman's letter:

"Where did you get it?" And without heeding her wordy answer, he fell to glancing over the epistle while three of his pupils made a scramble for the dust-covered inkstand on the mantelpiece.

"Silence, loafers you! Silence, or I'll break every bone in your Gentile bodies," the rabbi murmured to himself, from force of habit. Then putting down the letter with a bored air, he said, taking up pen and paper:

"Have you anything in particular to write, young woman?"

"Particular?" echoed the woman, blushing. "What can there be particular? Tell my sister that I am sending her ten American dollars, and that it makes more than twenty Russian rubles, and that I hope to the Uppermost that her husband will get well. Tell her also that I cannot send her any more now, but that after awhile I will. Mother sends her love. What else? Oh, tell her also that God has given me a crown for a husband and that he kisses my

301

footprints and treats mother like his own mamma, and—and—and—what else? Don't you know of anything else to write, rabbi?''

''I think you have got enough. You don't want me to be writing a whole year for five cents, do you?'' he grumbled.

''A whole year? You have only been writing ten minutes,'' his client protested, and then as if suddenly remembering something, she said with an ingratiating smile:

''Don't be angry, rabbi dear. You see, all my neighbors are writing to their parents about the war, so I should like to do the same. How much will you charge for writing it all up, just as it is?''

''I'll only charge you three cents extra,'' the rabbi replied, as he went to get a sheet of paper from his rickety old bureau. ''Here you have all about the war, young woman. Why do you make such a face? Don't you believe it's a description of the war? Am I a thief to rob you? If you think I am, then I'll tear the other letter to pieces and you can go with your five cents to where you came from.''

The poor woman turned pale. But the student of the ghetto interceded in her behalf, explaining the while that he was there for information and not as a client. Then it was the rabbi's turn to grow red and pale by turns.

''It is all fair and square, gentlemen,'' he said, as if answering charges. ''The description of the war is all true and carefully done, only I prepare several copies of it in advance. It spares me time, and I can do it in my leisure hours, in the evening. And what difference does it make to my customers? They get all about the war all the same, don't they? Besides, as you have seen, I only charge them three cents for it, while if I was to write a special one for each customer I could not do it for less than five cents.''

''All right, I'll pay you five cents extra and write me all about the war to order,'' struck in the woman.

''That I can't do unless you come in the evening, young woman,'' said the rabbi. ''The time is not mine. It belongs to these boys. Their fathers pay for it.''

But the woman was in a hurry, for her sister, who lives in Poland, needed the money, so it was decided at the rabbi's suggestion that the war letter be submitted to the stranger's judgment; whereupon the rabbi proceeded to read it in dramatic sing-song, a variation of the one in which his pupils had been studying their Hebrew books. The missive read, in part, as follows:

> And so the Lord of the World gave strength and power to the friends of the Jews, the American people, and they were victorious over our enemies, the fiends of the sons of Israel, at a place called Cuba. And much human blood flowed, and among those killed

were some children of Israel, for here it is not as it is in Russia. Here everybody goes to the war of his own will, and Jew and Gentile are alike. And two of the brave sailors who were wounded at the beginning of the fight, while cutting the enemy's telegraph under the sea, were Jews, and they had staked their lives of their own accord, for nobody compelled them to go. And they said to their captain: "We want to go," and he let them go. And a man named Dewey conquered a lot of Spanish islands called Manila, and burned their ships, and he was so brave, because the God of Abraham, Isaac and Jacob is with the Americans, because the Americans are good to the Jews. And we all pray in the synagogues that the war come to a speedy end and the Americans conquer their enemies completely, and that no more blood be shed in the world.

The visitor found the letter magnificent, much to the satisfaction of its author, whose wrinkled old face shone as he said:

"You should see my Hebrew! Yiddish is not much of a language. It does not come up to the holy tongue, the tongue of the law and prophets. You see, in Yiddish you can write no poetry, no lofty thoughts, but in Hebrew you can. Unfortunately very few of my customers have any use for it. 'What do I want with Hebrew?' they say. 'Write me a letter in plain Yiddish, so that my father can understand it.' Some want English, and they are mostly old people whose children have been raised here and are now in another American city. Russian letters I write for those of my customers who come from Moscow, St. Petersburg or other such cities. They can hardly speak Yiddish and they communicate with their friends in their mother tongue, which is the language of the Russians."

When the young woman was gone the rabbi resumed with a sigh:

"You see mine is a miserable life. It's hard work to teach these American loafers Hebrew. They don't care for it. In the forenoon they go to school where they learn Gentile wisdom, and that they like much better. They hate to talk Yiddish, and for the Bible they don't care half as much as they do for their school readers and the foolish stories they get there. Would at least their fathers could afford to pay me well for my labor. But they can't, for they are all poor workmen, and it is a good thing they send their boys to study the word of God at all. So all I get is from 75 cents to one dollar per boy, and how can you live on that? Small wonder we teachers of Hebrew must piece out our wretched living with side shows such as matrimonial agencies, letter writing, peddling, or the like. Still, thanks be God for what He gives us," he concluded with a smile.

Asked about his customers and the letters they want written, the rabbi said: "It's nothing to tell. Most of our Jews here can write their own letters. It's only those who come from the poorest families who need our services. Of course, most of the letters of these are written by their neighbors free of charge, but some would hate to bother a stranger or to let the housewives of their tenement know what they are writing about, so they come to us. Most of my customers are so simple-minded that they don't know what to communicate to their parents, wives or friends in Russia. 'Write that I am well, thank God,' they will tell you; 'and that I send my love to all, and for the rest, dear rabbi, you know better than I how a letter should be written.' With people of this class—and they are in the majority among my customers—I have little trouble. I have a form, of which I make twenty or thirty copies at a time, leaving space for the names and some particulars, and these I fill out in the presence of each client. Do they object? Not as a rule. They simply don't know what I am doing. It is a long time since you were an illiterate little boy, or you would know that the sight of writing makes their heads dizzy, and they can't tell the difference between the line that is being written under their noses and those that have been prepared beforehand. Besides, they don't care what you do, so they get a letter to carry to the Grand Street post office. When there is something of peculiar interest, like a big election or the war or some other sensation, I know that many of my clients will want to send home a description of it, and so I prepare a lot of such descriptions, copies of the same original which I make carefully—and the rest you have seen for yourself. Among the things that we usually have to describe are the furniture, the dresses, the meats, the Jewish theaters, and the general mode of living in this part of the city. Our customers are fond of boasting to their friends of the advantages America has over Russia and of showing that the poorest American workman eats and dresses better than a Russian nobleman, although sometimes, when the customer is out of work, the bragging may be turned into lamentations and curses upon Columbus for having discovered America at all. Such wailings are also characteristic of those who are afraid lest some undesirable relative might want to come over and ask for a passage ticket. But those are exceptional cases. The majority sing the praises of their new home and enclose in their letters views of New York to show what a grand city they live in. Sometimes we are told to add in the missive something like this: 'Do you see that beautiful tall palace on the picture, mamma? The street is called the Bowery and I live only a block or two from it.'

"Some of the letters which our customers receive from Russia or Galicia are full of English words, such as 'letter,' 'rooms,' 'moved,' 'picture,' and a dozen or two others which our Yiddish dialect has absorbed from the language of this country. You see, I hate to use these words in my letters. When I write Yiddish, it is pure Yiddish. But most other letter writers will write just as they speak here, and as their spoken Yiddish has got full of English words, their letters also are full of them. At first the recipients of these letters in Russia wondered what these words meant, but little by little they found out their meaning and came to use them, in their turn, in the letters which they wrote to America, till it has got to be fashionable to write 'letter' for *brief*, 'furniture' for *mebel*, or 'country' for *land*."

"IF IT'S ONLY A PAGE, IT'S FIVE CENTS"
November 22, 1901

A scrawny old Italian woman in a gay shawl and with a big pile of new knee-breeches on her head stopped in front of a cake stand on one of the Italian streets on the middle East Side and asked the proprietor whether he was the letter writer of whom she had heard.

"Of course I am," answered the stand-keeper, a fat, middle-aged man, with two dark little slits for eyes. "Do you want a letter written? Here, I have pen and ink and paper and envelopes all ready for you, *signora*. Who is it you want to write to—a son, a sister?"

"You're in too much of a hurry, *signore*," retorted the old woman, without removing the load from the top of her head. "You had better tell me how much you charge."

"I won't skin you, *signora*. You are not a rich American lady. It depends upon how long your letter is going to be. If it's only a page it's five cents; but if you have a great deal to say it'll be more."

"It won't be much this time. I must take this bundle to Bleecker Street before the factories whistle for lunch, so I haven't time for a long letter. Make it short. The man who used to write my letters on 104th Street was a great fellow at his trade. He could make you weep."

The cake vendor promised to try his best and proceeded to compose an epistle to the old woman's brother. It was a purely business letter. Her brother, who is in Italy, had bought some real estate with money which she had sent him from America, so she wanted him to pay the rent to a merchant who is in correspondence with a Mulberry Street banker.

"A dull letter!" exclaimed the stand-keeper, with a contemptuous shrug, when the woman had gone. "I often write eloquent ones. Those I like, and sometimes when I get going I write six or even eight pages, although I only charge for three or four. Most of my customers are old women, but I have some girls and young fellows who have love letters to write. That's the kind of stuff I like, especially when the customer is not bashful and wants to lay bare his heart to his girl. But old women are sometimes full of feeling, too. Some of them pour out their hearts to their children, and this gives me a pretty good chance for fine writing. There is nothing like a letter in which every word is ablaze with feeling, with real feeling, *signore.*"

As he said this his narrow little eyes became large and wide, and seemed to be ablaze, like the letters of which he spoke.

"I had an interesting case yesterday. A little bit of a girl wanted me to write her a love letter to a man in Boston. She didn't look more than fourteen, but she said she was eighteen, and the man I wrote to is her husband. Poor child, he doesn't care for her, the brute, and she cried so much, as she tried to tell me what she wanted me to say for her, that she could hardly speak, and I, I was so overcome I burst into tears, too. But you should have seen the letter I composed! If it does not melt the heart of that wretch he ought to be hanged or killed in the electric chair, the scoundrel."

The letter writer's neighbor, a cobbler, said that the ease with which the scribe could be made to weep was good for his business.

"The women who patronize him appreciate his tears," he added. "I know some who come here all the way from Elizabeth or Mott Street, and when you ask them why they can't get their letter writing done in their own neighborhood, they answer: 'Ah, but this man has so much soul!' "

Another professional letter writer, also an Italian, showed the reporter a letter which he had written for a client a few weeks ago, but which had been rejected because the description of America which it contained was not to the taste of the customer's daughter.

"When I first read it to her she liked it," he said. "But in the evening, when her girl came from work, she had a neighbor read it to her, and as the girl said it was no good she returned it to me. She wanted her five cents back, but, of course, she never got them."

Following is part of the missive in question:

America is a greater country than Italy, and Casimiro is making more money than he ever made at home. It is such a great country that sometimes you ride two hours in a big wagon which runs without horses (electricita they call it, but nobody can see it). The houses are so high that if you put two churches one on top of the other it would be like a big American house. That's all. There are railroads in the streets, and now they are digging out a big ditch for another railroad, which will run underground, that is to say, underneath America.

The author of the letter laughed at his own description. He was a school teacher at home and is quite an intelligent man, but the woman who ordered the epistle insisted on his writing every word she dictated.

"It was all I could do to keep from chuckling," he said. "She is a peasant woman, one of the most ignorant creatures you ever saw, but she had the courage of her convictions. Her daughter and their neighbors probably told her it was all nonsense, and, of course, she never confessed to them that the whole thing was of her own composing, and that she had compelled me to write it all down as it came from her lips. When she brought the letter back I put her in mind of the facts, but she screamed: 'What I told you to put in is all right. You didn't put it in right. That's the trouble.' Of course there is no use trying to reason with a virago like that."

In the ghetto the business is in the hands of keepers of cigarette and newspaper stands and teachers of Hebrew. Signboards announcing the fact that "here you can have your children instructed in the holy tongue and your letters written in Yiddish, English, German or Hebrew" are among the characteristic sights of the neighborhood.

One man told of his regular clients in the tenement houses, and how he goes from house to house writing letters for illiterate people.

"I'm just like a doctor," he said gayly. "You see, most of the people in my line of business are like lawyers. Their clients come to their offices. Mine—at least the regular customers—don't. I have a standing order to call on such-and-such a day; or, sometimes, a child will be sent to my house. 'Mister, mamma wants you to come and write a letter for her; hurry up.' This is the way they talk. Some children have no respect for older people. Of course, every tenement house is full of men and women who can write, so my clients could get some of their neighbors to carry on their correspondence for them. But then, a letter is apt to contain some secrets or private information of some sort or other, so they prefer to have it written by a man like myself, in whom they know they can confide. I am not the kind of fellow to give away professional secrets—not I.

"Most of the letters are about money that immigrants send to their parents or poor friends in their old home. The Grand Street branch of the post office is usually crowded with people who have some business at the money order department. Then there are the private banks of the neighborhood.

There are scores of them, and in each place you can see crowds of men and women waiting for a chance to hand in some money they want to send home. Well, all these people must write letters, mustn't they? In the first place, the money order must be accompanied by a few lines about the amount sent, and so forth and so on. In the second place, when a man, for instance, is so good to his parents at home that he will send them part of his hard-earned wages he cannot be a coarse-hearted man. He is sure to have some nice things to say to his father and mother.

"Many of my clients patronize me with the understanding that I won't tell anybody that they can't write. When I come in, they lock the door, so that no neighbor should discover me writing their letters, and when somebody knocks at the door I remove the paper as quickly as I can, while my customer goes to see who it is. It is foolish, but some people are too proud to let people know who they were at home. You see, some of my clients are pretty well fixed. They are in business and have fine carpets and expensive furniture. The women wear fine big bonnets and put on all the style they can. But some of these women are the daughters of poor shoemakers or chimney sweeps. They came over from the old country penniless, but their husbands have been successful here, and now your chimney sweep's daughter is playing the grand lady. Do you think she'll be anxious to have her neighbors know she can't even scribble? No, sir. She'll rather pay me an extra price, so as to make sure her secret is safe.

"Some of these rich people who put on airs but can't write take lessons in reading and writing. This they do in strict secrecy, just as their correspondence is done. I have no pupils of this sort, but a friend of mine has half a dozen of them.

"Some women send money to their parents unbeknownst to their husbands. These never have their correspondence done at home. There are other secrets which a woman may want to keep from her husband. For instance, one woman who used to patronize me two years ago was in correspondence with a man from whom she had been divorced. From the letters I knew that so far as the woman was concerned there was nothing wrong about it. It was a peculiar case of blackmail. That first husband of hers was a gambler and an all-around rogue. She married him in Odessa without knowing much about him, but she did not live long with him. As soon as she found him out she obtained a divorce and came to America. Here she married a most respectable man, whom she really loves. She told him she was a widow and that her first husband was a merchant, but she was always trembling for fear he might discover the truth. Somehow the gambler got on to it all—through some fellow-countryman of his, I suppose—and every time he needed a few rubles he would write to the poor woman, threatening to come here.

"You see, I wouldn't tell you all this two years ago, for then it was one of my professional secrets. But the woman's troubles are all over. One day her husband found a letter which she had left on the bureau by mistake. He soon knew the whole story, but it proved that the woman had been paying that man for nothing. Her husband is really fond of her and a good man, too, so he told her it was all right and that she needn't worry. Then I had a job to write a long letter to that gambler calling him all kinds of names and telling him that his former wife wasn't afraid of him."

One man, an elderly fellow, who rents a corner in a watchmaker's shop, was pointed out as a specialist in love letters. When he was asked for a specimen of his eloquence he said shyly:

"I keep no samples of my goods. Pay me for a letter for your lady love and you will have the sample you want. And if there is no such lady one can imagine one." The bargain was struck and the old man set to work. The letter ran as follows:

> The clear sky is blue, but your eyes are bluer; the birds of the air sing beautifully, but your voice is far more beautiful to the ear. Consolation of my life! My sweet vivifier! My sweet little crown! My heart feels like a chicken which wants to fly and has no wings. Alas, I am here, and thou art there! How can I live, how can I work, how can I be in peace while there is nothing but darkness around me—darkness which only the light of your consolation of a face could disperse.

"But how do you know her eyes are blue?" was asked.

"Well, I usually ask the customer what the color of the girl's eyes are. If they are black, I say nothing about the blue sky, of course, but there are lots of other things one can say about eyes."

"WOE AND JOY" FOR SALE
February 9, 1900

A prosperous-looking East Sider called at the Thalia Theatre while the actors were rehearsing an old play for the next performance. He applied at the box office, but in answer to a question as to what sort of tickets he wanted, he said resentfully:

"I don't want any tickets. I have a play to sell. Where are the actors?"

"It's a guy," whispered the cashier to the manager, who came in to inquire what was the matter.

The man was taken behind the scenes and introduced to the leading actor.

"I have got a play which I can let you use, provided you promise to produce it properly. Do you understand?" said the playwright, grandly.

A wink passed from eye to eye. The actors had not had a "guy" for a long time, and the old play they were rehearsing was dull. Besides, they knew it well, so they fell into line and sang out in chorus:

"All right, all right. Let us hear the gentleman read his drama."

The playwright flew into a passion.

"What do you mean by making fun of me?" he asked.

"They are not making fun of you at all," explained the star in his humblest manner. "This is the way every play is received, sir. If you object to it, we can't hear you read your drama, sir."

"That's all right. I thought they were taking me for a fool. But if this is part of the business, I don't mind. On the contrary, I wish to have my play treated according to the best rules of your profession. Otherwise how can you do it justice? But it is not a drama. It is a historic opera and comedy."

Here the guy took out of his pocket a small memorandum book, such as grocers give to their customers to keep their accounts in, and handed it to the star.

Another wink passed around the stage. The leading man opened the book and read:

"*Woe and Joy; or, Seven Years in the Dark Woods*. A historic opera in seven acts. In the first act the actors crack smart jokes and the public laughs. There are trees on the stage, and in one of them there is a canary bird which looks from the gallery to the orchestra as it chirps a beautiful song."

"Splendid! Beautiful! Can it be possible that you have never written dramas before?" the actors shouted. And, as they knew their business, the guy was in the seventh heaven.

"I swear that this is my first work," he said.

They exchanged looks, gestures and sighs of admiration, and expressed the desire to have him read his own play. He agreed.

"But in order to read it effectively, so that we can judge of its real beauty, you must make up as the characters are to look on the stage. Do you understand?"

"Of course I understand. Do you take me for a greenhorn?" answered the playwright with a touch of resentment. "The only trouble is that there are so many characters in the play, and I don't know how to make up."

"Why, like the whole lot of them!" replied the actors. "Every playwright does that. Else how can we know what effect his play may have?"

They also told him that they would have to take seats in the gallery or even in the corridors, while he was to read his play from the stage. How otherwise could they tell what effect the drama would have on the audience?

About an hour later a heavy figure, muffled up in beards, uniforms, and laden with crowns, swords, daggers, rifles, stood in the centre of the stage shouting at the top of its voice from the grocer's book. It was the guy. The sun came in through the windows in broad slanting bars, falling on the gilt of the chairs and illuminating the lumps of paint on the playwright's cheeks. The seats rose before him like a gigantic honeycomb. There was not a soul in sight, yet he read on. He dared not stir. He had been told to beware of marring the effect of his reading. When he got to the end of his manuscript he paused.

"Did you hear it all?" he shouted.

There was no answer.

The guy was frightened.

"Did you hear it, I say?" he asked again.

"Did you hear us laugh?" came a voice from the rear.

"Yes; why?"

"It's a very funny play. You may go home."

It took the guy an hour to undress. He never came to offer plays again.

"I SAW PARADISE OPEN BEFORE ME"
November 10, 1900

A little piece of humorous-pathetic life cut from Yiddish New York has recently been put into burlesque literary form in one of the ghetto newspapers. Leon Kobrin is the author, a man who writes many plays and short stories descriptive of the life of the Jewish quarter. This particular story made the whole Russian East Side laugh for two weeks, and the author is as proud of it as he would be of a play that ran three nights (a long time for a Yiddish theatre) in succession at the Thalia. It is the story of an old woman from Russia who has come to live with her children in New York. She is an orthodox Jewess and a greenhorn. By the latter term is meant somebody who is not "on to" the customs of the Russian Jews in New York.

The woman of Mr. Kobrin's sketch hates America. She is too old to learn new ways, and is shocked and puzzled at every turn. Her married daughter is so irreligious that the old lady won't stay with her at Easter, but goes to dine with an old countrywoman of hers who still does things in the old way, at whose house food is *kosher*, and prayer is devout and in correct form.

She has been there often before. She cannot read the names of the streets, and the system of blocks confuses her. She finds her way instinctively, with a few picturesque helps, one of which is the image of an Indian, before the door of a cigar store. When she arrives there she knows how to find her way. But on this particular occasion she cannot find the Indian, which she calls a Turk. She is confused and can't find her way, either to her old friend's house, or back home.

She sees a Jew on the street, with a beard. "Ah! that is an orthodox!" she thinks. "He will tell me where the Turk is." She seizes him by the arm. "Countryman," she cries, "where is the Turk" He stares and passes on. A *goy* (Gentile) with a shaved face attracts her attention. Perhaps he will know. "Where is the Turk?" she asks, in her Yiddish. But the Gentile does not understand. She grows more and more distressed, and asks everybody she meets about the whereabouts of the Turk. The young men crowd around her and derisively refer to her as "Grandma," and make fun of her Turk. She tells an Irish policeman in Polish that she wants to find the Turk. She uses Polish, for she thinks there are only two languages, Yiddish for the Jews and

Polish for the Gentiles, and the policeman she recognizes as a Gentile. He speaks Yiddish, however, and says: "Come to the station with me and perhaps we can find the Turk."

She thinks she is going to jail, and weeps violently. "Oh, I wish I were in Russia!" she cries to the jovial crowd of mixed "Jids" and Irish toughs who follow as the policeman drags her along. At the police station they hold a consultation about the Turk, and the store where the Indian originally stood, but from which it had been recently removed, was at last found, and the old woman returned to her daughter's house in safety.

But this was not the last of her adventures in New York. She had many of them, among the most amusing being her experience at the Yiddish theatre, where she behaved somewhat as Partridge did when he went to see Garrick with Tom Jones. She tells a neighbor afterward all about it. Her granddaughter was about to be married, so the whole family went to the theatre to celebrate.

"Before I went," she said, "I thought it would be a menagerie, where I could see some fine beasts. But it was not amusing at all. It was shocking. I will tell you, *Ach,* America!

"We went into a big building, where they played music just as if it was a *hochzeit* [wedding]. There were three or four stories to the house, and in front of the musicians was a wall, which suddenly disappeared through the roof. The lights went out, and the musicians, not being able to see, stopped playing. At the same time the people on the top roof began to yell and hiss. They were afraid when the lights went out, and I did not blame them, for it was very dark up there, and they thought they would fall down off the narrow roof.

"Then, suddenly, where the wall had been, I saw Paradise open before me, and all the people were quiet and looked at the spectacle. There was a real old Jew, such as you see him in the old country, with a long, long beard. He was rocking his body to and fro, chanting the Talmud, which he held before him. It was like heaven. I was very glad, and hoped my children would learn to be as pious as that. If there are such good Jews in America, America cannot be so bad, after all.

"Then the daughter of the rabbi appeared from behind another wall. She was as beautiful as seven suns. The rabbi kissed her, but I didn't think it was very decent to do it before the crowd, but he was a rabbi, so I guess it was all right.

"Then I was shocked to see a shoemaker appear, a very common man. And just imagine, the beautiful rabbi's daughter was in love with him—in love with a shoemaker! What a place is America! And he was a *goy,* too, for

313

he was shaved, a regular Gentile! America must be responsible for such things!

"And they kissed each other in public. And the people all laughed. And the rabbi didn't seem to notice, but kept on reading the Talmud. Ah, me! What will become of my children? I wanted to tell the rabbi what his wicked daughter was doing. I called to him, but he paid no attention. My children told me to keep quiet. They said it was not good to cry out in the theatre. But I struggled, and yelled still louder: 'Father rabbi, look at your daughter; she is kissing behind your back, and kissing a *goy*!' But he did not hear me. He must have been deaf. The people near me looked at me as if they were angry, and said: 'Keep quiet, will you?' But I cried till the wall closed up and the rabbi, the girl and the shoemaker disappeared. And then my children said they would never take me to the theatre again."

DIE ZWEI KUNELEHMELE
("THE TWO CLUNKS")
April 5, 1901

Not long ago, an old Jewish play was reproduced on the Bowery, written by Abraham Goldfaden, the founder of the Jewish stage, and to whom that stage is indebted for some of its classics. This particular play of Goldfaden's is a farce, but with a genuine quality of fun and delightfully expressive of Jewish character and customs. It is called *Die Zwei Kunelehmele*.

When the curtain rises, it is Friday night, the Jewish Sabbath. The rabbi, his wife, daughter and their neighbors have returned from the synagogue. The men, with their long beards, with the orthodox "locks" hanging down over their ears, their long black coats and tall silk hats, sit around a table, which bears two tall candlesticks, a flagon of wine and some glasses. At the other side of the room is another table, similarly set, around which sit the women, with their kerchiefs and their drab and homely apparel.

The guests depart, and the rabbi and his wife discuss the matrimonial prospects of their daughter, who has also left the room. The old man and his wife quarrel, because the rabbi wants the girl to marry one man and his wife wants her to marry another. The young man picked out by the rabbi is the son of another famous rabbi. That makes up for all his deficiencies, which are many, for the young fellow is lame, has only one eye, stutters and is half-witted. The mother has chosen, however, a handsome young fellow for her daughter, whom, moreover, the latter loves.

Then enters the *Vermittler*, the go-between, who, in orthodox Jewish communities in Russia, in which land these events are supposed to take place, is indispensable in all amatory matters. The young people never have anything to say about it. Love, if it comes at all, comes after marriage. The *Vermittler* describes to the girl's father the young fellow whom he has selected. The old rabbi strokes his beard reflectively, weighing the points. The *Vermittler* admits that the chosen one does not see very well out of his left eye, but that his right is pretty good. He also admits that the young man's walk is rather peculiar, but, then, he is rich and the son of a holy man. The *Vermittler* urges the fact that the Bible does not forbid marrying with the lame. If he is orthodox, it's all right. The inside is good, whatever the externals may be. The two arrange to meet soon and determine upon the engagement. They go out together and the young girl enters.

She sings a pleasing song, one of those Yiddish songs composed by Goldfaden before the Jewish stage was born. The stage is darkened, the curtain in the rear ascends, and the chorus, composed of Russian students, with her young lover, the handsome one, at their head, complete her wavering notes. The two lovers talk over the danger. She may have to marry the lame son of the rabbi! Cunning only can prevail. So the young student determines to disguise himself in the unattractive shape of the other wooer and palm himself off on the girl's father and the *Vermittler* as the chosen one.

This brings about a long series of farcical situations, some of them taking place in picturesque locations, among the congregations in front of the synagogue, or during the procession of the Maccabeans. The real cripple and the false one meet and gibe each other—make fun of each other's defects. The masquerading student exaggerates the other's limitations to such a degree that he frightens the old rabbi, the girl's father, who now wants to back out of the agreement, but the girl, knowing it is her lover, refuses to withdraw from the engagement. Then the student departs, and the real cripple enters. The girl, thinking it is still her lover, makes love to him, much to his astonishment. It results, naturally, in the girl's anger when she sees that he will not drop what she supposes to be a disguise. That, of course, brings about further trouble between her and her real lover, when he again appears.

The rabbi and his wife have another quarrel scene. Whenever the old man argues he speaks in a sing-song, moving his body to and fro, after the manner of the orthodox Jews. But his faith in the desirability of the union is nevertheless weakened, and the old woman begins to triumph, in her mild, wifely fashion.

315

In an ensuing interview between the girl and the cripple some of the popular superstitions are comically exploited. The one-eyed beau, who is very pious—so pious that he is always washing his hands in the air, in default of water—questions the girl about her religion, finds her, to his horror, very ignorant, and that she does not believe in ghosts and visiting angels. She laughs at him, jollies him, throws kisses at him. This is indeed horrible to his orthodox senses. It is not allowed to kiss, and he thinks her very wicked. He is afraid to be alone with her, and runs off the stage. Then the real one comes in disguise, and continues the scenes of misunderstanding. By this time the old parents think the girl has been bewitched to love such a monster.

In the next scene the lovers discover their mistakes and put up a joke on the old people, who now think the young man is a magician. He sends a note to his student friends, asking them to disguise themselves as ghosts. Then he disguises himself as a rabbi, chants, talks to his ancestors, looking up at the ceiling. He threatens to fly away through the air. All the while the real rabbi listens to him, terrified. He and his wife seize the young fellow to keep him from flying away. When he gets them thoroughly scared he extracts a promise from the rabbi that he will give his daughter to him. Then, with a wafture of the hand, he brings in dead souls (the students arrayed in white) to witness the rabbi's promise. The old rabbi puts the Bible on his head to ward off the evil spirits. The play closes with the engagement scene of the young lovers. The guests drink and dance, the cup is smashed upon the floor, signifying the permanence of the bond, and so everything comes out all right.

THE OPERA STANDEES

The Sun / December 21, 1902

That music has enough charms to make men and women—particularly women—stand for three hours and longer at a stretch without flinching is proved every Saturday afternoon at the Metropolitan Opera House. On Saturdays the feminine standees are out in full force.

At almost every matinée, long before the opera begins, there is a long line of women encircling the lobby and besieging the box office for admissions. It is noticeable that the first-comers seem to be in just as much of a hurry as those who arrive later—and for a good reason: every woman of them has in her mind's eye a particular brass railing on the other side of the entrance doors which divides the orchestra chairs from the standees' quarters, the five-dollar-a-ticket elect from the one-dollar-and-a-half cosmopolitans, and she is cherishing a determination to reach that railing among the first.

Once past the ticket taker, the rush begins, and the invaders who reach the coveted goal heave a big sigh of relief. Then, happy in the possession of a good, stout support to lean against and an unobstructed view of the stage, they contentedly settle themselves on their two feet for an afternoon's enjoyment.

And that the majority of the standees—even the unlucky ones who don't get anywhere near the sustaining railing and must content themselves with looking over other people's shoulders—do enjoy themselves, there can be no doubt; or why do the same people go over and over again?

"I feel as if my back was broken," faintly remarked a delicate-looking woman at the close of a *Tannhauser* matinée which lasted nearly four hours.

"Well, I hope you won't try it again," sympathetically returned a friend, who herself looked ready to drop. To her surprise, evidently, as well as the surprise of several bystanders, the quick answer was:

"Why, I mean to come next Saturday and the Saturday after that. I never feel a bit tired until the opera is all over "

Until this season, when the ungallant and much anathematized Fire Department interfered, it was quite customary at the opera house for women to flop down comfortably on the floor between the acts. Nothing, of course, could induce a woman who held a place at the rail to run the risk of losing it by going outside to camp on the stairs after the manner of some less fortunate standees. So they solved the problem by dropping down Turkish fashion just where they stood until the curtain went up again. But of late the awful edict has gone forth that no one may sit on the floor.

"It is against the rules of the Fire Department, madam," says an usher firmly.

Therefore the rail position is more in demand than ever, and women, young, old and middle-aged, are trying to adjust themselves to the new situation. Stand or not, there they are by the scores every Saturday afternoon, and the box office receipts from this source are as big as they ever were.

This (to the stockholders) satisfactory condition bears out the assertion of some opera house habitués that Mr. Grau's stars are far better appreciated by the standees than by either the box owners or the holders of orchestra chairs, and that the standees are by far the best-behaved part of the audience.

As a matter of fact not a whisper is tolerated behind that brass railing in an afternoon; stony stares greet the usher reckless enough to make a sound as he threads his way out and in; woe to the man or the woman who unwittingly drops an umbrella or an opera glass.

The suburbanite is there, a host of her, and suburbanites are not so well up in the art of talking and listening at the same time as are the fashionable of New York, nor do they enjoy the exercise so much—at the opera. As a rule the woman willing to go lunchless, as many of them do, in order to reach the opera house in time, willing, too, to stand the livelong afternoon, is there to listen to the music, and for nothing else.

She may, it is true, on occasion surreptitiously nibble at a biscuit, which as a prudent afterthought was tucked away in her jacket pocket, but she talks music, and music only, and that only between the acts.

"For goodness' sake, Jennie, do hold that cracker down; the usher is looking this way," piped a voice the other day just after the curtain went down on the first act.

"Well, I don't care if he is; I am just starving," was Jennie's reply. And she added: "Do hold your muff up a minute and shut off his view."

To hold a libretto and follow the score note by note from start to finish while standing would seem to any but an opera enthusiast a mighty hard thing to do, and yet behind the brass rail is the place of all others, it seems, where music scores are followed with an absorption wonderful to see. As every regular attendant at the opera knows, young women in the student stage are always the most enthusiastic in this particular. As a rule, two of them look on together, and every now and then hurriedly jot down certain private marks and comments for future reference.

This variety of standee is always brimful of satisfaction; always pleased, seldom critical, never hypercritical—she leaves that to a certain type of her elders, always in evidence at every performance, whose ear is so fine that invariably it discovers discords where, so far as the average hearing goes, none exists, and to whom the universe itself is "off the key." To all appearances these know-it-alls are more often men than women, though the woman is there, too, and they seldom remain in one spot for even one act. They must see the stage and the singers from every point of view. And they do. As a result a surprising number of flaws are discovered in the voice of even the highest-priced star, and, singularly enough, the more numerous the flaws the happier this style of critic seems to be. With an almost convincing air he will announce deprecatingly:

"Yes, Eames is in fairly good voice today; but did you notice that once or twice she was off the key?" or, "De Reszke sang that very well, even if he did flat a bit in the last aria"; and again, "I think Sembrich is a trifle hoarse today."

And when by chance one of these self-appointed critics gets anyone to agree with him, how he beams!

The lover of music for music's sake among the standees can almost always be spotted, not so much by an unconditional surrender to the charms of the music as by a remarkable oblivion to aught else—an oblivion which makes the less enthusiastic smile.

One day last spring when *Carmen* was the opera and Calvé the bright, particular star, and when almost every foot of standing room in the house was stood on, one of this type—a short man—stood wedged in the crowd some distance from the rail. He listened with rapture, he tried his best to see the stage. Finally, after much peering between hats and under hats, he settled down with his chin resting on the shoulder of the woman in front of him and stayed there to the end of the act. In that particular attitude evidently he had a view of the singers and, of course, he thought of nothing else. Nor, apparently, did the woman. It was not until the curtain went up that she seemed to become conscious that a man had his head on her shoulder. When she did find it out, if looks could have crushed, the man would have been ground to powder then and there.

Needless to say, he hurried to another part of the horseshoe as if he had no desire ever to see her again.

Perhaps one of the most interesting sights is the last moment of the opera when the curtain goes down on the final act, and women and men, too, grab their belongings and make a plunge for the ends of the standee quarters nearest the stage. The briskness of the plunge depends a good deal on what the opera is and who sings in it.

When, for instance, it has happened that Calvé or Jean de Reszke was the star of the afternoon, the stampede toward the stage was universal, for both artists are immensely popular with the matinée women. Now that neither is on this side of the Atlantic, the public has set up other idols, and none ever fails to receive an ovation from the standees at a matinée.

As the idols, after the fashion of their kind, emerge from the small door at the stage side to perambulate across the front of the curtain to the door on the opposite side, their admirers await them at both points with outstretched hands thrust over the brass rail. Sometimes the eager ones get a handshake for their pains—oftener they don't. But shake or no shakes, there they stand and crowd and push and wave as long as the little door is open and the idol in view.

"Sembrich shook hands with me!" ecstatically announced a pretty girl who was just leaving the opera house to a friend awaiting her, in a tone which indicated that her cup of bliss was running over. And behind the scenes the idol had forgotten all about it.

10

IDEOLOGUES

OF THE LEFT AND RIGHT

THE NEW NIHILISM
August 12, 1898

When Louis Miller, editor of the Yiddish *Vorwaerts* (*The Forward*), the daily organ of the East Side workingmen, was asked for news of the tailors' strike this morning he held out a page of a miniature Russian paper, and tapping it gently with his finger, said beamingly:

"This may not have any direct bearing upon the present strike of the New York cloakmakers, kneepants makers and children's jacket makers, but it is certainly very interesting in itself, and, when you come to think of it, the causes which give birth to papers like this and conditions such as find their upshot in strikes have more than one point of contact.

"The page I am showing you is from an underground nihilist paper. I do not know in what city it is published—indeed, you don't expect the Russian revolutionists to lessen the task of the Czar's police by giving to the world the name and address of their underground printing offices—but I do know that it is printed in Russia, and I should not be a bit surprised if the establishment were located next door to some chief of gendarmes. I received the paper only one hour ago, and the way it was mailed is rather peculiar. As I came to my little office this morning I found in my mail a bulky-looking thing which proved to be an old Russian calendar. At first I was rather perplexed, and as I fell to turning over leaf after leaf I could just feel a smile overspreading my face. I set it down for a practical joke, and the only thing that interested me was the name of the jester. And so I stood, turning the leaves of the ponderous calendar and cudgelling my brains about the identity of its sender, when, behold, a thin leaf like this one in my hand came fluttering out of the queer book and down to the floor. I picked it up with a fast-beating heart. It dawned upon me at once that it must be some nihilist document or publication, and so it proved to be. It is a paper called *Rabocheye Znamya* (*The Worker's Standard*), and, as the subtitle informs the public, it is 'the organ of the Russian Social Democratic Party.' Unless I am mistaken, this is the first organ of its kind ever published within the pale of Russia. It is well written and edited, and to judge from its tone and the information it contains, it is the mouthpiece of a healthy and growing movement.

"To send a paper like this by mail in the ordinary way is out of the question. The police sniff at everything that passes through the post offices, and it might be detected and traced to its sender. But then, our people are no fools, either. This paper has sixteen pages, so they tore it into eight parts, putting each leaf in different places in the calendar. A calendar is a rather innocent thing, isn't it? Well, but it has brought me the nihilist paper through the Czar's mails.

"Yes, Social Democracy is the modern phase of the revolutionary movement in Russia. It is the nihilists of today. Terrorism is a thing of the past. Our comrades in Russia do not preach any violence. All they are trying to do is what we are doing here under the protection of the Constitution of the United States. They educate the workingmen, they teach them the elements of science and they help them along in their fight for better wages and more humane treatment at the hands of their bosses. The motto of the underground paper I have just received is, 'Workingmen of all countries, unite!' So is the motto of the paper I edit, so is the motto of every Social Democratic paper in the world.

"Dynamite?" Mr. Miller echoed the question with a smile. "Come, you don't believe we have any use for it—unless it is the mental sort of dynamite, the sort of stuff that sets the workingman's brain in motion, that makes a thinking, progressive citizen of him? We teach the tailors of the East Side to become citizens of the United States and to look to the ballot box for adjustment of the various social difficulties. Of course, the strike is a very effective weapon in the struggle between capital and labor, but if you think strikes can be instigated by walking delegates or leaders, you are mistaken. Take the present strikes in this locality, for example. A more spontaneous and natural uprising of oppressed people against their taskmaster you never saw. If the bosses lived up to their agreements, as the men do, many of these conflicts would be obviated."

The general topic of conversation among the striking tailors this morning was the Pants-Makers' Union. At a special meeting of that organization, held last Tuesday, a motion to strike was defeated. A day or two after, however, a leaflet printed on red paper and calling upon the men to go out, was circulated in the sweatshops of the trade. Nobody knew whence the circular came, and as union people here are not used to underground literature, the appeal met with no response. At the meeting of the union last night it was decided to repudiate the nondescript handbill and to warn the men against obeying any order or call that does not bear the name of the union.

"We have no use for underground papers!" shouted some of the speakers. "Slaves as we are economically, the laws of this country guarantee us free speech. There is no censorship here and we can speak and print above-board!"

The kneepants makers are elated over the first victories of their union in its present strike, several of the bosses, including some of the leading "sweaters" in the trade, having asked for terms yesterday afternoon. The solid front of the bosses thus broken, the speedy ending of the strike is, in the opinion of the leaders of the men, assured.

"But what is the use of it all?" asked an elderly member of the union, removing a pipe from his lips to make a gesture of despair. "What good do all these victories do us? We strike every year, and yet we are just as wretched as ever."

"Old fool that you are!" cried a dashing fellow in a bicycle suit. "If you are so poor now, how much poorer would you be did you not strike at all?"

"Of course," assented a cadaverous man with a scrawny, reddish beard, "the bosses are like a bad boy; no matter how much you spank him he does not mend his ways, but let there be a let-up in the spanking and he'll get so bad that you won't be able to stand him at all."

A portly patriarch who stood in a corner smoking a cigarette was about to contribute to the discussion, but he changed his mind and confined himself to a philosophical sigh.

A USEFUL ACT OF PROPAGANDA
September 20, 1898

The anarchists of this city are chuckling over the despatch from Europe in which it was stated that the plot to kill the Empress of Austria had been hatched in New York. There is no regular organization of Italian anarchists in this city, they say, and, what is more, none of the German or English-speaking followers of Herr Most considers the murder of the Empress what they term a "useful act of propaganda."

"I for my part," said Johann Most himself, "would neither commit such an act nor encourage it. On the contrary, I should dissuade anyone from it. That vagabond of an empress never sought to play any role in politics; she lived with her husband like cat and dog, and was kept outside the sphere of political influence. The picking off of such a harmless old woman could therefore neither do any good to our cause nor even produce a useful effect."

Herr Most ridiculed the idea of the murderer being an anarchist at all. He characterized it all as one of the fakes of the capitalistic press and yellow journalism.

"If the young man who killed that old woman says himself that he is an anarchist (which is anything but certain) it makes not a bit of difference either, for one can call one's self anarchist without having the remotest conception what anarchism means."

This Most followed by a torrent of vituperation and overseasoned German at the expense of the Austrian Emperor in particular and emperors, kings and capitalists in general.

Isidor Rudash, a leader among the anarchists of the Lower East Side, was seen at his little bookstore on Grand Street. He is the most innocent-looking man on the block, and to judge from the opinion of his nearest neighbor, he is liked among the people who know him as a quiet, honest and good-natured man.

"He an anarchist!" said a woman who sells ribbons nearby. "He must have dreamed it. I know he talks about these things, but he cannot mean it. He could not touch a fly on the wall. It all comes from reading too much. He talks a lot of things out of his books, but he means no harm."

When Mr. Rudash was asked about the murder of the Empress and whether any of the New York anarchists had had anything to do with it, he said:

323

"It's the rankest nonsense. In the first place we have no permanent organization, because we do not believe in the tyranny of majority rule. We get together whenever there is anything to do in the way of agitation, and that's all there is to it. In the second place we don't approve of the killing of such persons as the Austrian Empress, because she was not in politics. I do not consider the whole thing any more of an outrage, however, than the murder of an ordinary person, and, what is more, I can understand the feelings that actuated the young anarchist. He was starved and writhing with sufferings of every sort, and his thirst for revenge happened to find vent in the stabbing of the woman. It was foolish—mind you, I insist that it was foolish—but considering the state of the poor man's mind it was not unnatural."

"Would you consider it foolish to kill the Emperor of Austria?" was asked.

"Of course not," was the answer. "He is the head of that Government which recently ordered the shooting down of hundreds of Hungarian peasants because they struck for more bread. To kill him would be an act of propaganda, one good for the cause."

————

ALL GOVERNMENT IS BASED ON FORCE
September 1, 1899

Errico Malatesta, the noted Italian anarchist, who arrived in this country a few days ago, is living with friends in Paterson, New Jersey. The house is crowded every evening with Spanish, French and Italian anarchists, who come there to pay their respects to the great man and listen with religious attention to the expression of his views.

Errico Malatesta is a man of about fifty years of age; his once robust body bears the marks of his prolonged and repeated residences in Italian jails. He is the descendant of an old Italian family and is highly educated. He speaks four languages fluently and has been a frequent contributor to Italian, French and Spanish magazines dealing with economic subjects. He was elected a member of the Italian parliament five years ago and took his seat as an outstanding anarchist. He played, during the bread riots in his land, a part so prominent that he was sentenced (without trial, he says) to four years' exile in the penal colony of the Isla Salvadore, on the African coast. Because of his failing health he was pardoned a few months ago, and has now come to the United States to propagate his ideas.

"The conditions of the people in Italy are in such a terrible state," said he to a reporter, "that one must have lived there in order to believe such misery possible. In spite of the fact that Italy has the forms of representative government every Italian is practically at the mercy of the officials. The constitution guarantees trial by jury in the French sense of the word, but this guarantee amounts to nothing. Years ago Crispi, then in the height of power, 'jammed through' (as you say) parliament a little insignificant-looking law, which introduced into Italy the Russian method of administrative dealing with political offenders. It was maintained in the beginning that this law was intended expressly for the repression of the anarchists, but later it was extended to include the socialists also, and today it is not rare that the government invokes that paragraph whenever it finds it expedient to rid itself of some opponent. This state of affairs alone would, perhaps, be sufficient to drive an English population to open revolt, but the Italian does not feel so greatly oppressed by it. To him the enormous burden of taxes is the one thing he will not submit to.

"And do you wonder that this is so, when I tell you that human ingenuity has been exerted to the utmost to increase the number of taxes and to take more and more from the poor laborer in the name of the state? The immense army and the costly navy which Italy has to maintain for the sake of the Triple Alliance have brought about a condition where fully two-thirds of the earnings of every Italian are taken by the tax collector. The rich, and Italy has her share of very rich people just as much as you have here, evade payment of taxes by various loopholes and subterfuges, but the poor have to pay them. Everything you can conceive of is taxed. The government has a monopoly on salt, which it sells at exorbitant prices to the poor, and they have the mill tax, the most oppressive tax ever invented. Think of it, every time the poor man brings his wheat or corn to the mill he has to pay to the government about 10 percent of its value for the privilege of transforming his wheat into flour. This is the monument Crispi erected for himself. Then there is the compulsory military service, which takes the young man from his work for three years—is there in all this no reason for a revolt?

"And once in a while the Italians do revolt. An especially obnoxious prime minister is killed or they rise in their hunger and help themselves to food from the stores. Then, of course, the government sends in its soldiers, and the killing is done legally and is applauded by every 'upholder of law and order.'

"How did I come to be an anarchist? I have studied the social question for a number of years. I had firmly believed that popular government was the

325

salvation of the race. I learned that parliament is a sham in Italy, and I went to England and to the United States to study the workings of popular government in its highest developments, and in both countries I saw that misery is ever on the increase. Then I became convinced that nothing short of a complete revolution would be of any avail.''

Malatesta became here very enthusiastic, and he left no doubts as to where he stands in regard to violence.

''Much has been said about we anarchists being bomb-throwers, assassins, cut-throats and so on. In a sense these accusations are true. I, personally (and no real anarchist can speak for anybody but himself), regret very much that deeds of violence are committed from time to time. But it seems to me that in the natural order of evolution human violence has as much place as has the eruption of the volcano. All great progress has been paid for by streams of blood, and I cannot see how the present conditions, based upon brutal force, can be changed in any other way but by force. Did it ever occur to those in power to stop the use of force on their part? Oh, no. The state and all government is based upon force, and as long as they are going to use force against us, we, in self-defense, must necessarily employ violent methods. Show me one anarchistic deed and I will point out to you the brutal oppression, the terrible crimes, which were responsible for it. Moreover, it is easy to raise the cry, 'Another anarchistic, dastardly outrage,' but how many take the trouble to investigate all the circumstances connected with the act. Not one in ten millions.''

Malatesta intends to stay in the United States permanently. He does not fear that the authorities will interfere with him; he is not afraid of being sent back. ''I have been convicted and sentenced a number of times, but never for a felony. All my crimes were of a political nature, and I understand that as a political offender I am not barred from this country.

''I have already addressed a few meetings of workingmen in this country and will go on to do so. I want to impress upon them the folly of all political actions. They only perpetuate the existing order of things, while the only hope lies in the absolute abolition of the system. I can see some good signs of progress here. Strikes are increasing in number, and while they are lost in most cases they are very valuable. A strike is a sort of revolt and it prepares the workingman for more serious fighting; every lost strike leaves a great bitterness in the hearts of the defeated workingmen. They learn to look upon the capitalist as their enemy, and once they become enlightened on this subject they will be ready to deal with their enemies as the Washington government deals with the Philippines.''

Mr. Malatesta said that he is not a rival of John Most nor of Emma

Goldman. He believes that they will work in harmony, though he admits that the so-called individualistic anarchists will have nothing in common with him. In due time he expects to go on an extended lecture tour over the country and to organize anarchistic groups wherever possible.

LAURENCE GRONLUND, SOCIALIST
October 28, 1899

In the course of a reminiscent conversation of some well-known persons, a man who knows every social reformer in town told the following story:

"It was in the fall of 1889, I was in Boston on business and had to stay over Sunday. On Sunday morning, as I took a stroll through the Common, my attention was arrested by a man who was reading a book as he sauntered along the walk. He was in the prime of life, blond, handsome, strong, and he was so absorbed in the book, which he held with both hands, that the passerby who stopped to look at him had an uncomfortable feeling lest he should run against a tree and hurt himself. But he did not. He walked on and in a perfectly straight line. Once or twice he raised his face—a good, intellectual face—but it did not look as if he were conscious of anything except the contents of his book.

"A few months ago, that is, nearly ten years after the scene referred to took place, as I was pushing and picking my way near the corner of Park Row and Chambers Street, I caught sight of a man reading a book as he walked leisurely through the medley of cable-cars, wagons and wide-awake pedestrians. In the hours of heavy traffic it is one of the most dangerous places to pass in town. Yet the man plodded along as leisurely as he would pace his room, without even raising his eyes from his book. The man was very poorly dressed. His hair and beard were gray, and altogether he looked underfed, sickly and decrepit. I followed him out of the jumble. My heart sank within me as I saw him pass between the trucks, delivery wagons and what-not. But he got out safely, as if some supreme power was guiding him. Then I saw him dig his hand into his pocket and pull out a water roll, which he began to eat without removing his eyes from the book in his hand. At last he paused to light his pipe. I started. It was the same man I had seen on the Boston Common. It was Laurence Gronlund, the author of *The Cooperative Commonwealth, Danton and the French Revolution, Our Destiny*, and *The*

327

New Economy; for in the interval between the meetings I had been introduced to him, and during his stay in New York some nine years ago I saw a good deal of him.

"I recalled myself to him, and we had a chat. He was happy. He had been out of a job for years, and now he wrote labor editorials for a newspaper. Of course, he was glad of the job, but he was still more delighted with the chance it gave him to speak to a large audience. He always had something to say about the way to make the world better than it is, and his great trouble was how to get large crowds to hear him. His books have a considerable circulation, but that was not enough for him. He had something to say every day.

"He was intensely religious. He found fault with French and German socialists for the atheism which accompanies their criticism of the present system. His thoughts were wrapped up in Jesus and in the brotherhood and divinity of mankind, which he preached. He was too religious to be a churchman, and too much of a socialist to be a member of a socialist organization. In worldly things he was a mere child. He did not know the value of money, and while his books show a powerful mind well stocked with important information, he was naive and guileless as a lamb. He lived in the future. A friend once met him in Chicago. He was hungry, and the friend invited him to have dinner with him. 'Ah, I've found a place where they give you a cup of coffee that big and three cakes for five cents,' Gronlund said, with enthusiasm. He had had many advantageous offers. He could have been a rich man, for he had brains, and there were rich men who were willing to hire his head and to pay well for it. But he only smiled. The work which they wanted him to do had nothing to do either with Christianity or with socialism.

"I saw him once when he was in the lowest depths of poverty. He was simply starved, yet when he began to speak of humanity he brightened up. His friends were anxious to do something for him, but all he wanted was that they should let him teach them his ideals.

"And so he worked until his death the other day."

———

HIGH PRIESTESS OF ANARCHY
ABANDONS AMERICA
November 22, 1899

Emma Goldman, known as "the high priestess of anarchy," has left this country. She has taken passage, under an assumed name, in a steamship sailing today, and is bound for England. Miss Goldman has been dissatisfied for a long time with the results—or, rather, lack of results—of her efforts, and her experiences in this country have slowly but steadily convinced her that the United States is not a soil adapted to the propagation of her anarchistic views. A few friends met Miss Goldman last night to bid her farewell, and she explained to them her reasons for leaving this country.

"Apathy on the part of the American workman and the ingratitude of my own comrades," said she, "have been about equally instrumental in making me disgusted. When Markham calls the workingman 'brother to the ox' he libels that animal. In my experience with the American workingman, during more than ten years, I have found him to be the most contemptible creature on earth. Even the ignorant Russian peasant, downtrodden and stupid as he is, will revolt some time when the outrages committed upon him become great. Here, in this country, the government is more despotic than that of the Czar. Crime after crime, outrage after outrage, is perpetrated in the name of 'law and order,' and the workingman goes on voting for his oppressors. Chicago, Hazleton, Coeur d'Alene, Idaho, are samples of what those in power do, and the workingmen of this country submit tamely, without even as much as a protest, and go on shouting for Bryan and free silver or for McKinley and expansion. Talk of liberty! Why, there is more of that in Russia than you have here. I have been imprisoned for one year because I insisted upon my right to talk in New York City, and in scores of other places the police would not let me enter the hall I had been hired to deliver a speech in. And not a single labor body dared to utter a protest. Only a few weeks ago I went to Providence, Rhode Island, and six big policemen forcibly prevented me from entering that town, upon order of the mayor. That is the freedom you hear so much boasting about on the Fourth of July. It makes me sick to think of it.

"I have spent years in an honest and conscientious effort to enlighten the American workingman as to the real causes of his misery and to show him

329

the remedy for it. What is the result? My very name makes him shiver; the newspapers have invented thousands of malicious lies about me, the parsons have denounced me from their pulpits and the fakirs who prey upon the workingmen, the so-called labor leaders, have pictured me as a sort of a grandmother to the devil himself. From reading all those ghost stories you would believe that I am in the habit of murdering a dozen people before breakfast, burning down a couple of blocks for lunch, and perhaps blowing up a whole county before I get my dinner. And the American workingman swallows all these lies and takes them for gospel truths. There is no hope nor help for him. He will not think, and he has always stabbed his best friend in the back and worshipped the man who makes a slave of him.''

Miss Goldman told of a number of incidents alleged to have happened during her frequent tours of agitation throughout the country, which she says bear out the truth of what she said. She spoke bitterly about the persecutions she said she had endured by the church, the state and almost every existing institution or social fabric. Someone asked her to say something about the ingratitude of her comrades, and at this she became highly excited.

"They call themselves anarchists," she exclaimed; "they are worse and more contemptible than the most brutal policeman. There are, perhaps, two dozen men and women in this country who deserve the name of anarchist; the rest of them are either cowards or hypocrites, many of them downright scoundrels. Look around you. A few years ago we were one solid mass, ready to fight to the very last against tyranny and oppression. At that time the men and women presented a solid front against the enemy, and some of them sacrificed their lives for the cause. How is it today? Split up in factions too numerous to count, without programme, without plans and with malice toward each other. There is a fight on between the Russian anarchists and the German, the French are at odds with the Spanish, and the English-speaking ones quarrel with all of them. Petty jealousies, personal abuse, detestable quarrels and constant warfare among the various groups drive out those few thoughtful people to whom anarchism means more than an empty word, to whom it is not a mere theory, but the only solution of the social question. I have been abused. Everybody knows that. I have been persecuted by the capitalists, the priests and the police. I have been lied about by the newspapers. But in their most venomous attacks these enemies have never resorted to such mean lies as have been circulated about me by so-called anarchists. It remained for them to accuse me of using money contributed for the anarchistic cause to my own personal benefit; they are the only ones who accused me of stealing. The lies they told about me, the infamous stories they circulated about my private life, and the tricks they played on me, the obstacles they put into my way make my blood boil. If that is not enough to make one disgusted with that crowd, I do not know what could.''

As to her plans for the future Miss Goldman said she had made no definite arrangements. She intends to visit England, Belgium, France, Germany and Switzerland, but does not know yet where her future home will be.

With Emma Goldman disappears an interesting character in her way. An apostle of destruction on the platform and in public, she has always been gentle and tender in private. Judging her from her public appearances, one was very much surprised to find her in her own home a sympathetic and womanly creature. She was a trained nurse by profession, and supported herself by nursing. Her little flat was neat, scrupulously clean, and had an atmosphere of domesticity that made the visitor gasp in astonishment when he saw the little woman in her role as hostess. The people in her neighborhood knew her well, and they liked her, for her sympathies were easily aroused, and she was always ready to help them in a quiet way. No beggar ever left her door without getting some help, and a number of persons were saved from starvation through her kindness. She was imposed upon frequently, but she never condemned anyone. "Society forced him to act in this way; society and not he is to be blamed for it," she used to say when others tried to persuade her to discriminate between men and men. But the moment she mounted the platform, the moment she began to address a crowd, her whole being underwent a change. She became inflamed, intoxicated by her own words, and at times she was ready to lead a mob into any kind of violence.

A POLISH REVOLUTIONIST'S LAMENT
March 24, 1900

A portly old man with majestic manner sat in an East Side "wine cellar" sipping claret and finding fault with old Europe. He spoke in a soft, voluminous bass, which did not quite harmonize with his stern gestures, and the three other men who sat at the same table, smoking and listening, often expressed hearty approval.

"Who is the greatest piano player in the world?" he asked, and after a pause he answered with an angry gesture: "Paderewski! Who is the greatest composer for the same instrument? Chopin—another Pole. Who is the greatest soprano in the world, now that Adelina Patti is practically out of the race?

Mme. Sembrich, a Pole! Who is the greatest tenor and the greatest operatic artist the world has produced? Jean de Reszke! Who is the greatest novelist? Sienkiewicz! Who was the greatest violinist? Veniavsky! All Poles! Yes, ours is the greatest nation in the world, and yet we are in bondage. Russia, Prussia and Austria have each a slice of our great kingdom; our glorious language is languishing under the yoke of foreign tongues; our children are persecuted, compelled to seek a home in strange countries, scattered all over the world.''

The old man waved his hand in despair, lit his pipe and was silent.

"But where does Europe come in?'' one of the three ventured, respectfully. "I blame Russia, Prussia and Austria, but—''

"But what?'' the old man interrupted him, impatiently. "The powers are all one syndicate, one gang. If England, for instance, were as pious as she says she is, she would have freed Poland long ago. She is strong. She could do it, if she would. But she doesn't care. It's somebody else writhing with pain, not she, so she can stand it.''

The old Pole was interrupted no more. He went on to picture what a glorious country Poland would be if she were freed from her oppressors. She would become the cradle of a new civilization, the great centre, radiating from which would be literature, music, the plastic arts, science, commerce. Its sunshine would bathe the whole world in light, fill every crevice of the globe with happiness, turn life into a poem.

"Ah!'' he sighed, getting up and beginning to pace up and down the cellar. "Talk of the millions spent in civilizing savages! Here is the greatest people God ever created, and it is allowed to perish; here is the greatest source of civilization the human brain can imagine, and it is allowed to lie fallow.''

Two hours later, when the old man and his friends were gone, the proprietor and another customer were talking over glasses of wine at the same table where the Pole had addressed his followers.

"He can't get it out of his mind,'' said the landlord. "His father and their whole family were active in the Polish rebellion of the sixties. He himself was a young man then, and his devotion to the cause gained for him the admiration of the district. They tell some interesting stories about him. He was engaged to be married, and he was so deeply in love with his sweetheart that often in the dead of night he would get up, dress himself and spend the rest of the night marching around the girl's house. Yet when her brothers refused to join the revolutionary forces he cursed their family and broke the engagement. 'The sister of cowards cannot be my wife,' he said.

"One day some secret arms were brought, and they had to be carried through the town. The young enthusiast undertook the task. Muskets, swords and pistols were covered up with sawdust, and the patriot, disguised as a peasant, went through the streets singing out his goods without stopping long enough to give a housewife a chance to ask what he had for sale. He safely reached the forest, where the older patriots were hidden. After he disappeared from the village it occurred to a Cossack that there was something suspicious about the peasant. Having delivered the arms, the young man cast off his disguise and went home. 'Didn't you meet a sawdust peddler?' a policeman asked him. Of course, he said 'No.' He is very proud of his revolutionary record, and tells these stories to everyone he meets, and sometimes he waits here for strangers, so that he might have a new listener.''

"IS SPENCER AN ANARCHIST?"
October 13, 1900

There is a successful and well-to-do physician uptown who styles himself a philosophical anarchist, and who often attacks what he calls the present system as one breeding vulgarity, crime and vice, predicting that sooner or later it will give way to "an order of things where there will be neither government nor tyranny."

The physician, whom we shall call Dr. X, says he derives his doctrines from the works of Herbert Spencer, which he knows all but by heart, and he condemns everybody who has read the English philosopher and yet fails to embrace "philosophical anarchy" as a blockhead. Is Spencer an anarchist? Yes, without being aware of it, says the well-dressed, prosperous-looking doctor, with a look of regret. Push his teachings to their logical conclusion and you get philosophical anarchy. Social statics alone is enough to convince you, but his whole synthetic system is in keeping with the same theory.

Dr. X brands everyone who does not agree with him that anarchy is the highest ideal of civilization as a socialist, and, according to him, the biggest socialists in the country are not the leaders of the "anti-capitalist" movement who bear that name, but Vanderbilt, Gould, Rockefeller, Havemeyer and Hanna—particularly Hanna, whom he calls the "active arch-socialist of the United States," while those millionaires who do not engage in politics he sneeringly characterizes as "the socialist rank and file."

As to the socialists who advocate the abolition of the "capitalist system," Dr. X says they are the only consistent socialists there are, and that while they have the courage and honesty of their convictions, the millionaires and the big politicians knowingly contradict themselves because, under modern conditions, they are on top of the heap. Not that he hates socialists less, for he considers the socialist adjustment of things the most barbarous system ever conceived by the human mind, and one of his favorite nicknames for Karl Marx is Strait Jacket Marx; but then the "consistent socialists" will never achieve any tangible power, he says.

When the news of the death of King Humbert was first published in the papers Dr. X spoke of the assassin and his friends in the most vigorous terms of condemnation, and when asked whether Bresci was not an anarchist like himself, his answer was:

"No, sir! No, sir! He's an idiot anarchist, while I'm a philosophical one. Bresci contradicts himself just as the big politicians do. The politicians go in for government, for tyranny, for a system where the majority tramples upon the minority, where the will of the individual is ignored, scoffed at; and at the same time they oppose compulsory cooperation, which is the system advocated by the socialists, and under which the bondage of the individual would be brought to the highest form of misery. So likewise anarchists of the Bresci type are a lot of tyrants, for they undertake to do violence to an individual or set of individuals, and yet they babble of the freedom of the individual and of the abolition of government. Johann Most and Mark Hanna are members of the same fraternity. Neither of them is an anarchist; both are socialists of the inconsistent sort."

"Would you have no government at all?" was asked.

"Not a bit."

"Then what would you do with the criminal class?"

"There would be no criminal class. It's all the result of government, of tyranny, of all those institutions which obstruct the working of the law of the fittest. And if there were some cases of atavism, we would organize for our self-protection. Mind you, we would organize in a voluntary way. There is no room for compulsory organization under anarchy. As to voluntary cooperation, it is the law of nature, for animals, too, often combine, in the form of flocks, troops, etc., for mutual protection or search of food. The great point is that human nature is much better than we think it is, and that if left to itself, unhampered by laws, legislatures, police, armies and all the other paraphernalia we call government, we would get along much better than we do now."

Dr. X said that the leader of the philosophical anarchists was Benjamin F. Tucker, editor of *Liberty*, which is the organ of the English-speaking anarchists of the "philosophical" type.

"Are there many anarchists like yourself?"

"I don't know, because we are scattered, and being individualists in the true sense of the term, each of us minds his own business and tries to spread the light in his own way, but I know dozens of men and women who are philosophical anarchists without knowing it."

THE RELIGION OF HUMANITY
March 13, 1901

Among the social reformers of this city there are a few men and women who derive their inspiration from the teachings of Auguste Comte. They profess what they call the religion of humanity, and regard themselves as members of the positivist movement, which in England has for its leader Frederic Harrison, the critic, who is now in this country lecturing in the various colleges. The home of English-speaking Comtism is in Newton Hall, a meeting place founded by Sir Isaac Newton in a little lane off Fleet Street, London. Here the Positivist Society, of which Mr. Harrison is a member, holds services every Sunday. Among the active members of the "Church of Humanity" are Edward Spencer Beesely, professor emeritus of modern history in the University of London, and several other persons of note.

The New York followers of the French philosopher look upon Newton Hall as a sort of positivist vatican, and now that Mr. Harrison is here and intends to spend a few days in this city the little group is all in a flutter of expectation. His chief address in New York will be delivered in Carnegie Music Hall, under the auspices of the Ethical Culture Society of Prof. Felix Adler.

The most active positivist in this country is Edward King, a Scotchman with a fine large head full of books and humor. He earns his living by teaching English to foreigners, and spends his leisure time reading, lecturing and joking. His jokes are so many lectures in positivism, however, while his lectures on the history of philosophy, the philosophy of history and scores of similarly "dry-as-dust" subjects, are interspersed with robust Scotch fun. His intellectual face, his laughing eyes and his waddling walk, which seems to be part of the undimmed good humor of the little philosopher, are familiar to thousands of reformers in this city. Some of these find fault with Mr. King because he has no enemies, but the only retort the merry Scotchman ever makes to such charges is an invitation to representatives of inimical reform groups to attend the same meeting where he calls upon them, in his gravely humorous way, to sink their differences in the common cause of humanity "for at least one day." Thus he manages to bring together socialists, anarchists, single taxers, members of philanthropic organizations, and people interested in work such as is done by the university settlement, and to assure them that they are all trying to do good, each in his own way, and that instead of fighting each other they should work in harmony.

Mr. King is a poor man, but his worldly needs are few, and whether he always finds the means to gratify them or not, his eyes are ever laughing and his compact little figure always bustling about on some mission in the "service of humanity." Like the other positivists he is an atheist, but his coreligionists speak of him as one of the most devout men in the world.

Another ardent follower of August Comte is a public school teacher, well known among the educators of this city as an authority on pedagogy and psychology, a passionate reader and an indefatigable debater on scientific and literary subjects. This man is often heard lamenting the scarcity of men who would devote their lives to lofty moral movements, but he invariably finds comfort in the reflection that there is not a human being so forlorn morally but there is some good in him or her, and that the sum total of purity and altruism is steadily increasing.

The New York positivists have no church of their own, but they all have the positivist calendar, composed by Frederic Harrison and others, and commemorate the "festival of humanity" each in his own informal way. This calendar includes holidays celebrating the births of Moses, Christ, Mahomet, as well as other religious leaders, scientists, artists, generals.

"We profess the religion of altruistic sentiment," said one of the New York Comtists the other day, "the religion of human progress. By 'humanity' we understand the past generations as well as the present and the future. We look upon the human race as an organism, and every man or woman who renders some important service to their organic being has a place in our shrine. The Christian calendar is filled with saints; ours is made up of members of the human family whose work has been beneficial to humanity."

When Mr. King was asked to sum up the principles of his church, he quoted the following from Mr. Harrison's twentieth century speech, delivered at Newton Hall on Jan. 1:

(1) Family, Country, Humanity.—No one of these without the rest, and humanity the dominant object of all.
(2) Live for Others.—The selfish instincts to be kept in check by the unselfish.

(3) Man Becomes More and More Religious.—If by religion we mean the harmony and rational service of man to replace a cloudy and distorted theolatry of our own fictions.

(4) The essential want of our age is to bring politics under the control of morals.

(5) All property is the accumulated product of society, and it must be held and used in the interest of society at large.

(6) Between each man and the world without we need the conception of humanity as the great organism whose kingdom is coextensive with our planet and coeval with the human race.

These are the moral and spiritual ideas which it is our task to bring to acceptance in the time to come. Few of us here are likely to see any large growth in this sense, for social and spiritual evolution is the silent progress of many generations. But if it were to come about in any marked degree in the century that opens today the new century would be recorded as the brightest that has appeared on earth since the rise of the Christian era.

Frederic Harrison is a man of seventy. He has a comfortable income and for the last forty years he has been giving all his time to the cause. When a reviewer spoke of him as one of the masters of English composition and a leading critic, Mr. Harrison remarked that it was not as a literary man but as a positivist that he worked with the pen. He does not believe in literature except as a moral factor, and the doctrines which he preaches from the pulpit at Newton Hall form the basis of his point of view as a literary critic.

CARNEGIE'S IDEA OF LIFE
March 15, 1901

Russell Sage was asked this morning what he thought of Andrew Carnegie's ideas regarding the duties of successful business men toward themselves, their employees and the community at large.

"It's an important question. It takes a great deal of thought to settle matters of this kind," he answered, seeming interested in the conversation. "If it's true that he is going to have $5,000,000 tied up and taken care of for the benefit of the workmen who need help and deserve it, it's a pretty good scheme—a good deal better than giving one man a million dollars for something and another for another thing without making sure that your money will be of real use to those who deserve help."

"Mr. Carnegie thinks that when a man has been in harness long enough and made a sufficient fortune he ought to retire and take care of his soul," the reporter put in.

Mr. Sage shook his head, smiling.

"I believe in staying in it until the end of the road," he said. "If a man wants to lessen his cares, well and good. But he ought to stick and control things, because he knows the business better than anybody else. I've been in my business from the start, haven't I? Well, shall I control my clerks or shall they control me?"

Mr. Sage asked the question with a broad, beaming smile, and he was going to say something else, but at this point the door flew open and one of his clerks appeared with some papers.

"I'm busy just now, excuse me," said Mr. Sage, and disappeared.

Abram S. Hewitt was asked by a *Tribune* reporter yesterday why he did not, like Mr. Carnegie, retire from business.

"Mr. Hewitt, you evidently do not agree with Mr. Carnegie's views on how a wealthy man's old age should be spent," began the reporter.

"I do most thoroughly agree with Mr. Carnegie on that point," replied Mr. Hewitt. "What makes you think I don't?"

"Because you don't get out of active business, and yet you are old and wealthy," said the reporter.

"I sincerely wish I had a chance to sell out like Mr. Carnegie had. I would jump at it," answered Mr. Hewitt. "Mr. Carnegie has been extremely fortunate. He is at last at liberty, but I am still in prison. I can't get out. At least I can't get out on terms which I feel it would be honorable to accept. I had a chance some time ago to sell out our Trenton works, but the condition was that they should be closed down permanently. This would have thrown about 500 of our people out of work—people who have been with us for years, and many of whom have bought their own little homes in Trenton. I could not accept such terms, so here I am with the burden yet on my shoulders. I suppose death alone will relieve me of it."

Mr. Hewitt's attention was next drawn to that clause in Mr. Carnegie's letter where he speaks of his failure so far to adjust to a manufacturing concern a pension system similar to the excellent one adopted by the Pennsylvania Railroad, and the old ironmaster was asked what were the difficulties in the way of such a step. Mr. Hewitt replied:

"My experience in my business has been the same as Mr. Carnegie's. Ironworkers shift so rapidly that a pension system is impossible. Railroad

338

employees remain for years with the same company, and their work and wages are steady. In our line the furnaces must frequently shut down temporarily, and that makes a vast difference. A beneficiary fund works better. We have had one for years. Our employees subscribe so much out of their wages—it may be a thousand dollars a year, or it may be ten thousand. Whatever it is, we duplicate it, and our employees get the benefit.''

———————

PRINCE KROPOTKIN HERE
March 19, 1901

Prince Peter Kropotkin, the anarchist and scientist, is expected to arrive in this city by the end of the month, and the anarchists have arranged for two large meetings where the Russian revolutionist is to expound the principles of their movement. The first meeting will take place at the Grand Central Palace, Lexington Avenue and Forty-third Street, on March 31, the second in New Irving Hall, corner of Norfolk and Broome Streets.

It was the Lowell Institute of Boston which invited Prince Kropotkin to this country for a course of lectures on Russian literature and scientific subjects. A similar series of lectures will be delivered by him in other cities under the auspices of colleges or institutions similar to the one which took the initiative in bringing the well-known Russian over, but while he is in this country, Prince Kropotkin will speak between whiles on the social question from the anarchistic point of view.

Prince Kropotkin belongs to one of the oldest families in Russia, and in his boyhood he was a favorite of Alexander II, at whose court he was sergeant of pages. When he grew old enough to think for himself and to analyze his surroundings the existing order of things proved out of harmony with his ideals. He left the army and devoted himself to science and to the spread of education. The movement which he joined was of the most peaceable character, yet he was arrested and kept in the fortress of Peter and Paul. There he was visited by a brother of the Czar, who tried to appeal to his sense of aristocratic pride, pointing out to him that his political associates were beneath his social dignity, but Prince Kropotkin, who was in prison because he had preached the equality of all men, scornfully declined to debate the question with his imperial visitor.

The anger of the Czar knew no bounds. Kropotkin's doom was sealed.

He was to be transported to Siberia, but the damp casemates of the fortress had so undermined his health that his days seemed numbered, when, by an elaborate scheme which was as ingenious as it was bold, he effected his escape from the prison hospital and across the frontier.

Prince Kropotkin is known in the history of geography and geology by some important scientific discoveries. He is the author of numerous scientific articles in the Encyclopedia Britannica, and is a regular contributor to the English reviews.

Prince Kropotkin is described by those who know him intimately as a kind-hearted, affectionate old man, whose two great interests in life are the progress of science and the happiness of humanity. "There are at this moment," says George Brandes, the critic, "only two great Russians who think for the Russian people and whose thoughts belong to mankind—Leo Tolstoy and Peter Kropotkin."

"YOU CAN'T MAKE
AN IRISH LANDLORD OF ME"
June 1, 1901

Russell Sage this morning showed and read to a reporter the following telegram, dated St. Paul, Minnesota:

> The five cases in Supreme Court of Minnesota were decided in your favor today. (Signed) Owen Morris.

"Morris," said Mr. Sage (in a tone of exultation which augured well for Mr. Morris), "is my lawyer. He is a very able man."

The suits which Mr. Morris has won for Mr. Sage concerned his ownership of about 30,000 acres of land in Stearns County, Minnesota, the value of which (so Mr. Sage told the reporter) could not be estimated offhand in a lump sum, "because it was variable." "Some," he said, "is worth $20 an acre, some $15, some $10. It would not average $15 an acre. Ten would be nearer."

The "human interest" in Mr. Sage's victory comes in through the fact that there are many settlers or squatters on Mr. Sage's tract of land; that some of them have been there from twenty to twenty-five years; that they never dreamed that they would ever be bothered by a rent-collector or even tax-gatherer, and that they believed that they had acquired "squatter sovereignty" in the land and could not be ousted. The land passed into the possession of Mr. Sage as assignee in trust of the lands of the Hastings and Dakota Railroad. Some fears have been expressed that Mr. Sage would follow up the court assertion of his ownership and his victory over "Dave" Crowley and the other old-time settlers or squatters, who disputed it, by wholesale eviction.

"Bah! That's all poppycock!" said Mr. Sage. "I'll treat them with consideration. Why should I evict them if they deal fairly with me? I simply wanted to make it plain that I owned the property, and I should think I do! I pay the taxes. That looks exceedingly like owning it, and the taxes are not inconsiderable at that. I am interested as a stockholder in the Hastings and Dakota road. In fact, I own a majority of the stock. We got a grant for the building of that railroad. I went on and built that road. That road earned that land, which was transferred to me by the stockholders. Do the tenants on that land who have just tried unsuccessfully to evict me, you see, instead of me evicting them—do the tenants on that land expect to live rent-free and have me pay their taxes besides? They must think I'm a—that I'm—ahem, very accommodating. Of course there was no doubt or hesitancy or dissent about the decision. Crowley had not a title. He had, I believe, a contract there or an agreement, and did not live up to his agreement. My lawyer tried to make him adjust matters; has been at him two years or more. He is an able man, that lawyer of mine. We had a contract in the land with a fellow by the name of Lamphrey. He made his contracts and did not meet his engagement with me. We had, of course, to bring suit against him and dispossess him. That's all there is to any eviction talk. All those men—those others—that treated us as the owners of the property, that recognized the fact that it was ours and that we were paying taxes on it, we treated, I tell you, with the utmost consideration. Wholesale evictions! Oh, no! You can't make an Irish landlord out of me. Of course, agreements must be kept and obligations must be met, according to their ability, by tenants. They must realize now that they are tenants and not owners, and I will treat them all with the utmost consideration."

JOHANN MOST IN COURT
September 16, 1901

The hearing in the case of Johann Most, the anarchist charged with printing an inflammatory article in his paper, *Die Freiheit*, on the eve of the assassination of President McKinley, was held before Magistrate Olmsted in the Centre Street Police Court at 10 o'clock this morning.

Assistant District Attorney Hermann, who appeared for the prosecution, presented an English translation of the article, which is entitled, "Murder vs. Murder," contending that it constituted a violation of public peace and decency. When Detective-Sergeant Krauch, who had put Most under arrest, began to tell his story, the prisoner interrupted him, saying:

"Didn't you take from my pocket a copy of my paper of fifteen years ago?"

Detective Krauch thereupon produced a worn-out copy of *Die Freiheit*, its front page enclosed in a border of glaring red, used, as Most explained, in commemoration of the French Commune of 1871, which the number referred to celebrated. The issue containing the article, which forms the subject of the present action, has no red on it.

"I kept this old copy in my pocket," explained Most, "because it contains the identical article, 'Murder vs. Murder,' and because there were rumors about that I would be arrested. You see, this article was reprinted in my paper fifteen years ago, and last week I reprinted it from my own paper as a filler, because I was short of copy. I carried it about ready to show that it was a reprinted article in case I was arrested."

Detective Krauch described how he obtained a copy of *Die Freiheit* and how he put Most under arrest.

"When I told him he was a prisoner," he added, "he said it was too bad that the article should have been published at such a time."

When Detective-Sergeant Steinbruch, who translated the article into English, had been sworn to the correctness of his translation, Most said:

"I want to ask you one question: Did you translate anything to the effect that presidents of republics should be killed?"

"I translated what I found in the article," was the answer.

Most conducted his own defense. When the prosecution had concluded

342

its case and he was told that the magistrate was ready to hear his side, he said in a low voice:

"This is a made-up case. It has all been made up for the sake of newspaper sensationalism. It was started by a man named Sanders, a reporter on a German paper. This fellow knew that the article was reprinted from a book published forty or fifty years ago by the Milwaukee Freethinker Society and that it was used by me as fill-up stuff when I was too busy to write an original editorial. Well, the yellow papers took it up and made a big noise about it just for the sake of sensationalism. Then they went to the police and asked them what they were going to do about it. The police made up their mind to make the most of Most and so I was arrested. When I asked the captain what the charge was he answered: 'The charge is that you are a suspicious character.' I said: 'This sounds very nice,' and they put me in a sweatbox with 50,000 cockroaches, so that I could not sleep at all.

"Now, this article is an academic one. It speaks of tyrants, despots, kings and rulers by the grace of God. It has nothing to do with presidents of republics. Why should violence be used against a president who may be removed by Congress? This article was printed on the day when the shooting occurred. There is no bad intention in it. It does not include anything which violates the law, and I should like to know where it contains a breach of the public peace. No X-rays could discover anything of the kind in it. This case ought to be dismissed."

All this Most said with an air of mild sarcasm and confidence, as if it was a mere trifle and he was sure of getting off.

Magistrate Olmsted asked the prisoner if he could prove that his paper was given to the news companies for circulation on the day of the shooting in Buffalo and not before.

"I can send somebody for witnesses," answered Most.

"You can go yourself," said the magistrate; "you are on bail." Whereupon the case was adjourned till 2 o'clock this afternoon, and the old anarchist, surrounded by his young wife and several of his admirers, jubilantly started on a search for the required witnesses.

At the afternoon session Most produced the proof asked for, but the magistrate decided to hold him for the grand jury. He reduced the bail from $1,000 to $500.

"WE FIND THE DEFENDANT GUILTY"
October 12, 1901

Johann Most, the anarchist who was arrested in the early part of September for having published an article in his paper, *Die Freiheit*, entitled "Murder Against Murder," was sentenced to one year's imprisonment in the penitentiary by Justice Hinsdale, presiding with Justices Holbrook and Wyatt, in the Court of Special Sessions, today.

Most was tried last week and was remanded for sentence until this morning. He was in the courtroom when court was opened, sitting with his counsel and bondsman. Neither seemed to expect a heavy sentence. When Most went to the bar, however, he displayed much of the nervousness which he showed when on the stand. When the case was called Justice Hinsdale, holding a roll of paper in his hand, spoke as follows:

"We have given this case careful consideration. You have been ably defended by an able lawyer, and we have given due weight to the importance of the case. We hold that the printing and publishing of such an article at such a time is a criminal act. Therefore we find the defendant guilty."

The justice then imposed the sentence, Mr. Hillquit, Most's counsel, having previously made the usual plea for mercy. Justice Hinsdale then presented an opinion on which the decision in the case was based. It covered a number of pages of closely written legal paper. After treating of the section of the penal code under which the charge was drawn, and quoting at length, with commentaries, from the translation of the article, it concluded as follows:

"It is impossible to read the whole article without deducing from it the doctrine that all rulers are enemies of mankind and are to be hunted and destroyed through 'blood and iron, poison and dynamite.' It is no answer to the evil and criminal nature of this article to claim that it was written for the purpose of destroying crowned heads. It inculcates and enforces the idea that murder is the proper remedy to be applied against rulers. The fact that it was published fifty years ago and again republished about fifteen years ago only emphasizes and gives added point to the criminality of republishing it at any time. It shows a deliberate intent to inculcate and promulgate the doctrines of the article. This we hold to be a criminal act. It is not necessary to trace any connection in this article with the assassination of the President. The offense here, in the eyes of the law, is precisely the same as if the bloody event had never occurred. The murder of the President only serves to illustrate and illuminate the enormity of the crime of the defendant in teaching his diabolical doctrine.

"Such articles and doctrines have no proper place in this free country. They stimulate the worst possible political ideas and passions, and, carried to their logical conclusion, would destroy the government. It was said by a distinguished English judge in the celebrated Somerset slave case that 'no slaves can breathe the free air of England.' It would be well if the laws of this country were such that it could be said truthfully that no anarchist could breathe the free air of America."

After the reading of the opinion, Mr. Hillquit made a motion for a certificate of reasonable doubt.

"Why, we had no doubt," answered Justice Hinsdale. "One of the Justices wanted to add the fine of $500, which would have been the full limit of sentence."

Motions for a new trial and an arrest of judgment were also made. They were denied. Throughout the proceedings Herr Most had stood at the bar visibly affected. When sentence was pronounced he clutched the railing and only by an effort saved himself from a collapse. After it was all over two big court officers took hold of his arms and hurried him over the bridge to the Tombs.

Most when seen in his cell seemed to take his sentence philosophically, but was, nevertheless, bitter in his remarks.

"The arrest was an outrage," he said, "and the conviction was another. There would seem to be something very incongruous in the movements of justice in the case. I was arrested and then allowed to go on $500 bail for five weeks. It was understood when I was arrested that the offense was only a misdemeanour—a technical charge. Now comes this extreme sentence. I cannot understand it. But there is nothing to be done about it, so far as I can see.

"I was imprisoned once before. The offense I was alleged to have committed was a speech in favor of anarchy. I was released on bail for three years. Then another district attorney came into office and I was brought to trial. This sentence I consider a great menace to the freedom of the press in this country."

The article which led to Most's arrest was printed in *Die Freiheit* on Sept. 7, the day after the shooting of President McKinley. Most was arrested on Thursday, Sept. 12, and after an examination in the Centre Street Police Court he was held for trial by the Special Sessions. He explained that he was short of matter on the night his paper went to press, and he had the article put in the forms without any idea of wrongdoing.

After several days he secured bail. A few evenings later he went to Queens Borough and was arrested in a raid on a meeting place of anarchists. It was alleged that he made a revolutionary speech. This case is still pending against him.

11
AFFAIRS OF STATE

EAST SIDE ORATORS
October 8, 1898

A German meeting was recently held in a large hall on Avenue A. The star orator was a successful young physician of German birth, but of American breeding, and as his oratorical powers were said to have won him laurels among the Yankees, a large crowd gathered to hear him. The doctor spoke excellent German, which, barring his rolling American "r," he pronounced to the entire satisfaction of the audience; and this foreign "r" of his, too, so far from detracting from the good will of the crowd, seemed to quicken it. It was the sole reminder that he was an American speaking good German and made his eloquence all the more striking. The men and women who filled the hall felt flattered, applauded him in season and out of season, and when he had stepped down from the platform, pronounced him the best German speaker they had ever heard.

The next speaker was an old shoemaker, who had lived some twenty years in New York without learning more than a hundred English words. He was a dignified old man. To be sure, you would have known him for a shoemaker at first glance, but for one of those who have a cheap edition of Heine in their little parlor. As he began, it seemed as if his chances of success had been ruined by his predecessor. The audience followed him as closely as they had the doctor, but there was not the same enthusiasm, and their eyes seemed to say: "You are all right enough on ordinary occasions, but you are only a shoemaker, after all."

However, the old man had not been at it ten minutes when all the men in the hall, at least, were absolutely in his power—far more so than they had been in that of his rival. There was this difference, however, that while the American had been applauded liberally, the shoemaker received few such expressions of approval. But, then, as he proceeded, the hall was every little while filled with shouts of "*Sehr richtig!*" (quite correct) and "Bravo!"

When the shoemaker had finished, a recess was taken, during which the comparative merits of the two speakers were discussed over glasses of lager. Opinions differed, but an aged man who was the centre of the largest circle in the hall and who was looked to as an authority on all questions of a bookish nature, said there could be no question about the shoemaker's having had the best of it.

"It's like this," he said, with a scholarly air, as he placed his glass of beer on the bar. "The doctor is certainly a first-class orator, but I am afraid he is too much of one for us Germans to like him. He got his training here in this country of practical common sense, as they call it, and rhetoric. But our German mind is not built that way. We are a lot of accursed philosophers, and nothing but abstract reasoning will serve our purpose. The shoemaker is a philosopher, and although he is rather fond of big words which he does not always use properly, his logic is clear and straight and has little or nothing to do with practical life. So you see, while the other fellow worked us up to a pretty high pitch of enthusiasm, this man got us more slowly but also more surely by his irresistible logic."

Whether the old philosopher was right or not, some testimony in favor of his view was offered a few days later at an open-air socialist meeting in the same neighborhood. The crowd was made up of Irishmen, Germans and Galician Jews, and each element was accommodated by a special orator. The first speaker was an American, and sure enough he was practical—so much so, in fact, that he confined himself to an attack upon the police and the politicians and the bad conditions of the schools, and left the chance listener wondering what all that had to do with voting a socialist ticket.

He was succeeded by a German, who had not been speaking five minutes before he had dived into the intricacies of the surplus value theory of Karl Marx, which he seemed to have at his fingers' ends, but which his audience apparently found too hard a nut to crack.

"What the deuce is he givin' us?" said a German-American, who had vainly tried to follow the argument.

The Jewish speaker scored the most decided success of the three. No sooner was his voice heard, than there was a rush, and hundreds of people came running to the truck which was the speaker's platform.

"Who is the orator? Is he a well-known man around here?" was asked of a bystander.

"I don't know whether he is or not, but our people are so fond of public speeches and debates, and anybody who can make himself understood and has the knack of holding their attention is sure of an overcrowded meeting."

"I wonder how they manage to deliver speeches in that gibberish," remarked a German Jew.

"Ah, but they do; and some of them use it with a considerable degree of eloquence. Of course, it is a crude, uncultured dialect, lacking in most of the words and phrases without which a civilized being could not convey his ideas, but then, its absorbing and expanding qualities are most unlimited, and an educated speaker who knows this lingo well will have no trouble in piecing it out with words of his own. The Yiddish speakers are as a rule educated young Russians, whose mother tongue is Yiddish. Some of them are well known on the East Side through the papers for which they write. They are the authorities on the Yiddish jargon in this country, where it has appropriated and assimilated so many English words. Yiddish oratory is nearly all of American and British origin, for in Russia meetings are not allowed; and it was in London and then in New York that the first attempts to deliver public speeches in Yiddish were made. As a consequence there is a certain English flavor to this eloquence of the ghetto."

HOLD NO POSTMORTEMS
November 9, 1898

Richard Croker today told how it happened.

"It was this way," he said. "A Republican landslide up the state carried Roosevelt through. I am satisfied with the vote in this county. I had every reason to hope that Roosevelt would not come to the Bronx with more than forty or fifty thousand, which would have elected Van Wyck by thirty-five or forty thousand. Of course, we could not overcome the 105,000 with which he came to the Bronx.

"But we made a better showing than last year. If Low and Tracy had got together in 1897, we would not have carried the boroughs of Manhattan and the Bronx by more than 25,000; now we carry them by 60,000 against combined opposition.

"The Republicans made a howl about an honest judiciary and they tried to force the sound money issue into the campaign, yet we elected our judicial ticket, all our congressmen in New York County, and we gained two congressmen in Brooklyn. I never knew of three candidates running so well together as our nominees for judges. Despite the attack made upon one of them, there was not more than a few hundred votes' difference between them.

"Roosevelt's military record pulled him through. It seems that any man with a Cuban military record can win this year. Captain Chanler beat Quigg."

When Tammany is in high feather election night, the ground-floor rooms of the Democratic Club, at Fifth Avenue and Fiftieth Street, are crowded at 6 o'clock. Last night it was 8 o'clock before the shining lights of the organization began to diffuse their radiance. Richard Croker was upstairs, and the room below, where Mr. Guggenheimer's private secretary read the returns, was measurably deserted. There were some twenty people present, but the downcast faces of these and the languid way in which they received the figures served to accentuate the depressing effect of the spectacle.

Toward 9 o'clock, however, the "result extras" cheered them up a bit, and immediately the number of braves present rose from twenty or thirty to more than a hundred. And it kept growing as long as the Van Wyck vote in the extras did. At about 11 o'clock it became clear that Roosevelt was to be the next governor and gradually the crowd thinned out.

As the returns were read, it was not necessary to pay attention to the exact figures, in order to know not only which of the two camps they favored, but also the approximate size of the majority. All that was needed was to listen to the applause, murmurs of disappointment, cheers, or yells which the figures would elicit. The gamut ran from the dead silence of crushing disappointment to the perfunctory outbursts of approval over the vote in Brooklyn, and every vote told its own tale.

Richard Croker was upstairs and did not appear on the ground floor, where the braves were gathered. His face had a gamut of its own. At about 9 o'clock, for instance, it was beaming, and when he was asked to make an estimate, the answer was:

"Twenty-five thousand majority for Van Wyck in the whole state and 90,000 in Greater New York." An hour or two later the same face was overcast, and in answer to the same question, Mr. Croker said:

"I can't make an estimate. The reports are conflicting." An hour after this Mr. Croker's countenance bore an expression of hope. He sat talking to his friends in a free and easy way, often smiling a good-natured fatherly smile, and seeking comfort in the defeat of Daly and Cohen. He found genuine consolation in the correctness of the forecast of the vote on the judiciary submitted to him by his district leaders on Saturday.

"What do you think of that?" he said, pointing to a paper containing that forecast. "We are not a thousand out of the way. This shows what a beautiful organization we have got."

Asked how he felt about the judiciary result, Mr. Croker said:

"The Republicans have misinformed the people, but the election of Leventritt shows that the voters did not believe them."

Some other questions were put, to which he answered:

"No, I can't be interviewed on the judges at all. As soon as they go on the bench we have nothing to do with them."

The other Tammany men in the room were trying to show that Van Wyck still had a fighting chance. Croker agreed with them.

"Why don't you claim the state?" said one man to him, speaking as a grandchild might to a grandfather.

"Why, that's what we are doing," answered the grandpa.

It was after 2 in the morning when he bade the reporters good night, retiring to his room, smiling and apparently as hopeful as ever.

Chairman McCarren was at the Hoffman House headquarters early this morning. He was as cool and unruffled as before the defeat of the Democratic ticket, and accepted the success of Colonel Roosevelt with good grace.

"I suppose Colonel Roosevelt won because he got more votes than Justice Van Wyck," he said. "Of one thing I am glad, and that is the good showing made in Brooklyn for Justice Van Wyck. He ran ahead of the vote it was estimated he would get.

"But I'm not holding any postmortems, and decline to be interviewed. It is probable that as all the upstate returns are not in yet, that their receipt will reduce Colonel Roosevelt's plurality very considerably."

The Hoffman House Democratic state headquarters will be closed for good shortly—just as soon as the odds and ends of the campaign work are disposed of.

The Democratic managers have not figured up their losses on bets. It is estimated that they lost $100,000.

THE BOLT OF ISRAEL
November 11, 1898

The celebrated Martin Engel birthday party, which cost Captain O'Keefe his life, is said to be claiming another victim. Martin Engel himself may lose his political head, and if he does, the famous banquet in his honor will have something to do with it. Croker says it is not true that he is going to turn the leader of "de Ate"* down, but some of the prominent Tammany men in the district say that he will have to. One of these admitted today that the Martin Engel dinner was a disgrace. And as "de Ate" failed to elect the Tammany candidate for assemblyman, the hero of the eventful dinner will have to step down.

The Tammany man in question had been one of the conspicuous guests at the birthday party, and when asked why he had attended what he now calls a disgraceful affair, he said naively:

"I couldn't help it. To stay away would have meant an insult to the others. There were many Tammany people who are opposed to Engel and who attended the dinner for the same reason. You see, Martin himself would not be so bad; but then, his associates, some of his most intimate friends and best workers on Election Day, are known to live upon the shame of the unfortunate women of Allen and Chrystie Streets. This is a respectable Jewish locality, and the people, at least those who are intelligent enough to understand what is going on, are bitterly opposed to this kind of thing. Then again, ex-Alderman Philip Benjamin has been working underground against Engel. Benjamin wants to supplant him, and although he will never see his ambition realized—for Croker will very likely give Engel's place to Florence Sullivan, a cousin of Dry Dollar Sullivan—yet Benjamin did all he could to knife the present boss. The result was that in Benjamin's election district, the Eighth, Louis Jaffer, Croker's candidate for assemblyman, pulled through by just one vote, while in the Seventh Election District, where Engel himself resides, he lost by sixty votes. Again, Lazarus Shapiro, who is the Tammany captain of the Seventh Election District, and who is an avowed enemy of Martin Engel, carried it for Jaffer by only ten votes. Last year Paul Wissig

---

*The Eighth Assembly District, at the heart of the Lower East Side.—*Ed.*

carried the same districts by considerable majorities. Now, Wissig is a Gentile, while Jaffer is a brother in Israel. So you see that the Jews are not as friendly to Tammany as they were last year.''

Speaking of Croker and the stress he laid on the assembly candidates, this man said:

''Well, Croker wants to be the leader of the state. That's an open secret. If he had won the election for governor and for the legislature, he would reach out for the United States senatorship. That he is dying to go to Washington and have a seat beside Thomas Platt is another thing that is the common talk of Tammany gatherings. That's why he was so anxious about Jaffer, his candidate for the assembly, and as instead of Jaffer the people here returned Charles A. Adler, the Republican candidate, Croker is sore, and Engel will have to quit.''

A Jewish merchant, who was asked how he accounted for the heavy Roosevelt vote in the neighborhood, said, with a shrewd smile,

''We are Jews, and Jews are a decent lot in the first place; we like fair play. One man from a family is enough. Two Van Wycks seemed to us unfair, hoggish. In the second place, we all like Roosevelt because of his work on the police force. In his time this neighborhood was a fit place to live in. Now, since Martin Engel and his henchmen obtained control, respectable working people must move from tenement house to tenement house, often without being able to find a place that is not infested with vice. Do you know what defeated Jaffer? The synagogue of which his father is a member and in which the young man himself celebrated his confirmation when he was thirteen years old. That synagogue, the congregation of Tifereth Israel, is on Allen Street, between Delancey and Rivington. This is the hotbed of vice. On last Yom Kippur, our holiest day, the inmates of the disreputable houses across the street stood on their stoops beckoning to the worshippers and passersby. The congregation was wild. It protested to the police and to the Tammany leaders of the district, but without avail. When young Jaffer subsequently wanted to deliver a political speech at the synagogue there was a row. He finally gained his point and spoke in behalf of Leventritt, but it cost him his own election.''

Other business men and two rabbis were interviewed, and while they all talked willingly, agreeing in the main with the statements quoted, they all did so on the condition that their names be kept out of print. ''We earn our bread and butter here,'' they said, ''and it takes all kinds of voters to make a neighborhood.'' One rabbi begged the reporter almost with tears in his eyes not to give him away.

''Oh, Lord of the World, what a place this is!'' he exclaimed. ''You cannot pass a dozen homes without seeing Yiddish girls gone to the bad. I am horrified to think what we have come to. But it is all because of Tammany. The fellows who ruin daughters of Israel and spread vice to this neighborhood; the fellows, accursed be they, who scoop gold from the mire of sin and shame are all Tammany heelers. They must be wiped out. The Jews will not brook them. Ah, Tammany was beaten! Roosevelt, the man of purity, the friend of the children of Israel, is elected! The Holy One—blessed be He!—will not let the wicked triumph. But you won't give my name to your printers; of course you won't,'' the pious man said, beseechingly.

"They call this place 'The Klondike,' " lamented another pious man. "It is worse than the Tenderloin; the police and politicians coin more money here. It is a gold mine for all kinds of vermin, and yet it is the Jewish quarter. Are we to blame for it? The leaders of Tammany are Gentiles. It is they who elevate every outcast to places of power; they who take up the scum of the Jewish community; they who bestow rank and gold on those whom no Jewish congregation would include in the *minyan* [the number of worshippers necessary to conduct the service]. In Russia these men are kept in the outskirts of the town, so that no decent man should disgrace his eyes by seeing them. Yet here they are the great and the mighty, and freely carry their diabolical works into the tenements of the respectable and righteous children of Israel.''

THE GOODNESS OF A BAD MAN
January 18, 1900

Osip Amolnick of 38 Eldridge Street got himself into trouble. He is new in this country. He left Russia, his birthplace, because he could not bear to see the persecutions of his race, and as "Zionism" seemed to him a dream, sweet but intangible, he went to the only place in the world where the Jews have a home.

"America is a strange land," he said a day or two after he was released from the detention pen of the Barge Office. "I don't know your tongue; your ways look queer to me; I seem to be a cripple; but you have no discriminative laws to make me feel like an outcast, a criminal whose crime is his nationality."

Recently he got into a quarrel with an East Side politician.

"The Jews have come here from all over the earth," he said to the Tammany man. "They have come in quest of a home. We enjoy the same rights as Christians here, so we ought to hold the franchise sacred. For centuries we have been begging to be treated like human beings; at last we have found a land where no line is drawn between Jew and Gentile. The day when a Russian Jew deposits his first ballot should be one of the dearest days of his life. Yet here you teach our poor people to pollute the holy privilege for which we have been clamoring for ages.''

The politician winked to the bystanders.

The passionate pilgrim did not desist. He could not see Tammany corrupt his neighbors and be silent. He complained to the police, he besought the sergeant to "join him in the fight for purity," and was told to "kick himself out."

Many citizens sympathized with him; almost everybody said he was right. Among the Tammany "workers" he came to be known as a nuisance. Hester Street is full of pushcart people. They do business on the street, on the corners and on the sidewalks. The policeman does not molest them, unless they refuse to pay. Amolnik was used to paying the Russian police officers, so he was not backward. Yet he was often arrested by the Hester Street policemen for peddling "beyond the pale." They have a "pale of Jewish settlement" in Russia.

Amolnik has a sweetheart. The wedding has been postponed until he is able to support a home.

"I can't live here. Let's go back to Russia," he said to her the other day. "When an honest man is persecuted there, it is only too natural. But this is a land of liberty and justice—I can't stand the outrage."

The girl did not quite understand him, but she was touched and went to see her friend, a grocer, who sent her to a "master of favors." She had known of the man in her native place. He had been a "stool-pigeon" there, an outcast among spies, well known because he was the only Jew of his kind. To New York he came about ten years ago. The Tammany policemen took him up. He became a hyphen between them and some of the ignorant Jews. He now wears a high hat and smokes Havana cigars, prefers his broken English to his good Yiddish, glistens with diamonds and smiles, and owns a liquor saloon and two tenement houses.

The liquor saloon hardly pays anything, yet the "master of favors" is said to be building another house. When one wonders how he makes his money, the people of the ghetto smile.

"Did you ever see the fellows who prowl about Allen Street?" a scholarly old book dealer asked this morning. "On Election Day they are all active Tammany hustlers, and the man you are speaking of is their head. He has the ear of Commissioner So-and-So and State Senator So-and-So. The police captain of the district keeps on the right side of him, which is on the wrong side of the decent people, of course. A man like Dr. Parkhurst 'ain't in it with him.' So Allen Street is Allen Street and 'de Ate' is 'de Ate.' It has gone completely Tammany, you know, and your man, who is a 'master of favors,' helped to carry it."

When the girl called at the house of the "master of favors," she found a man and a woman in the dining room. They were begging the host about something, and he was promising to do all he could for them, his florid, fleshy face beaming as usual. He greeted the girl effusively, and took her into his parlor, where the screaming carpet and the costly vulgarities of the furniture and the mantel set her head in a whirl. He had known her father, and he would be glad to be of use to her, he said.

"You never dared come near a respectable man like my father," was her answer—in her heart, of course. Aloud she told him the story. He smiled and told her that it would be all right.

"For your father's sake," he added, with another grin, in which there was some severity, and the girl left, feeling that the loathing with which she had entered his parlor was leaving her.

When the reformer heard of it, he took fire.

"I won't accept any favors from that creature!" he cried. He called on the politician, told him he was a scoundrel, but the politician only grinned that good-natured grin of his and told the young man to wait till his "greenhorn views" should wear away.

"You ain't no pratically. Dat de trouble mit all you fellars. In America you must be pratically," he said.

This morning the young man was describing it all to the old book dealer.

"The worst of it all is that he really has a good heart," he said, disconsolately. "His smile is irresistible, and he has more feeling than many an honest man. He really likes to do favors, the beast. He revels in it. He is quite in his element, and from his standpoint he is one of the best fellows in the world, and we, we are a lot of fools. Isn't that awful?"

———

THE SOCIALIST MAYORS
February 26, 1900

Trade union people and socialists in this city are busy entertaining their two distinguished guests, the pride and glory of the American labor movement, the two Socialist mayors of Massachusetts. John C. Chase, the municipal head of Haverhill, has been here before. During his last visit he expressed the hope that the next time he came to New York, he would not be the only Socialist mayor in the country. Charles H. Coulter has since been elected mayor of Brockton on a ticket of the same party, and as the two mayors made their appearance before a crowd of jubilant Socialists and trade unionists at the meeting of the Central Federated Unions yesterday afternoon, the realization of Chase's prophecy was cheered again and again, and the mayors, in great glee, promised to come next year accompanied by scores of other Socialist mayors.

Mayor Chase is a tall, spare New Englander of twenty-nine, with a pale, oval, thoughtful face and a simple earnest manner of speech. He looks like a scholarly young man with the polish worn off by years of physical exertion, but his diction, humor and oratorical habits suggest the self-educated, intelligent American workingman, who spends his leisure moments thinking, reading or discussing things rather than drinking, betting or quarrelling. Mr. Coulter, the mayor of Brockton, is as tall as Mr. Chase, but he measures a good deal more across the shoulders and around the waist. He is a robust-looking man with dark hair and a bushy moustache of the same hue—a black-eyed, kindly-faced giant, somewhat more phlegmatic and more formal than his "Comrade Chase," as he refers to the mayor of Haverhill.

They were seen on a train on their way to Newark, where they were to address another crowd of admirers yesterday evening. They were accompanied by quite a suite of Socialists, which included several professional men and a pretty young woman, who was described as "one of the privileged classes—an American college girl as deep in Socialism as she is in literature and the other fine arts."

"We are all Americans," said one of the party. "And the two mayors trace their descent to the old colonists. Their forefathers fought in the American revolution. Not that there are no foreigners in our movement, for there are many, and we are proud of them. But Socialism has been character-

357

ized as a foreign growth, as an exotic plant, and I wish to say that the Social Democracy which Coulter and Chase represent is a purely American movement. We are Socialists, but we are American Socialists. In Massachusetts the Yankee element prevails, and if in a city like New York our party includes many Germans and Russians, these are, or intend to be, American citizens like ourselves.''

Mayor Coulter said he had no objection to being interviewed, particularly when it gave him an opportunity to talk Socialism to millionaires.

"The readers of your paper are fond of dwelling upon the unity of capital and labor,'' he said, with a smile. "Well, that's precisely what we Socialists want. We expect to bring about an arrangement of things under which every man and woman will be at once a laborer and a capitalist. The trouble with the rich men is that they will not understand the meaning, the real meaning, of our movement. I think they had better try to understand it before it's too late. By making light of it, calling us a lot of dynamiters and unkempt anarchists, and cracking threadbare jokes on us, one only shuts his eyes to a tremendous power that is gathering head in this country as well as in every other part of the civilized world. We are not fools enough to talk of dynamite. We are Americans and we have something far more powerful. Our ammunition is the ballot, and our cannon is the glass box which stands in the polling place on election day. This is the kind of gun that has made the American people what it is; and this is the kind of gun that will unite capital and labor into a cooperative commonwealth.

"We believe in the organization of working people in the form of trade unions. If it is legitimate for capitalists to band themselves together in the shape of trusts, why should it not be proper for us to do the same? But what can our poor unions do against those gigantic trusts? We are so powerless, so helpless against them. It was this thought—the result of bitter experience— which made us introduce the mighty weapon of the ballot box as a mode of warfare. The capitalist congress and the capitalist legislature undo all we are trying to do for ourselves. Capital fights us politically, and now we are going to hit back.''

Mayor Chase complained of the stock questions which non-Socialists will persist in asking of Socialists in spite of the conclusive answers that have been given by the leaders of the movement all over the world.

"People tell me that Socialism is an unfeasible, impracticable scheme, a dream, because they cannot imagine a nation without rich and poor,'' he said impatiently. "Well, when our ancestors were told that Americans ought to be able to get along without George III, some of them pooh-poohed it all as a vision without substance. They could not imagine the colonists as members of an independent republic. When Fulton first offered to build a boat which would sail without sails, he was called a rainbow-chaser and a lunatic; when wise economists predicted that competition in trade would give way to consolidation, to trusts, business men smiled. Now we have a republic, steamboats and trusts, trusts, trusts, and almost nothing but trusts. Well, what is a trust, anyhow? It is Socialism, with a handful of capitalists reaping the benefit of it. We'll purge it of this excrescence. Perfect and extend the trust and you get the cooperative commonwealth. Dr. Heber Newton and Dr. Lyman Abbott are representatives of what is usually described as the better element. Yet both these reverend gentlemen view the trusts and the economical situation generally exactly in the same light as we do. And there are dozens of other well-known thinkers who take the same position.

"I remember the time when people would laugh at us, saying that we should never elect a single man. Well, I was elected once, and when I ran again the Democrats, the Republicans and even the Prohibitionists joined on a candidate to fight us. They raised an alarm. 'The community must be saved,' they said. Yet I was elected against the whole lot of them by the votes of typical American workingmen. It used to be predicted that our movement would be a thing of the past before we sent a single Socialist to the legislature. Well, we have two members of our party in the State House of Massachusetts—Carey and MacCartney—and we have, besides, six men on the Municipal Board of Haverhill—a town with 40,000 population—and three in the municipal body of Brockton, which is a centre of the shoemaking industry like my town, and has a population of about the same size.

"I'm a cool-headed Yankee, but I tell you it's growing like wildfire. Haverhill and Brockton and the surrounding towns are full of Socialism, and other places are catching on rapidly. It's Massachusetts, you know—the cradle of every great movement in America. It was the birthplace of the Revolution; it was the home of the first abolitionists, and now it is destined to become the fountainhead of the greatest emancipation movements the world ever saw.

"You may not agree with me," he continued, appealingly. "But I tell you the thing is getting hold of the people. There was a time when to be a Socialist in my old Yankee town was sure to place a fellow beyond the pale of social intercourse. He would be ostracised like a plague. Now the house of nearly every workingman in Haverhill and Brockton has some Socialist pamphlets alongside the family Bible.

"As mayor, and supported by the Socialist councilmen and aldermen, I have been able to raise the wages of car drivers and conductors in our city from $1.75 to $2.00 a day and reduce their working day to eight hours. This, of course, is only a trifle, but it has shown the working people what they can do through the ballot box. So far as their class is concerned it requires no self-sacrifice to be in our movement. On the contrary, they have everything to win and nothing to lose from Socialism. It's their movement, for ours is the party of class-conscious wage earners. Still, every great historical struggle calls for sacrifices, and our opponents wonder where we are going to get the people to hazard the bird in the hand for the two in the bush. As I say, working people have nothing to hazard. They have nothing but misery on hand. But I have alluded to men who belong to the privileged set whose hearts are with us. Look at our late war: think of the thousands of fellows, well-to-do and poor, who went to Cuba ready to be eaten up with the yellow fever and to die for their country. So you see, egoism, gross self-seeking egoism, has no monopoly of human nature. There is a soul in man. It is this soul which made heroes of our patriots, and this soul it will be which will make it possible for men to live like brothers, to love each other and to work for the good of all. Talk of the dream of having people get along well, without taking the bread out of each other's mouth, without being split up into rich and poor! If you don't deny our last war with Spain, how can you deny that altruistic spirit which is the pledge of human happiness—of Socialism?''

THE GERMAN VOTE
July 14, 1900

To ascertain the political views of German voters in this city in the national election, a reporter today canvassed several blocks of characteristic German neighborhoods—the upper Bowery, lower Third Avenue and lower Second Avenue. There the vote is a "German vote" undoubtedly, and if it could be accurately learned how each male adult in these sections intended to cast his ballot next November, the perplexing question in regard to New York's German vote would be answered. It was only along the upper Bowery, however, that the reporter found opinions already securely formed, minds made up concerning the issues, and the favorite candidates chosen. The other places reflected an atmosphere of considerable doubt.

"All the upper Bowery is solid for Bryan," said an old resident of that district. "I've watched politics here for fifteen years, and I've never seen a clearer case. It's not imperialism; they don't care anything about that; it's trusts. McKinley strikes us along here as the head of en enormous syndicate, which has Mark Hanna for its cashier and general manager. We believe Bryan would simplify things. He thinks a good deal more about giving the people an honest government, with protection for all classes and plenty of support for the laboring man in his struggles with the bloated capitalists, than he does of seeing after the interests of railroads and great corporations. He'd pay attention to the homes of the people. McKinley always tends to business," the speaker laughed, "business in the general sense of the word, I mean."

Franz Winkelmeier, a restaurant keeper at the corner of First Street and the Bowery, said that he voted for McKinley in '96 because he was afraid of free silver. Now he intends to vote for Bryan, because he believes that laws ought to be passed to disintegrate all existing trusts into the independent small firms which have been combined to form them.

"We haven't any restaurant combination, now, that is grasping enough to affect independent enterprise: but there is, indeed, a pie trust, which has either driven all the smaller pie bakers out of existence and forced them to bake on salary for the trust, or else make poor, cheap pie for lunchrooms. Free silver is settled by the gold legislation of the last Congress. I don't believe Bryan could upset that. He'll have too much else on his hands. The trusts and imperialism will keep him busy, even if he can control both houses of Congress, and that's not certain. But the issue of trusts comes home to every man that's trying to make a living. What has McKinley ever done to secure a man in his right to make a living by the business which he has learned to carry on but which the gigantic trade combinations grind to pieces like a grain of coffee in a mill? Yes, sir; Bryan will carry New York City, and the Germans will help him to do it."

The open-air cafés on Second Avenue that turn the broad sidewalk for a dozen blocks above First Street into a pleasant beer and coffee garden, contained numbers of easy-going Germans at their round tables. They were not talking politics. When the reporter approached a group and introduced the subject, they almost invariably answered:

"McKinley—yes, he is all right. I don't know," and relapsed into a reverie.

"Things were abundant and prosperous this year and last," said an old German, who was contemplating a great white cup of Vienna coffee with four lumps of sugar on a butter plate at its side, "but I cannot approve of McKinley. Yet I do not wish for a change lest our prosperity might change to some worse condition. We might grow poor, for instance—that would be not

361

so good as some other things—ha? I talk with my friend Miller and he says, 'Mr. McKinley is a bad President, who should receive rebuke at the polls for his misgovernment. He has blundered concerning our foreign possessions, and he puts low politicians into responsible office.' 'Well,' I say, 'business was never so good, why should I vote for Bryan when it might not be so good, eh?' Then we are afraid of the effect of the silver plank in the platform. It threatens to disturb the settled conditions of business. Why do we disturb what is so good already?''

"That is Mr. Freedman," said the waiter, as the reporter left the place. "He knows what he is talking about." Perhaps he did know what he was talking about, for his attitude of indecision was seen to be fairly universal in that quarter. Many of the men in the sidewalk cafés refused to think of politics. Life, the weather, with its delightful, cool breeze, was already so pleasant along the avenue that they would not enter into a wrangle to make it pleasanter. But one or two expressed themselves strongly on the subject of the President's "imperial" methods.

"A wiser leader of the American people," said Ernst Schultze of 78 Second Avenue, "would have established a coaling station somewhere in the Philippines and let the islands go to the great powers of Europe. That is their business—to govern colonies, and so compete with each other. It is not our business, but to make a great civilization, equalling the civilization already achieved in Europe. When we have that we shall be fitted to take colonies into our charge. Just now they are a burden, and absorb all the energies of Americans in commercial pursuits. America has been devoted to business too much to get educated. It is the price a young country must pay. But is it never to stop? Have we not land enough and business enough for all? Bryan is a patriot; he's an American who cares more for the United States than he does for all of Europe and Africa put together. I'd like to give him a chance to make this country self-centered, like it was thirty years ago.''

Various business men and German residents of the lower end of Third Avenue, from the Cooper Union up to Fourteenth Street, when asked to say how many men who voted for McKinley in 1896 intended to vote for Bryan this year on account of the President's alleged imperialism, said that a good many would vote for Bryan on account of trusts, not because of the plank against imperialism. But the majority, it was said, would be strong for McKinley. They said the German vote in general would go to McKinley on account of the prosperity which has existed ever since the beginning of his administration. "Bryan is a fakir," said one man, but he was promptly contradicted. "No, he's an honest man, but he's a fool," said his neighbor.

YOUNG SPELLBINDERS
November 3, 1900

There was a big crowd at the corner of Grand Street and Suffolk. An American flag fluttered; a huge picture of Governor Roosevelt loomed. It looked so much like the ordinary campaign meeting that the passerby, a stranger in the neighborhood, was about to go on, when the voice of the speaker stopped him. It was the thin voice of a boy of thirteen or fourteen.

"You say Bryan is the friend of the poor people, but if you stopped to think you wouldn't say so. If he was a friend of the poor people he would not be a friend of Dickie Croker, because Croker is a big enemy of the workingmen. That's what he is!"

The boy orator shouted it all out at the top of his schoolboyish voice, and as he said "That's what he is!" the crowd applauded and laughed. Some of his listeners were Democrats, but they joined in.

"What he says ain't right, but he's a smart fellar," said a bejewelled man, with his hands in his trousers' pockets.

"And now, fellar-citizens," resumed the thirteen-year-old spellbinder, "if you want a good President and good prosperity, go to work and vote for McKinley and Roosevelt, because McKinley and Roosevelt—because—because—" The speaker paused. Everybody laughed, but this only helped him out of his standstill. "What are you laughing at, anyway? If you was a lot of good Republicans, you would not laugh at all. You'd just go to work and vote for McKinley and Roosevelt, the best candidates you can get," he concluded in a sudden outburst of laughter, and was applauded again.

Another boy orator was holding forth on the corner of Cannon Street and Broome. This one was even smaller than the first. His voice could be heard but a few yards from the pushcart from which he spoke, but his gesticulations could be seen blocks away. They were the gesticulations of a trained, dignified speaker. Every once in a while he would raise his right hand, circle it in the air for some time, and bring it down upon the palm of his other hand with great force. Once or twice the stranger saw him throw up both arms and then thrust them forward appealingly. But all this was somehow lost upon his audience and he was not applauded.

At Madison and Montgomery Streets a young man with a Bryan badge, who presided over an "anti-trust" meeting, was found introducing a red-headed schoolboy named Charlie Kalmanovich as the next speaker. It was Charlie's maiden speech, and the flickering torchlights on either side of the cart lit up his pale, freckled face and his twitching lips.

"Speak up like a man, Charlie," a boy urged him from the rear. "Don't be afraid."

"I ain't afraid at all," answered Charlie, turning around.

"Well, go ahead," said the chairman, impatiently. "Joe and Ben will be around in ten minutes. They'll want to speak, too."

"All right. Ladies and gentlemen, er—I mean—I mean fellow-citizens." Then there was silence for a minute, during which the speaker tugged at the buttons of his jacket, while the audience stood smiling. He tried again. "Fellow-citizens—fellow-citizens." Then there was another pause.

"Pull him down!" said an old man.

"Send him to his mama," shouted a boy.

"Give him a chance. Can't you wait a minute?" pleaded a bonnetless young woman. "He's scared a little bit; that's all."

At this, the speaker screwed up his freckled face and began to cry. "Fellow-citizens—fellow-citizens," he said between sobs. It looked as if he had something to say at last, but the chairman would not let him go on.

"I am sorry to announce that Mr. Kalmanovich has a toothache," he said, placing himself in front of the orator. "We have other speakers who will address you tonight on the issues of this great campaign, and meanwhile, with your kind permission, I shall talk to you upon the subject of trusts—the great subject, the all-important subject of the present campaign."

———

THE POOR IN TERROR
October 24, 1901

The latest invention of the Tammany hustlers on the East Side is what they call "the illustrative method in politics." The innovation consists in a system of arrests, for the double purpose of showing how little life would be worth living under a reform city government and of enabling the Tammany heelers to get voters out of trouble.

Pushcart people, storekeepers, peddlers are being arrested by the score, and when they express surprise the Tammany men solve their riddle by saying: "This is the kind of life you will get if you vote them reformers into power.'' The next thing in order is to have a ''long argument'' with the policeman on the beat or with the Tammany bluecoats now in complete charge of the Eldridge Street station. The comedy is played well. The bluecoats first insist that the law must be enforced; they are obdurate, inflexible, but the Tammany hustler pleads, begs, cringes, until finally the bluecoat yields—very reluctantly and with an air which says more plainly than words that if it was not for the pressure of the Tammany man's appeal, the peddler, pushcart man or storekeeper would have to go before a magistrate or a judge of General Sessions.

In one instance, a man whose sidewalk has been crowded with boxes and barrels every day in the week except the Mosaic Sabbath ever since Van Wyck became mayor of the city, and who has been paying his protection money regularly, was suddenly told by the policeman on the block to go with him to the station house. The man took the arrest for a joke and congratulated his old bluecoated friend upon his good humor, but the policeman made a stern face and told him to hurry up.

''It's agin' the law,'' he said, pointing at the boxes. ''Come along.''

In this case, however, the illustrative lesson was a failure, for the policeman did not know his part quite so well as some of his brother officers of the precinct do, so that when the storekeeper took a side look at him he found that he was struggling hard to keep from smiling. Still, the storekeeper's wife was scared, and the first thing she did was to run to the politician of the block.

''You're a liar and a faker and a bad man,'' she said. ''You get us to pay our hard-earned money so that the police don't trouble us, and now my husband has been arrested.''

''Hush, don't make such a noise. Them reformers are all over these days. They might hear what you say,'' answered the Tammany politician. ''It's all on account of them your husband was pulled in. Tell him that if the reformers get in he'll be pulled in every day. His arrest is only a sample of the way reformers run a town. They just pull everybody in.''

The ignorant woman was frightened worse than ever and the result was that after her husband was ''pulled out'' by the same Tammany man, she started on a sort of agitation tour among her neighbors telling them ''to take pity upon themselves and their children'' and to see to it that the reformers did not run the city.

As a matter of fact, however, this sort of agitation and the entire ''illustrative method'' is a failure. The intelligent people of the district say there are scores of freelance agitators like that woman, but they add that their work is more than neutralized by the peculiar house-to-house canvass which is carried on by the enthusiasts on the other side.

"There are hundreds of people who talk scarcely anything but Low and Shepard these days," said an ardent follower of James B. Reynolds. "We are an active people, particularly in matters of an intellectual character, so many of our Low men go around agitating, discussing the issues of the campaign, and challenging Tammany men to a debate. I have lived many years in this district, and I can say that such a lively campaign, made up largely of freelance work in behalf of the fusion ticket, I have never seen before. The cafés, restaurants, tenements, synagogues—every nook and corner of the quarter is full of this discussion. Yes, the synagogues. I called at the study rooms, or vestry rooms, of one yesterday, and what do you think I saw? The old bearded men who sit with those big Talmud folios in front of them were not reading their books at all. They were discussing the campaign."

A good illustration of Tammany methods came up in the Centre Street Police Court today. Thomas J. Hayes, foreman of Engine Company No. 31, appeared to make a complaint against J. Annichiarico, a barber, 75 Mott Street, of having displayed a political banner in front of his place of business, in violation of the fire ordinances.

"What kind of a banner is it?" asked Magistrate Crane.

"It's a Seth Low banner," answered Hayes.

"I thought so," said the magistrate. "If it had been a Tammany Hall banner, you would not have been here. There are Tammany Hall banners all over the city, and we never hear any complaints against them. If you want to start into this business, why don't you bring in both sides?"

"Well, no one has made any complaints about any of the other banners," answered Hayes.

"And no one will," retorted the magistrate. "I will not see the Fire Department used for such purposes. I will issue a summons for Annichiarico, and have him in here to see what he has to say."

Magistrate Crane was very much exercised by Hayes's mission to court, and he denounced its purpose in severe terms.

A feature of this private propaganda is a series of quaint expressions which have been adopted by the fusionists for the purposes of their agitation. One man, for example, refers to the system of police blackmail as "the watchmaker's bill," and when his audience ask him what he means by it, he says, in mock surprise:

"Why, can it be that you have not heard what a shrewd, dishonest watchmaker does when you bring him a watch to fix? Suppose your watch is all right, except that you have just forgotten to wind it. Well, the watchmaker will break something and tell you it needs repairing. So also the Tammany heelers first 'pull a fellow in' so as to have a chance to 'pull him out,' and the fellow pays the bill and thinks the Tammany watchbreakers have done him a favor. That's the case with all the Sunday laws. The Democrats had a majority in Albany several times. Did they see to it that there should be no such laws? Not on your life. If you could keep your store open on Sundays under the law, where would the police and Tammany come in? So they wanted laws forbidding you to keep open, so as to be able to let you keep open and to charge you the watchmaker's bill.''

This man and several of his followers usually speak of Croker as the "head watch smasher.''

The Educational Alliance is doing energetic work for the fusion ticket in an informal way. The thousands of boys and girls who crowd the building daily learn lessons of moral and civic purity which turn them into an army of workers for the ticket which represents purity as against Tammanyism and such things as the "cadet" system. Nobody speaks to these children about the campaign, much less about the unspeakable evils which Tammany has been spreading in the neighborhood, but the ideas embodied in the fusion ticket are in the air, and these children who are brought in contact with good, public-spirited citizens, instinctively take the side of the fusion party and tell their fathers not to vote for Crokerism. That the work of this army of little campaigners is bearing fruit has been evidenced in many cases where old Tammany voters have come to pledge their votes for Low.

"I expected to vote for Shepard,'' said one man, "but my little girl begged me with tears in her eyes not to do so. 'They're all bad people, Papa. They're doing a lot of bad things. You mustn't have anything to do with them,' she said. Of course she's only a child, but I think she's right.''

A very popular candidate on the East Side is Samuel Greenbaum, who is running for justice of the Supreme Court on the fusion ticket. Mr. Greenbaum is one of the leading men on the board in charge of the Educational Alliance, and has been identified with some of the best work ever done by the rich uptown Jews for their downtown coreligionists. He is remembered by the earlier settlers of the present ghetto as one of the tireless workers in behalf of the Russian immigrants nineteen or twenty years ago, when the anti-Semitic riots in the south of Russia started that overflowing immigration from that country which has in a short time brought a quarter of a million of this class of immigrants to these shores. Mr. Greenbaum lays particular stress on the work of educating and Americanizing these foreigners. He was one of the originators of the first school founded for them by the uptown Jews, and the people of the quarter remember him for the lectures on American history which he delivered to the immigrants of those days.

Mr. Greenbaum's headquarters at the Gilsey House is one of the busiest and most interesting places in the present campaign.

Martin Engel knows but too well that the influences at work at the Hebrew Institute, or Educational Alliance, with which such men as Jacob Schiff and Mr. Greenbaum are connected, are anything but helpful to the "cadet" or "red-light" systems which Tammany has introduced into the neighborhood. His efforts, therefore, are directed against Mr. Greenbaum. But the neighborhood seems to be in revolt against Engel and Tammany.

12

THE RIGHTS OF LABOR

TAILORS AT PEACE
August 13, 1898

The children's jacket makers' strike is as good as ended. The first settlements were made yesterday, and one of the wits among the strikers entertained a crowd of his fellows by pointing out to them that the first agreement between a boss and the union had been signed at the same hour as the peace protocol was signed by the representatives of the United States and Spain. The settlement presented the same scenes which attended the conclusion of every tailors' strike, but there was a novel feature in addition, and that was the role played in them by the so-called boy agitator of the East Side, whose youthful personality is all the more interesting because his name happens to be Harry Gladstone. For an immigrant to Anglicize or Americanize his name upon arrival in this country is anything but an uncommon occurrence. Harry's father, however, was a Gladstone while yet in Lomzha, Poland, his native town, where Harry, too, was born, and when asked how he had come by the name of the English statesman, the old man answered with a melancholy smile:

"We are Jews, my son; we are Jews, and so God sends us from country to country that the Gentile may knock us about from pillar to post and trample upon us. My family has kept no pedigree, but there is a tradition handed down among us that once upon a time some two or three hundred years ago my ancestors lived in England or Scotland, and that one day the king of those lands took it into his head to banish some Jewish families. My ancestors were among them, and so they emigrated to Poland."

THE BRIDGE

The elder Gladstone is an invalid and passes his time in serving God, as he puts it, and playing with his canary birds, as Mrs. Gladstone, who supports the little family by her practice as a nurse, persists in adding. They have only two children, a daughter, Ida, and a son, Harry. Ida is said to be one of the prettiest young women in Essex Street between Broome and Delancey. She is only eighteen years of age, yet she has been married for more than a year, her husband being a ticket speculator on the sidewalk in front of the Windsor Theatre. When asked if he makes a living for her, Ida rolled her eyes and said, with exultation, that her husband netted as much as $2,000 a season and that he gave her every cent of it.

As to Harry Gladstone, who is about fifteen years old, he is a machine tender or "basting puller" in a sweatshop. He has been eight years in this country, only three of which he spent in the Chrystie Street Grammar School. Still he speaks English fluently enough, and prefers that tongue to his native Yiddish in addressing the boys, whom he is fond of referring to as his "fellow-workmen." His prominence in the children's jacket makers' strike was due to the initiative he took in organizing the boys and girls of the trade. The union he founded is seventy-five strong, the youngest boy in it being twelve years old. Asked about the age of the biggest girl in his organization, Harry said with a smile which looked ten years older than himself:

"We have very big girls, but they won't tell you their right age."

The average machine tender, or "turner," or "basting puller," gets from $2 to $3 a week, and the strike was for an advance of the scale of wages.

"What we wanted was $1 per machine," said Harry. "While the operators are workin' on them jackets we must keep turnin' the sleeves and the flaps and the collars, and sometimes three or four operators commence to holler at us, so that we get mixed up and nearly go crazy tryin' to attend to them all. But the boss, he don' care; he pays us the same. That won't go. We want a dollar for each machine and no more'n nine hours a day. It's enough, ain't it?"

"Sure!" put in one of the group of boys of Harry's union, who had been following their leader's talk breathlessly.

"Shut up! Let Harry talk to the reporter," whispered the others. "He is pannin' it out nice, ain't he, Mosey?"

The next meeting of the Machine Tenders' Union will take place this afternoon at 78 Essex Street, the headquarters of three of the striking tailor organizations. Young Gladstone will be the principal speaker, and when asked to give an outline of tonight's address, he said modestly that there was nothing to tell, that he was not much of a speaker, and that his "fellow-workmen'' were too worried about their bread and butter to have a mind for speeches, anyhow. Still, as he talked on, dilating upon the grievances of the basting pullers, he warmed up to the subject and became quite oratorical.

"I'll tell them to stick together and to think about their poor fathers and mothers they have got to support. I'll speak to them of the schools and how they can't go there to get their education, but must spend from fourteen to fifteen hours a day in a pesthole, pulling bastings, turning collars and sleeves and running around as if they were crazy. If you don't look out for yourself, who will? You have not had time to grow up, to get strength for work, when you must spend your dearest days in the sweatshop. Think of the way your mothers kiss you, how they love you, and how they shed tears over you, because they see their dear boys treated like slaves. Try to make a few dollars for them at least. Then you will come home and kiss your mammas and say, 'Don't cry, dear Mamma. Here I've brought you some money for rent, or for a Sabbath meal.' The only way to get the bosses to pay us good wages is to stick together, so let us be true to our union.''

As he spoke his voice now and then trembled with emotion, and his deep, dark eyes shone. He gave the impression of one who meant every word he said. There was not a trace of affectation about his manner, and the expression of his face bore that stamp of melancholy which is characteristic of much older representatives of his race.

STRIKES NATURALIZED
February 13, 1899

Trade unionism on the East Side is not what it used to be. It is fifteen years older than it was when it first came into being, and like some of its guiding spirits who joined the movement when they were beardless youths, it is less exuberant and noisy, and more practical and firm of purpose.

The sweatshop people of the "congested districts" for the most part come from a country where unions can exist only "underground," and where a strike for higher wages is treated by the government as a political conspiracy and a revolt. When the tailor comes to this country he rushes into the organization of his trade with the effervescent enthusiasm which is characteristic of his race. The first meetings he attends, the speeches he hears at these gatherings, and the first strikes in which he participates have for him a charm of novelty to which the English-speaking workingman is a stranger. These immigrants see themselves surrounded by conditions which they fail to find outside the Jewish quarter. Other workingmen earn their wages in factories comparatively well-ventilated and roomy, where they are kept a fixed number of hours daily, while the East Siders are huddled together in pest-breeding tenement houses with a workday of indefinite length. These impressionable men and women often make their way to their sweatshops at an hour when the streets they pass through, if these happen to be inhabited by Irish or German mechanics, are still in the silence of sleep; they often see themselves at their sewing machines with the end of their day's toil still far off, while the city is alive with the cheerful hum and buzz of working people returning from their tasks.

"Why should we be worse off than the rest of our class?" the prime movers of the labor movement on the East Side made the sweatshop hands ask. "Are we not as good as the Germans or the Irish? Behold, there is no race distinction in this country!"

The cry was taken up; it spread like wildfire, and the result was a great stampede from the sweatshops to the meeting halls; a fever of trade-union sentiment.

The first to organize these East Siders were educated Russian immigrants from the gymnasiums and universities of the Czar's empire. Most of them had been connected with the revolutionary movement at home. They had been drawn to this country by golden dreams. They would found agricultural colonies, turn a new leaf in the history of the wandering people, set an example to the rest of the world. They found here thousands of Jewish workingmen, and the number was swelling as fast as the steamers could cross and recross the ocean. The Gentile workingmen were organized into unions. The newcomers were not. A great strike broke out. The employers got some Jewish immigrants to take the places left by Irishmen or Germans. The former nihilists were horrified. What! Had their brethren come to this republic to put themselves in the way of poor men, clamoring for more bread? Israel must be among the best in the land—the land of promise of today.

A meeting was called—the first Yiddish labor meeting in this country— perhaps in the world. Those who had taken the place of the strikers had responded to the call with alacrity, and when the situation had been explained to them by the "students," as they usually called their educated brethren, they declared, some with tears in their eyes, that they had "scabbed it" in sheer ignorance, and that they would sooner starve than return to work.

A little later on, a meeting of tailors was called. The "students" drew pictures of the misery in which the children of the ghetto were kept by the sweating system, advocated assimilation with the Gentile workmen and started a union. The union was a success, and the first coatmakers' strike included every man and woman in the trade—some 8,000 persons in all. Not a "scab" man was there to take the place of a union man, and mothers of starving children kept up the courage of their husbands. The strike was won.

Other unions were formed, other strikes broke out. Wages were raised, the workday was shortened, and the general treatment of the men by their "sweaters" improved. But the unions were anything but a deep-rooted growth. They toppled over the moment they reached their highest point; they began to pall as soon as they had ceased to be a novelty. Few of the numerous labor organizations were strong enough to survive their own triumphant strikes.

Nothing daunted, the idealistic student would set to work organizing a new union, and so organization came and went, flaring up, soon to die down again, like a straw fire, to make room for a new union, new enthusiasm, new self-sacrificing struggles.

East Side trade unionism in those days was a religion rather than a movement for more money and less labor.

Years rolled by, the "students" have become busy physicians, lawyers, dentists. Many of them have remained true to their old ideals and give their spare time to the labor meetings, but the workingmen themselves have learned something—from experience as well as from the numerous publications with which the students have been flooding the ghetto—and the situation is changed. The workmen have learned to manage their affairs themselves, and their unions, while retaining their former educational function, are conducted in a cool, businesslike manner. Lecturers are invited as much as ever, and pamphlets and papers on the labor question, natural sciences or history still are distributed, but a line is drawn between business and intellectual pleasure, and the discussions at the "shop meetings" are less idealistic and more to the point.

The meetings at which political economy or sociology is expounded are as well attended as ever. Moreover, the "students" have founded an evening school where the East Side workmen are taught the elementary sciences, as well as English, and the lectures at this school are said to attract large numbers of trade-union people, but in all these undertakings the same change is noticeable as in the trade unions. There is less ecstasy and more system and common sense. When election time is approaching a lively agitation is carried on in the unions in favor of the Socialist candidates, but even the Socialist propaganda is conducted in a cool, methodical, businesslike way.

Compared to what it used to be, East Side trade unionism of today is "tremendously American," as one of the students put it.

"ALL IS QUIET ON HESTER STREET!"
March 11, 1899

A general tailor strike may break out at any moment, and if it does it will involve many thousands of men and women in Greater New York. Only a few of the sweatshop employees on the East Side are organized. Barring the Cloakmakers' Union, which is the one flourishing labor body in the Jewish quarter, the United Brotherhood of Tailors is the only trade union in the industry, and this, in its present regenerated state, is a very young and very feeble organization. Time was, when every branch of the trade had its union and when all these unions were powerful and filled the largest meetings with their enthusiastic members. This is now but a memory. The work in the sweatshops is going on without a hitch. Outside the cloakmaker shops, there are almost no walking delegates, no shop chairmen, no red cards, no membership stamps.

"All is quiet on Hester Street!" said a smiling sweatshop philosopher this morning, in answer to a question concerning rumored preparations for a general strike.

Upon further inquiry, however, it was revealed that the smiling philosopher was a "hand" no longer. Since the writer had seen him last he had become a "head," as he put it himself, or a "sweater," as his present hands would have it. Other men were seen—some of the old-timers and sages of the movement—and most of these agreed that although "all was quiet on Hester Street," it was only the calm that precedes the storm, that the tension was great and that a sudden outbreak of passion in the form of a big strike was inevitable.

One of these wiseacres of the sweatshops is an elderly man, with a short gray beard and moustache, which look as if he used his own teeth for scissors (another man explained that biting off your beard is not quite as bad a sin as shaving it). He would not give his name for publication—"I am only a poor tailor, and what do the Gentiles who read your paper care for my name?" he argued—but he was willing to talk.

"The present leaders of our union, Mr. Robinson and the other prominent men of the garment workers, are rather chary," he said in Yiddish. "They are going slow. They want to build up the organization as they build houses in old Poland. Do you know how they do it over there? A few men are engaged on the biggest building and they take it easy, so that a woman may give birth to a daughter, bring her up and see her under her wedding canopy before the structure is completed. This is the style of the old country. But here is a new world. Here is America, where everything is done on the 'hurry-up' principle; here a tower of Babel goes up in less time than it takes me to chant my evening prayer. Well, I do think the leaders will get up one morning and find themselves with a sweeping big strike on their hands. I know it is coming. I can smell it in the air. The position of our people in the sweatshops is simply unbearable. We are treated as the negro slaves used to be before God sent Abraham—Abraham Lincoln I mean—to free them. You hear the noise of the marketplace, but I, who am an insider, hear sighs of hunger and sobs of oppression. We are far worse off today than we were at any time before. We have stood it so far. But how long can it last. I know what is being said in the shops. 'Strike!' is the word. As yet it is only a whisper. But wait awhile. I have been through many a struggle. I know how they come on. Have patience.''

A bystander was even more emphatic than the old man.

"The leaders are trying to build up the organization peacefully," he said. "But it is slow work, and after they have tried every means they will have to play their last card—the card up their sleeve. They know that the masses are ready for it, and that the moment the call is issued the union will take a sudden spurt. They are bound to play their last card, mark my word.''

Adolph Kopelewitz, the general secretary of the Cloakmakers' Union, is undoubtedly the most intelligent and best informed trade-union man on the East Side. When the above statements were submitted to him at his office, corner of Clinton and Delancey Streets, he said that in the main they seemed to him to be a correct outline of the situation. He spoke in explanation of what he termed a partial revolution in the various tailoring branches which will be the sources of the trouble that is coming. Formerly the sweatshops were kept busy the year through, with occasional interruptions due to the general state of business. The only branch of the industry where this was not the case was that of the cloakmakers, who worked two or three seasons, from two to four months each, in the year. In proportion, however, as the mechanical facilities of the other branches increased, the season system invaded these trades until things became as bad among the coatmakers, for instance, as they were among the cloakmakers.

"You see, the manufacturer can now have all this summer stock, for example, done in two months, where formerly it would take six. This is due partly to the greater division of labor—larger sweatshops having supplanted the one-horse affairs—and partly to the great reserve army of labor, which stands ready to fill every shop at a moment's notice and do the work in a few weeks.

"And so, like the Pharaoh in his dream, we have fat kine and lean, busy months and slack. Of course, 'the slack,' as we say around here, eats up 'the busy.' Well, when the workman is out of a job, the union is powerless to help him. On the other hand, when he is busy he gets his price, and the union is useless. The only way in which the organization can make itself useful is by representing the workingman before his boss when he is so busy that he has no time to look after his own interests. This is what our union does, and it is the secret of our success. And we have got it so that in many instances the employers are friends of our union. Sometimes the employees may take it into their heads to strike at the height of the busy season, and we keep them from doing so because the men have a contract with their employer. But then, we have had the season system all along and time to adjust ourselves to it. In the other branches it is quite new. The injury it is working is great. The whole trade has been unbalanced. It is hard to make a living. The men are discontented, and I should not be surprised if a big stike—one like those we used to have—breaks out one of these days. Yes, a strike is very likely, and if it comes, the season system will be the main cause."

CLOAKMAKERS SPLIT CROSSWISE, NOT DOWN THE MIDDLE
May 8, 1899

Civil war has broken out among the 12,000 men of the Cloakmakers' Union of this city. At noon today excitement ran so high that none of the yelling, gesticulating crowd in front of the union's headquarters, at 158 Rivington Street, could collect himself enough to tell what it was all about. Man after man attempted to explain, but had to give it up. At last a philosophical-looking old man, with smiling blue eyes and a clay pipe, said:

"I tell you what, mister, it's like House of Representatives and the Senate. Suppose the two of them had a scrap, and the Senate said: 'You House of Representatives, you are no good, and I, the Senate of the United States, sack you, and you have got to look for another job.' What would you say to that? It would be funny, wouldn't it? Well, that's what the trouble is with our union."

Here the old fellow stuck his pipe into his mouth and went on smoking and blinking his eyes merrily. When asked to finish his explanation, he said:

"Why, didn't I say enough? I thought all you wanted was the parable and that you could catch on to the moral yourself. As I see, Gentile education doesn't do much for a man's brain. Well, our union has a senate—that's the executive committee—which is made up of fellows elected by the various branches, each branch being the same thing as a state; do you understand? Now we also have a board of walking delegates, whose members are elected by the whole union, so the two are having a fight and we fellows have got a big job on our hands deciding whether both are wrong or not. The senate claims that the representatives are lazy fellows, that they spend their time in 'café saloons,' and that's why it discharged the chairman of the walking delegates, Sam Cohen, while the delegates say they are also elected by the union and the senate has no business to discharge them."

The members of the union and the executive committee agree that the walking delegates are all honest fellows, and their accounts are all straight. Whether they spend their time walking from shop to shop or drinking coffee, is the question that has divided the cloakmakers, the strongest labor organization on the East Side, into two hostile camps.

"I often heard the delegates say to one another, 'Velvet!' " stormed one of the senate men. "At first I did not know what it meant, but then I found out. Oh, you can't fool me! You know that café on Houston Street, near Ridge. It's run by a fellow named Sammet, so they turned the Yiddish word into English, and made 'velvet' their password for drinks. What do you think of that?"

The senate called upon Sam Cohen to deliver up all the union moneys in his possession. This he refused to do until the whole organization decided the matter. He was then arrested on a charge of grand larceny, but got out on bail.

———

"HE IS RIGHT! HE IS RIGHT! HIS EVERY WORD IS HOLY!"
June 30, 1899

Eighteen clothing firms have signified their intention to settle the strike of the Pantsmakers' Union. All told about five hundred men are expected to return to their sewing machines by Monday. The employees of the shops where the conditions of the organization have been accepted would have resumed work this afternoon, but as tomorrow is Sabbath they will stay out a day or two longer. Not that all of the strikers are so devout as to be unwilling to break the holy day by working at their trade, but many of them are compelled to observe the Sabbath for the simple reason that their bosses keep their sweatshops closed on that day, while others are kept from violating it by their fathers, wives or mothers-in-law. A minority declared this morning that they would not start work on Saturday, lest they should forfeit the fruit of their victory. It would not do to celebrate their triumph with sin, they said, and while they expect to descecrate many a Sabbath to come, they have decided to be pious tomorrow.

By far, the greater part of the union, particularly the younger fellows, have no such scruples to stand between them and their machines. They wear four-in-hand neckties of the latest cut, smoke cigarettes, read newspapers—Yiddish or even yellow English—and generally consider themselves Americans. These are among the best members of the union and form the reserve picket army in the present strike. Their leaders are Joseph Sternberg and Jacob Lippman, two stalwart young fellows, who are described by their followers as willing to lay down their lives for the union. Sternberg spends most of his time with one of the bravest skirmishing committees of the organization. With these he charges many a tenement, taking sweatshop after sweatshop. His main weapon is eloquence.

"I never allow my men to use violence or even harsh language," he said this morning to a reporter while in the centre of a crowd of strikers on the sidewalk in front of their headquarters, 62 Pitt Street. "All we want is an opportunity to speak to the 'scabs.' Then we appeal to their sense of decency and self-interest, and in nine cases out of every ten the delinquents break down, drop their work as if it were forbidden by the law of Moses and join in our struggle. Often we come into a shop a handful—the committee and myself—and leave it fifty strong. Of course, the bosses shut their doors to us, but we have a secret by which we can get them to let us in in spite of themselves."

What that secret was Mr. Sternberg refused to disclose, but he cited several instances from which it was apparent that the "sweaters" are often afraid to deal with the pickets drastically for fear of arousing the sympathies of the "scabs" in their behalf.

Mr. Sternberg quoted the following dialogue as a specimen of picket oratory and the answer made by "scabs," when found working in time of strike.

"You are working, boys, aren't you? Woe to you and to your families."

"We wanted to join the strike, but the landlord threatened to put us out, and we haven't a cent for food."

"Are we living in our own houses? Are there no landlords to put us out? And yet we will starve and sleep in the street rather than be slaves and let the bosses trample upon us."

Then follows a tearful appeal in behalf of the wives and children of the scabs; the misery of life in tenement houses is described, the employers are likened to Pharaohs, and the non-union man is asked to be his own Moses, and to work out his own liberty.

"He is right! He is right! His every word is holy!" some "scabs" exclaimed yesterday. They reached out for their coats, when the boss asked them to wait awhile and listen to his side of the story. A debate ensued, the chief of the pickets speaking for the union and the "sweater" attacking it as the only source of poverty and wretchedness. Mr. Sternberg says the boss got the worst of it, that the "scabs" became good union men, and that the "sweater" then ate his own words and accepted the terms of the union.

The chief demand of the strikers is that the bosses should pay them regularly every week, and that a representative of the union should be allowed to visit the shop at any time when work is going on. The present pay is from four to twelve cents per pair of trousers, and, according to the new scale, the price is raised 30 percent.

THE NINTH DAY OF AV
July 10, 1899

The coatmakers of this city are talking of striking. If they do, the trouble will involve 20,000 men in Greater New York, and it may tie up the clothing business throughout the country. So far, the restlessness has not manifested itself in anything more formidable than a handbill depicting the misery of the coatmakers, applauding the pantsmakers for their recent victory and calling every sweatshop tailor to "take pity on himself, his unhappy wife and children," and to strike for "shorter hours, longer wages and less cruel treatment."

In order to strike one must have an organization, however, and as the coatmakers have not had a union for some time the old-timers have set about rallying their shopmates around the ledger of the old union. The pantsmakers and the kneepants makers won their strikes without much difficulty, and the average advance in wages which they gained is about $3 a week. It is argued, therefore, that by banding together and laying down work, the coatmakers, who are by far the most important and numerous in the tailoring industry, would easily gain a similar victory. As to the task of organizing 20,000 men in a week or two, the enthusiasts say, it could be done without any trouble. Some of these even predict that the entire trade will go out on strike on Sunday next, and when asked why on that day of all others, Wolf Misselsky, a gigantic old presser with a shaggy beard and hair, who stood in the centre of a large crowd of tailors on the corner of Essex and Broome Streets this morning, said:

"Because next Sunday will be the ninth day of the month of Av, when the faithful sit on the floor of the synagogue barefooted, bewailing the fall of the temple in the days of Titus, the fiend of Rome. We shed tears on that day, we lament the loss of our independence and glory, we sigh over the fate of the women and children who were outraged and tortured by the brutes of Rome. Well, it often happens that while we are at it we also weep over our own misery and utter groans for our own wives and children, who are starved and tyrannized by those brutal bosses of ours. Mark my words, the great strike will break out on the day of the fall of the temple. This was the case three years ago and several times before.

"All our great unions have been born of strikes, and many of these strikes broke out suddenly on the ninth day of Av."

Some of the bystanders nodded assent, and the general feeling in the crowd seemed to be in the direction of a big fight. To be buried is idiomatic Yiddish for being badly off, and most of the talk on the celebrated sidewalk, which has come to be considered as a sort of labor bourse on the East Side, turned upon the depth each branch of the trade has been buried. The finishers get the lowest wages, so they were said to lie "six yards in the earth." The operators, who can make as much as $18 a week, were described as having the topmost berth, although they, too, were covered with a thick layer of sod.

One of the bystanders, a young man wearing spectacles, who, it was said, attended college in the daytime and made coats in the evening, asked the reporter if he was not surprised to hear that a sweatshop employee was paid as much as $18 a week. The reporter said he was, and then the collegian-tailor offered to expound what he called the peculiar political economy of his trade.

"You see, we work under what is known as the task system. When we say an operator gets $18 a week it often means that his week is made up of ten or eleven days. In other words, he is paid $18 for six working days, the day being measured not by the number of hours, but by the number of coats. This quota rises and falls like stock on Wall Street. Just at present our 'day' is made up of twenty-two coats. This takes a little less than two solar days, so that one must work nearly two weeks in order to earn the $18 of which I speak.''

It is this task system which the coatmakers are trying to have abolished. Some of the younger and stronger fellows manage to do a full day's work every day, but this they accomplish by going to work at 4 o'clock in the morning and leaving at 8 in the evening. Some of them are even said to eat their lunch at their machines, "taking a bite between stitches." The great majority of the coatmakers are either too weak or too intelligent to put up with this kind of life. Hence the trade is said to be divided between those who are against a strike, because they are satisfied to work under the task system, and those who want to fight that system.

The only branch of the coatmaking industry which has its headquarters is the pressers, whose office is at 138 Delancey Street. Since last Saturday, however, this office has become the gathering place of representatives of the other sections. This morning the stoop of the house was crowded with eager-looking people. They all lay deep in the earth, they said, and wanted to know when the strike would begin.

SUMMER COMPLAINT: THE ANNUAL STRIKE
August 25, 1900

The shirtwaist makers' strike has accentuated the disappearance of the annual tailor strike. It was during the months of July and August that the cloakmakers, cutters or tailors, etc., used to break out, like a sort of summer complaint. It came every year, regular as the heat, unavoidable as malaria in swampy districts, and specialists came from as far away as Europe to study it. The phenomenon has disappeared. There was something like a children's jacket strike last year. The pantsmakers and the kneepants makers had a fight with their sweaters some few weeks after. But these were all small, one-horse affairs. The big annual tailor strike, *the* strike of the East Side, where hundreds of sweatshops were deserted, the streets of the ghetto were swarming with gesticulating, chattering, groaning men and women, and the newspapers were full of pictures of long-bearded patriarchs, has been gone now three years.

Where has it gone? What has become of the great annual tailor strike? The question has been asked by the curious, superficial observer, and it has been asked by the student of economics, but when it was put to the East Side labor leaders most of them only smiled and shrugged their shoulders, as if it were an idle query not worth racking one's brains over. Still, there are East Side labor leaders and East Side labor leaders. Some of them are said to have gone into the movement as philosophers, students of sociology, observers of human nature, workers for the cause of humanity, and what-not, and several of these took the question rather seriously. They had thought of it before, they said, and discussed it in Yiddish editorials and from the ghetto platform.

These labor philosophers did not quite agree as to some particular phases of the question, but they all seemed to endorse the opinion uttered by one of them, George Pine, that the contract system in the tailoring industries makes the old-time strikes futile, and that the experience of former victories has taught the tailors to attach no weight to such triumphs. They all failed in the long run.

A better mode of warfare has evolved from all these successes which have proven worse than failures, and organizations are in process of formation whose object will be to "open an era of rational and fruitful conflicts" between capital and labor. The seeming disappearance of the annual tailor strike is only the calm which precedes the storm, said one of the philosophers. A big fight is near at hand, and its great aim will be the abolition of the "un-American" sweating system.

Getting down to the gist of the subject, Mr. Pine pointed out that in all former strikes the "hands" did not come in direct contact with the clothing firms, their real employers, but dealt with the contractors or sweaters, a poor, irresponsible lot, who were willing to sign any contract and yield to any demand of the union simply because they knew their contracts were not worth the paper they were written on.

"During the busy season these 'cockroach capitalists,' as we call them, would give in to all our demands and sign any scale of wages we submitted. And we, inexperienced fools that we were, would celebrate our victory and go back to work with a flourish of trumpets. The busy season over, the sweaters would discharge all the good union men, leaving only such hands as were willing to work for less than the price which was paid before the strike broke out. This usually had a demoralizing effect on the organization, for there are always plenty of weaklings who, when jobs are scarce, will work for $4 a week rather than stick to the union and uphold the scale of wages.

"Thus a year would pass. By July or August, when the busy season set in in the many branches of our industry, these weaklings would recover part

382

of their dignity and ask for more wages. This would bring them back to our fold (the union), the general demand for better pay would infuse fresh life into our unions and find expression in a general big conflict between sweaters and their employees. The new strike met with the same sort of success as its predecessors; that is to say, we had an easy victory, but we soon found that we had conquered a lot of dead flies.

"Thus it was that what you call 'the annual tailor strike' used to make its appearance. It came and went regularly every summer, year in and year out. The first big strike of this kind broke out in 1883. Fifteen years elapsed. Fifteen 'great victories' had been recorded in the history of the East Side labor movement. The people began to ask themselves what they had to show for their trouble. Hours were as long as ever. Filth, misery of every kind— especially of that kind which is peculiar to the sweating system and is absolutely unknown to the American citizen outside the ghetto—every curse that goes hand in hand with the blessings of modern civilization reigned supreme in the pestiferous tenement houses of the tailoring district. We have opened our eyes. We have lost faith in victories over impecunious, irresponsible sweaters. Our next big fight will be directed against the clothing magnates of the Broadway warehouses. Let them sign the contracts, if they want their work done. And by and by the middleman must go altogether. Why can't we work in large, well-ventilated factories instead of in tenement house pestholes? Do away with the sweating system and all the filth of the East Side, physical and moral, will disappear, like the perennial strike."

"IF YOU JOIN THE STRIKERS, I'LL MARRY YOU"
September 8, 1900

A Bohemian family moved from a small Connecticut town to this city "to give the girls a chance to get married," as their father frankly put it. "I made a fine living there; I can't kick," he said to an English-speaking neighbor on Avenue B, "but the girls have only been two years in this country and the American fellows didn't take to them. Their ways are so different, don't you know. Well, I was for staying in Connecticut until my two daughters were Americanized, but my wife, she was afraid they might die old maids. Besides, they felt lonesome in that American town, so I sold out and moved to New York."

The conversation took place about a year ago. The family took apartments in the heart of the Bohemian quarter in the vicinity of Seventy-second Street. The old man found work at his trade, and his two daughters learned to make bunches and got jobs in a neighboring cigar factory. The income of the family increased; the girls joined a Czech dancing school; their mother gossipped or quarrelled with her neighbors who spoke the same language as she; the paterfamilias was elected doorkeeper of a Bohemian society; everybody was happy.

"All this comes from following my advice," the housewife often reminded her husband. "If it hadn't been for me we would still be rotting in that accursed Yankee town." And when a young fellow called at the house one evening, and the elder girl explained that he was one of the best rollers in her shop, the old lady's exultation knew no bounds. "He's in love with Marussy," she said. "He's dying to marry her. I can see it in his eyes. We'll soon have a wedding."

The head of the family is of a passive disposition and although he often wishes his wife did not talk so much, he accepts all her suggestions and prophecies. The young man called again. His visits became more frequent every week, and a proposal was expected by the girl's mother every day.

The old woman was getting impatient.

"Well?" she would say to her daughter.

"What do you mean?"

"I mean—you know what. He has been coming here now about two months."

"Oh, you are at it again," the girl would answer, blushing. "If you don't give it up, I'll tell him to stop coming."

The big cigarmakers' strike broke out. The two sisters joined the others, but their mother was shocked to lose $12 a week, and being a devout Catholic, she told her daughters that it was a sin to revolt, and that they must go back to work. The girls obeyed, but the young man was an active member of the union, and when he saw Marussy among the "scabs" he stopped calling at the house.

"It's because I'm scabbing," said Marussy, with tears.

"Well, let him propose to you if he would have you join the union," decided her mother.

"How do you know he cares for me at all? He never said he did. He only called."

"If he doesn't care for you, what business had he to kiss you? Do you think I didn't see it?"

"Shut up, Mamma. I'll drown myself, if you don't," implored the unhappy girl.

"That's all right. I'll settle it myself," snapped the old woman.

That evening Marussy's mother waylaid the young cigarmaker in front of Bohemia Hall, Seventy-third Street, between First Avenue and Avenue A, and asked him what he meant by kissing her daughter and then stopping to call.

"How do you know I didn't mean to propose to her?" he answered, flushing red.

"Then why don't you go to work and do it? Have you seen many girls like her? I have been here about half an hour now. I have seen hundreds of your striker girls. They look like cats, and Marussy is beautiful as a queen."

"I know she is. But she's a scab, and I can't marry a scab."

"You're a scab yourself, and if you don't come around and propose to her, I'll have you arrested for breach of promise."

"I never promised her anything," flamed out the cigarmaker.

"But you kissed her, and a kiss is as good as a promise. So the American lawyers say."

"How do you know I kissed her?"

"I saw it."

"But nobody else saw it. You have no witnesses, see?"

Next morning the young man saw Marussy on her way to work.

"I love you, Marussy," he said. "But you are a scab. If you join the strikers, I'll marry you."

"Will you? You're only fooling me. You only want to get me into the union."

The young man offered to pledge his word, in the presence of two witnesses, that he would marry Marussy if she joined the organization.

The engagement was celebrated the next evening.

"THOSE FOR CLEANLINESS AND
SELF-RESPECT, FOLLOW ME!"
January 12, 1901

Every member of the East Side Baker's Union, except the few whose employers have settled with their men, is out on strike, and the ghetto must live either on stale bread or content itself with Gentile rolls, cakes and loaves. The laws of Moses impose no special rules as to the preparation of this article of food. Every kind of bread, provided it contains nothing "impure," is *kosher*. But, like every other foreign colony in this city, the Russian and Polish Jews cling to their own methods and forms in the matter. So they miss their *bagels* (ring-shaped rolls), *challahs* (Sabbath loaves) and huge round loaves of rye bread keenly. They bear their privation willingly, however, so the strikers say, for the big bakers' strike which broke out again yesterday was initiated under circumstances which gladden the hearts of every house-wife in the tenement-house district.

The strike was ushered in with a long line of carriages, two bands of music and a free lunch, and the curious feature of it is that the festival, carriages, trumpets, free sandwiches and all, had been prepared and paid for by the "bosses," by the very people against whom the fight was started.

"Have you ever read the story of Esther?" asked Moses Lurie, one of the leaders of the strike. "If you have, you will remember how Haman had mapped out a plan by which Mordecai was to parade him through the streets, and how the tables were turned, so that it was Mordecai who rode the horse and Haman who played the footman. This is exactly what happened to our bosses. They had prepared a parade for themselves, but it turned out to be their funeral."

The strike, which originated some two weeks ago, after the union published a description of the shocking hygienic conditions of the East Side bakeshops, was making slow progress last week. The cadaverous-looking men who worked from thirteen to sixteen hours a day seven days a week in suffocating, pestiferous holes underground simply had not vitality enough left in them to stir. Their employers formed an association for the purpose of fighting the union, and one of the first things they did was to issue a circular denying all charges of uncleanliness and assuring the public that their "hands" were all happy. It was to show the neighborhood that the strike was a myth, that the association arranged for the parade yesterday afternoon. The members of this association, the "bosses," were to head the march in twenty carriages, while their employees, the "scabs" who had failed to join in the strike, were to follow on foot to the music of two bands.

The strikers have their headquarters at Zwieck's Hall, 86 Attorney Street, and to make the demonstration the more effective, the bosses gathered the "scabs" in Victoria Hall, 80 Clinton Street, which is a block or two away.

At about 3 o'clock yesterday the street in front of Victoria Hall was lined with carriages and crowded with people. Inside the two bands were playing lustily, while the 400 "scabs" were devouring free sandwiches and washing them down with beer or soda.

Presently there was a stir. Joseph Barondess, generally known as "The King of the Cloakmakers," entered the building. He is tall, broad-shouldered, smooth-shaven, and he speaks English in a rich, inspiring basso. He is the most popular man on the East Side and the dread of "cockroach bosses," as the ghetto people call an impecunious sweater.

Mr. Barondess said he wished to challenge the president of the association, E. Gottfried of 146 Essex Street, to a debate. The man in the chair, who was a workingman, not a boss, told him to go ahead. The "King of Cloakmakers" made a long speech portraying the misery of the bakers. The 400 men who were gathered to march nodded, sighed and groaned assent. The speaker told them that to work ten hours a day was enough; that one must not work more than six days a week; that if the bosses wanted some flour carried or some other outside work done they must get outside help; that to live without air and up to one's eyes in filth was bad. He wound up with the story of Moses.

"There were a few scabs in Israel," he said. "These smashed the tablets of the law and started the golden calf racket. Are you going to be scabs like them, or are you going to join the cause of cleanliness, health and decency. Moses said: 'Those who are with God, follow me!' So I say: 'Those who are for cleanliness and self-respect, follow me!' "

There was an uproar of enthusiasm and the four hundred voted to join the strikers. The bosses had the door locked, but the four hundred "followed" Joseph through the basement.

"And how about the free lunch?" asked a member of the bosses' association.

"Eat it yourself, and may it choke you," answered a striker.

"And how about the music?"

"And how about the carriages?"

There was no answer to these questions. The four hundred were on their way to Zwieck's Hall, and the strike is a real strike at last.

COCKROACH PHARAOHS
July 15, 1901

The big tailor strike, which Harry White, secretary of the United Garment Workers of America, declares to be imminent, will be the subject of a final and decisive discussion at a meeting of delegates representing the various tailor unions at 374 Grand Street tonight. Mr. White's fear is based on an unusual state of unrest among the people of the Lower East Side. They are tired of the sweating system and seem to be determined to make a strenuous fight for its abolition. That this system must go, all the labor elements concerned, including Mr. White and the central organization which he represents, agree. The only question at present is whether the East Side tailors are organized securely enough to retain the benefits of a victory in case the strike should come to a successful issue. Some of the leaders think they are; others share Mr. White's view of the situation. At all events the rank and file are said to be in a fidget, and a big strike involving from 40,000 to 50,000 men in Manhattan and the two tailoring districts of Brooklyn (Williamsburg and Brownsville) is the leading topic of discussion on the East Side today.

Should a strike be declared, the men will demand, first, the abolition of the contract system and the direct responsibility of the clothing firms for wages and the enforcement of all agreements affecting the "hands"; second, a minimum workday of ten hours; and third, a scale of wages to be worked out by the various unions.

Some of those who are in favor of a strike refer the others to the interest taken in the anti-sweatshop movement by men like Vice-President Roosevelt.

"Everyone who has eyes to see knows that the sweating system is the source of most of the misery of the East Side," said one seedy-looking, hollow-eyed man, speaking to a little crowd of tailors at the corner of Essex Street and Broome this forenoon. "They talk of 'red light' districts and 'cadets.' They spend thousands of dollars on anti-vice crusades. Let them help us do away with the sweating system and much of the evil will disappear. The wise men know it, so they will help us in our struggle.''

Similar impromptu open-air meetings were going on in many other places on the East Side. The strike was everywhere the all-absorbing subject of gossip and debate. One old man, who held forth in the centre of a fair-sized audience in front of a condemned building on Delancey Street, likened the sweating system to the ''Jewish exile in Egypt.'' He spoke of the ''sweaters,'' or contractors, as ''the cockroach pharaohs of the East Side,'' and wondered why a free country like this allows such a system of bondage to exist.

Another man—one of the leaders at the conferences which have been held to discuss the advisability and timeliness of a strike—put all the blame on the factory inspectors. ''If they do their duty things would not be half so bad,'' he said.

13
FEMALES AND FEMINISTS

"THINK OF A WOMAN'S HAIR IN THE
VESTMENTS OF THE HOLY SCROLLS!"
Undated

The curtain of red and gold was drawn aside; the carved doors stood wide open; the Holy Ark was deserted; for it was Simchat Torah and the scrolls of the Law were out for their yearly procession around the reading platform. Every synagogue in town celebrated the merry festival yesterday—the last and the brightest link in the long chain of autumn holidays—but nowhere was the service conducted with more pomp and more genuine Simchat Torah than by the Congregation Lovers of Justice, Men of Poland.

The twenty-odd scrolls of the Law, arrayed in their best silks and velvets, aglitter with their silver crowns and golden shields of David, were reverently carried by as many white-bearded patriarchs, led by the cantor. Then came a line of little boys, each with a paper flag, inscribed with the verses of the day and decorated with pictures of Moses and Aaron.

Young women stood on benches, touching the scrolls as they passed and kissing their own fingers, thus sanctified by contact with the holy parchment. It is the only day when the daughters of Israel are admitted to the main compartment of the house of God, and the damsels of the Lovers of Justice were out in full force.

One of the prettiest of them, a stately blonde with melancholy blue eyes, kissed the scrolls with unsmiling devotion. The other girls kept giggling and throwing glances at each other and at the young men; but she never unbent.

And once, when the cantor's voice rose to a higher pitch than usual, tears started to her eyes.

"What ails her?" asked a young woman in a whisper. "Crying on this merry day is even a sin, isn't it, Rabbi Nehemiah?"

"Don't judge her harshly, my daughter," answered Rabbi Nehemiah, hugging the scrolls as he passed. "She was the only and beloved daughter of a good father. Last year she touched his holy scrolls as he passed by her in the same spot. Now he serves God in the eternal world. It pleased the Uppermost to take him under the wings of His Presence. She misses her father, my daughter. And if the tears will come rolling down her fresh cheeks, don't judge her harshly, my child."

"Poor girl," said the young woman, as she dried her own tears. "But it is Simchat Torah and it is a sin to cry, and yet I am crying myself."

Presently there was a hitch. A buxom, dark-eyed sweatshop girl got entangled in the vestments and decorations of a scroll which she had stooped to kiss. The old man who carried the "purity" first blushed, then flew into a passion.

"It is a desecration of the Name!" he said. "Is it not enough that we let the girls into the synagogue? Think of a woman's hair in the vestments of the holy scrolls!"

But the other men took it less seriously, as merriment was the order of the day, and the synagogue soon rang with laughter. Even the blue-eyed girl could not help smiling.

"Are we not human beings?" asked a feminine voice.

"Yes, and are the beards of men more sacred than the beautiful locks of girls?" seconded the sweatshop girl, who had by this time disentangled herself from the holy vestments.

There was another outburst of mirth. The blonde was once more wiping her blue eyes, but this time they were tears of mirth, not of grief.

SERVANTS OF THE POOR
December 24, 1898

Most people hire servants because they can afford them. There are, however, some who keep a servant maid because they are so poor that they cannot afford to be without one. An East Side woman is employed in a large shirt-button factory. She earns from $8 to $9 a week. She is the mother of four little children. Her husband is sickly and his earnings are small and irregular. She is fond of cooking, but how can she afford it? The pleasure would cost her $5 a week, for it would lose her her wages at the factory, while a servant costs her only $12 a month. There are thousands of similar cases, and there are scores of agencies which do a thriving business furnishing servants to the poor.

The occupants of uptown flats complain of the tyranny of the servant. Can you imagine the martyrdom of the tenement-house "missus" who is compelled to hire a "domestic" because she is so poor that cooking her own dinner or scrubbing her own floor is a luxury beyond her means? And yet the comic papers of the East Side have no use for the subject. The fact is that the tenement-house "missus" has no tyranny to complain of. It is only your uptown housekeeper who is under the thumb of her Bridget. Her Cherry Street sister is treated by her servant as an equal. Not that all is sunshine in their relations, for it is not. But when a misunderstanding does occur, it is fought out there and then and in the open, with the result that the breach is healed as quickly as it opens, unless employer and employee at once "agree to disagree." Latent rancors and rankling ill-feeling between mistress and servant is a thing almost unknown on the East Side.

"Foot of a hog!" said a Hungarian woman to her servant maid the other day. "Is that the way you make a goulash? You ought to be a shoemaker, not a cook."

"And who are you?" retorted the maid, her arms akimbo. "I have served in houses where the dogs ate better than you. A 'missus' indeed! You had better pay me the half-dollar I lent you for meat yesterday, when the butcher would not trust you. A 'missus'! I can buy and sell and buy over again sixty such missuses as you are."

The "missus" offered her the alternative between shutting up and going where she had come from.

"You scare me out of my wits!" was the sardonic reply. "I could get a place in such a house uptown where my breakfast would be worth more than what you spend for food for the whole family."

And yet she preferred to stay in the tenement house and to share the scanty fare of her humble employers. Why? Because in the uptown house she would be a servant, while here she is one of the family. This is an exceptional case, however, for the majority of servants would rather be servants uptown than be treated as one of the family on Cherry Street. If it is not altogether pleasant to be regarded as an inferior, there are a thousand and one ways of avenging one's self for this slight discomfort. How we pay for keeping our servants on a separate floor is known to each of us in his own way. And when all is told, it may not be so easy to decide who is the superior and who the inferior as it may seem at first sight. You look down upon your cook. But then, you never played the eavesdropper when she and your chambermaid compared notes about yourself. No eavesdropping is necessary in the tenement house. Master and servant exchange opinions of each other in personal communion, as we have seen. And as both live on the same floor and break bread at the same table vengeance has no room.

Most of the servants in the tenement houses are peasant girls from the Slavonic provinces in Austria. The writer visited one of the agencies which furnish this class of help to the East Side restaurants and residences. The room, on the third floor of an old rookery, was crowded with jabbering peasant girls. The *zushickerke,* or servant broker, was a dishevelled, gaunt, black-eyed old crone, and as she picked up her bony self from the cavernous corner and stepped out to meet the visitor she reminded him of some of Shakespeare's witches.

"What do you want, mister—a servant?" she asked in a German dialect which she said was much better than Yiddish. The stranger said he wanted a servant, but could not understand either Polish or Ruthenian or Slavonic.

"Just now I have no girl who can speak English or German," answered the *zushickerke.* "But what matters it? I'll give you a servant who is so smart that she will learn to speak English or German in a week. Don't you believe me? Well, by that time you and your wife shall have picked up a little Ruthenian, and so between the two languages you will manage to get along."

Asked about the price, the *zushickerke* said:

"My girls are all first-class help. I should keep no other if they paid me a fortune. I can't afford to stake the reputation of my business, you know. Well, girls who can't cook, but are strong as oxen and willing to work, run from $10 to $12 a month, and girls who can cook charge from $12 to $16. It depends on what kind of cooking she can do. Yesterday I sent a girl to a doctor's family so she could make everything a mouth can name and eat, from barley soup to a Rumanian *mamulaga.* My charges?" the *zushickerke* asked, modestly. "I only charge $2. I don't care how much you are going to pay to the girl. And if you don't like her, let me know and I'll send you another one; and if the second does not suit you, you can have a third—all for the same $2. Of course I won't change your girl after the month is out. Then, if you wish a new servant, you must pay a new $2. But I never play my customers any tricks, and never take away a girl in order to recommend her to another place. Some *zushickerkes* do that when they are short of girls and there are families who want servants."

The old woman was asked what the *zushickerke* would do in case the servant refused to leave her place, but she answered with a smile that it did not matter. The girl's wish was not consulted. She was sure to obey and would follow her *zushickerke* to the end of the earth. They are only peasant girls, stupid, unable to speak English, and the *zushickerke* is the only friend she has in the new world.

One of the servant girls present was asked how she liked this country, the old Jewess acting as interpreter.

"When I get a good place, I like America," was the answer, "and when I get a bad place, I don't."

"What do you do with your money?"

"I save it for a marriage portion."

"Are you engaged?"

"Not yet. But a girl with a marriage portion is as good as engaged. There are plenty of fellows in Yonkers who will marry a lass if she is not a bugbear and her purse is not empty. Why in Yonkers? Where else can you find such a lot of Ruthenian fellows? There are some in Jersey City and other places, but I have never been there, so I don't know, and if I don't know I don't speak," she concluded, with a sly look at the other women in the room.

"HE LEAVES HALF OF WHAT HE MAKES
IN THAT DEN"
April 8, 1899

The two double tenement houses are still known in the neighborhood as Klein Mainz. The Mayence people who inhabited them ten or fifteen years ago have all moved uptown, but the old housekeeper is still there, and she struggles hard to keep herself and the old name alive. The grocery is located in one of the twin houses, and the beer saloon in the other.

The grocer is a middle-aged widow with three little children. She is a big, clear-eyed woman. She never gossips of anyone except herself, though she takes a sincere interest in the troubles of her customers. The women of Klein Mainz like her, patronize her store and confide their secrets to her. They speak of her as "the widow." Of herself she tells everybody that she had married "Papa" when she was an old maid, and that she would not mind marrying again provided she found a man as good as "Papa" was. "Maybe you know somebody?"

The saloon-keeper is an old raw-boned, florid-faced Bavarian, with a black chin-beard, brass-rimmed spectacles and a bad temper. Whenever his wife (she is rather dumpy, but her spectacles are brass-rimmed like his) clambers down the first flight of stairs and comes into the saloon, his bad temper breaks out. "I have told you more than once," he reminds her in the language of the Munich Bowery, "that the right place for a hen is her coop. Shuffle back! Shuffle back!" The fat little thing with brass-rimmed spectacles like her husband's drops her eyes and arms, and shuffles back, and shuffles back.

Recently two of the women complained to the widow of the saloon-keeper. If it had not been for him the figures in their little grocery books would have been stricken out long ago, they said. The widow did not gossip, but the two women liked the wording of their complaint, and repeated it to their neighbors. It made a hit. A third housewife came to tell the widow that she could not pay her bill because her husband had spent all the money in the beer saloon, and then a fourth and a fifth. The grocer looked glum. In her heart she cursed her five customers and their husbands, but in her head she agreed with them that the "old terrier" was the cause of all her troubles. She did not gossip but one of the five did, and the next afternoon she assured the Bavarian that he was a blood-leech and that the good widow was of the same opinion.

"Did you say I was a blood-leech?" he asked, dashing into the grocery store and glowering down upon the quailing widow.

"I call you a leech! When?" she stammered.

"When! If I knew when, it would mean that I heard it, and if I could hear it you would not dare call me a leech. Mind that you hold your tongue the next time. You want all the wages the tenants bring on Saturday to go into your cash box, don't you?" he sneered.

"And you want it all to go into your pocket," she flamed out. "It's you, you old miser, who bleed the poor people of Klein Mainz, you who make drunkards of them, you who have ruined many a good family."

The old man was shivering with rage. He offered to throw a ten-pound weight at her head, and she tearfully threatened to try some bad eggs on his face and call a policeman into the bargain. The old man made a grumbling retreat.

The news spread through both tenement houses, and that evening a meeting was held at the grocery store. Enthusiasm ran high. Some of the women who had kept quiet, opened their mouths. The extent of the evil was much greater than it had been supposed.

"It's no use hesitating to tell the truth. My old one spends more than a third of his wages in that cur's pesthole."

"One-third! I wish my ruffian would spend as little as that," broke in another housewife, with poetical license. "My old reprobate, he leaves more than half of what he makes in that den."

While this was in progress in the grocery store, the husbands of these women, and some others, were peacefully singing and chatting at the tables of the beer saloon.

"They are there now," said a tall, plump enthusiast. "They are there, and that worthless dog is pouring glass after glass into their stupid brains. I tell you what. Let us send word to them. 'If you don't quit and go home at once there will be no supper tomorrow. The widow and the butcher want their money. No more tick.' "

The motion was carried and the mover delegated to carry it out. She wavered, but she had to go. She was long in coming back—so long that the other housewives lost their patience.

"What can be the matter with her?"

The matter was simply this: Her husband could not have kissed her forehead without standing on tiptoe. He weighed quite a number of English pounds less than she. As to looks, the women of Klein Mainz (and they ought to know) were all of the opinion that the couple looked like a monkey and a princess when side by side. And yet when the princess entered the Bavarian's saloon and the monkey raised a questioning, frowning look to her blue-eyed face, that face turned red and then white.

"What devil has brought you here?" snarled the monkey.

"I only wanted to ask you for the keys," muttered the princess.

She did not leave by the street door through which she had come, but by the "Sunday entrance," which was a shortcut to her room, kitchen and bedroom, on the third floor, right-hand side, back.

Another housewife volunteered to go and see what was the matter with the plump enthusiast. This one was a pink-cheeked old Silesian. A quarter of an hour had passed, and neither of the two was coming.

"What is the matter?"

This time it was quite another matter. The Silesian with the pink cheeks was not afraid of her husband. Neither was he of her. She cursed him, and he replied by calling her *Liebchen* and dear little treasure; she tried to wrench him away from the table, and he answered by throwing his arm about her and ordering *Eins* for her. *Das Ewig-Weibliche* was no match for his arm.

Delegate No. 2 sank into a chair; the lager sank in her glass, and the pink cheeks grew pinker.

The good women in the grocery store were making nominations for a third delegate to ascertain what had become of the first and the second. But this is as far as the oral minutes of the meeting go, and how it all ended is unknown. It was all confused and vague.

———————

"LET'S DANCE"
June 30, 1900

This is the sixteenth week since the cigarmakers' strike broke out, and the faithful members of the union are celebrating it today with a dance. The music is supplied by amateurs, members of the organization, and the dancing is all done by the women, as most of the men who stopped work sixteen weeks ago have since procured other jobs and are too busy rolling cigars to hop around with the girls. The older women, particularly those who have babies in their arms, begrudge the dancers their fun, so they declare it out of order.

"You do well to frisk about like that," grumbled one matron with six-month-old twins on her lap. "What do you care if your mamma has got to pawn her wedding ring to pay the milkman?"

"Go'n pawn yourself. You don't know what ye talkin' about," was the retort. "I never made more'n five dollars a week, anyway, an de union, it pays me de same."

"That's right," put in another girl. "This strike is the first vacation I ever got. It's too hot to work for $5 a week, and if the bosses don't want to give us a raise we can afford to dance and get strike money."

"Shut up, girls. Money is coming from all over the country, and the manufacturers know it, so they won't let you dance long." This was delivered quite oratorically by one of the leaders, and the 200 girls in the hall broke off their dancing to listen to him, and when he told them he had nothing to say, a Bohemian woman of about forty-five years of age got up on a bench and asked the many-colored crowd whether she had the floor.

"Yes, ma'am! Go ahead! Speak nice!" yelled the girls. The amateur musicians were fidgeting about, but they had to wait. The Bohemian woman was a favorite, and, moreover, the dancers say her voice is more musical than the tones produced by the amateur fiddlers, so she clasped her hands and began:

"Girls, it's nearly four months since the present strike began. Four months is a third of a year [wild applause] which means that we have been striking the third part of a year [cheers]. But thanks to the prosperity enjoyed by this free republic [applause] and to the Divine help which we have enjoyed in this strike [the girls rolled up their eyes toward the ceiling] our brothers and sisters in the other cigar factories are working steadily and making fine wages. So they send us part of their earnings in order that we may hold out and win the fight. [Applause and the cry of babies.] And when we have beaten the bosses, wages will rise throughout the entire trade. I tell you, sisters, it is hard to defeat labor when God is on its side. It's the will of heaven that we win, and that's why the shops are so busy; why everybody is earning good wages; why we get enough strike benefit to fight our employers until they are compelled to give in. [Cheers.] Will you be true to your union?"

"Yes!" shouted the girls.

"All right. And now let's dance."

THE SCHOLARLY WAISTMAKERS
August 24, 1900

The shirtwaist makers who went out on strike two weeks ago have all gone back to work, more or less victorious, but about a hundred other members of the trade left their sewing machines yesterday. Most of these were girls, and as one of them, a young woman in eyeglasses and with a big Russian book under her arm, explained to the reporter, the majority of the new strikers are well-educated immigrant girls come to seek higher education in the American colleges.

The conversation was held in the meeting hall at 77 Essex Street, which is the headquarters of the striking shirtwaist makers, and the young woman with the voluminous book was the centre of a small crowd of other strikers, who nodded approval to all she said. She would not give her name for publication, because "in Russia one is taught to keep himself in the background, not to seek notoriety." Besides, she was not the leader of the fight, but "a common soldier in the ranks."

The big book under her arm proved to be Gray's *Anatomy*, for the bespectacled shirtwaist maker expects to enter the Woman's Medical College. Others of the strikers are studying law, still others are preparing for the Dental College or the College of Pharmacy, and all of them have learned to make shirtwaists as a temporary occupation to support them and to pay their way through college.

George Pine, a good-looking young man with broad shoulders, who was pointed out as an authority on East Side labor matters, confirmed the statement that the Shirtwaist Makers' Union contained a considerable number of educated men and women.

"This accounts for the intelligence with which the strike has been conducted and the easy victory gained by the hands," he added. "These students or would-be or will-be students all come from Russia, where the higher schools are practically closed to Jews. They come here in quest of learning. Not that America has the best colleges in the world, but because here one may find something to do to keep his pot boiling, while he is at college. Some American boys work their way through college by serving as waiters in summer hotels. Well, the great majority of ghetto collegians make their living and their tuition fee by kicking the treadle of a sewing machine. When you walk along East Broadway you often come across a dazzling carriage with a bewhiskered, pompous-looking doctor grandly leaning back behind the coachman. Well, the chances are that no further back than five or six years ago, this shining star of the ghetto was a poor, hard-working shirt maker. In those days our impecunious students usually took to ordinary shirt making. Now shirtwaists pay much better, or ought to. So our educated immigrants flock to that industry."

"MADAM, YOU HAD BETTER LEAVE THE ROOM"
June 1, 1901

There is an unwritten law in the Court of General Sessions that mothers, sisters or wives of defendants about to be sentenced should be asked to leave the courtroom in which the proceedings are taking place. This law was recently tried on a Bohemian woman, but it proved inoperative. Her husband had been found guilty of an offense where a good-looking girl of seventeen was the complaining witness. The prisoner's wife was a middle-aged woman, sallow-faced and pockmarked. She was sure her husband was innocent.

"How do you know?" asked one of the interpreters.

"I know because I know," she answered, sullenly.

After a little time she broke out:

"You don't mean to tell me he would care for that ugly thing?"

The interpreter, who is the favorite of all the clerks and attendants in the building, was moved and said nothing.

"You're silent, sir," the woman went on, excitedly. "I see you don't think I know what I am talking about. But my husband is crazy for me. I know he is. Perfect beauties have tried to get a mash on him, and it did not work. The idea of such a horrid thing cutting me out of my husband's love— me!" And she laughed so heartily that the interpreter could not help joining in.

When her husband was arraigned for sentence, the same interpreter said to her, gently:

"Madam, you had better leave the room."

"Why? Oh, I see, they're going to send him to Sing Sing, and you're afraid I'll faint. But I shan't. You may be sure I shan't. He is innocent, and yet they're going to punish him. But he's not the man to break down. If you know him you would know what a brave fellow he is. I want to see him bear up under this woe of his. My heart will weep, but I just want to see my hero hold up his head while they're sending him, an innocent man, to his doom."

There was a peculiar gleam of exultation in her eyes as she said all this. The interpreter advised the court attendants to let her stay in.

"She's a crank," he said to a bystander.

On another occasion, an Italian woman, whose son was to be sent to state prison for grand larceny, clutched at the bench and refused to stir.

"Murderers, that you are!" she screamed. "Isn't it enough that you are going to rob me of the shining star of my life? Will you have the heart to turn out a mother so that she can't see her boy walked out of this world?"

"But he will come back to you," the interpreter shouted at her, angrily.

The old woman shook her head and burst into tears. "Something tells me I'll never see him alive. You're a lot of murderers."

She clutched at her seat with might and main, but the combined strength of two attendants proved more than a match for her.

Another Italian woman could not understand why she should not be allowed to see her husband discharged.

"The *signori* were kind enough to let me sit here all through the trial, and now that my Giacomo has been found by the twelve *signori* to be innocent and he is going to take me home, you won't let me wait to hear the judge say: 'Giacomo, you are an honest man. Go home with your wife.' "

When she found out her mistake and that her Giacomo had not been found an honest man, she fainted.

"SHE CAN TALK LIKE A LAWYER"
August 1, 1901

Ninety of the sweaters who belong to the Contractors' Association have withdrawn from that body and granted the demands of the striking tailors on the East Side. This, however, does not terminate the fight of the other contractors against the union. What the Association loses in numbers it makes up in energy and resourceful men. The latest innovation in this sort of warfare is a band of persuaders, corresponding to the walking delegates or pickets of trades unions. These persuaders are going from tenement house to tenement house talking to the wives of the strikers. Proceeding on the theory that the housewives have a keener appreciation of the loss sustained by them through the strike than their husbands, these "walking orators," as they are called by some, are making an effort to win the women of the tailoring district over to the contractors' side. So far, however, the attempt is said to have met with no success. Only in two or three cases, where the persuader was reinforced by the oratorical help of the sweater himself, did the strikers' wives get into a row with their husbands because they wouldn't return to work on the old terms.

One red-haired little man told a crowd of strikers this morning of the victory which his wife scored over the persuaders.

"She can talk like a lawyer," he said in Yiddish. "And when she is in the women's compartment at the synagogue she reads the Commentary aloud and the other women sit listening and sighing. That's the kind of woman my wife is. You ought to hear her talk to the janitor in German! Whenever any of the tenants wants something done or said they call upon her. She can talk, and she isn't afraid of anybody. Well, when that fellow, my sweater's persuader, came around I just waited to see what was going to happen. I knew there was going to be fun. Well, he started to get in his fine work, to tell my wife how poor she was and how the sweater was crazy to let me make a living, and all that sort of rot, but she cut him short and delivered such a lecture that even Joseph Barondess isn't in it with her. She told him that we didn't want any sweating system, and that the sweaters must go, and when he got mad she gave him a piece of her mind and got hold of the poker. You should have seen the fellow scoot!''

Meanwhile the number of clothing firms who sign the union agreement is growing steadily. Up to this forenoon 160 manufacturers had settled.

General Secretary Harry White announced today that the cutters employed by an uptown firm, numbering about sixty men who cut the cloth for 1,000 tailors, had met last night and resolved to notify the firm this afternoon that unless it complied with the demands of the striking tailors every cutter would go out. The reply of the firm is expected by tomorrow. Similar action was taken by the cutters, forty in number, representing work for 700 tailors, employed by a firm on Waverly Place. Reports from Bayonne to Secretary White indicate that great excitement reigns there among the strikers. Three New York firms have their work done there. The shops in which these men are employed were established, Mr. White said, by the Baron de Hirsch Society with a view that the work of making garments could be done more easily and better in the suburbs of New York. In Bayonne there are 600 men on strike.

General Secretary Guyer of the Cloakmakers' Union said in all there were less than 3,000 workers on strike, and that it was in no sense a general strike, but an affair to be settled by each shop. The executive committee of the union, he said, had not taken any action in the strike except to approve in cases where individual shops struck. At no time, he said, has there been any thought of a general strike. Each shop has its own grievances and rights them as best it can, with the assistance of the union. The question of ''ordering'' cloakmakers on strike, he stated, did not lie with the union in the present trouble, but with the committee of each shop.

WOMEN OF VALOR
June 29, 1902

The East Side housewife is misunderstood and misinterpreted. She is pictured as living without a murmur in squalor and filth, her favorite pastime is stated to be to gossip and quarrel with her neighbors, or, better still, with her unfortunate janitress. Her children are declared to be physically impoverished, because she either cannot or will not prepare food according to the latest hygienic rulings of American cooking clubs.

Not being able, as a rule, to speak English, she cannot refute these charges, and only those who come into close, neighborly relations with her can appreciate her true worth. She is at once the joy and the despair of the typical settlement worker of fine theories and high ideals.

In reality, she wages perpetual warfare on the common enemy of all housekeepers, dirt, and under the most exasperating conditions. Her landlord does not set her a shining example of sanitation and cleanliness, nor does he provide for her use the simplest of modern conveniences.

Any woman who attempts to keep house in three rooms, even in the simplest fashion, for a family of six, with perhaps a lodger or two, must either pick up continually or take refuge on the fire escape from sheer lack of foot room. Hence she has little time for gossiping or quarrelling.

For the sake of her children she will go hungry if necessary, and in the preparation of dishes peculiar to her race or nationality, she could win out, hands down, against the average head of an American cooking school.

And her husband, far from considering her as an obstacle to his progress, regards her as a beacon light, leading him ever onward to a bank account and competency. She it is who carries the family purse, purchases every article in the family wardrobe and deposits the family savings in a bank of her own selection.

Summer lays on her shoulders only fresh burdens. In her vocabulary there is no such word as vacation.

The babble of a thousand voices rises, along with fetid odors and heat glare, from the street below. Even had she money to invest in luxuries like screens and awnings, they would be impossible, because they would obstruct the entrance of what little fresh air reaches her apartments.

The cooking of the meals, a comforting process in winter, now converts her flat into a furnace room. The gradual shrinkage in the five-cent chunk of ice has long since converted the ice man into a deadly enemy.

And through and over it all hangs the fear that her husband may be overcome by the heat in the great factory where he is pressing winter suits and overcoats for twelve terrific prostrating hours each day. Then he would be taken to the hospital from which she would be barred by the blue-coated guardians whose language she has not mastered.

Yet all this she faces with a dim philosophy that it is a mortal ill to be borne, not combatted, and that somehow she and her offspring will survive the torrid wave.

The East Side, as it is popularly known, covers a comparatively small area, something less than half a square mile, wherein is crowded a little city of its own, the ghetto, with a population of 500,000 souls. Half a million men, women and children, almost exclusively Polish and Russian Hebrews, crowded into what might be described as four good-sized city blocks.

That they live and thrive and become decent citizens is the greatest proof of the ability of the East Side wife and mother.

Monetary conditions set the limit of her apartment at three rooms. In the modern tenement each of these must have access to an open court or airshaft, but there still stand hundreds of houses erected before the present tenement laws went into effect.

In these the best room will overlook the street, or court, according as it may be a front or a rear tenement. There will be two windows, from one of which runs the fire escape.

A room ten feet square is considered spacious, and a shallow clothes press in this apartment is regarded by its mistress with proper appreciation akin to gratitude. A door and a window cut through the partition afford light and air for the middle room, where the cooking is usually done.

Beyond is a still smaller room, so designed merely by courtesy, and here there is neither ventilation nor light—only Stygian darkness.

The average American housewife making her first trip through the East Side is impressed by the almost entire absence of carpets, the pretentiousness of whatever pieces of furniture her East Side sister may possess and the peculiar arrangement of her china closets. The landlord or his representative looks at none of these.

The all-important question with him is whether the tenant keeps her stove and copper utensils in good condition. If this be the case, he feels himself assured that he has secured a thrifty tenant who will meet her rent promptly.

Personal neatness, apparently, counts for little with the real East Sider, and judgment is never pronounced on a newcomer in the neighborhood until the janitor's wife and perhaps the woman next door have caught a glimpse of the stove and reported its condition to the older residents.

The East Side matron regards the installment house as an institution of the evil ones and buys her furnishings only as she has cash in hand and to spare. In this case she is apt to splurge a trifle, buying furniture quite out of proportion to the size and general appearance of her room.

If there is only one bed in the house, it will be of white iron with as much brass ornamentation as her purse will permit. At night this is occupied by the father and mother, and during the day it is piled with the bedding used in making shakedowns for the other members of the family.

This pile may reach to a height almost on a level with the top rail of the headpiece, but once in place it is carefully hidden from view by a lace bedset, or a priceless old counterpane brought over by her family as immigrants.

A combination sideboard and refrigerator fills the ambitions of the East Side housewife, also a good portion of the room; and a massive pier glass between the two front windows is regarded as an essential. Lace curtains, the more obvious the pattern the better, she does not regard as incompatible with a sanded floor.

Draperies of imitation cretonne in vivid colorings give life to the dun-hued surroundings and are retained the year round, along with the lace curtains. Bureaus and chiffoniers seem unpopular.

But however many or meagre be such furnishings, the china closet of the genuine East Side woman is a thing of beauty and a joy forever. Each shelf is hung with a pleated curtain of stiffly starched linen trimmed with homemade lace and insertion.

Behind these, on the shallow shelves, are ranged two distinct sets of dishes, according to the Mosaic law that the animal products, such as meats, gravies, soups made from meat, etc., shall not be eaten from the same dishes as milk, cheese and butter. Separate sets of knives, forks and spoons also are provided, and two distinct sets of cooking utensils.

In the hand-to-mouth existence she leads, little does the East Side housekeeper know of store room, linen room and pantry; but her china closet is a part of her religion and is guarded with a jealous eye.

The thrifty East Sider invariably has a lodger or two who pays 50 cents a week for a shakedown on the floor and a peg whereon to hang the suit he wears to the synagogue. He may also arrange with her for his morning coffee and roll at 5 cents or more, according to the market prices.

Her day begins early, as the men must be at their shops by 6. For a family of six, where the daily income is $2, the breakfast will consist of coffee, bread and butter, with occasionally an egg.

Directly after the departure of the men, the woman begins tidying up. The shakedowns are hung on the fire escape to air, if the weather permits. If not, they are piled one on the other on the bed, if there is one, or in a corner of the room.

The children are prepared for school with watchful care. The Hebrew regards the education of his children as a profitable investment, and sends them to both the public summer schools in the morning and the Hebrew schools in the afternoon.

Moreover the mother will stint herself to provide for at least one member of the family a musical training, paying 25 cents for piano lessons, with the privilege of practicing a certain time each day at the teacher's home.

The children disposed of, the woman is ready for her shopping tour. It may consist merely of a trip down the two, three or four flights of stairs for the daily wrangle with the ice peddler, whose wares she must herself carry the weary flights back to her rooms. The delivery system on the East Side is in the embryonic stage.

If she has a refrigerator, the disposition of her purchase is simple. If she cannot boast this much-desired possession, the ice is kept in the stationary washtub, wrapped in heavy paper or clothes.

In either case, it is used principally to cool off the drinking water and not as a means to keep perishable supplies. The latter she purchases only as they can be used.

She buys a few ounces of butter at a time, which brings it up to a figure that would make her West Side sister wince. This is one of the conditions that confront the East Sider.

There is absolutely no provision in her tenement for storing table supplies, and she spends a good part of her time each day running back and forth between her home and the various shops.

Her children learn early to shop, and that thriftily. There is practically no credit on the East Side, and the tradesmen thrive.

The ghetto housewife is clannish, seldom roaming far from Hester Street, with its array of pushcarts, for her trading, which may include anything from a bunch of onions to a new dress. Of the great department stores beyond Broadway she knows nothing.

Over the remnants displayed on the Hester Street curb she haggles until she wins her point. The unyielding bargain placards of the West Side shops would try her thrifty soul.

She has solved the fuel question partly by purchasing a portable, two-hole gas stove, which she mounts on a table or a box. This costs her $1.50 new, or considerably less if she finds a trustworthy second-hand dealer.

She avoids the monthly visit of the gas company's collector by using the slot machine meter. The company places in her house a slot machine, into which she drops a quarter and the gas is turned on. When she has burned a quarter's worth of gas, the flow stops abruptly and is not resumed until a second quarter is dropped in the machine.

An ordinarily good manager uses 25 cents' worth of gas a week, which is considerably cheaper and infinitely more comfortable than coal at the rate of 10 cents a scuttle or 35 cents a 100-pound sack.

Once a week, on Friday, she starts her coal fire to do the baking for her Sabbath day.

Meat is the item of living which strikes dread to the heart of the East Side provider. It must be purchased from a *kosher* shop, it must be cut from the most expensive portions of the animal, the forequarters and breast, and it must be absolutely above suspicion. No *kosher* butcher may keep meat more than three days.

The breast of beef sells at 18 cents a pound, the cut known as chuck bringing 14. Meats not *kosher* sell as low as five and six cents a pound, but the Gentiles living on the East Side patronize the *kosher* shops largely, to be assured of getting clean, untainted meat.

Only the best poultry is offered in the East Side, where it brings from 18 to 25 cents a pound. The finest fish goes to the Hester Street shops and wagons, commanding from 18 cents to 30 cents a pound. Pike is regarded as the greatest delicacy.

So minutely and thoroughly does the East Sider's religion enter into his domestic life that he eats either the best there is in the market or nothing. Better black bread and coffee than savory meats that are open to suspicion. The housewife may offer but one dish at a meal, but that will be carefully prepared according to the law and traditions.

The East Side child when he gets a cent does not run to the nearest candy shop. The money represents to him actual food and is spent usually at fruit stands.

Diminutive baskets of strawberries in season sell for two cents, bananas in good condition and of reasonable dimensions can be had for one cent, but oranges are practically unknown here during the summer months.

All vegetables are now sold by the pound, as false bottoms in measures and a skilful arrangement of potatoes in other measures more than once have nearly caused riots. Potatoes bring two cents a pound, beets, an East Side staple, have risen to seven cents a pound, and cabbage is considered cheap at five cents a head.

Onions, which are used in immense quantities, command five cents a pound. Cucumbers sell here for a cent when five cents are demanded uptown.

All this the housewife has not discovered on a single trip, but at various times during the day she has sallied forth, basket on arm, to watch the rise or fall of the market.

Her luncheon has been a simple matter, for the man at work a sandwich and some cheese, for the children and herself perhaps only bread and butter, with fruit if there were cents for the little ones.

The one meal of the day is dinner, which she prepares with infinite care and which is served at about 6:30 o'clock. For this there will be soup, meat, potatoes, radishes or cucumbers, and if times are good with the family, there may be a pie made of prunes or rhubarb. If business at the shop is dull, there will be only one or two dishes, in which case extra care must be taken to provide nourishing qualities.

A never-failing staple for the East Sider is herring, which can be purchased at the rate of two for three cents. From these she concocts a peculiarly satisfying salad.

The fish is soaked, chopped and then mixed with finely minced onions, boiled egg, pepper and just enough vinegar to give flavor, but not to make the mixture mushy.

The East Side cook prepares fish after fashions that other housewives have tried in vain to copy. A recipe that sounds simple enough and yet which baffles the uninitiated calls for seven pounds of the best white fish such as pike.

This is cleaned, rubbed well with salt and laid on the ice to cool. The bones and heads are used to form a false bottom in the agate pot used for cooking. This prevents burning.

The fish is then taken from the ice, washed free of salt, cut into portions sufficient for one person each and laid in cold water to the depth of two inches, to which has been added sliced onions, pepper and salt. It is permitted to simmer quietly for at least two and a half hours. Just before serving, a tablespoon of butter is added.

This is a popular dish for Friday night, being served cold for the Sabbath-day lunch, when it will be found that the broth in which the fish was cooked has formed round it like a jelly.

Another characteristic East Side dish is made from fish skinned and cut fine while raw and then mixed with finely ground cracker crumbs, minced onion, salt, pepper, and one or two raw eggs, the whole made into balls which are stewed, not fried. These, too, are eaten cold for the Sabbath-day luncheon.

Friday is the busiest day of the week for the East Side housewife, for she cannot so much as strike a match in her house on the next day. No matter what the weather on Friday, the coal fire is started, great loaves of bread, twist, and coffee cake, glistening with a varnish of beaten egg, and made dishes such as those described here are prepared.

When this supply of bread gives out, she buys at the Hester Street market, paying four or five cents a loaf for white bread and two cents a pound or three pounds for five cents for the black bread similar to that used by the Russian peasants in their native land.

The wife of the man who earns $3 a day, and has a family of five, calculates to spend about 56 cents a day on her table. The rent will be $10 a month, and out of the remainder she will manage to save not only the coveted deposit against a slack season, but sufficient to send her family decently clothed to the synagogue.

The children each may have only a single garment to don during the week, but on the Sabbath day they will sally forth arrayed like the flowers of the field, every garment fashioned by the untiring fingers of the under-rated East Side mother.

Aside from her cooking, which, by reason of the Mosaic law, is a complicated process, the East Side housewife conducts her house on simple lines. Bathrooms are unknown in the cheap tenements, but the children can linger round the nearest hose house until the good-natured firemen turn on a freshening stream.

The few garments worn by the East Side child can be quickly dried on the roof or the ever-convenient fire escape. The cleaning goes on eternally. Her only storeroom is a single trunk, which holds the few family treasures and is hidden from view by a friendly if gaily flowered curtain. The heaviest contribution to her wash comes in the form of the inevitable Nottingham window curtains and the china closet curtain, which are a source of pride.

When the weather becomes unbearable, even the shakedowns do not have to be prepared. The suffering family betakes itself to fire escapes, areaway or roof.

When a four-story tenement is divided into sixteen apartments and each apartment or flat shelters at least six persons, the picture presented on a hot night can readily be imagined.

As the exhausted housewife drops off into uneasy slumber, the chances are that she dreams of successive rises through ten, fifteen, twenty-dollar apartments until her husband, now a baster or presser, may become a clothing contractor of importance; then they will lease a large private house and sublet two floors, and the children will have silk frocks to wear to the synagogue.

But as for leaving the East Side when the wave of prosperity strikes them, that would be quite absurd, quite impossible.

The East Sider who has $300 in the bank is ready to start on an independent business career. With a deposit of $500 at his command, he considers seriously the purchase of real estate.

But to the end of the chapter his wife will continue to haggle over the food supply, make her children's clothes and contribute of her blood to the family exchequer.

PART FIVE
The Arena

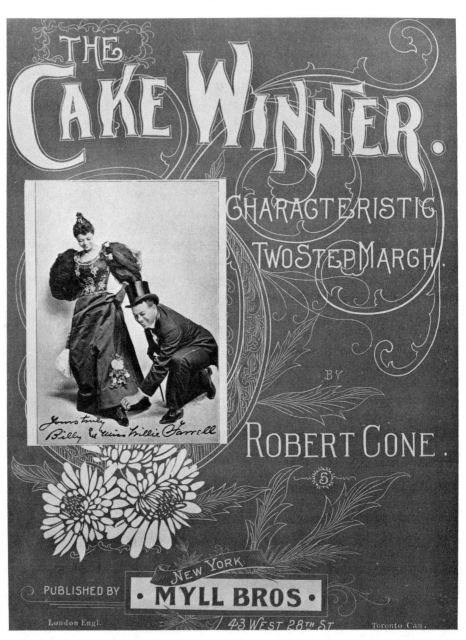

Sheet music cover, c. 1897. (Landauer Sheet Music Collection. *Courtesy of the New York Historical Society, New York City.*)

14

FANCY FREE

TWO BOYS FROM ASIA
March 12, 1898

It was recess time, yet the sidewalk in front of the Norfolk Street school did not have the usual look of recess. Instead of romping and frisking about adding their yells to the thousand and one sounds of the markets nearby, the children who had not scampered home for lunch stood in knots, motionless, silent, grave, their glances converging on two queer-looking lads who stood on the same sidewalk. These lads wore huge top-boots, and their loose sack coats were tightly gathered at the waist with wide leather belts, each with a heavy buckle of gleaming brass. They were apparently brothers and looked like well-groomed fellows of twelve and eleven years. As they stood gazing at the street the older of the two would now and then begin to smile—a profuse, hearty, lovely smile—wherewith his dark eyes would grow fidgety, a dimple would form in each of his plump, rosy cheeks and the dazzling whiteness of his teeth would show like two rows of pearls. His brother's round apple face never relaxed. With his eyes half shut and his red lips puckered up he was viewing the crowd over his shoulder, as if in grim readiness to pounce upon the first intruder and rend him to pieces.

The policeman, who had been gossiping with the janitor, happened to face about. As his eye fell on the two boys his lips parted. Few sights are out of the ordinary on Norfolk Street, yet the two odd-looking brothers attracted his attention. And chewing at an imaginary quid, by way of suppressing his look of amusement, he approached the little foreigners.

"What's that? Klondike boots?" he asked, raising one of the younger boy's legs and feeling of the leather in which it was encased.

"*Nyet Klondaika! Nyet Klondaika!*" was the angry reply, as the little fellow wrenched himself free.

The bluecoat looked embarrassed. He was not used to such retorts, and before he recovered from the rebuff he sheepishly took hold of one of the older boy's boots.

"What in ———— is it, anyhow?" he asked. "Are you from the Klondike or Siberia?"

"*Nyet Klondaika! Nyet Siber!* Turkestan," the older boy shouted as if answering a question by his teacher, and as he did so there came those dimples into his cheeks and he smiled upon his questioner a cherubic smile, which seemed to go straight to the cop's heart.

"Yes, they come from Turkestan, Asia," a Norfolk Street–born little Semite interposed, "an' dey don't speak no English an' nobody don' know vat dey're talkin' about."

"Get out!" thundered the bluecoat, venting on the American boy his belated sense of frustrated ambition.

No language is Greek to Norfolk Street, however, and so it was not long before an interpreter was found and the two little strangers could be interviewed.

"What is your religion, my lad?" was the first question.

"We are Christians, of course!" the older boy replied, half lifting his arms in surprise. "What, then, should we be?"

"How long have you been in this country?"

"Two months, but it seems so long!" he added, intimately.

The young fellow gave him a sneering look, as if he would say, "Can't you send them about their business, fool you?"

"How do you like America? Is it as good a place to live in as Turkestan?"

"Pretty good, only there are no mountains, nor large open fields. The houses are like mountains," he added, with a giggle. "Still, when I get used to it and learn to speak English, I think I shall like it." As he spoke he gesticulated in the same hearty, winsome way in which he laughed or smiled, and altogether he impressed his interviewer as an intelligent, well-informed boy, with the tact of a man of thirty and the manner of a child of six.

"What is your teacher's name?"

"Miam!"

"Miam? Is there a teacher by that name in the school?" one of the school boys was appealed to.

"No, sir; but I know what he means," a bright little boy proceeded to explain. He was interrupted by his Turkestan classmate, however, who said

414

to his interpreter: "What is the matter? Doesn't the gentleman believe me? Why should I tell him a lie? Don't I hear the boys say, 'Yes, Miam!' 'No, Miam!' "

"How long have you been at school?"

"This is our first day."

"Do you like it?"

"Very much. We like the marching in the morning and on going out, and the singing and the way the chief reads from a big book, when all the boys were quiet—oh, so quiet! you could have heard a fly buzz through the room—and—and everything! Only we don't understand English, so we do and say everything the other boys do. This morning we came near getting punished. When it was quiet and Miam was watching the class, a boy whispered to us: 'Yes, Miam!' So we thought we had to repeat, and at once shouted at the top of our voices: 'Yes, Miam!' The other boys began to laugh, and the Miam looked so angry! She told us to rise. We obeyed. Then she said something and stamped her foot. But we did not know what she meant, so I gesticulated and gesticulated to her—of course, I would not give away the boy who had put up that job on us—till she was not angry any longer and little by little she began to smile and I smiled, too, and then she laughed, and I also laughed and all the other boys laughed. And then she got angry again and shouted: 'Keebquied!' "

MIKE AND MIKOVA
June 4, 1898

A Long Island bicyclist, who devotes his wheel to the exploration of what he calls the "terra incognita" of Greater New York, has discovered a Polish village in the big city. It is situated midway between Flushing and Jamaica and consists of fifty or sixty shanties, scattered among the farms which yield the peasants their livelihood. These farms do not belong to them, however, being owned or rented by Americans or Germans, by whom the Poles are hired. Their pay is about a dollar a day, but potatoes, which constitute the principal part of their food, they get from their employers free, and as every able-bodied man and woman works, the little community knows no want, while many of its members carry savings bank books in their breast pockets.

The village certainly would not be quite so well off as it is were its people given to drink, but they are not, as a rule, and the German whose inn is within a stone's throw of the settlement has to rely for his custom upon his fellow-countrymen and English-speaking farmers rather than upon his Polish neighbors. The latter are all good Catholics, and every Sunday morning, rain or shine, they may be seen plodding along in groups, on their way to Newtown, where they have their church.

The population of the village is made up of immigrants from the Polish kingdom, Austria, Galicia and Posen. They are all peasants, and although some of them have been here some time, they have retained many of the essential traits of life in their native villages.

No Polish village could do without a Jew, much less in America, where he is so badly needed as a means of communication with the strange people who speak English. "Russian sounds so much like Polish," said one of the denizens of the village in question, "yet if it was so hard to learn to speak it even when one was in the Czar's army, where the tongue of the accursed Muscovites is taught with kicks and cuffs, how much harder would it be to pick up English! But a Jew is different. He will learn anything. That's what he is a Jew for."

And so the Long Island village has its Jew, and he is the social center of the colony and the connecting link between it and the rest of the world. His name is Michael Harris, and the Polish peasants call him, not Meechalka, as they would at their native place, but Mike, as they heard some Irish laborers address him. "Mike" seems more up to date, and they are willing to be abreast of the times wherever they can. But then, "Mrs. Harris" is altogether too difficult and too funny a name to pronounce, so they have dubbed her Mikova (the wife of Mike).

Mike deals neither in vodka (whiskey) nor in beer, but, barring these commodities, his store contains everything the peasant's mouth can name, and many an article of which he never so much as heard in the old country— luxuries with which noblemen alone may be familiar.

It was a late hour on a Saturday afternoon when the writer visited the peaceful little village in company with the wheelman who claims immortality for having discovered it. Dusk was gathering over the sloping stretches of vegetable gardens and the gray row of cottages on the hillside. The doors of the store, which overlooks the crossroads from a raised platform, were wide open. A company of chickens was raking the ground underneath or saunter- ing about with a preoccupied air. Two peasants in American clothes, out of keeping with the simple-hearted look of their sturdy faces and the huge Polish pipes between their teeth, sat on a porch watching the strategic movements of a warlike dog and a scared cat. A boy, barefooted and with a soldier's cap on his blond head, stood in the middle of the road, now talking to a little girl in broken English, now addressing himself to the two belligerents in Polish.

Mike was found in the store behind the counter, waiting upon a woman who wanted a loaf of rye bread, a few yards of calico, and a spool of cotton. Two other women, with uncovered heads, like the first, came in. One wanted to know the price of a pair of shoes, and the other held a big jug, which she wished to have filled with vinegar, and a muslin purse from which she was anxious to pay an old bill. The two strangers seemed to make the peasant women ill at ease, for they spoke to the storekeeper in subdued tones, and as they made their exit, each hugging her purchase as though afraid lest the two Americans should take them away, they kept their eyes on the floor. Not so Mike. He received his visitors with a cordiality and ease of manner which seemed to say: "Well, what can you expect of a peasant woman? But they are human beings, after all, are they not?" He is a big, husky man of thirty-five, and his features have little or nothing to indicate his race.

"I have lived sixteen years in this place," he said. "But I go to New York every day in the week—every single day. The Gentiles here are so helpless! I must speak English for them, read their mail, write their letters, lend them a dollar or two when they are short—but they are excellent pay—and go their bail when they get in trouble. Do they like me? Not half so much as they like my wife. Her they would die for. The women come to tell her their tales of woe, and all the gossip of the village is first brought to her. Very often this gossip will lead up to a quarrel, and then my wife—oh, she has the head of a minister, I tell you—will decide who is right and who is wrong, rebuke the gossip-monger and make peace. She is their judge and their *rebbitzen* [the wife of a rabbi].

"Most of the peasants hereabouts have their own fiddles, and they often come with them to my house, where they spend the evening playing, dancing, singing and making merry, just as they do in the village inns in Poland. We have a school half a mile away, and they send their children there. When they grow up they will all be Americans, but by that time there will be other immigrant peasants, so the village will still be in need of me."

"Mikova" was away visiting some friends in a neighboring town, but her absence did not prevent a number of peasants from assembling in the back room of the store, which is their usual gathering place, and where the storekeeper's wife reigns. The conversation turned on the priest, work, and the gossip of the settlement. The war was not mentioned, and when one of the strangers asked a young fellow, through Mike, what he thought of the fight, the peasant grinned, blushed, dropped his eyes, and shrugging his shoulders, he finally ventured to say:

"How should I know? The *pan* [nobleman] can read, so he ought to know all about it."

"Would you like to see Spain whipped?"

"Why not?" was the answer.

"Would it make any difference to you if it was America that was licked?"

The young peasant was opening his mouth for another broad grin, when an older man broke in: "God will not let America be beaten. America is a good land. One can make a living here, and there is no Czar to drag you into the army, either."

"Sure, there isn't," a little old fellow asserted. "Who can doubt that America is a better place to live in than Poland? Over there one wears bark shoes and eats rough bread and lard; but here, if you are in luck and get a good job, you dress like a nobleman, and get meat for dinner every day in the week. The war? Oh, I know. America is having a fight with the people called Spaniards, isn't it? You see, I know all about it. But I cannot see why they should be fighting. Are they little children or are they drunk that they should have come to blows? America is such a smart country. It has a machine for everything. Look at the way they work their farms—so smart, so smart! And yet they fight like little boys."

"Oh, you are a fool to be talking like that to the *pan*," a man interposed. "War isn't like a plain fight. It is—well, it is war; that's what it is, and if God wants to have it, it must be, and that settles it. Am I right, Mike?"

With a knowing look at the strangers, Mike said that he was.

THE CAKEWALK:
STRAIGHT, FANCY, AND BURLESQUE
November 3, 1898

The big cakewalk, which took place on the main floor of Madison Square Garden last night, was preceded by some "littler" cakewalks on the stage, as one of the participants put it. One of these was performed by a thirteen-year-old negro boy in knee breeches and a negro girl of the same age. Both were jet black and both thin. As their cadaverous, sombre little figures launched out swaying, bobbing, floating, tripping, there was something extremely touching as well as amusingly fascinating in their movements. At any rate, the few elderly darkies among the spectators who stood near the stage looked on and applauded with a smile of pathetic exultation.

It was after 11 o'clock when the great "international" cakewalk was started. The band struck up a slow march and little by little, as couple after couple emerged from behind the stage, the big garden seemed all afloat with sound and movement. The walking seemed to lend grace and spirit to the music, and the music seemed to heighten the charm of the walking. There were all tints and types in the crowd, "from the comedy of the pure black," as Mr. Howells would have said, "to the closest tragical approach to the white." Each pair moved with its own step and its own gestures, yet there was unity and harmony to the chaos of color and movement. An invisible hand seemed to be controlling and guiding the whole restless disorder according to a plan known only to itself, and the mystery of it added to the fascination of the spectacle.

A young mulatto woman, powdered and painted, and looking more like the patent medicine pictures of Emma Calvé than Emma Calvé herself, swam past the observer with a fellow who looked like a parlor stove wreathed in smiles. With her arms akimbo and her plump body thrown back, she was plunging and bucking, nodding and winking in a way which set the black crowd nearly swearing with admiration. A tall, lean young negro with dreamy eyes and with coffee-colored companion, fleshy, genial and happy, went by on a straight walk. They were both full of grace and fluency, and at once became popular. A young woman with the color of a white girl and the features of a negress was performing a "grotesque" with a pitch-dark young fellow, who had a straight nose and thin lips.

A young negro in a black fur cap and a sable face all bandaged up in a kerchief of the same hue had a toothache and was querulous. A Hebrew spectator said he looked like a certain type of orthodox rabbi. He was the supreme authority of the walk.

"Out!" he would say through his bandages to a couple whose steps were not up or not down to the standard, and out they would slip—shamefacedly, forlornly, but with perfect resignation to their fate.

"Why did you reject that couple?" he was asked.

" 'Cause they didn't do it wid—what do you call it?—science—no, that ain't de word."

"Skill?" his questioner suggested.

"No, that ain't it, neither," the rabbi answered, gruffly.

"Grace?"

"That's it. You've got to walk swell and nice, you know, jes' like a swell guy on de street. No foolin.' "

The first prize was awarded to Luke Blackburn, but the crowd was yelling for Pickaninny, the tall man with the dreamy eyes. Blackburn, who ran the whole show and who looks like an Italian barber, made his bow, medal in hand.

"Pickaninny! Pickaninny!" came from all sides, amid jeers, groans and applause.

"Ladies and gentlemen!" Blackburn shouted at the top of his lungs. "Some of you don't t'ink de decision is right. Well, I am willin' to walk anyone for $1,000."

The crowd hooted. "The people give it to me," said Pickaninny, and he went over to the judges to ask if there was not a second prize.

There was none for the "straight" walk, so Pickaninny gave his name and his wife's, William Hill and Eva Hill, and uttered a challenge to the world. His friends, Ridley and Foster, accompanied by Tommy Lloyd, offered to back him for $500 against $1,000, to outwalk Blackburn or anybody else, on condition, however, that either the people decide or that the contest be held in Illinois.

"Oh, are you from Chicago?" asked a spectator who had howled at the award to Blackburn. That seemed to explain all to him, but another spectator said that it was Blackburn's prize just as it was Blackburn's show.

"MAY THE LORD BLESS OUR GUEST, THE GRAND DUKE KIRILL VLADIMIROVICH!"
January 3, 1899

The Russian Church at 323 Second Avenue seemed too small to hold all the splendor of the service which was held in it at noon today in honor of Grand Duke Kirill Vladimir, the cousin of Nicholas, Czar of all the Russias. Father Chotovitsky, the regular priest of the church, was arrayed in purple and silver as usual, but today he only assisted in the service, for Bishop Nicholas was there, and the bishop conducted the service.

The latter, who was until recently at the head of the orthodox Greek congregations of Alaska and the Aleutian Islands, will sail for Europe tomorrow, together with the Grand Duke Kirill.

Archimandrite Raphael of the Syrian Church, at 77 Washington Street, also participated in the devotional ceremonies. The bishop and the archimandrite wore robes of yellow silk and gold brocade and tall mitres set with diamonds. Bishop Nicholas's breast was aflame with red ribbons and gold medals. He is a tall, sturdy-looking man of fifty with a small beard on a face beaming with health and genial kindness. His deep bass, as he chanted the service, seemed as much out of proportion to the size of the room as the imposing ceremony.

The little church and the bit of corridor leading to it were crowded with men and women. Most of them were Russians, the others were Americans and Germans from the neighboring houses, and nearly all of these were rather poorly clad. They formed a prosaic background to a spectacle of dazzling picturesqueness.

Standing in front of the commonplace and somewhat dingy-looking throng was a well-dressed man of thirty or thereabouts. He was tall, slim, stately and interesting. There was nothing striking in his face, but his figure outlined itself rather boldly upon the crowd of worshippers and sightseers. The man was Grand Duke Kirill, whose father was brother of the late Czar Alexander III, and who is one of the possible successors to the throne of Russia. He stood erect, but his oval head was slightly bowed and his eyes shut in prayer.

The room was filled with the soft odors of incense and the heavy but pleasing peal of the bishop's voluminous voice.

"And may the Lord bless our Czar, Emperor Nikolai Aleksandrovich!" sang the bishop.

"O Lord, be merciful!" chimed in the chorus of juvenile and feminine voices.

"And may the Lord bless our guest, Grand Duke Kirill Vladimirovich!"

"O Lord, be merciful!"

"And all the dukes and princes of Russia!"

"O Lord, be merciful!"

In his address of welcome, the bishop apologized for the small size of the church. "But the spirit of God is omnipresent," he added, "and so the Lord is with us here this afternoon while we are welcoming your Imperial Highness to our little church."

The Grand Duke answered by bowing to the altar, making the sign of the cross and kissing the hand of the bishop. Gospodin Pankevich, the president of the congregation, welcomed the imperial guest with bread and salt.

421

"I thank the congregation of the orthodox church from the bottom of my heart," said the young Grand Duke as he received the gift and passed it to his secretary.

The service over, the Grand Duke started for his carriage, but his progress was arrested by a young woman in white with a large bouquet in her hand, who curtsied to him, saying in melodious Russian:

"In the name of our humble Russian community, your Imperial Highness, permit me the honor of expressing our respect and love, and to present you with this humble token of our loyalty."

The woman was the wife of Father Chotovitsky of the Russian Church in which the service had been held. The Grand Duke received the flowers with a graceful bow, and taking off his high hat, he said:

"My profound regards and thanks to yourself and all the others whom you represent, little mother."

"We crave the pleasure of having your Imperial Highness honor our humble abode with a visit."

"With the greatest pleasure," was the gallant answer.

The party then proceeded upstairs, where they remained for five minutes.

Bishop Nicholas, Father Chotovitsky, Count Cassini, Russian ambassador at Washington, and others followed the Grand Duke to the carriage, and when it had rolled away amid a large crowd of bystanders, the bishop returned to the private rooms of the local priest.

THE LAST AMERICAN
February 14, 1899

The only American on a certain block on the Upper East Side is a tall, gaunt, bespectacled old man, with a flowing white beard and a high, shining forehead. The block is occupied by Germans, Czechs, Hungarians and Italians, and, barring the children, the old man is the only person who can speak English. He does not speak any of the languages he hears around him, and as his landlady is an old Czech, who speaks nothing but her native tongue, the two communicate by signs.

The neighbors speak of him as the "Yankee gentleman," or "that American." They treat him with reverence, and when groups of them meet at the beer saloon in the middle of the block, comparing notes on the faults of their adopted country and its people, exception is made of the old Yankee, who is conceded by all to be a fine old fellow, almost as good as a Czech or a Hungarian.

The people of the block do not know what the American does for a living, or how he spends his time. All they do know is that he leaves his room at 9 in the morning and returns to it at 7 in the evening. As he passes along the sidewalk, everybody greets him respectfully, the old people taking off their hats and the housewives nodding their heads and smiling, as they shout from the windows, "Goot morn, mister!" or "Goot evenik, mister!" There is something patronizing in the reverence they show him. He is a foreigner among them. They are perfectly tolerant, but they are not unaware of it.

"You are a Yankee," they seem to say, "yet we like you. To us all men are alike."

As to the old man, he feels like a foreigner on the block, too, and that is one of the reasons why he prefers to live in that neighborhood. It was from a friend of his, a resident of another district, that his story was learned.

"The funniest part of it is that he was born in the same place where he now feels like a foreigner," said the friend. "Yes, he was born in a shanty which stood on the very spot where now stands the big tenement house in which he boards. That was many years ago, and the place was then beyond the limits of the city proper. My friend left New York when he was a boy. He went west and made money and lost it. Then he went south and got married and made new money and lost it, too, together with his wife.

"He returned to New York to find himself friendless and lonely. The place where his cradle once rocked was an empty lot. He visited it, but felt indifferent. He settled somewhere on the West Side, near a large warehouse in which he had procured employment as a packer. He lived frugally, saving more than half of his wages against the rainy day. Twelve years rolled by. He was too feeble to work, but by this time he had a little money of his own, and he had it so invested as to be able to live on his income, provided he lived more modestly than he had been used to. Somebody advised him to look for a room on the East Side. Everything was much cheaper there, he was told. The suggestion brought him to his birthplace once more. The vacant lot was occupied by a towering tenement house now. The people were all foreigners. Only the little children could understand what the old man wanted. And yet everybody seemed to look down on him, as if it were their native country and he a mere stranger who could not speak the language of the place.

" 'A foreigner in my own birthplace!' the old man said to himself, bitterly. He felt like pulling down every tenement house in the neighborhood, and for a few days he never ceased inveighing against 'the invasion of our good country by people in a state of semi-savagery.'

"His native spot grew dear to him. He felt as if a lot of vandals had seized the most sacred spot on earth and as if it was his duty to free it from their hands. The first thing he did was to get a room in the house which stood on that holy spot. He wanted to gain a foothold in the place, he thought, and then—what he then would do he did not know himself, but he thought he did, and so he went on living in the Czech's room and hating his neighbors. He had not lived three months in the house, however, before he warmed first to his landlady, then to some of the other people on the block.

"He is a queer old fellow," his friend says of him. "He is still sure he hates all his neighbors and that he wants all foreigners expelled from the country. He spends his time reading at Cooper Institute or the Astor Library and worrying the life out of himself over his little investment. Nothing seems to give him greater pleasure than to curse the monopolists, whom he charges with conspiring to bring down the incomes of poor old men like himself, and the foreigners who, he says, have turned the richest country in the world into a land of beggars. And yet watch him going home and returning the salutations of his neighbors. If you think he hates them you are mistaken, or he is."

"WE ARE NOT COSSACKS"
April 10, 1899

It wanted an hour of the beginning of the evening performance of Buffalo Bill's Wild West when Colonel Cody's private secretary took a visitor behind the scenes at the Madison Square Garden. The visitor could speak Russian, and Private Secretary Fellows was glad of the opportunity to communicate through him with the nine Cossacks in the show. The space behind the big canvas partition at the eastern end of the huge arena was dimly illuminated, the twilight thickening in the direction of the stables, where glittered a lone electric lamp amid a mass of blackness. Presently, the neigh of a horse was heard; then a sabre flamed and a white figure glimmered out of the gloom.

"Hey! Choo!" said a voice.

The horse disappeared, while the white figure came up, bowing to the ground, in front of the private secretary and his visitor. More electric lights were turned on. The white figure turned out to be a tall, handsome man. His beard was blond and his face shone with a manly smile. He wore a cassock of white worsted gathered in at the waist by a narrow girdle of leather and enamelled silver. A white fur cap, in the shape of a truncated cone, its top covered with red silk and gold lace, was jauntily tilted back on his head. A shirt of white silk trimmed with gold showed through an opening at the bosom of the coat, while dangling from the girdle were a dagger and a sabre. A silver cross and four silver medals glistened under two rows of what looked like silver cartridges at the man's breast. Things gleamed and glittered all over him, and yet there was nothing obtrusively dazzling. The white and the red, the silver and gold blended into a quietly pleasing effect, not unlike that of his face.

"*Govorite po-russkiy* [Do you speak Russian]?" asked the visitor.

"*Da, da* [Yes, yes]," said the man in white, in a fever of joyous excitement. "It is not my tongue; it is the tongue of the people who have conquered us, but the Russian Czar is our Czar now, and his faith is our faith, and so I have learned to speak Russian."

He then said his name was David Kadzbaya, that he was a Georgian nobleman, and that the American consul at Batum, province of Kutaisi, Russia, had chosen him to be the chief of the Caucasians whom he sent to Buffalo Bill's show.

"Please ask the American gentleman why they insist upon calling us Cossacks," he said, with a pained look. "The Americans are educated people, and yet they persist in mixing us up with a race that differs more from ours than does the English race. You know we are not Cossacks. We are much better. Could a Cossack wield a *khinzbul* [dagger] as we do? Or sit in his saddle, or *dzhigit* [play tricks on horseback] like a Georgian?"

Five of the other Georgians emerged from the darkness. They were dressed like their chief, except that their coats were salmon-colored instead of white. They were all dark and nearly all handsome.

"I wear the white *chokha* [cassock] because I am the chief," explained Kadzbaya, with his pleasant smile. "Look at me and think of several fellows like myself, all in snow-white and all on noble steeds galloping after the Czar's carriage, as it flies through the streets of some provincial town. The sun plays on our gold and silver mounting, on the red silk of our caps and on the gilt lace of our shirts; we spur our horses to a fiery pace; their heads almost touch the Emperor's carriage. We ourselves hang over him, striking terror into the hearts of the hidden enemy. Ah, it is a beautiful sight, sir. Look at these medals, sir. I won them in the Turkish war, where I fought under the Russian flag, even as my fathers fought for their liberty against the Russians.''

Asked about the rows of curious silver ornaments projecting from pockets across his breast, the chief of the Georgians said:

"Oh, these are relics of our glorious past. They are mere sticks of wood, covered with silver at one end. But they represent the powder boxes which we used to carry in the mountains. That was before 1801, when our people lost their independence. Yes, we have lost our independence, but our valor is the same as old.''

As he warmed up, Kadzbaya grew eloquent. There was a sparkle in his eye, and he often gnashed his white teeth as he spoke of his horse, his *khinzbul* and his *eusredi* [sabre].

"See this steel?'' he said, unsheathing his sabre and cutting a swath in the air. "How much do you suppose it cost? Four hundred rubles, sir! Four hundred rubles—about two hundred American dollars. Yes, sir! What is a man without a good *eusredi* and a brave *khinzbul*? A Georgian who is worth his salt will rather be without a wife than without a good steed and good steel. 'Speed, my oak!' we say to our horse; 'run like a lion, tear the mountains asunder for me, darling! Fly like a swallow, my love! Sweep over sea and waste, over mountain and dale. Can there be any obstacle where the freedom and the glory of your brother, your master, is at stake? Fly, birdie, fly!' That's what we say to our comrades, our horses, each in his own way. But how can you realize the beauties and the thunders of our tongue, the great Georgian tongue, unless you hear its echo among the Caucasian mountains, where the gales, our horses, carry their brave riders up and down, back and forth? I was twelve years old when I first mounted a horse and drew a *khinzbul*, and they have been my chums and counselors ever since. Have you heard of Irakly, our youthful king, who led our people against the Persians? He was a boy of thirteen then, but he crumbled the Persians into powder. Why? Because his men knew how to make friends of steeds and steel, sir.''

"Ask him if he knows the nature of the part he and his men are playing in the show,'' suggested Mr. Fellows. When the question had been rendered into Russian, Kadzbaya smiled.

"We know that we are playing the Spaniards in the recent war. We are told to be licked, and we are. It is only a game, anyhow. The Americans see us on horseback. They know what we could do in dead earnest, though. It took the Czar centuries to settle us,'' he added with a wink. "The American Rough Riders? They are pretty good. But let them come to the Caucasus and court a Georgian girl with their riding. There is no fire in them, and nothing

426

sweet, either, even if they do know their business. No, sir, a Georgian girl would not fall in love with a fellow who has a clumsy seat in his saddle and who carries his head as if it were tied with ropes to his shoulders. But they are good people, these Americans, they are good people."

A REVOLUTION OR A JOKE
May 12, 1899

The mysterious revolutionary proclamation, signed "Young Syria," which was distributed among the Arabic-speaking population of lower Washington Street yesterday was the all-absorbing topic in the cafés, stores, and tenement houses of the Syrian quarter this morning. The neighborhood seems to be about evenly divided between those who are wondering when the underground parts will invade Constantinople, and those who are trying to guess the name of the fellow who played such a capital practical joke on the colony. The believers speak of a vast correspondence carried on by Young Syria with the patriots in Europe and Asia. The skeptics, on the other hand, wink their black eyes merrily and declare "Young Syria" a myth.

"Just address your letter 'Young Syria' and it will reach the president," said an enthusiast over a glass of arak this morning.

"Just do that, and your letter will land in the dead letter office," retorted a skeptic.

People who believed in what they called the "terrible movement" could be found by the dozen, but they all carefully keep their names out of print.

"You ask me why I am afraid to let you print my name?" asked one of the educated members of the colony. "It is not for my sake that I am afraid. There are no cowards in our family, sir. But then, I have an old father at home, and should the Turkish spies get wind of my revolutionary sympathies—" (there he gripped his own throat and stuck out his tongue).

"What do you mean? Would the government strangle your father because you were suspected of disloyalty?"

"S-s-sh! S-s-sh! Don't talk so loud, sir. The ceiling and the floor have ears," he whispered. "Of course, the government would kill my father; of course it would."

"Are you a member of Young Syria?"

"I don't say I am," he answered, half shutting his eyes. "It is a great movement, sir, though I don't say I know anything about it. All the members are educated people like myself—mind you, you must not print in the paper that I am one of them, for I don't say I am.''

The reporter observed that he could hardly put him in his paper without getting his name, but this was not enough; he had to give a solemn pledge of secrecy. Then the man became more fluent and warmed up to his talk.

"Our men fly around like birds in the mountains of Syria. Armed with fiery leaflets and pamphlets, each hot enough to set the soul ablaze, our noble agents dart from village to village, spreading the combustibles of the revolution. The hearts of the people catch fire. The conflagration is spreading like a freshet of flames. Another few months and all Syria will be up in arms. And what then? Then the death knell of tyranny will be sounded. Away with you, Abdul Hamid!'' the patriot gasped into the reporter's ear.

His eyes had a wild look in them, and his fist was clenched and quivering. After he had cooled down a little he went on:

"I'll tell you a secret. You may print it, but don't put my name in your paper. Before Sultan Murad was deposed because he was insane, a delegation of Syrian patriots called on his brother, the present sultan. 'Be my friends and you shall have a parliament,' said he. Well, they thought he would be a gentleman, so they helped him to the throne. He did give us a parliament, but only for three months. He fooled the people, but now we are going to fool him. Did you read *Underground Russia*? It's about the nihilists. Well, these fellows got rid of Alexander II, their tyrant, and we will know what to do with ours. But, mind you, I don't say I am one of them.''

———

"CATS, RATS, AND MATS"
October 5, 1901

The public evening schools for foreigners are open, and the little comedies and tragedies of the classroom in which immigrants of all ages grapple with the language of their new country are in full swing. A typical case was pointed out in one of the schools on the Upper East Side, where a fourteen-year-old Swede and a grey-headed Czech were studying the mysteries of c-a-t, m-a-t, and r-a-t in the copy of *Butler's First Reader*. As the two followed the teacher, the boy's face wore an absorbed, self-satisfied expression, while his neighbor stared at the letters before him in a puzzled, shamefaced way. When it was the old man's turn to spell the words aloud he dropped his eyes and shrugged his shoulders.

"C-a-t—cat," the boy whispered, pointing out the letters with his dirty index finger and looking from his elderly partner to the teacher triumphantly.

After a short pause, the old man threw his head back and said resentfully:

"I'll bet you this fellow can't read his own language. If my father had sent me to school when I was a boy I would be smarter than he now."

The teacher, who is a Bohemian himself, explained that there were not enough Swedes in that school to form a class, and that this was the reason why the boy had been placed in a Bohemian class.

"There are evening classes for Swedes and Norwegians in some of the other schools," he said. "Anyhow, we use comparatively little of the language of our scholars. We speak as much English as possible, and they learn to understand it quite fast."

In another classroom a neat man of forty was explaining the use of "shall" and "will" in good English which he uttered with a strong Bavarian accent. By way of illustrating the distinction between the two words, he told the time-honored story which the visitor subsequently heard in two other evening schools, of the Frenchman who was drowning in an American river and who cried to the people on the bank: "I will drown and nobody shall save me."

Several members of the class nodded their heads appreciatively, while one man, a red-faced, bald-headed fellow, shouted out:

"Dat ees false. Correct ees: 'I shall drown and nobody veel safe me.' "

When the same room was visited again, about an hour later, the teacher was writing on the blackboard a list of words used in the same form as noun and verb. Finally he wrote "Pocket your watch and watch your pocket" and asked his class what it meant.

"It means," answered the bald-headed scholar, enthusiastically, "dat it ees a danger and dat a tief can steal de watch. De foisht 'pocket' means 'put it in de pocket' and de second 'pocket' means plain pocket."

In one room a cadaverous-looking man of thirty-five was struggling with the "th" in bath.

"Stick your tongue against your teeth and utter the 't' sound," commanded the teacher, in Bohemian. "This way."

The pale-faced man nodded assent, impatiently, and signaling to the teacher to let him try, he proceeded to screw his face for the task. Suddenly he shouted: "Bat!" and stuck out his tongue.

The teacher said his tongue was "a couple of seconds too late," and told him to try again, whereupon the sickly immigrant called out "ba!" put out his tongue, and after hurriedly withdrawing it, added: "t t t t" with might and main.

This man had no trouble with the "w," which was an insurmountable obstacle in the way of his neighbor, a fat, near-sighted young man in a huge necktie of German make.

"Say 'well,' " the teacher urged him.

The fleshy scholar said "vell" and opened his short-sighted eyes wide.

"But you say 'vell' whereas I say 'well,' " the teacher explained.

The stout man failed to see the difference.

"Don't shut your lips when you utter the 'w,' " said the teacher in German. "Keep them slightly apart—like that."

"Ouell," muttered the young man, with a questioning look.

The visitor was seated by the side of a shaggy middle-aged fellow whose clothes emitted a strong odor of oil paint. He was a rather communicative man, and he soon found an opportunity to whisper to the stranger, in bad German, that he was a Pole from Galicia, Austria, and that his listener must not get the idea that Czolgosz* is really a Pole. Speaking of the evening school, he said:

"Why should Poles hate a president? America is a better friend to them than any other country in the world—better even than Galicia. At home I was a common painter and nobody ever bothered his head to teach me to read and to write, while here the President is so kind that he makes schools for old fellows and common people like myself. Here everybody is a gentleman and must know how to read—even a common laborer."

Similar comment was made by a middle-aged tailor whose acquaintance the writer made in one of the evening schools of the Jewish quarter.

"It is not in vain that Columbus is considered to be a big man," he said. "I was born and raised in Russia, and lived there until I was the father of six children. Do I speak Russian? Not a bit; only Yiddish. Can I write? No, sir. I can read the holy books, but write I can't—not a dot, sir. Why? Because I am a poor man. Well, but here is America, sir. This is not Russia. This is America, and that's all. So although I have only been a year and a half here, yet I understand everything my niece says to me. She is an American girl, my niece, and now I am going to school. Why? Because I wrote to my brother, who is still there at home, that in America everyone is an educated man and reads a newspaper every day and that I, too, was going to become an educated man and to read a newspaper every morning."

*Leon Czolgosz assassinated President McKinley on September 6, 1901.—*Ed.*

430

One of the teachers in this school narrated to the writer some of his experiences in enrolling applicants a week or two ago.

"One fellow asked me how long it would take him to master the language so as to be able 'to read and to write like an educated man,' and when I burst into laughter he said, beseechingly: 'Don't laugh at me, sir. My heart is broken. I love a good maiden, but she does not care for me because she is of good family and I am only a cigarmaker. "If you were an educated man it would be different," she says.' I explained to him that all we could do for him in a month or two was to get him to read, write and speak English a little. He was grievously disappointed, but he decided to try.

" 'When she sees me read or write she may give in, after all,' he said. 'I make nice wages, and if she were mine I should kiss the ground she walked on.' We enrolled him. The teacher in whose class he is tells me he is very diligent. He comes before the lights are turned on, and he hangs on his teacher's every word; but he is too anxious to learn, in too much of a hurry to become what he calls an educated man, and 'rather stupid,' as his teacher puts it.

"I had a similar case last year, only instead of being in love the man who wanted to become an educated man in one evening school season had a son-in-law to curry favor with. He was a poor, illiterate buttonhole-maker, and his daughter had married a young man who subsequently became a lawyer, so he was anxious to be fit company for that son-in-law of his. 'He treats me nicely,' he said, 'only I can see through it all. When there is company in the house he is ashamed of his father-in-law. I know he is. Well, when I have learned to speak English, grammar and all, he won't have to feel ashamed. I won't speak Yiddish then. Won't he and my daughter be surprised when they hear me speak English? I don't tell them I am going to school, you know.' "

In another classroom of the same school a gaunt old man with a white forked beard was seen alongside a lad of fifteen or sixteen, his grandson. Asked how he liked learning English, he said with a good-humored sigh:

"I am afraid it's too late for me to start. It takes a young head like his [pointing at his grandson] to master these queer words and rules. Still, I must try. If I could read and write English I might get a good job. One thing seems very funny. Americans are said to be a smart people, and yet they bother their heads about all kinds of nonsense. Why, look at the book they have given me. You find nothing but stories about cats, rats, dogs, little boys and such-like foolishness. Can it be that they want an old man like myself to be interested in things of that sort?"

The teacher explained that the books used by his class were originally intended for children, and that they were given to adults because there were no other elementary readers, but the gaunt old man only sighed dubiously.

"Sometimes a scholar will get tired of 'cats, rats, and mats,' as they call it venomously, and stop coming altogether," said the teacher, "but then the number of such old fellows is comparatively small. The bulk of our attendance is made up of young men from twenty to thirty years of age, and the majority of these come to stay. As a rule, they learn to speak and to read tolerably well in a relatively short time. To be sure, all we can hope to do is to get them started, but once they get the foundation of the language, contact with their English-speaking neighbors does the rest pretty quickly. In the higher classes we teach them grammar, composition and American history. We also get up debates among them. Last year, for instance, one of my scholars made a successful argument in fluent and fairly correct English on the subject of protection. Yet he had only attended school two seasons, and when he first enrolled he could not say a word.

"There are schools of almost every nationality, and in each case the teacher must adjust himself to the peculiar difficulties which his class finds in trying to learn English. The Italians, for instance, have a tendency to add a vowel at the end of a final consonant sound. They say 'cata' for 'cat,' 'tabla' for 'table,' and so on. This is due to the fact that their native tongue does not permit a consonant sound at the end of a syllable. Again, some sounds they drop altogether, as for instance, the 'c' in 'victory.' The Germans, on the other hand, insist on pronouncing the 'l' softly, and in the majority of cases they confound the 'v' with the 'f,' the 'd' with the 't,' to say nothing of the 'w' or the 'th,' that everlasting bane of the evening school teacher's life. All this must be taken into consideration and special methods must be devised to suit each case."

In one of the evening schools for immigrant women an intelligent-looking Armenian woman sat between her two daughters.

"I am too old to learn a new language myself," she said, with a smile, "but then, the girls must not be deaf and dumb in the land, and how can one let one's daughters go through the streets alone at night? Of course, while I am at it, I, too, pick up a word or two. I had to enroll anyhow. When my girls get through with their studies here they'll go to evening high school. I wish I could send them to college, but we are poor in this strange land and must work for a living during the day."

Teachers and scholars are jubilant over the increase in the length of the school season. Instead of ninety nights it will be 120.

"There is every reason to hope that it will be made longer still," said one principal. "Another thing talked about is an increase in salaries. The great point is to make it worth one's while, so that the teachers can look upon work as a permanent and well-paying occupation. This will insure better teachers and better work. When the season was only ninety nights it was impossible to achieve any substantial results. Many a scholar would drop out in the middle of the season because the whole affair did not seem to be taken seriously enough by the city. Now it will be different.''

15

PASSIONS ON TRIAL

THE MORE MODEST OF THE TWO HATS
December 20, 1898

The roll call of talesmen and some other routine business which preceded this morning's session of the trial of Fayne Strahan Moore left a humdrum air about Recorder Goff's courtroom. It was about 11 o'clock before all this was disposed of.

"Fayne Moore to the bar!" the clerk then called out. His words were drawled lazily, but they at once aroused the spectators from their dreamy apathy. There was a stir and a craning of necks toward one of the two doors at the further end of the room. The door opened and a streak of red came gleaming from the obscurity of the little corridor. It was the usual spectacle which greets the people who attend the trial in question, daily, but it never seems to pall on them. Fayne Moore made her appearance in her green dress with red facings and fur trimmings, and the more modest of the two hats which she has worn in court since the beginning of her husband's first trial. She walked up to her seat with a graceful, well-bred gait, her eyes now raised, now lowered with something like embarrassment. As she reached her place by the side of Mr. Hill, her lawyer, she greeted the lawyers and some of the reporters with a beaming smile. Some artists at once set to work sketching her face. They found it an uncommonly difficult job, they said. The reason is that the woman looks like the stereotyped picture of a pretty girl in the fashion weeklies, and that her likeness is all in a certain something in her expression which is hard to locate.

Altogether she looks like an overgrown schoolgirl, bland and credulous and easy to be made a catspaw of. She keeps her eyes on the jurors, scanning each one of them, and now and then leaning over to communicate her impressions to her counsel, rejecting this man and accepting that. She is picking out her own jury. And yet she looks as if she did not realize the meaning of the whole proceeding and enjoyed it all as she would a theatrical performance in which she occupied the centre of the stage. She does not seem to be capable of realizing anything beyond the occurrence of the moment, and her smiling answers to the questions of her polite counsel make her look like a girl conversing with her cavaliers in an opera box rather than a defendant charged with robbery in the first degree. Her eyes, which have been described as "hypnotic," bear out the impression of an inexperienced, light-minded schoolgirl. There is nothing hypnotic about them, and if some of the jurors in Moore's first trial found it difficult "to keep their eyes off of her" it was simply because she is a pretty woman and because the crime of which she is accused adds a morbid element to the interest which she commands as the central figure in a courtroom.

"This woman is charged with the crime of robbery in the first degree!" says Abraham Levy to every talesman, and the well-dressed young woman to whom he refers looks straight before her, sometimes with a smile in her eyes and about her lips, as if her counsel were merely joking and she were getting tired of the joke.

Both sides were anxious to dispatch matters as much as possible, and show far more leniency in examining talesmen than they did during the two trials of William A. E. Moore for the same offense. The result is that by noon today, which is the second day of the present trial, there were six men in the jury box, while at the second trial of William Moore there were only two jurors at the same time.

Michael Hosh, of 681 East 142nd Street, one of the talesmen called, infused some merriment into the otherwise monotonous work of the morning session. He was an elderly Irishman with a paddle-shaped chin beard, a ruddy face, a thrust-out nose and a look in his eyes which seemed to defy all efforts to draw him out. Asked whether he was worth $250, he shifted uneasily, then smiled slyly, and, the usual look coming into his eyes, he murmured, "I guess so." He looked like a man who is worth many times that sum, but whose capital is all in a stocking carefully hidden in his wife's trunk.

"Did you read of this case?" Mr. Levy asked.

"No, sir."

"What? You don't read the newspapers? You cannot read and write?"

"That I can."

"So you do read the daily newspapers, don't you?"

435

"Yes; but only twice a week, sir."

He was excused.

Augustus Feverel, 501 West 156th Street, asked the lawyers to speak loud to him.

"I can't hear well," he pleaded.

Mr. Levy said that he was speaking in a low voice on purpose to test the talesman's hearing.

"It is necessary," declared Recorder Goff. "I notice that when it comes to serving as jurors, defective hearing becomes quite epidemic in our city."

The talesman could hear Mr. Levy, who stood at quite a distance from him, but he was not acceptable to McIntyre, and was discharged on a peremptory challenge by the state.

Quite a number of talesmen, all of the Mosaic faith, were excused by mutual consent because of their acquaintance with Mr. Levy. In one instance, the latter asked a talesman, who seemed to be a Catholic, whether he belonged to the same society with Mr. McIntyre, and receiving a negative answer, he pursued, with a smile:

"I do not wish to ask the name of the organization to which you belong, but is it one to which I would be admitted?"

Court adjourned at 1:30 o'clock. As Recorder Goff has a meeting of the board of directors of the Sailors' Snug Harbor to attend this afternoon, no afternoon session was held. By the time court adjourned, there were nine men in the jury box.

MOLINEUX AT THE BAR
March 2, 1899

The corridors of the Court of General Sessions were swarming with men and women this morning. They seemed to represent all classes, from tailor-made girls and their well-dressed escorts to rusty-looking denizens of the slums nearby. The crowd kept swelling. The hum and buzz grew louder and louder. Lawyers and assistant district attorneys were hovering about with their papers. Now and then a prisoner was conveyed past the chattering clusters, but these attracted little attention. "Molineux!" was the word on all lips. No other name excited interest.

This well-bred young man, the pampered son of a brave and wealthy general, had been indicted for murder in the first degree, and it was to catch a glimpse of him that the throng was waiting. Only a few days ago, he was seen in the same building walking about with the free and easy air of a man above suspicion. He was a free man then, and all but lionized by the district attorney's office. This morning he was to appear with detectives by his side, a defendant, a prisoner, charged with having poisoned one person and suspected of having poisoned two. The crowds in the criminal building cannot do without a star, and Molineux was a star among stars. Mrs. Vermeule was forgotten. Fayne Moore was eclipsed. Dr. Kennedy, whose trial is expected to begin one of these days, had lost notoriety.

"Molineux! Molineux!" The crowd had no eye, no ear, no patience for anybody or anything else.

Those who were admitted into Part I, General Sessions, where Molineux was to be arraigned before Recorder Goff, made a rush for vacant seats as shipwrecked passengers would for the boat ready to carry them ashore. Some of the women were flushed and restless, as if the fact that they were within a few minutes of seeing Molineux was too good to be true. Artists were sketching the courtroom—the setting which was to contain the great picture of the day. Reporters were making themselves comfortable for their work. "Special men" were writing introductions to the news to follow. Court officers looked bored, as if assuring the spectators that no sensation can be big enough to disturb their official dignity.

General Molineux was early on the ground, as yesterday. But instead of the dreary, yearning look with which he entered the coroner's court yesterday morning, he looked bright and chipper. He was at once surrounded by friends and proceeded to talk and laugh, as if his son's acquittal were not merely a hope in his heart but an accomplished fact. Everybody is glad to see the brave old general in a cheerful frame of mind, and as he stood talking and smiling the many eyes that were fixed upon him were smiling, too.

Then Molineux's lawyers, armed with bulging hand-valises, made their appearance. Mr. Weeks's aspect was grave. Mr. Battle, his partner, who looks like a young priest, wore the sympathetic expression characteristic of his face. The general shook hands with them heartily, and the three stepped aside to hold a whispered consultation.

At that moment the side door flew open and District Attorney Gardiner, accompanied by Mr. Osborne, his assistant, made his appearance. As the two proceeded down the aisle shaking hands and smiling right and left it looked like a sort of extemporaneous ovation. Their faces shone. They took their places in front of the rail like two horses trying to be modest.

"Hats off in court!" roared a voice. The side door flew open again. A hush fell upon the room. A rustling of silks was heard, and in came the tall, stately figure of Recorder Goff, in his flowing silk gown, bowing, smiling and happy.

A minute later, necks were craned toward the further end of the room. Eyes were riveted to the door which leads from the prisoner's pen. There was another hush. The women in the audience looked nervous. Some of them turned pale with excitement. The door opened. Walking at a brisk step came a smoothly shaven young man in a well-fitting dark Newmarket. Everything about him was neat and fresh. He looked like a man born to be well-dressed and well-fed.

It was Roland B. Molineux. His face was slightly flushed. The light-hearted smile with which he was wont to make his appearance at the coroner's inquest was lacking. He looked as though the situation had begun to dawn on him. He shook hands with his father and the lawyers. A smile broke out upon his face, but instantly vanished, and the next moment he found himself at the bar, the centre of a semi-circle of brass buttons and blue cloth.

"Roland B. Molineux!" said the clerk, "the grand jury has indicted you for murder in the first degree!"

Molineux looked straight ahead of him, mute and childlike. The happy-go-lucky air was gone. He was a new man.

Mr. Weeks moved that the pleading be adjourned for a week or two.

"We want time, your Honor," he said. "This defendant was indicted while he was asking the coroner for the examination which the law grants him. The examination was refused and he was indicted before he was given an opportunity to be confronted with his accuser."

The recorder at once granted the motion, adjourning the hearing to Tuesday next.

"In a case like this," he remarked, "where a man is charged with a serious crime, every opportunity should be given him to prepare his case."

"Another thing, your Honor," resumed Mr. Weeks; "we ask the district attorney to inform us for what date he intended to move the trial. I understand from the newspapers that he expects to have it on the April calendar. If so, every minute will be precious to us. We must see the exhibits of the handwritings and prepare photographed copies, and we also want to see the minutes of the indictment."

To all of which the recorder said that the matter lay with the district attorney, and that it could be moved later on, after the pleading.

Roland B. Molineux was then taken back to the Tombs. He made his way with the same quick step and air of agitation with which he had come in.

438

As he approached the back door through which he was to disappear, a tall, well-dressed man standing by the wall grasped his hand. Molineux paused. The two smiled and shook hands heartily. The door opened. Molineux nodded to his friend and proceeded on his way into the darkness of the little corridor. The door closed upon him. The crowd rushed for the side doors.

IT WAS JACOBS' DAUGHTER
March 6, 1899

A little man of sixty, sallow-faced and nervous, was arraigned before Judge Blanchard in Part I of the Court of General Sessions this morning. He was charged with having been the principal actor in a "gold dust" swindle of which a man named Bernstein of Cleveland, Ohio, was the victim. The go-between in the transaction was Solomon Jacobs of Chicago. Jacobs was tried in the Court of General Sessions here and sentenced to eight years' imprisonment. He is serving his term in Sing Sing. Recently, Coppelman was arrested in Chicago on a similar charge, and while he was confined in a police station of that city he made a written confession, declaring himself guilty of the crime for which Jacobs was sentenced, and asserting the latter's innocence.

It was Jacobs' daughter Minnie who obtained this confession from Coppelman, and this morning she was the central figure in Judge Blanchard's courtroom. She was pointed out as a heroic daughter, who had travelled from city to city and stood all sorts of privations, in an effort to set her father, whom she thought an innocent man, free. There was some delay in the proceedings in the court, and Miss Jacobs had time to talk about the case. She is a tall, dark young woman of twenty-five or six, dressed in mourning for her mother, who died of grief after her husband was sent to state prison. Miss Jacobs was born in London, but was brought up in this country. She is a music teacher, and her English, though not altogether free of the cockney accent, bespeaks a woman of culture. To all questions concerning her fight for her father's liberty she answered with a modest, well-bred smile, endeavouring to strip the case of every element of sensationalism. She was also trying to look calm and to discuss the matter in a businesslike, matter-of-fact way, but her flushed face and her general manner betrayed the nervousness and anxiety which she was taking pains to conceal.

"I do hope I won't be disappointed," she said. "Bernstein, the victim of the swindle, was so nice to me this morning. He and father were school-boys together in Russia, and he knows that father is innocent. Still, I hear he now says he is only interested to see Coppelman convicted, and that he could not testify either for or against papa. But then, what matters it so long as Coppelman, who knows all about the case, says father is absolutely innocent, and that's all that is necessary to set him free, isn't it?

"Why, look at this," she said, unfolding a typewritten copy of Coppelman's confession and pointing to the last two pages. The passage indicated read as follows:

> That the said Jacobs all the time acted, as he supposed, in the interest of his friend, Bernstein, as well as with a view to earning the commission promised by both parties, namely, the sum of $350 from each. That said Jacobs at no time knew that the transaction was a criminal one, or that the said goods were any-thing but genuine gold. That said Jacobs was at no time a confeder-ate of this affiant (Coppelman) in this crime, or in any other crime. That this affiant is of the firm belief that the said Jacobs, during the entire time of the transaction, was innocent of the commission of a crime, and was ignorant of any criminal intent on the part of this affiant, or either of his confederates.

The affidavit further states that the affiant had "worked the gold dust swindle for years," and that he had often employed men as agents who were utterly unaware of the criminal nature of the transaction.

Asked to tell how she obtained the confession from Coppelman, Miss Jacobs said evasively:

"Oh, he is a soft-hearted little Jew. He broke down and told the truth." After a while, she reluctantly added some of the details of the scene in the Chicago police station.

"Well, I can speak Yiddish—the language of the ghetto, you know. It's my father's mother tongue, and it is the only language Coppelman speaks well. His English is so badly broken that you can hardly understand it. Well, I addressed myself in Yiddish to him. 'Do you know me?' I asked him. 'Do I look like my father?' People say I look the very picture of my father, you know, and that's why I asked him that question. He took a good look at me and turned pale. 'Yes, I know who you are,' he said, with emotion. 'You are Jacobs' girl.' I then proceeded to describe to him how I had been hunting him in several cities, and how mother had died of grief. As he heard of mother's death, the tears started to his eyes. 'This girl's father is as innocent as a child!' he cried out. 'Captain, her father is an innocent man!' He kept repeating it to every policeman that was around, and when I asked him to make a written statement he agreed cheerfully.

"Coppelman is a good-natured man. He admits having been engaged in the fraudulent business for many years, but he was anxious to settle down to an honest life, he says. At any rate, here is his confession. My father is innocent."

Maurice Gottlieb, a lawyer, appeared for Coppelman. The assistant district attorney who conducted the prosecution during the trial, which resulted in Jacobs' conviction, was on hand to represent the people in the case of Coppelman as well as that of Jacobs. The original case against Jacobs was so strong that the prosecuting attorney secured his conviction without making an argument to the jury. Notice of motion for a new trial was served on the district attorney, and the formal pleading in Coppelman's case was adjourned until tomorrow.

"COULD YOU SEE
ANY PART OF THE LIMBS?"
April, 4, 1900

The courtroom of the criminal branch of the Supreme Court was crowded today with actors, managers of theatres and dramatic critics. A play was on trial in the person of an actor, an actress and two managers, and members of the profession and the business were on hand to watch or to testify. Olga Nethersole, better known to the crowds in the lobbies of the criminal court building as Sappho, came into the room, followed by Hamilton Revelle, Marcus Meyer and Theodore Moss, her codefendants, at 10:30 o'clock. Unlike yesterday she was perfectly calm and seemed to be alive to the humor of the situation.

The trial on the charge of misdemeanor and maintaining a public nuisance was begun in earnest five minutes later, but the opening speech for the prosecution was made not by Assistant District Attorney Le Barbier, who has charge of the case, but by his associate, Assistant District Attorney Hennesy, and his was a brief, very formal and almost non-committal address, which he read in a hesitant voice from notes.

The first witness for the state was Henry Brevoort Kane of 253 West Seventy-sixth Street, who began by saying that he went into Wallack's

Theatre and saw *Sappho* without a ticket. Witness described the ball in the first act.

"Did you notice the costumes?" asked Mr. Le Barbier, who conducted the examination.

Witness colored, made a gesture of regret, and said: "Yes."

"Did you see any actress in that ball scene that you can remember?"

"I did. I saw a man pick up a young woman in his arms and carry her out of the room. I think it was supposed they were going to supper," witness added with the air of a man who wants to be accurate.

"Anything else?"

"I saw a man encircle the limbs of a woman with his arms and raise her up in his arms."

"In what way was she raised up to the pedestal?" asked Mr. Le Barbier after witness described the scene.

"She was just raised up and placed there," was the answer.

"How was she dressed?"

Mr. Hummel objected that there were photographs of Miss Nethersole in the part referred to, but the question was allowed, and witness said:

"I think the costume could best be described by the word 'diaphanous.' It was a very loose thing."

"Did you ever see an ancient Greek robe?" put in Justice Fursman.

"I did," was the reply.

Mr. Le Barbier asked whether any portion of Sappho's body was visible, but the question was excluded as leading.

"Could you see any part of the limbs of Sappho?"

"No, I could not."

"Did the lights go out?"

"I think not."

"Did you hear any conversation between Sappho and Jean Gaussin?"

"I did. She asked him what he was doing and why he had left the country."

"What happened when Sappho came near Jean?"

"Well, she embraced him—"

The witness was interrupted by an outburst of laughter, in which Miss Nethersole joined with a smile, and the court restored order with a severe admonition.

"I object to the witness characterizing it as an embrace," Mr. Hummel was heard protesting when silence was restored.

"What next?" asked Mr. Le Barbier.

"Well, they waltzed," answered the witness, who was by this time all flushed and perspiring with excitement.

"Yes, and did not Sappho's head rest on Jean's shoulder?"

The question was ruled out.

"The music," the witness went on, "was slow and hesitating. The other performers went out by different exits, and I think that was the end of the scene."

"What next?"

There was a craning of necks at this. The staircase scene was coming. Miss Nethersole leaned back in her seat and prepared to listen with an air of calm attention.

"It was the staircase scene," answered Mr. Kane. "I saw Sappho and Jean come in. They had a few minutes' conversation and he offered to carry her upstairs. He then took her in his arms and carried her upstairs. He had one arm underneath her shoulders and the other under her knees. They talked while they were going upstairs. They would go up a little way and then the curtain would drop. Then it would go up again and they would go a little further upstairs. At last they disappeared altogether," witness concluded with a perplexed look.

Speaking of the second act, witness told how he saw a room which seemed to be a bachelor's lodgings. It belonged to a young man, and the young man was no other than Jean Gaussin, he declared. "He was on the stage with a character called Uncle Cesaire. Enter Sappho. She had some flowers. She said, 'Sweet dreams.' Jean looked frightened. Uncle Cesaire was accompanied by his wife and a young girl. Jean and the girl remained on the stage together, uncle and aunt having gone out together. Jean helped Sappho on with her coat and hat, and then suddenly she took off her coat and hat and threw her arms around Jean Gaussin's neck."

"Next?"

"The next thing I remember was that Jean Gaussin sat in a chair and Sappho sat on his lap. She spoke in endearing terms to him, and after some more talk the act was closed."

Miss Nethersole smiled. The third and fourth acts were recited in a similar way.

"Then the curtain fell," said the witness with an air of great relief, as he reached the end.

"Your witness, Mr. Hummel," said the assistant district attorney.

"Not a question!" returned Mr. Hummel. "Call your next witness!"

"All right," answered Mr. Le Barbier, in a spiritless way.

"William Inglis," and the reporter of the newspaper which started the

Sappho sensation as one of its "features" took his seat on the witness stand. He had represented his paper in the proceedings in the same case before Magistrate Mott, and this forenoon he only repeated the story which formed his "copy" on that occasion. His description of the staircase scene was far more expressive of pious indignation than that of the preceding witness.

The reporter described the whole play, reciting passages and acting parts, to the amusement of the crowd. He gnashed his teeth, mouthed, gesticulated, and it was a comical scene for a courtroom, especially when the witness glanced at Miss Nethersole and expressed his shocked feelings. The witness was interrupted by the recess, taken at 1 o'clock.

HAPPY ESSEX COURT
October, 10, 1900

When Magistrate Pool took his seat in the Essex Market Police Court yesterday the narrow, high-ceilinged, squalid courtroom was filled with cheerful-looking men, women and children. It was a better-dressed and better-fed crowd than the one usually seen in police courts, and the happy faces among it were in contrast with the wet, dingy outlook which the tall windows offered to the white-haired magistrate on the bench.

Every police court in town has its individuality. One of the distinctive features of the one on Essex Street is that the proportion of "drunks" to "rows between respectable business people," as one of the lawyers of the place put it, is much smaller than it is in any other police court in town. Many of the complainants in this busy place spend whole days and plenty of five-dollar bills on the pleasure of "getting square." The gigantic rows of tenement houses in the neighborhood are crowded with people with swift blood in their veins. Their tongues are kept busy and their tempers have many a chance to break out. Hence the large number of well-groomed, prosperous-looking litigants and prisoners.

This is true of every day in the year, but yesterday was the Feast of Tabernacles, and the sons and daughters of Zion were dressed in their new holiday clothes. So the rickety old courtroom looked festive, comparatively.

One of the prettiest and best-dressed women on the benches outside the enclosure was a black-eyed, pale-faced young matron in a dark hat. She kept smiling and gesticulating to her lawyer, who stood on the bridge in front of the judge. On Yom Kippur she was the heroine of the neighborhood. Her husband was a cantor, and she had him driven from the synagogue in the middle of the solemn service he was conducting.

"Why?"

"Because he had abandoned her," answered the lawyer, as a matter of course. "The president of the synagogue told him a fellow who wouldn't support his wife couldn't stand forth before God as the representative of a whole congregation."

"And what is she doing here?"

"Oh, she wants her husband arrested. His being chased out of the synagogue didn't do him much good."

The first case was a fight between two young men.

"I saw them in the doorway of a saloon," began the policeman who had arrested them, but he was checked.

"It was a saloon, was it?" waving the officer aside. "I don't want any cases of fighting in saloons. Discharged. Next!"

"Next" was an Irishwoman charged with intoxication.

"Is it true?" asked his Honor.

"I was working for a Jewish family, and it's their holiday, sir."

"So you were celebrating the Hebrew holiday? One dollar."

The next "drunk" said the officer told the truth, but that he was "loaded" only once a month, and Monday was his drinking day. He was fined $2.

He was followed by another Irishwoman.

"Yes, your Honor, I took a drink. I met a lady friend—"

"Are you sure it was a lady? What did you drink? Whiskey? Two dollars."

Next came a good-looking boy. His mother, who appeared against him, said he stole some money from her pocket.

"I want him sent to prison, but don't make it too long, your Honor," she said, stealing a glance at her son. The case was adjourned.

The boy's place in front of the rail was taken by a stout young woman. She had been seen accosting men on the Bowery, and everybody within the enclosure seemed to have seen her in court before, but the policeman who arrested her said he was sorry, very sorry; he hadn't sufficient evidence against her; so the magistrate had to let her go.

The next prisoner was accused of cutting the window cords and disfiguring the walls of the rooms from which he was dispossessed.

"What have you got to say?"

"I want to tell the whole truth, your Honor," began the prisoner, bringing the tips of his thumb and index finger together and starting into an oratorical attitude.

"You tell your story, and then we'll see whether it's true. Be quick."

"The landlord, I paid him his rent regularly, your Honor. I've witnesses."

"But did you cut the ropes?"

"He raised the rent $6."

"So you did cut the ropes?"

"They were my own ropes. I paid 45 cents for them, and I wouldn't let him have them for nothing. I paid my rent regular, and he raised it $6."

"Ten dollars!" said his Honor.

Then a little woman described, with a great deal of pathos, how the prisoner, a short, hatchet-faced fellow, had hit her with a flatiron.

"Here is the wound, your Honor," she concluded, baring her stout arm and showing a pink scar.

"What did he say when he came into your house?"

"He said nothing," answered the little woman. "He went right to work and began to beat me."

The prisoner pointed to his bared chest, inviting the magistrate to see the wound the complainant had inflicted there. The magistrate tried hard, saw nothing and fined the man $10.

By this time the courtroom was so crowded that his Honor, looking up from the lawyers and witnesses in front of him, exclaimed:

"What's this? What brings them here? Officers, open the doors and windows and let's see whether that won't drive some of them home." The throng remained compact, immovable. "I want this room cleared," declared the magistrate. "Put out every person who isn't seated. Put them in the yard." He was obeyed this time.

The next case was a fight between a man who came too early to collect an egg bill and the customer who told him to come later in the day. The egg man's face was all bruised, and the customer, who was the prisoner in the case, asked the magistrate to do him a favor and look at the red spot on his cheek. It was the trace of a blow, he said, but his Honor said his other cheek was just as red and fined him $10. As the egg dealer was leaving the enclosure he stuck out his tongue at his enemy.

Most of the lawyers spoke good English, but there were some who asked their clients questions like, "Did you vent up to him?" or "Do you know dis complainer?" But those were among the "old-timers" of the place, so it was all taken as a matter of course.

Sometimes the magistrate would say: "Show us where he hit you," and the answer would be, "In Ridge Street."

As the reporter was making his way out, the lawyer of the cantor's wife stopped him.

"There will be a tip-top seduction case at 2:30."

"And how about the cantor's wife?"

"Oh, she'll get him all right."

The woman who sat several yards away smiled approvingly.

"I CAN'T STAND HIM"
October 12, 1900

One of the prisoners who were arraigned before Magistrate Hogan in the Essex Market Court yesterday morning was a red-haired boy, seventeen years old, who was accused by his mother of calling her names and breaking her furniture. The complainant in the case was a neatly dressed, though bonnetless woman of about forty-five, with iron-gray hair, a pale face and sad, intelligent, deep dark eyes.

"When he wants something and I refuse to give it to him he becomes wild, your Honor," she said, through an interpreter. "I can't stand him."

The boy was bound over to keep the peace for three months, and as there was nobody to bail him out he was taken out through the door leading to the cells.

"Serve him right," said his mother, following him out with her black eyes. "These American boys are beyond us, poor foreigners that we are. They have no respect for us. I suppose if I could speak English he wouldn't dare make fun of me and call me vile names. As it is, I am like the hen that hatched out ducklings. It'll do him good. I am not sorry a bit." Her face seemed to show that she was, and she wanted to continue her talk to the bystanders, who listened to her with interest, but her place was needed for another complainant, so she was told to go home.

It was one of the typical Essex Market cases, which grow out of the chasm between immigrant parents and their American-born children. The neighborhood is full of these chuckling-hatching hens, and the gulf between the fathers and the sons is much wider than difference of language alone could make it.

"The trouble is that most of the people of the tenements hereabout," said an East Side physician who happened to be in court, "come from primitive towns in Russia, Poland or Rumania. They are clever, and in their own antediluvian way, even intellectual, but they know nothing of those ways and facts of civilization which the poorest American boy regards as part of his everyday life. Their children pick up these things at school and on the street, so that in many cases they gradually come to look down upon their fathers and mothers as inferior creatures. The average East Side boy is sure that America is the only place in the world where the people, that is, those who can speak English, amount to anything. On the other hand, the poor, ignorant, helpless old folk learn to look upon this country as a land of loafers and rowdies.''

One of the following cases was a fight between two sweatshop tailors. The defendant insisted upon telling his story at length. The interpreter told him he couldn't do so, and that he was to answer questions only.

"Is that justice?" shouted the prisoner. "If you want to judge straight you must hear both sides, and if you want to hear my side you must let me tell you my story. It's all very well for you to ask questions, but suppose your question is one of those which cannot be answered by yes or no?"

"Stop; you are talking too much."

"All right, I'll stop, with pleasure, sir. It will be very funny to watch you hear both sides, without giving one of them a chance to open his mouth."

"I ask you whether you struck this man. Did you or did you not?"

"But how can I answer it, seeing that you told me to stop?"

"Say yes or no."

"It's both 'yes' and 'no,' see?"

"What do you mean?"

"I'll tell you what I mean, only you must let me do it."

The man's story was finally heard by one of the policemen who speaks German. He was discharged.

Next came a man who was accused of appropriating $10 which the complainant said he had collected for him, his employer.

"Did you vent to vork and made dis contract?" asked the defendant's lawyer, as he slapped down a typewritten paper in front of his Honor. "Dis contract shows de defendant and de complainer vere partners."

"No, it doesn't," said Magistrate Hogan. "It's only a contract of employment. According to it your man was to work for a commission. I'll hold the prisoner in $200 bonds to behave himself."

While the lawyer was examining the contract with a crestfallen air, a stranger asked the American-born lawyers present whether the salesman's advocate had passed his regent's examination in English.

"Oh, he has been admitted to the bar all right," they answered gaily.

A YIDDISH PARROT

February 27, 1901

The case of Yetta's parrot came up in one of the East Side district courts the other day. The bird is here referred to as Yetta's in accordance with the decision of the justice who presided over the trial, for, indeed, Leah-Golde insists that Polly is hers, and will be with her sooner or later. She is tall and dark, Leah-Golde, with prominent black eyes which seem to be on the verge of tears for the hundreds of young men who are madly in love with her—so, according to her neighbors, she says to herself—and to whom she is unable to give a look of encouragement. Being in love with none of the young men she knows, Leah-Golde is saving a marriage portion and otherwise preparing to meet the unknown predestined one for whom she is sure God has been saving her heart. She is a finisher-girl in a sweatshop, but she can read a Yiddish newspaper, so she has made up her mind that that predestined one of hers shall be an educated man, and to be worthy of him she goes to evening school and takes piano lessons of a teacher who lives in the same tenement where Leah-Golde makes her home at present.

Yetta is blonde and short. She met her predestined one long ago in Russia, and as the couple found it difficult to pay $14 a month for three rooms, they took in a boarder. That Leah-Golde was this boarder some six months ago is not denied, but what is denied by Yetta is that she ever sold her parrot to Leah-Golde. A description of this parrot was given by Yetta herself on the witness stand.

"I sell my Polly!" she exclaimed, as she dug her index finger in her heart, in a gesture of East Side dismay. "I sell my treasure, my joy, the light of my eyes!"

"Stop! Answer questions," commanded Leah-Golde's lawyer. "Did you receive $22 from the plaintiff?"

"From whom? From Mrs. Plentoff? May I be choked with my own words of truth if I ever knew such a woman. It's a lie."

"Stop! Did you or did you not?"

The justice explained to the defendant that the plaintiff was Leah-Golde, whereupon Yetta shrugged her shoulders and said:

"I take $22 from her? Twenty-two dollars for my Polly? You never saw such a Polly, Mr. Judge."

She was stopped again, but she said it was necessary for her to show why the plaintiff's story was untrue, and as there was no objection she was told to go on.

"First, Mr. Judge, my Polly is nothing but green, gold and red. She is so beautiful that people stop on the other side of the street to admire her. You wouldn't believe it, Mr. Judge, but some people eat her up with their eyes. They actually give her the evil eye by admiring her so much, and then I must spend money to have some master of wonders take off the evil. She is a regular beauty, Mr. Judge. She is just shining like the sun, so that one of my neighbors hurt her eyes looking too much at her." There was a roar of laughter. "Don't you believe it?" Yetta retorted. "That neighbor of mine is in court. She'll be a witness. Well, Polly is much nicer-looking than some old maids, anyhow. [This with a side glance at Leah-Golde.] As to speaking, why, she is the greatest talker on Stanton Street, Mr. Judge. She can talk English almost as well as the janitor, to say nothing of Yiddish. She talks so quickly that my boy—he's an American kid—can't understand what she is talking about."

"Does she know the Talmud, too?" asked the lawyer on the other side, with something like a smile.

"A sight better than you, anyhow," snapped Yetta. "I tell you what, it's no use to make fun of the holy Talmud, either. If some people knew a little bit of Talmud they would make better lawyers than they do—some people."

"Hold on. The question is whether you took $22 for which you promised to deliver the parrot when you moved out of your former apartments. Did you or did you not?"

"Did you or did you not," Yetta mocked the lawyer, screwing up an expression of impatience as she did so, which brought forth a new guffaw from the crowd. "I have told you I didn't. How many times shall I repeat the same? Can't you remember? You have no more memory than my cat and yet you're a lawyer. Well, I never took any money nor promised to sell anything, and to prove it to you I will say that when Leah-Golde came to claim Polly I burst into tears and said: 'I'll let you cut out my tongue [another outburst of merriment], cut off my arm, take my children, take everything in the house, only don't take Polly, my sunshine, my happiness, the sweetness of my heart.' "

Leah-Golde was called to the witness stand in rebuttal. She was grave, dignified, but instead of being filled with pity for a hundred hopeless suitors, her big black eyes were brimful with tears which rolled down her dark lean cheeks in glistening beads.

"May I not live to stand under my wedding canopy with my predestined one by my side, your Honor," she said, "if I did not pay this woman $22 for her Polly."

"But what do you want a parrot for?" asked counsel for the defense.

"What for?" and Leah-Golde dropped her big streaming dark eyes. "I had taught that parrot to say 'good luck' to me, so I thought it would be bad luck for the two of us to part."

Unfortunately, however, Leah-Golde had no witnesses, while several details in the case were favorable to her enemy, so the parrot is still talking two languages in Yetta's parlor.

AN OVERCOAT—THE REAL WITNESS
July 1, 1901

Coroner's Physician Dr. Albert T. Weston was called to the stand at the opening of proceedings at the McDonnell murder trial today, but the real witness, while he was testifying, was a heavy black overcoat which was worn by the defendant at the time of the fracas, which, according to the prosecution, was the cause of the death of George Price; for Dr. Weston could only give his opinion, as an expert, while the coat, with two holes for mouths, spoke of facts. Unfortunately, however, the language of this silent witness was not clear enough to be understood by all alike, so that the meaning of its testimony was interpreted by each of the two sides in its own way.

Dr. Weston said that the holes showed that the shots were fired from under McDonnell's coat. The defense, on the other hand, contended that the coat caught fire on the outside, and that it was Tom Kennedy's pistol, not McDonnell's, which singed and punctured the material. From the questions asked by Abraham Levy, McDonnell's lawyer, it was plain that, according to his theory, Kennedy, his client's enemy, took out a pistol and fired it close to the defendant's coat.

Police Sergeant Petty, the next witness, was called as an expert on shots. He said he had experimented with McDonnell's revolver, firing from it at a piece of sheet iron.

"The dent produced by this revolver is exactly the same as that found in the ceiling of the Onawa Café, where the shooting took place," he said.

The section of the ceiling containing the bullet mark and the piece of sheet iron used in the witness's experiment were put in evidence. Sergeant Petty then put on McDonnell's overcoat, and, while his face was streaming with perspiration, he showed how, in his opinion, the punctures were made by the pistol. He understood the speechless testimony of the garment in a way which agreed neither with the construction put upon it by Dr. Weston nor with the interpretation of Mr. Levy. He was sure that the holes were made by the defendant holding his revolver outside his coat, but with its muzzle close to it when he fired the alleged shots.

McDonnell's wife was by his side, as usual, and his daughter occupied her customary seat at the opposite side of the room. The two looked calm and patient today. So far from bubbling over with the expectation of seeing the prisoner released without having to put up a defense, as they were last Friday, they said they were anxious to have him take the stand and "show the whole world that Myles McDonnell is not the man he has been made out to be," as the defendant's wife put it.

The prisoner himself spoke of his eagerness to have the whole affair cleared up. "I don't want to slip out of them," he said. "I want all the facts known. There were several respectable people in the Onawa Café when the fight took place. They could testify how I was set upon by a lot of enemies bent upon killing me. The trouble is that, being respectable people, they probably hesitate to appear in a case like this, naturally being averse to having it come out that they were in the Onawa Café at a late hour. One of these is a man named Wesley; another is a retired piano maker named Mathushek; a third is a buyer for D. M. Williams, who told the story to one M. Robbins. I don't know their addresses, but I hope they will realize that it is their duty to come forward and tell what they know in a case where a man's life is at stake."

Antonio Bosto, a bootblack, identified the part of the ceiling containing the bullet mark referred to. He was followed by Joseph Josephson, who was questioned regarding the conversation he had with McDonnell after the defendant's arrest, but his testimony was apparently a great disappointment to Deputy Assistant District Attorney Garvan.

"Did McDonnell say to you: 'I put two bullets in Kennedy'?" Mr. Garvan asked. According to the prosecution, McDonnell intended to shoot Kennedy, but his bullets hit the wrong man, George Price, who happened to get between McDonnell and Kennedy.

"No, sir," answered the witness.

"Didn't you tell me he told you he put two bullets in Kennedy?"

"No."

The state then rested, and Henry Unger, the former assistant district attorney, who is Mr. Levy's partner, proceeded with his motions. He first moved that the piece of ceiling in the case should be discarded. This denied, he moved that the jury be instructed to bring in a verdict of "not guilty" on the ground of insufficiency of evidence.

"Nothing has been thus far adduced to connect this defendant with the death of Mr. Price," he said, "further than the inconsequential testimony of the experts and the identification of McDonnell by Price, to which we have objected as improper legal evidence."

"Oh, there is a good deal of evidence besides that," said Justice Fursman. "Eliminating Price's testimony and taking the other evidence, assuming it to be true, McDonnell and Price were in the saloon. Price was trying to get in between Kennedy and McDonnell, while the latter had a pistol in his hand; two witnesses tried to seize his hand; five or six shots were fired; no one else exhibited a pistol; Price was seen staggering home, and a bullet was taken from his body which bears the same indications as are found on bullets used in the defendant's pistol. There is evidence here upon which a jury might bring in a verdict of—no, strike that out—evidence upon which the jury might infer that Price was shot there."

The motion was denied, and Mr. Unger opened the case for the defense. It was an elaborate address, rather in the nature of a final plea than of a mere outline of the case to be presented, and as Mr. Unger, who is one of the best-known figures in the criminal courts, had never before been seen in the role of an advocate pleading with a jury, his speech attracted the largest crowd seen in the courtroom since the beginning of the hot spell. He not only told the twelve men what the defense proposed to do, but attacked the case of the other side, going over it in detail, arguing, ridiculing, appealing. The keynote of his speech was a contention that McDonnell was the victim of foul play, and that "if he had not been put on trial someone else—and the right person, too—would be here today."

Mr. Unger spoke of his client as a citizen of eminent respectability and usefulness to the community. "If we are proud of $1,500,000,000 worth of goods we export to other countries, this man has participated in this growth of our foreign trade, for, being one of the most successful commercial travellers in this country, he has done a great deal to introduce our manufactures in Australia. He is a gambler, too—we won't deny that—but he is one of our best citizens all the same, an honest man, a loving father and husband, a man with spotless reputation."

The first witness called by the defense was Richard A. Craig, a city surveyor, who identified a diagram of the Onawa Café that he had prepared for the trial.

PART SIX
The Frame of Soul

Leo Tolstoy. Portrait by Ilya Repin, 1901. (*Courtesy of The New York Public Library.*)

16

LIFE IN RUSSIA:
A BACKWARD GLANCE

THE YOUNG POMESHCHIK
February 26, 1898

Ah, snow! Thank God! My heart swells with joy; memories crowd my soul. For once, New York looks like my birthplace. Sweet illusion—how sweet to indulge it! I slip on my ulster, button it up to the chin, and imagining the frost to be many times stronger than it is, I hurry out to the avenue. A delightful morning, isn't it? Only those passersby make me laugh. Look at them huddling themselves and shrugging and puffing! No; I am not at home; it is New York, after all. But the flakes—dear little souls—never cease falling; and as one after another they let themselves down on my bosom, on my chin, on my eyebrow, scenes of home rise in my mind and a yearning takes hold of me.

Snow, snow, snow—almost nothing, but snow! I can see the white mountains on our farm, the half-buried hovels in the village nearby, the frozen river behind the church. I can hear the peasant sleds crunching past, the distant tinkling of a nobleman's sleigh bell, the merry cawing of the black feathered host. To be sure, as the *pomeshchiki* (lords of the manor) of the place, we lived in the beautiful farmhouse. Yet I had many an opportunity to play with the peasant boys in the village, as well as at my home. Well do I remember the pale face and large frightened-looking eyes of little Vaska, my favorite. I need scarcely mention that he never addressed me otherwise than *barin* (master, lord); but this did not prevent him from telling me something like "Go to the deuce, *barin,* will you?" He never dared touch his lordly playmate, however; and, beat him as I would, he was sure to take it all without a murmur, and upon the whole we got along nicely and, in our respective ways, were attached to each other.

Vaska was one of the few village boys who went to school. The school, however, was distant about two English miles, and as the snowflakes fall on me and on my walk along the beautiful American street, I see him trudging along the snow-covered road on his way thither. You would scarcely have taken him for a human being. Muffled up in his mother's rough jacket, with his father's cap hiding his head from view and his father's birch-bark shoes tied around his feet, he looked like a moving bundle rather than my ten-year-old playmate.

I remember one day, as I saw him start off for school, my own English governess came out to call me to my classroom on the second floor of the mansion. "If I have got to learn to read and write," I asked her, "what business has a peasant boy to do the same?"

"Well," she answered, "he learns to read and write only Russian, while you are taught French, German and English."

There were other differences. My classroom was a pretty little sanctum, warm and cozy, and fitted up with the latest school furniture—maps, pictures and what-not. On the other hand, the school to which Vaska had to plod through three *versts** of snow was a squalid, chimneyless shanty, with nothing but a carpet—the teacher's property—for furniture. Seated on this carpet, with a crowd of dirty peasant boys around her, I once saw a pale, haggard girl. She was the daughter of an impoverished family of *pomeshchiki,* and she taught school for some few rubles a month. The upper part of the room was full of smoke, so that the necessity of sitting on the ground was not without its advantages. As Vaska spent the day at school and in his journeys there and back, his mother would, on fitting him out for the expedition, shove a lump of rye bread into the bosom of her jacket. This was his lunch and dinner, unless, in a burst of generosity, I stole something in the kitchen for him.

When Vaska was free from school and from work and I was through with my tasks, we would play *babki,* our equivalent to the American game of marbles. In *babki* the place of marbles is taken by knuckle-bones, and instead of being arranged in a circle they are placed in a row, either in pairs or at equal intervals.

*See p. 10.

When we grew older we played towns. We would place the ends of two chunks of wood close together on a third of the same size, their other ends resting upon the ground and the three forming the letter "T." On the top of the two parallels we would place, lengthwise, a fourth piece of wood, leaving room for a fifth, which was to stand erect at the point of meeting of all the four. These chunks of wood we would hit with a club, crediting the performer with the number of chunks he knocked out of the goal. Vaska was a great hand at both games, and won many a victory over me. Sometimes his skill would tighten the bonds of my affection for him, but more generally I felt humiliated and swore off playing with the peasant boy. The idea of my servant being my superior was more than my keen sensibilities could bear.

The church stood in the middle of the village, and our family attended the Sunday service with the utmost regularity. As there are no pews, nor seats of any kind in the Greek Church, we had to stand, like the peasants who crowded it. When we entered the throng fell aside, to make a passage for us, and I can almost see them staring at our butler, carrying the carpets and cushions upon which we were to kneel. After prayer we would all kiss the priest's cross, which he presented first to the members of our family and then to the peasants.

The following well-known passage in one of Nekrasov's poems depicts a scene with which every Russian brought up in the country is familiar from personal observation:

> Once, on a cold winter's day, as I came out of the woods, I beheld a peasant's team slowly climbing the hill. The sleigh was laden with twigs, and dignifiedly marching in front and holding the animal by the bridle was a little bit of a boy. He wore large top boots, a huge sheepskin coat and enormous mittens—all apparently his father's.
>
> "Good morning, my lad," I greeted him.
>
> "Go your way, sir!" he said.
>
> "Oh, what a stern gentleman!" I said. "Where did you get the wood, my little man?"
>
> "In the forest, of course. Pa is cutting it down—can't you hear?—and I am taking it home. Why?"
>
> "How big is your father's family?"
>
> "Big enough, only there are no more than two men peasants among us—pa and myself."
>
> "I see. And what is your name?"
>
> "Vlass."
>
> "And how old are you, pray?"
>
> "Goin' on six. Get up, dead jade, you!" the child roared in a

bass, as he gave the bridle an angry jerk and mended the horse's pace. And such was the sunlight which fell on the picture, and so comically small was the child, that I felt as if it were a scene represented in cardboard, or that I had strayed into a children's theatre, with tin figures on the stage before me. But the boy was a boy—a living, real boy—and the sleigh with the faggots, and the snow reaching to the windows in the village, and the cold flame of the sun—all that is genuinely Russian was there, all that bears the stamp of our bleak, deadly winter was there; all that is torturingly dear to the Russian heart; all that instills Russian thoughts in one's mind—honest thoughts, unblessed with liberty but uncursed with death; living thoughts, immortal thoughts, which, strangle as one would, are so full of life, so full of pain, so full of hatred, so full of love!

———

THE SPY*

A Story by I. N. Potapenko

Translated from the Russian by Abraham Cahan

August 13, 1898

When I entered the University, Litvitsky was in the third class.

I came from a remote province and knew no one. My classmates in the gymnasium had all gone to other universities. It so happened that Litvitsky was the first man I had met within the walls of the University.

His outward appearance rather surprised me. I had known college students who used to come to our town for their vacation. They all dressed carelessly, most of them wearing colored blouses, which made neckties unnecessary, and black, wide-brimmed soft hats. Many of them had thick curly hair, which they preferred to keep in a chaotic state; they spoke loudly and affected a blunt, harsh manner. Such was the fashion in those days, just as it was the fashion to carry an extremely stout cane.

To be sure, one occasionally came across a dude or two who sported a stylish sack coat, spacious trousers and a tawdry cravat; there were some few high hats, too; but I knew that these were the outcasts of the University, and

*A story of student life in Russia during the height of the nihilist movement of the 1870s. —A.C.

so I had scarcely shed my gymnasium uniform and had not yet started for the university town when I got into a colored blouse and high top-boots and made a point of combing my hair into a bushy mane.

When I first met Litvitsky, I had some doubts whether he was a student at all. He was of medium stature, lean and pale-faced. His looks had something womanish in them, though this may have been due to his habit of shaving his moustache as well as his beard. He wore a long, black, tightly buttoned coat, a white linen collar, and a black necktie. All this, as well as the kettle-shaped hat, which he would hold in his hand so as to cover his slender walking stick with it, while it scarcely made the impression of freshness, was presentable enough. His smooth, colorless hair was carefully combed from right to left, and upon the whole he suggested a well-behaved *chinovnik* (governmental clerk), rather than a college student.

He was the first to speak.

"Are you looking for the clerk's office?" he accosted me.

I answered in the affirmative, and he pointed out the door to me. When I emerged, I found him in the corridor, waiting for me, as I thought.

He began to ply me with questions as to the city I came from, the school I was going to choose, what I was going to make my specialty, and the like.

His voice was soft and rather feeble, as though it came from a somewhat diseased chest. We came out into the street and proceeded on our way side by side.

"And you—are you also a student here?" I ventured to inquire.

"Yes; I am in the third philological class."

"What a queer student!" I said to myself.

However, we got to talking, and he offered me some friendly suggestions as to lodging, board, books, and gave me an idea about some of the professors. We parted on terms of some familiarity and friendship.

Such was my first meeting with Litvitsky. A whole week had passed before I saw him again. During that period, I made the acquaintance of a multitude of other students. At first I was introduced, or introduced myself, to my classmates, and then to practically the entire University.

One day I was one of a crowd of students on their way from the University to the restaurant where we all took our dinner. The crowd consisted of men of all sorts of colleges and classes. The conversation, now and then interrupted by a crossing cabman or truck driver, was more or less general.

By this time, I felt myself quite student-like, having at once mastered all the conventions and requirements of my new environment and gained the intimacy of my schoolmates.

THE FRAME OF SOUL

Emerging from a side street some two hundred feet ahead of us was the spare, insignificant figure of a man in a long coat, in whom I recognized Litvitsky.

Our company deployed till we occupied the whole width of the street, and as Litvitsky passed us, I saw him lift his kettle-shaped hat. Some of the men returned his salute; others did not. It struck me that this was not the kind of greeting one would give one's classmate and chum. There was no cordiality in the way some of my companions raised their hats, nor did they utter a single word of welcome. It was as if Litvitsky was a stranger to the University and its people.

As his eye fell on me, however, he paused with a smile.

"How are you, how are you?" he said. "I have not seen you for a whole week. I have not been quite well, you know."

I also paused and shook his hand. Not one of my companions followed my example. It even seemed to me as if they gave me a look of surprise as they proceeded on their way.

Litvitsky asked me a few questions—all of a perfectly natural and ordinary character—as to how I had established myself, whether I liked my board, which of the professors I liked best.

I answered all his questions, until I noticed that the other students had disappeared around the corner, when I bade Litvitsky a hasty good-by in order to catch up with them.

"Drop in on me once in a while, do, please," he said to me. "I shall really be glad to see you."

He gave me his address, and we parted.

I found the company at the restaurant. Four of us, including myself, usually occupied the same table, so I took my seat which had been kept vacant for me, but I noticed that the other three, who had been engaged in a lively conversation, cut it short at sight of me, while the students at the other tables threw glances at me, as if I had suddenly acquired a novel interest for them.

A few minutes had passed. I was beginning to feel rather awkward. At last one of my neighbors broke silence.

"Have you known Litvitsky long?" he asked.

"About a week," I answered. "He was the first man I had met here when I came to the University. Why?"

"Nothing. I am just asking."

That was all they would say about Litvitsky.

Meanwhile, Litvitsky had completely rallied from his illness, began to attend the lectures, and we met at the University almost daily; but I never saw

462

him with the crowd or talking to any one of the older students. Some novice would accost him, perhaps, with some questions and stand conversing with him for some time, but even this was never repeated by the same man. At first I thought he was simply a reticent man, but in my personal relations with him I found him quite talkative. He was fond of history, and when we met and our conversation touched upon the lectures at the University, he would talk upon his favorite subject with enthusiasm and eloquence.

"When will you look in upon me at last?" he once asked me, in a casual sort of way.

In point of fact, there was no reason why I should not call on him, and I determined to do so. He lived high up in a humble little room with a single window. He seemed sincerely glad to see me, and having lit a candle, he went to order tea.

A few of the most trivial questions on my part at once drew him into willing conversation, and I soon learned that his home was in a remote out-of-the-way town where his father served in the local post office; that the old man doted upon him, that his mother was dead, and that he had sisters whom it was hard to marry off, for the reason that there were no suitable young men in the town. His father sent him $15 a month, which is quite sufficient to pay his small bills. He did not care to give lessons, because he needed the time for his own studies.

His room struck me as exceptionally well kept. He had a number of historical books, and they all lay in a corner, arranged in excellent order.

"You must be a great reader?" I asked.

"Oh, yes; I am always reading," he answered. "Only my health is rather poor. My chest is weak and my eyes get tired quickly."

"By the way, Litvitsky, what makes you keep aloof from the students? That's the way it strikes me, at least."

His countenance fell.

"I don't care for them," he said.

"Why?"

"Because they are unjust."

"Unjust? What do you mean?"

"I don't wish to disenchant you. Besides, I hate to obtrude my views on other people. Wait till you see for yourself. Maybe you will soon come to think as they do. Indeed, it does not take much observation to form opinions such as theirs; you may fall in with their notions before you are aware of it. Well, the long and the short of it is—let us talk of something else."

We did change the subject, but his answers now seemed to me queer and left my curiosity unsatisfied.

On the next day I did not see him at the University. He seemed to have had a relapse. In the afternoon Stroganov, who had become my most intimate friend at college, came to see me.

"Look here, old man," he said, "you seem to be quite thick with that fellow."

"What fellow?" I asked, not in the least suspecting whom he meant.

"Why, that man—what you may call him—Litvitsky."

"Thick? I don't know him well enough to be thick. Still, we are acquainted and get along quite well."

"Do you? That's strange."

"Why?"

"Because Litvitsky is a suspicious man."

"Suspicious? What do you mean?"

"I mean what I say. He is a suspicious fellow and that's all there is to it."

"I'll be hanged if I understand what you mean."

"Ask the other students, and they'll tell you the same. Some even say he is a spy."

"Who says so? What grounds have they?"

"Why, everybody says so. It's the general opinion of the University."

Litvitsky a spy! The declaration shocked me. I began overhauling my own impressions, but could not rid myself of the influence which the suspicion lodged in my mind by Stroganov began to exercise over my reason. It made no difference that Stroganov had not advanced a single reason for that suspicion. The word he had dropped was beginning to color everything in my imagination and to present Litvitsky in a novel aspect. What had formerly seemed only odd suddenly became suspicious. His manner, his clean-shaven face, his long coat, the way he combed his hair, his voice—everything was now against him. But all this lasted only a minute. I shook off these silly and utterly unfounded thoughts and began to reason like a man. What have they seen? Where are their facts? I spoke to other students and the answer was the same.

"Yes, Litvitsky is a suspicious character."

"What leads you to think so?" I would insist. "What facts have you? What do you know against him?"

"I don't think there have been any definite facts, but—but such is the general opinion. Why, look at his eyes and his insinuating voice!"

"But you forget that he is no more responsible for having such eyes and such a voice than you are."

"Ah, but one's eyes and voice reflect one's soul. You had better not trust him too much."

In point of fact, I had nothing to keep from anybody, because I did not go into politics and was a member of no "circle." I was simply loath to part with the notion that Litvitsky was an honest fellow.

"That won't do!" I once shouted in the smoking room to a dozen students. "You must tell me once for all. What has Litvitsky done to give you cause for your opinion?"

Everybody shrugged his shoulders. "How naive! Things like that are done on the sly, don't you know," said Bochagov, a shaggy young man who had considerable influence among the students.

"Consequently, none of you have any facts whatever against him, have you?"

A general sneer was all the answer I got. I seemed to be talking altogether naively, so that to argue with me was as hard as it was useless.

But my sense of justice would not rest there. It demanded something positive. That day, I saw Litvitsky only for a moment. He was busily taking notes, and as I passed by him, he raised his eyes, and after greeting me with a nod, he asked:

"Why don't you drop in?"

"I will—this afternoon."

"On business?" he asked. He looked disappointed.

"His eyes do seem to have something searching in them," I said to myself. "There is something penetrating and cold in their look."

In the evening I called at his lodging. He was seated at the window. The grave things I came to speak about made me feel awkward, and I fell to pacing the floor nervously.

"You seem to be agitated, are you not?" he asked.

"Yes, I am agitated. Listen, Litvitsky," I began firmly, determined to come to the point at once. "You must excuse me, but it is my moral duty to speak to you. You see, they all say so—it is the general opinion—I don't believe it—not for a second—I first wish to hear what you have to say about it."

Litvitsky jumped to his feet.

"Scoundrels that they are!" he shouted, his eyes glaring. "It is not enough for them that they are unjust themselves. They cannot bear to see justice in anybody else, either. It is too bad you gave in. I am sorry, awfully sorry—still, I am not forcing myself on anybody. You are free to turn away from me. You won't be the first man to do it. I am used to it."

He resumed his seat. His head shook, his shoulders quivered, his knees were knocking against each other, he breathed heavily and loud.

"Come, Litvitsky," I began, reassuringly. "I have not yielded in the least. I have told you I take no stock in what they say. Only, I thought it was my duty to tell you about it. I wanted to know how this sort of rumor could have originated, for, as I say, the opinion seems to be general."

"The general opinion! The general opinion!" said Litvitsky, quivering from head to foot. "That's always the most unjust opinion. You are young and inexperienced, or you would know that the general opinion is always based upon some accidental, meaningless symptom. The mob has no reason. It is only capable of belief, and nothing will it believe more readily than slander. Run someone down, tell something nasty about him or her, and they will all hail it with joy. Tell them something good about somebody, and I shouldn't be a bit surprised if they refused to believe you."

"Consequently what they say about you is absolutely without foundation?"

"No foundation? Why, lots of it, old man. Here I am cleanly shaven, for example; my face is pale and I cut my hair, which is against the rule, don't you know. You must look like a highwayman if you would be accounted an honest man. I attend my lectures regularly—that is, as much as my poor health will permit—and I try to do my work properly, and that's another point against me. Again, I don't care for political economy. History I am fond of, and I devote as much time as possible to it, but they think one must read political economy—it has got to be a symbol of faith with them. They are opposed to all sorts of uniforms and conventions, and yet what are their blouses and top-boots and broad-brimmed hats if not a uniform? Well, I don't care to put on that uniform of theirs. I prefer to dress in my own way."

He spoke with so much bitterness that I scarcely recognized his voice. His usual mildness of accent and insinuating softness of intonation were gone. His words rang with determination and firm conviction, while his eyes, calmly observant, as a rule, were now aglow with passion.

As I stood listening to him and looking at his transformed face, I felt a change coming over myself. The so-called "general opinion" had already produced its effect on me. I had begun to look upon Litvitsky from a preconceived point of view, and when in answer to my question he broke out upon the students, I had said to myself: "Well, he is excited; consequently he is not innocent." But the more he spoke the clearer it became that he was undergoing the most cruel agonies, until there came a moment when, contrary to my will, as it were, contrary to my reason and the dictum of my senses, I suddenly began to feel that he was absolutely innocent, and that all that was said about him was calumny of the most detestable sort.

I stepped up to him.

"Well, don't be excited, Litvitsky; don't be excited. If I knew that my friendship could redeem the terrible injustice of the other students I should be happy to offer it to you."

He looked me fully in my face, as though to ascertain whether my words were sincere; then grasping my hand, he said:

"It can; it can. Thank you. Maybe it's because I feel the need of a friend so keenly, I have made so many attempts at getting one. Often a young man new at the University, whose brain has not yet been poisoned by the 'general opinion,' would conceive a liking for me. But two weeks hardly passed before he would grow cold and suspicious of me. Oh, how difficult it is to live without friends, all alone among so many people who hang together and are happy in being together! I must confess, many of them I cannot help liking in spite of the cruel injustice they do me. I know they are good fellows. It's the accursed 'general opinion' that is responsible for what they do to me. Oh, what tortures I have undergone! Can it be that they are indifferent to it all?"

I grasped his hand once more and we parted.

A year had passed. The summer I had spent in the country, and now I was a member of the second class, while Litvitsky was in his last year, preparing for his final examinations. The professors thought a great deal of him, and it looked as though there was a future chair for him, too.

We were on terms of warm friendship, as usual, and I must admit my intimacy with him did me good. I was extremely young, and Litvitsky, thanks to his inborn tact and well-balanced mind, unknown to myself guided me in the right direction. He taught me to love the science which he loved himself, and I took up history with a zeal and devotion for which I am now grateful to him.

As to the students' attitude toward me, they seemed to forgive my friendship with the suspect. True, they never discussed their secrets in my presence, but my position was never made intolerable.

In the course of that winter, a young scientist, who shortly before had defended his thesis, ascended one of the vacant chairs of the University. He had not occupied his dignified post many days when half of his thesis proved to have been copied from some foreign publication. The plagiarism proved, the students assembled in the young man's lecture room gave him a round of hisses, whistling and all sorts of cries. The other colleges joined in, and the revolt embraced the whole University. Lecture rooms became deserted; the students were busy holding meetings. The courtyard, the corridors and the lodging houses were crowded with indignant students listening to speeches delivered from chairs or tables.

It was at one of these meetings that the following episode took place: I was in the crowd and saw Litvitsky enter the room. He looked agitated. As a rule, he took no interest in the affairs of the students, but in this instance he felt offended in common with the rest. History was his favorite subject, and his heart revolted at the idea of a plagiarist occupying its chair. He had expressed his indignation to me, and I was sure that his feelings in the matter were sincere.

At the moment he entered the room, the improvised platform was occupied by a student with a dishevelled mane whose speech was full of fire. Suddenly I heard a whisper:

"Sh—sh! Let's be more careful, gentlemen."

Everyone looked around. The speaker was every little while interrupted.

"Look out! There is a spy in the room. Look out!"

My heart was wrung. I hardly believed my senses. Have they really said it? As if by previous agreement, the crowd pressed to the walls, so that the middle part of the room was vacant, and standing all alone in its center was Litvitsky. The situation at once became clear to everybody, including himself.

He stood staring at the crowd with stupid eyes. His head shook and his shoulders trembled just as they had on that evening when I had had my explanation with him. The orator had left the table and everybody was silent, when suddenly Litvitsky leaped upon the table and began to speak—not on the point which had brought the students together, but on something queer, out of the ordinary, which made everybody feel awkward and nervous.

"Somebody has shouted 'Spy!' here," he began. "Well, I know to whom the word refers. . . . It's a question of honor. . . . Do you understand what a question of honor means? I demand proofs. . . . Yes, at last I am here before you to demand your proofs. Let those who uttered that word come forward and advance their proofs. I allow them to burrow in my soul, to ransack my whole life. . . . Otherwise I shall have the right to say, and to say aloud, to shout so that the whole world will hear me, that you—all of you—all those present in this room at this moment, are scoundrels!"

There was a murmur, an outcry and hisses, but Litvitsky went on.

"Screams and hisses are no arguments. So none of you will say openly what he knows against me, none of you can prove the mean calumny with which you have been persecuting me now for four years? Not a single man? I am waiting. . . . Nobody is coming forward? Nobody?" roared Litvitsky, whose voice, usually soft and meek, now rang like thunder. "Nobody? Then I declare—I declare you all a lot of rogues, scoundrels! . . ."

The last word was cut short abruptly. Litvitsky fell to the floor.

Silence ensued. Litvitsky lay senseless. Another student and myself carried him into a cab and took him to his lodgings.

He fell ill with fever, and his illness dragged on. A few days after the memorable meeting his father arrived, and what used to impress me as queer and suspicious at once became natural to me. The point is that father and son have a striking resemblance to each other and that the elder Litvitsky shaved his beard, combed his hair and buttoned his coat, spoke and bore himself exactly as his son did. Even the hat the old man wore was kettle-shaped, like my friend's.

"It is from him that he got all these habits and tastes," I said to myself. The other students also saw him, and the truth at once began to dawn on them. A sudden reversal of feeling followed. The students began to inquire about his health, and, instead of mistrust and contempt, showed respect and love.

When Litvitsky became convalescent and I told him of the present feelings of the students toward him, he said:

"I don't care. They have proved to me that their respect, like their disrespect, is not worth much. I have no respect for them."

His illness did not prevent him from passing his examinations with honors, and a tutorship was offered him at the University, but he declined it, and when I asked him why he did so he said:

"I want to go away from here—from everything that suggests my tortures during these four years. The students have inflicted a wound on my soul which can never be healed."

He returned to his native place, where he entered the civil service in some one of the provincial tribunals.

————————

THE FUNCTIONARY

A Story by Anton Chekhov
Translated from the Russian by Abraham Cahan
October 22, 1898

One pleasant evening a pleased functionary sat in the second row of the orchestra circle with his opera glass trained on the performance of *The Bells of Corneville*. As he followed the play, he felt something exceedingly sweet and blissful pervading his whole being. Then all at once (this "all at once" is quite a favorite phrase with storytellers; they seem to think that life is full of the unexpected, and I agree with them, too) his face became all wrinkled, his eyes rolled up, his breath suddenly stopped, and withdrawing his opera glass from the actress, he bent his head and—pardon the word—sneezed.

Now, there is no injunction whatever in any of the laws of the Russian Empire against sneezing, and a common peasant will sneeze as heartily as a Chief of Police or even a Privy Councillor. Nothing daunted, therefore, Cherviakov wiped his face with his handkerchief, and, good citizen as he was, looked about to see whether his sneezing had attracted anybody's attention. Presently he blushed. An old man in front of him was wiping his bald head and neck with his white glove and muttering to himself as he did so. Great heavens! It was General Bryzhalov of the Department of Transportation.

"I have sneezed all over him!" said Cherviakov to himself. "Of course, he is not my chief, but it is too bad, all the same. I must apologize."

With a preliminary hem and cough, Cherviakov leaned forward and whispered into the General's ear:

"I am very sorry to have sneezed on your Excellency. I did not mean it. I beg your pardon."

"That's all right," answered the General.

"I hope you'll excuse me," Cherviakov resumed anxiously. "I am sorry it happened. Do forgive me, sir."

"Keep still, please," said the General. "Let me follow the play, will you?"

Cherviakov was crushed, and with an embarrassed simper he turned his eyes upon the stage. His former beatitude was all gone out of him. He was anything but happy.

During the next intermission he came up to General Bryzhalov's row, paced up and down the aisle, and finally mustering courage, stopped by the General's side and began muttering and stammering:

"I sneezed on your Excellency—beg pardon—you know—I assure you, it was not because of—"

"Oh, don't mention it! I have forgotten all about it," the General said impatiently.

"He says he has forgotten all about it, but at the same time his eye is full of malice," Cherviakov thought to himself as he looked at the General. "Why, he would not even speak to me. I should have explained to him that I never meant to sneeze on him, that I could not help it, because sneezing is one of the involuntary acts of nature. As it is, he may suspect that I did it on purpose. If he does not think so now, it will occur to him afterward."

Arrived at home, Cherviakov told his wife of his rudeness to a high functionary, to General Bryzhalov of the Department of Transportation. But she made light of the matter, he thought, and not only did she fail to be alarmed by the incident, but even declared that the incident did not amount to anything, seeing that Bryzhalov was not his chief, and was not even connected with his department.

"Still, it will do you no harm to call on him and apologize," she said, upon afterthought. "He might think you have no manners."

"Exactly! You see, my dear, I did apologize, in fact, but somehow I failed to put it right. There was so little time."

The next day Cherviakov put on his uniform, had his hair cut and betook himself to General Bryzhalov's quarters to explain the unfortunate accident and to apologize.

In the General's reception room he found a number of men and women and the General himself, who was already receiving petitions. Presently his eyes fell upon Cherviakov.

"Last night at the theatre, your Excellency," said the functionary, "I happened to sneeze, and as your Excellency had a seat in front of me I sneezed on your Excellency. I therefore come to beg . . ."

"What nonsense!" the General exclaimed. "The idea! What can I do for you?" he asked, turning to the next man.

Cherviakov grew pale. "He does not care to speak to me at all!" he thought. "He does resent it, then. I knew he did. But it would not do to let the matter go. He is General—General Bryzhalov of the Department of Transportation. It is no laughing matter. I must explain to him that I did not mean to sneeze on him."

When the General had disposed of all his petitions and was about to withdraw, Cherviakov took a stride toward him and said:

"Your Excellency, if I may trouble your Excellency for a moment, I wish to say that it is from a deep sense of remorse that I have come here. I never intended to sneeze on your Excellency. Never, sir, never!"

His Excellency made a wry face and, with a despairing wave of his hand, cried out:

"Why, why it looks as if you were making fun of me, sir. What's the matter with you?" And with a shrug of his shoulders, he disappeared.

"Making fun of him!" said Cherviakov to himself on his way home. "I don't quite see where the fun comes in. Strange, a general should fail to see a point so plain. Very well, then, I'll not bother him with my apologies any more—not I. The deuce take the pompous old fogey. I am going to write him a letter, but call in person again—I'll be hanged if I do."

Day after day passed, and Cherviakov wrote no letter to General Bryzhalov. He somehow could not find the time or the mood for it, until finally he made up his mind to risk calling upon the General in person again. To speak seemed so much easier than to make a written explanation.

"I called here the other day, your Excellency," he began, the moment the General raised his questioning eyes to him. "I did so not for the purpose of making fun of your Excellency, as you were pleased to suspect. Not at all. I was simply anxious to apologize for having sneezed on your Excellency. It never entered my thoughts to make fun. How dare I? If we were to allow ourselves fun at the expense of our superiors, why, then, there would be no respect for . . ."

"Get out!" the General roared, growing livid and trembling with rage.

"I beg your pardon?" queried Cherviakov in a whisper, his heart sinking within him with terror.

"I say get out of here at once!" the General shouted, stamping his foot.

Something seemed to break in the functionary's heart, and without hearing or seeing anything about him, he staggered out into the street and dragged himself home.

Once arriving there, he took to his bed and died.

————————

THE RETURN OF SOFIYA ROGOVA
April 15, 1899

The soirée at Everett Hall was a decided success. The vast dining room was crowded with Russian-speaking (or yelling) men and women. The intellectual elite of the colony was gathered in full force "to show one's self and to have a look at others," as the Muscovite phrase goes. There were physicians and lawyers and dentists galore, including an odd dozen of female members of the three professions. The concert was over and the ball was in full blast. Yet only part of the main hall was taken up by the dancers, the majority of the multitudinous gathering promenading or bustling about, in couples or singly, or standing about in groups, some watching the dancers, others chatting, still others making merry around tables in the large side room. A noisy crowd it was—more noisy, perhaps, than gay, and with a higher percentage of good looks and bookish faces than of evidences of prosperity or fashion.

A well-shaped young woman came along the main hall, her expressive hazel eyes wandering about wistfully as she picked her way through the surging throng. She wore a gray woollen dress. It was brand-new and became her prettily. The consciousness of this beamed out of her pink and white face. Her advent created a little stir.

She had gone back to Moscow, and her return to America was an agreeable surprise. Her name was Sofiya Vladimirovna Rogova, but she was more generally known as Sonya.

Mrs. Basin was presiding over the tea counter and a group of young women. She was a well-dressed, important-looking matron of forty. Her face spelled Duty and Decorum. This, however, did not prevent Gossip and Malice from occupying every available bit of space in her soul. Tonight, she was looking somewhat below her best. She knew it, and was out of spirits. She was dying to inquire about Sonya's dress, but would not give the newcomer the satisfaction. Still, a remark upon the garment was due, in common decency. So she said, with studied indifference, as she threw a commiserating side glance at the skirt:

"A new dress, isn't it? Made in Russia?" But the subject was too painful, and she passed to another before Sonya answered her question. "And so you have actually been there, and it is not a dream? Well, well! You know, it seems to me, if I went there I should not come back."

"That was the way I felt at first, too," answered Sonya. "I was so homesick—it came upon me all of a sudden, you know—I thought I should die unless I went to Russia at once."

Other listeners joined the knot around the tea table.

Mrs. Basin was getting interested, and there was a tremor of unfeigned feeling in her voice, as she said:

"I can imagine how your heart beat when you got over the frontier." And effusively inviting Sonya to a seat beside her throne, she asked her to describe in detail her return to her native place.

"Tell us every bit of it. Omit nothing, Sonya," implored a doctress, as she moved up closer to Mlle. Rogova.

Sonya started reluctantly, but soon warmed up to her story and thrilled the group by a spirited, simple account of her arrival in her birthplace. When she described her meeting with her former classmates and bosom friends, some of her audience were shocked to hear that Sonya's experience had been of a disenchanting nature.

"You are expecting, God knows what. Yet when you meet at last, there is nothing stirring about it; you feel that there is very little left between you two—that you are strangers. You kiss each other and keep saying good things, but—well, it now seems to me as if it was all a farce.''

A Miss Geffen gave Sonya a look of reproach.

"Again," Mlle. Rogova went on, "things somehow seemed to have shrunk in size, to have grown less interesting and inspiring than I had pictured them to be. One of the streets in the neighborhood of my home, which had always seemed to me an important thoroughfare, swarming with people, proved to be much narrower and all but deserted. I visited the scenes of my childhood. Well, I had expected to burst into tears at sight of them. Nothing of the kind! No, I did cry, but it was artificial. I had worked myself up to it, consciously—as if following a programme," she added, with a timid little laugh. "Everything looked the same as of old, and yet, somehow—" She was fumbling for words, and then, brightening up, continued: "It is as if the things themselves remained unaltered, but the halo which had formerly surrounded them had faded away. Only the Russian tongue, the dear Russian tongue, sounded sweeter than ever. Well, I had not been a month there before I began to feel bored. You see, after you get used to the rapid flow of life in America, the world seems to be just creeping along over there.''

"Don't say that, Sonya," the doctress begged her, distressed.

"I see you are quite Americanized," put in a sallow-faced lawyer, with a touch of resentful irony.

"Well," Sonya resumed, in an apologetic way, "maybe my attachments lack steadfastness—although I don't think they do—maybe I belong to those natures with whom an interruption breaks the spell forever. At any rate, it was not long before it came home to me that I was a stranger there. Yes, the aureoles have faded away. The thread is broken, and you can't put it together again," she said pensively, as if speaking to a spot on the wall. "It drew me back here and I could not help returning. Did you say I was Americanized? Well, now that I am here I feel that this is not my home, either. But one thing is certain, Russia can never be to me what it once was. Perhaps, it is because we are Jews—a persecuted, wandering people without a home. When I walked in the streets of my native town every policeman and the meanest tramp in the gutter would make me feel that I was a mere *Zhidovka**—a hated, inferior being. Perhaps it was because it was here in New York that I had first tasted life on my own hook. Take it as you will, the thread is broken. At times I feel like weeping—not for my country, for I have none any longer—but for this very loss, irretrievable loss, of it.''

Tears glistened in Mrs. Basin's eyes, but a detachment of younger

*Russian in a contemptuous sense for Jewess.—A.C.

people came up and forced Sonya, Miss Geffen and the doctress into the adjoining hall, where the chorus was forming under the direction of a cadaverous little man with flaxen curls, eyes almost completely white and coatsleeves an inch or two too long.

The chorus was slow in coming to order. Spirits were too buoyant to take anything seriously, and meeting the beseeching gestures of the sickly man with merriment, the crowd went on jarring and grating his poor nerves.

Little by little, however, those with music in their souls began to take it more seriously; the others desisted, reverently, and from a hundred hearts forth poured itself a song, a sad, a stirring song, a mighty song, a Russian song.

It was an ancient piledriver's tune, one of the prettiest of folk airs. The words speak of zestful toil at the birch-bark rope, of winding and unwinding it, of "letting her go"; but the melody seems to be telling quite another tale—one at once of world-dazzling glory and black woe, of a great unbending spirit, pining away in iron-barred captivity:

> Yo-ho! Yo-ho!
> Once more, once more,
> Yo-ho! Yo-ho!

Everybody fell grave. The hall was filled with far-away echoes that spoke of home and exile, of faces that were dear and things that would not be forgotten.

Sonya sang with religious fervor. She heard the story of crushing, heart-wringing separation in the voices, but she also heard a note of pensive indifference, tender and ever a chord that moaned to her:

"The thread is broken, the thread is broken!"

———

NESTOR OF NIHILISM
February 24, 1900

Two hundred Russian-speaking men and women assembled in one of the meeting rooms at 209 East Broadway the other evening. The chairman was a broad-shouldered man of forty-five, with a thick blond beard and a typical Slavonic face. His name is Vladimir Aleksandrovich Stalechnikov. At his home, which is near St. Petersburg, he belonged to the oldest nobility and was the owner of a large estate, but he was actively interested in the nihilist movement, and was about to be arrested when he fled to Switzerland. He then went to Italy and France, and finally settled in this country, where he has lived for more than twelve years.

There were other nihilists in the room, some of them old-timers, like the chairman, who participated in the "underground circles" of the seventies and eighties, when the movement was at its height and when members of the highest aristocracy in Russia were scheming against the monarchy. Peter Lavrovich Lavrov was one of the Nestors of nihilism, and the speakers at the East Broadway meeting dwelt on his career and his personality with peculiar tenderness and affection, as if the deceased had been their beloved grandfather.

"Imagine a tall, stalwart man of seventy-six, military of aspect and bearing," said Mr. Stalechnikov, "a nobleman, every inch of him. Kindly and gentle like a dove, polite and gallant like a knight, a walking cyclopedia, a dreamer who lived and suffered for the good of humanity in the sincerest sense of the phrase—imagine such a man and surround him in your mind by thousands of admirers; place him in a suite of tiny rooms at rue St. Jacques, Paris, with a samovar at his table, with almost every inch of every wall covered with books; picture him writing during the day and talking to a small circle of visitors in the evening—writing and talking of the woes of Russia and the rest of the civilized world, and of the time when they would all be happy; picture all this and you will have the picture of a man like Peter Lavrovich Lavrov.

"He was a professor of philosophy at the military academy of St. Petersburg and a contributor to the best magazines of the capital. In the seventies, when the revolutionary movement was spreading among the educated classes, he was found in the front ranks of the movement. He wanted to see his country free—free to develop its resources and the faculties of its children. He was arrested and sent north to one of the coldest provinces in Russia. But the young revolutionists could not spare him. There were hundreds who stood ready to be imprisoned so that the great teacher might regain his liberty and his work of enlightenment.

"Several young men went to the place where Lavrov lived in exile, and, at the peril of their own liberty, they brought about his escape. He wanted to return to St. Petersburg to live "under ground." But the nihilists would not let him take chances. 'You are too valuable to run the risk of an arrest,' they said to him. 'Go to Switzerland, to France, anywhere where you will be safe. Go and teach us while we are facing the dangers of the work here. We shall read your articles, your pamphlets; we shall hear your voice from afar, and it will inspire us to sacrifice our lives for the good of our country.'

"He settled in Paris and his residence began to attract pilgrims from every part of his country. There were thousands of men and women who were willing to die for the cause, and to all of these the name of Peter Lavrov was a name to conjure with.

"Counts and princes visiting the French capital would call at his place incognito and leave contributions to the movement. There were many such persons in those days. They were good at heart, but too weak to sacrifice their social position and luxuries to their convictions. They were glad to help the revolution without being known as nihilists. Turgenev, the great Russian writer, was one of Lavrov's admirers, and he, too, kept this secret, although for different reasons. The novelist's influence was so great that it would have been a pity if his books had been proscribed on account of his friendship for the great revolutionist.

"There is a considerable Russian colony in the Latin quarter. Most of these are nihilists, including some runaways from Siberia or candidates for the gallows. Lavrov's 'at home' was on Thursdays, and you should have seen the old man in the company of his guests on those evenings! There were sure to be several student girls in the gathering, and Lavrov's gallant attentions to them would shock the nihilistic sensibilities of the very recipients of these attentions. 'Why should we be petted as if we were babies?' they would protest. 'We are emancipated women, as good as men!' But gallantry was Lavrov's second nature. He could not help it.

"He was one of the greatest Russians that ever lived," concluded the speaker. "Yet the very mention of his name would get a subject of the Czar into trouble."

TOO LATE

A Story by I. N. Potapenko
Translated from the Russian by Abraham Cahan
October 14, 1899

It all came about quite unexpectedly. The feeling had been ripening in Nikolai Ivanovich's heart for some time, but he well knew his own indecision and bashfulness (strange as this may seem for a man of forty), and he was sure that it would all wear off in course of time, when one day, when he least intended to, he blurted it all out to her. This is the way it happened:

The evening before, Antonina Sergeyevna had looked in on them just for a moment, to kiss Sashenka, as she put it. Sashenka is his daughter. She is eighteen. The poor girl was used to passing the time with her mother and now feels lonely. Since Nadya died, two years ago, the house has become quiet and dreary. So Antonina Sergeyevna drops in quite often to keep Sashenka company. Often she takes her out, sometimes to her house, sometimes to the theatre. She is like a second mother to her, Antonina Sergeyevna, and Sashenka loves and respects her.

The night before, Sashenka was not at home. She had gone to Pavlovsk, to Zinaida Ivanovna, her father's sister. She had stayed overnight there and was not expected back until late the following afternoon. Antonina Sergeyevna stepped in on her way from her shopping tour.

"So you will have to dine all alone, poor man!" she said with a smile.

"Yes, all alone, all alone, Antonina Sergeyevna!" he answered, with playful declamation.

"Well, I am in the same boat. I tell you what. Come and dine with me, and instead of two lone souls there will be one pair."

She burst into laughter. He colored the least bit. It goes without saying that he accepted the invitation, and so, at 5:45 he took a cab and drove off to the Kirilechnaya.

It was a warm spring day. The weather made one think of summer resorts, but the St. Petersburgers had not as yet the courage to leave the city. Only a few brave ones, like Nikolai Ivanovich's sister, had made haste to go to the country, but then, her residence in Pavlovsk was a solid brick building, good for a winter house. Nikolai Ivanovich felt in unusually good trim, in mind as well as in body. Of late he had often had moments of ennui, which was natural enough, for he had lived with Nadya for nearly twenty years, and how happily they did live! Not a quarrel, not a misunderstanding; so that the habit of this sort of life had become a second nature with him. Well, Nadya died. At first his heart was torn with pain. His woe was too fresh to calm down. Little by little, however, it had become dulled, as though enveloped in mist, and instead of the former pang, Nikolai Ivanovich would simply feel lonesome. Sashenka was a great comfort to him, of course, but then, she had her own interests to occupy her mind. She was only eighteen, while he was a man of forty.

Little by little, he became aware that each time Antonina Sergeyevna called at the house his spirits would rise. At first, he set it down to her gay disposition and the tactful, interesting chat with which she would fill the house. But later on he perceived another thing which he thought queer. When he was alone, he would catch himself thinking of her charming eyes with their long lashes. He could hear ringing in his ears her soft, melodious voice, and somehow he often felt a strong desire to kiss her hand. Such were the symptoms of the feeling which he considered a queer one for him to experience. Indeed, it was only two years since Nadya died, only two years since they had lived like a pair of doves. To think that he could feel toward another woman the way he did! Still, even this strange feeling he got used to, and so it kept growing, imperceptibly, until it assumed harrowing dimensions. The company of Antonina Sergeyevna became a necessity with him. Often he was so wild to see her that he had to invent some pretext or other to call at her house.

This time he came on the stroke of 6. The table was set for three, for with Antonina Sergeyevna lived a distant relative, a rickety old creature, blind, deaf—a bag of bones of singular vitality. She was somewhere in the neighborhood of ninety, and she was expected to live at least ten years longer.

The meal over, the human wreck was sent off to its room. Antonina Sergeyevna's home was full of comfort and taste, although her last husband had left her but a very moderate income. On 5,000 rubles a year she managed to live better than some people do on twelve. She received on Thursdays, entertained excellently, went to the theatre, dressed well—in short, she enjoyed life perfectly. She was thirty-four, looked less, and told people her exact age.

Nikolai Ivanovich made himself comfortable in an easy chair in the drawing room, and with the permission of the hostess he lit a cigar. Antonina Sergeyevna was seated on the sofa in front of him, and in her society, amid these graceful and commodious surroundings, as he sat looking into her smiling eyes and listening to her gay talk, he felt in a state of indescribable bliss.

Unbeknown to himself he shut his eyes.

"Are you sleepy?" she asked.

He gave a start.

"Not at all, not at all," he said.

"What, then, is the matter?"

"What is the matter?" he echoed, musingly, removing the cigar from his mouth. "Shall I tell you?"

"By all means," she answered, egging him on with a prolonged look of her beautiful, languid eyes.

"I am happy, Antonina Sergeyevna; that's what's the matter."

"How do you mean?"

"Simply that your company makes me happy; that it is indispensable to me. There!"

She broke into a laugh and said:

"Bravo, Nikolai Ivanovich!"

"Don't laugh. It is not a laughing matter. It's quite serious, Antonina Sergeyevna."

"Is it?"

"Yes, it is."

Of course, she saw it was something serious. Indeed, had she not noticed it of herself, had she not thought of it before!

She had become a widow some time before Nikolai Ivanovich lost his wife. She had the art of arranging things to her own satisfaction. She was pleased with her life and with herself. Being no dreamer, there were no visions of handsome young fellows, much younger than herself, to obtrude themselves upon her imagination in the lonely silence of the night. She was thirty-four, and a similar marriage would have seemed to her vulgar and foolish. Nikolai Ivanovich, on the other hand, she liked. He seemed to have in him everything that thirty-four years and her sober view of life wanted. He was a man of solid habits, not at all too old. Tall, slender without being gaunt, he held himself erect and was apparently free from any of the ailments from which men begin to suffer at that period of their life when you hear them say, half humorously: "Getting old! Forty years is no laughing matter!" No, there was nothing in him to show that he was getting old, neither a suspicious floridity of complexion nor habitual apathy, nor yet that so-called "skepticism" which really means a lack of vitality. In his younger days Nikolai Ivanovich had lived a regular life, so he was well preserved in body and in spirit. He was capable of the enthusiasm of youth, but he never lost his head. In short, he was just the kind of husband she wanted. She had made his acquaintance shortly after the death of his wife, and they had soon become warm friends. To be sure, the fact that Antonina Sergeyevna struck Sashenka's fancy had something to do with it, for, indeed, since the death of Nadya, Sashenka's interests controlled everything he did.

"Well, then, why don't you speak out, Nikolai Ivanovich? Is it that you don't think I could—I could understand anything serious?" she asked.

"I really don't know whether you will understand me," he answered with a sort of desperation.

"And yet you call yourself my friend!" she reproached him.

"Antonina Sergeyevna! Isn't it plain to you that—oh, well—that I simply can't live without you?"

She colored deeply, as she asked with a tremor in her voice:

"How do you mean?"

Once he got going, as he used to put it, he could not check himself.

"If I cannot live without you it means that I wish to live with you." He crossed over to her and took her by the hand which rested on the round little table in front of her. "We are children no longer. Why not call a spade a spade? Marry me, Antonina Sergeyevna."

He kissed her hand and then he stood looking in her eyes. He was waiting for an answer. Her hand she did not withdraw, but signed to him to take a seat by her side.

"Sit down here, my friend, and let us talk it over. As you say, we are children no longer, so we needn't hesitate to discuss it frankly and simply, need we? When—well, when one's heart won't beat calmly, as usual, there is no use mincing matters."

He sat down by her side, overflowing with happiness. She continued:

"I am an egotist, Nikolai Ivanovich, and my own interests are the first consideration with me. I am contented with my present mode of life, and I could go on living like that until I die. But I am willing to change it, provided the change is not for the worse. Do you think it won't be?"

"How shall I answer this question?" he exclaimed. "You know me well. That's all I can say."

"Yes, I do know that you are one of the best men in the world, or my heart wouldn't beat as fast as it does, but you have a daughter."

"She loves you as she did her own mother."

"That may be true as long as I haven't taken her mother's place. You and I are not the only egotists, Nikolai Ivanovich. Oh, those younger hearts, full of poetic dreams, sometimes have in them an egotism of which people of our age are seldom capable. Well, let us decide the question conditionally. Tell Sashenka about it. Not that you are to ask her permission: 'May I get married, Sashenka?' Of course not. But you ought to inform her of the matter as something decided and see how she takes it. Then we shall talk it over."

He kissed her once more, this time gratefully. He came away in ecstasy over her tact and practical good sense as well as over his own happiness. In the evening he went to see a play. He slept excellently that night, and the next day he worked with a clear head and with unusual relish. Toward evening he took a cab and went to meet Sashenka at the Tsarskoe Selo station. Of course, he postponed the important conversation till later in the evening.

They were having tea. Sashenka, fresh, well-made, pretty, was telling her father the news of her aunt's country house. Aunt was so glad she had moved to Pavlovsk early in the season. The weather was simply superb. Only the day before yesterday it had been windy so that it was necessary to make a fire. Yesterday there was a misfortune. Terenty, the old tomcat, died. Aunt had been awfully fond of him, and she was so worried. Still, in the evening they went to hear the band at the railway station. That was all the news she brought from Pavlovsk, but she told it with so much spirit and grace that it acquired a peculiar interest.

Nikolai Ivanovich listened musingly. Each time Sashenka burst out laughing he would smile assent. Her story touched his consciousness but slightly. He was taken up with himself: he was casting about for a way to bring the conversation round to the subject which filled his mind. At last he said:

"And I had a call from Antonina Sergeyevna."

"Had you? It's too bad I was away. It's quite a while since I saw her," exclaimed Sashenka, with sincere regret.

"She asked me to dinner."

"Did you go?"

"Yes."

"I should think you did. I can imagine how lonesome you felt, and she is so jolly, so clever, isn't she?"

"Oh, yes; Antonina Sergeyevna is a very clever woman, indeed."

Sashenka fell silent and the conversation on this subject might have been considered closed, but that was not what Nikolai Ivanovich wanted. He was fumbling for a way to the main point.

"Tell me frankly, Sashenka," he began, and forthwith checked himself, for she looked up at him in surprise. Then he resumed. "Are you very fond of Antonina Sergeyevna?"

"What makes you ask such a strange question? Of course I am very fond of her. You know I am."

"Of course I do; but is it really a strong attachment? That's what I mean."

"Oh, Papa! How queer you are tonight! Whatever makes you ask such peculiar questions?"

"Well, I suppose I have some reason for asking them," he answered, with some vexation. It was with himself that he was vexed. It suddenly came over him that he was acting like a schoolboy who is afraid to answer his teacher's question in plain, straightforward language. He forced himself to come straight to the point.

"The fact of the matter is that I think I could explain it to you, Sashenka. . . . You see, you are so young, you will hardly understand it. . . . It's like this: Solitude is the hardest thing to bear, especially at a period of life when one is getting old. Well, each man is bound to come across some person who could make him a warm friend, an intimate friend, don't you know? I doubt whether you can understand it. . . .''

"Certainly I don't. I don't know what you are talking about, Papa.''

"I thought you wouldn't. It's like this, my child. It often happens in life that two lonely persons meet and come to the conclusion that they ought to unite their lives, and then . . . they are lonely no longer.''

"Yes, such things will happen. Well?''

"I am still playing the schoolboy,'' he thought to himself.

"To make a long story short,'' he then said resolutely, "what would you say if I was to marry Antonina Sergeyevna?''

"You marry! What do you mean?'' she asked, in bewilderment.

"Why, can't I marry? I am not so old. . . . I love Antonina Sergeyevna.''

"How can you say that, Papa—how can you say that?'' she repeated, tapping the table with her fist.

His face darkened.

"I don't understand what you mean,'' he said, sternly. "Is there something strange in my loving Antonina Sergeyevna?''

"And how about Mamma?''

He fixed her with a sad, reproachful glance. Could it all be conscious cruelty on her part? Indeed, could there be anything more heartless than to mention poor Nadya at this moment? But no, she did not mean it. Sashenka was not as hard-hearted as all that. But the worst of it was that Nikolai Ivanovich was utterly unprepared for this sort of objection. He was at a loss for an answer.

"The memory of your dear mother is sacred to me, my child,'' he began.

"Sacred!'' she interrupted him.

"Yes, sacred. It means—''

"It means that you have forgotten her so entirely that you fell in love with somebody else. That's what it means.''

Nikolai Ivanovich winced. What was the meaning of all this? Was she really making a schoolboy of him? How dare she carp at his every word, and take that hostile tone with him? Why should she have torn open the wound which had almost healed up in his heart? Perhaps he had only himself to blame. He had no business to talk of such an important psychological problem to a mere child. All he should have done was to announce to her his decision and to tell her that it was final.

"I'll ask you not to speak to me like that, Sashenka,'' he said. "You

483

have touched upon something which you had much better have left alone. There are some things in life which you are too young to understand.''

She moved her teacup from her and got up. There were tears in her eyes, and her shoulders quivered.

"I don't care. You shan't get married and that's all there is about it,'' she said in a voice shaken with sobs. "You—you cannot do it—you have no right to—I'll cease to respect you, if you do—I'll hate you.''

"Sasha!'' he exclaimed, authoritatively.

"Oh, how unhappy I am!'' she said, and, covering her face with her hands she ran out of the room.

Nikolai Ivanovich grew thoughtful. Where did Sashenka get that tone, those words and that sentimentality of hers? To be sure, it would be foolish to attach any importance to the words of a girl hardly out of her teens, who knows life from books; and yet he felt that his plan was shattered. He loved Sashenka with all his soul, and he could not so much as think of losing her respect. Besides, what business had he to put that bitter drop into her young life, to overcast the clear sky which fate had not as yet darkened by a single cloud? Sashenka was wrong, a thousand times wrong, but her feeling in the matter sprang from a love for the memory of her mother so perfectly legitimate that it seemed wrong to oppose it. Moreover, as the matter stood now, his whole plan was hardly feasible. His new happiness could not be ushered in except by disturbing Sashenka's peace of mind. A cloud of ill-feeling would enter his house. The marriage would mar his own life and that of Antonina Sergeyevna.

He sat motionless, his head despondently bent, when suddenly a servant came in and said excitedly:

"Miss isn't feeling well.''

"What's the matter?'' Nikolai Ivanovich asked, starting.

"She is crying all the time. She has buried her face in her pillow and won't stop crying, sir.''

He leaped to his feet and rushed into his daughter's room. He found it lit with two candles burning on the dresser. Sashenka lay with her face downward, convulsed with sobs.

"Don't distress yourself, my child,'' he said, tenderly, putting his hand to her head.

"Leave me alone! Oh, I am so miserable, so miserable!'' she said, pushing him from her roughly.

"But you are taking it all too hard, Sashenka. You look at it in the wrong light. I will do as you wish.''

She raised herself.

"Papa, darling!" she said, regaining some composure, "you won't get married, will you?"

"No, my child, since you don't want me to—"

"Upon your word of honor?"

"Yes," he yielded, sadly. He felt as if something very dear to his heart were wrenched from him. She threw her arms around his neck impetuously, and clung close to his side.

"Dear, good, golden Papa mine! However did it enter your mind? You know you are not as bad as all that."

"There was nothing bad about it," he retorted, softly. "I have promised to do as you wish, but that doesn't mean that there was anything wrong about the matter."

"Papa, dear, but you know how you used to love Mamma. I used to see you caress her, and call her all kinds of pet names, and kiss her hands, and how could I bear to see you love somebody else?"

"Maybe you are right, but just put yourself in my position. I am getting well on in years, and sooner or later I shall be left all alone."

"But I am with you, Papa."

"You will get married, my child."

"Oh, I never think of that. I'll always be with you, Papa darling."

Nikolai Ivanovich could not work that evening. He went early to bed, but he was slow to fall asleep. He pictured his coming loneliness and old age. A chill touched his heart.

At 11 o'clock the next morning Nikolai Ivanovich came out of his house for his usual morning stroll. He never thought of going to see Antonina Sergeyevna. Sooner or later he would have to explain the situation to her, but the task was by no means a pleasant one and he was in no hurry to perform it. He had yielded to Sashenka, and under the circumstances that seemed the only thing he could have done. Indeed, he should have had a similar explanation with her before he proposed to Antonina Sergeyevna. However, his friend was such a good woman, such a sincere friend, that she was sure to realize the painfulness of his position and sympathize with him. He was going to take a turn or two across the bridge and then to return home, but somehow his feet took him to the Kirilechnaya, and he found himself in front of Antonina Sergeyevna's house.

She received him with a gay smile, but as she scanned his face she divined all and her eyes took on a melancholy expression.

"Good morning, my friend," he greeted her, with a sad note in his voice.

"Be seated, and never mind telling me what has transpired. I can see it all for myself."

He sat down with a sigh.

"Oh, you must let me tell you all about it."

"Wait till I tell you all about it," she returned, with a faint smile.

"I don't think you could, quite. You would never think of the motive, of the inconceivably cruel motive."

"Yes, I could. As if I hadn't predicted it! Youth is egotistic, Nikolai Ivanovich! It will tease one's old wounds without knowing it. Indeed, what does a young person know about heart wounds? Later on, when one becomes acquainted with these things, one grows more considerate of others, but unfortunately this often does not happen until it is too late."

"You do know everything," admitted Nikolai Ivanovich.

"Not only do I know it now, but I foresaw it all from the outset. I could have told you all this yesterday. Well, you had to take an oath, hadn't you?"

"Pretty nearly. I had to give my word of honor."

"I don't blame your daughter a bit. From her own point of view she is perfectly right. So far her love for her mother is the strongest, the most fervent, the deepest feeling she has ever experienced. When she falls in love herself she will realize that to love a living person does not necessarily imply any lack of faith to the dead. I speak frankly and without hesitation, because our positions are similar. I loved my husband as devotedly as you did your wife, but once fate has chosen to take them away, all that is left of them to us is their memory, which we cherish and keep enshrined in the depths of our hearts. Yes, their memory is sacred to us, but we are weak and sinful mortals. The living cannot content themselves with memories of the dead. They are looking for the living. That's the way we found each other."

"Let us wait, Antonina Sergeyevna. The future will be friendlier to us, perhaps."

"Oh, well, I fancy the best thing we can do is to dismiss it all from our thoughts."

He came away depressed, and yet, at the same time, he felt tranquilized and restored to his former mental equilibrium. After all, he was glad of what had transpired by mere accident, as it were, between himself and the good woman. True, it cost him a considerable amount of anguish, but this was not unaccompanied by certain rewards. Antonina Sergeyevna and himself had drawn closer to each other, their friendship had been confessed, legitimized.

Sashenka knew how to take herself in hand, and when Antonina Sergeyevna called, she bore herself with irreproachable tact. To the widow's house she now went but seldom, and for a prolonged visit never. Indeed,

Antonina Sergeyevna avoided to invite her. The relations between the two women were of that subtly decorous sort which usually establish themselves between two persons for the sake of a third. Things went on smoothly, and the uninitiated eye would have been unable to detect the slightest hitch. The heartiness of their former affection for each other was gone, however. All her good sense notwithstanding, and try as she would to look at the matter from Sashenka's point of view, Antonina Sergeyevna could not shake off a certain feeling of resentment. Be it as it might, Sashenka had played a decisive part in her life. If it had not been for her, or if she had taken a more sensible view of the whole thing, Antonina Sergeyevna's life would have assumed a new, and a better, course. Nikolai Ivanovich was just the man who could give her quiet, undisturbed happiness. Indeed, how much longer would she be entitled to that kind of happiness at all! Time presses onward. It does not pause to wait for human misunderstandings to adjust themselves, for the obstacles which prevent one from enjoying life to be removed. And so each time she met Sashenka she experienced an access of ill-feeling for the girl which she tried in vain to repress.

Sashenka, on her part, was scarcely conscious that her manner toward Antonina Sergeyevna was not the same as it used to be. As to her father, who was not much of an observer, things seemed to go in the most satisfactory manner. To his fate he had reconciled himself completely, and he sought additional comfort in what he regarded as the failure of the recent occurrence to mar the mutual relations of the two women.

Five years passed.

There are people of whom fate seems to take unceasing care, seeing to it that nothing about them is disturbed or changed in any abrupt way; that their lives flow on ever in the same peaceful and smooth channel. Some people seem to be doomed to a life of vicissitudes and upheavals, to change in a short time to the point of losing their former identity; others, on the other hand, pass through the world without any sharp changes, without any jolt-ings, remaining ever the same, day in, day out. Our friends belonged to the latter category. Sashenka had grown up and developed into riper womanhood; Antonina Sergeyevna had slightly gained in flesh, and there was an additional wrinkle or two about her eyes; Nikolai Ivanovich's hair was ever so faintly sprinkled with silver. That was all. Now, as in the life of people of this class, things will shape themselves according to a well-established rule, in the most ordinary, everyday way, there occurred to Sashenka that which occurs to most girls of her age. She fell in love with a young man, and the young man fell in love with her. He proposed and was accepted, and the two were to be married.

Sashenka's choice was perfectly worthy of her. He was quite handsome, young, with a university diploma and with an estate in the same province where the lands of Nikolai Ivanovich were situated. Otherwise, indeed, it would have been impossible for her to fall in love with him, or for her father to bless the marriage.

Nikolai Ivanovich watched the preparations for the wedding with an amused smile, underneath which lurked a vague sense of yearning. Something was going on in his soul. This could be seen in his face when he looked at his daughter. Reproach shone out of his eyes. But then, Sashenka was too absorbed in her happiness to take notice of such things.

Once, when they were alone, they fell into conversation.

"And so you are going to be married, Sashenka," said Nikolai Ivanovich. "Well, what are you two going to do with yourselves after the wedding?"

"We'll travel."

"And then?"

"And then we'll live in the country some time," she answered languidly.

"Well, you have my best wishes. As to myself, I shall be left all alone and will end my life in solitude."

"But, Papa, dear . . . you remember you wanted to . . ."

"What do you mean, my daughter?" asked Nikolai Ivanovich, who understood only too well what she was hinting at.

"Why, you wanted to marry. . . . Only . . ."

All at once she got up, and crossing over to him, she threw her arm around his neck.

"I was awfully cruel at that time, Papa darling," she said with a sob in her voice. "Why did you mind me?"

"Well, the nature of your objection was such as to make it impossible to ignore, my child," he said with sad meekness.

"Oh, that was terrible. I can hardly believe it possible. It is really too bad that one who knows absolutely nothing of life should be allowed to pass upon questions of such importance. I am willing to do anything to repair it, Papa. How will I ever be able to enjoy anything while you are languishing in loneliness? You don't think it's too late, do you? She doesn't feel hurt, does she? It was I who hurt her—well, I'll go and ask her forgiveness. I'll beg her; I'll implore her."

Nikolai Ivanovich smiled.

"No, my child, you mustn't do that," he said, stroking her hand. "It will all arrange itself somehow or another. Don't let it disturb your happiness, my darling. Well, I must leave you. I have some pressing work to do."

He retired to his room, but he did not work. The scene which had just taken place had completely upset his peace of mind. He did not regret it, however. He did well to remind her of what occurred five years ago, he said to himself. It was as well that she should know how cruel she was on that occasion. Let her regret it.

Spring came. The young couple set out on their wedding tour. Nikolai was overcome by a crushing sense of loneliness. It was as if the house had suddenly become empty. He could neither work nor stay indoors. He was afraid of becoming a sit-at-home lest he should grow fat and bloated. Hitherto unmindful of the flight of time, he suddenly began to count his years, and was shocked to find himself well on toward fifty. There were moments when he was literally seized with terror. Could it be that he was really doomed to end his days in solitude, in hopeless solitude?

It was in a moment of despair like this that he one day hastened to call on Antonina Sergeyevna. In her presence he felt relieved. The tie which adjusted itself between them five years ago had never been loosened. She was ever the same friend and comrade to him. This time, however, he looked dejected. Sombre thoughts had got a firm hold of his mind, and he was powerless to expel them.

"What makes you so downhearted this morning?" she asked.

"Some melancholy thoughts are bothering me, Antonina Sergeyevna."

She burst into laughter.

"Can't you get rid of them?"

"I can't, Antonina Sergeyevna."

"Then let me share them with you and relieve you of your burden."

"Well, if you could only stamp out of your mind a certain sad episode which took place five years ago. . . . If you could forget it as though it had never happened. . . . As to myself, I am the same as I was then, and I am ready to repeat the same words, the same prayer. . . ."

She heaved a sigh.

"It is not necessary to forget everything, Nikolai Ivanovich," she said. "What happened at that time is not anything that we ought to wish to forget. As to what you have said just now, I'll tell you frankly that everything must be done in season. To make a fool of myself is what I have always feared more than anything else. It is enough to appear ridiculous once to lose people's respect forever. From forty to fifty is the swiftest period of a woman's life. What would have been quite natural and simple at thirty-four would be found absurd and ludicrous at thirty-nine. I don't know how you feel about it, Nikolai Ivanovich; as to myself, it's too late. I have grown stout. I feel that to stand before the altar under such circumstances wouldn't be quite—how shall I put it?—quite an aesthetical performance," she said, with a smile. "In short, it is too late, Nikolai Ivanovich. There is such a thing as better never than late. Don't you think I am right?"

"You are always right, Antonina Sergeyevna," he answered dejectedly, kissing her hand.

They continued warm friends.

THE SHARE OF COUNT BRANTSEV

A Story by Abraham Cahan

Ainslee's Magazine / March 1901

It was about a year before his arrest that Count Brantsev learned to spell words by tapping on his table as political prisoners do in communicating through the walls of their cells. He was a spare, dark-complexioned young man, with a scholarly face which usually wore the expression of one straining to recall something. He had heard of captives who tapped out incoherent sentences in their sleep; and there was a story among the nihilists of two brothers who emerged from the fortress in such a state of mental excitement that during the first minutes of their meeting they could not speak except by knocking on the wall.

Brantsev knew that this was the one joy in the life of solitude and silence which was, sooner or later, to be his; and the reddish building where some of his dearest friends had been buried alive, with those sounds stealing their way from grave to grave, had an agonizing fascination for him. For the rest, his personal case appealed to him in an impersonal way.

When he found himself alone in a prison cell at last, his first feeling was one of relief. His simple, artless Russian nature had always revolted against the simulations and conspiracies of his revolutionary career, and his delicate nerves were so worn out by this incessant struggle with danger that to be powerless to continue it seemed a comfort. Here, at least, there was no arrest to fear, no spies to outwit.

Presently something seized his throat and his brain with a huge, massive grasp. He began to pace the stone floor, listening to his anguish as if it were something audible; but the grating noise of his own footfalls seemed to make common cause with that pang in his throat, and he stopped at the window. All he could see was a colorless stretch of wall and a square yard of sky. After a little he caught himself harkening to the stillness of his cell as though it, too, were sound. Finally he bethought himself of his signal code and hastened to spell on the wall.

"Who is there?"

There was no reply. He tried the opposite wall, and again his question remained unanswered.

Brantsev was seized with horror. His solitude seemed suddenly to have increased in size. He tapped again and again, now at this wall, now at that; but the adjoining cells were apparently empty. He seated himself on his cot. As his eye fell upon the fresh long hand upon his knee he exclaimed, inwardly: "I am so young! I have not yet begun to live!" The thought that he had had no chance to love or to be loved had hung about his brain ever since he became the quarry of political detectives. The thousand and one little tricks he had to play on the enemy, and all the exciting details of his "underground" life, had left him no mind for "affairs of the heart." Moreover, when one is ever expecting to be torn from all that one holds dear, why open a new source of pain in one's life? Indistinctly, however, he had always remembered that there was something, the sweetest blessing of existence, to which his soul was a stranger; and now, as he sat on his cot and it flashed upon him that he might be doomed never to know that happiness which was the gift of every being, his heart cried out to the whole world to take him back to the life in which everybody outside was rejoicing.

He beheld his revolutionary friends. They were speaking of him in subdued heartbroken accents. It was their manner rather than their words which implied admiration for his courage and devotion. Whereupon his bosom swelled with joy, and as he took another turn about the cell, he felt ready to mount the scaffold. He tried to picture himself with the noose tightening about his neck. One moment and the ordeal was over. It seemed the easiest thing in the world to go through. After a while he paused. That ponderous agony gripped him once more; and again he fell to walking backward and forward, in great, rapid strides.

More than three months had dragged away their tantalizing lengths. Brantsev's days of black misery alternated with periods of exuberant good spirits, which usually disappeared as suddenly as they came. Once or twice he fell into a stupor, sleeping day and night for a week together or sitting for hours in a state of mental and physical apathy. The three great themes of his daydreams were: his escape, his fancied love affairs, and the victory of the revolutionary party.

It was as if all his faculties had been transformed into imagination. The things he envisioned stood out with growing vividness. He made declarations of love now to this, now to the other young woman of his acquaintance; he threw open the cell door of every political prisoner in the empire; turned into a bird, he was flying about the land and chirping words of hope and light into the ears of the people. The stillness of his cell assumed all sorts of shapes and conditions in his mind. Sometimes it was a kind of alcohol evaporating on the flat of somebody's hand; at other times it impressed him as a living thing, hiding from him now in this corner, now in that. The place beyond the colorless prison wall, upon which he had never set his eyes, loomed in the form of a precipice, with a brook trickling at the bottom; and in some unaccountable way he took it into his head that this brook kept whispering:

"The sixth! The sixth! The sixth!"

Or he would fancy a company of blue butterflies sailing past his cell window.

"Where are you off to, little butterflies?"

"To our sweethearts, sir. We're in love! We're in love!"

And for long hours together he would hear the echo:

"We're in love! We're in love! We're in love!"

The whole world was in love. Every creature came in for its share in an abundance of joy—every creature but himself. Was he ever to receive that share of his?

It was early in the morning. The bit of sky up above was growing brighter and brighter. Count Brantsev was walking to and fro, his heart straining and struggling as a bird struggles to disengage itself from a boy's grasp. For some moments the terrible pang in his throat and his brain seemed something enjoyable. Then, in his helplessness, he had a fancy that if he pressed the top of his head hard against the wall and stood howling like a wounded beast, it would relieve him.

Suddenly, hark! a series of muffled sounds fell upon the wall across the room from his cot:

"Tup-tup; tup-tup—"

Brantsev trembled, as he looked round. His pain was gone.

"Who are you?" he hastened to spell.

"Sonya Malinina. And you?"

"Brantsev," he answered, with a fast-beating heart.

"Really?"

"Do you know me?"

For a minute or two the wall was silent. Then it murmured:

"I have never seen you. But how do you know I am not a spy?"

The question set his teeth on edge. It was like suggesting to a weary traveller that the well he has come upon may contain poison.

"Is this but another way of ascertaining whether I am one," he tapped,

492

with a pained look. "But neither of us would say anything which might be of interest to the rogues, anyhow. So where is the danger?"

"That's so," she assented.

She explained that she had been transferred from another cell the night before. Then they talked of their health, and she told him that she felt surprisingly well.

"I can't complain, either," he rejoined. "The only thing that worries me is the idiotic interest the meals are beginning to have for me. I am simply ashamed of myself. Of course, sometimes I do feel rather blue."

"When you do, just imagine the gendarmes prying into your soul and gloating over your low spirits. You will be sure to brace up. It always works with me. Another thing, set yourself to work on some psychological problem. Put your friends in all kinds of situations and determine what each of them would do or say. I find it good sport."

They compared notes about the size of the sky each of them could see, the guards, the commonplace books in the prison library, the promenade yard, their dinners. At this she asked Brantsev whether he took care to chew his food well.

"You must not think I bothered about these things when I was at large," she said. "But here one must look after one's health. Besides, it helps to kill time."

He told her of his former passion for mathematics and how he had suddenly lost all interest in it; and she described her grandfather, an impoverished, old-fashioned magnate, who would not let her read books "unbecoming a real lady," such as a history of Russian literature or Darwin's *Descent of Man*.

Mlle. Malinina proved to be familiar with the history of humanity's struggle for liberty. She spoke of Danton, Washington and Delescluze* as she would of personal friends, and dwelt on the Social Republic in a matter-of-course way which Brantsev thought at once amusing and touching.

He lay down on his cot with glowing cheeks. A whisper fluttered through his veins. The personified silence of the cell had vanished. The meaning of life was centered beyond the wall; and the better to contemplate his vision of Mlle. Malinina he shut his eyes. The general contour of a feminine figure was growing more distinct every instant, and at the same time its features were getting vaguer and vaguer. He strained his imagination until it seemed to hurt him. He opened his eyes. Compared to the other three walls, the one which divided him from the girl was like an animate creature now.

*Louis Charles Delescluze (1809–1871), a leading French radical.—*Ed.*

493

The next morning he awoke to the thought that a greater delight was in store for him; and no sooner had he regained full consciousness than he jumped out of bed and made for "Sonya's wall." He checked himself, however, for fear of waking her in case she was still asleep. The scrap of sky was his clock, and as he looked up its delicate tint told him it was between six and seven. He washed himself, and started to go back to his cot, when the wall saluted him.

"Good morning!" it said—the first greeting he had received since he was placed in this tomb of his.

The soft, muffled sounds went to Count Brantsev's heart, suffusing it with warmth and mystery.

"Good morning," he returned. "How long have you been up?"

"About an hour."

"Listen. It is perfect torture to talk without having the least idea what you look like. Describe your appearance and I shall describe mine. That will give our minds something to address themselves to as we converse."

Sonya went into raptures over the plan.

"To begin with, I am twenty-four and blond—very," she said. "But how am I to tell you what I look like? There is no danger of my flattering myself. On the contrary, I am afraid I may paint the devil blacker than he is, out of false modesty."

Brantsev blushed before the wall as he begged the young woman whom he neither saw nor heard not to do herself any injustice, and biting his lips shamefacedly, he waited for her reply.

"Well, I don't think I am bad-looking, for at the gymnasium, where the girls used to pass upon each other's looks as our teachers did upon our studies, I was rated rather high. But every time I look at my flat face and narrow eyes in the glass I feel awfully discouraged. Do you think you have enough? Well, a relative of mine who is a painter says I would make an ideal model for a picture of a *muzhik* girl of the vivacious type. I am a great giggler, you know."

She was anxious to convey to his mind a complete likeness of herself, but she gave up the attempt in despair. As well she might undertake to describe a melody. It was clear, however, that in her own brain there was a vivid picture. Not so the count. When he essayed to sketch his features for her he was surpised to find that he had but a very vague idea of them himself.

Sonya suggested that if he stood at a certain angle his window might serve him as a looking glass. He did, and the result was a minute description.

The next morning she asked him to pass his finger over his lower lip, and to tell her what sort of curve it formed, and when he had complied, she said:

"Now I think I can see you. Of course, it may be all nonsense. I might not be able to pick you out on the street after all. But such as my picture is, it is almost perfect. That lip of yours bothered me all night. Strange, isn't it?"

She inquired if he sang, and when he had transmitted an affirmative answer, she asked him how he would like to hum "Nechaev," a revolutionary song, in duet, she beating time.

Singing was strictly forbidden, so Brantsev scarcely uttered a sound; but as he whispered the words of the poem to the slow rhythm of her tapping, and mentally followed the doleful tone, tears came to his eyes.

"My heart is yearning for you, Sonya," he fingered out on the wall. "I cannot behold your lovely face as clearly as you think you see mine. But I can look at your beautiful spirit as if it stood smiling upon me. I am happy to be entombed by your side. I love you, I love you, dearest."

"And I love you, too," she returned.

They discarded the formal "you" for the familiar singular, and with their souls winged, they went on raving of their bliss. That brook beyond the prison fence seemed more real than ever. "The sixth! The sixth! The sixth!" it murmured to the count, as he beheld his spiritual self force its way through the pores of the wall which stood between him and Sonya.

"Listen," he said. "Suppose we invented some sort of lasting fireworks by means of which a proclamation, written in gigantic letters of gold, could be produced on the sky, calling upon the people to free themselves. Wouldn't that be fine?"

They dwelt upon the fantasy with delight, exchanging jokes at the expense of the police who were vainly trying to put out the fiery letters.

"Or suppose a golden trumpet were to appear from the clouds. I can see it burst into song. I can hear its words. They are no ordinary words. They can be seen and felt. And the people turn out in throngs and bare their heads as they look and listen. And those words drop from the trumpet's mouth in a shower of pearls, and the peasants gather them up, and although they are unlettered sons of the people and cannot read, yet they know what the words mean."

Sonya asked him if he could set it to verse. He confessed that he had done so weeks before, and at her exultant request, he spelled his crude lines again and again until she had them all safely by heart. He knew scores of celebrated poems, particularly from Nekrasov, which he recited to her by the hour.

"You must be an excellent declaimer," she said.

"What makes you think so?"

"I feel it. It may appear funny, but the sounds of your finger, as you telegraph poetry, are more expressive than when it's prose. I can feel the cadences, the rising and falling inflections. You put soul into your strokes, as though the wall was a piano. But, of course, it may be all pure imagination.''

A few weeks after this conversation Sonya said:

"There is a new 'political' on the other side of my cell.''

Brantsev turned pale.

"Who is he?''

"Ivan Pavlovich Panutin. He says he does not know you. Wait, he is calling. Don't be jealous, dearest. I am in earnest; don't be jealous. Nobody in the world could ever give my heart a feeling like that which has been there since I made your acquaintance. Nobody, nobody, dearest.''

He did feel jealous, and the pang it gave him was a novel torture. It came over him every time she spoke, or he fancied her speaking, to her new neighbor. He often paced up and down the cell gloomily, but he never thought of freedom in such moments. He could not leave this dungeon if he had his choice, he thought. But this state of his mind was not to last long. One morning, when his finger signalled, "Good morning, Sonya!'' there was no answer.

"Sonya!''

The wall made no reply. He reflected that she might be out for her walk, although he knew that it was too early in the day for that; but another hour had passed, and his tapping still remained unanswered.

During the following month Count Brantsev was transferred to a sub-aqueous cell in the fortress of Peter and Paul, St. Petersburg, whence, after a lapse of three years, he was transported to the remotest parts of Siberia.

THEODORE AND MARTHA

A Story by Abraham Cahan
September 25, 1901

One of the men whose acquaintance I made in the Austrian quarter was a lank, beardless German of forty or fifty, with the features of an old maid. He was from the Baltic provinces of the Czar, an excellent engraver, but a restless nomad (at the time I was introduced to him he had made three tours around the world) and one of the queerest fellows I had met in the neighborhood of Tompkins Square. He was insanely honest, quick-tempered, and jealous as a woman and vindictive as a savage. His name was Beneke. When I asked him whether his people were related to the famly of the celebrated psychologist, he answered:

"No, but an aunt of mine once rented a room to Richard Wagner, the composer. That was when he lived in Riga and was a poor man."

However, it is not of Beneke, but of Theodore Gerasimov, his Russian friend, that I wish to tell here. The German was full of stories and not without a certain insight into human nature. I think it was because I seemed never to get tired of listening to him that he conceived a liking for me. Of Theodore he spoke so often that I became familiar with every detail of the episode in which Beneke played an amusing part. It was at Philadelphia where he met him, but the strange tale opens in a Russian village during the last days of serfdom.

Fedka—as Theodore was then called—was the only serf in the village who wore leather boots. The others all tramped around in bark shoes. It was his master, Ivan Makarovich Pevtsov, a landowner of many souls, as the phrase went in those days, who kept him in showy clothes. Whenever Ivan Makarovich was in company and the serf-holders got to boasting of their subjects (much as American farmers do of their pumpkins) Pevtsov would sound the praises of Fedka.

The peasant lad was handy with all sorts of tools, and when he had a piece of chalk, he drew pictures of horses, cows or pigs which brought many a curse of admiration from the villagers. The nobleman's pompous old aunt, who had given Fedka lessons in reading, often went into ecstasies over his "capacity and love for learning." The pastime, however, had palled on her before Fedka was able to spell his name, and so he would have grown to be an illiterate, ignorant peasant like his father had not fate suddenly turned the flow of his youthful life into unforeseen channels.

One summer afternoon as Pevtsov was sauntering about the village, drowsily gazing from under the vast brim of his hat, his eye fell on Marthutka, the prettiest girl on his estate. She was eighteen, tall and strong, with yellow hair, a blood-and-milk complexion and eyes of the kind which speak of peace and good will. Her step and the swing of her arms as she walked had an effect of calm vigor. A few paces off Pevtsov saw his favorite, whom he recognized by his top-boots and the neat cut of his red blouse.

"Fedka? Marthutka?" he growled, lazily, pausing by a fence.

The lad marched up briskly and drew himself up in the dashing military fashion which his tedium-stricken proprietor had taught him. The girl crossed the road and smiled—a broad smile of repose and of something like humbled assurance. Fedka also grinned, in his thoughtful, pensive way, for, indeed, his dark face was clouded with sorrow, even when he laughed.

"Kiss her!" the nobleman commanded, in the manner of a boy setting a dog on his enemy.

Martha dropped her eyes and colored, but she dared not dodge, and Fedka bent over and smacked her flaming cheek, with the air of a man performing his duty.

"Do you call that a kiss? You can't fool your master, rogue that you are. None of your scamping. Now, then, little devil."

Fedka kissed Martha once more, this time with might and main.

"That's different. Begone!"

The two had not proceeded many steps when the *muzhik* lad was called back.

"How would you like to marry her?" his master asked.

"I'm too young to be married, sir."

"Silence, impudent thing. It's none of your business whether you are young or old. You're going to marry Marthutka. She is the prettiest lass in the village, and you're going to be her husband. Away with you."

Fedka did not stir.

"Away with you, I say."

"Take pity, little father; I don't care to be a married man."

"Nobody asks you whether you do. You don't know what is good for you. Go tell your father to make ready for the wedding."

Fedka did not dislike the girl, but he had an independent little spirit. Had he been allowed to follow his own taste he might have chosen her of his own free will some day. As it was, his heart revolted. He went down on his knees, kissed his master's feet, cried, begged. But this only made things worse. Pevtsov was anything but a hard-hearted man. People of his class were accustomed to unreasoning obedience, however, and the most respectful resistance was apt to make a tyrant of the best of them. He flew into a passion and told the peasant boy that unless he married Martha that very week he would be flogged to death.

Fedka had no choice but to do his lord's bidding; and his misery began at once. He lamented his lost youth as though he had suddenly become an old man, and was ashamed to show his head among the other young fellows of the village, as if his marriage had been inflicted as a penalty.

Martha now seemed the homeliest creature in the world. Everything she did or said was loathsome to him, and he blamed her for their compulsory union as if it had all been her doing. What repelled him more than anything else was her prominent gums. Often when he was in the grip of his anguish and she chanced to open her mouth, those big, gleaming gums of hers made his head swim with disgust. At the same time he was almost thankful to them for being so large, thus giving him a pretext to hate her.

Another thing for which Martha was obnoxious to Fedka was the good-natured evenness of her disposition. She bore her woes without a murmur, forever serene, forever ready to smile and to expose those blood-red gums which he had taught himself to abhor so acutely.

He did everything he could think of to make life a burden to her; but so far from showing any resentment she took it all with a certain air of indulgence—like a mother forgiving the irritableness of a sick child. And this was another source of venom for Fedka.

One day, shortly after the emancipation of the serfs, as Theodore walked along the road, with Martha dragging herself behind him, he caught sight of their former master. To spite the nobleman, he turned upon his wife with words of abuse. Ivan Makarovich became furious.

"I'll have you flogged!" he said. And to prove that although serfdom had been abolished his authority was not yet a thing of the past, he hastened to have the constable put his threat into execution.

Theodore slept in the woods that night. His native village never saw him again.

Thirty-three years had elapsed. It was a winter evening in 1894. Theodore Gerasimov sat in a spacious, bleak-looking room in one of the humbler quarters of Philadelphia. One of the walls was covered with books. The cheap lamp on the table lit up the absorbed face of a man of fifty. When he looked up from his book he fixed on the lamp a pair of sad, wistful eyes.

Unlike some of his fellow immigrants, he had made no money in America. Instead, circumstances had put him in the way of something which he now sincerely placed above wealth. Some educated Americans who took an interest in the melancholy young Russian had made an intelligent man of him. He had dreamed of a learned career, but the indolent Slavic blood in him stood in his way. The result was a penniless jack-of-all-trades with a valuable library, a passionate reader with a mind full of unsystematized information.

The older he grew, the lonelier he felt. When he thought of the wife he had deserted, it was as if he were charged with a crime which had been committed before he was born. He had never been able to throw off a vague feeling that somewhere, far away, there stirred something which was an inexhaustible source of discomfort to him. He did not write to his birthplace, because the courage failed him to recall the dead past to life; and yet the burden of that past lay on his soul, its weight increasing as the years wore on.

He made a crude sketch of his native village, and sometimes, when he was alone in his room, he would take it out of the huge volume which was its shrine and sit gazing at it until his solitude began to frighten him. He often whispered to himself in Russian. He had not used his mother tongue for thirty-three years, and all he remembered of it was a score or two of broken phrases and words. But then, his present horizon was so much wider than the one which had surrounded him in his birthplace that the entire vocabulary which made up his mother tongue would strike him as a sorry affair now. Besides, most of his ideas were of American birth, so that his English was really as much of a native language to Theodore as his Russian. The songs of his childhood he had retained much better than he had his language, and recently, when he hummed one—for the first time in many years—there was a lump in his throat.

He had grown impressionable and sensitive as a prisoner. The images of his mind were full of life. When he was absorbed in soliloquy he heard the sound of his own voice. The place of his birth, with Martha for a central figure, scarcely ever left his brain now. "If I were only sure she was alive," he often sighed.

One day, in his reverie, he had fancied Martha drowning herself to put an end to the life of loneliness and disgrace to which he had condemned her. He could almost see the livid corpse floating along the native brook. The ghastly picture was growing more vivid and more importunate every day. He saw it in his shop, and he saw it when he was intent on his reading. At night, when the room was dark and he lay in bed courting sleep, the floating corpse would seem so real that he often had to get up and light the gas to dispel the hallucination. His burden grew and grew, and the keener his misery the fainter was his heart when he thought of writing to his old home.

It was during this period that he had met Beneke. An intimacy had sprung up between the two. Theodore had unbosomed himself to the German and invited him to share his room with him.

"I hate to sleep alone," he had said. "I am getting to be a big fool."

As Gerasimov now sat gazing at the lamp, the door swung open and in came Beneke.

"Is that you?" the Russian inquired without removing his eyes from the light.

"Yes, but don't let me disturb you. Go on with your reading," answered the beardless man, tenderly. A minute or two later he said: "Excuse me, Theodore, only one question: how do you feel?"

"I'm all right," the other replied, reluctantly. By degrees, however, he let himself be drawn into conversation, and for the hundredth time he was made to describe his feelings with regard to his past. "Yes, the whole thing interests me like something read in a book. At times I feel as though it had all happened yesterday, but even then I don't seem to have any personal connection with it. I have forgotten my native tongue and I am an American, yet my heart is Russian: it's so sad most of the time."

My German friend remembered this conversation and the whole scene surrounding it with particular vividness, because it was the last heart-to-heart talk the two men had at that period of Beneke's story. The engraver was madly attached to his roommate. He drank in his every word and overwhelmed him with attentions, but Theodore was beginning to weary of him.

"Oh, how I loved him!" Beneke exclaimed, with something like fury, as he described his first quarrel with Gerasimov to me. "I knew his weakness. Believe me, I understood him through and through. Indeed, if you know anything about me you ought to know that I am no fool, that I have eyes to see. Don't you think so?"

I had to assure him that I did before he went on:

"Well, the worst thing about him was his vanity. He was always taken up with the fact that he was well-read and full of wisdom, don't you know. I think all self-educated people are like that. They keep reminding themselves that there are others who are not educated. It's like a poor fellow who becomes rich. He can never forget that he has lots of money. Why? Because he was not born to comfort and can never get used to it. Don't you think this is a good point?"

I said I did, and he continued, beamingly: "Well, if he had not been so conscious of his education he would have written to his wife long before I met him. 'How can I?' he once said to me. 'She is a peasant woman, so ignorant, so uncivilized, while I am a man of the nineteenth century.' That was his favorite boast—'I am a man of the nineteenth century.' Well, that let the cat out of the bag. He was simply afraid she might come to claim him, and how could he live with a peasant woman? Ha, ha, ha! But wait till you hear the end of it. He was a good fellow all the same; else I would not have loved him. He had a warm heart, and that's what I like more than anything else in people, don't you?"

By degrees Beneke discovered that his idol thought him a bore. The beginning of their rupture came one evening when Theodore went out for a walk without asking the German to join him. Beneke's ecstatic devotion then turned to a fervor of hatred.

"You're a false man," he once said to Theodore. "I was a fool, but now I have found you out. Do you know what you are? The biggest scoundrel in the world. I'll fix you."

Beneke then found himself in Moscow. To be sure, it was not for the express purpose of "fixing" his enemy that he had gone there, but once in central Russia he could not help visiting Gerasimov's birthplace, a moderate distance from the ancient capital of the Czars.

A few weeks later Theodore received a letter from Martha which informed him, in a matter-of-fact way that "the wife given him of God was praying for his health and welfare"; that she was well and had never abandoned the hope of being reunited to "him whom God had appointed to be her companion and master."

"When he received this letter, he came near dropping dead," Beneke said to me. "He told me all about it when I saw him again. You see, it seemed as if he was going to become the husband of a peasant woman who was a perfect stranger to him, but little by little he became interested. He told me how he used to go to the looking glass to study his own weary face and to think of Martha's. The past had arisen from its grave, you know. He thought of his wife 'as a fountain of peace' and all that sort of thing. He was going to do his duty and gave himself no end of credit for being so good. He was a saint, a martyr, and all because he was going to live with his legal wife. Ha, ha! Well, he was counting without the hostess. Ha, ha, ha! Look here, have you ever come across a truly religious person? I don't mean one who spends a lot of time praying and all that sort of thing. I mean a man or a woman whose heart is full of it; who believes deeply and truly and makes no fuss about it, either. Well, Martha was that kind of person. When I saw her for the first time I was astounded by the way she looked. She was strong and fresh and her face was at least fifteen years younger than her years. When I told her I had a message from her husband she only smiled and grew pale a little. She asked me for details. Then she said in a whisper: 'God is merciful.' You would not believe it, but she made me blush, as if I was only a fool, and she, although a peasant woman, my superior.

"When Theodore stood waiting for the train that was going to bring her to him from New York, he kept saying to himself that he must forget the difference between him and her, and try to treat her like an equal, but when she came—they recognized each other at once, and she made the sign of the cross and was shocked to find him struggling with his native tongue—he felt as I had when I first met her. She really looked bigger than the 'man of the nineteenth century.' He blushed and stammered, and finally his old days came back to him and he burst into tears and sobbed and begged her to forgive him, and all that sort of thing. As you see, my revenge turned out to be a blessing. Ha, ha! Of course I had acted as a scoundrel, and to tell you the truth I felt so wretched that I had to go back to this country to ask Theodore's forgiveness. He forgave me quickly enough. Ha, ha! I saw them together. He told me he felt young again. Of course she was an ignorant peasant, and he—'a man of the nineteenth century,' but she was a moral force. Her presence soothed him—she was 'a fountain of peace,' after all. Oh, how happy he was. Only his happiness in this world was not to last long. He died about a year and a half after that!''

REVOLUTION THREATENS RUSSIA
April 26, 1902

An educated young Russian, who is said to be one of the active figures in the revolutionary movement which is spreading in the southern districts of his native country, has arrived in this city on a short visit. His stay here has nothing to do with the political struggle with which he is connected at home, and his friends have taken every precaution to conceal his identity.

"He is here on business of a purely private character," the man with whom the nihilist is stopping explained. "It is a family affair, in fact, and he must get back to his native town as quickly as he can, so it would not do to have some of the Czar's spies shadowing his movements and causing his arrest the moment he sets foot on Russian soil, would it?"

The young revolutionist is a college student and one of the victims of the recent conflict between the men of a certain university and the local authorities. He has been in touch with the revolutionary propaganda and speaks of these matters in a tone of authority and personal experience.

He was found sorting some newspapers and magazines which a friend in this city had obtained for him from a fellow revolutionist.

"Most of these papers are printed in Russia," he said. "The underground press of our party has never been so active before. Several of the larger factory towns print a revolutionary paper each. The police and the gendarmes are straining every nerve to discover these printing offices, of course, and in some instances they are successful, but in almost every case a new establishment takes the place of the detected one within a few days after the raid. Our leading 'underground' organ is called *Iskra* ["The Spark"], and has been coming out regularly and circulating throughout the country during the last few months."

Speaking generally, the nihilist said, the movement was getting hotter every day, and to judge from appearances Russia was "trembling on the verge of a revolution." By way of illustration he told how in the theatres of a certain southern city revolutionary songs were sung by the audience at every performance, the authorities being powerless to interfere.

"The day before I left I went to see a play. While we sat looking at the stage a rain of revolutionary leaflets came pouring from the galleries, accompanied by cries of 'Down with despotism! Long live liberty!' The police made a dash for some of the men who did the shouting, but in the commotion that followed they were worsted by the audience. Scenes of this sort were utterly impossible about five years ago. Now they are quite a common occurrence.

"The treatment of the revolutionists by the authorities is a mixture of medieval brutality and timidity of the kind which characterized the French government on the eve of the great revolution. On the one hand the prisons are overcrowded and men are being slowly killed in isolated cells for the most ludicrous trifles; on the other hand, the police are often attacked by bands of revolutionists in broad daylight without anybody being arrested as a result of the conflict. One morning a crowd of university students and workingmen unfurled some revolutionary flags in front of a public place in Odessa. They burst out singing revolutionary hymns and calling the authorities all sorts of names. The police charged them with bare sabres, but in this particular case nobody was injured, and the guardians of law and order left the scene without making a single arrest.

"The point is that every passerby and many of the people who had come out of the neighboring houses to look on expressed remarkable sympathy with the paraders. On another occasion a number of revolutionists were all but hacked to pieces by a detachment of cavalry, but then, there have been numerous examples where the soldiery has refused to shoot at our people.

"The most significant feature of the present movement is the open sympathy which hundreds of army officers have evinced for our party. It stands that without the army our movement would have to wait a long while before anything in the form of a big open demonstration would be possible. Indeed, one must not lose sight of the fact that our strength is concentrated in the cities, being mainly embodied in the factory population, while the peasantry is for the most part still too ignorant to appreciate the meaning of our agitation, except in a crude and naive way. Now, as the army is largely made up of this element of the population, there would be mighty little hope for us were it not for the fact that the thing is in the air, so that the soldiers, and more particularly their officers, imbibe our ideas from the very atmosphere that surrounds them.

"I suppose you know from the dispatches that have been printed in the newspapers how in several instances the authorities have been rather reluctant to call out the military. The revolutionary sentiment of which I speak has become so general that the government is loath to command soldiers to fire at a crowd of revolutionary students and workingmen for fear of having them disobey orders. An interesting story is told of the colonel of a certain regiment in a western province who on visiting the barracks one morning found some of the young officers reading the *Spark*. He was thunderstruck, but when he ordered some sergeants to lock them up they refused to comply. One of the officers, a good-natured young fellow, then invited his superior to a discussion of politics, the upshot being that the colonel declared himself a revolutionist. The matter somehow came to the ears of the governor of the province, who communicated it to the general in command of the local division, whereupon the latter dropped his hands in despair, saying: 'These are awful times. One can't trust his own self. I am afraid to think of these things lest I, too, should become a republican.'

"The movement is headed by a compact organization known as the Social Democrat Party of Russia. Its programme is practically the same as that of every socialist party in Europe. Mind you, I say 'socialist,' for, indeed, there is not a single anarchist in our ranks. The anarchists are opposed to government in any form. They are opposed to parliaments, voting and what they call majority rule, whereas these things are just what we are fighting for. The socialist system of universal cooperation, based on the principle of representative government, is our goal, but for the present we want those popular institutions, which every civilized country in the world enjoys as a matter of course.

"If you hear of some of our fellows shooting a minister or a general or a chief of police, you must not run away with the idea that we believe in violence as a system—as a regular method of warfare. If you were familiar with the conditions which led up to the shooting of Bogolepov, Sipyagin, or to the attempt on the life of Trepov, you would admit that there was no other way out of the situation. You have read in your papers how every class of the population made merry over the death of Sipyagin. This shows you the feeling of the country in cases of this sort. The ministers are a lot of lawless brutes, and the indignation aroused by their methods, particularly by the summary way in which innocent people are thrown into prison or literally butchered, beggars description.''

The young revolutionist was asked whether the present movement was a continuation of the ''terroristic'' crusade which resulted in the assassination of Alexander II in 1881. He shook his head and then, upon reflection, he said:

''It is, and yet is not. A few days ago, on April 15, we commemorated the death of Sofiya Perovskaya, Zhelyabov and the other three men who were executed as the result of the trial which was held over the persons implicated in the great plot on the life of Alexander II. Well, at that time, or rather a few years later, some of the revolutionists of those days lost heart. People thought these men and women had thrown away their lives on a lost cause. Sofiya was the daughter of a former governor of St. Petersburg, you know. She belonged to one of the best families in the land, yet she gave her life to the movement. So it was thought that the sacrifices which she and hundreds like her were making were all doomed to be fruitless. Yet now one cannot help seeing that the movement for popular institutions and personal liberty has made tremendous headway. It is a new movement with new methods, but the sacrifices borne by the revolutionists of twenty years ago have borne fruit.

''The old terrorists looked upon terror as a systematic and leading mode of warfare. The Social Democrats of today have no such idea in their programme. If a man makes up his mind to kill an obnoxious official it is his own business. He does not do it in the name of any party, but upon his own responsibility. As a matter of fact, we don't believe in such methods. Our movement is so strong that we don't need them. We believe in agitation and in open demonstrations.

''The terrorists expected the revolution to come from a handful of well-organized, fearless and self-sacrificing fellows. We look forward to the day when the working classes will make a bold and decisive stand for free institutions. The college students and the educated classes generally go hand in hand with them, but it's the workingmen who are regarded as the bulwark of our real strength.

''The student troubles usually originate in some conflict between the young men and the authorities arising from some oppressive piece of university legislation, but in almost every instance these outbreaks have a revolutionary significance and are associated with the political propaganda of the Social Democrats. You see, the despotic regime with which the Russian student is expected to put up at the university is a miniature picture of the political conditions which are weighing down the whole country. So in protesting against these oppressions the university man inevitably feels in touch with the greater movement, with the one tending to the emancipation of the whole people. Of course, a great many of our college boys are members of the secret party and take an active part in its agitation.

"Scores of educated young men of my acquaintance spend much of their time among the workingmen, teaching them, reading books on political economy and kindred topics to them. The gendarmes and the spies are active, but we are far more active and alert than they are, and while thousands of our men and women go to prison and to Siberia, the army of such secret teachers and their pupils is growing rapidly. The working people are getting to be quite an intelligent class with us. They have unions, and in many cities they are well organized. Now, as unions are forbidden, all these organizations are 'underground' revolutionary societies affiliated with the Social Democratic Party.

"At the time Alexander II was assassinated, the movement was almost confined to a handful of students. Now it embraces the urban population of thirty or forty provinces. I recently had a talk with one of the old-timers. He took part in some of the plots of the terrorists and spent many years in prison and in exile. He said that the revolutionists of his day were self-sacrificing dreamers, while those of today represented a living and swiftly rising cause.

"Finland is getting bolder and bolder; the south is fidgety; the universities are hotbeds of revolution; the factories are so many barracks, drilling soldiers for the coming great conflict between the government and people; ministers are being shot and those who still survive turn cowards; the Czar himself has lost his head; the court is in a perpetual panic, in a flurry of general distrust; the virus of the revolutionary propaganda is eating its way to the hearts of the best people in the land. Verily, things in Russia are beginning to look much as they did in France at the time Louis XVI felt constrained to convoke a legislative assembly representing the various classes of the people.

"The father of a friend of mine is connected with large manufacturing interests in the south. In a talk I recently had with him he dropped a remark which sizes up the situation better than volumes of sociology would do it. 'The business of the country is developing in fine style,' he said. 'Our industries are growing, so we'll have to get a parliament, I suppose. You see all nations that are powerful in business have parliament. It's all very well for a slow, indolent people to be ruled in the good old way; but when the country people know enough to hustle and do things, the people begin to feel like taking a hand in their own government.'

"The same man said that the great Siberian Railway was going to do more for Russian liberty than a whole army of propagandists could ever expect to accomplish. This is true. It tells the story of the present situation in a nutshell.

"Russia has made great progress during the last decade or two. It has developed wonderfully along economic lines, and this development is bound to find its reflection in politics. People have better chances of hearing what is going on in other lands nowadays. Try as the government will, it cannot keep the population from contact with the current of life in the civilized world at large. In the first place, the number of common people who can read is getting larger every day, all the efforts of the authorities to the contrary notwithstanding. In the second place, the increasing industrial resources of the country throw larger and larger masses of the village population into the cities, where one quickly learns what is going on in France, England or America, for instance. All this has the effect of widening the horizon of the lower classes and opening their eyes to the fact that they are living under a regime which in other places has long since been discarded. Still more important is the experience which the masses get with the police in their struggle for better wages and more humane treatment at the hands of their employers.

"A few months ago the operatives of a mill asked me to deliver a course of lectures to them on political economy and politics. It had to be done in secret, of course, but this only whetted their appetite for our gatherings. We met in a large barn in the very heart of the city, several of our friends playing their accordions and banjos outside to ward off 'snoopers.' They would play their instruments lustily, with pretended rapture, so as to drown the voices within. Well, I was curious to know what had led my pupils to revolutionary ideas, and asked each of them to answer that question. Some of them hesitated, being unable to trace out the successive steps by which they had reached their new views and proclivities. Upon the whole, however, they all spoke quite intelligently, and it became clear that the stand taken by the government in every conflict between capital and labor is one of the greatest sources of popular discontent. 'When I was a boy,' said one elderly man, 'I used to think the Czar was the bigger father of the two.' When I asked him what he meant, he said with a gesture of impatience, 'Why, don't you know what I mean, sir? You're an educated man; you know everything, yet a trifle like this you don't know. Every man has a father, hasn't he? Well, that's his own father, the husband of his mother. Now, besides this one we all have another father who takes care of the whole bunch—that's the Czar. So every man has two fathers, hasn't he? At least that's the way I used to think when I was a fool; and I was sure the Czar was the greater and more important father of the two. Later on I found out my mistake. I had a chance to see for myself

508

the kind of fathers the officials are to us poor fellows. When I asked for a raise the boss of the shop knocked two teeth out of my mouth, and had me arrested in the bargain, and when my shop mates went out on strike soldiers beat them with the butt ends of their rifles till many of them fell bleeding on the pavement. They called us rebels, the officials did, and said that when a man won't work unless he gets better pay he is an enemy of the Czar. That settled me. I made up my mind there and then what sort of father he was, the Czar. We got a good deal of help and money from students and other educated people. Then I said to myself: 'These gentlemen are our brothers. They and we poor wretches ought to stick together and see to it that we get a little more liberty and justice.'

"I have quoted that elderly workingman, because his words have clung to my memory and because they are so typical of what one hears from people of his class these days. What he said is perfectly true. The educated classes, the well-informed and refined men and women who fraternize with the factory people, teach them and follow their lead in the struggle for liberty. I say 'follow their lead' advisedly. It is these working people who stand at the head of the movement. All we do is to keep track of them to fall into line when something breaks loose. Of course, university riots have often precipitated a general conflict between the authorities and the rest of the population, but then, in some instances these riots would scarcely have occurred had it not been for the fact that the university students were confident of support on the part of the masses.

"No revolution could be brought about by students alone. The keynote to the present situation is the awakening of the working people and the ties of sympathy which bind them and the educated classes into one solid revolutionary army.

"That the government is becoming aware of all this is evidenced by its present anxiety to parade as the friend of the working people. The governor of one of the northwestern provinces, for instance, recently issued an order compelling every employer of labor to post a notice in his shop to the effect that he was not allowed by the authorities to keep his hands longer than ten hours a day. Circulars are being sent out to the police enjoining them not to maltreat working people. But this only tends to impress the population with the strength of the revolutionary movement.

"During the early stages of the movement, great stress was laid on the importance of the agricultural population. The revolutionists of those days firmly believed that the solution of the country was going to be worked out by the peasant. All that was necessary, so they argued, was to arouse him to a sense of the great wrong of which he was the victim. Hundreds of well-bred, cultured young men and women would don peasant garb and try to mingle with the village people, affecting their speech and leading their life. The result was a few thousand arrests and all sorts of atrocities, but no revolutionary movement among the peasants. The Russian tiller of the soil has been kept in a state of abject misery and bondage too long to have any backbone or intelligence left in him.

"Here is an amusing incident which will give you an idea on this particular point: A political prisoner in charge of two gendarmes jumped out of the window of a flying train. The scene took place recently near the town of Pskov, the revolutionist being on his way from Minsk to St. Petersburg, where he was to be put in prison. The train was stopped too late. After hiding in the woods for some time, the runaway made his appearance in a nearby village. There he was arrested by some peasants in compliance with an order from the local authorities directing them to look out for a runaway prisoner. The appearance of the man they had caught was a puzzle to them, however. 'Look here,' they said, 'you are dressed like nobleman, like an educated man, while here we have been ordered to catch a criminal. You don't look like a thief, do you?' The revolutionist admitted that he did not, and began to tell them what sort of prisoner he was. He drew a picture of the suffering of the people under the present regime which drew tears from the eyes of his captors. 'How true! How true!' they said. He delivered quite a lecture to them, and they listened with bated breath. Yet at the end of the impromptu meeting one of the crowd said: 'You are right, and we can see that you are our friend, and that you are sacrificing yourself for the good of the people, but what are we going to do? We have wives and children. We can't afford to be locked up, and if we let you go the police will put us in prison.' So with tears in their eyes, they tied the revolutionist hand and foot and delivered him up to the authorities.

"About the same time the employees of a factory in St. Petersburg attacked two gendarmes who were taking a student to a railway station, and after a fierce fight liberated him. Things of this sort are quite a common occurrence these days. In one case two runaway 'politicals' were concealed in a shop. When the foreman threatened to call the police the operatives told him that if he did his life would be in danger. In another place a student girl was taken care of by the employees of a well-to-do seamstress. When the proprietress of the place refused to let her stay at her place, for fear of bringing the gendarmes down on her establishment, the girls threatened to go out on strike, and the prosperous seamstress had to submit."

17
LITERATURE AND TRUTH

HOWELLS ON ZOLA
February 26, 1898

A representative of this paper called on William Dean Howells, the novelist, for an interview on the Zola trial. The two writers have much in common, not alone in their views upon the art which they serve, but also in their broad and warm devotion to the cause of humanity, in their self-denying sympathy for the suffering and the downtrodden of the human race, in their readiness to take up cudgels against everything that is unjust or untrue. Mr. Howells is fond of characterizing realism as truth in fiction. If so, then the two novelists are brothers in arms in their struggle for the truth in life as well as in letters.

Mr. Howells, who will next month celebrate his sixty-first birthday, looks considerably younger than his age. He entered his library with a brisk and elastic step, and as he welcomed his visitor his voice and smile had the heartiness of youth.

It was an informal chat on one of the absorbing topics of the day rather than what is ordinarily understood by an interview, and during the greater part of the conversation the distinguished author seemed to be deeply interested in the subject.

"The encouraging part of the whole affair," Mr. Howells said, "is the fact that it was brought to a trial at all. The trial of Emile Zola means, of course, a second trial of Esterhazy and Dreyfus, and, although justice had no more chance this time than it had at the court-martial, still it was a good thing to compel the Government to give Zola a hearing. Imagine the same thing on

511

German or Russian soil. No matter how gross the injustice, the Government would not have allowed the case to be reopened. It takes a country like ours, a Republic, for that. Monarchies cannot afford to establish such precedents.

"Take the case of Mrs. Maybrick.* I am not familiar with the details of the trial, but it is well known that the judge who had charged the jury afterward died in a lunatic asylum.

"Zola's trial? Why, of course, it was amusing," Mr. Howells said, with a hearty laugh. "We here can hardly realize such scenes in a law court. The only instance I remember where one of the actors in a trial was allowed to talk back to the lawyers and judges was in the case of Guiteau.† Guiteau's talk was not stopped by the judge, and so much the better for justice on this particular occasion. Why, Guiteau was a madman, and I can't see how they could hang him. No, there was not much justice at the Zola trial. But is not Zola's an enviable position to be in? What a glorious thing it is to have a chance to fight for justice as he does! The whole country is against him. His enemies have triumphed; but they know as well as Zola that the real victory is on his side."

Mr. Howells said this in the simple way which characterizes him, but as he spoke a light of admiration came into his eyes and there was a tremor of enthusiasm in his voice. "Voltaire," he continued, "had a similar experience. He fought the French Government on behalf of a poor outraged family. There is this difference, however. Voltaire carried his point, while Zola must go to jail for the boldness with which he proclaimed the truth. But victory in the higher sense is the result in his case as it was in Voltaire's."

Speaking of Zola's works, Mr. Howells said: "In point of fact his recent novel, *Debâcle,* foreshadowed the whole episode of which Zola is now the hero. Ah! what a great novel that is! In it, as in all his stories, Zola builds upon such a broad, solid foundation—the truth. After Tolstoy, I consider him the greatest creator of modern fiction. He is an epic poet, and his works contain overwhelming arrays of facts presented in the manner which the highest art alone can attain. His stories throb with life and truth. Indecent? Yes, he is indecent—I admit that—but not immoral. The truth presented as it is in his novels cannot be immoral."

Asked about the part the Parisian students have taken in the anti-Zola demonstrations, Mr. Howells said, with a merry laugh: "Whoever took college boys seriously? They are mere children, and to attach importance to what they do in a matter like the anti-Dreyfus affair would be ridiculous."

* Florence Maybrick poisoned her husband.—*Ed.*

† Charles J. Guiteau assassinated President James A. Garfield on July 2, 1881.—*Ed.*

The conversation then turned upon other authors and books, whereupon, speaking of the present vogue of *Quo Vadis,* Mr. Howells said: "I have not read any of Sienkiewicz's historical novels, but I know his *Children of the Soil,* and as I was reading that story of modern Polish life I felt in the presence of a great master."

ZANGWILL AND GARLAND
February 24, 1899

Israel Zangwill and Hamlin Garland spoke on the novel before the Nineteenth Century Club at Delmonico's last night. It was Mr. Zangwill's farewell discourse, as he is to sail for England on the *Campania* at 3 o'clock tomorrow afternoon. He expects to return to this country at an early date, however. His *Children of the Ghetto* and *The King of Schnorrers* are to be played by Richard Mansfield, and Mr. Zangwill will in all probability assist in their production. He was given a most cordial reception last night.

Chairman Taylor of the Nineteenth Century Club introduced the English novelist as "a gentleman whom William Dean Howells characterizes as one of the most brilliant minds of this age." Mr. Zangwill's subject was "The Novel," and what he said comprised his well-known lecture on "Fiction as the Highest Form of Art," which he has delivered here several times. It was adapted to the occasion, however, and contained some new matter. "I have been so often accused of brilliancy," he said, "that tonight on my last appearance in this country, so far as my present visit is concerned, I want to be dull.

"When a London paper warned its readers not to take me seriously I wondered where I could give vent to my irrepressible earnestness.

"Every form of art has its parasites," Mr. Zangwill further said, by way of preface: "Almost as much has been written on the novel as in it. I propose to glorify as a critic what I am trying to practice as a novelist. The novelist is underrated by the critics and overrated by the tax collector. We all know that fools rush in where angels fear to tread. Sometimes the angels fear to tread because fools rush in to criticize. But then, angels have no need to tread. They can fly, and the higher and wider their flight the better. My friend, Max Nordau, says artists are mad. He forgot to define two things, however: 1. What is art? 2. What is insanity?"

513

The central idea of Mr. Zangwill's lecture was that while the sciences are each taken up with a special class of phenomena and treat life in a lifeless way, fiction alone deals in life in all its varying aspects, presenting it as life. "Fiction is the only science that is complete. It includes all sciences plus life and beauty. The novelist deals in everything, from theology to codfish. The scientist pigeonholes the universe. The novelist paints it in all its glory and greatness. The scientist classifies the fly, but the fly does not know it has been classified. The scientist impales the butterfly. The novel lets it flutter full of life and beauty. The truth lies in the butterfly. In fiction everything is true except names and dates. In history nothing is true except names and dates. The great law which fiction follows is the law of attention. Nothing but what attracts attention and is retained by memory is taken by the artist. Art deals in essences, not in accidents."

Mr. Zangwill spoke as an unqualified realist. "Truth is beauty, beauty is truth," he quoted. "But truth without art is not enough to make good fiction."

The next speaker was Hamlin Garland.

Mr. Garland began his address by paying some graceful compliments to Mr. Zangwill. Continuing, he said:

"I do not believe the fictionist can take his art too seriously. An artist may take himself too seriously, but his art, never! The painter has been called the man with the seeing eye, the musician the man with the hearing ear, but the novelist must both see and hear. The great novelist approaches the omniscience of an archangel. He must know something about all arts and all about his own. He must have the cold exactness of science, and he must have also a sympathy quick and all-embracing as flame. He must condemn, without despising, and exalt, without sentimentality. He must not preach, and yet it is his high office to instruct in the highest ways of living. His work must make for justice, and consequent good will among men; but he must not preach.

"The novel, what is it? It is a poem, a song, a history, a drama, a studio of sculpture, a gallery of paintings, a message of light. It is the *book;* all other arts are merely its illustrations and accompaniments. Consider the void, the silence, the monotony which would result were the fiction of the world suddenly to be swept away! There are novels (and romances) which we could spare; but fiction, the art preservative of all arts, is seen to be the dominant and ever-expanding, all-inclusive art of our day. It commands the present, it will possess the future in some form. It is, as Mr. Zangwill has said, the highest form of truth, because it is synthetic. It fuses and blends. That is to say it creates.

"The great novels of America have always had truth for their motive. *The Blithedale Romance, Silas Lapham, Hugh Wynne,* and *Theron Ware** have been marked examples of the synthesis which forms the highest form of truth; but to expect any novelist to bring together and fuse into one work all the diverse and widely separated types of American citizenship is to expect the impossible. The 'great American novel' of which we endlessly talk is as impossible as the great British novel. If it were to appear no one would read it. Our present stage of fiction is one of recording with the keenest insight and wealth of detail the significant and characteristic life in various sections of our nation. Just as in England, Barrie, Jane Barlow, Rudyard Kipling and Israel Zangwill are celebrating the peculiar phases of provincial or city life in Great Britain. This stage may pass, but for the moment it is most vital and characteristic, both in England and in America. In my judgment it should be encouraged.

"Our aim should be to supplement the English novel, not to imitate it. Sincerity and rugged devotion to a high purpose are good foundations for any art, and to believe that fiction is the highest form of truth will go far to sever us from pettiness and imitation. We need self-unconscious and deeply earnest artists, not copyists content to write in a form prescribed for them. Doubtless this phase called "local color in fiction" is passing, for the customs and habits which gave it birth are passing. They will soon be gone. The ghetto is breaking up. The Irish are acquiring English customs and the Scotchman is losing the burr on the end of his tongue. Fifty years from now a thousand of these interesting costumes and customs will have passed away. The tendency of the world is toward what the cowboy calls 'hard-hats,' the all-conquering derby and cutaway coat displacing the eagle feather Sioux, the Scotch plaid and the Mexican sombrero.

"It is the novel that explains the motives of a community because it adds the emotional element, without which statistics are vain. It presents the other half of the globe. The fiction of England enables us to comprehend English life. So our fiction should present American life—and on the whole does so, but we need wider sympathy with and deeper insight into the habits, customs and the emotions they subtend. We need more men without prejudice—men who are willing to wait patiently for appreciation and reward.

"Fiction as Mr. Zangwill has set it forth is not to be written by children, nor by clubmen. It must be the work of truth-seekers as well as of lovers of

*The Blithedale Romance by Nathaniel Hawthorne, *The Rise of Silas Lapham* by William Dean Howells, *Hugh Wynne, Free Quaker* by S. Weir Mitchell, and *The Damnation of Theron Ware* by Harold Frederic.—*Ed.*

art forms. Did any one of you think the novelist a man who writes to please people? Undeceive yourself. If his work is acceptable he has a house—if it isn't he returns to his six-by-nine hall-room and wears an overcoat and mittens, while he works out his rebellious idea.

"The spirit of the great novel must be large, though the material may properly be local and exceeding humble. The subject may be eastern or western or southern, but the method and the spirit must be national—or international. Local color and local prejudices are distinctly subjects for American fiction, but the novelist should not stoop in them to the belittling of the artist that is in him. To be true, to feel the dignity and importance of his art, these are essentials to the novelist.

"The sincerity of the artist is the saving grace of art. Our fiction will not be fantastic so long as men study life. It will never be literal reproduction so long as the novelist is true to his own angle of vision. The fact will correct the fantasy, the artist will color the fact. Life is the model, truth the master, and the heart of the artist the motive for work.

"To one who believes each age to be its own best interpreter the idea of decay of fiction never comes. That which the absolutist takes for decay is merely change. Life means change. The American novel will take care of itself. It will deepen with our convictions and widen with our sympathies.

"America is the most majestic and creative of nations. Its mountains, its huge buildings, tunnels and bridges prove that. Only in literature and art has it been bound by the old and the false. Its inventive constructive genius was developed by needs which made tradition of no avail. The great national inventors, builders, engineers roll out of common American life. American literature—the American novel—must come in the same way from the free soil and the open air. An epoch of such invention, I believe, is upon us."

DOSTOYEVSKY THE MAN
Vera Mikulich
Translated by Abraham Cahan
April 29, 1899

Mme. Mikulich,* a Russian writer of short stories, has published in *Zhenskoye delo* ("Woman's Interests") her reminiscences of Dostoyevsky, the novelist. Mme. Mikulich's sketches have met with marked success, and

*Vera Mikulich was the pen name of Lydia Veselitskaya (1857–1936), a popular writer who also authored a valuable memoir of Tolstoy.—*Ed.*

she is accorded by the Russian critics a place among the prominent young writers of her native country. Dostoyevsky's acquaintance, however, she made before the temptations of literary fame had entered her life, and it is to that period that her reminiscences relate.

"The natural life of woman," says Mme. Mikulich, "with her affection for her husband and children, with her peaceful domestic cares, clean kitchen, well-lighted nursery and comfortable drawing-room, appeared to me as something so delicious and so full of poetry that, compared to it, every occupation to which men devoted themselves seemed to me coarse, commonplace, prosaic. Writing material and printer's ink—what dirt it all was beside baby's crib, baby's bathtub and the air of cleanliness and freshness they exhaled! To be sure, I could excuse a certain degree of enthusiasm over literature. Indeed, I myself was not altogether barren of it, but reading somebody else's work is one thing and being a writer one's self is quite another. Of course, poverty might drive one to almost anything, but God is merciful, I would say to myself, and I hoped to be spared the necessity of writing. If my son were a famous writer—ah, that would be another matter. But myself—never!

"At the same time I would think of the great names in our literature with infinite reverence. I knew, of course, that men of genius like Tolstoy (the dearest of all), Dostoyevsky, Goncharov or Turgenev were still alive and writing, and that they were realities, beings of flesh and blood; but the notion of my ever meeting one of them without being thunderstruck seemed impossible.

"I had read of a young writer's first impression of Lamartine, to whom he had recently been introduced. 'What do you think of him?' he was asked. 'Well,' he said, disappointedly, 'he did not seem to be as much impressed by me as he might have been.' As to myself, I think Lamartine might have had every reason to be pleased with me, for upon finding myself in the presence of Dostoyevsky, my teeth were fairly chattering and my brain reeled. I saw him several times without being introduced to him, and it was some time before I actually made his acquaintance. I do not remember him arguing or disputing with the other guests at S———'s, where we met. When somebody happened to express an opinion contrary to his he would declare his disapproval in a straightforward, brusque way; but I have no recollection of anybody contradicting him, although none seemed quite to agree with his views. Whenever he spoke at S———'s he had 'the floor' all to himself, only now and then interrupting himself to answer some question by one of the ladies. He talked well, with eloquence, fervor and the confidence of firm conviction. He would assail the Catholic church and papacy, the 'rotten West' and its culture, which was undermined, shaking, on the eve of destruction. It was only a matter of time when the so-called Western civilization would disappear and something new, unheard of, something unlike anything we know, would come in its place. 'Who knows but our poor land may be destined to convey a new message, to say a new word, to humanity?' was one of his favorite sayings. He had ardent faith in what he termed the high mission of the Russian people. He saw in its patience and endurance a source of invincible power and greatness. It was his favorite topic and he recurred to it very often. 'The mission of our people,' he said, 'is one which concerns the destinies of all Europe, of the whole world. Its goal is the happiness of humanity. The genius of the Russian people embraces the idea of the universal brotherhood of men, and that sober view of things which teaches one to forgive and to discern between inconsistency and logic.'

"Dostoyevsky was sure that the salvation of the intelligent classes in Russia lay in their acceptance of the true national spirit, which is the spirit of truth. In the course of its endless martyrdom the Russian people had received Christ into its soul, and Christ had saved it from despair. The essence of the teachings of Christ was the essence of true enlightenment. He distinguished enlightenment from science. The salvation of mankind lay in enlightenment, rather than in science, and the Christianity of the Russian people was to constitute what he called the life-foundation of its intellectual development.

"When I looked at his nervous, agonized face, with his burning eyes, I could see the man who was sacrificing himself to bring about a better state of things. It was a delight to hear his quiet voice as he spoke of Christ, Christianity, the church, the mission of the Russian people. Catholicism had degenerated into idolatry, Protestantism was giving way to atheism. Where, then, was the truth? Where was the key to humanity's salvation? In Russia, of course. 'Our poor land may be destined to utter a new word.'

"At last I made his personal acquaintance, and we played a game of 'fools,' of which he was very fond. As was to be expected, he played in his own queer way. Elena Andreyevna, who was looking on, warned Dostoyevsky against me.

" 'Look out for yourself, or she'll beat you to pieces,' she said. 'If you think she is a fool like myself, you are mistaken.'

" 'I see, I see,' Dostoyevsky replied, frowning upon his cards. 'Well, if you really beat me, I shall not forgive you—never.'

"I did beat him, and asked his pardon. Elena Andreyevna left and we two remained alone. I was exceedingly happy to play with him, and felt in a solemnly excited mood. We played silently, only now and then exchanging some trivial remark upon the cards. Then he said: 'You are coughing, like myself. Only your cough will pass away, while mine won't. God save you

518

from such a cough.' 'But the doctors are curing you, are they not?' said I. 'They are, but what is the use? Some things won't be cured. It's your turn. If you beat me again—well.'

"This time he won. I was for going home, but he continued to shuffle the cards, and I had not the heart to get up. He looked me over with unceremonious intentness.

" 'Are you capricious?' he asked. 'Are you good-natured? Magnanimous? Religious? Do you pray much? Are you vindictive? Do you forgive an offense? How do you do it?'

"I tried to answer as truthfully as possible. After a while my curiosity got the better of me and I asked him how he began to write, whether he had ever attempted verse, and whether *Poor Folk* was the first thing he had published. No, he had never written any verse—that is, he had, too, but only in a light, comical vein. Serious poetry he never could compose. *Poor Folk* was the first thing he had brought out. Before that he had produced nothing original and he had begun his literary activity by translating novels which he liked himself, particularly those by Balzac. He went into ecstasy over Balzac, and, hearing that *Eugénie Grandet* was all I had read, he told me to be sure and read *Père Goriot, Les parents pauvres* and *Un grand homme de province à Paris.*

" 'Read these novels,' he said. 'If you like them I'll recommend you some more, and tell you what I like in them.'

"I asked him how he liked Zola as compared with Balzac. He said he had only read *Nana* and *La fortune de Rougon,* and that this was as much of Zola as he would ever read, because he found him uninteresting. He thought Zola's stories dull and overburdened with detail.

" 'So that you place Balzac higher, don't you?' I asked. 'Infinitely so. He is much the wiser and the more interesting of the two, for one thing.' 'And whom do you think the greatest, yourself or Balzac?'

"Dostoyevsky did not laugh at my childish simplicity, but reflected seriously and then said: 'Each of us is of value only in proportion to the amount of original, individual matter he has contributed to the world's literature. The question is, How much one has done that is fresh, original, new, that belongs to himself, and is not a rehash of what has been said by others. That's the great point. As to drawing comparisons between Balzac and myself, I cannot do that. I think each of us has done our share.'

"The conversation then passed to our Russian writers. Unfortunately, I did not hasten to commit his words to paper. As far as I can remember, however, he said that the life of our society was bound to undergo a material change, that we were marching onward (it was the common Russian people who furnished the motive power), that our ideals would develop and that we should look back to our present joys and amusements with a feeling of shame. The change in life was to be accompanied by a corresponding change in literature. Never mind that we saw no new men of talent just now. New conditions were sure to find new exponents. Thought was immortal and the work of each generation was continued by its successor. God would not shut His lips and His light would not go out.

"All this he expressed in his earnest, animated way. I drank in every word, never removing my glance from his exalted, fervent eyes, and feeling myself in the 'temple of truth.' When Dostoyevsky grew silent it came over me that it was a piece of impertinence on my part to have been sitting so long with this great man. I hastened to get up, saying: 'I was so timid about speaking to you, Fyodor Mikhaylovich, and yet here I have sat talking with you and listening to your conversation. I am so glad and so much obliged to you! To you it is nothing, it does not cost you anything, while I shall have something to remember as long as I live. I am very much obliged to you, but I don't wish to abuse—' Here I became so confused that I could not explain what I was afraid of abusing. Dostoyevsky also rose and said: 'Well, I don't know how I shall feel afterward, but the first impressions of you are very pleasant ones indeed.'

"God, how happy I was! Unable to conceal my joy, I said: 'Are they, really? How glad I am!' "

RESURRECTION CENSORED
May 19, 1899

A well-known Russian, who has lived in New York for many years and has written several books in the English language, speaking today about the American version of Tolstoy's latest novel, said:

"It is shocking to see how liberal the Russian censor is compared to public opinion in America. Why should not this most strict of censors—the Anglo-Saxon sense of decency—draw a distinction between the 'pornography for pornography's sake' of a Paul de Kock and the great moral agencies in the form of the highest art such as Hardy's *Jude the Obscure* and *The Awakening* of the greater realist, Tolstoy?

"The editor of the American magazine which is now serially publishing, in mangled form, Tolstoy's novel, is a man of advanced views, broad-minded and catholic, and I consequently am convinced that what he does to the story in the way of suppression and perversion he does because he deems the magazine to be the mouthpiece of the country rather than the mouthpiece of his own opinions. I believe that he has made the changes reluctantly, for such changes are certainly detrimental to the moral as well as the literary excellence of the work. They mar the effect of truth that characterizes all of Tolstoy's work in general, and this in particular. No one can help seeing the gaps. Tolstoy himself deems it the most moral novel he has written. He treats a most important social question, a question having many ramifications, touching the military and economic system of Russia. He handles it, indeed, without gloves, but he does not preach. He lets life tell its own tale of woe.

"The original version will come out in England, printed in the Russian language, and will be sold among the educated Russians in this country, as well as in the Russian colonies in the university cities of Europe. It will also be smuggled into Russia, where the cultivated classes are waiting for it impatiently. Some of them will read it at the price of their liberty, but it will be so eagerly read that the limited number of copies for each town will soon be reduced to crumbling tatters. Were the author other than Count Tolstoy, he would be sent to Siberia, but Tolstoy is too great for the Czar to tackle him."

TOLSTOY, THE ARTIST*

February 2, 1901

These twelve volumes contain all that Count Tolstoy has done in the field of imaginative literature, as well as the more important of his essays in religion, art and social problems—the result of his work as a portrayer of human life and as a moral teacher covering a period of nearly half a century. It is Tolstoy the man and the prophet, Tolstoy the aged Russian nobleman, who works in the fields with his peasant neighbors and who has been excommunicated by the Holy Synod, rather than Tolstoy the creator of immortal images, that is present to the popular mind as one of the great personalities of our time. And this is to be deplored. For important as is his

*A review of *The Works of Count Lyof N. Tolstoy,* 12 vols., ed. Nathan Haskell Dole (New York: Thomas Y. Crowell, 1900).—*Ed.*

work as a reformer and a preacher, it seems to be conceded on all sides that it is as an artist and not as an apostle that he is destined to leave his mark on the history of culture. It is quite natural that the personal qualities of the aged novelist, his gigantic individuality and his quaint life should prove a more tempting source of "copy" to the newspaper man than his high position in the world's literature. And this is all the more to be deprecated because there seems to be ground for thinking that if Tolstoy's reputation as a story-teller were not partly eclipsed by his fame as a champion of a religious and social creed, the beneficial influence which his fiction cannot fail to exercise on the taste of the reading public would be much more palpable than it is.

But if it is as a story-teller rather than as a moral teacher that he will be known to posterity, the stories which he tells are all the embodiment of moral lessons, not, indeed, preached by the author "in cold blood," but mutely taught by life itself.

When Maupassant was asked why he wrote, he said: "To make money." This was apparently his way of conveying the idea of one's freedom from hobbies or moral doctrines as the basis of one's creative activity—the idea of "art for art's sake." However that may be, were the same question expressed to Tolstoy, he would reply (as he does, in fact, in his volume on *What is Art?* and in his *Confession,* and as has been borne out by everything he has done in the line of fiction): "I write to express my views." In other words, Tolstoy thinks best when he thinks in images, and all his images are born of what he has to say on the various social phenomena which appeal to his *Weltschmerz.* He never writes except when it is "inevitable," as Wordsworth used to put it; not a line in all his numerous stories but is the upshot of artistic thirst.

As a moralist, Tolstoy is the champion of truth and simplicity in all things, and this is characteristic of his fiction as well as of his work as a publicist or preacher. Everything that bears the slightest taint of affectation is revolting to his frank, sincere and broad Slavic nature, and one of the qualities which have led some of the foremost critics in France to proclaim him the greatest master of the modern novel lies in the artistic truth which forms the soul of all his productions, in the convincing force of his fiction, in the absolute sincerity in which it is conceived and executed.

"I have now said," he remarks in concluding one of his Sevastopol stories, written at the very beginning of his career, "all that I wish to say at this time. But a heavy thought overpowers me. Perhaps it should not have been said, perhaps what I have said belongs to one of those evil truths which, unconsciously concealed in the soul of each man, should not be uttered, lest they become pernicious, as the lees of wine should not be shaken lest it be thereby spoiled. Where is the expression of evil which should be avoided? Where is the expression of good which should be imitated in this sketch? Who is the villain, who is the hero? All are good, and all are evil. Neither Kalugin . . . nor Praskukhin . . . nor Mikhaylov . . . nor Pest . . . can be either the heroes or the villains of the tale.*

"The hero of my tale, whom I love with all the strength of my soul, whom I have tried to set forth in all his beauty, and who has always been, is and always will be the most beautiful is—the truth."

These words are the keynote to all that is contained in the twelve thick volumes before us. They are full of immortal beauty, because they are full of truth.

Matthew Arnold, in his enthusiastic essay on Count Tolstoy, dwells on the lifelike visions which form the basis of his literary work. "The author saw it all happening so," he says, "saw it and therefore relates it; and what his novel in this way loses in art it gains in reality. For this is the result which, by his extraordinary fineness of perception and by his sincere fidelity to it, the author achieves; he works in us a sense of the absolute reality of his personages and their doings." It is evident that by art the English critic here means technique or the sense of proportion, for he certainly could not have spoken of art as the antithesis of the gift of making things real.

This "sense of absolute reality" is largely due to the depth of psychical penetration which marks Tolstoy's stories and which is the secret of their unparalleled effect as an educational agency. "He is the greatest living moralist," as Boyesen† once said of the Russian novelist, "because he pierces deeper into the heart of things than any contemporary writer."

Literary analysis is associated in the mind of the average novel reader with the notion of a "dry-as-dust" argument as to the why and the wherefore of everything the characters do or say. Particularly has this been the case with us since the advent of what is usually called our romantic revival. Realism is commonly burlesqued as fiction overburdened with commonplace detail, on the one hand, and with a wearisome examination into motive on the other. But Tolstoy's psychology does not argue. It paints. It is by portraying what is going on in the human heart and mind, by seizing upon the salient points in the mental or emotional activity of his personages and presenting them to us

---

*Kalugin and the others are all characters in Tolstoy's war story "Sevastopol in May" (1855).—*Ed.*

†Hjalmar J. Boyesen (1848–1895), Norwegian-American novelist.—*Ed.*

in the form of vivid pictures, that he produces the overwhelming effect of reality which we get from his stories. These soul-images often appear in the nature of psychological discoveries, recalling as they do to our mind facts of our inner consciousness of which we are not aware ourselves, but which we recognize in the artist's picture; and the joy of this sort of recognition is the highest form of esthetic pleasure known to readers of fiction.

The pseudo-realistic novels of the last decade are responsible for the curious opinion quite current among a certain class of reviewers that a faithful transcript of life cannot make interesting reading. "What excitement can there be in following experiences with which we are all familiar?" asks the irreconcilable romanticist. The absurdity of such a question becomes apparent when it is applied to the portrait of a man of ordinary flesh and blood made with brush and paint by a master. Indeed, it is sufficient to read a few pages in any story by Tolstoy to be thrilled by the same sort of emotion which we get while standing in front of a masterpiece in oils. When a man finds a book like *Anna Karenina* or the *Death of Ivan Ilyich* dull reading, it means that he lacks one of the finest senses given to the human race. His misfortune is as great as that of the man who is entirely devoid of the sense of music.

Another impression which seems to be common among people who devour the well-written and high-priced dime novels of today by the score is that to describe life as it is requires no special talent. Since the tale contains no ingenuity of plot, nor anything out of the ordinary, the average reader of popular fiction is inclined to believe—and the tenor of a good deal of our criticism encourages him in this belief—that anybody could write such a story. Those, however, who can tell literary gold from literary tinsel know that it takes imagination of a far higher order to produce a convincing picture of everyday experience than it does to invent the most cleverly entangled and disentangled plot. Besides, the writer of those stories which mainly depend on incident for the interest of his work has a free hand. He can marshal his puppets as he pleases. Not so an artist like Tolstoy. As he tells us himself, he often spends hours over a single sentence. Not that he is worried over the rhetoric of the troublesome passage, for Tolstoy's is the simplest and most unsophisticated Russian in the literature of his country. It is to determine the precise feeling or state of mind of his character, and to find words which will convey it truthfully and clearly to the reader, that he is usually at pains. Lies are innumerable; truth is one. Therefore, the writer of fictitious adventure stories has a carte blanche, while he whose business it is to create truthful fiction like Tolstoy's is tied and fettered by his own artistic veracity. Now, as it is much easier to detect a dissonance than to strike the right tone, Tolstoy often fills up his waste basket before he lights upon that word or phrase which reproduces the truth of life to the entire satisfaction of his sensitive ear.

Every situation, every relationship between man and man, every question and answer, look, smile or gesture, has an inner meaning which in most cases is distinct from and of far more importance than the outward appearance of things. To be forever searching for this inner meaning and to convey it in irresistible pictures is one of the characteristic features of Tolstoy's genius. In this indefatigable quest of truth he probes the deepest recesses of the human soul ever visited by an artistic eye.

The writer of plot stories has all he can do to invent incident. Tolstoy is wholly devoted to the study of human nature. The average critic is wont to speak of a literary study of everyday life patronizingly. "While the author cannot boast any extraordinary inventive facility," says one reviewer, for example, "he has succeeded in making his simple tale interesting." Would the same critic deem it necessary to apologize for the man who found pleasure in studying the life of butterflies or ferns? Can it be that our own hearts and minds are less interesting than the nerves of an insect or a leaf?

Realists are commonly charged with superabundancies of detail, but there is detail and detail. There is the kind that says nothing—the species of description that does not describe; and there is the vivifying kind of detail which fills Tolstoy's works, every stroke of which adds a life throb to the character, scene or situation. Those whose ambition it is to paint life in the colors of a golden sunset usually meet with the fate of the man who prayed for and was cursed with the golden touch. Human beings are turned into a dazzling mass of inanimate metal in their hands. Tolstoy belongs to the chosen few who are blessed with the life-giving touch which converts dreams into pulsating reality.

When a respectable man reaches a stage of jealousy where he stabs his wife, the frenzied state of mind in which he commits the murder is commonly supposed to preclude the possibility of his being clearly aware of what he is doing. Such is the conventional idea of a situation of this sort, and the average novelist proceeds upon this idea, taking it on trust from the popular mind, and calling upon his own art to help him take this all-forgetting frenzy as glaringly as possible. Not so Count Tolstoy. He takes nothing ready-made; he subjects everything to the most rigorous examination of his wonderful artistic instinct. So when Posdnishev (of *The Kreutzer Sonata*) stabs his wife, the author feels that the conventional notion of the jealousy-crazed mind, under conditions such as he portrays in his famous sketch, is false. He thinks, and, thanks to his unusual artistic memory, which retains the merest trifle in his own consciousness, he arrives at the conclusion that, although of a high-strung, nervous temperament, and in a frame of mind verging on insanity, Posdnishev yet remembers every detail of his fatal act. And this the artist represents in a striking picture:

"I remember every detail," says Posdnishev in the course of his story which he tells in the railroad car, "and not for a second did I fail to remember. The more violently I kindled within me the flames of my madness the more brightly burned the light of consciousness, so that I could not fail to see all that I did. I knew every second what I was doing. I cannot say that I knew in advance what I was going to do, but at the instant I did anything, and perhaps a little before, I knew what I was up to, as if for the purpose of being able to repent, in order that I might say to myself: 'I might have stopped.' I knew that I struck below the ribs first and that the dagger would penetrate. At the moment I was doing this I knew that I was doing something, something awful, something which I had never done before and which would have awful consequences. But this consciousness flashed through my mind like lightning and was instantly followed by the deed. The deed made itself conscious with unexampled clearness. I felt and I remember the momentary resistance of her corset and of something else, and then the sinking of the blade into the soft parts of the body. She seized the dagger with her hands, wounding them, but she did not stop me.

"Afterward, in the prison, while a moral revolution was working itself out in me, I thought much about that moment— what I might have done—and I thought it all over. I remember that a second, only a second, before the deed was accomplished, I had the terrible consciousness that I was killing a woman—a defenseless woman—my wife. I recall the horror of this consciousness, and therefore I concluded—and indeed I dimly remember—that having plunged the dagger in, I immediately withdrew it, with the desire to remedy what I had done and to put a stop to it. I stood for a second motionless, waiting to see what would happen—and whether I might undo what I had done."

That Posdnishev remembers "the momentary resistance of her corset, and then the sinking of the blade into the soft parts of her body," or that he immediately withdrew the blade with the desire to remedy what he had done, is only a "detail," but it is one of those details which illumine a whole world of human life, just as the miniature arc of electric light illuminates a room full of people and things. That corset and the soft sinking of the blade into the body and Posdnishev's "immediate" withdrawal of the dagger haunt the reader as long as he lives and infuse into the whole scene a vividness unknown to the most vigorous class of romantic storytelling. "Amid all the shouts of the fighters and the clash of their swords"—to quote again from Boyesen's essay on "The Great Realists and the Empty Storytellers"—"there is to me a deadly silence in the popular novel of adventure. The purely artificial excitement leaves me cold and a trifle fatigued. I see everywhere the hand that pulls the wires. . . . There is, on the other hand, a vast murmur of human activity in his [Tolstoy's] novels, a busy clamor of human voices, a throbbing turmoil of human heart-beats—so much so that one appears to have lived through his books rather than to have read them."

Add to all that has been said of the above scene that Mme. Posdnishev looms before the reader like a living creature, an intimate friend of his, a woman whom he seems to have known all his life, and the effect of such a "detail" as the resistance of her corset becomes still more striking, still more appalling.

Another such detail, although one belonging to a different category, is to be found, for instance, in the description of the way Ivan Ilyich's colleagues, the judges, learned of his death from a newspaper paragraph which one of their number reads out to the rest in his chambers in the courthouse. The first thought that flashed through their minds as they heard the news was:

"Well, he is dead, and I am not."

Their interest in the promotions and changes which the death of Ivan Ilyich will cause, their feelings for the widow, thoughts for the dead man and the entire life, prolonged illness and the last moments of Ivan Ilyich himself—everything is portrayed with the same sort of detail, and the result is a simple story of life and death, which, when it was first published in an English version, some fourteen years ago, produced a veritable sensation in this country as well as in England.

And when Tolstoy paints "the shouts of the fighters and the clash of their swords," as he does on the vast canvas of his *War and Peace* (three volumes) or in his short Sevastopol stories, the fighters are real fighters, the clash of swords is a real clash, and the blood is real human blood.

Tolstoy's pen had been active for some thirty years, he had written all of his more important novels, including *Anna Karenina* and *War and Peace,* before France discovered that Russia possessed a great literature and that Tolstoy was the most real of realists.

At home his genius was recognized at once. The following is from an essay on Tolstoy, written in 1856 by Nikolai Chernyshevsky, the leading Russian critic of that time:

527

This talent belongs to a young man full of fresh energies and with a long road before him. Many are the new experiences which are to meet him on this road; many new feelings are to stir in his heart, many new problems to engage his mind. What splendid hope for our literature! What a wealth of new material life is to furnish to his poetry! We predict that all Tolstoy has given us so far is merely pledge of what he will do in the future; but how rich, how glorious are these pledges of his!

This was written when *Childhood, Boyhood, Recollections of a Billiard Marker,** *Lost in the Steppe, Two Hussars* and his three Sevastopol sketches made up the sum total of Tolstoy's works. When the gifted critic returned from Siberia after many years of exile and enforced silence, he found Tolstoy at the head of the realistic literature of the world. And now that forty-five years have elapsed from the time when Chernyshevsky made the above prediction, the then young hero of the Crimean War is an aged prophet, one of the most remarkable personalities in Europe. The twelve volumes which form the subject of this review testify that the prophecy of the great Russian critic and martyr has come true. Only instead of realizing the hope of Russian literature alone Tolstoy has become the pride and the glory of all cultured civilization.

THE SOUL OF THINGS
November 9, 1901

By Bread Alone† is a novel with a serious purpose and a big canvas. In its spirit there is something quite admirable—a desire to get down to the soul of things, to be significant and important. There is not a frivolous line in the book and none of the "little ways," the minor virtues of the affable novelist. Mr. Friedman has attempted to do a big thing. Has he done it?

We do not know whether the author of *By Bread Alone* has been influenced by Count Tolstoy or not. Very likely not, for Tolstoy is not the only writer of his school. But the hero of Mr. Friedman's novel is in many

*Cahan means *Notes of a Billiard Marker.—Ed.*

†By I. K. Friedman (1870–1931), published in New York in 1901.—*Ed.*

ways quite similar to the hero of *War and Peace*—to Pierre, that physical, moral, religious, dreamy, human character, burly, big and charming—one of the greatest characters in all fiction. Throughout *By Bread Alone* is noticeable also the same kind of religious feeling, feeling for nature and the troubles of the poor, as in the work of the great Russian. This is only to indicate what the new book has attempted, leaving for the moment the question as to the success unanswered.

Blair Carrhart, the hero of *By Bread Alone*, is a young American, who thinks strongly and feels strongly, and for himself, unconventionally. He is filled with problems of the soul, goes through successive and excessive crises. He is misunderstood, but remarkable at college. His father wants him to go into business, but Blair, after a revelation in the fields, *à la* Tolstoy, decides to become a minister, preaches for awhile, but his scientific-religious soul cannot for long endure the empty forms of theology, and he decides to work for the great poor people, to get near their lives and understand their problems. He is engaged to a sweet girl, whom he incidentally throws over, finding her inconsistent with his great projected career. She suffers in noble silence, while he goes out into the rough world to develop his soul.

His destiny takes him to Chicago and vicinity, where he becomes a steel worker in the great factories. He is gigantic of frame, as big physically as he is soulfully. He becomes a leader of the working people, lives in the home of one of them, preaches to them the doctrine of socialism and of industrial cooperation, shares their passions and their interests, and pities fiercely their wrongs. He has a towering faith in and a towering love for the people, the people who before the book is over are represented as brutal, passionate butchers. Blair not only teaches and inspires them, but with his own fists punishes their bullies and shares in their elemental interests. The great strike comes, there are many chapters full of blood and carnage—chapters where the artistic attempt is realism. People are slain on every hand, women are rendered soulless in their rage, Blair is disgusted and crushed, and, seriously wounded, goes through another crisis. He sees that he has tried to help the people from the wrong end. He marries the sweet girl, therefore, and determines to try for the legislature, in order to help the people by laws.

In detailed description, in character sketches of the poor working people, in glowing accounts of the factories and processes of the making of steel, in the fights between the workingmen and the Pinkertons, in Blair's personal encounters with the gigantic Pole, there is a great deal of vigor. The realism of it is striking—too striking—and now we suggest the quality which makes the book really a failure, in spite of its interesting attempt and in spite of much that is strong and individual in detail.

For *By Bread Alone* has a strong melodramatic element, is sensational and extravagant in incident and in language. This distinguishes the volume eternally from a "book of the soul." Realism is attempted, but riotism is attained. A far greater artist than Mr. Friedman—Thomas Hardy—sins in the same way in books like *Tess,* where by the atmosphere of nature and of sympathy with common people he suggests a large, religious treatment and then ruins the whole thing by lurid, melodramatic detail. It is not because of the unusual and violent things that happen—unusual and violent things happen in *War and Peace*—but because of insistence on the sensational detail. Nobody would call *War and Peace* sensational. *Tess of the d'Urbervilles* is sensational and *By Bread Alone* is sensational. Mr. Hardy's pen is delicious and never shocks in language. Mr. Friedman's pen is too violent and shocks continually. In style the book is as bad as it is in specific incidents. An adjective is seldom enough; a stronger and a stronger, even if it must be coined, is sought. "Soul" is not pretentious and is spontaneous. Effort, effort rather than easy and inevitable accomplishment is what is felt in this book. It is the frame, not the reality, of a soul novel. It is what the critics in the ghetto call "onion" or "garlic" literature. An example of what is not unusual is: "The woman seemed transformed into a wild animal; her black eyes glowed like those of a carnivorous beast about to seize its prey; her long hands were like claws, strangling, merciless."

Perhaps if Mr. Friedman had not tried for so much, his failure would not have been so apparent. It ought to be said, however, in justice, that the purpose was excellent, and that the book is more interesting to us than four-fifths of the novels against which not so much can be said, being negative, that come to our hand.

THE MANTLE OF TOLSTOY
Bookman/December 1902

The reading public does not content itself with selecting its several favorites among the representatives of literature. It does not rest satisfied until it has chosen some one novelist or poet upon whom to confer the rank of the greatest living writer. It is as though each country had a literary throne which could be occupied by only one man in a generation, and which the reading public could not bear to see vacant for any length of time. Critics may agree upon two or three contemporary story-tellers as coordinately the foremost masters of their art, each taking precedence in some special field or quality; the public, however, seems to be loath to be dominated by any such oligarchy. While writers are fond of referring to the world of letters as a commonwealth or republic, their readers, much like the Jews of the time of Saul, hate to be left without a king. And if this is apparently the case with Anglo-Saxons, is there anything astonishing in the fact that in a country like Russia the highly centralized political regime under which the people live should find its reflection in the domain of art?

During the sixties and seventies of the last century, it was Ivan Turgenev who filled the office of the greatest Russian novelist. Although the chief works by which Tolstoy is best known to the civilized world were published during the same period, it was not until the death of the author of *Rudin* that "the sage of Yasnaya Polyana" came to be rated not only as the leading novelist of his own time, but as the most important writer in the entire range of Russian fiction. And now that Count Tolstoy is an aged and sick man, the question is often asked, Who of the younger representatives of Russian literature is to be regarded as heir-apparent to the throne which he has filled so grandly during the last two decades?

The question is one not easily answered, and the facts with which it is connected disclose a situation unparalleled in the history of Russian literature since the days of Gogol and Pushkin.

Maxim Gorky occupies a position analogous to the one enjoyed by Kipling in English-speaking countries. Every new story from his pen is hailed as an event of prime importance, and his appearance in public is greeted with the most exuberant ovations. This noisy success of his would certainly seem to point him out as the unanimous popular choice for the place of the supreme story-teller of the present generation. Certain elements in the character of his work, however, when viewed in the light of deep-rooted Russian conditions and tastes, prevent one from taking his clamorous vogue seriously. One well-known critic speaks of him as a writer who was "quick to reach the pinnacle of his reputation, but who has already set out on his downward journey"; another writer describes Gorky's stories as the over-seasoned, but ephemeral dish served to a dyspeptic public; while almost all of his most enthusiastic admirers among book reviewers of note conceded certain faults in his art which in a country like Russia must be regarded as fatal to lasting preeminence.

That Gorky is gifted with an active imagination, and that his stories possess originality and unusual vigor, no one disputes. These virtues alone are not enough, however, to make literature of the kind which the educated

Russian has been accustomed to exact from his leading writers. It should be borne in mind that popular recognition in the country under consideration is not synonymous with a large circulation among the typical novel-devouring part of the population. To be sure, Russia has her Georges Ohnets and Marion Crawfords,* whose stories keep the wife of many a provincial office-holder awake nights; but even this class of readers know that the novels in which they are absorbed are not considered literature, while those who follow the book reviews in the magazines or newspapers scarcely ever come across the names of these authors at all. As to that peculiar species of dime novel which is well written and well printed and sells for $1.50, it never sails under false colors. It is frankly a "dime novel," and one would no more think of calling it literature than one would a popular soda cracker that sold at the rate of so many hundred thousands a day.

Now Gorky's stories are certainly literature, but his talent is not made of the stuff that characterises the genius of men like Tolstoy, Turgenev, Dostoyevsky, Goncharov or Pisemsky. Gorky is a child of the slums, and of these slums he writes in a novel and forcible way. He is a clever story-teller, and running through all his tales is a clear-cut message, a well-defined central idea, that has never been promulgated through the medium of Russian fiction before. Such a writer, amid the conditions which surround Gorky and his constituency, could not fail to seize the public eye.

The prevailing order of things, added to the psychological peculiarities of the Slavic reader, have worked out literary ideals which in the United States or England would scarcely meet with acceptance at the hands of an appreciable minority. The cultured Russian yearns for political freedom. Living as he does the life of the enlightened Frenchman or Englishman, he naturally misses those liberties the enjoyment of which has so long since come to be looked upon as part and parcel of civilization. The university-bred subject of the Czar casts upon the parliaments of Western Europe furtive glances full of envy. By rendering politics forbidden fruit his government makes it the dream and passion of nearly everyone who can read and think. Words like "party," "political programme," "constitution," or "free speech" are invested with a charm which the Anglo-Saxon of modern times could scarcely realize. In other words, the Russian reader of good literature considers himself a member of a downtrodden languishing nation. As a consequence, every victim of oppression or poverty—of misery in any form—appeals to him as a fellow sufferer. On the other hand, a senseless censor system lends to every

*French novelist Georges Ohnet (1848–1918) and American novelist Francis Marion Crawford (1854–1909).—Ed.

book championing the cause of "the degraded and the insulted" the relish of forbidden fruit. To elude the vigilance of the censor, therefore, to make literary images say things which in the form of an essay or editorial would be likely to bring publisher and writer under the ban, is the kind of art which is sure to attract attention in the land of the Czars.

The upshot has been an ironclad aesthetic theory, under which the talented artist who does not lay bare some form of human misery is looked upon as something like a public officer who neglects his duty. A tax-gatherer seizing the famished cow of a famished peasant family is the sort of pastoral that makes the surest appeal to the imagination of the educated Russian reader.

The salient feature of the best Russian literature, the one directly traceable to the movement which resulted in the abolition of serfdom, is the sympathetic attention paid to the tillers of the soil and the poor, ignorant, weak and defenseless common people generally. "The idealisation of the peasant" is one of the staple phrases in essays and editorials of that period.

The novelist, then, is expected to have something to say, and his theme must have some social iniquity to accentuate, or at least be taken from the life of the disinherited and of the "poor in spirit." Now the peculiarity of Gorky's position in the literature of his country lies in this, that while his art has a moral lesson to inculcate and seeks its images in the lower strata of society, preferably among those who have altogether been dislodged from the regular current of life, his message is a persistent panegyric of strength and backbone, of the master-spirits of the human race, not of its victims, nor of those who are poor in spirit. He advocates the basic ideas of Nietzsche through the medium of "over men" in the form of drunken peasants or social waifs.

"A fellow must be sized up, to begin with," says the hero's father in his *Foma Gordeyev*. "You must find out the kind of stuff he is made of, find out whether there is anything in him. If he is a smart chap with some backbone to him and a mind for business, then you might as well give him a lift. But if you run up against a weak-kneed fellow without a bit of ambition, and that sort of thing, then spit at him and pass on. This is what I want you to bear in mind: When a fellow is always complaining and sighing and wailing, he is not worth a rap, is not worth your pity. Help only those who won't back down even when they are in trouble. Suppose a rotten plank and a sound one dropped into the mud. What would you do? Why, of what earthly use is a decayed piece of wood? So you had better let it stay where it is, down in the mud, so that people may tread upon it and keep the dirt off their shoes. As to the sound plank, pick it up, put it in the sunlight, let it dry up, for, indeed, it may be of some use, if not to yourself, to somebody else.''

Such is the ethical doctrine which Gorky preaches in almost every one of his numerous stories and sketches, in season and out of season. It is quite a novel doctrine in Russian literature. As a *leit-motif* it has never been utilized in Russian fiction before; but if it is only too natural that this motive, coupled with Gorky's resourcefulness and vigour, should have brought him into instant vogue, it is equally inevitable that a philosophy of this sort, as a basis of a literary message, shall sooner or later pall upon the Russian reader and gradually arouse opposition.

The average Russian bookman looks upon his government as the embodiment of undue strength and upon himself as an underdog, as one of the weak. The theory of the survival of the fittest applied to human beings in the crude, brutal form in which Gorky applies it through his Napoleons of the gutter is scarcely calculated to meet with lasting favour among a people who are always "complaining and sighing and wailing," always complaining of their own "Hamletism" (as Turgenev calls it) and of being ruled by a bureaucracy of misfits. The typical Russian does not regard those who whine and have no turn for business as so many decayed planks for the stronger citizen to trample under foot. He pities these weaklings, and, indeed, himself, for being victims of an effeminating, enervating social system. It is to depict this very shiftlessness that Turgenev wrote his *Rudin,* that "epic of Russian phrasemongery." But then, *Rudin* is instinct with human pity, and this all-forgiving pity is what makes it one of the most characteristically Russian novels ever written. The modern Hamlet, the man of great words and small deeds, is quite a common type in Russian literature, and in every case he has been treated with the same human sympathy and philosophical leniency as that which pervades Turgenev's masterpiece, and which is in keeping with the popular character. It is a noteworthy fact that Russia sees a greater relative number of acquittals in criminal cases than any other civilized country in the world. Tolstoy portrays this inclination of the common people in his *Resurrection,* where the tradesman in the jury box readily votes in favor of the defendant. Not that he thinks Maslova innocent of the charge, but because "Who is free from wrong-doing?" Indeed, so characteristic is this tendency in the average Russian that it has been accentuated as the keynote to the whole psychology of this curious people in whom the world is so keenly interested these days, but whom it seems at a loss to make out.

Rudin, then, is a distinctly Russian novel, and if it is, Gorky's stories are decidedly un-Russian, all his "atmosphere" and the vividness of his characters notwithstanding.

A still graver drawback is Gorky's lack of artistic sincerity. The point is that with all his undeniable skill as a character painter, his tales do not ring true. They are not marked by that freedom from consciousness which another trait of the national character, as well as the best traditions of the country's literature, make a necessary condition to enduring fame. The average Russian has been correctly described by foreign observers as a naive, unsophisticated creature with a profound sense of human motive; as one in whom the simple-minded sincerity of the child is combined with the intuitive human wisdom of the prophet. Born to be sad, mere cleverness for its own sake would be lost upon him, and a work of art, which is straining for effect, be it ever so lofty or subtle, is sure to weary him. This is as true of music and painting as it is of literature. The overwhelming seriousness and melancholy of Tolstoy is paralleled in the canvases of Vereshchagin and in the symphonies of Tchaikovsky. When we pass to Gorky, in the same connection, we find once more that, although a child of the very heart of his people, he is essentially the least Russian of all writers of note in the history of the modern Russian novel.

Scarcely an image in all his works but is marred by artifice, by an effect of cunning and of premeditation. His illiterate, semi-savage, yet strangely intellectual and heroic tramps are quite an up-to-date set of philosophers of the decadent school; and, while they may be found interesting, one cannot resist a feeling that the ideas they embody are not theirs, but have been crammed into their heads in order that their author may parade his own paradoxes. Try as Gorky will to translate the piquant views which he professes into the logic and speech of peasant or vagabond, his characters and the high sentiments they are made to utter will blend no more than the sandwich man will blend with the signboards he is made to carry around.

With all his apparent earnestness, Gorky is a good deal of a sensationalist. He is not interested in life in the way which is characteristic of a Tolstoy or a Turgenev. He does not listen to its undertones with the rapt attention of the man with whom artistic study is its own reward; he is not searching for the fundamental meaning of things, for the hidden importance of seeming trifles. What he really does is to hunt for effects of the kind which are apt to catch the eye of the cultured, and these he finds by the score.

The greatest truly Russian writer among the younger story-tellers of today is Anton Chekhov, the man to whom Gorky dedicates *Foma Gordeyev*, his most ambitious novel. Judged from a purely artistic point of view, Chekhov is the Tolstoy of the Russian short story. Of all the other representatives of the recent fiction of his country (leaving out the author of *Anna Karenina* as belonging to a former generation) he alone has the art of making his characters and their surroundings strikingly, irresistibly real. His unfailing grasp of the evanescent detail of life and his incisive sense of motive, added to the tremendous earnestness and maturity of his humour, compel the admiration even of those critics who impeach him for what they call his lack of any definite moral purpose. Having no "unifying idea" to convey, but painting life's bitter comedies and tragedies wherever he finds them, his triumph is of a purely literary character, without any admixture of that educational element which in a country like Russia takes the place of politics.

Keen as the general appreciation of Gorky's talents is, the most enthusiastic praise of his stories is not altogether free from a certain patronizing note. His most ardent friends among critics do not seem to applaud him except with a condescending smile on their lips; and, upon the whole, one seems to admire him as a writer who is not to be taken seriously, but whose work is entitled to special recognition because he is an under-educated, crude son of the masses.

To be more explicit, the hysterical popularity of the "peasant-litterateur" is the outcome of all that peasant-worship which has grown out of the humanitarian movements of his country. It is true that the agricultural population has since been supplanted in the sympathies of Young Russia by the factory proletariat of the cities; but then, this proletariat is largely made up of former peasants, and besides, Gorky's parents stand in closer relationship toward this element than they do toward the peasantry. The element in question, the wage-workers, have especially endeared themselves to the hearts of the magazine-reading public by their participation in the political demonstrations of the university students, by having become the mainstay and the chief hope of the radical movement; and Gorky, who belongs to them by birth and early breeding, is known, in addition, as an outspoken radical and reformer. In other words, his overwhelming vogue is largely due to the fact that he is of the common people, and to the open secret that he is a bitter enemy of the present regime.

The case is altogether different with Chekhov. He is neither a revolutionist nor any other sort of "ist"; as to his antecedents, he is a nobleman by birth and education.* He owes his success to his talent and to nothing else, and his stories are received with that mixed feeling of admiration and reverence which is the share of the truly great. Nor is his success restricted to

---

*Cahan is mistaken on both counts. Chekhov was the grandson of serfs, and Gorky a son of the provincial middle class.—*Ed.*

a comparatively small number of devotees, as is the case with a writer like George Meredith. His several volumes have had enormous sales, and library statistics show them to be among the most popular books in almost every section of the empire.

Chekhov began his literary career as a writer of *feuilletons* for newspapers. These were, for the most part, burlesque sketches, full of the irrelevancies of life, but displaying a depth of insight into reality which attracted immediate attention. There was an echo of sadness to his fun, and an intensity of human interest of the kind which leaves the reader's consciousness divided between a hearty laugh and a subtle sense of pity. He gradually lapsed into more serious moods and began to write longer stories, every one of which has been hailed unanimously as art of the highest order and at the same time condemned as barren of any "social idea." He has been known to fame for some twelve years, yet he has never felt tempted to leave the short story for the full-fledged novel. He is particularly interested in the Russian capacity for being bored and melancholy, a propensity which seems to be growing on him as the years pass.

Mikhaylovsky, the leading Russian critic of today, omits no opportunity to assail Chekhov's lack of any moral message, but even he does not dispute his genius as a portrayer of the kaleidoscopic, capricious trifles in our everyday experience. Nor does he deny his supreme position as a knower of men. He simply begrudges him his talent as something "worthy of a better cause," as a great literary gift in the possession of a man who fails to put it to the use which the aesthetic theory of his country proclaims the only justifiable goal of artistic effort.

This violation of the traditional maxim which condemns art for art's sake, and perhaps also his being confined to the short story, may stand between Chekhov and the mantle of Tolstoy.

Vladimir Korolenko, known to Anglo-Saxon readers as the author of *The Blind Musician,* is an artist of high merit. For several years he held the palm of precedence uncontested. He is still a great favorite by virtue of his charming personality and the ardent human sympathy which animates his stories, as well as on account of the years of suffering he passed in exile. His style has been likened to Turgenev's, and the high artistic finish of his tales once gave him the foremost place among the younger generation of writers. If one had asked ten years ago upon whom the mantle of Tolstoy was destined to fall, Korolenko would have been named as a matter of course. Since then he has been gradually eclipsed by Chekhov. He may safely be called the best living writer of fiction after Chekhov, although the sensational vogue of Maxim Gorky had the temporary effect of diverting some attention from both.

THE FRAME OF SOUL

Russia has quite an array of other young writers of recognized force, all of them realists in the inoffensive Russian sense of the term. Of these, Veresayev, whose *Memories of a Physician* is "all the rage" just now, and Andreyev,* who was "discovered" only about a year ago, are still mere apprentices in the art of story-telling. The critics are forever bewailing the absence of talents like those of the middle part of the last century. This decline in the quality of the literary output is often ascribed to a lack of anything like the moral ideals which vitalized Russian letters about the time of the emancipation of the serfs. But then, Russia is living a rather rapid life these days. The completion of the great Siberian railway and the general stimulus given to Russian industries, on the one hand, and the frequency and boldness of political demonstrations in which college students make common cause with the masses, on the other—all this is looked upon as something pointing in the direction of a new moral uplifting. And if the crusade against serfdom produced a Turgenev, a Tolstoy, and a Dostoyevsky, the present struggle for popular institutions will give birth, so it is prophesied by the enthusiasts, to a new great literature, one which will mirror the new era even as the splendid fiction of the sixties mirrored the public-spirited ideas of those days.

*V. Veresayev (1867–1945) and Leonid Andreyev (1871–1919).—*Ed.*